MACROECONOMIC THEORY

Economics Handbook Series

Anderson: *National Income Theory and Its Price Theoretic Foundations*
Atkinson and Stiglitz: *Lectures on Public Economics*
Carlson: *Economic Security in the United States*
Chacholiades: *International Monetary Theory and Policy*
Chacholiades: *International Trade Theory and Policy*
Gapinski: *Macroeconomic Theory: Statics, Dynamics, and Policy*
Hansen: *A Survey of General Equilibrium Systems*
Hansen: *The American Economy*
Harris: *The Economics of Harvard*
Harris: *Monetary Theory*
Harrod: *The British Economy*
Henderson and Quandt: *Microeconomic Theory: A Mathematical Approach*
Hirsch: *The Economics of State and Local Government*
Hirsch: *Urban Economic Analysis*
Jones: *An Introduction to Modern Theories of Economic Growth*
Kendrick: *Stochastic Control for Economic Models*
Kindleberger and Herrick: *Economic Development*
Maddala: *Econometrics*
Nourse: *Regional Economics*
Ott, Ott, and Yoo: *Macroeconomic Theory*
Quirk and Saposnik: *Introduction to General Equilibrium Theory and Welfare Economics*
Taylor: *A History of Economic Thought*
Taylor: *Macro Models for Developing Countries*
Theil, Boot, and Kloek: *Operations Research and Quantitative Economics*
Walton and McKersie: *A Behavioral Theory of Labor Negotiations*

MACROECONOMIC THEORY
Statics, Dynamics, and Policy

James H. Gapinski

Florida State University

McGraw-Hill Book Company

New York   St. Louis   San Francisco   Auckland   Bogotá   Hamburg
Johannesburg   London   Madrid   Mexico   Montreal   New Delhi
Panama   Paris   São Paulo   Singapore   Sydney   Tokyo   Toronto

To
Gerri, Missy, and Susie
for moments lost

This book was set in Times Roman by Science Typographers, Inc.
The editors were Diane D. Heiberg, Bonnie E. Lieberman, and Jonathan Palace;
the production supervisor was Charles Hess.
R. R. Donnelley & Sons Company was printer and binder.

MACROECONOMIC THEORY
Statics, Dynamics, and Policy

234567890 DODO 898765432

ISBN 0-07-022765-9

Library of Congress Cataloging in Publication Data

Gapinski, James H.
    Macroeconomic theory.

    (Economics handbook series)
    Includes indexes.
    1. Macroeconomics.   2. Statics and dynamics
(Social sciences)   3. Economic policy.   I. Title.
II. Series: Economics handbook series (McGraw-Hill
Book Company)
HB172.5.G36   339   81-20688
ISBN 0-07-022765-9   AACR2

CONTENTS

Preface   ix

Part 1   Inquiry into Statics

1   **From the Classics to Keynes**   3

1.1   Legacy of the Classics   4
1.2   Solving the Classical System   11
1.3   The Keynesian Perspective   12
1.4   From the Ruins   20

2   **Anatomy of a Static Keynesian Macro System**   24

2.1   The Model Structure   24
2.2   Amplifying the Equilibrium Relationships   27
2.3   Diagraming the Interrelationships   35
2.4   Emergence of the Bond Market   38
2.5   Autonomous Displacements and Policy Implications   41
2.6   Interdependent Shifts and Kinked Curves   45

Part 2   Elementary Dynamics

3   **Toward Dynamics: Theory and Practice**   51

3.1   Temporal Movements in a Static System   52
3.2   Model Metamorphosis: From Statics to Dynamics   54
3.3   Effects of Alternative Lag Structures   60

3.4   Taxonomy and Terminology of Temporal Responses   65
3.5   Dynamic Multipliers and Econometric Models   70
3.6   Dating Business Cycles in Practice   75
3.7   Constructing Composite and Diffusion Indices: An Example 79
3.8   An Indicator Approach to Anticipating Business
      Cycle Turns   83
3.9   The Scope of Harmonic Motion within Business Cycles   87

4   Popular Models of Cyclical Response   94
4.1   The Acceleration Principle   94
4.2   Frisch's Theory of Erratic Shocks   99
4.3   A Samuelson-Type Interaction Model   99
4.4   The Contribution of Hicks   106
4.5   Metzler's Perspective on Inventories   108
4.6   On Consumption and Investment   115

Part 3   Dynamics Extended

5   Lagged Effects in Consumption   119
5.1   Keynes' Law of Consumption: A Fall from Grace   119
5.2   A Tenuous Reconciliation   128
5.3   Habit Persistence and the Consumer   131
5.4   Discontinuous and Continuous Habit Persistence   138
5.5   The Coming of Wealth Theories   142
5.6   The Permanent Income Hypothesis   143
5.7   From Permanents to Measureds and Beyond   148
5.8   The Life Cycle Hypothesis   154
5.9   Shortsightedness: Similarities within a Principal Difference 156
5.10 Recapitulation and a Comment on Partial Adjustment   160

6   Investment, Inertia, and Temporal Motion   163
6.1   Contrapuntal Principles of Profits and Acceleration   164
6.2   Marginal Product and Marginal Efficiency   167
6.3   The Flexible Accelerator   177
6.4   On the Financial Side of Investment   183
6.5   An Inertial Multiplier-Accelerator Model   186
6.6   Lessons and Thoughts from Dynamics   192

Part 4   Mechanism of Policy

7   Policy Decisions under Certainty and Uncertainty   197
7.1   An Analytical Framework   199
7.2   Pairing Instruments and Targets   205

7.3	Instruments as Targets	208
7.4	Consequences of Uncertainty: Random Exogenous Variables	210
7.5	Enter Uncertainty Regarding Multipliers	213
7.6	Summing Up	219

8 **Policy Discretion and Rules** 221

8.1	A Challenge to Functional Finance	221
8.2	Feedback Controls and Their Effects	228
8.3	Feedbacks in Combination	235
8.4	Further Endorsement of Feedbacks	238
8.5	Rational Expectations: Completing the Circle?	243

Part 5 Equilibrium Dynamics and Policy

9 **Celebrated Paradigms of Economic Growth** 251

9.1	Dimensions of Technical Progress	252
9.2	The Model of Harrod	257
9.3	Professor Domar's Effort	260
9.4	The Neoclassical View of Growth	263
9.5	Neoclassical Growth under the CES	269
9.6	Cambridge Growth, Kaldor Style	273
9.7	The Cambridge of Robinson	279
9.8	Neoclassical Growth with a Cambridge Saving Function	283

10 **Growth under Vintage Capital** 286

10.1	From Vintages to Aggregates	287
10.2	Neoclassical Growth despite Embodiment	290
10.3	Basics of Aggregation Amplified	296
10.4	The Putty-Clay Hypothesis	300
10.5	A Model with Embodied Progress and Putty-Clay Capital	304
10.6	The Steady Growth Solution	308
10.7	Further Properties of Steady Growth: Comparative Dynamics	313
10.8	Reformulation under Adaptive Rationality	319

11 **Growth and Policy: The Speed of Adjustment** 325

11.1	Some Determinants of Adjustment Time	328
11.2	Linkage with the Elasticity of Substitution	334
11.3	An Apparatus for Examining Adjustment when Putty-Clay Rules	337
11.4	Response Paths: The Case of Static Expectations	342
11.5	Response Paths and Adaptive Rationality	346
11.6	Determinants Reconsidered under Putty-Clay	350
11.7	A Concluding Thought	357

Appendixes

A Quantitative Tools of Economic Analysis   359

A.1 The Limit   359
A.2 The Derivative   361
A.3 Indeterminate Forms and l'Hospital's Rule   364
A.4 Differential Calculus of Several Variables   364
A.5 Homogeneous Functions   368
A.6 Maxima and Minima of Functions: One Independent Variable   369
A.7 Maxima and Minima: Several Independent Variables   371
A.8 Constrained Maxima and Minima   374
A.9 The Integral   377
A.10 Two Natural Functions: The Log and the Exponential   380
A.11 Linear and Convex Combinations   384
A.12 Mathematical Expectation and Its Arithmetic   385
A.13 Regression Analysis: Ordinary Least Squares   387

B Mathematics of the Composite Indices of Leading, Coincident, and Lagging Indicators   393

C Functional Forms in the CES Production Family   396

C.1 The Elasticity of Substitution and the CES Function   396
C.2 The Leontief Function   398
C.3 The Cobb-Douglas Function   399
C.4 The Linear-Isoquant Function   399

D Outline for Solving Linear Difference Equations   400

D.1 The Solution Mechanism   400
D.2 Solution for the Basic Multiplier Model   402
D.3 Solution for the Interaction Model   404

Indexes   407
   Name Index
   Subject Index

PREFACE

It was September 1976 when this project began in earnest. I recall the date quite well because I had only then settled into a temporary reassignment from Florida State University to the U.S. Department of Commerce in Washington, D.C., as part of the Economic Policy Fellowship Program of the Brookings Institution. The euphoria of celebrating the Bicentennial in the nation's capital had finally waned, and the time seemed ripe for turning to a serious academic pursuit. That was five years ago—to the very month as I prepare this preface. To be sure, other endeavors were started and completed during the half decade, but it is safe to say that *Macroeconomic Theory* dominated the period.

As the subtitle *Statics, Dynamics, and Policy* suggests, this book is intended to lead the student in an orderly manner from an analysis of statics to an examination of dynamics and then to a study of attendant problems of policy. It begins by reviewing the classical model of income determination and against that backdrop presents the main contributions of Keynes. Those contributions find expression in Chapter 2, which explores the various properties of a static linear model. The static system is made dynamic in Chapter 3. That chapter shows how temporal behavior depends upon the specific lag structure adopted, and along the way it introduces the concept of dynamic multiplier. Chapter 4 continues the study of dynamics by presenting several models premised on the simple accelerator, one of them being a variant of Samuelson's interaction paradigm. Chapters 5 and 6 revisit the consumption and investment specifications used in earlier stages of the discussion and conclude that inertia affects both spending streams. This conclusion urges that the consequence of inertia on temporal motion be considered. The closing segment of Chapter 6 obliges. It develops a dynamic model which includes inertia in consumption and investment and which contains the Samuelson paradigm as a special case. The impact of inertia on motion is then analyzed by varying the magnitudes of inertial parameters.

The inquiries into statics and dynamics note that policy formulation is a difficult business. *Macroeconomic Theory* pursues this point by examining the mechanism of policy. In Chapter 7 it focuses on theoretics of policy decisions and discloses how those decisions are influenced by uncertainty. It extends the exposition by addressing in Chapter 8 the question of whether policy should be conducted on the basis of discretion or rules. Here Lerner's doctrine of functional finance is confronted by Friedman's precept of a constant growth rate rule. That discussion dissolves into a comparison of the dynamic movements prompted by active feedback controls and by the passive rule. Implications of rational expectations for the efficacy of countercyclical feedbacks are also treated.

After completing the investigation of disequilibrium dynamics and the accompanying policy issues, *Macroeconomic Theory* turns to equilibrium dynamics. In Chapter 9 it reviews the growth models of Harrod, Domar, the neoclassicals, Kaldor, and Robinson. In Chapter 10 it gives a detailed account of growth under capital embodiment. There the issue of capital aggregation is raised, and the conditions for aggregation are explored. The putty-clay hypothesis then comes to the fore, and the properties of a growth model containing putty-clay capital and Harrod-neutral embodiment are established. Chapter 11 concludes the presentation by considering policy in a growth setting and by analyzing its impact on the speed of adjustment for models encountered in Chapters 9 and 10.

As might be inferred from the foregoing remarks, *Macroeconomic Theory* examines a menu of topics which is standard for an advanced undergraduate or a first-year graduate course in macroeconomics. For example, it derives IS and LM curves from a linear system and presents multiplier expressions implicit in that paradigm. It looks at the popular consumption and investment theories and attends to the effects of policy. Moreover, it investigates models which focus on business cycles and those which address economic growth.

But *Macroeconomic Theory* goes beyond the standard menu as well. With the aid of a macro budget constraint, it extracts the implications for the bond market from the usual IS-LM framework and deduces the status of the *three* markets (commodities, money, and bonds) for all combinations of interest and income. It discusses the method used by the National Bureau of Economic Research to uncover the dates of business cycles and extends that exposition by studying the harmonic motion of key economic series over recent cycles. It works through an example showing how composite and diffusion indices are constructed; it also describes the anatomy of the composite index of leading indicators and reports the index's performance history. Rather than summarily stating that the Keynesian consumption function received setbacks at the hands of Kuznets and others, *Macroeconomic Theory* reproduces evidence which led to those setbacks. In addition, it highlights the microeconomic foundations of the permanent income hypothesis and of a polar opposite, the shortsightedness hypothesis. For each model it derives the macro consumption function from the micro underpinnings. *Macroeconomic Theory* likewise goes beyond the typical bill of fare in treating topics such as dynamics given inertia, optimal policy decisions under uncertainty, the efficacy of feedback controls, the problem of capital aggregation, the ramifications of putty-clay, and the speed of adjustment.

The quantitative skill required for the first half of this volume is mainly algebra. Calculus appears only sporadically, and when it does it is usually relegated to footnote presentation. This format should allow students sufficient time to learn or to refresh those basics of calculus presumed in the second half,

Section 5.6 and beyond. In preparing for that latter disquisition, students might consult Appendix A. It reviews the specific elements of calculus on which the text draws, and its examples come principally from the textual discussion itself. Appendix A also takes up a few rudiments of mathematical expectation and econometrics helpful in assimilating the material.

Throughout the development of the book, I have had the pleasure of working with very talented people. Rose Ciofalo was my first editorial contact with McGraw-Hill; she generously supplied the initial encouragement and direction. Thereafter Diane Heiberg became editor of the project and, along with Clare Hogan, provided the continuing guidance needed to keep it on course. The congenial environment which Diane and Clare fostered certainly contributed much to sustaining the enthusiasm necessary for seeing the project to its completion on schedule. Bonnie Lieberman, who assumed editorial responsibility for the final phase of the work, continued that cooperative spirit.

To the reviewers of the many installments of *Macroeconomic Theory*, I extend my thanks for their comments and suggestions, which combined to appreciably improve the substance and form of the book. Victor Cholewicki of Catholic University; Kathleen M. Langley of Boston University; and Carl G. Uhr of the University of California at Riverside are due a score of kudos in this regard.

Transforming manuscript pages into galleys and then into a bound volume requires prompt attention to a long list of details. During the metamorphosis an index must be composed and—at least in the present case—a preface must be written. Content changes must be finalized, footnotes and graphics must be joined to the text, and style consistency must be verified. Everything seems to occur at once. Jon Palace, the editing supervisor, brought order to this period by coordinating all production activities and by expeditiously resolving the eleventh-hour problems. Careful encoding by the copy editor coupled with fast and accurate typesetting by Science Typographers, Inc., greatly eased the burden of the production stage.

Others involved in the development process deserve special credit. Linda Zingale typed most of the manuscript and never missed a deadline despite having to decipher my hieroglyphics without benefit of a Rosetta stone. Jim Anderson, Craig Hewitt, and Peter Krafft did an outstanding job on the artwork. Since I can neither type a word unless a keyboard schematic is chiseled into the wall nor draw a straight line unless a ruler is bolted to the desk, I can truly appreciate their talents. I owe a sizable debt of gratitude to Terry Gets, the mild-mannered representative of McGraw-Hill. It was Terry who, after sifting through an early draft of *Macroeconomic Theory*, suggested that it be sent to McGraw-Hill for consideration. That particular visit by Terry to Florida State is recorded indelibly in my mental ledger.

Finally, on a personal level, I deeply thank my parents Henry and Helen and my courageous sister Nancy for their long-standing support and encouragement. I also, and especially, thank my wife Gerri and my daughters Missy and Susie; to them I dedicate this effort.

James H. Gapinski

PART
ONE

INQUIRY INTO STATICS

FROM THE CLASSICS TO KEYNES

According to the model of income determination which prevailed in the early 1900s, full employment characterized the normal condition of the economy. Shocks to the system might result in periods of unemployment, but unemployment would be a temporary phenomenon. Furthermore, said the model, prices would change slowly if at all. This quiescent setting suggested laissez faire as an appropriate rule for policy guidance.

Then came October 24, 1929—Black Thursday—the day which ushered in the great crash of the stock market. Then came 1930 and for the United States unemployment amounting to 9 percent of the labor force, a dramatic rise from the 3 percent rate of the previous year. Then came 1931 and an unemployment rate of 16 percent. The situation grew even worse. Year 1932 saw 24 percent; 1933, 25 percent. Not until 1941, more than a full decade after the crash, did the unemployment rate fall below 10 percent.[1] One of the unmistakable lessons learned from this tragic experience was that a developed economy could have substantial unemployment for a prolonged period of time. In defiance of conventional wisdom, unemployment was not temporary; rather, it seemed to describe the equilibrium of the economy. In the midst of this distress, and hardly by coincidence, John Maynard Keynes introduced his pathbreaking book *The General Theory*.[2] It described a model capable of generating equilibria where the labor force was less than fully employed.

---

[1] A lucid account of the events associated with the crash appears in John Kenneth Galbraith, *The Great Crash, 1929* (Boston: Houghton Mifflin Company, 1954), especially Chapters 6–10. The unemployment statistics are cited from U.S. Department of Commerce, *Historical Statistics of the United States: Colonial Times to 1970*, part 1 (Washington, D.C.: U.S. Government Printing Office, 1975), p. 135.

[2] Keynes, *The General Theory of Employment, Interest, and Money* (New York: Harcourt, Brace and World, Inc., 1936).

This chapter first presents the macro model at which Keynes took dead aim and accepts his terminology by calling it "the classical system."[3] Afterward, the discussion turns to his modifications of key classical postulates, and through those alterations the Keynesian paradigm emerges. Since this review is primarily intended as background for subsequent chapters, both models are treated in a stylized fashion often free from complicating nuances.[4] All markets are assumed to be perfectly competitive. Moreover, the economy is viewed as a single sector. Only one type of good is produced, and it can be either consumed or accumulated as capital.

1.1 LEGACY OF THE CLASSICS

The classical model can be segmented into a production section, a money section, and a saving and investment section. Each is examined in turn.

Production

A principal element in the production section is a production function, which may be defined as a purely physical-technical relationship indicating the maximum amount of output which can be produced from alternative combinations of inputs. This function relates inputs to output, and it is independent of prices. Note that the production function is a boundary function: it describes the maximum amount producible. While production could occur below the boundary level, such inefficiency is ignored.

The production function applicable to the entire economy can be written as

$$Y = f(L, K) \tag{1.1}$$

Y denotes real output, the quantity of the good produced. It also represents income since in a macro context the production of output generates an equivalent value of income payments for the factors of production.[5] L represents the number of workers employed; K, the stock of capital in service.

---

[3] Keynes considered the classics to be "the *followers* of Ricardo, those...who adopted and perfected the theory of Ricardian economics, including (for example) J. S. Mill, Marshall, Edgeworth and Prof. Pigou." He acknowledged, however, that this interpretation might involve a solecism inasmuch as "'the classical economists' was a name invented by Marx to cover Ricardo and James Mill and their *predecessors*,...the founders of the theory which culminated in the Ricardian economics." In short, Keynes used the term "classical" to identify the neoclassical economists. See Keynes, *The General Theory*, p. 3n.

[4] A more comprehensive treatment of the classical and Keynesian schools of thought appears in Gardner Ackley, *Macroeconomic Theory* (New York: The Macmillan Company, 1961), Chapters 5–9, 10 (pp. 208–220), 14–15; in Ackley, *Macroeconomics: Theory and Policy* (New York: Macmillan Publishing Co., Inc., 1978), Chapters 4–5, 9–10, p. 534; and in Lawrence R. Klein, *The Keynesian Revolution* (New York: The Macmillan Company, 1949), especially Chapter 3, pp. 199–213. The following exposition draws from those presentations.

[5] Barry N. Siegel, *Aggregate Economics and Public Policy*, 4th ed. (Homewood, Ill.: Richard D. Irwin, Inc., 1974), pp. 6–11.

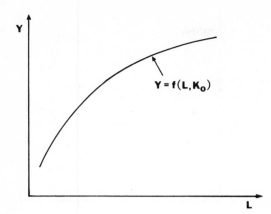

Figure 1.1

Equation (1.1) is presumed to be well-behaved. It displays positive but declining marginal products along with positive cross-marginals, the latter meaning that an increase in one input causes the marginal product of the other to increase when the quantity of that second input remains unchanged. These characteristics hold for all positive and finite input levels.[6] Figure 1.1 illustrates the production function with capital fixed at the level K_o. For higher K_o values, the entire curve would lie above that indicated; the converse also applies. In what follows the capital input will stand at K_o, thereby rendering the macro model descriptive of a short-run situation.

Coupling the production function with some optimization rule observed by entrepreneurs leads to the demand curve for labor. Entrepreneurs might be profit maximizers, their profit function being

$$\pi = pY - wL - qK_o \qquad (1.2)$$

p symbolizes the price of the good being produced; w denotes the money wage; q denotes the input price of capital, namely, the unit capital rental. Maximization of profit π with respect to labor subject to the production function generates a rule which advises entrepreneurs to employ labor to the point where its marginal product MP_L equals the real wage w^*:[7]

$$MP_L = w^* \qquad (1.3)$$

with $w^* = w/p$. The real wage can be viewed as worker compensation expressed

---

[6] The properties of (1.1) can be expressed concisely in mathematical format: For $0 < L < \infty$ and $0 < K < \infty$, $f_L > 0$ with $f_{LL} < 0$, $f_K > 0$ with $f_{KK} < 0$, and $f_{LK} (= f_{KL}) > 0$. f_i and f_{ii} denote, respectively, the first and second partial derivatives of Y with respect to input i. Likewise, f_{ij} represents the partial of f_i with respect to input j. Thus $f_L > 0$ says that the marginal product of labor is positive, while $f_{LL} < 0$ says that it declines. $f_{LK} > 0$, or equivalently $f_{KL} > 0$, signals positive cross-marginals.

For a review of quantitative tools used in economic analysis, refer to Appendix A.

[7] From (1.2) the partial derivative of π with respect to L is $\pi_L = pf_L - w$, where f_L abbreviates MP_L. Setting π_L at zero to find the stationary points discloses only one, that associated with (1.3). The second partial of π with respect to L reads $\pi_{LL} = pf_{LL}$. Since $f_{LL} < 0$ for positive and finite input values, $\pi_{LL} < 0$, assuring that (1.3) identifies a global maximum. (*continued*)

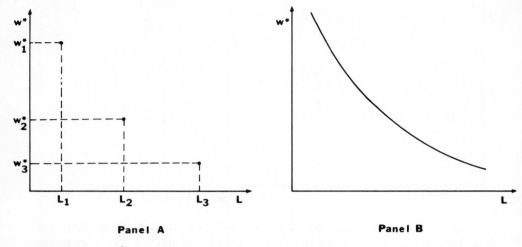

Panel A   Panel B

Figure 1.2

in terms of goods; it indicates in effect the quantity of output received by workers for each unit of their input into the productive process.

The labor demand curve follows directly from the marginal productivity condition (1.3). At real wage w_1^* that condition would be satisfied if entrepreneurs were to employ, say, L_1 workers. Panel A of Figure 1.2 locates the relevant point. For (1.3) to hold at a lower real wage w_2^*, MP_L must fall. Given the property of diminishing marginal productivity, this decline would occur only if the quantity employed were increased. Therefore, at w_2^* more labor would be employed, say L_2. Similarly, at a still lower real wage w_3^*, L_3 would be employed. These points begin to reveal the labor demand curve, a completed version of which appears in Panel B of Figure 1.2. It should be clear that this demand curve is simply labor's marginal product curve. At each real wage the demand locus gives the labor input needed to equate the marginal product to that wage. Each wage level, therefore, is identical to the marginal product. It should also be clear that entrepreneurs maximize profit only at points on the demand curve. In functional notation, labor demand Ld may be written as

$$Ld = Ld(w^*) \tag{1.4}$$

Labor supply Ls varies directly with real wages. It rises when real wages rise; it falls when they fall. The supply curve, depicted in Figure 1.3, provides a convenient standard for establishing full employment. Full employment means that all those willing and able to work at the prevailing wage are in fact working.

An assumption underlying this optimization process is that the production function does not impose technical limits on f_L which prevent satisfaction of (1.3). A ceiling or floor might restrict f_L, but not to the extent that maximum $f_L < w^*$ or minimum $f_L > w^*$.

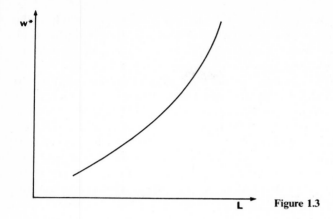

Figure 1.3

Since the supply curve pertains precisely to that group of individuals, full
employment occurs when the curve is satisfied—when the economy lies "on" the
curve. Under this interpretation the full-employment mark is not stationary; it
changes with the real wage. Mathematically,

$$Ls = Ls(w^*) \tag{1.5}$$

Equilibrium real wage results from the interplay of supply and demand forces
in the labor market. It is the wage for which

$$Ld(w^*) = Ls(w^*)$$

At that wage all individuals willing and able to work are working, and entrepreneurs are maximizing profit. No pressure exists from either side of the
market to alter the wage. Figure 1.4 identifies the equilibrium wage w_E^*; L_E
denotes the corresponding level of employment. Full employment prevails.

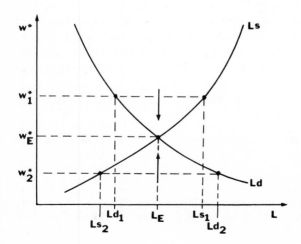

Figure 1.4

Figure 1.4 also illustrates the wage determination process. According to the classics, money wage is flexible both upward and downward. If the real wage were initially w_1^*, there would be an excess supply of labor, in the amount of $Ls_1 - Ld_1$. Workers would bid down the money wage rather than remain unemployed. As the money wage fell, the real wage would fall too, and it would continue to decline until it reached w_E^*. If the real wage were initially at w_2^*, labor would be fully employed. Entrepreneurs, however, would be unhappy because they would not be maximizing profit; that maximum requires Ld_2 workers, not the Ls_2 being supplied. As an inducement to attract the extra workers needed for a profit maximum, entrepreneurs would offer a higher money wage, and this increase would pull the real wage toward w_E^*. Arrows in Figure 1.4 show the movement of the real wage in disequilibrium. Money wage flexibility is crucial for the attainment of full employment.

Once the level of employment is determined by this *tâtonnement* process, the level of output becomes known from the production function since the other input, capital, remains fixed. The output which results, $Y_E = f(L_E, K_o)$, can be dubbed "full-employment output." Flexibility of the money wage, by maintaining employment at L_E, maintains output[8] at Y_E.

Money

Classical economists championed the quantity theory of money, which asserted that price was proportional to the quantity of money in circulation. Money demand was regarded as proportional to nominal income; namely,

$$\text{Md} = kpY \qquad (1.6)$$

Md represents the number of paper dollars demanded for transactions purposes. An economic unit receives income and pays expenses in different temporal patterns. Because of this difference in timing of receipts and disbursements, money must be kept on hand, but it is reserved exclusively for transactions. Such money balances may be called "active." Proportionality coefficient k depends upon institutional characteristics and remains fixed for any particular set of characteristics. Price, however, is flexible both upward and downward.

A fundamental proposition of the classical school states that no rational person would hoard—that is, hold idle money balances, those being dollars over and above the amount designated for transactions. Hoarding is unreasonable because it means forgoing interest income. Money is a sterile asset. It earns no

---

[8] The production function might pivot through time, prompting a shift in the labor demand curve. Alternatively, the labor supply curve might shift. In such cases the point of labor market equilibrium would move, but the money wage would propel the real wage to that new location. Full employment, of course, would then occur at a new level; so would full-employment output.

As will become obvious shortly, a change in full-employment output would change price. This price response, however, would not prevent the money wage from bringing its real counterpart to the full-employment mark. The direct relationship between the money wage and the real wage envisioned under classicalism is reviewed and criticized by Keynes in *The General Theory*, pp. 9–13.

interest itself, and consequently it would be retained only to the extent needed to meet expenses.

The supply of money Ms comes from the monetary authorities:

$$\text{Ms} = M_o \tag{1.7}$$

where M_o is the exogenously determined number of paper dollars in circulation. Equilibrium in the money market therefore requires that

$$M_o = kpY \tag{1.8}$$

Since k is constant and Y remains stationary at a level associated with the full employment of labor, money supply and price are proportionally related.[9] Doubling money doubles price. Hence the quantity theory.

Saving and Investment

Income received by households may be partly consumed and partly saved. As the rate of interest rises, postponement of present consumption becomes more attractive, and consequently real saving S depends positively upon the rate of interest r:

$$S = S(r) \tag{1.9}$$

As interest rises, saving rises; as interest falls, saving falls.

How can saving be accomplished? One option calls for the accumulation of idle money balances, but such action would constitute hoarding. Alternatively, a household intending to save could do so by purchasing bonds. This strategy appears to be the sound one because the household would exchange a sterile asset for an interest-earning asset, a swap ostensibly promising sure gain.

Bonds are offered by businesses usually to secure the finance needed to acquire capital goods in excess of the amount permitted by their internal funds. The interest on bonds represents to business a cost of borrowing, and the quantity of capital goods acquired reflects this cost. Thus real investment I may be written as

$$I = I(r) \tag{1.10}$$

When interest rises, the cost of investing rises and investment declines. When interest falls, the reverse happens.

The schedules for saving and investment are both regarded as highly interest-elastic. Both are also presumed to be stable; they remain fairly stationary through time. Figure 1.5 graphs the two functions. Like money wages and prices, interest is flexible upward and downward. It gropes toward the equilibrium rate r_E, which occurs at the intersection of the two curves,

$$I(r) = S(r)$$

I_E designates the equilibrium level of saving and investment.

---

[9]k can be recognized as the reciprocal of the velocity of circulation.

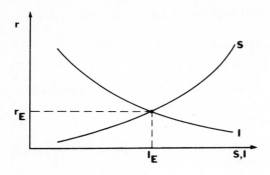

Figure 1.5

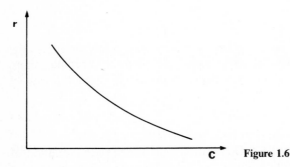

Figure 1.6

Details of the saving function portrayed in Figure 1.5 enable articulation of the consumption function. Since

$$Y = C + S(r)$$

where C denotes real consumption,

$$C = Y - S(r)$$

With income being constant at a full-employment level, consumption must depend upon interest alone. It varies inversely with interest and evidences an interest sensitivity which mirrors that of saving.[10] Figure 1.6 illustrates.

---

[10] "For the classical theory of the rate of interest,... it was convenient to suppose that expenditure on consumption is *cet. par.* negatively sensitive to changes in the rate of interest, so that any rise in the rate of interest would appreciably diminish consumption." Keynes, *The General Theory*, p. 93.

It deserves mention that consumption and saving exhaust *disposable* income, the income available to households after taxes. However, since the taxation power of government is not formally modeled in this chapter, all income Y may be construed as disposable and therefore as completely exhaustible by consumption and saving.

1.2 SOLVING THE CLASSICAL SYSTEM

The classical model lends itself to easy solution. The production section first determines the real wage and the level of (full) employment. With employment known, so is output, which, in turn, enters the money market to determine price. Price can be viewed as resulting from the collision of nominal and real forces, namely, nominal money supply and full-employment output. With price established and with real wage determined from the production section, nominal wage becomes known. Interest comes from the saving and investment section, as does the allocation of output between consumption and investment. Figure 1.7 portrays the various steps in this solution process; the sequence begins in Panel A. From the network of interrelationships depicted by the figure, it should be evident that shifts in either the saving or the investment schedule affect only the saving and investment section. The rate of interest changes, the allocation of output changes, but nothing else changes. The effects are purely local.[11]

Classicalism generates sanguine conclusions. Full employment results from the natural functioning of the economic system. Furthermore, given a constant supply of money, any change in price would evolve slowly through time. Institutional features of the economy might undergo transformation, thereby altering the parameter k. Societal attitudes might change, as might the population size, thus shifting the labor supply curve. Or modifications in the production process might pivot the production function and shift the labor demand curve. Hence full-employment output might not remain stationary through time.[12] All these occurrences, however, would transpire slowly, and their effect on price would be gradual. Price stability could therefore be preserved by leisurely changing the money supply. Full employment and stable price can be achieved in the classical model, and monetary policy is sufficient for their attainment.

[11]If the capital stock were allowed to change in the face of investment, a given volume of investment and hence any adjustment in that volume would move the production function and would trigger the response sketched in footnote 8. However, since a change in the capital stock tends to be small relative to the level already extant, the admittedly awkward assumption of stock constancy despite investment is retained, and the aforementioned bridge from the saving and investment section to the rest of the model is allowed to collapse. Content lost by that assumption is negligible. For a long-run setting, however, the loss would be more pronounced, as the discussion of the Domar growth model in Section 9.3 indicates.

[12]J. R. Hicks chooses to treat saving in the classical model as dependent upon interest *and* income: $S = S(r, Y)$, with $S_r > 0$ and $S_Y > 0$. Under this interpretation a change in output shifts the saving schedule mapped against interest and alters equilibrium interest. The saving and investment section may react to changes originating elsewhere in the system, but nevertheless changes originating in the saving and investment section do not spread to other parts of the system. Hicks' view of classical saving can be found in his paper "Mr. Keynes and the 'Classics'; A Suggested Interpretation," *Econometrica*, **5** (April 1937), pp. 149, 152, 156.

Since $C = Y - S$, a change in income would shift the consumption function drawn against interest if the saving function read $S(r)$; the shift would likely occur if the saving function read $S(r, Y)$.

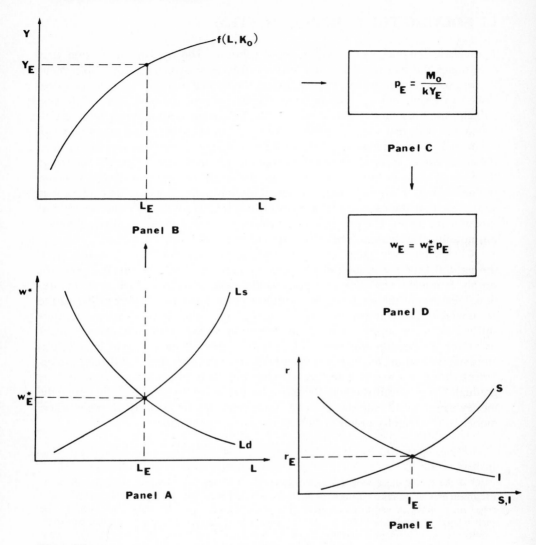

Figure 1.7

1.3 THE KEYNESIAN PERSPECTIVE

Keynes took exception to key tenets of the classical philosophy. His view of the money wage differed dramatically from the orthodoxy, although other elements of classical production were preserved. In order to enhance the flow of presentation, discussion of Keynes' amendment to the production section follows the discussion of the amendments pertinent to the money and the saving and investment sections.

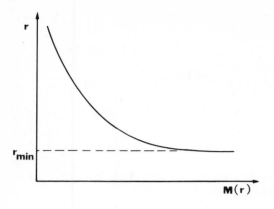

r

rmin

M(r)   Figure 1.8

Money

Unlike the classics, Keynes believed that economic units had an intrinsic tendency to hoard and dishoard. They would hoard to avoid expected losses in the bond market; they would dishoard to take advantage of anticipated capital gains. Hoarding was rational.

The tendency to hoard translates into a schedule of liquidity preference. It describes the economywide demand for idle money, money earmarked for speculative purposes.[13] As Figure 1.8 indicates, the liquidity preference schedule betrays an inverse relationship between the quantity of idle money demanded $M(r)$ and the rate of interest: demand falls when interest rises and rises when interest falls. Furthermore, the schedule displays a horizontal region, which theorists subsequent to Keynes called the "trap."

The shape of this speculative demand curve can be explained in two ways.[14] One deals with opportunity cost. As interest rises, the cost of holding idle money, measured in terms of forgone interest income, rises. Consequently, a rising interest rate should provide an inducement to reduce the quantity of money held in idle form. A falling rate should do the opposite.

A more compelling explanation presents itself, however. It is based on the notion of a "normal" rate of interest. Keynes believed that there was an interest rate which speculators regarded as normal and toward which the actual rate was expected to return.[15] The consequence of this perception becomes apparent by reviewing the relationship between bond price p_B and interest.

[13] "There is ... a necessary condition failing which the existence of a liquidity-preference for money as a means of holding wealth could not exist. This necessary condition is the existence of *uncertainty* as to the future of the rate of interest. ... Thus ... there is a risk of a loss being incurred in purchasing a long-term debt and subsequently turning it into cash, as compared with holding cash." Keynes, *The General Theory*, pp. 168–169.

[14] Ibid., pp. 171–172, 201–204.

[15] "What matters is not the *absolute* level of r [the rate of interest] but the degree of its divergence from what is considered a fairly *safe* level of r. ... If the general view as to what is a safe level of r is

(*continued*)

Bond price is the present value of the future dollar payments produced by the bond. It can be expressed as

$$p_B = \frac{R}{1+r} + \frac{R}{(1+r)^2} + \cdots + \frac{R}{(1+r)^{n-1}} + \frac{R}{(1+r)^n} + \frac{R'}{(1+r)^n}$$

R represents the dollar yield in each of n periods, the bond's life. R' represents principal, which is repayable when the bond matures. As interest rises, bond price falls, and as interest falls, bond price rises.

This inverse relationship can be made more transparent under the simplifying assumption that the bond never matures. Its life is infinite , and the repayment of principal ceases to be a consideration. p_B therefore becomes

$$p_B = JR$$

where

$$J = \frac{1}{1+r} + \frac{1}{(1+r)^2} + \frac{1}{(1+r)^3} + \cdots$$

Manipulating J gives

$$(1+r)J = 1 + \frac{1}{1+r} + \frac{1}{(1+r)^2} + \cdots$$

$$(1+r)J - J = 1$$

and

$$J = \frac{1}{r}$$

Hence

$$p_B = \frac{R}{r}$$

The price of a bond which pays a fixed dollar amount per period forever is the ratio of yield to interest. A British consol exemplifies this type of bond. Again, bond price and interest are inversely related.

At a high interest rate speculators may expect that in the future the rate will fall back toward the normal level, driving up the price of bonds. Consequently, if they bought bonds now (when the interest rate is high), they would expect to

---

unchanged, every fall in r reduces the market rate relatively to the 'safe' rate and therefore increases the risk of illiquidity. ... *Any* level of interest which is accepted with sufficient conviction as *likely* to be durable *will* be durable; subject, of course, in a changing society to fluctuations for all kinds of reasons round the expected normal. ... [The rate of interest] may fluctuate for decades about a level which is chronically too high for full employment;—particularly if it is the prevailing opinion that the rate of interest is self-adjusting, so that the level established by convention is thought to be rooted in objective grounds much stronger than convention." Ibid., pp. 201–204.

enjoy a capital gain in the future (when interest falls).[16] Their idle balances would therefore be low. At a still higher interest rate even more speculators come to believe that interest will subsequently fall. Thus even less idle money is held. As interest rises, speculators move from idle money into bonds.

The reverse applies at a low interest rate. At a low rate speculators may feel that the rate of interest will rise in the future and, consequently, that the price of bonds will fall. If they bought bonds now, they would expect to suffer a capital loss in the future. Under these circumstances their holdings of idle money would be large. At a lower interest rate, more speculators come to expect a subsequent rise, and larger money hoards result. As interest falls, speculators move from bonds into idle money.

The trap corresponds to that rate of interest r_{min} at which all speculators believe that the next change in the rate must be upward. In other words, at r_{min} there is unanimous belief among speculators that capital losses would be suffered by anyone caught holding bonds. At this rate the demand for the safe asset money becomes insatiable.[17]

This speculative demand for money $M(r)$ is added to the transactions demand, making[18]

$$Md = kpY + M(r)$$

With money supply exogenously given,

$$Ms = M_o$$

and equilibrium in the money market entails

$$M_o = kpY + M(r) \tag{1.11}$$

What effect would insertion of the speculative demand into the classical model have on equilibrium? The answer hinges upon whether or not the trap is binding. If the trap is ineffective, price and money wage are affected. Interest continues to be determined in the saving and investment section, where it maintains its earlier role. But now it also fixes the amount of speculative holdings, as Figure 1.9 depicts. Since money wage is flexible, output remains unchanged at the old full-employment level. Thus adding a speculative component to money demand in the face of a given money supply must lower price. Price falls to enable a transfer of transactions balances to the speculative hoards. In response

[16] Quite apart from the expectations about future interest rates engendered by a high current rate, a high current rate implies that bond price is presently low and thus reinforces the attractiveness of bonds. This reinforcement becomes transformed into an impediment at a low rate.

[17] "Opinion about the future of interest may be so unanimous that a small change in present rates may cause a mass movement into cash. ... [Speculative holdings] may tend to increase almost without limit in response to a reduction of r below a certain figure." Keynes, *The General Theory*, pp. 172, 203.

[18] Keynes also postulates a precautionary demand for money: balances reserved for emergencies. These, however, are merged with transactions balances, and the combination is regarded as dependent upon income. Ibid., pp. 196, 199–200.

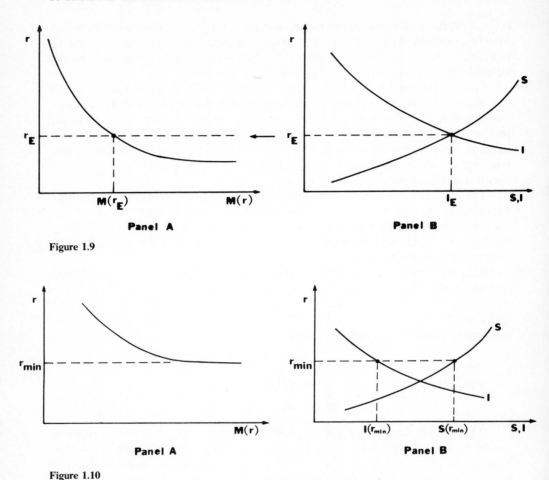

Panel A

Panel B

Figure 1.9

Panel A

Panel B

Figure 1.10

to oppose successfully

to this fall in price, money wage falls to thwart the onset of unemployment that otherwise would result if the real wage rose. Full employment persists.[19]

Seemingly, little has changed. Yet insertion of the speculative demand establishes new linkage. Unlike the situation in the pure classical paradigm, changes in the rate of interest due to shifts in either the saving or the investment schedule now impact the money section (price) and the production section (money wage). Liquidity preference provides a conduit that transmits to the rest of the system any change originating in the saving and investment section.

An effective trap makes the presence of liquidity preference devastating. Figure 1.10 shows that the interest rate is prevented from reaching its equilibrium

---

[19]Franco Modigliani, "Liquidity Preference and the Theory of Interest and Money," *Econometrica*, **12** (January 1944), pp. 70–72.

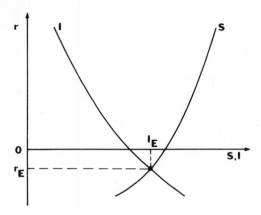

Figure 1.11

level. At the trap rate, planned saving exceeds planned investment; there is deficient aggregate demand. Output cannot be sold, inventories begin to accumulate unintentionally, and entrepreneurs eventually cut back production and employment. Unemployment develops. Any attempt by workers to preserve full employment through a reduction in money wage would prove futile, since the fundamental malady is that entrepreneurs cannot sell all the output forthcoming from the existing level of employment.

Saving and Investment

In contrast to classical doctrine, Keynes argued that both the saving and the investment schedules were quite inelastic with respect to the rate of interest.[20] This property suggests that the schedules might cause a negative equilibrium rate, as Figure 1.11 illustrates. For all positive rates, planned saving exceeds planned investment, and consequently traplike pressure pervades the economy. Aggregate demand is deficient, inventories accumulate, and eventually output and employment fall. The economy slides toward depression.[21]

---

[20] "The main conclusion suggested by experience is, I think, that the short-period influence of the rate of interest on individual spending out of a given income is secondary and relatively unimportant, except, perhaps, where unusually large changes are in question." Keynes, *The General Theory*, p. 94. The influence of interest on saving should therefore be relatively unimportant as well.

  With respect to the investment schedule, also designated the marginal efficiency of capital schedule, Keynes wrote, "When there is a change in the prospective yield of capital or in the rate of interest, the schedule of the marginal efficiency of capital will be such that the change in new investment will not be in great disproportion to the change in the former; *i.e.* moderate changes in the prospective yield of capital or in the rate of interest will not be associated with very great changes in the rate of investment." Ibid., p. 250. The marginal efficiency could become negative. Ibid., pp. 317–318, 321–322.

[21] The saving schedule depicted in Figure 1.11 claims that households have the same basic attitude toward saving whether the interest rate proves to be positive or negative. The investment function there speaks analogously about the attitude of entrepreneurs toward investing. An alternative

(*continued*)

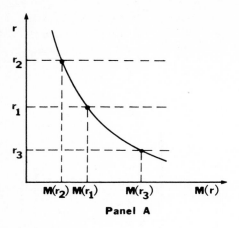

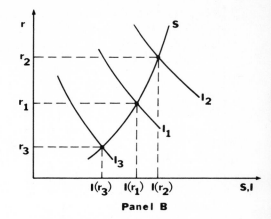

Figure 1.12

Keynes challenged the classical investment function not only regarding its elasticity but also regarding its stability. He considered the investment function to be highly volatile; it would shift upward and downward.[22] The ramifications of this phenomenon can be clearly seen by disregarding the two anomalies discussed to this point, the trap and a perverse equilibrium rate of interest. As the investment schedule shifts upward and downward, say from I_1 to I_2 to I_3 in Panel B of Figure 1.12, the interest rate rises and falls, from r_1 to r_2 to r_3. Accordingly, this rise and fall in interest causes speculative balances to fall and rise. Equilibrium in the money market [equation (1.11)] requires price to rise and fall respectively, since under a given money supply transactions balances must be altered to accommodate the pulsating speculative hoards. Furthermore, money wage must rise and fall respectively if the real wage is to remain at its full-employment equilibrium level. Full employment is still possible, but the system

---

possibility imagines that households are far less willing to save and entrepreneurs are far more willing to invest at negative rates than at positive ones. In this circumstance the saving and investment functions would exhibit kinks at zero interest. An extreme kink finds both the saving and the investment functions becoming coincident with the horizontal axis as interest tends toward zero. At negative rates, households refuse to save while entrepreneurs want to invest without bound. Neither alternative, however, amends the fundamental conclusion that the imbalance between saving and investment leads the economy into depression.

[22] "It is important to understand the dependence of the marginal efficiency of a given stock of capital on changes in expectation, because it is chiefly this dependence which renders the marginal efficiency of capital subject to the somewhat violent fluctuations which are the explanation of the Trade Cycle." Keynes, *The General Theory*, pp. 143–144. The marginal efficiency schedule is "fickle and highly unstable," reflecting in part "animal spirits— . . . a spontaneous urge to action rather than inaction." Ibid., pp. 161, 204.

hardly resembles the tranquility envisioned by the classics. Interest, price, and money wage are all fluctuating together in response to a vibrating investment schedule. Rising price and money wage accompany rising interest; falling price and money wage accompany falling interest.[23]

Money Wage

Now comes the *coup de grace*. As the investment schedule shifts up and down, interest shifts up and down, price shifts up and down, and money wage shifts up and down. Full employment can be maintained, but only if money wage fluctuates in concert with price. Keynes, however, contends that money wage does not exhibit the necessary flexibility; instead, he argues, it is essentially rigid. While it might respond somewhat to economic conditions, it might *not* adjust sufficiently to preserve full employment before a fluctuating investment schedule.[24]

The Triple Threat and Its Policy Implications

Keynes identifies three separate and distinct sources of unemployment. First, an effective liquidity trap would activate depressionary forces by creating a deficiency of planned investment relative to planned saving. Second, a perverse equilibrium interest rate, a possibility generated by the inelasticity of saving and investment with respect to interest, would do the same. Third, a rigid money wage would prevent the real wage from adjusting to preserve a full-employment equilibrium. Each possibility, taken alone, poses a threat to full employment; with all three possibilities working simultaneously, persistent full employment becomes quite doubtful.

The propositions championed by Keynes lead to policy implications much different in spirit from those of the classics. Full employment is no longer a matter of course. It is more a matter of chance, and therefore policy assumes a

---

[23] Pulsations in price and money wage caused by a vibrating investment curve might be intensified if the liquidity preference schedule also vibrated. The position of that schedule reflects a "given state of expectations," and consequently modifications in the expectations held by speculators would move it, perhaps in a jerky fashion. "Changes in the liquidity function itself, due to a change in the news which causes revision of expectations, will often be discontinuous." Ibid., pp. 198, 202. A movement in only the liquidity preference schedule would likewise alter price and money wage if full employment were to be preserved.

[24] "This struggle [for money-wages] is likely, as employment increases, to be intensified in each individual case both because the bargaining position of the worker is improved and because the diminished marginal utility of his wage and his improved financial margin make him readier to run risks. Yet ... these motives will operate within limits, and workers will not seek a much greater money-wage when employment improves or allow a very great reduction rather than suffer any unemployment at all. ... Experience shows that some such psychological law must actually hold." Ibid., p. 253.

vital role unimaginable in the classical framework. Furthermore, as is suggested by an effective trap, monetary policy on occasion can be totally inadequate for propelling the economy toward full employment. Under a binding trap, all money injected into the economy becomes absorbed into the speculative hoards without stimulating output and employment. Keynesian economics thus reveals the patent need for utilizing an additional type of policy, one which directly affects aggregate demand. It is fiscal policy, its instruments being government expenditures and taxes.

1.4 FROM THE RUINS

Having rejected the classical model, Keynes offered a substitute which recognized that the natural functioning of the economy could result in prolonged unemployment. The new model embraced liquidity preference and other unorthodox postulates, including a different hypothesis about consumption.

In Keynes' view, consumption depends upon income; more precisely, real consumption is a function of real income. Furthermore, the function is stable. While other factors may affect consumption, they serve in a secondary capacity, and hence the function tends to remain stationary. The marginal propensity to consume, which refers to the change in consumption due to a small change in income, lies between zero and unity. Some but not all of an increase in income would be consumed; so mandates a fundamental psychological law. Differently stated, the response of consumers to income changes has a psychological basis. The marginal propensity, in addition to ranging between zero and unity, may decline as income rises. Moreover, the average propensity to consume, which identifies the ratio of consumption to income, falls as income rises. This property implies that the consumption function has a positive intercept. Figure 1.13 offers a curvilinear locus portraying these characteristics of the consumption function; the dashed line represents a linear approximation.

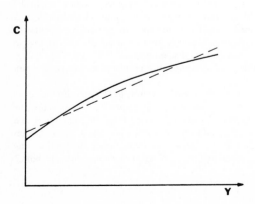

Figure 1.13

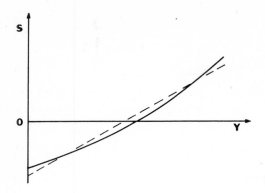

Figure 1.14

Since saving is the complement of consumption, it too must be principally determined by income; interest, as Figure 1.11 illustrates, does not constitute its main determinant. Other properties of the saving function must also be linked to those of the consumption function. Figure 1.14 displays the curvilinear and linear saving schedules that correspond to the consumption schedules appearing in Figure 1.13.[25]

The complete Keynesian system can be conveniently summarized in equation form.[26]

[25] The following quotations are Keynes' specific statements about the nature of the consumption function. The page numbers in parentheses cite *The General Theory*.

On the included variables (p. 90): "We will therefore define what we shall call *the propensity to consume* as the functional relationship χ between Y_w, a given level of income in terms of wage-units, and C_w the expenditure on consumption [in wage-units] out of that level of income, so that $C_w = \chi(Y_w)$." Also (p. 91): "Consumption... is obviously much more a function of... *real* income than of money-income."

On the stability of the function (pp. 95–96): "We are left therefore, with the conclusion that in a given situation the propensity to consume may be considered a fairly stable function, provided that we have eliminated changes in the wage-unit in terms of money. Windfall changes in capital-values will be capable of changing the propensity to consume, and substantial changes in the rate of interest and in fiscal policy may make some difference; but the other objective factors which might affect it... are not likely to be important in ordinary circumstances." Also relevant here is the first quotation listed in footnote 20 of this chapter.

On the marginal propensity to consume (p. 96): "The fundamental psychological law... is that men are disposed, as a rule and on the average, to increase their consumption as their income increases, but not by as much as the increase in their income. That is to say,... dC_w/dY_w is positive and less than unity." Further (p. 120): "The marginal propensity to consume is not constant for all levels of employment, and it is probable that there will be, as a rule, a tendency for it to diminish as employment increases; when real income increases, that is to say, the community will wish to consume a gradually diminishing proportion of it."

On the average propensity to consume (p. 97): "These reasons will lead, as a rule, to a greater *proportion* of income being saved as real income increases."

[26] Similar summaries appear in Ackley, *Macroeconomic Theory*, p. 403; R. G. D. Allen, *Macro-Economic Theory: A Mathematical Treatment* (New York: St. Martin's Press, Inc., 1968), p. 127; Michael K. Evans, *Macroeconomic Activity: Theory, Forecasting, and Control* (New York: Harper & Row, Publishers, Incorporated, 1969), p. 347; Hicks, "Mr. Keynes," p. 153; and Klein, *The Keynesian Revolution*, pp. 199–200.

Production section

$$Y = f(L, K_o) \tag{1.12}$$

$$Ld = Ld(w^*) \tag{1.13}$$

$$w = w_o \tag{1.14}$$

Money section

$$Md = kpY + M(r) \tag{1.15}$$

$$Ms = M_o \tag{1.16}$$

$$Md = Ms \tag{1.17}$$

Saving and investment section

$$S = S(Y) \tag{1.18}$$

$$I = I(r) \tag{1.19}$$

$$I = S \tag{1.20}$$

Aggregate production function (1.12), with its fixed stock of capital, stands as a reminder that the model has a short-run posture. Equation (1.14) expresses the view that the money wage is basically rigid; there it remains constant at the level w_o. Noticeably absent from the production section is the labor supply relation (1.5). As the economy converges to its equilibrium solution, it may be forced to sacrifice that curve. In other words, while the solution dictates that the economy stay "on" both the labor demand curve and the production function, it may require the labor supply schedule to remain unsatisfied—precisely the meaning of unemployment. Hence its omission.

Money demand, equation (1.15), consists of transactions and speculative components. However, under a binding trap the speculative component dominates, thereby in effect reducing money demand to a function of interest alone.[27] Saving equation (1.18), mirroring the consumption function, concentrates only on income; it ignores secondary factors. Investment schedule (1.19) contains the same argument as the classical twin, but it is appreciably less elastic and more volatile than its predecessor. Finally, equilibrium condition (1.20) represents, in disguised form, the equality between aggregate demand and supply.

In the classical system output is determined by technical considerations, such as the height of the production function and the position of the labor supply

---

[27]Hicks, "Mr. Keynes," pp. 152–153.

curve. In the Keynesian system, by contrast, output is determined by aggregate demand. Supply accommodates, rather than creates, demand.[28] Discussion of the Keynesian legacy continues in Chapter 2.

[28] Keynesian policies for controlling aggregate demand failed to cure the later economic ailment of stagflation: jointly high rates of unemployment and inflation. This failure and an increasing awareness, sharpened by an interruption of the international flow of oil, that supply elements crucially affect macro performance gave birth to a school of thought which asserts that policy should address the supplies of the factors of production. Supply-side economics looks at the marginal tax rates underlying supply and at the consequences which policy action has for a distant future. In one sense, then, Keynesian demand-side economics and contemporary supply-side economics differ in their time horizons, the short run versus the long run, respectively. Their policy prescriptions, however, could be merged to advantage. For discussion of these and other aspects of supply-side economics, see Michael J. Boskin, "Some Issues in 'Supply-Side' Economics" (mimeograph, Stanford University, April 1980), pp. 1–2.7, 6.1. See also *The Wall Street Journal* articles by Lindley H. Clark, Jr., "Long-Term Economics," April 22, 1980, p. 24; Martin Feldstein, "Inflation and Supply Side Economics," May 20, 1980, p. 22; Walter W. Heller, "Can We Afford the Costs of Kemp-Roth?" February 10, 1981, p. 26; Irving Kristol, "Of Economics and 'Eco-Mania,'" September 19, 1980, p. 28; Paul Craig Roberts, "Supply-Side Economics," February 28, 1980, p. 24; and Herbert Stein, "Some 'Supply-Side' Propositions," March 19, 1980, p. 24.

CHAPTER
TWO

ANATOMY OF A STATIC KEYNESIAN
MACRO SYSTEM

Now that the fundamental precepts of Keynesian economics have been reviewed, attention turns to a simple model based on them. The model is static. It focuses on equilibrium positions, although it does permit some inferences about disequilibrium states. Its equations exclude lagged terms, and each assumes a linear form.[1]

2.1 THE MODEL STRUCTURE

Consumption follows the rule

$$C_t = C_o + cYd_t \tag{2.1}$$

C_t denotes real consumption at time t, and Yd_t denotes real disposable income at

[1] This system closely resembles that of Warren L. Smith and Ronald L. Teigen, eds., *Readings in Money, National Income, and Stabilization Policy*, rev. ed. (Homewood, Ill.: Richard D. Irwin, Inc., ©1970), pp. 8–25. To broaden the implications, however, it includes a slight reformulation involving commodity price introduced in James H. Gapinski, "A Comparison of the Impact Multipliers of the Truncated vs. the Original Forecasting Model and the Effect of a Restricted Output Supply on These Multipliers" (mimeograph, State University of New York at Buffalo, September 1967), p. 14. A further reformulation undertaken in Section 2.6 below renders the model a generalization of the one considered by William E. Mitchell, John H. Hand, and Ingo Walter, *Exercises in Macroeconomics: Development of Concepts* (New York: McGraw-Hill Book Company, 1973), p. 273.

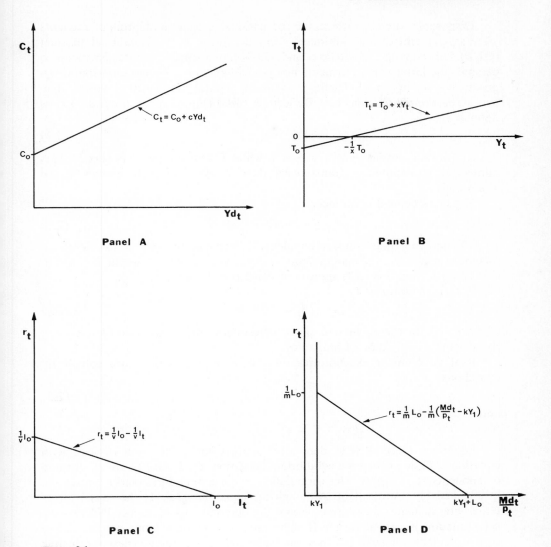

Figure 2.1

time t. C_0 represents exogenous, or autonomous, consumption: that portion of consumption determined outside the system by a *deus ex machina*. c denotes the marginal propensity to consume out of disposable income, $0 < c < 1$, and cYd_t represents that portion of consumption induced by income. C_t is endogenous; it constitutes an unknown to be determined within the system. Panel A of Figure 2.1 portrays this consumption function.[2]

---

[2] The model does not require time subscripts, but their use serves to facilitate comparisons with the dynamic models which follow later.

Disposable income surfaces in the national income and product accounts after several entries are subtracted from or added to gross national product (GNP). Subtractions include taxes and additions encompass transfer payments to persons, the latter being payments not associated with a current contribution to productive activity. The benefits from social security and unemployment compensation exemplify transfers. Reflecting this computational process, Yd_t is defined as

$$Yd_t = Y_t - T_t \tag{2.2}$$

Y_t denotes total output (GNP) at time t, while T_t denotes net taxes (tax receipts minus transfer payments). Transfers can thus be viewed as negative taxes. Y_t and T_t are reals.

Net taxes depend upon income:

$$T_t = T_o + xY_t \tag{2.3}$$

$T_o < 0$, implying that transfer payments exceed tax receipts at low levels of income. x symbolizes the marginal propensity to tax out of total output, $0 < x < 1$. The graph of equation (2.3) appears in Panel B of Figure 2.1.

For real investment I_t,

$$I_t = I_o - vr_t \tag{2.4}$$

where $v > 0$. In the Keynesian spirit, investment falls as the rate of interest r_t rises.[3] Panel C of Figure 2.1 illustrates.

Real government expenditures on goods and services G_t are completely exogenous

$$G_t = G_o \tag{2.5}$$

and

$$Y_t = C_t + I_t + G_t \tag{2.6}$$

Equations (2.1) to (2.6) define the market for goods and services, with equation (2.6) describing the equilibrium condition. C_t, I_t, and G_t are all demand components; Y_t is supply. This formulation of the commodities market presents it in a noticeably uneven light. Although the equations identify the causal forces underlying demand, they totally ignore the determinants of supply. No production function is provided, nor is there any clue about a labor market. These supply elements do exist, but they can be omitted under the Keynesian principle that supply accommodates demand in a slack economy. According to equations (2.1) to (2.6), demand drives the commodities market and supply adjusts to the extent necessary to satisfy that demand.

In addition to the commodities market, a money market exists, and the item exchanged there is paper dollars. Money demand observes the formula

$$\frac{Md_t}{p_t} = kY_t + (L_o - mr_t) \tag{2.7}$$

where $k > 0$ and $m > 0$. Md_t denotes the number of paper dollars demanded.

---

[3] The volatility of the investment schedule discussed by Keynes and noted in Section 1.3 could be incorporated into equation (2.4) by presuming that autonomous investment I_o fluctuates.

These dollars might be regarded as having uniform denomination; for example, they might all be \$1 bills. p_t denotes the price of goods and services in the system. Although price could be made endogenous, this model takes it as exogenous. There is no price-determining equation. Md_t/p_t, which measures the demand for paper dollars in terms of the goods and services exchanged, can be viewed as the quantity of real balances demanded. kY_t represents real transactions demand. $L_0 - mr_t$ notates real speculative demand, and because the speculative demand is linear, a liquidity trap does not arise. Money demand is free from money illusion. A change in price has no effect on the quantity of *real* balances demanded; instead, the demand for nominal balances changes proportionally.[4] Panel D of Figure 2.1 portrays the total demand for money at some income level Y_1.

The number of paper dollars supplied Ms_t is exogenously determined, and consequently

$$\frac{\mathrm{Ms}_t}{p_t} = \frac{M_o}{p_t} \tag{2.8}$$

where Ms_t/p_t represents real supply. For equilibrium in the money market,

$$\frac{\mathrm{Ms}_t}{p_t} = \frac{\mathrm{Md}_t}{p_t} \tag{2.9}$$

In sum, then, the model contains seven endogenous variables (C_t, Yd_t, Y_t, T_t, I_t, r_t, and Md_t), seven exogenous variables (C_o, T_o, I_o, G_t, p_t, L_o, and Ms_t), and five parameters (c, x, v, k, and m). Parameters are constants having no specific, preassigned values.

Interest is the price of credit, and its presence in the model means that a debt instrument such as a bond circulates along with commodities and money. Yet no equations delineate the bond market. Rather, that market remains suppressed. The rationale for this suppression lies in Walras' law, which states that if n markets exist, $n - 1$ of which are in equilibrium, then the nth market must also be in equilibrium. The model, being static, focuses on equilibria, and for statements about equilibria an explicit treatment of the bond market proves unnecessary. It should be recognized, however, that the market chosen for exclusion is arbitrary. Commodities could be deleted with attention given to money and bonds, and the same conclusions would be reached.[5]

2.2 AMPLIFYING THE EQUILIBRIUM RELATIONSHIPS

The nine-equation model, albeit simple in structure, is somewhat clumsy to manipulate when retained in full-blown form. It can be written, however, far

---

[4] Further comment regarding the absence or presence of money illusion in the demand for money is offered by Don Patinkin, *Money, Interest, and Prices*, 2d ed. (New York: Harper & Row, Publishers, Incorporated, 1965), p. 254. A money demand equation similar to (2.7) can be found in Michael K. Evans, *Macroeconomic Activity: Theory, Forecasting, and Control* (New York: Harper & Row, Publishers, Incorporated, 1969), p. 347.

[5] Patinkin, *Money*, pp. 35–37.

more compactly, and in the process relationships hidden by the original formulation become apparent.

Equation (2.6) expresses the equilibrium condition for commodities. All other equations in the commodities market elaborate various elements of (2.6), and hence equations (2.1) to (2.5) naturally substitute into (2.6). The transformed equation still retains its equilibrium character, but it explicitly summarizes all relationships in the commodities market. To produce this single summary equation, first insert (2.2) and (2.3) into (2.1) and obtain

$$C_t = C_o - cT_o + c(1 - x)Y_t \qquad (2.1a)$$

$c(1 - x)$ signifies the marginal propensity to consume out of GNP. Since $0 < 1 - x < 1$, this propensity must be smaller than the propensity applicable to disposable income. The explanation, of course, is that as Y_t changes by one unit, Yd_t responds by less than one unit because taxes absorb part of the Y_t change. Yd_t adjusts by $1 - x$ units.

Substituting (2.1a), (2.4), and (2.5) into (2.6) gives

$$Y_t = C_o - cT_o + c(1 - x)Y_t + I_o - vr_t + G_o \qquad (2.6a)$$

This version of the equilibrium condition embodies all relationships in the commodities market. Rewriting it with r_t expressed in terms of Y_t yields

$$r_t = \frac{1}{v}(C_o + I_o + G_o - cT_o) + \frac{1}{v}\left[c(1 - x) - 1\right]Y_t \qquad (2.10)$$

Equation (2.10), like (2.6a), indicates the various combinations of interest and income needed to maintain equilibrium in the commodities market. Convention designates (2.10) "the IS equation" since commodity equilibrium entails the equality of investment and saving. That equality can be easily demonstrated.

In equilibrium,

$$Y_t = C_t + I_t + G_t$$

But from (2.2),

$$Yd_t + T_t = C_t + I_t + G_t$$

After rearrangement,

$$I_t = (Yd_t - C_t) + (T_t - G_t)$$

The difference between disposable income and consumption is personal saving S_t (S_t being real). Thus

$$I_t = S_t + (T_t - G_t) \qquad (2.11)$$

$T_t - G_t$ constitutes government surplus, or government saving. Hence the right-hand side of (2.11) represents total saving. In equilibrium, investment equals saving.

Incidentally, the equation for private saving can be readily deduced.

$$S_t = Yd_t - C_t$$

and from (2.1)

$$S_t = -C_o + (1 - c)Yd_t$$

which shows that the marginal propensity to save out of disposable income is $1 - c$. By using (2.2) and (2.3),

$$S_t = -C_o - (1 - c)T_o + (1 - c)(1 - x)Y_t \tag{2.12}$$

As with the propensity to consume, the marginal propensity to save out of GNP is smaller than the propensity applicable to disposable income. The earlier explanation again applies.

Paralleling the case for commodities, the relationships in the money market collapse into a single equation. Substituting (2.7) and (2.8) into (2.9) produces

$$\frac{M_o}{p_t} = kY_t + (L_o - mr_t)$$

or equivalently

$$r_t = -\frac{1}{m}\left(\frac{M_o}{p_t} - L_o\right) + \frac{k}{m}Y_t \tag{2.13}$$

Equation (2.13) provides a comprehensive restatement of the equilibrium condition for the money market. It gives the various combinations of interest and income needed to maintain equilibrium in that market. Since the traditional symbols for money demand and money supply are L and M, respectively, (2.13) might be dubbed "the LM equation."

The IS and LM expressions, (2.10) and (2.13), each contain two endogenous variables, Y_t and r_t. Y_t can be determined by combining the two equations to eliminate r_t:

$$\frac{1}{v}(C_o + I_o + G_o - cT_o) + \frac{1}{v}\left[c(1 - x) - 1\right]Y_t = -\frac{1}{m}\left(\frac{M_o}{p_t} - L_o\right) + \frac{k}{m}Y_t$$

which eventually simplifies to

$$Y_t = \frac{C_o + I_o + G_o - cT_o + (v/m)(M_o/p_t - L_o)}{1 - c(1 - x) + vk/m} \tag{2.14}$$

From (2.13) and (2.14), r_t becomes

$$r_t = \frac{(k/m)(C_o + I_o + G_o - cT_o) - (1/m)\left[1 - c(1 - x)\right](M_o/p_t - L_o)}{1 - c(1 - x) + vk/m}$$

$$\tag{2.15}$$

Expressions (2.14) and (2.15) each constitute a reduced-form equation, which may be defined generally as an equation that states a single endogenous variable solely in terms of predetermined quantities consisting of parameters, exogenous variables, and lagged endogenous variables. This last category, however, remains empty here. With Y_t and r_t known, all other endogenous variables can be determined; more precisely, from (2.14) and (2.15), reduced-form equations for the remaining endogenous variables come into view.

Predetermined variables entering a reduced-form equation linearly have coefficients which represent multipliers.[6] To demonstrate, let G_t change from G_o to $G_o + \Delta G_o$—Δ meaning "change in"—and let ΔG_o be either positive or negative. Then the level of income corresponding to the new level of government expenditures is

$$Y'_t = \frac{C_o + I_o + G_o - cT_o + (v/m)(M_o/p_t - L_o)}{1 - c(1 - x) + vk/m} + \frac{1}{1 - c(1 - x) + vk/m}\Delta G_o$$

Subtracting Y_t from Y'_t yields

$$Y'_t - Y_t = \Delta Y_t = \frac{1}{1 - c(1 - x) + vk/m}\Delta G_o$$

The coefficient of G_o in reduced-form equation (2.14) is that multiplier which indicates the effect of a change in government expenditures on equilibrium income. It might be called the equilibrium government expenditures multiplier on income. Its value is unaffected by the size of the expenditure change.

Calculating multipliers for the exogenous price variable, which enters the reduced forms nonlinearly, follows the same basic pattern but results in a slightly more awkward expression. For example, a change in price from p_t to $p_t + \Delta p_t$ changes income by

$$\Delta Y_t = \frac{v/m}{1 - c(1 - x) + vk/m}M_o\left[\frac{1}{p_t + \Delta p_t} - \frac{1}{p_t}\right]$$

with the bracketed expression converting to $-\{1/[p_t(p_t + \Delta p_t)]\}\Delta p_t$. The equilibrium price multiplier on income becomes $-(v/m)[1 - c(1 - x) + vk/m]^{-1}M_o N$, $N = [p_t(p_t + \Delta p_t)]^{-1}$. Because of the nonlinearity associated with price, all price multipliers depend upon the magnitude of the price change. These multipliers, however, owe their existence to the model's naiveté: A more sophisticated system which treats price as endogenous would instead contain multipliers *on* price.

Scrutiny of equation (2.14) reveals the presence of seven equilibrium multipliers on income. Similarly, there are seven for interest and for each of the other five endogenous variables. In all, then, the system contains 49 multipliers, which appear in Table 2.1. Any particular entry there gives the multiplier relating the exogenous change identified at the top of the corresponding column to the endogenous change identified at the left of the corresponding row. For convenience,[7] $h = 1 - c(1 - x) + vk/m$.

---

[6] The notion of multiplier was introduced not by Keynes but by R. F. Kahn in "The Relation of Home Investment to Unemployment," *Economic Journal*, **41** (June 1931), pp. 173, 182–190. Keynes acknowledges this contribution in John Maynard Keynes, *The General Theory of Employment, Interest, and Money* (New York: Harcourt, Brace and World, Inc., 1936), pp. 113–116.

[7] Endogenous variables constructed from the ones explicitly contained in the model and exemplified by personal saving also command multipliers. Those multipliers are withheld.

Table 2.1 Equilibrium multipliers embedded in the static macro model, (2.1) to (2.9)

	ΔC_o	ΔI_o	ΔG_o	ΔT_o	ΔM_o	ΔL_o	Δp_t
ΔC_t	$1 + \dfrac{c(1-x)}{h}$	$\dfrac{c(1-x)}{h}$	$\dfrac{c(1-x)}{h}$	$-c\left[1 + \dfrac{c(1-x)}{h}\right]$	$\dfrac{vc(1-x)}{mh}\dfrac{1}{p_t}$	$-\dfrac{vc(1-x)}{mh}$	$-\dfrac{vc(1-x)}{mh}M_oN$
ΔI_t	$-\dfrac{vk}{mh}$	$1 - \dfrac{vk}{mh}$	$-\dfrac{vk}{mh}$	$\dfrac{vkc}{mh}$	$\dfrac{v[1-c(1-x)]}{mh}\dfrac{1}{p_t}$	$-\dfrac{v[1-c(1-x)]}{mh}$	$-\dfrac{v[1-c(1-x)]}{mh}M_oN$
ΔT_t	$\dfrac{x}{h}$	$\dfrac{x}{h}$	$\dfrac{x}{h}$	$1 - \dfrac{cx}{h}$	$\dfrac{vx}{mh}\dfrac{1}{p_t}$	$-\dfrac{vx}{mh}$	$-\dfrac{vx}{mh}M_oN$
ΔYd_t	$\dfrac{1-x}{h}$	$\dfrac{1-x}{h}$	$\dfrac{1-x}{h}$	$-\left[1 + \dfrac{c(1-x)}{h}\right]$	$\dfrac{v(1-x)}{mh}\dfrac{1}{p_t}$	$-\dfrac{v(1-x)}{mh}$	$-\dfrac{v(1-x)}{mh}M_oN$
ΔY_t	$\dfrac{1}{h}$	$\dfrac{1}{h}$	$\dfrac{1}{h}$	$-\dfrac{c}{h}$	$\dfrac{v}{mh}\dfrac{1}{p_t}$	$-\dfrac{v}{mh}$	$-\dfrac{v}{mh}M_oN$
Δr_t	$\dfrac{k}{mh}$	$\dfrac{k}{mh}$	$\dfrac{k}{mh}$	$-\dfrac{kc}{mh}$	$-\dfrac{1-c(1-x)}{mh}\dfrac{1}{p_t}$	$\dfrac{1-c(1-x)}{mh}$	$\dfrac{1-c(1-x)}{mh}M_oN$
ΔMd_t	0	0	0	0	1	0	0

Why does, say, C_o exert a multiplier effect on T_t and I_t even though it does not enter the structural equations for those variables [(2.3) and (2.4)]? The answer is that a change in C_o means a change in demand, which in turn influences supply Y_t. A movement in Y_t alters the transactions demand for money, and with a given money supply, money market equilibrium requires that the speculative demand be amended to exactly offset the modified transactions demand. This alteration in speculative demand proceeds through interest rate adjustments. A change in C_o, therefore, begets changes in Y_t and r_t, thereby affecting T_t and I_t. These multipliers arise because of the induced effects of a change in C_o.

The exactly offsetting changes between transactions and speculative demands necessary to preserve money market equilibrium in the face of a fixed money supply explain the zero entries posted for the multipliers on Md_t. When the money supply remains fixed, money market equilibrium insists that total money demand stand fixed as well: changes in, say, C_o can have no influence on Md_t, and therefore there are zeros. When the money supply does change, however, equilibrium insists that total money demand match that change dollar for dollar, and the multiplier on Md_t must then be unity. Changes in money demand must precisely equal those in money supply, and consequently the multipliers on Md_t can manifest no induced effects. They exhibit only autonomous effects.

Some multipliers mirror both autonomous and induced effects; the equilibrium consumption multiplier on consumption is an example. A one-unit change in C_o autonomously changes C_t by one unit, which must be added to the induced response propagated by the C_o change. The same is true for the investment multiplier on investment and the tax multiplier on taxes. In those cases, however, the induced effects counteract the autonomous effects. An increase in I_o increases Y_t and hence r_t to maintain a constant money demand. The higher r_t, however, causes some reduction in investment, forcing the investment multiplier on investment below unity. An increase in T_o lowers income; this induced effect makes the "own" multiplier less than unity.

Government expenditures and taxes have multipliers which typically carry opposite signs in accordance with the opposite functions of those variables. Government expenditures act as an injection into the system; taxes serve as a leakage. Since the reduced-form equations are linear in the policy variables G_o, T_o, and M_o, the total effect of any particular policy package can be determined by adding the multiplier effects of the separate policies. One package, known as "balanced budget policy," calls for equal changes in government expenditures and taxes ($\Delta G_o = \Delta T_o$). Thus

$$\Delta Y_t = \frac{1}{h}\Delta G_o - \frac{c}{h}\Delta T_o = \frac{1-c}{h}\Delta G_o$$

$(1-c)/h$ signifies the balanced budget multiplier. It is positive and, except for trivial possibilities like $v = x = 0$, less than 1. Balanced budget policy is therefore expansionary. A rise in government spending by a unit initially boosts total spending by that amount. A tax increase of a unit, however, initially causes total spending to fall by less than a unit because consumers pay part of the tax increase

Table 2.2 Estimated values of the equilibrium multipliers

	ΔC_o	ΔI_o	ΔG_o	ΔT_o	ΔM_o	ΔL_o	Δp_t
ΔC_t	2.169	1.169	1.169	−1.735	3.102	−2.389	−413.839N
ΔI_t	−.271	.729	−.271	.217	1.934	−1.489	−257.977N
ΔT_t	.436	.436	.436	.651	1.158	−.892	−154.518N
ΔYd_t	1.461	1.461	1.461	−2.169	3.878	−2.986	−517.298N
ΔY_t	1.897	1.897	1.897	−1.518	5.036	−3.878	−671.816N
Δr_t	.053	.053	.053	−.042	−.377	.290	50.288N
ΔMd_t	.000	.000	.000	.000	1.000	.000	.000

by reducing saving. Consequently, aggregate demand expands. The reverse also holds. For an expenditure and tax policy to have no effect on income, taxes must change more than expenditures; namely,[8] $\Delta T_o = (1/c)\Delta G_o$.

All M_o multipliers, except that on Md_t, contain the price level—more precisely, $1/p_t$. These multipliers relate nominals to reals, and to do so, they must include a "conversion factor." $1/p_t$ indicates the bundles of goods and services which one paper dollar can buy; it is the relative price of nominal money holdings.[9]

Table 2.2 presents estimates for the multipliers. The individual parameter values comprising the multipliers were obtained by fitting the model to recent annual data for the United States, with the following results.

$$C_t = 6.90 + .80Yd_t \tag{2.16}$$

$$T_t = -13.80 + .23Y_t \tag{2.17}$$

$$I_t = 211.75 - 5.13r_t \tag{2.18}$$

$$\frac{Md_t}{p_t} = .07Y_t + (176.78 - 2.51r_t) \tag{2.19}$$

Values for the exogenous variables M_o and p_t were set at the sample means; namely,[10] $M_o = 173.25$ and $p_t = .77$.

---

[8]If the budget begins in balance, with $G_t = T_t$, enacting a balanced budget policy $\Delta G_o = \Delta T_o$ does not preserve that balance. Equal increases result in a budget surplus, while equal decreases create a deficit. An initial balance survives when $\Delta T_o = [(h - x)/(h - cx)]\Delta G_o$. Since $1/c > (h - x)/(h - cx)$, an expenditure and tax policy which is neutral on income becomes surplus-producing for increases in the policy variables and deficit-producing for decreases.

[9]Patinkin, *Money*, p. 28.

[10]The estimation process attempted to capture the spirit of the model. Definitions for the data series read as follows.

C_t: real personal consumption expenditures on durables, nondurables, and services
Y_t: real GNP
T_t: real federal, state, and local government tax receipts net of transfer payments and of federal grants-in-aid to states and localities   (*continued*)

The table reports a government expenditures multiplier on income of 1.897 and a corresponding tax multiplier of -1.518. These combine to make the balanced budget multiplier .379. Monetary policy gives rise to a stronger effect on income than does fiscal policy. Even apart from the boost imparted by price ($p_t < 1$), the money multiplier on income exceeds the expenditures multiplier by a factor of two. Since monetary policy influences income through adjustment in investment induced by interest rate changes, the interest sensitivity of investment and money demand crucially affects the money multiplier. In the present case, that sensitivity renders $v/m = 2.04$. The price multipliers are large, reflecting the size of M_o. As established in Chapter 1, price and interest move in the same direction.[11]

The values assigned to the parameters and variables in equations (2.16) to (2.19), joined by a G_o of 250, produce from the reduced-form equations the

---

Yd_t: $Y_t - T_t$
I_t: real gross private domestic investment
r_t: yield on Moody's corporate bonds, industrials
$Md_t (= M_o)$: currency plus demand deposits
p_t: implicit price deflator for GNP (1.00 in 1972)

All dollar magnitudes were expressed in billions, and the real variables emerged by deflating the corresponding nominal series with p_t. An annual time scale prevailed with ordinary least squares providing all estimates. The sample initially covered the period 1950–1975, but because of sign problems, (only) the investment equation was reestimated over the period 1968–1975. The likelihood of specification biases and the modest intention of the experiment suggested that an appeal to a more advanced regression methodology should be avoided. Those same reasons urged omitting statistics of the equations' econometric performance. A brief review of ordinary least squares and of related econometrics appears in Section 13 of Appendix A.

Averages for M_o and p_t apply to the 1950–1975 period.

[11]An experiment involving money illusion in the speculative demand deserves brief mention. The money demand equation (2.7) is respecified as

$$\frac{Md_t}{p_t} = kY_t + \left(\frac{L'_o}{p_t} - mr_t \right)$$

which, in contrast to (2.7), says that a price change alters the demand for real speculative balances. Estimation of this equation observes the ordinary least-squares rule and uses annual data. To avoid perverse signs, it addresses the abbreviated period 1968–1975, giving

$$\frac{Md_t}{p_t} = .16Y_t + \left(\frac{68.23}{p_t} - 1.44r_t \right)$$

The revised policy multiplier expressions relevant to income read $\Delta Y_t = 1.048\Delta G_o$, $\Delta Y_t = -.839\Delta T_o$, and $\Delta Y_t = 4.850\Delta M_o$, with $p_t = .77$. Fiscal policy has become feeble, losing most of its induced effects; monetary policy, however, remains virtually uncompromised.

This experiment demonstrates a principal difficulty faced by policy makers. Although responsible policies cannot be developed without information about multipliers, knowledge of their true values lies beyond reach. Information which does exist takes the form of estimates, but these are affected by theoretical design, sample period, and a host of other factors. Policy decisions necessarily entail uncertainty.

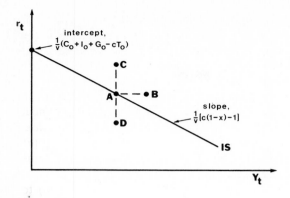

Figure 2.2

equilibrium levels for all endogenous variables.[12] Specifically, $C_t = 693.75$, $Yd_t = 858.56$, $T_t = 238.53$, $I_t = 153.34$, $Y_t = 1097.09$, $r_t = 11.39$, and $Md_t = 173.25$.

2.3 DIAGRAMING THE INTERRELATIONSHIPS

Additional insight into the workings of the model can be gained from graphs of the IS and LM equations. Figure 2.2 presents the IS locus. For points along the line, $Y_t = C_t + I_t + G_t$; equivalently, investment equals saving as demonstrated earlier.

The IS locus displays a negative slope. Why? The answer can be found with the aid of a slightly elaborated version of equation (2.11):

$$I(r_t) = S(Y_t) + [T(Y_t) - G_t] \qquad (2.11a)$$

As is evident from equations (2.3) and (2.12), private and government saving both rise when income increases. Consequently, total saving must rise also. Maintenance of equilibrium in the commodities market therefore dictates that investment rise to meet the higher saving level. Since investment depends negatively on interest, this adjustment occurs only if interest falls. *Voilà*, a negatively sloped IS curve!

The explanation involving equation (2.6) proceeds in a similarly straightforward fashion. As income increases by one unit, consumption demand rises by only c units, and thus additional commodity demand is needed to perpetuate

[12]$G_o = 250$ affords computational convenience and approximates the mean (249.76) of real federal, state, and local government purchases of goods and services pertinent to the period 1968–1975.

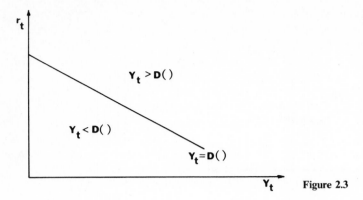

Figure 2.3

equilibrium. Interest must fall to permit that added demand to materialize from investment.

Equilibrium lies along the IS curve. What, then, is the condition of the commodities market for points off IS? Consider first points above the line, in particular point B compared with A in Figure 2.2. The same interest rate applies to both. When income increases from its equilibrium level at A, supply increases accordingly. As already noted, however, consumption demand changes by a smaller amount, precisely $c(1 - x)\Delta Y_t$. Since interest remains unchanged, investment is the same at B and at A; so are government expenditures, which do not respond to income or interest changes. Thus a movement from A to B increases supply Y_t more than demand $C_t + I_t + G_t$. Excess supply of commodities exists for points above IS.

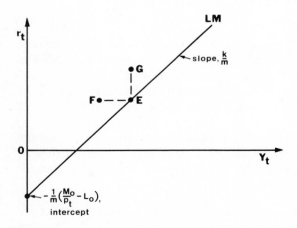

Figure 2.4

An identical conclusion, of course, ensues if the comparison involves points A and C. Both have the same supply of commodities and hence the same level of consumption, C_t. Moreover, G_t is the same. But the higher interest at point C forces I_t to fall relative to its value at A. Although Y_t, C_t, and G_t each bear identical values at both points, I_t is smaller at point C, leading to excess supply.

A converse argument concludes that there is excess demand for commodities below IS. Y_t, C_t, and G_t are the same for points A and D, but since lower interest prevails at D, investment must be greater there: hence excess demand. Figure 2.3 summarizes the three states; $D(Y_t, r_t) = C_t + I_t + G_t$.

Figure 2.4 portrays the LM equation. LM exhibits a positive slope, because as income increases, the transactions demand increases. But with a fixed supply of money, the additional transactions dollars must be drawn from speculative hoards. For this swap to occur, interest must rise.

Along the LM curve there is equilibrium in the money market, $M_o/p_t = kY_t + (L_o - mr_t)$. Above the line there is excess money supply. Points E and F, having the same interest rate, have the same speculative demand. But with Y_t lower at F, transactions demand, and therefore total demand, is less there than at E. A given supply of money applies to both points, and consequently excess supply arises above LM. A comparison of points E and G leads to the same conclusion. E and G give identical transactions demands, but point G has a lower speculative demand. The same money supply applies to both, and hence point G signals excess supply. Conversely, points below LM represent excess demand for money. Figure 2.5 illustrates, with $L(Y_t, r_t) = kY_t + (L_o - mr_t)$.

The confrontation of the IS and LM curves takes place in Figure 2.6. The values of Y_t and r_t at the intersection, point A, are given by equations (2.14) and (2.15). Quadrant I identifies an excess supply of commodities and an excess demand for money. Quadrant II reveals excess supply of both. Quadrant III evidences excess commodity demand with excess money supply, while quadrant IV shows excess demand for both.

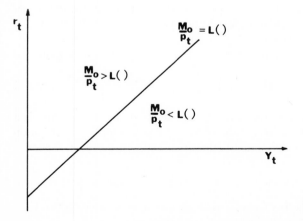

Figure 2.5

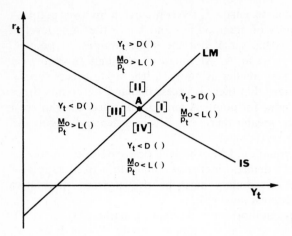

Figure 2.6

2.4 EMERGENCE OF THE BOND MARKET

Inferences about the status of the bond market are now possible. At the intersection point A in Figure 2.6, that market must be in equilibrium consonant with Walras' law. The law remains silent, however, about its condition at other combinations of interest and income, because at any of those points commodities and money do not achieve equilibrium simultaneously. To determine the status of the bond market at locations away from A, one might appeal to a budget constraint which equates total supply of all items circulating in the system to total demand:[13]

$$Y_t + \frac{M_o}{p_t} + \text{Bs}_t = D(Y_t, r_t) + L(Y_t, r_t) + \text{Bd}_t \qquad (2.20)$$

Bs_t and Bd_t denote the supply of real bonds and the demand for real bonds, respectively. This budget constraint says that the economy's "endowment" of commodities, real money balances, and real bonds provides the sole means for satisfying, or financing, total demand.

Rewriting equation (2.20) in terms of excess demands and supplies gives

$$\text{Bd}_t - \text{Bs}_t = \left[Y_t - D(Y_t, r_t) \right] + \left[\frac{M_o}{p_t} - L(Y_t, r_t) \right] \qquad (2.21)$$

The element on the left-hand side identifies excess demand for bonds; the first bracketed component on the right-hand side identifies excess supply of commodities; and the second bracketed component identifies excess supply of money.[14]

---

[13] Patinkin, *Money*, pp. 24, 227. His thoughts regarding the bond market are described on pp. 213–221.

[14] Negative excess demand for an item means an equal amount of excess supply of that item; likewise, negative excess supply means an equal amount of excess demand.

The economy's endowment at a given interest-income combination might render both excess supplies zero, thereby imparting a zero value to excess bond demand in accordance with Walras. That interest-income pair, which creates equilibrium in each of the three markets simultaneously, corresponds to point A of Figure 2.6. For the other interest-income pairs, which do not simultaneously equilibrate all markets, the budget constraint implies that excess bond demand must exactly offset excess commodity and money supplies.

Quadrant II of Figure 2.6 evidences excess supplies of commodities and money. Consequently, the budget constraint mandates that there be excess demand for bonds in that quadrant. In quadrant IV excess demands for commodities and money imply excess supply of bonds. But in quadrants I and III, where commodities and money display opposite symptoms, the condition of the bond market seems to be ambiguous. It really is not. According to the budget constraint, bond market equilibrium requires that

$$0 = [Y_t - D(Y_t, r_t)] + \left[\frac{M_o}{p_t} - L(Y_t, r_t) \right]$$

or that

$$(C_t + I_t + G_t) - Y_t = \frac{M_o}{p_t} - [kY_t + (L_o - mr_t)]$$

Inserting the consumption and investment equations (2.1a) and (2.4) makes

$$r_t = -\frac{1}{v + m} \left(\frac{M_o}{p_t} - L_o \right) + \frac{1}{v + m} (C_o + I_o + G_o - cT_o)$$

$$- \frac{1}{v + m} [1 - c(1 - x) - k] Y_t \qquad (2.22)$$

In strict analogy with the IS and LM expressions, this equation indicates the various combinations of interest and income needed to maintain equilibrium in the bond market. Designate it the BB equation. BB breaks the seeming ambiguity because it passes through quadrants I and III, explicitly dividing each into regions of excess bond demand and supply. The logic that BB resides in quadrants I and III follows.

Consider any interest-income pair which equilibrates the bond market. For such a pair constraint (2.21) says that the commodities and money markets must be "balanced." If each of those markets does not enjoy equilibrium, then the excess demand in one of them must exactly cancel the excess supply in the other. Now let interest rise while income remains unchanged. $D(\ )$ and $L(\ )$ both decline and force the commodities and money markets, taken together, into an excess supply position. Bonds therefore must evidence excess demand above BB. Conversely, they must show excess supply below BB.[15] If the BB line were to pass

---

[15] This behavior pattern of bonds conforms to the conventional picture of demand and supply, where excess demand prevails below the equilibrium price and excess supply above. Since the reciprocal of interest measures bond price, a rise in interest from the BB line implies a fall in bond price from its equilibrium level and the onset of excess demand. The reverse is also true.

into quadrant II, then it would split that quadrant into two sections, one having excess supply in all three markets. If BB were to enter quadrant IV, then excess demand would develop in each market. The budget constraint rules out both possibilities.

A mathematical proof that BB lies exclusively in quadrants I and III involves two steps. One confirms that BB contains point A of Figure 2.6. This exercise entails replacing r_t and Y_t in (2.22) with their reduced forms and leads to $0 = 0$. The other step shows that the slope of BB falls between those of the IS and LM lines; namely,

$$\frac{1}{v}[c(1-x)-1] < \frac{1}{v+m}[c(1-x)-1+k] < \frac{k}{m}$$

Rewrite $[c(1-x)-1+k]/(v+m)$ as

$$\frac{c(1-x)-1}{v+m} + \frac{k}{v+m}$$

The first of these two terms is less negative than is $[c(1-x)-1]/v$, and since the second term is positive, the left-hand inequality must be satisfied. Furthermore, since the second term is less than k/m while the first is negative, the right-hand inequality must also hold. BB therefore passes through point A and inhabits quadrants I and III.

Why does the relative magnitude of $1 - c(1-x)$ and k determine the sign of the BB slope? Suppose all markets initially display equilibrium and income increases by one unit while interest remains unchanged. $1 - c(1-x)$ thus represents the net increase in commodity supply; it signifies the excess supply of commodities. k represents the excess demand for real money. When $1 - c(1-x) = k$, the excess supply of commodities precisely offsets the excess demand for money, and hence the new higher income level does not disturb the bond market equilibrium at the given interest rate. In other words, the slope of BB is zero. But when $1 - c(1-x) > k$, the excess supply of commodities exceeds the excess demand for money at the given rate of interest: commodities and money in combination exhibit excess supply. For bonds to maintain equilibrium, interest must fall to raise the demand for commodities (reduce commodity excess supply) and to raise the demand for money (increase money excess demand). In this case BB reveals a negative slope. A similar argument holds for $1 - c(1-x) < k$, with BB being positively sloped.

The remaining task is to determine which of the three slope options applies to BB. To do so, suppose again that income expands by one unit while interest remains unchanged. The economy's endowment rises by one unit and, by virtue of the budget constraint (2.20), occasions a one-unit increase in total demand. From the consumption function (2.1a), the demand for commodities rises by $c(1-x)$ units; from the money function (2.7), the demand for real money rises by k units. Consequently, the budget constraint implies that the demand for real bonds must change by $1 - c(1-x) - k$ units, because only then can total demand grow by exactly one unit. Like commodities and real money, real bonds

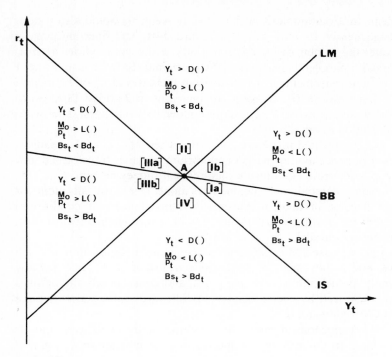

Figure 2.7

are presumed to be normal goods. Their demand varies directly with income, thereby making $1 - c(1 - x) - k$ positive. It follows that BB has a negative slope.[16] Figure 2.7 superimposes BB on the IS-LM map portrayed in Figure 2.6, and it registers the state of each of the three markets in the various quadrants and subquadrants.

2.5 AUTONOMOUS DISPLACEMENTS AND POLICY IMPLICATIONS

Shifts in the IS, LM, and BB curves occur when the exogenous variables change value. Consider the IS. As Figure 2.2 indicates, an increase in G_o raises the IS intercept and propels the curve rightward. Why? At the new (greater) G_o, each interest-income pair previously associated with equilibrium—namely, each point on the original IS—now reflects excess demand. To reestablish equilibrium, income might rise while interest held constant, thereby increasing supply relative to demand. Alternatively, interest might rise while income remained unchanged,

---

[16]Estimating $1 - c(1 - x) - k$ from the fitted equations (2.16) to (2.19) happily gives .314 and a negative slope of $-.041$ for BB.

thus reducing demand. Combinations of those two movements would also restore equilibrium. Consequently, IS undergoes a rightward shift. And since an increase in G_o does not alter the income or interest sensitivity of the commodities market, that shift appears as a parallel displacement of the original IS; slope is unaffected by the change. Similar movements in IS result from increases in C_o or I_o or from decreases in T_o. Decreases in G_o, C_o, or I_o or increases in T_o drive IS leftward since the original curve represents excess supply under these changes. A leftward shift permits restoration of equilibrium.

The LM curve, highlighted in Figure 2.4, shifts when M_o, p_t, or L_o changes. As M_o increases, a previous money market equilibrium becomes transformed into excess supply, and a return to equilibrium requires that money demand rise. This adjustment in demand materializes if income rises alone, if interest falls alone, or if those changes happen in tandem. Succinctly, reinstatement of equilibrium necessitates a rightward shift in LM. A decrease in M_o engenders a leftward shift. Both displacements are parallel.

Price shifts LM, because LM summarizes money market equilibrium in terms of real balances, and a movement in price alters real supply. A price increase reduces real supply at each interest-income point, and consequently the original LM becomes characterized by excess demand. A leftward shift results. A price decrease pushes LM rightward.

L_o denotes the exogenous demand for real speculative balances, and its changes reflect swings in the attitudes of speculators. An increase in L_o signifies eroding confidence in the bond market; speculators adopt a more bearish position and retreat from bonds at all interest rates. A decreased L_o signals heightened enthusiasm for bonds, speculative attitudes taking a tone more bullish than before. When L_o increases, excess demand arises along the original LM, and with real money supply fixed, that extra demand must be extinguished by a reduction in income, a rise in interest, or both. LM moves leftward. A more bullish attitude forces LM rightward.

Most shifts in IS and LM prompt an accommodating displacement of BB since (in the manner of Walras' law) BB must pass through each intersection point of IS and LM. The intercept of BB reveals this reconciliation: It contains all exogenous variables affecting either IS or LM. The only exceptions to an accommodating shift occur for joint equal changes in autonomous commodity and real money variables having bond effects in opposite directions; for example, $\Delta G_o = \Delta M_o / p_t$. The change in commodities demand just balances the change in money supply, thus requiring no adjustment in the bond market at zero income. In these cases the intersection point of IS and LM slides along a stationary BB. Given the redundancy of BB for determining equilibria, it will be ignored henceforth.

The IS-LM apparatus permits elementary yet informative policy experiments. In particular, it suggests fiscal and monetary policy actions for reducing unemployment, and it provides clues about how the system might adjust to inflation. Figure 2.8 presents a framework for analysis. Y_{FE} indicates the full-employment level of income, the amount of output forthcoming each period under full

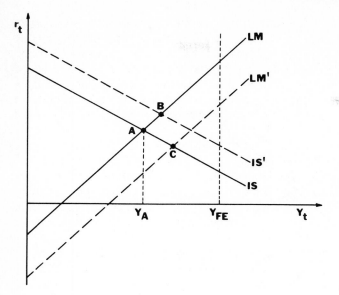

Figure 2.8

employment of labor. It is presumed constant through time. Point A locates the original equilibrium position of the economy. Output Y_A falls below Y_{FE}, and since the production function [equation (1.12)] imposes a direct relationship between output and employment, the difference $Y_{FE} - Y_A$ can be interpreted as a measure of unemployment. Greater differences imply greater unemployment levels, and smaller differences imply the opposite.

How can fiscal policy be used to reduce unemployment? Clearly, government purchases G_o might rise, taxes T_o might fall, or both actions might be implemented together. These initiatives shift the IS rightward, say to IS' in Figure 2.8, reducing unemployment. The increased demand pulls up output and, from the production function, employment. Interest rises: under a constant real money supply, the extra transactions demand associated with an increased income level must come at the expense of speculative hoards.[17] Greater income and interest levels induce, respectively, greater consumption and less investment than are extant at point A.

Reducing unemployment through monetary policy calls for increasing the nominal money supply. LM shifts right, say to LM' in Figure 2.8. Interest falls from A as a portion of the added money becomes absorbed into the speculative hoards. Investment, income, and consumption rise. These fiscal and monetary scenarios corroborate the signs of the corresponding multipliers in Table 2.1.

---

[17]A more appealing explanation of interest behavior emerges from the bond market: An issuance of bonds needed to finance the increased government spending or the decreased taxation forces the price of bonds downward and, concomitantly, the rate of interest upward.

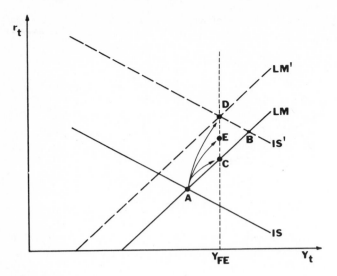

Figure 2.9

For the policy actions pictured in Figure 2.8, the attainment of equilibrium is not obstructed by the ceiling income level Y_{FE}. This situation may not always prevail, however. For example, fiscal policy intended to reduce unemployment could prove to be overcorrective. One possible reason concerns multipliers: In attempting to determine the amount of fiscal stimulus needed, planners require knowledge of the relevant multipliers. Only estimated values are available, however, and those estimates could easily be inaccurate, as suggested in Section 2.2. Thus policy action might unwittingly be too strong (or too weak) and produce unintended results. Another possibility is that other autonomous shocks unexpected by planners may arise adding to the fuel of fiscal stimulus. The overcorrection is reflected in Figure 2.9, where IS shifts to IS'. Equilibrium switches from A to B, but B cannot be attained since it lies beyond the full-employment ceiling. The output level necessary for equilibrium simply cannot be produced.

How might the system adjust in the absence of subsequent policy maneuvers? Several options involving price present themselves. First, income and interest might travel the path which leads to point C and to money market equilibrium. At C, however, commodities exhibit excess demand since C lies below IS'. Price therefore might rise, shifting LM leftward to LM' and forcing it through point D. Second, income and interest might follow the designated path to point D on IS' while LM remains in its original position. Equilibrium obtains in the commodities market, but excess supply characterizes the money market. Price might rise to bring money into equilibrium by driving LM to LM'. This response resembles the classical case of too many dollars chasing too few goods at full employment. Third, a compromise movement might result. Output and interest first reach point E, where there is excess demand in the commodities market and excess supply in the money market. Price rises, shifting LM leftward until it passes through E, but since excess commodity demand still persists, price continues to rise until LM′ evolves.

From these alternative price patterns, it should be clear that static analysis alone cannot predict how the economy adjusts to a disruption of equilibrium. The *disequilibrium* relationships among variables must also be articulated. That task in turn involves an introduction of lags into the model. Dynamic analysis, the study of the adjustment path traversed by a system, lies just ahead. But before the discussion turns to dynamics, two aspects of the present investigation merit further consideration.

2.6 INTERDEPENDENT SHIFTS AND KINKED CURVES

It was postulated that policy action prompted independent shifts in the IS and LM curves. Fiscal policy displaced only IS; monetary policy, only LM. Interdependent shifts can be introduced in several ways.

One procedure envisions real money holdings as an additional argument in the demand functions for commodities, real money, and real bonds. When consumers' real money holdings rise, their wealth position improves and they spend more. Conversely, they spend less when real balances fall. Investors may be similarly influenced.[18] These real-balance effects can be incorporated into the consumption and investment functions (2.1) and (2.4) by revising their intercepts to reflect an exogenous term and a real-balance term:

$$C_o = C'_o + c'\frac{M_o}{p_t}$$

$$I_o = I'_o + v'\frac{M_o}{p_t}$$

Total money balances enter these formulations under the assumption that both consumers and investors hold a constant proportion of the total; $0 < c' < 1$ and $0 < v' < 1$. This amendment converts the intercept of the IS equation (2.10) to $[C'_o + I'_o + G_o - cT_o + (c' + v')M_o/p_t]/v$; the slope of IS remains unaffected since the revisions do not involve income or interest. Money demand contains the extra term $m'M_o/p_t$, $0 < m' < 1$, and the LM intercept in (2.13) becomes $-[(1 - m')M_o/p_t - L_o]/m$. Because of the real-balance effect, an increase in M_o drives IS rightward along with LM; a decrease drives both leftward.[19]

A second avenue for linking the IS and LM curves emanates from an accommodating monetary policy. Table 2.1 shows and Figure 2.8 intimates that

---

[18] Patinkin, *Money*, pp. 19–20, 205–206.

[19] Budget constraint (2.20) imposes an additional, but not unexpected, restriction on the real-balance propensities. It says that a unit increase in M_o/p_t changes real bond demand by $1 - c' - v' - m'$ units. For this quantity to resemble in sign the real-balance coefficients assigned to commodities and real money, the inequality $c' + v' + m' < 1$ must hold.

fiscal policy by itself induces perverse investment behavior through the rate of interest. Fiscal stimulus elevates the interest rate, causing investment to fall; it exerts a "crowding out" effect on investment. Conversely, fiscal restraint lowers the interest rate and causes investment to rise; it has a "luring in" effect. These adverse investment responses can be prevented or weakened by monetary policy. For example, interest would be lower and investment and income would be higher if an increased money supply accompanied a rise in government purchases. Pictorially, the intersection point of IS' and LM' in Figure 2.8 would be operative, rather than point B. Observe, however, that a rigid rule of continuous accommodation divests monetary policy of its autonomy and reduces it to a simple extension of the fiscal instruments.

A third source of IS-LM linkage stems from price, as suggested at the close of the previous section. A shift in IS destroys commodity equilibrium and leaves either excess commodity demand or supply at the original interest-income level. The movement of price associated with such imbalance would displace LM and could be made endogenous through the expedient

$$p_t = p_{t-1} + a\left[D(Y_t, r_t) - Y_t\right] \tag{2.23}$$

where p_{t-1} denotes price last period and the constant a is positive. However, for (2.23) to work meaningfully, $D(\ )$ must not equal Y_t, and consequently their disequilibrium relationship must first be established. Introducing real-balance effects along with (2.23) quickly complicates the shift interdependency.

Another matter deserving amplification concerns the shape of the LM. The LM has been portrayed in this chapter as possessing a negative intercept along with a positive slope which remains the same at all interest-income combinations. This shape differs from that advanced by J. R. Hicks when he introduced the IS-LM apparatus.[20] Hicks visualized that for low levels of income, the LM would have a floor at a positive rate of interest. As income increased beyond some point, LM would bend upward with steadily increasing slope and would eventually become vertical. The horizontal segment reflected the liquidity trap while the vertical portion reflected the belief that a given supply of money set a limit to the level of income which could be sustained.

An LM curve more in keeping with the Hicksian spirit can be extracted from equations (2.7) to (2.9) by restating the speculative demand for money. Equation (2.7) posits the speculative demand Z_t as

$$Z_t = L_o - mr_t \tag{2.24}$$

This equation, as it stands, imposes no restrictions on the level assumed by the interest rate or by the speculative demand itself. Negative interest is entirely acceptable to the formula, and so is negative speculative demand, which would result if interest took a sufficiently large positive value. These peculiarities can be

---

[20]J. R. Hicks, "Mr. Keynes and the 'Classics'; A Suggested Interpretation," *Econometrica*, **5** (April 1937), pp. 148–149, 153–154. Hicks defined the IS and LM curves in terms of nominal, rather than real, income.

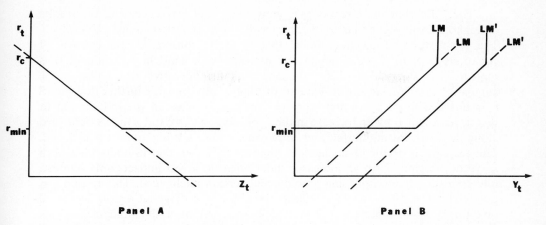

Figure 2.10.

avoided by rewriting the speculative demand as

$$Z_t = \begin{cases} 0 & \text{if } r_t \geq r_c \\ L_o - mr_t & \text{if } r_c > r_t > r_{\min} \end{cases} \qquad (2.25)$$
$$Z_t \geq L_o - mr_{\min} \qquad \text{if } r_t = r_{\min}$$

where $r_c = L_o/m$ and $r_{\min} > 0$.

Panel A of Figure 2.10 shows liquidity preference schedule (2.24) with a dashed straight line. The angular locus, which is drawn with solid lines and which includes the vertical axis when $r_t \geq r_c$, represents schedule (2.25). Panel B of the figure illustrates the linear and angular LM loci associated with the linear and angular liquidity preference schedules, respectively, in Panel A. For the moment ignore the LM' configurations. The horizontal segment of the "bent" LM reflects the trap; at $r_{\min}$ the speculative demand for money proves to be an overwhelming force in total money demand and causes LM to lose its income responsiveness. For interest at or above the critical mark r_c, the speculative demand ceases to operate and the transactions demand becomes the exclusive force in total money demand. Accordingly, LM loses its interest sensitivity and becomes vertical.

Panel B also shows the effect of increasing M_o or decreasing p_t. Previous rightward shifts in LM to LM' now translate into rightward pivots around $r_{\min}$. Decreasing M_o or increasing p_t pivots the angular LM leftward.[21] A change in L_o likewise pivots LM—rightward for a decrease in L_o and leftward for an increase. However, a changed L_o also modifies the length of the LM diagonal inasmuch as it alters the value of r_c.

---

[21]Expressions (2.25) and the angular liquidity preference and LM configurations depicted in Figure 2.10 resemble the corresponding offerings by Mitchell et al., *Exercises*, pp. 273, 275, 286–287, 295–296. See also pp. 255, 258, 260.

The "Hicksian" LM serves as a convenient tool for comparing the results obtainable from Keynesian economics with those expected under classicalism. The formulation of Keynes' model that is to be considered still consists of equations (2.1) to (2.9), although the speculative demand in equation (2.7) is replaced by expressions (2.25). Imagine that the operative LM curve is the angular one designated LM in Panel B of Figure 2.10. Imagine further that the IS cuts this LM in its horizontal segment. Then an increase in the inducement to invest, represented by an increase in the I_o of relation (2.4), shifts the IS rightward along the floor, raising output and employment while leaving interest unchanged. This response is decidedly unclassical. Suppose, however, that IS intersects LM in its vertical region. Then an increased inducement to invest impacts only interest: interest rises while output and employment remain unchanged. This response is purely classical. When an IS intersects the LM in the diagonal region, increased investment boosts interest, but it also boosts output and employment. This scenario is partly classical and partly unclassical. Keynesian economics thus stands as the polar opposite of classicalism only when the trap prevails; beyond the trap Keynesian economics could be viewed as merely qualifying established classical doctrine. It was this perspective which prompted Hicks to label Keynesian economics as the economics of depression.[22]

[22] Hicks, "Mr. Keynes," pp. 154–155.

TWO

ELEMENTARY DYNAMICS

Part

TWO

ELEMENTARY DYNAMICS

THREE

TOWARD DYNAMICS: THEORY AND PRACTICE

The discussion now turns to dynamics, the study of temporal movements exhibited by an economic system. Unlike statics and comparative statics, which locate, describe, and compare equilibrium positions, dynamics investigates motion and asks, How does a system behave through time? Does it manifest fluctuations, or does it evolve in a unidirectional fashion? Does it eventually reach an equilibrium?

A hallmark of dynamics is the presence of lags. The model enunciated in Chapter 2 ignores lags and instead treats all relationships as simultaneous; all variables are determined at the same time. Economic relationships, however, might be viewed as sequential. Households receive income *before* they consume. Businesses ascertain the interest rate and *then* invest. GNP rises *after* implementation of a new government spending program. In short, something happens and then something else happens. Interactions might be recursive, not simultaneous.

Of course, while economic relationships may be truly recursive, data are collected, compiled, and published only for various well-defined units of time such as a month, a quarter, or a year. Consequently, relationships recursive within a given time frame may appear simultaneous when applied to data. Those involving a month lag appear simultaneous when viewed from quarterly data; similarly, those with a quarter delay become simultaneous in an annual perspective. Thus, even if interactions are recursive, simultaneity occupies an important niche in economic analysis.

Important, but not exclusive, and much information about the functioning of an economic system can be gained by explicitly recognizing the underlying lags. Dynamics promises many insights necessarily missed by statics and comparative statics.

3.1 TEMPORAL MOVEMENTS IN A STATIC SYSTEM

The static model considered previously lends itself to easy translation into a dynamic framework. However, before this metamorphosis occurs, it is instructive to examine the temporal movements implicit in the model's original formulation. For convenience, that version is reproduced here:

$$C_t = C_o + cYd_t \qquad\qquad C_0 > 0, 0 < c < 1 \qquad (3.1)$$

$$Yd_t = Y_t - T_t \qquad\qquad\qquad\qquad (3.2)$$

$$T_t = T_o + xY_t \qquad\qquad T_o < 0, 0 < x < 1 \qquad (3.3)$$

$$I_t = I_o - vr_t \qquad\qquad I_o > 0, v > 0 \qquad (3.4)$$

$$G_t = G_o \qquad\qquad G_o > 0 \qquad (3.5)$$

$$Y_t = C_t + I_t + G_t \qquad\qquad\qquad (3.6)$$

$$\frac{\text{Md}_t}{p_t} = kY_t + (L_o - mr_t) \qquad k > 0, L_o > 0, m > 0 \qquad (3.7)$$

$$\frac{\text{Ms}_t}{p_t} = \frac{M_o}{p_t} \qquad\qquad M_o > 0 \qquad (3.8)$$

$$\frac{\text{Ms}_t}{p_t} = \frac{\text{Md}_t}{p_t} \qquad\qquad\qquad (3.9)$$

C_t denotes real consumption expenditures at time t. Likewise for t, Yd_t represents real disposable income; Y_t, real output (say, real GNP); T_t, real net taxes; I_t, real investment; r_t, the interest rate; G_t, real government expenditures on commodities; Md_t, the nominal money demand; p_t, the price of commodities; and Ms_t, the nominal money supply. Symbols with a subscript o denote exogenous magnitudes. Equation (3.6) is the equilibrium condition for the commodities market; it says that aggregate supply Y_t equals aggregate demand D_t $(= C_t + I_t + G_t)$. Equation (3.9) indicates equilibrium in the money market: real money supply and demand are equal.

As explained in Chapter 2, all relationships within the commodities market [equations (3.1) to (3.6)] are summarized by the IS equation

$$r_t = \frac{1}{v}(C_o + I_o + G_o - cT_o) + \frac{1}{v}[c(1 - x) - 1]Y_t \qquad (3.10)$$

The LM equation summarizes the relationships within the money market [equations (3.7) to (3.9)]:

$$r_t = -\frac{1}{m}\left(\frac{M_o}{p_t} - L_o\right) + \frac{k}{m}Y_t \qquad (3.11)$$

From these two equations a value for Y_t emerges; namely,

$$Y_t = \frac{1}{h}\left[C_o + I_o + G_o - cT_o + \frac{v}{m}\left(\frac{M_o}{p_t} - L_o\right)\right] \qquad (3.12)$$

where $h = 1 - c(1 - x) + vk/m$. The corresponding r_t reads

$$r_t = \frac{1}{h}\left\{\frac{k}{m}(C_o + I_o + G_o - cT_o) - \frac{1}{m}[1 - c(1 - x)]\left(\frac{M_o}{p_t} - L_o\right)\right\}$$

$$(3.13)$$

These Y_t and r_t represent equilibrium values since both satisfy equilibrium conditions (3.6) and (3.9). With Y_t and r_t established, equilibrium values for all other endogenous variables can be determined.

The temporal movement of output can be deduced from equation (3.12). Clearly, if the exogenous variables and parameters remain unchanged through time, then so does Y_t. Suppose, however, that government purchases increase by an amount ΔG_o at a specific point in time $t = t_o$ and remain at the new level $G_o + \Delta G_o$ permanently. What happens to Y_t? It increases at t_o by an amount $\Delta Y_t = \Delta G_o/h$. Observe that Y_t assumes its new value instantaneously; its increase does not lag behind that in expenditures.

A graphical account of this adjustment process appears in Figure 3.1. Panel A presents the customary IS shift, to IS′. Prior to time t_o, Y_t assumed the value Y_A. At t_o, however, G_o rises, and consequently Y_t becomes Y_B. Correspondingly, r_t rises from r_A to r_B. Panel B indicates the movement of Y_t through time. Y_t remains constant at Y_A prior to t_o, but at t_o it switches permanently to the higher level Y_B. Interest, not depicted temporally, behaves similarly. Had government expenditures declined instead of increased, responses exactly the opposite of those described would have resulted.

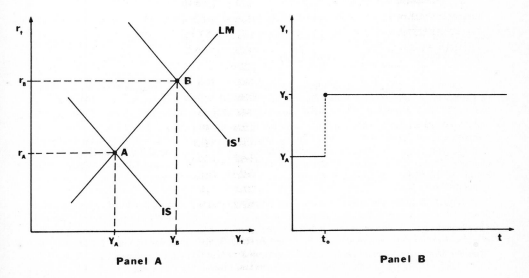

Panel A　　　　　　　　　　　　**Panel B**

Figure 3.1

Panel B indicates the path of *equilibrium* output. What about the behavior of *actual* output? How does it respond to the increased government expenditure? The static system cannot address this question in any meaningful way because it generates only equilibrium solutions. If one wishes to argue that actual values always equal their equilibrium levels, then one can interpret the single-step adjustment in Panel B as tracing the actual path of the economy. However, treating actuals and equilibria as equivalent appears naive given the complexity of developed economies.

3.2 MODEL METAMORPHOSIS: FROM STATICS TO DYNAMICS

Actual values become clearly divorced from their equilibrium counterparts by inserting lags into the system. Numerous types of lags can be identified, and they may assume a variety of lengths. For simplicity, however, consider only a lag between aggregate commodity demand and supply, which can be introduced into the static model by altering equation (3.6) alone. Reflecting the one-period delay studied by Professor Erik Lundberg, that equation appears as

$$Y_t = C_{t-1} + I_{t-1} + G_{t-1} \tag{3.6a}$$

which says that commodity supply in any period depends upon and equals commodity demand in the previous period.[1] Supply lags behind demand; phrased differently, demand changes and then supply changes. Unlike the static twin (3.6), equation (3.6a) is not an equilibrium condition; it is a behavioral relation describing how entrepreneurs respond to demand changes.[2] All other equations of the earlier system remain intact, and consequently the dynamic model consists of equations (3.1) to (3.5), (3.6a), and (3.7) to (3.9).[3]

Inserting the commodities equations into relationship (3.6a) leads to

$$Y_t = \left[C_o - cT_o + c(1 - x)Y_{t-1} \right] + \left[I_o - vr_{t-1} \right] + G_{t-1} \tag{3.14}$$

where the first and second bracketed expressions after the equality represent lagged consumption C_{t-1} and lagged investment I_{t-1}, respectively. Since no

---

[1]Lundberg can be credited for adding dynamic life to John Maynard Keynes' *The General Theory of Employment, Interest, and Money* (New York: Harcourt, Brace and World, Inc., 1936). Dennis Robertson, who postulated a lag between the receipt of income and the expenditure of income, also embellished *The General Theory* dynamically. See Erik Lundberg, *Studies in the Theory of Economic Expansion* (New York: Kelley and Millman, Inc., 1954), foreword and Chapter 9, especially pp. 188–192, and Dennis H. Robertson, "Some Notes on Mr. Keynes' General Theory of Employment," *Quarterly Journal of Economics*, 51 (November 1936), pp. 171–175. See also Lloyd A. Metzler, "The Nature and Stability of Inventory Cycles," *Review of Economic Statistics*, 23 (August 1941), pp. 113–114.

[2]Equation (3.6) also may be viewed as describing the way entrepreneurs react to changed demand. It says, however, that they respond instantaneously and completely to always satisfy demand. Thus, equation (3.6) represents an equilibrium condition as well.

[3]A prototype of this model can be found in Warren L. Smith and Ronald L. Teigen, eds., *Readings in Money, National Income, and Stabilization Policy*, rev. ed. (Homewood, Ill.: Richard D. Irwin, Inc., ©1970), pp. 30–40. The following discussion draws from that work.

alterations have been made to the money market, equation (3.11) still summarizes the relationships there, and consequently it can be used to write r_{t-1} of equation (3.14) in terms of Y_{t-1}. Substitution into (3.14), with the time sequence of real money balances noted, gives

$$Y_t = C_o - cT_o + I_o + \frac{v}{m}\left(\frac{\text{Ms}_{t-1}}{p_{t-1}} - L_o\right) + \left[c(1-x) - \frac{vk}{m}\right]Y_{t-1} + G_{t-1}$$

$$(3.15)$$

Clearly, output in any period t depends *inter alia* upon its value in the previous period. Contrary to equation (3.12), which comes from an equality between aggregate demand and supply and which therefore describes equilibrium output for the static system, equation (3.15) describes actual output for the dynamic model.

Introduction of a lag into the relationship between the demand for and supply of commodities causes the usual condition for equilibrium in that market to vanish. The notion of equilibrium in commodities can be preserved, however, by defining equilibrium as a *path* along which a balance of forces exists. Such a tack in effect constitutes a temporal extension of the customary static definition of equilibrium as a point. Two possibilities quickly come to mind. Equilibrium may be taken to mean the state in which a system replicates itself: in the absence of shocks, the endogenous variables assume unchanging values through time, and this type of equilibrium may be termed a stationary state. Alternatively, endogenous variables may expand smoothly through time. This type of equilibrium, known as a steady state, is characteristic of growth models, which will be discussed in Part 5. For present purposes the stationary state provides particular conveniences, and hence it is adopted here.

In a stationary state, endogenous variables duplicate their earlier levels; for example, $Y_t = Y_{t-1} = Y_{t-2} = \ldots = Y_E$. Confronting equation (3.15) with this constancy criterion yields, after simplification,

$$Y_E = \frac{1}{h}\left[C_o + I_o + G_o - cT_o + \frac{v}{m}\left(\frac{M_o}{p_o} - L_o\right)\right] \qquad (3.16)$$

All parameters and exogenous variables are presumed to be stationary through time, and p_o denotes the fixed price level. From equation (3.11) it should be evident that since output is constant at Y_E, interest is constant as well. So are the other endogenous variables. A stationary state does exist.

Equation (3.16) has a form identical to equation (3.12) of the static model, and thus the behavior of equilibrium values must be the same for both. As G_o increases to $G_o + \Delta G_o$ at time t_o, equilibrium output for the dynamic system rises at t_o to $Y_E + \Delta G_o/h$. Unlike the static model, however, the dynamic system can articulate the movement of actuals. An example might be helpful.

All parameters and exogenous variables adopt the values appearing in equations (2.16) to (2.19) and in the related discussion. In particular, $C_o = 6.90$, $c = .80$, $T_o = -13.80$, $x = .23$, $I_o = 211.75$, $v = 5.13$, $k = .07$, $L_o = 176.78$, $m = 2.51$, $M_o = 173.25$, and $p_t = .77$. These assignments never change through time. $G_t = 250$ for time prior to t_o, but at t_o it increases by 25 to 275 and stays there forever.

Two equilibrium values for output apply: one prior to the change in government expenditures and one afterward. For any period before t_o, $Y_E = 1097.09$ according to equation (3.16). At time t_o, however, the equilibrium jumps permanently to 1144.53.

How does actual output behave? Equation (3.15) provides the answer. Written for the specific example under study, it becomes

$$Y_t = 6.90 - .80(-13.80) + 211.75 + \frac{5.13}{2.51}\left(\frac{173.25}{.77} - 176.78\right)$$

$$+ \left[.80(1 - .23) - \frac{5.13(.07)}{2.51}\right]Y_{t-1} + G_{t-1}$$

or more compactly

$$Y_t = 328.24 + .4729Y_{t-1} + G_{t-1} \qquad (3.17)$$

For time t_o, equation (3.17) reads $Y_{t_o} = 328.24 + .4729Y_{t_o-1} + G_{t_o-1}$. But $G_{t_o-1} = 250$, and since equilibrium prevailed in period $t_o - 1$, $Y_{t_o-1} = 1097.09$. Therefore, actual output at t_o equals the old equilibrium value, $Y_{t_o} = 1097.09$. Even though government expenditures rise from 250 to 275 at t_o, thereby making current demand 1122.09, actual output does not change because it depends upon previous, not current, demand.

If production does not expand to accommodate the added government purchases, then how is the increased spending satisfied? By sales from inventories, which fall by 25 units. This decline can be easily observed. Let K'_t denote the level of inventories at the end of period t. Then

$$K'_t = K'_{t-1} + (Y_t - D_t)$$

Namely, the inventory level at the end of period t equals the level at the end of the previous period plus the excess production in the current period. With a rise in aggregate demand of 25 units unmatched by any increase in supply, the inventory level falls by that amount.[4]

This entire adjustment process repeats itself in the next period. For time $t_o + 1$, equation (3.17) gives $Y_{t_o+1} = 328.24 + .4729Y_{t_o} + G_{t_o}$. Since $Y_{t_o} = 1097.09$, the first two right-hand terms assume exactly the same numbers that they did in the prior step. However, government expenditures equaling 275, not 250, now enter the equation, and thus production at time $t_o + 1$ becomes 1122.09. It rises by 25 over its value at time t_o. Inventories still decline, now by 11.83 since aggregate demand at $t_o + 1$ equals 1133.92.

Table 3.1 records the movement of output and inventories throughout the adjustment process. Actual output converges to (approaches and reaches) the new equilibrium level 1144.53, and it does so unidirectionally—without oscillation.

---

[4] For the static case a change in demand is satisfied instantly, and hence the inventory level does not adjust.

Table 3.1 Temporal response of output, inventories, and interest due to a permanent increase in government expenditures

Calendar date	Actual output	Output change	Inventory level	Inventory change	Interest rate	Government purchases
t	Y_t	$Y_t - Y_{t-1}$	K'_t	$K'_t - K'_{t-1}$	r_t	G_t
$t_o - 1$	1097.09	0.000	3000.00	0.000	11.385	250.00
t_o	1097.09	0.000	2975.00	−25.000	11.385	275.00
$t_o + 1$	1122.09	25.000	2963.18	−11.823	12.082	275.00
$t_o + 2$	1133.92	11.823	2957.59	−5.592	12.412	275.00
$t_o + 3$	1139.51	5.592	2954.94	−2.644	12.568	275.00
$t_o + 4$	1142.15	2.644	2953.69	−1.251	12.642	275.00
$t_o + 5$	1143.40	1.251	2953.10	−.591	12.677	275.00
$t_o + 6$	1144.00	.591	2952.82	−.280	12.693	275.00
$t_o + 7$	1144.28	.280	2952.69	−.132	12.701	275.00
$t_o + 8$	1144.41	.132	2952.62	−.063	12.705	275.00
$t_o + 9$	1144.47	.063	2952.59	−.030	12.706	275.00
$t_o + 10$	1144.50	.030	2952.58	−.014	12.707	275.00
$t_o + 11$	1144.51	.014	2952.57	−.007	12.708	275.00
$t_o + 12$	1144.52	.007	2952.57	−.003	12.708	275.00
$t_o + 13$	1144.52	.003	2952.57	−.001	12.708	275.00
$t_o + 14$	1144.53	.001	2952.57	−.001	12.708	275.00
$t_o + 15$	1144.53	.001	2952.57	0.000	12.708	275.00
$t_o + 16$	1144.53	0.000	2952.57	0.000	12.708	275.00
$t_o + 17$	1144.53	0.000	2952.57	0.000	12.708	275.00

Convergence proceeds at a decreasing rate, the successive output increments becoming continually smaller. Inventories travel in the opposite direction. From an assumed initial level of 3000 units, they unidirectionally decline at a decreasing rate and fall to the same extent that output rises. Obviously, at the heart of the model lies an assumption that inventories react passively to market conditions. Entrepreneurs take no action to maintain inventories at some target level, be it defined as an absolute quantity (such as 3000 units) or as a quantity expressed relative to another variable (for example, sales). Table 3.1 also reports the movement of interest rates. Interest, like income, responds in a unidirectional manner, moving from its old equilibrium of 11.385 to a new equilibrium of 12.708.

Figure 3.2 compares the movement of equilibrium and actual output for the permanent increase in government expenditures. Equilibrium output, indicated by horizontal dashes and the triangular point, rises at t_o—when expenditures rise—but actual output does not begin rising until $t_o + 1$, after which time it increases to the new equilibrium continually but at diminishing speed. Actuals never overshoot that equilibrium. A more technical examination of the temporal path traversed by actual output appears in Section 2 of Appendix D.

The behavior of the system under a "one-shot" increase in government expenditures is recorded in Table 3.2 and Figure 3.3. Expenditures rise to 275 at

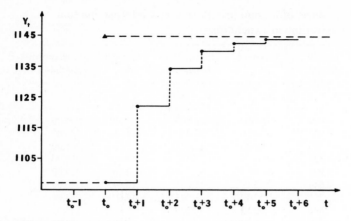

Figure 3.2

Table 3.2 Temporal response of output, inventories, and interest due to a temporary increase in government expenditures

Calendar date	Actual output	Output change	Inventory level	Inventory change	Interest rate	Government purchases
t	Y_t	$Y_t - Y_{t-1}$	K'_t	$K'_t - K'_{t-1}$	r_t	G_t
$t_o - 1$	1097.09	0.000	3000.00	0.000	11.385	250.00
t_o	1097.09	0.000	2975.00	-25.000	11.385	275.00
$t_o + 1$	1122.09	25.000	2988.18	13.177	12.082	250.00
$t_o + 2$	1108.92	-13.177	2994.41	6.232	11.715	250.00
$t_o + 3$	1102.69	-6.232	2997.36	2.947	11.541	250.00
$t_o + 4$	1099.74	-2.947	2998.75	1.394	11.459	250.00
$t_o + 5$	1098.35	-1.394	2999.41	.659	11.420	250.00
$t_o + 6$	1097.69	$-.659$	2999.72	.312	11.402	250.00
$t_o + 7$	1097.37	$-.312$	2999.87	.147	11.393	250.00
$t_o + 8$	1097.23	$-.147$	2999.94	.070	11.389	250.00
$t_o + 9$	1097.16	$-.070$	2999.97	.033	11.387	250.00
$t_o + 10$	1097.12	$-.033$	2999.99	.016	11.386	250.00
$t_o + 11$	1097.11	$-.016$	3000.00	.007	11.386	250.00
$t_o + 12$	1097.10	$-.007$	3000.00	.003	11.385	250.00
$t_o + 13$	1097.10	$-.003$	3000.00	.002	11.385	250.00
$t_o + 14$	1097.10	$-.002$	3000.00	.001	11.385	250.00
$t_o + 15$	1097.10	$-.001$	3000.00	0.000	11.385	250.00
$t_o + 16$	1097.10	0.000	3000.00	0.000	11.385	250.00
$t_o + 17$	1097.09	0.000	3000.00	0.000	11.385	250.00

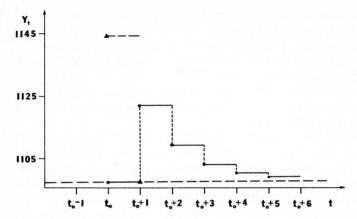

Figure 3.3

time t_o but remain there only until time $t_o + 1$, when they permanently return to the 250 level. Because of this shock, equilibrium output rises to its 1144.53 value instantaneously at t_o, and then it falls back to its original 1097.09 value instantaneously at $t_o + 1$, as the triangular points show. Actual output takes a giant step upward at $t_o + 1$, declining afterward at a decreasing rate. Inventories continue their passive behavior. They first decline but then increase following the return of government expenditures to their original level and the consequent onset of excess

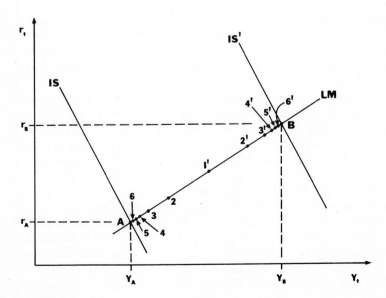

Figure 3.4

aggregate supply. Inventories eventually recover the initial loss and end the adjustment period at their original level of 3000.

The temporal movement of output and interest under either a permanent or one-shot disturbance can be plotted on an IS-LM map. Since no modifications were made to the money market in devising the dynamic system, the LM equation (3.11) must hold at each point of time, and hence the response of output and interest to any change in government expenditures must generate points which lie along the LM line. Figure 3.4 illustrates.

For a permanent increase in government expenditures, the IS shifts to IS', and equilibrium output and interest rise instantaneously from Y_A and r_A to Y_B and r_B, respectively. The actual values which subsequently evolve are designated by the points numbered $1', 2', \ldots, B$. At time $t_o + 1$ actual output and interest locate at point $1'$; at time $t_o + 2$ they reside at point $2'$. Note that the spacing between adjacent numbered points narrows as the adjustment advances toward point B. For the temporary increase in expenditures, the IS shifts to IS' at t_o and returns to its initial position at $t_o + 1$. Actual output and interest move to point $1'$ at time $t_o + 1$ and then gradually return to point A via points $2, 3, \ldots, A$.

3.3 EFFECTS OF ALTERNATIVE LAG STRUCTURES

Equation (3.6a) says that production lags demand by one period. The length of lags in a system crucially affects its temporal response, and this sensitivity can be demonstrated by rewriting (3.6a) to reflect a lag of length i:

$$Y_t = C_{t-i} + I_{t-i} + G_{t-i} \qquad (3.6b)$$

With this formulation a change in government expenditures at time t first impacts output i periods later, at $t + i$. In the following experiment the refinement captured by equation (3.6b) constitutes the only modification to the original specification of the dynamic model, which therefore consists of equations (3.1) to (3.5), (3.6b), and (3.7) to (3.9).

Figure 3.5 illustrates the temporal response of the system to a permanent increase in government expenditures for lags of alternative length. Specifically, $i = 1, 2, 3,$ and 10. Although the example of a one-period lag has already been studied, it is considered again for comparison purposes. Convenience dictates that consecutive points be joined without recourse to the "steps" noted in Figure 3.2.

As Figure 3.5 shows, the reaction of the system becomes more protracted as the lag length increases. For a two-period lag, each value of Y_t occurs twice; for a three-period lag, thrice; and for a ten-period lag, ten times. These repetitions coincide with multiple declines in inventory levels. For instance, when $i = 10$ the increase in government expenditures beginning at $t = 0$ generates no additional output over the time interval $t = 0$ to $t = 9$. In each of those periods, therefore, aggregate demand exceeds aggregate supply by 25 units, and inventories must be drawn down each period by that amount. This logic suggests that the total decline in inventories over the entire time of disequilibrium should be greater for a longer

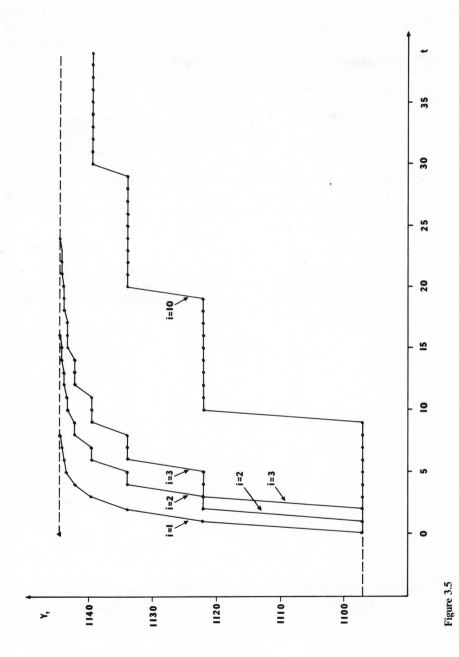

Figure 3.5

length of lag. For $i = 1$ the decline equals 47.43 units and matches exactly the increase in actual output between equilibria acknowledged by Table 3.1.[5] For $i = 2$ the inventory decline amounts to 94.86, while for $i = 3$ and $i = 10$ it totals 142.30 and 474.32, respectively. Of course, the increase in actual output remains the same across the various cases.

Though differing in their pace, all response paths depicted in Figure 3.5 have a basic feature in common: they all converge to the new equilibrium in a unidirectional fashion at a diminishing rate. Fluctuations in output do not arise as the system accommodates a single shock. In short, cyclical fluctuations are not inherent in the model. For cycles to occur it must be impacted by phenomena that cause the equilibrium level to fluctuate. One shock might drive equilibrium output upward, thereby prompting actual output to rise. A later shock, however, might force the equilibrium downward, leading actual output to fall.

Cyclical oscillations can be made inherent in the response pattern of the system by introducing a second lag structure. This time a lag, of length j, is added to the investment equation (3.4):

$$I_t = I_o - vr_{t-j} \qquad (3.4a)$$

Equation (3.4a) says that investment spending in the current period depends upon the interest rate prevailing j periods earlier. Investment decisions, and the consequent spending, may be subject to delays, and equation (3.4a) reflects those delays. With this change the complete model becomes

$$C_t = C_o + cYd_t \qquad (3.1)$$

$$Yd_t = Y_t - T_t \qquad (3.2)$$

$$T_t = T_o + xY_t \qquad (3.3)$$

$$I_t = I_o - vr_{t-j} \qquad (3.4a)$$

$$G_t = G_o \qquad (3.5)$$

$$Y_t = C_{t-i} + I_{t-i} + G_{t-i} \qquad (3.6b)$$

$$\frac{Md_t}{p_t} = kY_t + (L_o - mr_t) \qquad (3.7)$$

$$\frac{Ms_t}{p_t} = \frac{M_o}{p_t} \qquad (3.8)$$

$$\frac{Ms_t}{p_t} = \frac{Md_t}{p_t} \qquad (3.9)$$

Substitution of the commodities equations into relation (3.6b) gives

$$Y_t = \left[C_o - cT_o + c(1-x)Y_{t-i} \right] + \left[I_0 - vr_{t-i-j} \right] + G_{t-i} \qquad (3.18)$$

which generates the movement of actual output. The first bracketed term refers to

---

[5] Close examination of Table 3.1 shows that actual output rises by 47.44 while inventories fall by 47.43. This discrepancy is due to rounding error.

the consumption component of output, C_{t-i}; the second bracketed term refers to the investment component, I_{t-i}. Since no change has been made in the money market, the earlier LM equation (3.11) continues to hold:

$$r_t = -\frac{1}{m}\left(\frac{M_o}{p_t} - L_o\right) + \frac{k}{m}Y_t \qquad (3.11)$$

From these two equations the evolution of output and interest can be monitored.

As before, the system begins in a stationary-state equilibrium where output and interest have been constant throughout the relevant past. All parameter and exogenous values considered previously apply, and government expenditures increase from 250 to 275 at time zero and remain at the higher level forever. From equations (3.11) and (3.18) the old and new equilibrium values emerge and exactly equal their counterparts for both the static and the preceding dynamic models. The question which remains is, How do the actual values for the new system behave temporally?

In reacting to the shock of increased government spending, the system must traverse the LM curve, but the movement may not be "one-way." An intuitive explanation runs thus: If investment were not interest-induced, then the progress of output recited by equation (3.18) would have to be upward, unidirectional, and decelerating. For instance, an increase in Y_{t-i} of one unit, caused by an earlier increase in government spending, prompts an increase in Y_t of $c(1-x)$, which is less than unity. This increase of $c(1-x)$ causes another in $t+i$ of $[c(1-x)]^2$, which must be less than $c(1-x)$. The process repeats itself. Incidentally, interest does rise in this scenario; but with no interest-induced investment present, that change merely leads to a reallocation of money balances. There are no output ramifications.

Now introduce investment into equation (3.18). Output begins expanding because of the shock of government expenditure. Interest too must expand to preserve equilibrium in the money market, and the increased interest causes investment to fall j periods later, thereby counteracting (i periods after that) some of the upward stimulus to output arising from consumption. If j is large, the decline in investment enters the sequence of events when the increases in output from consumption have become small, and this circumstance tends to cause a decline in actual output. It follows that output should observe fluctuations at least for large j.

Figure 3.6 displays the motion of the system for four combinations of lags: $i = 3, j = 1$; $i = 3, j = 2$; $i = 1, j = 5$; and $i = 1, j = 10$. Although in practice the output lag i would likely be longer than the investment lag j, the latter two lag combinations are considered for the sake of exposition. These, in fact, generate the more interesting time profiles.

Consider first the case of $i = 1, j = 5$. Since $i = 1$, the increase in government expenditures at $t = 0$ increases output and interest at $t = 1$. The increased income excites consumption at $t = 1$ and thus the consumption component of equation (3.18) in the next period ($t = 2$). The higher interest rate of $t = 1$, however, does not affect investment at $t = 1$ or the investment component at $t = 2$. Instead,

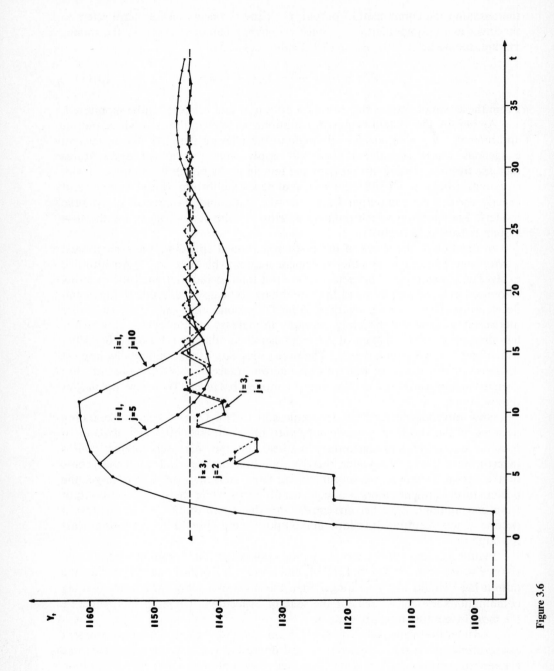

Figure 3.6

investment remains unchanged. The consumption component rises again at $t = 3$, while the investment component stays dormant. Therefore, in the initial stages after the increase in government spending, only a multiplier effect arising from consumption operates, and as Figure 3.6 illustrates, expansion proceeds at the decreasing rate typical of a pure consumption-induced adjustment. At $t = 6$, five periods after interest first rose, investment falls. This decline materializes when the consumption-induced rise in income wanes, and therefore output falls in the following period. The fallen output in turn redirects consumption, which joins depressed investment in furthering output's decline. The initial output decline at $t = 7$, of course, forces interest to decrease in the same period, and this reduced interest eventually prompts investment to rise, pulling output upward.

Mapped in the IS-LM framework of Figure 3.4, the adjustment process first yields two points, those for $t = 1$ and $t = 2$, on the LM line between equilibria A and B. It then places the next four points on the LM to the right of B successively further from it. Afterward, the points retreat along the LM, proceeding back to the left of B. Thus, the oscillations around $Y_t = 1144.53$ in Figure 3.6 translate into right-left pulsations around point B along the LM line in Figure 3.4.

The case for $i = 1, j = 10$ unfolds similarly. There, however, output continues to rise beyond $t = 6$ because the investment restraint does not become effective until much later. Furthermore, the initial decline in output is more severe than that for the case of $i = 1, j = 5$, because the investment decrease comes when the consumption-induced effect is almost spent: little consumption increase remains to offset the investment decline. Both examples of shorter lags—$i = 3, j = 1$, and $i = 3, j = 2$—also evidence fluctuations, although in both instances the movements are jerky and the first decrease occurs before attainment of an output value equal to the new equilibrium level.

Inventories for each of the four cases yield an inverted image of the corresponding output path. In particular, they fall when actual output remains below the new equilibrium, and they rise when it exceeds that level. Jerkiness therefore characterizes two inventory profiles, while smoothness characterizes the other two. As in the prior family of experiments without an investment lag, inventories converge to alternative levels depending upon the lag structure. For $i = 3, j = 1$, and $i = 3, j = 2$, they settle at 2864.49 and 2871.28, respectively; for $i = 1, j = 5$, and $i = 1, j = 10$, they settle at 2986.50 and 3020.43, respectively.

3.4 TAXONOMY AND TERMINOLOGY OF TEMPORAL RESPONSES

Different lag structures generate different patterns of cyclical response, as Figures 3.5 and 3.6 illustrate. Alternative configurations may also emerge from variations in parameter values, as Chapter 4 will demonstrate. However, while the paths followed by a system may show marked differences across cases, they tend to exhibit fundamental similarities and therefore lend themselves to classification according to several basic types. Figure 3.7 provides a convenient taxonomy.

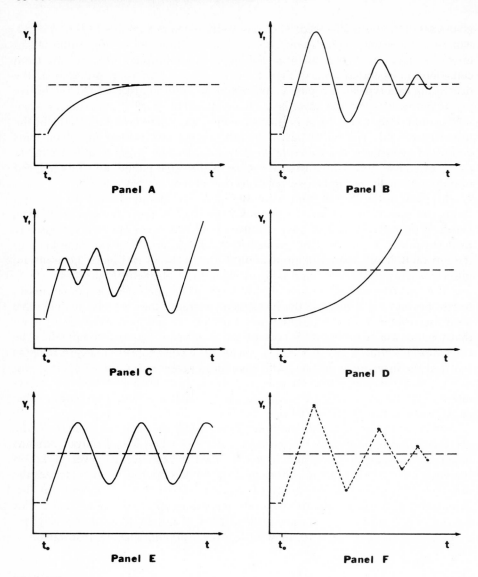

Figure 3.7

Underlying this figure is the presumption that government expenditures increase permanently at time t_o. The dashed horizontal lines again represent the old and new equilibrium output levels, and for convenience time assumes noninteger values. It is treated as a continuous variable rather than as a discrete variable.

Panel A indicates unidirectional movement of actual output and resembles the paths presented in Figure 3.5; the actuals converge to the new equilibrium without oscillation. Panel B shows damped oscillations. Actual output rises above the new equilibrium and then oscillates around that level. The fluctuations become smaller through time, and the system eventually settles at the new equilibrium. The two responses in Figure 3.6 for $j = 5$ and $j = 10$ qualify as damped cycles. In both Panels A and B, a new equilibrium exists, and it is stable. The system does converge to that level.

Unstable movements appear in the next three graphs. Panel C displays fluctuations which grow larger through time, a pattern known as "explosive oscillation" or "antidamped oscillation." Panel D illustrates direct explosion—no fluctuations occur. Panel E exhibits regular cycles, fluctuations which neither grow nor diminish in size. In all three cases a new equilibrium exists, but it is unstable. The system does not converge to that level.

Panel F portrays a damped cobweb. Cobwebs refer to cycles composed only of alternating high and low values, and the two time paths in Figure 3.6 for short j lags reveal cobweblike movements. Cobwebs need not be damped.

The anatomy of a cycle for actual output is examined in Figure 3.8. Turning points occur at years $(t =)$ 0, 8, 13, and 19. The upper turning points, each labeled by a P, are peaks; the lower points, each designated by a T, are troughs. Cycles are customarily measured from peak to peak or from trough to trough. Under the former rule the cycle runs from year 8 to year 19 and hence has a length, or period, of 11 years. By the latter criterion, its length is 13 years. The amplitude of a cycle refers to its height, measured as an average of the greatest

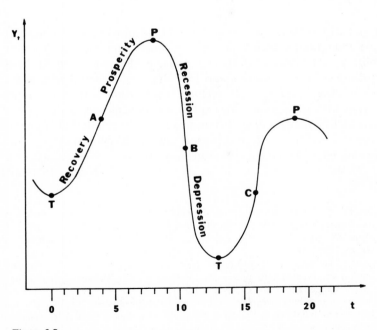

Figure 3.8

and smallest values in the cycle. Under either the peak-to-peak or trough-to-trough norm, the amplitude of the cycle in Figure 3.8 equals the average of those peak and trough values at years 8 and 13. As Figures 3.7 and 3.8 suggest, both the period and the amplitude can vary across consecutive cycles.

Various phases of the cycle may be discerned. According to Professor Joseph Schumpeter, a cycle can be partitioned into the four phases shown in Figure 3.8 between the two troughs. Segment TA represents a recovery period. Segment AP depicts prosperity and PB indicates recession. Segment BT identifies a depression. A similar schematic can be found in the earlier work of Wesley C. Mitchell, whose contributions to dynamic analysis are discussed more fully anon.[6] Recovery and prosperity together form the expansion phase of a cycle, while recession and depression make up the contraction phase.

Certain types of cycles bear the names of researchers who "discovered" their existence. For instance, cycles with a period of approximately 60 years were observed by N. D. Kondratieff, an economist writing in the early 1900s, and have come to be called Kondratieffs in his honor. Similarly, cycles having approximately 10 years' duration are known as Juglars in recognition of the pioneering work in the middle 1800s by the scholar Clement Juglar. Kitchins refer to cycles roughly 40 months long and are named after Joseph Kitchin for his findings in the 1920s. W. L. Crum, a contemporary of Kitchin, also noted the 40-month cycle, but he failed to gain the broad acknowledgment that Kitchin enjoyed. Fluctuations of intermediate duration, longer than Juglars but shorter than Kondratieffs, have been detected separately by Arthur F. Burns, Simon S. Kuznets, and C. A. R. Wardwell. Of 15 to 25 years in length, they are commonly called Kuznets cycles.[7]

Schumpeter viewed the temporal evolution of the economy as a cumulative result of multiple fluctuations occurring simultaneously and having different periods and amplitudes. To make his discussion manageable, he focused on three types of cycles—those of short, medium, and long duration—and dubbed them Kitchins, Juglars, and Kondratieffs, respectively. It is important to note, however, that three cycle types were chosen only for expository convenience; reality is not necessarily constrained to that number. Schumpeter also postulated an integral relationship among the cycles, based on historical and statistical review of data: one Kondratieff contains six Juglars, and one Juglar contains three Kitchins. This relationship is depicted for actual output in Figure 3.9, which ignores trend

---

[6]Mitchell's taxonomy of 1913 is reprinted in his *Business Cycles and Their Causes* (Berkeley: University of California Press, 1941), pp. 149–162. See also Joseph A. Schumpeter, *Business Cycles: A Theoretical, Historical, and Statistical Analysis of the Capitalist Process*, vol. I (New York: McGraw-Hill Book Company, 1939), pp. 208–209.

[7]Moses Abramovitz, "The Nature and Significance of Kuznets Cycles," in *Readings in Business Cycles*, Robert A. Gordon and Lawrence R. Klein, eds. (Homewood, Ill.: Richard D. Irwin, Inc., 1965), pp. 519–524, and Schumpeter, *Business Cycles*, pp. 161–174.

Different types of cycles may be associated with different causal phenomena. Kondratieffs, for example, are typically linked to major innovations such as the advent of the locomotive; Kitchins, by contrast, are often attributed to minor shocks such as inventory adjustments.

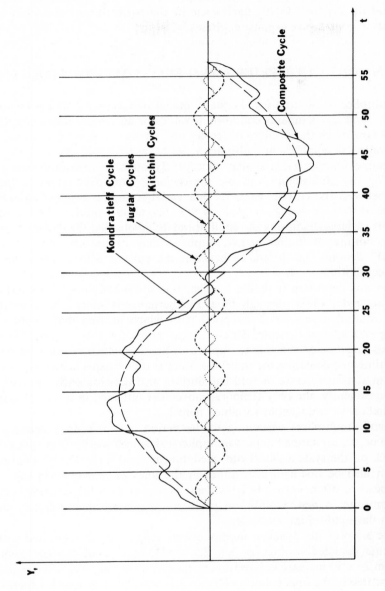

Figure 3.9 *Source:* Schumpeter, *Business Cycles*, p. 213.

movements and midyear fluctuations due to seasonal factors including weather and holidays. Again, t is measured in years. Figure 3.9 also displays the cumulative effect of all three cycles. This composite wave exemplifies the empirical movement in, say, real GNP. Each cycle in the figure begins and ends at the midpoints of consecutive expansion phases.[8]

3.5 DYNAMIC MULTIPLIERS AND ECONOMETRIC MODELS

Each multiplier considered for the static model of Chapter 2 and presented in Tables 2.1 and 2.2 compares equilibrium values of an endogenous variable and indicates how much those values differ per unit change in an exogenous variable. Each is called an equilibrium multiplier.

Dynamic analysis has a similar concept: dynamic, or disequilibrium, multipliers. For any endogenous variable the dynamic multiplier refers to the difference between the current value of that variable and its original equilibrium level, the difference being divided by the magnitude of the change in the exogenous variable disrupting the equilibrium. Symbolically, the dynamic government expenditures multiplier on, say, output at time t can be written as $\Delta Y_t' / \Delta G_o$, where $\Delta Y_t'$ denotes the difference between the current actual output and the original equilibrium level.

From this definition it should be clear that a dynamic multiplier, unlike its equilibrium twin, varies through time. Furthermore, it should be clear that a dynamic multiplier registers a temporal path which mirrors that of the corresponding endogenous variable. This analogue arises for two reasons. First, the exogenous impetus, ΔG_o in this example, is a number which remains unchanged through time in calculating the multiplier even if the impetus is merely one-shot. Second, in stationary state the old equilibrium also remains unchanged through time. Consequently, the only temporal movement reflected in a dynamic multiplier is that of the endogenous variable,[9] here Y_t.

Dynamic multipliers pertaining to the period in which an exogenous perturbation occurs are termed impact multipliers; they indicate the immediate effect of a shock on the system. Short-run, medium-run, and long-run dynamic multipliers can also be distinguished, although the lines of demarcation separating these types are often vague. It is evident, however, that for dynamic systems which converge to new equilibrium positions, the long-run multipliers should approach the equilibrium multipliers.

Table 3.3 presents dynamic multipliers on actual output associated with six experiments depicted in Figures 3.3, 3.5, and 3.6. Five of the six involve a permanent 25-unit increase in government expenditures, $\Delta G_o = 25$; the remaining case, presented in the final column of Table 3.3, presumes a temporary increase in

---

[8]Schumpeter, *Business Cycles*, pp. 161–162, 169, 172–174, 213.
[9]In mathematical terms a dynamic multiplier simply translates and scales the axis of the endogenous variable.

Table 3.3 Dynamic government expenditures multipliers on output under alternative lag structures and durations of exogenous impact

	Duration of increase in government expenditures					One period
	Permanent					
Time	$i = 1, j = 0$	$i = 3, j = 0$	$i = 3, j = 1$	$i = 1, j = 5$	$i = 1, j = 10$	$i = 1, j = 0$
0	0.000	0.000	0.000	0.000	0.000	0.000
1	1.000	0.000	0.000	1.000	1.000	1.000
2	1.473	0.000	0.000	1.616	1.616	.473
3	1.697	1.000	1.000	1.995	1.995	.224
4	1.802	1.000	1.000	2.229	2.229	.106
5	1.852	1.000	1.000	2.373	2.373	.050
6	1.876	1.473	1.616	2.462	2.462	.024
7	1.887	1.473	1.473	2.373	2.517	.011
8	1.893	1.473	1.473	2.231	2.550	.005
9	1.895	1.697	1.852	2.089	2.571	.003
10	1.896	1.697	1.676	1.968	2.584	.001
11	1.897	1.697	1.697	1.873	2.592	.001
12	1.897	1.802	1.930	1.801	2.453	0.000
13	1.897	1.802	1.767	1.770	2.280	0.000
14	1.897	1.802	1.805	1.771	2.119	0.000
15	1.897	1.852	1.946	1.792	1.986	0.000
16	1.897	1.852	1.813	1.822	1.884	0.000
17	1.897	1.852	1.859	1.855	1.808	0.000
18	1.897	1.876	1.941	1.885	1.754	0.000
19	1.897	1.876	1.838	1.908	1.716	0.000
20	1.897	1.876	1.886	1.922	1.689	0.000
21	1.897	1.887	1.929	1.927	1.671	0.000
22	1.897	1.887	1.855	1.927	1.658	0.000
23	1.897	1.887	1.899	1.921	1.671	0.000
24	1.897	1.893	1.919	1.914	1.703	0.000
25	1.897	1.893	1.866	1.906	1.746	0.000
30	1.897	1.896	1.904	1.890	1.926	0.000
35	1.897	1.897	1.905	1.898	1.972	0.000
40	1.897	1.897	1.893	1.898	1.916	0.000

expenditures of the same amount. All shocks occur at $t = 0$. i and j denote the length of the output and investment lags, respectively. Of course, $j = 0$ for the output configurations in Figures 3.3 and 3.5.

With $i = 1$ and $j = 0$, a permanent injection forces the dynamic multiplier for output continually upward at a decreasing rate, rising from an impact level of zero and culminating at the value of the equilibrium multiplier (1.897). No overshooting occurs. This pattern, as suggested, reflects the temporal response of actual output itself. When $i = 3$ and $j = 0$, a similar sequence develops, but because of stuttering the approach to the equilibrium magnitude 1.897 proceeds more slowly. For $j > 0$, the dynamic multiplier oscillates after assuming an impact value of zero. When $j = 1$, it always stays below two; but when $j = 5$ or $j = 10$, it exceeds that mark in the short to medium runs. For all three cases, however, the long-run multipliers can be shown to eventually equal the equilibrium level. The example of a temporary injection shows the dynamic multiplier declining from unity to a long-run level of zero. Its magnitude at impact equals zero as well.

The model underlying this series of dynamic multipliers—specifically, equations (3.1) to (3.3), (3.4a), (3.5), (3.6b), and (3.7) to (3.9)—provides a convenient framework for discussing the basic concepts of dynamics. It is especially helpful because it has a direct static counterpart which can be cited for comparison purposes. As it stands, however, the model is hardly a reasonable representation of a developed economy; it is too simple. It claims that consumption can be properly treated by a single function even though consumption actually encompasses automobiles, other durables, nondurables, and services, each of which may have causal determinants markedly different from the others. It also ignores lagged effects in consumption. Furthermore, the model fails to provide a meaningful separate focus on the various categories of investment (notably plant, equipment, housing, and inventories), and it has nothing to say about the role of output, existing capital, internal funds, and expectations on investment decisions.[10] Employment functions are absent, as are price determining equations. Moreover, no consideration is given to the different industrial sectors of an economy such as manufacturing, mining, and trade. In these and many other respects the dynamic model studied remains deficient for pragmatic, albeit not for pedagogic, purposes.

A number of macroeconomic models have been formulated to help describe and understand the complicated interactions within an economy and to help forecast its future course. These econometric[11] models consist of equations derived from theory and estimated empirically and thus come complete with "known" coefficients. These models vary greatly in detail and size. Some are highly aggregated, involving fewer than 10 equations. Others evidence appreciable disaggregation and entail hundreds of equations. Many fall between those guides.

The dynamic multipliers underlying such econometric macro systems are often constructed in a manner slightly different from that discussed earlier. Rather than being calculated with reference to a stationary equilibrium level, they are determined by referencing a baseline, or control, solution: namely, the path traversed by the economy in the absence of some contemplated policy action. For instance, if a policy initiative to be proposed is a permanent government program requiring an annual expenditure of $2.5 billion on nondefense goods and services, then the baseline solution traces the economy's motion in the face of all currently effective policies and programs while excluding the suggested $2.5 billion hike. This baseline may display cycles. The proposed program is then introduced into the model, and the resulting path can be compared against the baseline. For each endogenous variable the comparison gives the change in its magnitude across the

---

[10] Consumption and investment are revisited in Chapters 5 and 6.

[11] As mentioned in Section 13 of Appendix A, econometrics refers to the quantitative study which combines economics, mathematics, and statistics.

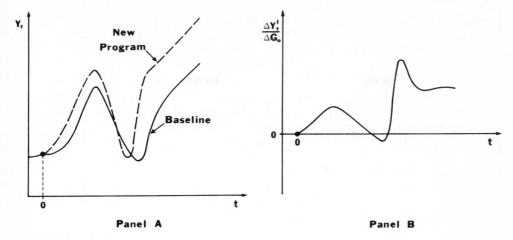

Panel A   **Panel B**

Figure 3.10

paths at any instant, a change which when divided by the $2.5 billion expenditure yields a value of the dynamic multiplier for that variable. Panel A of Figure 3.10 graphs hypothetical profiles of actual output from the baseline solution and from the solution evoked by the new program, which is anticipated to begin at time zero. Panel B shows the dynamic multiplier on output; that locus reflects the difference in the output paths generated with and without the nondefense program.

Dynamic multipliers for any endogenous variable differ across econometric models, and these discrepancies can be traced to a host of factors including the form of equations, the length of lags, the sample period used in the estimation process, and the estimation method itself. Table 3.4 illustrates this disagreement by reporting for seven quarterly econometric models of the U.S. economy the dynamic multipliers on real GNP due to a permanent increase in real government nondefense expenditures. Represented there are the models of the Bureau of Economic Analysis (BEA); the Brookings Institution; Data Resources, Incorporated (DRI); the Federal Reserve Bank of St. Louis; and the Wharton School of the University of Pennsylvania. Also considered are the DHL III model of the University of Michigan and the joint venture by the Massachusetts Institute of Technology, the University of Pennsylvania, and the Social Science Research Council (MIT-PENN-SSRC or, more succinctly, MPS).[12] Quarter 1 records the impact multipliers.

---

[12] For a detailed discussion of these and other econometric models, see Gary Fromm and Lawrence R. Klein, "A Comparison of Eleven Econometric Models of the United States," *American Economic Review*, **63** (May 1973), pp. 385–393, and the symposium on econometric model performance appearing in the *International Economic Review*, **15** (June, October 1974) and **16** (February 1975). Of the symposium papers, see especially Carl F. Christ, "Judging the Performance of Econometric Models of the U.S. Economy," **16** (February 1975), pp. 65–72.

Table 3.4 Dynamic multipliers on real GNP due to a sustained increase in real government nondefense spending, from alternative econometric models

	Econometric model						
Quarter	Bureau of Economic Analysis	Brookings Institution	Michigan DHL III	DRI Version 71	Federal Res., St. Louis	MIT-PENN-SSRC	Wharton Mark III
1	1.1	1.8	1.4	1.4	.5	1.2	1.3
2	1.7	2.4	1.6	1.7	1.0	1.5	1.6
3	2.1	2.7	1.7	1.7	1.0	1.9	1.8
4	2.2	2.8	1.7	1.6	.5	2.2	2.0
5	2.3	2.8	1.6	1.4	−.1	2.3	2.1
6	2.3	2.8	1.5	1.2	−.2	2.4	2.2
7	2.3	2.8	1.4	1.0	−.2	2.4	2.3
8	2.2	2.7	1.4	.9	−.2	2.2	2.4
12	1.8	2.4	1.0	.6	−.2	.7	2.6
16	1.6	2.0	1.0	.3	−.2	−.5	2.4
20	1.3	1.5	1.1	−.1	−.2	na	1.9
24	0.0	1.2	1.1	−2.5	na	na	1.2
28	−3.8	1.1	.7	−1.4	na	na	.3
32	−7.4	1.0	.2	2.2	na	na	−.8
36	−11.2	1.0	.1	2.7	na	na	−1.9
40	−23.2	.9	0.0	2.5	na	na	−3.0

na: not available.
Source: Fromm and Klein, "Eleven Econometric Models," p. 391.

For each model the multipliers oscillate through time, although in all but two systems they simply rise to a peak and then fall. The exceptional cases, DHL III and DRI-71, betray an extra rise and fall in the later stages of the adjustment process. The impact multipliers appear fairly uniform across the models, ranging from a low of .5 for the St. Louis paradigm to a high of 1.8 for the Brookings version. The remaining five lie in the interval 1.1 to 1.4. Medium-run multipliers, however, exhibit less conformity. For instance, the MPS model has in quarter 16 a multiplier of −.5, while the Brookings system has a multiplier of 2.0. Put equivalently, MPS claims that a $5 billion increase in nondefense spending *decreases* real GNP by $2.5 billion in the sixteenth quarter under the policy action, while Brookings argues that such action *increases* GNP by $10 billion. The long-run multipliers are even more divergent. In quarter 40, for example, the BEA value equals −23.2, which substantially understates the DRI level of 2.5. Either GNP falls by $116 billion or it rises by $12.5 billion!

Discrepant multipliers are just one explanation of why forecasts of the effects associated with a given policy move vary across models. Another explanation lies in the need for a forecaster to assign future values to the exogenous variables. Forecasting the temporal response of real GNP may require predicting future movements of, say, the money supply, and thus two researchers relying on the same model would likely generate different forecasts because of different assumptions about the subsequent behavior of money. A model may produce optimistic predictions only because the researcher has a felicitous "hunch" about a few key exogenous variables. As experience has shown, optimistic and pessimistic forecasts can exist simultaneously.

For a policy maker, econometric models and the forecasts emerging from them are helpful in formulating and assessing current and prospective initiatives. However, given the disparate forecasts conceivable from alternative models and the possible absence of a clear consensus among pundits, policy makers must regard such information as clues to be supplemented by other evidence. Doing otherwise could easily result in a policy maneuver that actually worsens an already acute economic situation.

3.6 DATING BUSINESS CYCLES IN PRACTICE

Developed economies have experienced frequent fluctuations in activity: it rises then falls, only to rise again. The introduction to Chapter 1 provided a glimpse at one of the most pronounced declines in economic fortune witnessed by the United States in over a century—the great depression. That episode, however, can be interpreted merely as an example, albeit a dramatic one, of the uneven movements which typify the maturation of established economies.

Scrutinizing fluctuations in the economic activity of the United States has been a principal endeavor of the National Bureau of Economic Research (NBER). Founded in 1920 by Wesley Mitchell and others, the NBER is a private nonprofit research organization which has an extensive and diversified list of study areas but which, since its inception, has been a leading authority on the temporal path traversed by the economy.

According to the NBER, a business cycle is a fluctuation in aggregate economic activity covering a wide range of economic processes.[13] It refers not to a swing in a single specific series but rather to the common movement evidenced by a large collection of them. It is therefore a somewhat amorphous concept. Cycles last from 1 to 12 years,[14] and they are measured by the NBER from trough to trough or from peak to peak. In the NBER's view, an individual cycle can be segmented into nine stages. Stage I embraces the three months centered on the

---

[13]Arthur F. Burns and Wesley C. Mitchell, *Measuring Business Cycles* (New York: NBER, 1946), p. 3.

[14]A fluctuation in a single series observing this time scale is termed a specific cycle of that series.

Although differing in scope of coverage, business and specific cycles both refer to absolute increases and decreases in activity. Another cycle concept has recently evolved, prompted by the much milder character of fluctuations since World War II. Known as a growth cycle, it refers to fluctuations in the growth rate of aggregate economic activity. Its comprehensiveness resembles that of a business cycle. Ilse Mintz discusses growth cycles in her "Dating United States Growth Cycles," *Explorations in Economic Research*, **1** (Summer 1974), pp. 1–113. So does Geoffrey H. Moore in his *Business Cycles, Inflation, and Forecasting* (Cambridge, Mass.: Ballinger Publishing Company, 1980), pp. 21–24, 444.

initial trough; stage IX does likewise but for the terminal trough. A middle stage, V, applies to the three months centered on the peak. The rise in activity occurring between stages I and V forms the expansion phase of the cycle and is divided into three segments of equal length: stages II, III, and IV. Similarly, the decline in business activity occurring between stages V and IX is partitioned into three equal segments, stages VI, VII, and VIII, each of whose length may differ from that of an expansion segment.[15] Figure 3.11 outlines this taxonomy, with Z_t denoting hypothetically general economic activity at time t. Th and Pk designate trough and peak periods, respectively; T and P, as before, represent trough and peak points, respectively. While the figure shows that expansions and contractions are separated by turning *periods*, the NBER often prefers to separate those phases simply by *points*.

Central to tracking the course of business cycles is the siting of their peaks and troughs. Locating these extreme points correctly is important both for descriptive purposes and for analytical inquiry. For instance, evaluating the severity of a recession or the strength of a recovery requires a comparison of actual magnitudes in those periods with some base. An appropriate base figure is the previous turning point, but improper diagnosis of its location can appreciably affect conclusions about the intensity of the fluctuation. Furthermore, determining the cause of a cycle and the effectiveness of countercyclical policy in ameliorating its consequences is inexorably tied to an accurate mapping of the cycle's course. A true profile can result only if the turning points are properly detected.

Describing the NBER's method for dating the peaks and troughs of business cycles, Mitchell and Burns in 1938 likened the process to one of successive approximation involving the review of cyclical movements evidenced by hundreds of separate series.[16] Over the decades, however, emphasis for pinpointing reference dates—dates of the business cycle turns—seems to have narrowed to a small set of series representing four dimensions of activity: production, income, employment, and sales. Nonetheless, information continues to be sought from other economic indicators, and some of the data consulted may be studied by means of composite and diffusion indices to be described anon. Work by the NBER in locating recent turning points exemplifies the streamlined analysis.[17]

Table 3.5 presents the NBER's chronology for all business cycles witnessed by the United States from December 1854 to July 1980. The chronology has been amended through time because of data revisions *inter alia*, and Table 3.5 embodies those amendments. Reference dates appear by month, by quarter, and

---

[15] Burns and Mitchell, *Measuring Business Cycles*, pp. 29–30.

[16] Wesley C. Mitchell and Arthur F. Burns, "Statistical Indicators of Cyclical Revivals," reprinted in Geoffrey H. Moore, ed., *Business Cycle Indicators*, vol. I (Princeton, N.J.: Princeton University Press, 1961), p. 163; Wesley C. Mitchell, *What Happens During Business Cycles?* (New York: NBER, 1951), p. 11.

[17] A clear presentation of the dating process appears in the comprehensive inquiry by Victor Zarnowitz and Geoffrey H. Moore, "The Recession and Recovery of 1973–1976," *Explorations in Economic Research*, **4** (Fall 1977), pp. 471–557.

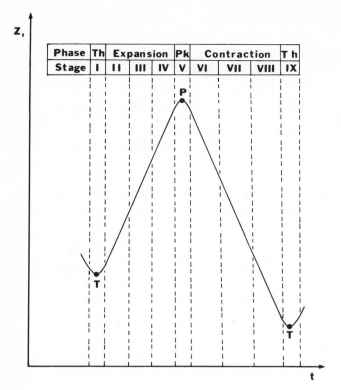

Figure 3.11

by year. Dates are first identified by month. In selecting the quarter to which a turning point applies, the NBER follows the principle that a turn is matched to the corresponding quarter unquestionably if the month occurs midquarter— February, May, August, or November. If not, then it applies either to that quarter or to the adjacent one, whichever seems more suitable in the quarterly setting. Annual turning points are set by a similar procedure.[18] Notice that a quarterly or annual turn may not coincide with the quarter or year of the monthly reference. For example, the peak in April 1865 translates into a peak at 1865:1 and 1864 on the quarterly and annual scales, respectively; likewise, the trough of January 1912 locates at 1911:4 and 1911 in the alternative formats. Clearly, the temporal pattern established on the basis of monthly data may not transfer to another time framework exactly.

Table 3.5 also records the duration of each expansion, contraction, and cycle. The length of a contraction is computed using the peak date in the given tabular line and the trough date in the following line. Cycles are measured from trough to trough, and the terminal trough of a particular cycle appears in the line succeed-

---

[18]Burns and Mitchell, *Measuring Business Cycles*, pp. 80–81.

Table 3.5 Reference dates and lengths of business cycles for the United States

Reference date perspective

Monthly		Quarterly		Yearly		Duration* of		
Trough	Peak	Trough	Peak	Trough	Peak	Expansion	Contraction	Cycle
December 1854	June 1857	1854 : 4	1857 : 2	1855	1856	30	18	48
December 1858	October 1860	1858 : 4	1860 : 3	1858	1860	22	8	30
June 1861	April 1865	1861 : 3	1865 : 1	1861	1864	46	32	78
December 1867	June 1869	1868 : 1	1869 : 2	1867	1869	18	18	36
December 1870	October 1873	1870 : 4	1873 : 3	1870	1873	34	65	99
March 1879	March 1882	1879 : 1	1882 : 1	1878	1882	36	38	74
May 1885	March 1887	1885 : 2	1887 : 2	1885	1887	22	13	35
April 1888	July 1890	1888 : 1	1890 : 3	1888	1890	27	10	37
May 1891	January 1893	1891 : 2	1893 : 1	1891	1892	20	17	37
June 1894	December 1895	1894 : 2	1895 : 4	1894	1895	18	18	36
June 1897	June 1899	1897 : 2	1899 : 3	1896	1899	24	18	42
December 1900	September 1902	1900 : 4	1902 : 4	1900	1903	21	23	44
August 1904	May 1907	1904 : 3	1907 : 2	1904	1907	33	13	46
June 1908	January 1910	1908 : 2	1910 : 1	1908	1910	19	24	43
January 1912	January 1913	1911 : 4	1913 : 1	1911	1913	12	23	35
December 1914	August 1918	1914 : 4	1918 : 3	1914	1918	44	7	51
March 1919	January 1920	1919 : 1	1920 : 1	1919	1920	10	18	28
July 1921	May 1923	1921 : 3	1923 : 2	1921	1923	22	14	36
July 1924	October 1926	1924 : 3	1926 : 3	1924	1926	27	13	40
November 1927	August 1929	1927 : 4	1929 : 3	1927	1929	21	43	64
March 1933	May 1937	1933 : 1	1937 : 2	1932	1937	50	13	63
June 1938	February 1945	1938 : 2	1945 : 1	1938	1944	80	8	88
October 1945	November 1948	1945 : 4	1948 : 4	1946	1948	37	11	48
October 1949	July 1953	1949 : 4	1953 : 2	1949	1953	45	10	55
May 1954	August 1957	1954 : 2	1957 : 3	1954	1957	39	8	47
April 1958	April 1960	1958 : 2	1960 : 2	1958	1960	24	10	34
February 1961	December 1969	1961 : 1	1969 : 4	1961	1969	106	11	117
November 1970	November 1973	1970 : 4	1973 : 4	1970	1973	36	16	52
March 1975	January 1980	1975 : 1	1980 : 1	1975	1979	58	6	64
July 1980		1980 : 3		1980				

*Entries are expressed in months.
Source: Moore, *Business Cycles and Forecasting*, pp. 438–439. Copyright © 1980, NBER. Reprinted with permission from Ballinger Publishing Company and NBER. Supplementary information obtained in part from U.S. Department of Commerce, *Commerce News* (Washington, D.C., July 29, 1981), p. 2.

ing the cycle's duration entry. For example, the initial and terminal troughs for the cycle lasting 78 months occurred in June 1861 and December 1867, respectively.

Two contractions have endured longer than 40 months: those of October 1873–March 1879 and August 1929–March 1933. The latter plunge, commonly associated with the collapse of the stock market in 1929, actually began *before* the fateful day on Wall Street.[19] Expansions have been more protracted than contractions; seven have survived beyond 40 months. That which began February 1961 proved to be especially long and caused some researchers to wonder if the notion of a 10-year business cycle had become obsolete.[20] However, the contractions since December 1969 seem to constitute ample evidence that the business cycle is not dead.

3.7 CONSTRUCTING COMPOSITE AND DIFFUSION INDICES: AN EXAMPLE

To decide the exact month of a business cycle peak or trough, economic series are studied individually; they can also be examined collectively by means of composite and diffusion indices. An example demonstrating the construction of such indices might help to explain their properties.[21]

Consider four indicators with the following temporal behavior:

		Recorded data, in dollars			
Series	January	February	March	April	May
A	10	20	35	10	5
B	2990	2995	3000	2995	2990
C	150	155	160	155	170
D	1.00	.85	1.20	1.10	1.25

Series A first expands, peaks in March, and then contracts. Series B, like A, rises to a March peak and falls afterward; however, its fluctuating movement, measured by the difference between "highs" and "lows," is much milder than that for A. Indicator C increases through March, decreases briefly, and then resumes its upward trek. Series D traces a sawtoothed pattern. It declines, rises, declines, and finally rises. Thus three of the four series expand continually from January to March, all peak in March, and all decline from March to April. From April to May two series expand while two contract. Observe the wide range in magnitudes across the four indicators: series B exceeds series D by a factor well in excess of 2000.

---

[19]John Kenneth Galbraith explores the relationship between the decline in economic activity and the crash of the stock market in *The Great Crash, 1929* (Boston: Houghton Mifflin Company, 1954), pp. 179–193.

[20]A conference addressing the possible extinction of the business cycle was held in 1967. Conference papers and the associated discussion appear in Martin Bronfenbrenner, ed., *Is the Business Cycle Obsolete?* (New York: John Wiley & Sons, Inc., 1969).

[21]Blueprints for these measures are offered by Ilse Mintz, "Dating Growth Cycles," pp. 22–24; Julius Shiskin, *Signals of Recession and Recovery: An Experiment with Monthly Reporting*, Occasional Paper 77 (New York: NBER, 1961), pp. 123–125; and U.S. Department of Commerce, *Handbook of Cyclical Indicators: A Supplement to the Business Conditions Digest* (Washington, D.C.: U.S. Government Printing Office, May 1977), pp. 73–76.

A composite index looks at both the amplitude and the direction of changes in all component series. Its value at the start of a period under investigation, January in this example, is set at 100, and consequently its level for each of the other months may be established from the percent changes relevant to consecutive months. The traditional manner of calculating percentages, however, treats increases and decreases asymmetrically because the value chosen as the base differs accordingly. Symmetry can be obtained by calculating percentages in the fashion used to determine arc elasticities: the average of the initial and terminal points becomes the base. Consonantly, for any series the percent change equals $100(S_g - S_f)/[(S_f + S_g)/2]$, where S_f and S_g denote the values assumed by the series at initial and terminal points f and g, respectively. Percent changes thus computed for the four series appear as

	Percent changes			
Series	January–February	February–March	March–April	April–May
A	66.67	54.55	− 111.11	− 66.67
B	.17	.17	− .17	− .17
C	3.28	3.17	− 3.17	9.23
D	− 16.22	34.15	− 8.70	12.77

Indicator C clearly shows symmetry in the percentages. February–March evidences an increase of 3.17 percent and March–April a decline of 3.17 percent. Had the traditional expression for percentage been adopted, the figures would have read 3.23 and − 3.13 percent, respectively.

An exception pertinent to the computational step just outlined deserves mention. If a series may evidence zero or negative values—as might one which refers to changes in the levels of some other variable—or if it is defined initially as a ratio or percentage, then the algebraic differences in the monthly magnitudes are calculated, instead of the symmetric percent changes. For example, series D might have measured dollar changes and followed the sequence − 1.00, − 17.22, 16.93, 8.23, and 21.00 from January through May. Calculation of its algebraic differences would then have resulted in the same figures entered above as percent changes.

The percentages recorded above for indicator A substantially exceed those for indicator B, and thus the informational content of the B changes would be lost in combining the two series into a single composite index unless the amplitude of the percent changes for the two were somehow reconciled. This process of adjusting amplitudes, called standardization, is quickly accomplished. For a given series the percent changes, with signs ignored, are averaged over the entire period January to May. The average is then divided into each of the percent changes for that series. This procedure causes the adjusted percent changes to average to unity over the entire period. Signs are ignored when computing the average because standardization attempts to correct the *amplitude* of the changes, and signs are irrelevant from the standpoint of amplitude. They indicate the *direction* of change. Averages for the four series are 74.75, .17, 4.71, and 17.96 percent, respectively, and hence the standardized rates become

	Standardized rates			
Series	January–February	February–March	March–April	April–May
A	.892	.730	− 1.486	− .892
B	1.000	1.000	− 1.000	− 1.000
C	.696	.673	− .673	1.960
D	− .903	1.901	− .484	.711

Obviously, series A no longer dominates series B.

Since all indicators now enjoy equal rank in terms of amplitude, amalgamation can proceed meaningfully across series. Consolidation occurs separately for each month by averaging the standardized rates across all series. In this stage of the calculations, averaging is conducted with full recognition of signs to incorporate into the final index the different directions of change characterizing the various series. Unweighted averages of the standardized rates register as

Average rates			
January–February	February–March	March–April	April–May
.421	1.076	− .911	.195

When some composite indices are constructed, weighted averages are formed.

The sequence of rates obtained departs from the standardizing rule; its four entries (signs disregarded) average to .65, not to 1. The sequence is therefore standardized, in this example by dividing the average into each element. What emerges are standardized average rates:

Standardized average rates			
January–February	February–March	March–April	April–May
.648	1.655	− 1.402	.300

From these numbers the values of the composite index result.

A composite index CI observes the same percent change expression as do the individual series. With ζ_{fg} denoting the standardized average rate relevant to initial and terminal points f and g, that expression gives

$$\zeta_{fg} = 100 \frac{CI_g - CI_f}{(CI_f + CI_g)/2}$$

and consequently

$$CI_g = CI_f \left(\frac{200 + \zeta_{fg}}{200 - \zeta_{fg}} \right)$$

Assigning 100 to the composite index for January and utilizing the standardized average rates .648, ... , .300 produces

Composite index				
January	February	March	April	May
100.00	100.65	102.33	100.91	101.21

This index rises continually to a March peak and falls in April, thereby confirming the suggestion gathered from casual inspection of the recorded data for series A through D. But it also makes some sense of the confused signals emanating from the four indicators during the April–May period. It says that, on balance, economic activity rose then.

Unlike a composite index, which addresses both the amplitude and the direction of changes implicit in a collection of series, a diffusion index DI focuses on direction alone. To construct a diffusion index for the four series A through D, each is designated in any given month as expanding ($+$) or as contracting ($-$). Peak months belong to the expansion, trough months to the contraction. Making the appropriate translations for the four series leaves

Phase description					
Series	January	February	March	April	May
A	+	+	+	−	−
B	+	+	+	−	−
C	+	+	+	−	+
D	−	−	+	−	+

Underlying the designations for January is the presumption that a movement between January and February continues an earlier pattern. Thus, the December value for series A lies below 10 while that for D remains above 1.

A diffusion index may be defined simply as the percent of the component series expanding. Alternatively, it may be taken as the net percent expanding: the percent expanding minus the percent contracting. This latter measure might also be expressed in cumulative fashion, where its value in any single month equals the sum of all current and previous net percentages. Each variant, however, conveys information on the extensiveness of a fluctuation in economic activity. In effect each asks, How widespread is the expansion or contraction?

Regarding the example under study, the sequences for the diffusion index calculated under the three definitions read

Diffusion index					
Definition	January	February	March	April	May
Percent expanding	75	75	100	0	50
Net percent expanding	50	50	100	− 100	0
Cumulative net percent expanding	50	100	200	100	100

Although the specific configurations displayed by the diffusion index differ across its alternative formats, all versions point to March as the peak month and hence support the conclusion deduced from the composite index. Observe that the cumulative net form continues to rise as long as more series are expanding than are contracting. It falls when the opposite occurs and remains stationary when the number of component series expanding just equals the number contracting.

3.8 AN INDICATOR APPROACH TO ANTICIPATING BUSINESS CYCLE TURNS

The reference chronology of NBER identifies turning points of aggregate economic activity. Some individual economic series coincide with those turns; they reach troughs approximately at business cycle troughs and peaks approximately at business peaks. Other series are tardy in their pattern; they turn only after the reference dates. Still others anticipate those dates. Their troughs and peaks occur before the turns of general activity, and they rise and fall before general activity does. A final group of series bears little or no systematic timing relationship to the business cycle.

Of the series which move in sympathy with business activity, several do so quite devoutly and hence can be used as a barometer of economic conditions. For instance, a few series which have turning points roughly coincident with those of business cycles lend themselves to gauging current business activity. Similarly, a few indicators which notoriously lag behind reference turns lend themselves to corroborating signals obtained from the coinciders. Of special interest, however, are those series which lead the cycle turns because they contain information that anticipates the future performance of the economy. Their decline constitutes a warning of a possible subsequent economic contraction, while their rise augurs a possible expansion. Interest in leading indicators is not new; it traces back at least four decades.[22]

Many series lead the reference dates but with differing degrees of consistency. To help select a convenient set of reliable leaders, the NBER established criteria by which a candidate is evaluated, and those criteria identified for the United States the following 12 series as leaders:[23]

1. Average length of workweek for production workers in manufacturing, in hours
2. Layoff rate in manufacturing, inverted
3. New orders for consumer goods and materials, in 1972 dollars

[22] Mitchell and Burns, "Statistical Indicators."

[23] Norms used in the selection process are described by Victor Zarnowitz and Charlotte Boschan, "Cyclical Indicators: An Evaluation and New Leading Indexes," in U.S. Department of Commerce, *Business Conditions Digest* (Washington, D.C.: U.S. Government Printing Office, May 1975), pp. vi–viii. "Cyclical Indicators" is reprinted in U.S. Department of Commerce, *Handbook of Cyclical Indicators*, pp. 170–184. Data on the leaders can be found in *Business Conditions Digest*; see, for instance, the April 1981 issue, pp. 60–61, 64–69, 71.

4. Index of net business formation
5. Index of stock prices for 500 common stocks
6. Contracts and orders for plant and equipment, in 1972 dollars
7. Index of new building permits for private housing
8. Vendor performance, percent of companies receiving slower deliveries
9. Net change in inventories on hand and on order, in 1972 dollars and smoothed
10. Percent change in sensitive crude materials prices, smoothed
11. Percent change in total liquid assets, smoothed
12. Money supply M2, in 1972 dollars

As notated, some measures are smoothed, meaning that their basic data are converted into moving averages. The layoff rate is registered in inverted fashion because this rate, as published by the Bureau of Labor Statistics, moves opposite to the business cycle. The index of net business formation addresses business incorporations and failures; it captures changes in the total business population. Sensitive crude materials prices refer to the prices of items, except agricultural products, entering the market for the first time. Captions for the remaining indicators are self-explanatory.

Each individual leader supplies information on one feature of economic activity. However, as the analysis in Section 3.6 suggested, each business cycle has characteristics unique to itself, and consequently allegiance to a single indicator, even that with the most impressive performance history, may miss key symptoms of an impending cyclical reversal. In short, crucial information might escape if reliance is placed on a single series.

Additional reasons can be offered for avoiding a focus on a single leader. Each series is subject to measurement error. While inaccuracies customarily reside in economic data, they become compounded for the leaders which, of necessity, must be based on preliminary figures. Taking the 12 indicators together allows any offsetting errors to cancel. Furthermore, treating the collection of indicators as a single unit tends to suppress the effect of erratic movements which contaminate the separate series.[24]

This single unit or composite index is formed largely in the manner described in Section 3.7. A few new wrinkles can be detected, however.[25] First, the differences or percent changes in each leader are standardized to unity (approximately) by an adjustment factor determined from a preassigned historical period. These standardized rates are then averaged for a given month across indicators not with equal weights but with weights that reflect the performance of the respective series. Leaders which perform more reliably receive greater weight. Next, the monthly average rates undergo standardization. However, rather than being set relative to unity, the standardized values are determined relative to the

---

[24] Zarnowitz and Boschan, "Cyclical Indicators," pp. viii–ix. Similar arguments can be mustered to defend the use by NBER of many series, rather than one, to establish reference dates.

[25] U.S. Department of Commerce, *Handbook of Cyclical Indicators*, pp. 73–76.

average of the absolute monthly rates of a group of coinciders. Tying the adjusted amplitude of the leading indicator index to that for coincident indicators makes the leading index more reflective of the magnitude of economic developments than does a link to unity. Finally, the standardized average rates of the leading index are modified to capture the secular drift of aggregate economic activity as approximated by the average trend for the coinciders. That trend is forced into the standardized average rates, and consequently it is the one observed by the leading index. Thus calculated, the composite index of leading indicators reflects both the amplitude and the trend of general business activity, but, of course, it leads that activity. The mathematics of the leading index appears in Appendix B.[26]

Performance of the leading index is depicted in Figure 3.12, which superimposes the movement of the index for the period from 1948 to early 1981 onto business cycle reference dates registered in Table 3.5. The shaded regions identify contraction phases. Each number in parentheses represents the total months by which an index turn leads the corresponding reference cycle turn, the latter being marked with an arrow. Clearly, the index led every peak and trough mapped. For instance, it peaked and turned down 15 months before business activity followed suit in January 1980. Likewise, it bottomed and rose 2 months before activity did in July 1980.

On the negative side of the ledger, the index has a tendency to give false signals. Figure 3.12 reveals that from mid-1950 to mid-1951 it warned of a decline in economic activity which never happened. Similarly, in 1962 and again in 1966 it incorrectly foretold of a contraction. These misses, coupled with sobering conclusions from several studies investigating the index's forecasting ability, advise caution in accepting the index as a predictive tool.[27]

---

[26] Coincident and lagging indicators also have composite indices. The index for the coinciders consists of four series: the number of employees on nonagricultural payrolls, the Federal Reserve Board index of industrial production, deflated personal income less transfers, and deflated manufacturing and trade sales. It emerges from the same steps followed in generating the composite index for leaders except that its average monthly rates are not standardized. The index of laggards entails six series: the average duration of unemployment, deflated manufacturing and trade inventories, the index of labor cost per unit of output in manufacturing, commercial and industrial loans outstanding, the ratio of consumer installment credit to personal income, and the average prime interest rate. Formation of the composite index of lagging indicators proceeds exactly as for the index of leaders. The aforementioned coinciders are the ones used in constructing the leading and lagging indices.

See Appendix B for the mathematics of the coincident and lagging indices. See also U.S. Department of Commerce, *Handbook of Cyclical Indicators*, pp. 73–76, and Victor Zarnowitz and Charlotte Boschan, "New Composite Indexes of Coincident and Lagging Indicators," in U.S. Department of Commerce, *Business Conditions Digest*, November 1975, pp. vii, xi. "New Composite Indexes" is reprinted in *Handbook of Cyclical Indicators*, pp. 185–199. Data on both indices are posted in *Business Conditions Digest*; consult, for example, the April 1981 issue, p. 60.

[27] A sampling of the disenchantment with the index's 1962 performance appears in George W. Cloos, "More on Reference Dates and Leading Indicators," *Journal of Business*, **36** (July 1963), pp. 360–361. Thoughts urging diffidence in utilizing the index come from Saul H. Hymans, "On the Use of Leading Indicators to Predict Cyclical Turning Points," *Brookings Papers on Economic Activity*, no. 2 (1973), p. 358, and from H. O. Stekler and Martin Schepsman, "Forecasting with an Index of Leading Series," *Journal of the American Statistical Association*, **68** (June 1973), p. 295.

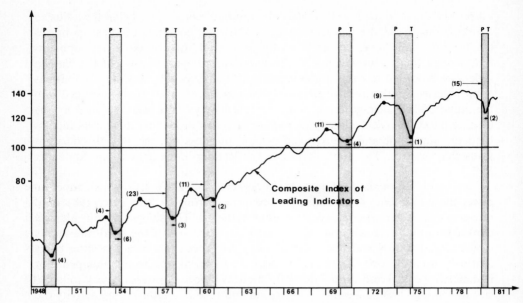

Figure 3.12 *Source*: Series 910 (equal to 100 in 1967) reported by U.S. Department of Commerce, *Business Conditions Digest*, April 1981, p. 10. Supplementary information obtained from U.S. Department of Commerce, *Commerce News*, July 29, 1981, p. 2.

It bears mentioning that graphical displays such as Figure 3.12 somewhat misstate the forecasting ability of the composite index. The version of the index profiled there did not exist prior to 1979 (although its separate components did), and consequently that temporal configuration largely depicts values which the index *would have* assumed on data revised since their original publication. In practice, however, an initial report of the index for a given month is based on preliminary and incomplete information. Hence, a signal from the index in any instance may reflect data error more than it does a true movement in economic forces despite the error offset possible from the index's format. To guard against the possible erratic behavior of the index, some economists reserve judgment about the prospects of a future reversal in economic fortune until a new direction taken by the index persists for several consecutive months.

The composite index of leading indicators is subject to ongoing refinement. This evolutionary process has as its goal the development of an indicator which is the most reliable possible in the face of exogenous shocks and a changing structure of the economy. The composite index and the econometric models now extant attempt to extract information on the future path of the economy, information which would enable policy makers to adjust that path to temper cyclical fluctuations. Efficacy of policy action is therefore tied to forecasting, which regrettably still remains an art in search of a science.

3.9 THE SCOPE OF HARMONIC MOTION WITHIN BUSINESS CYCLES

According to the NBER, business cycles consist of sympathetic movements in series which cover many different dimensions of economic activity. A glimpse at the extensiveness of this harmonic response is provided by Table 3.6, which summarizes for the United States the temporal behavior of 30 economic series over all business cycle phases from the end of 1948 to mid-1980. Albeit hardly exhaustive, the table does sample a fairly wide range of segments making up the macro system.

Column designation C49 identifies the business contraction which terminated October 1949 or 1949 : 4, the monthly or quarterly scale being decided by the time dimension of the particular series under examination. In a like manner E53 identifies the reference expansion which expired July 1953 or 1953 : 2. Table 3.5 lists the reference dates pertinent to the other column designations with one exception—C80. While that abbreviation does represent 1980 : 3 in the quarterly format, it stands for August 1980, not July 1980, in the monthly setting.[28] Seasonal fluctuations have been removed from all variables normally subject to them.

The direction of movement in each series during a given business cycle phase was determined by comparing its values at the corresponding reference turns. A minus sign represents a decline in the series; a plus means an increase. For instance, the minus applicable to the Federal Reserve Board (FRB) production index in the C49 column signifies that the index's value at the reference trough of October 1949 fell below its value at the reference peak of November 1948. By contrast, the plus pertinent to real GNP in E53 says that the level of GNP for 1953 : 2 exceeded that for 1949 : 4. A posting of zero indicates that a series held the same value at the beginning and end of the relevant reference phase. The last column of the table reports a synchronous ratio. For any series it expresses the number of consonant movements relative to the total number of reference phases. A phase with an entry of zero is ignored in calculating the ratio. For the two unemployment variables and the two "failure" variables in the business climate group, the ratio is calculated from their inverted movements since those series measure inactivity and should on theoretical grounds respond in a contracyclical fashion.[29]

The historical profiles for many series match the reference phases very neatly throughout the three decades examined; 18 of the 30 measures show synchronous ratios above .90. GNP and the production index fall during business contractions and rise during expansions. Capacity utilization follows a like pattern, as do

---

[28]August serves as endpoint because it seemed to be a strong candidate for the trough month when this inquiry was being conducted. July was declared the trough only after the study had been completed.

[29]Table 3.6 strongly resembles Table 21 in Burns and Mitchell, *Measuring Business Cycles*, pp. 98–99. The present analysis may be viewed as updating that earlier investigation.

Table 3.6 Expansions and contractions for selected series during consecutive business cycle phases: the United States experience

Series	Business cycle phases													Sync. ratio
	C49	E53	C54	E57	C58	E60	C61	E69	C70	E73	C75	E80	C80	
Production														
Gross national product*	−	+	−	+	+	+	−	+	−	+	+	−	−	1.00
Industrial production index, FRB	−	−	−	+	−	+	−	+	−	+	+	+	−	1.00
Capacity utilization rate, FRB	−	+	−	+	+	+	−	+	−	+	+	+	−	1.00
Income														
Personal disposable income*	−	+	−	+	+	+	+	+	+	+	+	+	−	.85
Corporate profit after taxes*	−	+	−	+	+	+	−	+	+	+	+	+	−	1.00
Employment														
Civilian employment	−	+	−	+	+	+	−	+	−	+	−	+	−	1.00
Civilian unemployment	−	−	+	+	−	−	+	−	+	−	+	−	+	1.00
Unemployment rate	+	−	+	+	−	−	+	−	+	−	+	+	+	1.00
Sales														
Retail sales*	+	+	−	+	−	+	−	+	−	+	−	+	−	.92
Manufacturing and trade sales*	−	+	−	+	+	+	−	+	+	+	−	+	−	1.00
Aggregate demand														
Personal consumption expenditure*	+	+	−	+	−	+	−	+	+	+	−	+	−	.77
Gross private domestic fixed investment*	−	+	−	+	−	+	−	+	−	+	−	+	−	1.00
Inventory investment*	−	+	−	+	+	+	−	+	−	+	−	+	−	1.00

	Inventories		New orders			Interest rates				Prices					Business climate				
Manufacturers' finished goods inventories*†	+	+	+	−	+	+	+	+	+	−	+									.46
Manufacturing and trade inventories*	+	+	+	−	−	+	+	−	+	+	−									.77
Plant and equipment contracts and orders*	−	+	+	−	+	+	+	−	+	+	+									1.00
New orders with capital goods industries, nondefense*	−	+	+	−	+	+	+	−	+	+	+									1.00
New orders for consumer goods and materials*	−	+	+	−	+	+	+	−	+	+	+									1.00
Treasury bill rate	−	+	+	−	+	+	+	−	+	+	+									1.00
Average prime rate	0	+	+	−	+	+	+	−	+	+	+									1.00
Corporate bond yields	−	+	+	−	+	+	+	−	+	+	+									.77
Municipal bond yields	−	+	+	−	+	+	+	−	+	+	+									.77
Implicit GNP price deflator	−	+	+	−	+	+	+	+	+	+	+									.54
Consumer price index	−	+	+	−	+	+	+	+	+	+	+									.54
Producer price index	−	0	+	−	+	+	+	0	+	+	+									.64
Producer price index of crude materials	−	+	+	−	−	−	−	−	−	+	+									.77
Stock price index, 500 common stocks	+	+	+	−	+	+	+	+	+	+	+									.69
Net business formation index	−	+	+	−	−	−	−	−	−	+	−									1.00
Business failure rate	+	−	+	+	+	+	+	+	+	−	+									.92
Liabilities of business failures*‡	−	+	+	+	+	+	+	+	+	+	+									.62

*Series is expressed in constant dollars.

†Nominal figures are deflated by the implicit price deflator for personal consumption expenditures.

‡Nominal figures are deflated by the implicit price deflator for gross private domestic fixed investment.

Source: Author's findings based on data appearing in various issues and supplements of U.S. Department of Commerce, Business Conditions Digest and Survey of Current Business (Washington, D.C.: U.S. Government Printing Office).

Table 3.7 Annual percent changes for selected series during consecutive business cycle phases: the United States experience

Series	Business cycle phases												
	C49	E53	C54	E57	C58	E60	C61	E69	C70	E73	C75	E80	C80
Personal disposable income, real (Q)	−1.52	5.29	−.83	4.64	−.88	3.88	.60	5.41	3.13	5.21	−3.00	4.07	−3.08
Personal consumption expenditure, real (Q)	2.21	4.04	.49	4.11	−.13	4.74	−.09	5.20	.92	4.89	−.91	4.74	−3.01
Manufacturers' finished goods inventories, real (M)	2.52	6.61	3.94	5.51	−4.34	1.74	4.13	3.87	5.31	−1.65	11.81	.62	4.53
Manufacturing and trade inventories, real (M)	1.27	8.95	−4.38	2.91	−4.99	4.06	−.06	6.61	1.80	3.58	.44	3.32	−.03
Implicit GNP price deflator (Q)	−2.06	3.54	1.36	2.94	.82	2.13	.39	3.27	5.08	5.73	11.16	8.10	9.63
Consumer price index (M)	−2.25	3.49	.30	1.60	3.18	1.10	1.08	2.99	5.41	5.37	11.01	9.89	11.91
Producer price index (M)	−7.09	3.53	0.00	2.10	1.12	.26	0.00	1.59	2.31	8.51	16.81	10.26	12.24

Producer price index of crude materials (M)	−12.85	2.54	−.93	−.06	−.88	−1.82	−.73	1.70	−.10	22.80	−2.47	13.28	18.37
Stock price index, 500 common stocks (M)	4.28	14.10	21.93	18.32	−11.45	15.81	13.87	5.27	−8.18	7.02	−13.42	6.69	19.53
Gross national product, nominal (Q)	−3.39	12.51	−1.90	7.35	−2.47	7.57	.16	10.06	4.51	12.00	5.38	14.86	4.93
Personal consumption expenditure, nominal (Q)	1.29	7.90	1.91	6.37	1.89	6.82	1.06	9.32	5.37	10.86	9.85	14.83	6.42
Gross private domestic investment, nominal (Q)	−27.55	19.42	−10.16	13.06	−28.41	18.76	−18.70	13.07	−1.54	21.39	−18.59	23.64	−21.51
Addendum: phase duration													
In months	11	45	10	39	8	24	10	106	11	36	16	58	7
In quarters	4	14	4	13	3	8	3	35	4	12	5	20	2

Source: Table 3.5 and author's findings from the publications cited in Table 3.6.

after-tax profits, civilian employment, and both sales variables. Also responding in accord with the business cycle are the two major components of gross private domestic investment—fixed and inventory investment—along with the three measures of new orders, the Treasury bill and average prime interest rates, and the business formation index. Three of the four barometers of inactivity register an equally impressive performance record, the lone exception being the liabilities of business failures. That variable, when inverted, agrees with reference cycles poorly.[30]

Personal disposable income has a synchronous score of .85. It does not mesh with 2 of the 13 reference phases, but each miss coincides with a business contraction. Business expansions are observed faithfully. An analogous history characterizes personal consumption, which registers .77 on the synchronous scale. Manufacturing and trade inventories move sympathetically with economic activity through the fifties and sixties, but they do not conform in the contractions of the seventies. Nonetheless, they resume their sympathetic behavior in 1980. Finished goods inventories are much less congruent with reference cycles. Interest rates on corporate and municipal bonds track business phases well until the mid-seventies, when they lose step. Far more obvious departures from the reference cycle pattern, however, occur for the GNP price deflator and for the consumer price index. With the exception of the first contraction period, these variables never decline. Or do they?

A string of pluses connotes that a series continues to expand absolutely; it says nothing about the *relative* movement of the series over different phases of the cycle. A variable which expands throughout successive business phases might on a systematic basis grow more slowly during some; yet such information would not be transmitted by consecutive pluses. Consecutive minuses might withhold similar information. Table 3.7 addresses this subtler issue by presenting the annual percent changes for those variables which Table 3.6 listed as having at least four uninterrupted occurrences of the same sign.

All percentages appearing in Table 3.7 for a series were determined by expressing the difference between values at adjacent references turns relative to the value at the earlier turn. Depending upon the time dimension of that series, the resulting "raw" percentages were converted into monthly or quarterly rates and then annualized. An M or Q in parentheses following a descriptor of a series marks the dimension as either monthly or quarterly, respectively, and the addendum records the duration of each cycle phase. These latter entries enabled computation of the monthly or quarterly percentages.

Of the four nonprice variables repeated from Table 3.6 in the first four rows of Table 3.7, three display a distinct pattern: their lower rates of growth always

---

[30] In view of the perfect synchronous scores for the industrial production index, manufacturing and trade sales, plant and equipment orders, new orders for consumer goods, the average prime rate, and the business formation index, it is not surprising that these series find their way into the composite indices of leading, coincident, and lagging indicators. The synchronous ratio measures the ability of a series to match its phases with those of the business cycle, and that ability falls under the conformity criterion used to evaluate a series for inclusion in any of the indices.

correspond to business cycle contractions.[31] Real disposable income, for example, increases at a .60 percent annual rate during the contraction ending 1961 : 1, but it grows at a 5.41 percent rate during the subsequent expansion. It rises at 3.13 percent in the next contraction and at 5.21 percent afterward. The maverick series, real finished goods inventories, rises more slowly during contractions but only prior to the sixties.

The GNP price deflator, the consumer price index, and the producer price index generally show slower increases during business slumps until the end of 1969. For them, however, the seventies give birth to a dramatically different sequence. Specifically, each of the three contractions beginning with the one which expired in 1970 has an annual inflation rate higher than that in the preceding expansion, and the contractions of 1973 to 1975 and of 1980 evidence the greatest inflation rate since World War II: it assumes double-digit proportions! Resistance of these price indices to moderation during contraction combined with the simultaneous growth in unemployment reported in Table 3.6 manifest the anomaly of stagflation: high rates of inflation and unemployment occurring together.[32]

Table 3.7 also presents the temporal response of three popular series not reported in Table 3.6, namely, GNP, consumption, and investment all expressed in current dollars. With the three, absolute or relative declines always occur during business cycle contractions.

Two lessons emerge from Tables 3.6 and 3.7. First, many individual economic series exhibit consistent patterns over the course of business cycles. Those which directly measure economic activity tend to rise during reference expansions and tend to fall absolutely or relatively during reference contractions. Interest rates and prices behave likewise. Series which measure inactivity tend to move in an opposite fashion. A definite repetitiveness can therefore be discerned in business cycles. Second, while strong tendencies persist, departures from them are not infrequent, and differing nuances can be perceived. As Wesley Mitchell observed back in 1913, business history repeats itself, but always with a difference.[33]

---

[31] Such relative declines are symptomatic of the growth cycles mentioned in footnote 14 earlier in this chapter.

[32] The causes, consequences, and controls of stagflation are topics pursued in James H. Gapinski and Charles E. Rockwood, eds., *Essays in Post-Keynesian Inflation* (Cambridge, Mass.: Ballinger Publishing Company, 1979).

[33] Mitchell's remark is reprinted in his *Business Cycles and Their Causes*, p. ix.

FOUR

POPULAR MODELS OF CYCLICAL RESPONSE

Several dynamic macro models highlight the search for a theoretical explanation of cyclical behavior. Four are considered here, namely, those of Frisch, Samuelson, Hicks, and Metzler. All share a close kinship in that they crucially involve the acceleration principle or accelerationlike phenomena. Before the models themselves are discussed, a theoretical justification of the acceleration principle seems appropriate. Of special interest are the conditions required for its representation in linear form since linearity is imposed by each model.

4.1 THE ACCELERATION PRINCIPLE

Following the tradition of Keynes and the classics, the previous two chapters treated investment as dependent upon the rate of interest. Higher interest rates induce smaller investment *ceteris paribus*, while lower rates induce greater investment. An alternative description of investment, known formally as the "acceleration principle," postulates that net investment depends positively upon the change in income and may be written as

$$I_t = f(\Delta Y_t)$$

where I_t denotes real net investment at time t and Y_t denotes real income (real output) at t. The change in income is understood to pertain to a single time period.[1]

---

[1]Discussion in this section uses discrete changes to help express relationships even when a relationship is derived by calculus. A review of calculus and of other quantitative tools appears in Appendix A.

The acceleration principle is often represented linearly, a formulation referred to as the simple accelerator:

$$I_t = v(Y_t - Y_{t-1})$$

or perhaps

$$I_t = v(Y_{t-1} - Y_{t-2})$$

More distant income changes might be invoked instead. The constant v (≥ 0) is called the "acceleration coefficient." Empirical evidence on this linear version is hardly impressive, providing little support for it.[2] These findings must be viewed in perspective, however. While they cast grave doubt on the simple accelerator, they do not necessarily deny the *principle* of acceleration, which is grounded in theory.

The basis of acceleration is the theory of the firm.[3] Consider the case of a profit-maximizing perfect competitor. The expression for profit π reads

$$\pi = pQ - wL - qK \qquad (4.1)$$

where Q denotes the quantity of the firm's output and L and K represent its quantity of labor and its stock of capital, respectively. Output and inputs are tied together by some type of production function. p and w denote the prices of output and labor, respectively, while q denotes the capital rental. From equation (4.1) the conditions necessary for a profit maximum are

$$\text{MP}_L = \frac{w}{p} \qquad \text{and} \qquad \text{MP}_K = \frac{q}{p}$$

where MP_L and MP_K signify the marginal products of labor and capital, respectively. Therefore, at the profit maximum point,

$$\frac{\text{MP}_L}{\text{MP}_K} = \frac{w}{q} \qquad (4.2)$$

[2] Several experiments were conducted on a simple accelerator which reflected alternatively the current income change ($Y_t - Y_{t-1}$) and the previous change ($Y_{t-1} - Y_{t-2}$). Gross private fixed investment less capital consumption allowances served as net investment; net national product (NNP) and GNP served as income. Annual deflated figures were gathered on all variables, and the equations were estimated by ordinary least squares both for 1950–1975 and for 1968–1975. The resulting regressions always displayed low explanatory power, the r^2 being essentially zero, and their residuals frequently appeared autocorrelated. Both findings suggest that important variables had been omitted from the equations.

Debate between accelerationists and profiteers—those who believe that profit (or, more generally, finance) considerations are important determinants of investment—prompted additional experiments. Real net investment was postulated as linearly dependent upon real income. One equation contained an intercept; the other did not. Again NNP and GNP were adopted along with annual time frames for the periods 1950–1975 and 1968–1975. The least-squares equations evidenced a quality similar to that for the simple accelerator. Their explanatory power proved low and autocorrelation seemed operative.

[3] The following derivation generalizes that by Daniel Hamberg, *Models of Economic Growth* (New York: Harper & Row, Publishers, 1971), pp. 21–24.

The left-hand term in this equation is the marginal rate of technical substitution (MRTS).

More information is required about the production function to proceed further with the derivation. Let it be the constant elasticity of substitution (CES) function, developed independently by Arrow, Chenery, Minhas, and Solow, and by Brown and de Cani.[4] As the name suggests, it imposes the same value for the elasticity of substitution at each point of every isoquant. That elasticity is the percent change in factor proportion divided by the percent change in MRTS when output remains fixed; factor proportion means the capital-labor ratio K/L. Since MRTS is the negative of an isoquant's slope, the elasticity can be viewed as a measure of an isoquant's curvature.

The CES may be written as

$$Q = \gamma [\xi_1 K^{-\rho} + \xi_2 L^{-\rho}]^{-\zeta/\rho} \tag{4.3}$$

Parameters γ and ζ are positive and finite, while parameters ξ_1 and ξ_2 are positive and sum to unity. Parameter ρ can assume any value from -1 to infinity inclusive. The elasticity of substitution, symbolized by σ, is $1/(1 + \rho)$. Three special cases of the CES can be identified: the Leontief fixed-proportion function ($\sigma = 0$), the Cobb-Douglas function ($\sigma = 1$), and the linear-isoquant function ($\sigma \to \infty$). These formulas are derived in Appendix C.

From (4.3) MRTS can be expressed as $(\xi_2/\xi_1)(K/L)^{1+\rho}$, and thus (4.2) reduces to

$$\frac{\xi_2}{\xi_1} \left(\frac{K}{L} \right)^{1+\rho} = \frac{w}{q}$$

and to

$$K = \left(\frac{\xi_1}{\xi_2} \right)^{\sigma} \left(\frac{w}{q} \right)^{\sigma} L \tag{4.4}$$

Equation (4.4) describes the optimal (profit maximizing) factor proportion. However, since this inquiry seeks the acceleration principle, (4.4) should be rewritten to express capital in terms of output, thereby enabling the connection between their changes to be deduced. Equation (4.4) is transformed by solving the production function (4.3) for L under the rule of constant returns to scale, $\zeta = 1$:[5]

$$L = \left[\frac{1}{\xi_2} \left(\frac{Q}{\gamma} \right)^{-\rho} - \frac{\xi_1}{\xi_2} K^{-\rho} \right]^{-1/\rho}$$

---

[4] K. J. Arrow, H. B. Chenery, B. S. Minhas, and R. M. Solow, "Capital-Labor Substitution and Economic Efficiency," *Review of Economics and Statistics*, **43** (August 1961), pp. 225–250, and Murray Brown and John S. de Cani, "Technological Change and the Distribution of Income," *International Economic Review*, **4** (September 1963), pp. 289–309.

[5] A constant returns production function and perfect competition render the objective function (4.1) linearly homogeneous in K and L. Profits can be expanded without limit by simply increasing capital and labor in the same proportion, and consequently the optimization process does not determine the levels of output and inputs. However, while levels cannot be solved without recourse to an extraneous constraint, such as market size or labor availability, the optimization process does determine proportions, notably the capital-labor and capital-output ratios.

Thus (4.4) becomes

$$K = \left(\frac{\xi_1}{\xi_2}\right)^{\sigma}\left(\frac{w}{q}\right)^{\sigma}\left[\frac{1}{\xi_2}\left(\frac{Q}{\gamma}\right)^{-\rho} - \frac{\xi_1}{\xi_2}K^{-\rho}\right]^{-1/\rho}$$

Raising both sides to the $-\rho$ power and collecting the $K^{-\rho}$ terms make

$$K^{-\rho}\left[1 + \left(\frac{\xi_1}{\xi_2}\right)^{1-\sigma\rho}\left(\frac{w}{q}\right)^{-\sigma\rho}\right] = \left(\frac{\xi_1}{\xi_2}\right)^{-\sigma\rho}\left(\frac{w}{q}\right)^{-\sigma\rho}\frac{1}{\xi_2}\left(\frac{Q}{\gamma}\right)^{-\rho}$$

Simplification yields

$$K = \Lambda Q \tag{4.5}$$

where

$$\Lambda = \gamma^{-1}\left[\xi_1 + \xi_2\left(\frac{\xi_1}{\xi_2}\right)^{1-\sigma}\left(\frac{w}{q}\right)^{1-\sigma}\right]^{1/\rho}$$

Equation (4.5) shows that the optimum capital stock is proportional to the quantity of output, and hence the notion of acceleration is close at hand. The proportionality term Λ, however, involves the wage-rent ratio, and consequently two cases must be examined. The first is straightforward: $\sigma = 0$. Because of technical characteristics of production, the factor proportion is fixed and all isoquants are right-angled. In this case Λ reduces to

$$\Lambda = \gamma^{-1}\left[\xi_1 + \xi_1\frac{w}{q}\right]^0 = \frac{1}{\gamma}$$

Thus from (4.5)

$$\Delta K = \frac{1}{\gamma}\Delta Q$$

Since ΔK can be identified as net investment, this equation is the simple accelerator.

In the more general case, the factor proportion is not fixed by technical circumstances—that is, $\sigma > 0$—and therefore a change in the wage-rent ratio can alter the factor proportion. To examine this possibility, write (4.5) more generally as

$$K = K\left(Q, \frac{w}{q}\right)$$

Capital may change either because output changes or because the wage-rent ratio changes, the linkage being

$$\Delta K = \Lambda\Delta Q + \Omega\Delta\left(\frac{w}{q}\right) \tag{4.6}$$

with $\Omega = \Omega(Q, w/q)$.

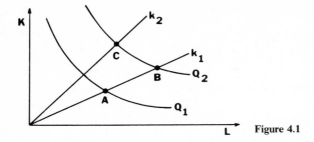

Figure 4.1

When variable factor proportions are permitted, the theory of the firm does give rise to an acceleration component for net investment. There is, however, a second component which reflects a change in relative factor prices. Equation (4.6) therefore generates two separate movements, as Figure 4.1 illustrates. k_1 and k_2 denote factor proportions; Q_1 and Q_2, output levels. One movement occurs for a given proportion: for example, that from point A to point B in the figure. This response represents the acceleration effect $\Lambda \Delta Q$; there is no substitution between inputs. The other movement occurs along a given isoquant, from B to C. It represents the substitution effect $\Omega \Delta(w/q)$, where changes in relative factor prices force the substitution of inputs. Only if relative prices remain fixed does the acceleration principle operate without compromise. If $\Delta(w/q) = 0$, then (4.6) becomes

$$\Delta K = \Lambda \Delta Q$$

This analysis reveals two important points. First, there is an acceleration phenomenon in investment, but it is not the only determinant if factor proportions are variable and if relative factor prices are changing. In that instance relative price changes lead to a substitution effect which contaminates the pure acceleration effect and invalidates the simple accelerator. The change in relative factor prices which has characterized factor markets provides one, though not the only, explanation for the poor empirical performance of the simple accelerator.

The second point complements the first. The simple accelerator is valid in two cases: either when the factor proportion is fixed by the nature of the production process—it is Leontief in fact—or when the factor proportion is variable but relative prices are fixed. In the latter circumstance, even though alternative factor proportions are technically possible, they do not arise because of price considerations. The production process is Leontief in effect. It should be obvious that under the simple accelerator, labor is assumed to change to accommodate the changed capital stock. Labor adjusts to preserve constancy in the factor proportion.

Although the simple accelerator can be justified only under rather stringent conditions, its linear form affords substantial convenience in exposition. Furthermore, it may be regarded as providing a crude approximation to more sophisticated investment functions. In any event, the dynamic models to be discussed next adopt the simple accelerator as a fundamental premise.

4.2 FRISCH'S THEORY OF ERRATIC SHOCKS

Frisch develops dynamic macro formats which express net investment as a constant proportion of the change in consumption.[6] Assorted time profiles are generated for the variables depending upon model formulation and parameter values, and those profiles include unidirectional convergence, linear trends, and damped oscillations. Frisch's preferred model, when coupled with his appraisal of parameter values, gives rise to damped oscillations. Any shock to the system therefore sets into motion cyclical fluctuations which eventually fade away provided that no other disturbances arise in the interim. Because of the economy's intrinsic structure, the cyclical effect of a single perturbation is transmitted (or propagated) temporally.

Shocks are unlikely to synchronize themselves to assure that each one arrives only after the effect of its predecessor has vanished. A more plausible prospect envisions a system that is bombarded erratically by shocks which strike at different times, in different directions, and with different strengths. Shocks occur while the influence of earlier ones still operates. It is this succession of disturbances which provides the force (or impulse) required to sustain cycles. The cyclical movement of variables reflects the cumulative effect of separate perturbations, and although the fluctuations may display varying amplitudes and periods, they can reasonably be viewed as regular, claims Frisch.[7] Figure 4.2 presents a sketch.

Y_E denotes the equilibrium level of income. For convenience each shock is assumed to cause only an instantaneous displacement of equilibrium, and consequently the Y_E depicted can be understood to apply uniformly through time. A disturbance at time t_0 propels the system away from Y_E and starts the dampening process, as the solid line shows. Before the system totally recovers from that shock, another occurs at t_1, renewing the disruption. Again dampening sets in but only to be upset at t_2. The cumulative effect of these disturbances produces a temporal pattern which resembles regular cycles (the dashed line).

4.3 A SAMUELSON-TYPE INTERACTION MODEL

Samuelson postulates a dynamic macro system which combines the multiplier process with acceleration effects originating from the simple accelerator.[8] The

---

[6]Ragnar Frisch, "Propagation Problems and Impulse Problems in Dynamic Economics," in *Economic Essays in Honour of Gustav Cassel* (London: George Allen and Unwin, Ltd., 1933; reprinted, New York: Augustus M. Kelley, Bookseller, 1967), pp. 171–205. The derivation of the simple accelerator in Section 4.1 can be amended to relate investment to a change in consumption rather than to a change in income by treating equation (4.3) as the production function for consumer goods.

[7]Frisch's emphasis on regular cycles reflects his observation that actual fluctuations displayed approximate regularity. Ibid., pp. 202–203.

[8]Paul A. Samuelson, "Interactions Between the Multiplier Analysis and the Principle of Acceleration," *Review of Economic Statistics*, **21** (May 1939), pp. 75–78.

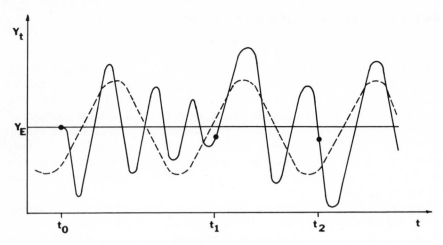

Figure 4.2 *Source*: Frisch, "Propagation Problems," p. 202.

following model closely parallels his.

$$C_t = cY_t \qquad (4.7)$$

where c denotes the marginal propensity to consume, $0 < c < 1$. Equation (4.7) says that real consumption is proportional to real income. For real investment

$$I_t = b(C_t - C_{t-1}) \qquad (4.8)$$

$b \ (\geq 0)$ represents the acceleration coefficient pertinent to consumption. Since consumption depends upon income, equation (4.8) can be rewritten to explicitly reflect an income change; namely,

$$I_t = bc(Y_t - Y_{t-1}) \qquad (4.8a)$$

Real government spending is exogenously determined,

$$G_t = G_o \qquad (4.9)$$

and production observes a simple rule which prescribes equating current supply to last period's demand:

$$Y_t = C_{t-1} + I_{t-1} + G_{t-1} \qquad (4.10)$$

The difference between this model and Samuelson's is that here a lag enters the output relationship (4.10) but not the consumption function (4.7). Samuelson poses the reverse. The presence of an output lag implies that the path followed after a disruption of a long-run equilibrium features the inequality of current demand, $D_t = C_t + I_t + G_t$, with current supply. It is a disequilibrium path, and consequently inventory levels can vary through time. In the Samuelson model, where an output lag is absent, the path followed is one of short-run equilibrium, and hence inventory levels do not change.

Collapsing equations (4.7), (4.8a), and (4.9) into (4.10) yields

$$Y_t = cY_{t-1} + bc(Y_{t-1} - Y_{t-2}) + G_o \tag{4.11}$$

or

$$Y_t = c(1 + b)Y_{t-1} - bcY_{t-2} + G_o \tag{4.12}$$

In a long-run equilibrium of the stationary-state variety

$$Y_t = Y_{t-1} = Y_{t-2} = \cdots = Y_E$$

and thus from (4.12)

$$Y_E = c(1 + b)Y_E - bcY_E + G_o$$

or, more simply,

$$Y_E = \frac{G_o}{1 - c} \tag{4.13}$$

At first glance equation (4.13) appears odd. While consumption and government spending affect equilibrium through c and G_o, respectively, the third component of aggregate demand, investment, has no effect whatever. The explanation readily presents itself, however. Long-run equilibrium is characterized by constancy in income. From equation (4.8a), therefore, investment must be zero in equilibrium; it cannot exert an influence.[9]

For (4.13) to identify a legitimate equilibrium, it must imply that saving equals investment. It does. As indicated in Section 2.2, the expression for total real saving with government present is $S_t + (T_t - G_t)$. Under (4.13) private saving becomes

$$S_E = Y_E - C_E = \frac{G_o}{1 - c} - \frac{cG_o}{1 - c} = G_o$$

Thus, with taxes absent from the model, total saving under (4.13) is $G_o - G_o = 0$, the value of investment.

In addition to permitting the determination of equilibrium income, equation (4.12) gives the time path that arises for actual income due to a disruption of equilibrium.[10] Figure 4.3 shows the paths corresponding to five pairs of b and c values. The original G_o is 250, and with $c = .68$ the original equilibrium[11] is 781.25. G_o jumps to 275 at $t = 0$ and remains there permanently. Equilibrium income does likewise; it rises instantaneously and permanently from 781.25 to 859.38 at $t = 0$. Since c and G_o assume the same values for all (b, c) pairs, the same equilibrium values apply to each pair.

---

[9]Insertion of a constant autonomous component into the investment equation would allow investment to influence equilibrium. That adjustment, however, would be inconsequential for the temporal behavior of the system. The same applies to autonomous consumption.

[10]Equation (4.12) is identical to Samuelson's income equation, and hence both models occasion identical income movements. Samuelson, "Interactions," p. 76.

[11]The G_o value repeats the benchmark which appeared in earlier chapters. Estimating c from equation (4.7) by ordinary least squares using annual data on real consumption and real NNP for the period 1950–1975 yields .69. Computational ease prompts the minor adjustment.

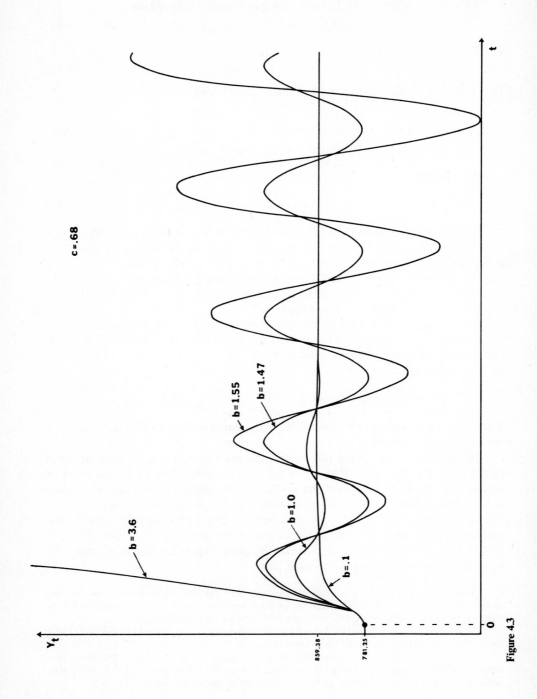

Figure 4.3

The temporal movements crucially depend upon the combination of b and c. For example, the duo $b = .1$ and $c = .68$ produces unidirectional convergence to the new equilibrium, while $b = 1.0$ and $c = .68$ generates damped oscillations about that equilibrium. These patterns are stable in that convergence results. The remaining three (b, c) pairs evoke unstable movements. $b = 1.47$ with $c = .68$ fosters regular cycles, and $b = 1.55$ with $c = .68$ engenders explosive oscillations. $b = 3.6$ with $c = .68$ leads to direct explosion; income rises beyond the new equilibrium and never returns.[12]

Figure 4.4 presents the profiles for inventory stock corresponding to those for income previously shown. At the heart of the stock profiles lies an equation whose derivation is rather straightforward. Section 3.2 noted that since $Y_t - D_t$ gives the change in inventories during period t, the inventory stock at the end of the period, K'_t, must be

$$K'_t = K'_{t-1} + (Y_t - D_t)$$

In the present case, therefore,

$$K'_t = K'_{t-1} + (1 - c - bc)Y_t + bcY_{t-1} - G_o$$

As Figure 4.4 reveals, the inventory paths, which begin at a stock level of 3000, reflect their income counterparts. Damped inventory oscillations accompany damped income oscillations; explosive oscillations accompany explosive oscillations. The directions of movement differ, however; inventories decline when income rises and inventories rise when income declines. Changes for both series display the same absolute magnitudes. For example, when $b = 1.0$, income ultimately rises by 78.13 and inventories ultimately fall by that amount, rounding error excepted.

More insight into the link between the parameters b and c on the one hand and the temporal behavior of income on the other can be obtained by solving (4.12) after recognizing that it is a difference equation in income. Solving this equation means translating it into a form which makes the dependent variable a function of time alone. The mathematical gymnastics, outlined in Section 3 of Appendix D, give

$$Y_t = A_1 \left[\frac{c(1 + b) + \sqrt{c^2(1 + b)^2 - 4bc}}{2} \right]^t$$

$$+ A_2 \left[\frac{c(1 + b) - \sqrt{c^2(1 + b)^2 - 4bc}}{2} \right]^t + \frac{G_o}{1 - c} \qquad (4.14)$$

A_1 and A_2 denote arbitrary constants. $G_o/(1 - c)$ is the equilibrium value for income, and consequently (4.14) can be interpreted as separating the movement of actual income into an equilibrium component and a component representing the deviation from equilibrium.

[12] Since time is a discrete instead of a continuous variable, the temporal paths in Figure 4.3 should actually be depicted as "steps." Continuous curves are chosen to facilitate the graphing process; this tack will continue henceforth.

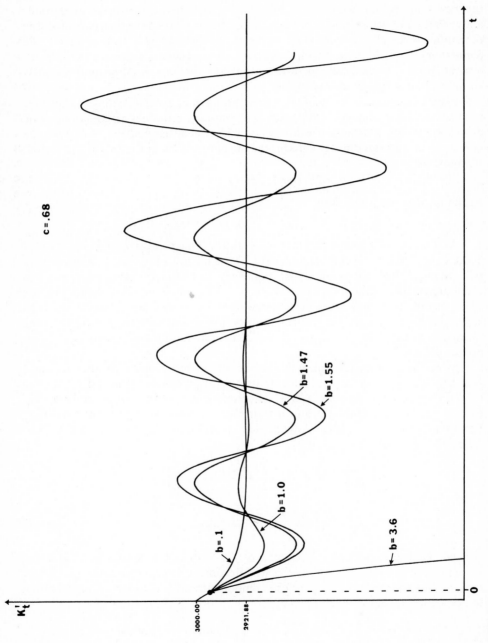

Figure 4.4

Equation (4.14) clearly shows that the time path of income under disequilibrium conditions depends exclusively upon b and c, and it explains the configurations exemplified in Figure 4.3. From the bracketed expressions in (4.14), it is possible to determine the range of b and c values associated with any particular type of time profile for income. Fortunately, Samuelson has already done this. His work is reproduced in Figure 4.5. Region A corresponds to unidirectional convergence; region B, damped oscillations; region C, explosive oscillations; and region D, direct explosion. Points on the B-C line, where $bc = 1$, are associated with regular cycles.

A subtle asymmetry can be detected from this graph. Larger b values always lead to greater instability. As b increases, for given c, the system becomes more unstable, because a larger b forces any change in income to exert a greater impact on investment and thus on income in the next period. However, an increase in c, for given b, does not always impart more instability. A rise in c does increase instability when $b > 1$; but when $b < 1$, it decreases instability. Specifically, the income profile changes from damped oscillations to unidirectional convergence. Why this disparity?

The multiplier, acting alone, evokes stability. For $b = 0$, equation (4.12) becomes virtually identical to equation (3.15) or its illustration (3.17), and equation (4.14) simplifies to

$$Y_t = A_1 c^t + \frac{G_o}{1 - c}$$

As time assumes consecutive values $0, 1, 2, \ldots$, the factor c^t continually shrinks, thereby giving rise to unidirectional convergence. The multiplier by itself is stabilizing. But with an operative accelerator, changes in c—unlike those for b—affect two equations: the consumption function *and* the investment function, through bc. Thus increases in c strengthen both the stabilizing multiplier effect

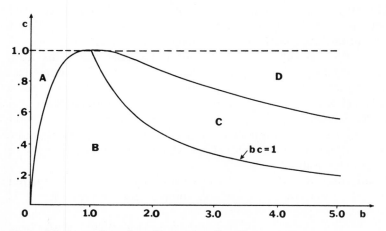

Figure 4.5 *Source*: Samuelson, "Interactions," p. 78.

and the destabilizing acceleration effect. Which is strengthened more? The answer depends upon the size of b. For $b > 1$, the accelerator gains relatively; for $b < 1$, the multiplier does.

4.4 THE CONTRIBUTION OF HICKS

Figure 4.5 illustrates that the marginal propensity to consume and the acceleration coefficient play crucial roles in determining the system's behavior. It also provides a convenient framework for classifying several dynamic paradigms. The multiplier model discussed in Section 3.2 corresponds to (b, c) points along the vertical axis. Frisch's theory of erratic shocks, with its underlying "best guess" premise of stability, might be loosely associated with region B. Region B must also be the home of the interaction model for it to be compatible with observed history. J. R. Hicks, on the other hand, takes a different tack.[13] He claims that the economy is inherently unstable. The system, which includes a simple accelerator, possesses a structure that tends to produce either explosive oscillations or relentless deflection when an equilibrium becomes disrupted. In terms of Figure 4.5, the parameters lie in regions C or D.

Hicks' hypothesis seems faulty at first, for if true, then why has the economy not exhibited instability? The explanation, says Hicks, is that the economic system is subject to limits which cannot be exceeded. This view contrasts with the notion of free or unconstrained response implicit in the multiplier, Frisch, and interactive models. Two bounds (also called "buffers" or "nonlinearities") can be identified: a ceiling and a floor.

The ceiling prompts resurrection of the full-employment output considered in Section 2.5. During any period there is a limited amount of resources available for use in the production process. Corresponding to that limit is a maximum level of output: output cannot expand beyond the level permitted by the full employment of resources. This interpretation of ceiling assumes added meaning since fixed factor proportions preface the simple accelerator. Consequently, a finite labor supply can constrain the amount of output forthcoming in any period.

Explaining the floor is slightly more involved. Its existence stems from another Hicksian innovation, an asymmetric accelerator. Symmetry characterizes the accelerator in the interaction model—equation (4.8a), where a given increase in income causes net investment to rise by the same amount that an equal decrease in income causes it to fall. A possibility associated with symmetry envisions that the negative net investment called for during a downswing might be achievable only if entrepreneurs destroy capital which would otherwise survive the toll of physical deterioration.

Instead of endorsing symmetry, Hicks proposes an accelerator which, put simply, assumes one form for upswings and another for downswings. It is

---

[13]J. R. Hicks, *A Contribution to the Theory of the Trade Cycle* (London: Oxford University Press, 1950), Chapters 6–8.

expressible as a branch function:

$$I_t = \begin{cases} bc(Y_t - Y_{t-1}) & \text{if } bc(Y_t - Y_{t-1}) > -\delta K_{t-1} \\ -\delta K_{t-1} & \text{otherwise} \end{cases} \qquad (4.15)$$

According to equation (4.15) the conventional simple accelerator operates on upswings and on that portion of downswings for which the investment numbers produced are not "too negative." "Too negative" is determined by the amount of capital deteriorating that period, where deterioration is treated as proportional ($\delta \geq 0$) to the existing capital stock at the start of the period, K_{t-1}. When the accelerator requires more scrapping of capital than would arise from natural causes, it ceases to operate and the decay function takes effect. Convenience suggests making the toll of natural decay independent of the actual level of capital, and therefore the lower branch of (4.15) is replaced by $-\Phi$, Φ being a positive constant.

The consequences of this asymmetric accelerator for the floor and for the behavior of the system given disequilibrium are readily detected by modifying equation (4.11) of the interaction model to accommodate (4.15). Consonantly,

$$Y_t = cY_{t-1} + \begin{cases} bc(Y_{t-1} - Y_{t-2}) \\ -\Phi \end{cases} + G_o \qquad (4.16)$$

Now two alternative equilibria exist, each of which corresponds to one branch of the investment function. For the acceleration component, the equilibrium expression previously encountered [equation (4.13)] holds:

$$Y_E = \frac{G_o}{1 - c} \qquad (4.17)$$

Net investment is zero. But for the deterioration component, equilibrium becomes

$$Y_E' = \frac{G_o - \Phi}{1 - c} \qquad (4.18)$$

This equilibrium applies to much of the downswing, and since it manifests negative net investment, it must lie below the equilibrium described by (4.17). Equation (4.18) defines the floor which Hicks pictures. It is the level of income associated with the lower equilibrium. Furthermore, when the deterioration effect replaces the simple accelerator on a downswing, the multiplier rules alone, and because of the multiplier's stability property, the economy converges to the floor in a unidirectional fashion.

Figure 4.6 displays the progress of the economy under Hicks' buffers. Y_{FE} denotes the full-employment ceiling, while Y_E' denotes equilibrium adjusted for capital deterioration. It is the floor. The economy begins in equilibrium and remains there until $t = 0$, when G_o jumps to a new higher level but returns immediately to its original value. Y_E therefore represents the customary equilibrium level throughout the subsequent evolutionary process. Because of the increased G_o, income rises until the ceiling is reached. Along the ceiling, however, income remains unchanged, thereby driving net investment to zero. This decline

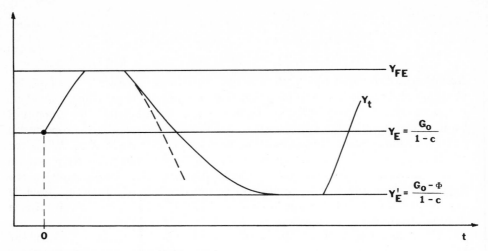

Figure 4.6 *Source*: Hicks, *Contribution*, p. 97.

in investment causes income to fall and activates the deterioration component of the investment function. The depressed equilibrium becomes operative, and an uncompromised multiplier effect propels the system to converge with the floor. Net investment remains negative along the floor, and consequently the economy witnesses a continual reduction in its capital stock. Eventually there is a burst of investment initiated by entrepreneurs to acquire the capital needed to maintain production at the Y_E' level. Alternatively, the government might boost G_o temporarily. In either case the system departs the floor, and the sequence repeats itself.[14] The dashed curve in Figure 4.6 indicates the path that income would follow if the accelerator operated throughout the downswing. Since acceleration effects strengthen the forces of recession, the descent would be more rapid.

It should be noted that the shape of cycles depends upon the time profiles of the ceiling and the floor. Horizontal buffers, as Figure 4.6 reveals, can lead to roughly regular cycles. A horizontal floor coupled with a growing ceiling, due perhaps to an increasing labor force, can produce explosive cycles.

4.5 METZLER'S PERSPECTIVE ON INVENTORIES

All dynamic models considered thus far presume passive inventory behavior. A shock to the system disrupting an equilibrium state changes inventory levels, but inventories react in whatever manner necessary to accommodate the discrepancy

---

[14] The economy can leave a stationary-state floor only through exogenous shocks. Hicks, while first postulating a stationary state, later introduces progressive equilibria and buffers. A growing floor induces through the accelerator a recovery in the economy; exogenous shocks are unnecessary.

Hicks examines several refinements to the basic scenario portrayed in Figure 4.6. Ibid., pp. 99–100, 106–107.

between current supply and demand. No effort is made to recover inventory depletions or to eliminate accumulations. A fundamental premise of those models contends that inventories are plentiful initially and that they are never exhausted. Since the models dismiss price adjustments, exhaustion would prevent the reconciliation of supply with demand.

Metzler provides a different perspective.[15] Inventory behavior is permitted to be active, with entrepreneurs incorporating into their production plans the attainment of some desired level of inventories. They therefore produce to satisfy anticipated sales and to adjust existing inventory levels. The inventories held consist exclusively of consumer goods.

Entrepreneurs attempt to maintain inventories at a constant level Ξ; they also attempt to correct any departure from the target level entirely within a single period. The quickness of this adjustment process may not be unreasonable since inventories of consumables typically do not face the lags pertinent to heavy capital goods. Under these conditions, in period t the production for inventories I_t' becomes

$$I_t' = \Xi - K_{t-1}' \tag{4.19}$$

where K_{t-1}' is the actual inventory stock at the end of the previous period. Equation (4.19) is not especially informative; a more transparent and helpful form lies close at hand, however.

What happened in period $t - 1$? Entrepreneurs adhered to the same principle regarding inventories: adjust their level to Ξ by the period's end. Therefore, in $t - 1$, decision makers modified their production plans to attain Ξ. They produced enough to satisfy anticipated consumption in $t - 1$ and to reach the inventory target. Had entrepreneurs correctly guessed the amount consumers would purchase in $t - 1$, Ξ would have been attained at the close of that period. Correct "guesstimates" come infrequently, however. If actual sales exceeded anticipated sales in period $t - 1$, then entrepreneurs had to divert to sales output originally intended for inventory. Thus, the actual inventory level at the end of $t - 1$ necessarily fell short of Ξ by the amount of the discrepancy between actual and anticipated consumption. It follows that the amount which entrepreneurs must plan to produce in period t to restore inventory levels to the Ξ target at the end of t is the discrepancy inherited from $t - 1$:

$$I_t' = C_{t-1} - C_{t-1}^* \tag{4.20}$$

where C_{t-1} and C_{t-1}^* denote, respectively, actual and anticipated real sales (consumption) for $t - 1$.

The same reasoning applies for the opposite occurrence in $t - 1$. That is, if actual sales fell below the anticipated level, the output which entrepreneurs produced for sales was not completely sold and the balance found its way into inventories. But since enough was produced to bring inventories to the target level under accurate sales expectations, inventories must exceed Ξ by the difference

[15]Lloyd A. Metzler, "The Nature and Stability of Inventory Cycles," *Review of Economic Statistics*, **23** (August 1941), pp. 113–129.

between actual and anticipated sales. Thus in the next period t, entrepreneurs desire to *reduce* inventory levels by $C_{t-1} - C_{t-1}^*$. Again (4.20) applies, but this time I_t' is negative, not positive. A negative I_t' implies, in effect, that entrepreneurs plan to satisfy current demand partly by drawing down inventory levels. Total production is less than otherwise.

As equation (4.20) clearly shows, sales expectations form an integral part of inventory plans. To determine expected sales, Metzler introduces what is called the "coefficient of expectation":

$$m = \frac{C_t^* - C_{t-1}}{C_{t-1} - C_{t-2}} \tag{4.21}$$

m relates the anticipated change in sales to the actual change witnessed for the previous period. From (4.21), C_t^* becomes

$$C_t^* = C_{t-1} + m(C_{t-1} - C_{t-2}) \tag{4.22}$$

According to equation (4.22), expected sales depend upon past sales, and m is the weight which entrepreneurs assign to the previous change. $m = 0$ means that they expect current sales to equal last period's sales. Rather interesting cases arise for $m < 0$. Negative m imply, from (4.21), that the anticipated change and the previous actual change display opposite signs. Put differently, entrepreneurs expect sales to reverse direction in the current period. If sales increased last period, they are expected to fall this period; if they decreased last period, they are expected to rise this period.

The Metzler model is derived by inserting his innovations of active inventory policy and entrepreneurial expectations into a standard macro framework:

$$C_t = cY_t \tag{4.23}$$

$$I_t = I_o \tag{4.24}$$

$$I_t' = n(C_{t-1} - C_{t-1}^*) \tag{4.25}$$

$$Z_t = C_t^* \tag{4.26}$$

$$C_t^* = C_{t-1} + m(C_{t-1} - C_{t-2}) \tag{4.27}$$

$$Y_t = Z_t + I_t' + I_t \tag{4.28}$$

I_t denotes the demand for machines; it is autonomously determined. The parameter n enters (4.25) to facilitate subsequent classification of various versions of Metzler's model. n assumes either zero or unit value. $n = 0$ implies passive inventory behavior, while $n = 1$ indicates active behavior. Z_t represents production for consumption sales; it equals sales expected for the same period. Total output Y_t consists of production for consumption sales, inventories, and machine sales. Its equation, (4.28), describes the production criterion. It does not constitute an equilibrium condition.

For this model, total demand D_t is simply $C_t + I_t$, and inventory stock at the end of the period is

$$K_t' = K_{t-1}' + (Y_t - D_t) \tag{4.29}$$

This expression, introduced earlier, discloses an inventory change which differs fundamentally from that described by (4.25). Equation (4.25) gives the planned or ex ante change; equation (4.29) gives the realized or ex post change. It reflects not only entrepreneurs' plans but also any error embedded in those plans. This relationship can be easily established. Rewrite (4.29) as

$$I_t^* = Y_t - D_t$$

where I_t^* denotes the ex post change $K_t' - K_{t-1}'$. Expansion yields

$$I_t^* = Z_t + I_t' + I_t - C_t - I_t$$

which simplifies to

$$I_t^* = I_t' + (C_t^* - C_t)$$

Ex ante and ex post inventory investment are equal only if entrepreneurs correctly anticipate consumer sales.[16] If sales exceed expectations, then ex post investment falls short of its ex ante counterpart. If sales are deficient, then ex post investment exceeds the ex ante mark.

Substituting equations (4.23) to (4.27) into (4.28) results in

$$Y_t = c(1 + m + n)Y_{t-1} - c(m + n + mn)Y_{t-2} + mncY_{t-3} + I_o \quad (4.30)$$

Under stationary-state conditions the equilibrium level of income becomes

$$Y_E = \frac{I_o}{1 - c} \quad (4.31)$$

m and n do not affect equilibrium, because consumption, like income, remains fixed through time in stationary state. I_t' and the change component of C_t^* therefore vanish.

By manipulating m and n, various versions of the Metzler model emerge. $n = m = 0$ corresponds to the multiplier model considered in Section 3.2 and to the interaction model for $b = 0$. This case needs no further discussion; three others, however, do deserve amplification.

$n = 1, m = 0$

Active inventory behavior prevails, and expected sales equal actual sales last period. Equation (4.25) conveniently reduces to $I_t' = c(Y_{t-1} - Y_{t-2})$ with planned inventory investment taking the form of a simple accelerator. But in this instance the acceleration effect cannot cause unstable movements because the acceleration coefficient, played by the marginal propensity to consume, is constrained to values less than unity.[17]

Income equation (4.30) simplifies to

$$Y_t = 2cY_{t-1} - cY_{t-2} + I_o \quad (4.32)$$

---

[16] Metzler's model blesses entrepreneurs with perfect foresight regarding machine sales: they always anticipate them correctly.

[17] Metzler also considers an inventory accelerator whose coefficient may exceed unity. Metzler, "Nature of Inventory Cycles," pp. 125–126.

112

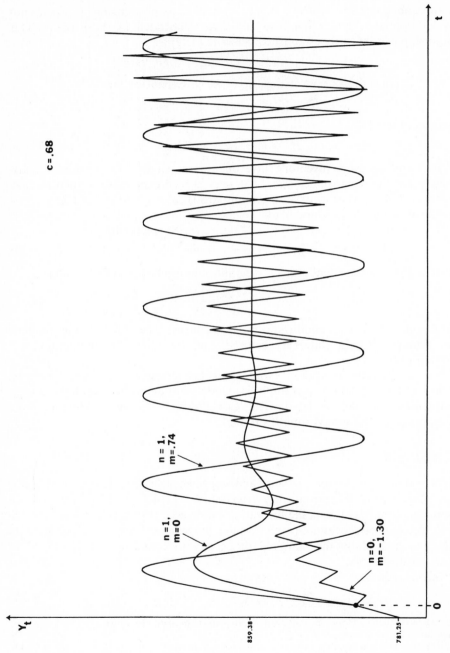

Figure 4.7

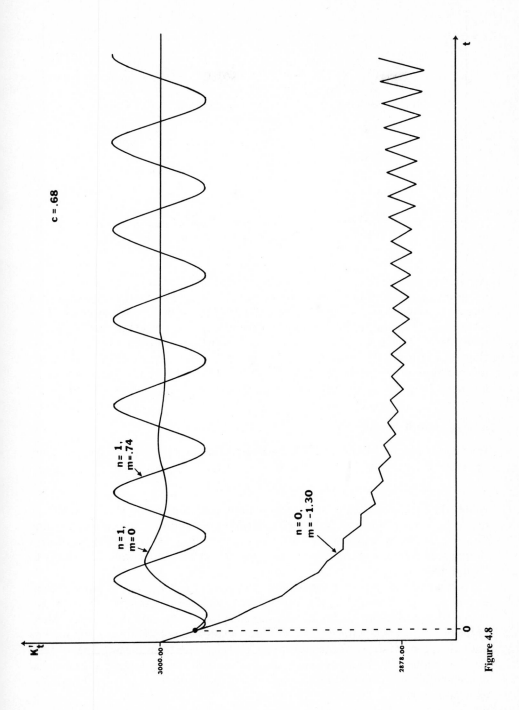

Figure 4.8

113

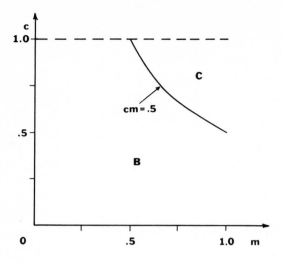

Figure 4.9 *Source*: Metzler, "Nature of Inventory Cycles," p. 125.

An exogenous shock to the system generates damped oscillations about a new equilibrium for any value of c in the usual range. Inventories also evidence damped oscillations, but they eventually return to their original level. This restoration of the initial stock stands in dramatic opposition to the case of passive inventory behavior. Figures 4.7 and 4.8 illustrate these profiles for $c = .68$. I_o changes permanently from 250 to 275 at $t = 0$, and consequently equilibrium income rises instantaneously from 781.25 to 859.38 via (4.31). Inventory stock begins at 3000. These conditions replicate those underlying Figures 4.3 and 4.4.

$n = 0, m \neq 0$

Inventories respond passively, but sales expectations reflect past changes. Here the income expression (4.30) becomes

$$Y_t = c(1 + m)Y_{t-1} - mcY_{t-2} + I_o \tag{4.33}$$

which should look familiar. It repeats income equation (4.12) of the interaction model by substituting Metzler's coefficient of expectation for the earlier acceleration coefficient. In other words, Metzler's expectation scheme (4.21) acts like a simple accelerator. The solution of (4.33) for $m \geq 0$ therefore graphs identically to Figure 4.5.

Unlike the acceleration coefficient, however, m can assume negative values, and in that range several configurations are possible. For example, with $c = .68$, $m = -.5$ generates unidirectional convergence for income and inventories. Alternatively, $m = -1.30$ with $c = .68$ produces explosive cobweb cycles for income and, after a slight delay, for inventories. Cobwebs stem from the anticipated sales reversal implied by the expectation rule, and for sufficiently large m that reversal is transmitted to income and hence to inventories. Figures 4.7 and 4.8 display the explosive cobweb.

$n = 1, m \neq 0$

In this case both Metzler innovations operate: inventory behavior is active, and expectations follow an acceleration format. From (4.30),

$$Y_t = (2 + m)cY_{t-1} - (1 + 2m)cY_{t-2} + mcY_{t-3} + I_o \qquad (4.34)$$

An abbreviated solutions map for this third-order difference equation appears in Figure 4.9. Region B identifies damped cycles; region C, explosive cycles. Similar inventory movements correspond to each region. Points along the B-C line, where $cm = .5$, yield regular cycles both for income and for inventories, as Figures 4.7 and 4.8 illustrate. The regular inventory oscillations, contrary to those in Figure 4.4 for a passive response, are centered around the original stock level. Negative m can create cobwebs.

4.6 ON CONSUMPTION AND INVESTMENT

The dynamic macro systems examined in this chapter and in Chapter 3 involve consumption functions patterned after Keynesian economics: consumption depends only upon income. Investment is determined either by the interest rate or by an acceleration phenomenon. A third formulation renders investment purely autonomous. These consumption and investment functions provide an expedient framework for analysis, but they ignore major theoretical and empirical advances which have become ingrained in conventional economic wisdom. These advances and their consequences for dynamic models make up the subject of Part 3.

THREE

DYNAMICS EXTENDED

LAGGED EFFECTS IN CONSUMPTION

Discussion in Chapters 2 and 3 assumed that the consumption function was Keynesian, with real consumption expenditures being dependent solely upon real disposable income, with the marginal propensity to consume lying between zero and unity, and with the average propensity to consume declining as income increased. This formulation is conveniently transparent for expository model building, but its simplicity comes at a price: other determinants of consumption necessarily remain beyond its field of vision, and some may dramatically affect the dynamic response of macro systems.

This chapter is principally concerned with the role of lagged factors in current consumption. It reviews theoretical arguments justifying the inclusion of various lagged terms in the consumption function, and in the process it traces the evolution of consumption theory since Keynes' tour de force.[1] The next chapter considers lagged influences on investment and examines the impact of lags in the consumption and investment functions on the temporal adjustment of macro paradigms.

5.1 KEYNES' LAW OF CONSUMPTION: A FALL FROM GRACE

Early tests of the Keynesian consumption hypothesis, known later as the "absolute income hypothesis," met with apparent success and seemed to confirm that the psychological law truly did apply to consumer behavior. However, the adulation enjoyed by Keynes' function proved to be short-lived, for several reasons.

---

[1]John Maynard Keynes, *The General Theory of Employment, Interest, and Money* (New York: Harcourt, Brace & World, Inc., 1936).

119

In 1942 Simon Kuznets published time-series estimates of consumption and national income in the United States for overlapping decades from 1879 to 1938; each estimate represented the average for a particular decade. These data suggested that the average propensity to consume remained roughly constant through time even though income rose appreciably. In 1946 Kuznets published alternative estimates for a longer historical period, 1869 to 1938, and these revealed the same basic pattern.[2]

Table 5.1 presents pertinent data from both studies. The 1942 inquiry revealed that, with the depression decades 1924–1933 and 1929–1938 excepted, the average propensity to consume out of national income ranged from a low of .852 to a high of .899 based on constant dollars and from .880 to .896 based on currents. In contrast to these narrow bands lie the vistas for national income. Real income rose by a factor in excess of 4, from $15.2 billion to $68.6 billion; its nominal counterpart's increase was an even more startling factor of 7, from $10.3 billion to $71.9 billion. Similarly, the 1946 study showed that exclusive of the depression experience, real income expanded 7-fold, from $9.3 billion to $69.0 billion, while the average propensity ranged between .838 and .898. Nominal income swelled 11 times, from $6.5 billion to $72.2 billion, while the corresponding propensity stood between .859 and .891. Succinctly, although national income rose to a considerable degree over a historical period of at least 50 years, the average propensity to consume national income remained quite stable, at a value of roughly .87. Since personal taxes and transfer payments over the periods studied by Kuznets were small, a similar relationship was implied for disposable income and the average propensity to consume disposable income. It was also implied for data expressed in per capita terms.[3]

Thus, the average propensity to consume, despite Keynes' precept about it, did not vary in the face of expanding income. Its constancy, in turn, signaled a proportional consumption function—one which passed through the origin—rather than the nonproportional model of Keynes. Since Kuznets' data embraced a half century or more and focused on decade averages, thereby tempering cyclical fluctuations, it might be said that Kuznets discovered a long-run, or secular, consumption function which was proportional. This finding received corroboration in the mid-1950s from Raymond Goldsmith and associates, who studied *inter alia* the relationship of personal saving to personal disposable income for the United States.[4] A subset of their comprehensive data appears in Table 5.2, where

[2] Simon Kuznets, *Uses of National Income in Peace and War*, Occasional Paper 6 (New York: National Bureau of Economic Research, 1942), pp. 31, 35, and *National Product since* 1869 (New York: National Bureau of Economic Research, 1946), p. 119.

[3] See James S. Duesenberry, *Income, Saving and the Theory of Consumer Behavior* (Cambridge, Mass.: Harvard University Press, 1967), p. 56, and Arthur Smithies, "Forecasting Postwar Demand: I," *Econometrica*, **13** (January 1945), p. 6.

[4] Raymond W. Goldsmith, *A Study of Saving in the United States*, vol. I (Princeton, N.J.: Princeton University Press, 1955), p. 76, and Raymond W. Goldsmith, Dorothy S. Brady, and Horst Mendershausen, *A Study of Saving in the United States*, vol. III (Princeton, N.J.: Princeton University Press, 1956), pp. 427, 429.

Table 5.1 Series on consumption, national income, and the average propensity to consume national income, from studies by Simon Kuznets

	Date of investigation: 1942						Date of investigation: 1946					
	Based on 1929 dollars			Based on current dollars			Based on 1929 dollars			Based on current dollars		
Decade	Consumption, in millions	National income, in millions	Average propensity to consume	Consumption, in millions	National income, in millions	Average propensity to consume	Consumption, in millions	National income, in millions	Average propensity to consume	Consumption, in millions	National income, in millions	Average propensity to consume
1869–1878	na	na	na	na	na	na	8,056	9,340	.863	5,706	6,489	.879
1874–1883	na	na	na	na	na	na	11,649	13,601	.856	7,230	8,312	.870
1879–1888	13,411	15,175	.884	9,237	10,310	.896	15,260	17,875	.854	8,632	9,941	.868
1884–1893	15,563	18,087	.860	10,179	11,527	.883	17,660	21,042	.839	9,410	10,953	.859
1889–1898	18,045	21,189	.852	10,936	12,425	.880	20,248	24,170	.838	10,021	11,671	.859
1894–1903	22,617	26,126	.866	13,337	15,084	.884	25,356	29,751	.852	12,398	14,350	.864
1899–1908	28,292	32,402	.873	18,286	20,615	.887	32,265	37,324	.864	17,252	19,740	.874
1904–1913	33,936	38,744	.876	23,722	26,640	.890	39,114	44,992	.869	23,099	26,273	.879
1909–1918	39,217	45,034	.871	32,776	36,934	.887	43,970	50,560	.870	31,799	36,341	.875
1914–1923	47,576	53,826	.884	49,460	55,949	.884	50,719	57,269	.886	48,478	55,324	.876
1919–1928	61,694	68,598	.899	64,095	71,887	.892	62,031	69,047	.898	64,298	72,160	.891
1924–1933	69,070	73,316	.942	65,412	70,064	.934	68,900	73,265	.940	65,428	70,139	.933
1929–1938	69,501	71,110	.977	60,344	61,274	.985	71,002	72,045	.986	60,036	61,274	.980

na: not available.
Source: See footnote 2.

Table 5.2 Relationship between personal disposable income and the average propensity to consume personal disposable income, from Raymond Goldsmith et al.

Reference cycle, trough to trough	Personal disposable income, in millions of		Average propensity to consume when consumption	
	1929 dollars	current dollars	includes durables	excludes durables
1896–1900	27,753	12,847	.919	.906
1900–1904	33,842	17,103	.910	.895
1904–1908	40,533	22,225	.896	.880
1908–1911	45,580	26,161	.909	.895
1911–1914	46,895	29,725	.910	.897
1914–1919	56,619	46,591	.848	.839
1919–1921	58,098	67,050	.916	.912
1921–1924	61,924	62,886	.910	.890
1924–1927	71,172	72,729	.894	.861
1927–1932	74,471	70,867	.929	.926
1932–1938	71,685	57,842	.980	.980
1938–1946	102,760	110,782	.815	.806
1946–1949	121,501	172,777	.915	.866

Source: See footnote 4. Figures on personal disposable income were derived from the device used by Goldsmith (vol. I, p. 76) to compute the average propensities, namely, an arithmetic average over a given cycle with the trough years receiving half weight. Data for 1896, being unavailable, were assumed equal to those for 1897.

each entry represents a mean for a complete business cycle and therefore filters the effect of cyclical variations. All trough references come from the National Bureau of Economic Research (NBER) and match those presented earlier in Table 3.5. The average propensities to consume disposable income which are cited reflect consumption treated as alternatively including and excluding consumer durables; although they were calculated from current-dollar magnitudes, deflation of the underlying series would likely yield comparable results. As the table shows, neither average propensity series exhibits much movement in the predepression years 1896 to 1927, even though personal disposable income rises then from $27.8 billion to $71.2 billion in reals and from $12.8 billion to $72.7 billion in nominals. Proportionality prevails and intimates proportionality in per capita terms as well.[5]

[5] Curiosity impelled the author to use the Kuznets and Goldsmith data reported in Tables 5.1 and 5.2, supplemented where necessary, for regressing consumption on income and an intercept, both series being measured variously as reals, nominals, real per capitas, and nominal per capitas. Population figures for the Kuznets regressions came from his *National Product*, p. 120; for the Goldsmith regressions, from U.S. Department of Commerce, *Historical Statistics of the United States*:

(*continued*)

A second failure of the Keynesian consumption function regarded predictions of economic conditions for the period immediately following World War II. Forecasts based on that function spoke of a slump, and the logic underlying those gloomy prospects was simple. The higher income anticipated as necessary to sustain full employment after the war would generate saving in excess of the amount absorbable by investment because of an average propensity to save which presumably rose with income. Realized investment would then exceed its planned counterpart, and a downturn would ensue.[6] In reality, however, the expected decline in economic fortune did not transpire.

This second failure can be viewed in greater detail by focusing on forecasted values of consumption for the postwar period: consumption was underpredicted by a sizable margin. Tom Davis and Robert Ferber conducted systematic analyses of these errors for the United States by fitting several Keynesian equation forms for consumption and for its strict complement saving to the then latest set of consistent data available. Table 5.3 summarizes selected results; there, forecast error equals the predicted nominal consumption minus the actual nominal consumption.[7] C, S, and Y stand for consumption, saving, and disposable income, respectively, in real terms at the aggregate level. Their counterparts, with asterisks, denote real per capita magnitudes, while p denotes the price level. Thus pC and pY designate nominal consumption and nominal disposable income, respectively. Since all variables hold contemporaneously, subscripts are suppressed. The Ferber study concentrated on saving predictions, but these translate quickly into values for nominal consumption; for instance, from a forecast of per capita real saving, nominal consumption emerges via $(Y - S^*N)p$, N being population. It should be noted that all predictions appearing in the table are of the ex post (after-the-fact) type: magnitudes of income, price, or population needed to forecast nominal

---

Colonial Times to 1970, part 1 (Washington, D.C.: U.S. Government Printing Office, 1975), p. 8. This source updates that cited by Goldsmith in his Study of Saving, vol. I, p. 262. Cyclical averages for head counts were calculated by the same procedure adopted for the entries in Table 5.2, although data equivalence for 1896 and 1897 was unnecessary since the 1896 figure existed.

For the predepression period 1896–1927 and with consumption first including and then excluding durables, the Goldsmith regressions always, save once, gave positive intercepts, but no intercept was significantly different from zero even on a 10 percent one-tail test. The Durbin-Watson and von Neumann statistics indicated that all eight equations escaped autocorrelation. With the depression decades 1924–1933 and 1929–1938 omitted, the eight Kuznets regressions (four for the 1942 study and four for its 1946 mate) evidenced negative intercepts, thereby supporting on a one-tail test the hypothesis of zero intercept. However, both real equations for the 1946 data set had autocorrelation problems. All estimation work was conducted by ordinary least squares.

[6]Glenn E. Burress, "Who First Proposed the Habit Persistence Hypothesis: Keynes or Duesenberry and Modigliani?" Indian Economic Journal, **20** (January/March 1973), p. 472.

[7]Tom E. Davis, "The Consumption Function as a Tool for Prediction," Review of Economics and Statistics, **34** (August 1952), p. 277, and Robert Ferber, A Study of Aggregate Consumption Functions, Technical Paper 8 (New York: NBER, 1953), pp. 64–65. The equations in Table 5.3 represent reestimates of equations fitted by others in studies published circa World War II. Their coefficients and forecasts differ from the originals, but the equations nevertheless serve to demonstrate the forecasting inadequacy of the earlier expressions. See Ferber, pp. 8–10.

Table 5.3 Annual postwar forecast errors for nominal consumption arising from Keynesian-type consumption or saving functions, in billions of dollars

Estimated equation†	Sample period	Year to which the forecast error applies			
		1947	1948	1949	1950
(1) $C = 10.69 + .80Y$	1929–1940	−12.9	−8.8	−12.9	−11.9
(2) $C^* = 11.45 + .78Y^*$	1929–1940	−11.9	−7.5	−11.0	−9.6
(3) $pC = 7.77 + .85pY$	1929–1940	−13.8	−10.0	−14.0	−12.2
(4) $S = -10.68 + .20Y$	1929–1940	−13.0	−8.5	−10.8	−9.1
(5) $S^* = -95.27 + .22Y^*$	1929–1940	−12.0	−7.4	−9.2	−7.6
(6) $pS = -7.89 + .15pY$	1929–!940	−13.9	−9.8	−12.0	−9.7
(7) $S = -6.61 + .14Y$	1923–1940	−9.7	−4.6	−6.9	−4.6
(8) $S^* = -85.66 + .21Y^*$	1923–1940	−11.7	−7.1	−8.8	−7.2
(9) $pS = -6.77 + .14pY$	1923–1940	−12.4	−7.9	−10.1	−7.7
	Addendum				
(10) Actual nominal consumption		165.6	177.5	178.8	184.2

†All estimates of the marginal propensities differ significantly from zero, the smallest Student's t value being 3.48. Likewise, all intercepts in the saving equations display significance, the smallest t registering 22.33. Information on the significance of the consumption intercepts was not available. However, reestimation by ordinary least squares of the three equations, using data published in U.S. Department of Commerce, *The National Income and Product Accounts of the United States, 1929–1974: A Supplement to the Survey of Current Business* (Washington, D.C.: U.S. Government Printing Office), shows significant intercepts in each case, the lowest t being 4.69. Moreover, the consumption propensities listed above are reproduced exactly, the lowest t for the reproductions being 23.06. However, the equation corresponding to that in line 1 evidences autocorrelation; according to Ferber, so do the saving functions in lines 7–9.

Source: See footnote 7. Entries in the first three rows come from Davis; all others, including the *Addendum*, from Ferber.

consumption for any period equal those which actually occurred in that period. The errors reported, therefore, are those attributable solely to difficulties inherent in the estimated equations. Generating a forecast of a dependent variable in practice—ex ante—would require predicting the future values of all independent variables, and hence the resulting forecast errors would typically differ from those determined in ex post experiments.

As Table 5.3 reveals, the extent of underprediction is large regardless of whether the consumption or saving function involves reals, per capita reals, or nominals. The size of these errors can be more fully appreciated by expressing them in 1980 terms. For instance, the $13.0 billion understatement for 1947 (line 4) constitutes 7.85 percent of actual 1947 nominal consumption. Applying that percentage to the $1672.8 billion nominal consumption for the United States in 1980 gives $131.3 billion. Even to the most optimistic of spirits, such a projected "deficiency" in consumption would spell trouble for the economy. Prediction errors derived from the sample period 1923–1940 are, on balance, smaller than those founded on the shorter interval; their mean, however, never falls below $6.5 billion or, in 1980 values, $59.0 billion.[8]

The inability of Keynes' function to explain the proportionality relationship uncovered by Kuznets and its poor predictive performance suggested that it ignored important determinants of consumer behavior. But which determinants? And how should they be included? On the other hand, the Keynesian relationship *did* enjoy successes regardless of these shortcomings. When applied to short-run annual data (those covering, say, a decade or two), it gave estimates of the marginal propensity which fell within the hypothesized range. Furthermore, its intercept estimates supported nonproportionality and the tenet that the average propensity declines with increasing income. The estimated equations appearing in Table 5.3 demonstrate these points. Thus, economists in the mid-1940s actually faced a paradoxical question. How is it possible for both a short-run nonproportional consumption function and a proportional long-run function to be compatible with the empirical observations on consumption and income? Asked equivalently, is there a theoretical explanation for this bifurcated relationship? A corollary question also deserved an answer: Can theoretics explain why the long-run marginal propensity to consume exceeds the short-run propensity? In this connection it bears observing that the Kuznets estimates based on real national income and reported in Table 5.1 suggest a long-run value in excess of .87 when disposable income rules. By contrast, the six real equations in Table 5.3 suggest a short-run value of .80; so does equation (2.16), estimated for the United States from annual data over the period 1950–1975.

Before the discussion turns to several theories prompted by these mysteries of consumption, it seems judicious to note that according to Keynes' function, consumption and income are positively related; consumption rises as income rises and falls as income falls. In other words, the two variables should not move in opposite directions nor should one remain stationary while the other changes. This dictum provides the background for Table 5.4, which presents a historical account of real consumption and real personal disposable income for the United States by year from 1929 to 1980. It omits the 20-year period 1951–1970 because both variables always increased during that span. Asterisks mark the entries which represent decreases in a series. Consumption and income decrease together on 6 occasions. For 1942, however, consumption falls while income rises, and in 3 instances it rises while income falls. That trio of cases applies to the successive years 1945 to 1947. Temporary constancy of a series never develops for this data set.

---

[8] Davis calculates the forecast errors for nominal consumption pertinent not only to the years 1947–1950 but also to 1946; it amounts to −$4.9 billion, −$4.4 billion, and −$4.1 billion, respectively, for the first three equations listed in Table 5.3. Actual nominal consumption that year may be taken as $146.9 billion. Besides the sample periods 1929–1940 and 1923–1940, Ferber uses 1923–1940, excluding the worst depression years, 1931–1934. Forecast errors associated with that sample, albeit generally much smaller than those reported in Table 5.3, are withheld because the corresponding estimated saving functions have insignificant income coefficients.

Table 5.4 Annual data on consumption and personal disposable income, in billions of 1972 dollars

Year	Consumption	Personal disposable income	Year	Consumption	Personal disposable income
1929	215.1	229.5	1945	270.9	338.1*
1930	199.5*	210.6*	1946	301.0	332.7*
1931	191.8*	201.9*	1947	305.8	318.8*
1932	173.9*	174.4*	1948	312.2	335.8
1933	170.5*	169.6*	1949	319.3	336.8
1934	176.9	179.8	1950	337.3	362.8
1935	187.7	196.8	1971	696.8†	779.2†
1936	206.2	220.5	1972	737.1	810.3
1937	213.8	227.7	1973	768.5	865.3
1938	208.8*	212.6*	1974	763.6*	858.4*
1939	219.8	229.8	1975	780.2	875.8
1940	229.9	244.0	1976	823.7	907.4
1941	243.6	277.9	1977	863.9	939.8
1942	241.1*	317.5	1978	904.8	981.5
1943	248.2	332.1	1979	930.9	1011.5
1944	255.2	343.6	1980	935.1	1018.4

*Entry represents a decrease in a series.
†Entry is not chronologically contiguous with its predecessor.
Source: Rebenchmarked data furnished to the author by the U.S. Department of Commerce during the first quarter of 1981.

Quarterly data for the United States from 1947 to 1980 reveal similar configurations, as Table 5.5 confirms. The period 1962–1969 is excluded for the reason cited above—consumption and income continually increase during that interval—and asterisks now indicate a drop or no change in a series. Consumption and income decrease jointly on 7 occasions, but on another 7 consumption declines during an income expansion. In 14 instances it rises during an income contraction, and such episodes relate to two consecutive quarters twice, 1954:1–1954:2 and 1974:2–1974:3. Constancy in only one series happens thrice. Again, in disagreement with Keynes' assertion, the two variables have not always exhibited a positive relationship. The renegade movement observed most frequently on quarterly data has consumption rising and income falling even over consecutive quarters. In this regard the parallelism with the annual time scale should be obvious.

Per capita real data engender temporal configurations which may differ from their aggregate counterparts, and the cause can be quickly deduced. A change in a per capita variable, say, income, may be expressed as $Y^*_t = Y^*_t(\dot{Y}_t/Y_t - \dot{N}_t/N_t)$, where the dots signify time derivatives such as $\dot{Y}^*_t = dY^*_t/dt$. Even if the aggregate income series rises, its per capita version falls when the aggregate does not rise fast enough (the target speed is the positive rate of population growth).

Table 5.5 Quarterly data on consumption and personal disposable income, in billions of 1972 dollars and seasonally adjusted at annual rates

		Quarter				Quarter				
Series	Year	1	2	3	4	1	2	3	4	Year
Consumption	1947	302.3	307.0	307.2	306.8*	308.8	312.1	312.6	315.4	1948
Income	1947	321.5	314.6*	321.6	317.6*	324.8	334.6	341.2	342.7	1948
Consumption	1949	315.8	319.8	319.3*	322.5	327.7	333.6	348.0	339.9*	1950
Income	1949	336.2*	336.2*	336.5	338.2	361.5	359.4*	362.2	368.2	1950
Consumption	1951	345.7	337.8*	340.7	342.1	342.7	348.6	350.2	358.8	1952
Income	1951	365.7*	373.7	375.6	375.6*	375.1*	379.0	387.3	391.2	1952
Consumption	1953	362.8	364.6	363.6*	362.6*	363.5	366.2	371.8	378.6	1954
Income	1953	395.5	401.2	399.7*	400.1	399.8*	397.5*	403.9	411.7	1954
Consumption	1955	385.2	392.2	396.4	402.6	403.2	403.9	405.1	409.3	1956
Income	1955	414.8	423.7	430.8	437.8	441.0	444.5	446.9	452.5	1956
Consumption	1957	411.7	412.4	415.2	416.0	411.0*	414.7	420.9	425.4	1958
Income	1957	452.7	455.5	457.7	456.2*	452.2*	454.9	464.7	471.0	1958
Consumption	1959	434.1	439.7	443.3	444.6	448.1	454.1	452.7*	453.2	1960
Income	1959	474.4	482.2	479.2*	483.0	488.2	490.9	490.9*	489.0*	1960
Consumption	1961	454.0	459.9	461.4	470.3	667.4†	670.5	676.5	673.9*	1970
Income	1961	493.6	500.6	505.8	515.0	737.4†	752.5	760.1	756.2*	1970
Consumption	1971	687.0	693.3	698.2	708.6	718.6	731.1	741.3	757.1	1972
Income	1971	771.1	779.9	780.7	785.2	792.0	798.7	812.4	838.1	1972
Consumption	1973	769.0	766.8*	770.5	767.4*	762.1*	764.9	770.1	757.3*	1974
Income	1973	855.6	862.9	868.8	874.1	861.2*	860.6*	860.1*	851.8*	1974
Consumption	1975	764.0	776.3	786.3	794.2	810.6	817.7	827.1	839.4	1976
Income	1975	845.8*	892.2	879.2*	886.1	900.3	904.7	909.5	915.1	1976
Consumption	1977	851.9	856.0	866.4	881.3	884.1	900.6	911.2	923.4	1978
Income	1977	918.7	931.6	948.1	960.9	966.8	975.5	985.9	998.0	1978
Consumption	1979	925.5	922.8*	933.4	941.6	943.4	919.3*	930.8	946.8	1980
Income	1979	1005.7	1006.9	1015.7	1017.7	1021.0	1008.2*	1018.5	1025.8	1980

*Entry represents a decrease or a constancy in a series.
†Entry is not chronologically contiguous with its predecessor.
Source: See Table 5.4.

An implication, therefore, is that a per capita measure must exhibit no fewer, and probably more, declines than does its aggregate cousin.

In an annual setting for the period 1929–1980, real per capita U.S. data (not reproduced here) show that consumption and disposable income decline together 9 times, that consumption falls when income rises 2 times, and that consumption rises when income falls 4 times. Constancy of either series never occurs. In a quarterly context for the period 1947–1980, with adjustment for seasonality and conversion into annual rates, U.S. real per capitas have mutual consumption and disposable income declines in 17 instances. They evidence consumption decreases coupled with income increases in 15 instances and the reverse movement in 16. Constancy in only one series happens 3 times. In terms of per capitas, the anti-Keynesian match occurring most prevalently continues to be consumption increases and income decreases.

The negative relationship between current consumption and current income underscores the incompleteness of Keynes' formulation. Variables other than current income influence consumption, and at times their combined effect outweighs the force of the income. Hence, although income may be falling, these additional factors may provide sufficient boost to allow consumption to rise nonetheless. Conversely, they might become a depressant strong enough to cause consumption to fall despite an income expansion. Broadening the consumption specification to capture determinants besides current income therefore seems to be an essential requirement for any theory which hopes to improve on the original Keynesian postulate.

5.2 A TENUOUS RECONCILIATION

In forecasting the composition of full-employment real GNP applicable to the United States for the years following World War II, Arthur Smithies adopts a consumption function which expresses per capita real consumption expenditures C^* in terms of per capita real disposable income Y^* and a time trend, the latter being included to capture the effects of structural changes in the American economy.[9] Use of per capita magnitudes, witnessed in footnote 5 and in Table 5.3, can be defended as an effort to reflect the tone of the microeconomic model of consumer behavior in a context of macro data. That model talks about a single household, and per capitas convert aggregate quantities into measures relevant to an individual. In effect, they report on the behavior of an "average" household.[10]

The trend term in Smithies' function represents the influence of three factors: the migration of people from farms to cities, a shift in the distribution of income toward greater equality, and a rise in the perceived standard of living. *Ceteris paribus*, each of these agents should increase per capita consumption. Households migrating from rural districts lose access to production for own consumption and yet face new needs which cannot be satisfied within the family unit itself; consequently, their spending from given income levels increases. Similarly, greater equality of the income distribution should increase aggregate and hence

---

[9]Smithies, "Forecasting Postwar Demand," pp. 3–7.

[10]Strict rendering of the various consumption theories under consideration demands that the discussion in this and subsequent sections preserve the distinction between aggregate and per capita measures found in the original works. However, conclusions and implications deducible from one quantification scheme should apply to the other, and in contemporary econometric efforts the measures are often used interchangeably.

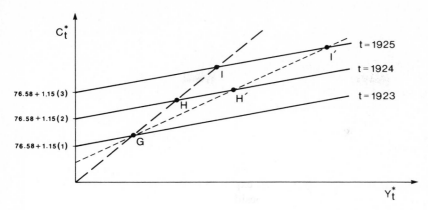

Figure 5.1

per capita consumption, because income is transferred from richer households (those with lower marginal propensities to consume) to poorer ones (those with higher propensities). While consumption by the former group declines, that of the latter rises to more than compensate for the loss, and on balance total and per capita consumption rise. Regarding the third factor, as consumer items previously deemed luxuries become reclassified by households as necessities,[11] the amount of income spent increases at the expense of saving. Because of these considerations, the time argument t in the consumption function should have a positive coefficient.

When applied to the United States for the years 1923 to 1940, Smithies' equation emerges as

$$C_t^* = 76.58 + .76Y_t^* + 1.15(t - 1922) \qquad (5.1)$$

Time has a subtrahend 1922 merely for benchmarking purposes. With it, the year 1923 becomes 1 to the consumption function, the year 1924 becomes 2, and so forth. In short, all temporal comparisons are made relative to 1922 conditions. The time coefficient says that if income were held constant, consumption would rise each year by $1.15 per person. Clearly, the marginal propensity to consume equals .76.

This function is sketched in Figure 5.1. For any given year it looks typically Keynesian, but advancing time causes it to shift upward, as the solid lines indicate. More would be consumed from each level of disposable income.

According to Smithies, the upward drift in the nonproportional function (5.1) can explain why Kuznets detected proportionality. Since each consumption line remains effective for only one year, only one observation for consumption and

---

[11]For a discussion of a possible force provoking this change in attitude, see E. Ray Canterbery, "Inflation, Necessities and Distributive Efficiency," in *Essays in Post-Keynesian Inflation*, James H. Gapinski and Charles E. Rockwood, eds. (Cambridge, Mass.: Ballinger Publishing Company, 1979), p. 98.

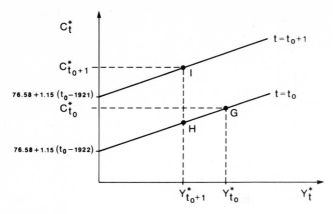

Figure 5.2

income can lie on each. Thus, the consumption-income point for 1923 falls on the lowest solid line in Figure 5.1, say at G. The point for 1924, H, occupies the middle rung, and that for 1925, I, occupies the top. When connected, these empirically observed points reveal a proportional relationship between consumption and income, thereby explaining Kuznets' finding. The nonproportional consumption function shifts upward through time in such a way that the observed consumption-income points happen to trace a line through the origin.

Happen is a key word in this reconciliation. For points G, H, and I to fall on a proportional line, the upward drift in the consumption function, due to Smithies' $1.15t$ term, must be synchronized with the long-run pace of income. Too slow a shift, for instance, would result in points G, H′, and I′ and in a nonproportional long-run locus. The shift coefficient, however, is calculated from only a fraction of the history examined by Kuznets in 1942, and hence synchronization with the long-run pattern might be viewed as a chance occurrence. In fact, estimation of Smithies' relation over a different time period can be shown to disrupt the cadence.[12] Furthermore, time used as an argument in the equation conceals more than it reveals. It enters as a surrogate for true causal entities, but its movement remains entirely independent of economic conditions. In keeping with this blindness to economic circumstances, the equation claims that with income held constant, households *must* consume more, never the same or less, each period. Thus Smithies' hypothesis, while representing an important thrust in the proper direction, advises that additional thought be given to the consumption paradox.

Mention should be made here that equation (5.1) can explain the negative relationship between current consumption and current income observed most

[12] Franco Modigliani, "Fluctuations in the Saving-Income Ratio: A Problem in Economic Forecasting," in *Studies in Income and Wealth*, vol. 11, Conference on Research in Income and Wealth (New York: NBER, 1949), pp. 373–378.

frequently: a fall in income coupled with a rise in consumption. Figure 5.2 illustrates. At time $t = t_0$, per capita income $Y_{t_0}^*$ applied to the relevant consumption line generates per capita consumption $C_{t_0}^*$, point G. Structural changes then prompt the line to ascend, and although income declines to $Y_{t_0+1}^*$, the upward drift is more than sufficient to allow consumption to rise, to $C_{t_0+1}^*$ at point I. This movement from point G to point I can be viewed as consisting of two steps: that from G to H attributable to reduced income and that from H to I attributable to structural changes.

5.3 HABIT PERSISTENCE AND THE CONSUMER

A set of theories more sophisticated than Smithies' can be grouped under the banner of "habit persistence," according to which households try to continue prior consumption patterns because of habits acquired from experiences related to consumption. Smithies himself provided a clue about the force of habit, but an earlier statement on the role of habits in consumption behavior can be found in *The General Theory*. Specifically,

> The fundamental psychological law... is that men are disposed, as a rule and on the average, to increase their consumption as their income increases, but not by as much as the increase in their income....
> This is especially the case where we have short periods in view, as in the case of the so-called cyclical fluctuations of employment during which habits, as distinct from more permanent psychological propensities, are not given time enough to adapt themselves to changed objective circumstances. For a man's habitual standard of life usually has the first claim on his income, and he is apt to save the difference which discovers itself between his actual income and the expense of his habitual standard....[13]

Two hypotheses of habit persistence, developed independently by James Duesenberry and Franco Modigliani, made their debut literally at the same time —at a meeting of the Econometric Society held January 1947.[14] Since both works contain marked similarities, only one, Duesenberry's, will be considered in some detail. Modigliani's will be treated afterward in abbreviated fashion.

---

[13] Keynes, *The General Theory*, pp. 96–97.

Glenn Burress and Thomas Mayer discuss Keynes' impetus to the notion of habit persistence. Burress even interprets Keynes as recognizing that two different consumption functions might emerge because of habits, the short-run variant having a shallower income slope. He concludes that Keynes anticipated the theoretical propositions which were to be articulated later. See Burress, "Habit Persistence," and Thomas Mayer, *Permanent Income, Wealth, and Consumption: A Critique of the Permanent Income Theory, the Life-Cycle Hypothesis, and Related Theories* (Berkeley: University of California Press, 1972), pp. 18–19.

[14] James S. Duesenberry, "Income-Consumption Relations and Their Implications," in *Income, Employment and Public Policy: Essays in Honor of Alvin H. Hansen* (New York: W. W. Norton & Company, Inc., 1948), pp. 54–81, and Duesenberry, *Theory of Consumer Behavior*, Chapters V, VII; and Modigliani, "Fluctuations," pp. 379–388. On the timing of the hypotheses' appearances, see Duesenberry, "Income-Consumption," footnote 1, and Modigliani, footnote 23.

Duesenberry examines two budget, or cross section, studies: those for 1935 and 1941. He notes that in 1935—during the depression—dissaving out of given levels of income was much greater than in the more prosperous year 1941. How can this behavior of dissaving be explained? To him, quite easily, if one supposes that households sacrifice saving to protect and maintain their standard of living. As income declines, households attempt to sustain previous consumption levels by reducing saving; if income falls sufficiently far, the reduced saving manifests itself as dissaving. This notion of saving forfeiture, while compatible with the budget data, also has a psychological appeal; namely, "it is harder for a family to reduce its expenditures from a high level than it is for a family to refrain from making high expenditures in the first place."[15] In terms of the bromide, it is more difficult to take candy from a baby *after* the baby tastes its sweetness.

Which standard of living would households try to defend? Their highest standard: that associated with the highest level of income or, alternatively, consumption.[16] Consequently, when (say) income declines from a peak level, it triggers a reduction in saving as households strive to emulate earlier consumption. Current saving behavior therefore depends upon *relative* income, current income relative to the previous peak level.

Mathematically, the relationship which Duesenberry contemplates reads

$$\frac{S_t^*}{Y_t^*} = F\left(\frac{Y_t^*}{Y_{\text{Pk}}^*}\right) \tag{5.2}$$

S_t^* and Y_t^* represent, respectively, per capita real saving and per capita real disposable income at time t; Y_{Pk}^* represents the previous peak level of per capita real disposable income. This equation says that the average propensity to save depends upon relative income, and from the earlier argument the dependency should be positive. As income falls relative to the previous peak level, saving should be sacrificed and the proportion of income saved should fall. Equation (5.2) contrasts with Keynes' view that the propensity responds to absolute income, $S_t^*/Y_t^* = G(Y_t^*)$, because it implies that the average propensity to save would not change in the presence of changing income if the ratio of current to previous peak income remained intact. Keynes' formulation implies that the average propensity always changes in the face of changing income. Acknowledging that there is little reason for championing any particular form for the function F, Duesenberry accepts linearity as a satisfactory approximation. Thus, equation (5.2) becomes

$$\frac{S_t^*}{Y_t^*} = a_D + b_D \frac{Y_t^*}{Y_{\text{Pk}}^*} \tag{5.3}$$

with $b_D > 0$. Since very low income levels would likely be characterized by dissaving, $a_D < 0$.

---

[15] Duesenberry, "Income-Consumption," p. 70.
[16] Ibid., p. 74.

Hidden within this saving equation rests a consumption function, which can be quickly exposed. Since real disposable income equals the sum of real consumption and real saving, a similar relationship holds in per capita terms: $Y_t^* = C_t^* + S_t^*$, C_t^* being per capita real consumption expenditures. Thus, $1 = C_t^*/Y_t^* + S_t^*/Y_t^*$, and $C_t^*/Y_t^* = 1 - S_t^*/Y_t^*$. Substitution from equation (5.3) yields

$$\frac{C_t^*}{Y_t^*} = (1 - a_D) - b_D \frac{Y_t^*}{Y_{Pk}^*} \tag{5.4}$$

The average propensity to consume changes only when income changes relative to its previous peak level. As this relative falls, the consumption propensity rises. From (5.4),

$$C_t^* = (1 - a_D)Y_t^* - b_D \frac{Y_t^{*2}}{Y_{Pk}^*} \tag{5.5}$$

Alternatively expressed, equation (5.5) becomes

$$C_t^* = \left(1 - a_D - b_D \frac{Y_t^*}{Y_{Pk}^*}\right) Y_t^* \tag{5.6}$$

While equivalent mathematically, equations (5.5) and (5.6) offer different advantages for elucidative purposes. The latter lends itself especially well to the case of smoothly rising income; the former, to that of fluctuating income.

Suppose first that income increases steadily through time, as it might in a long-run perspective. Then previous peak income Y_{Pk}^* is the income level of the preceding period; namely, $Y_{Pk}^* = Y_{t-1}^*$. Furthermore, the ratio in equation (5.6), now Y_t^*/Y_{t-1}^*, can be treated as fixed. Specifically, since $(Y_t^* - Y_{t-1}^*)/Y_{t-1}^* = v^*$, v^* being a constant, Y_t^*/Y_{t-1}^* must be constant at $1 + v^*$. Thus when income grows steadily through time, equation (5.6) reduces to

$$C_t^* = [1 - a_D - b_D(1 + v^*)]Y_t^* \tag{5.7}$$

The consumption function is proportional with a marginal propensity to consume of $1 - a_D - b_D(1 + v^*)$. Higher growth rates v^* beget lower propensities, and lower v^* beget higher propensities. For the special circumstance of stationary state, where no growth occurs, $v^* = 0$ and the propensity simplifies to $1 - a_D - b_D$.

Fitting equation (5.3) to annual U.S. data for the period 1923–1940, Duesenberry obtains $a_D = -.066$ and $b_D = .165$. Hence, for any reasonable income growth rate, equation (5.7) transforms itself into approximately[17]

$$C_t^* = .90 Y_t^* \tag{5.8}$$

Voilà, the Kuznets result!

---

[17]For simplicity the assumption of stationary state underlies this and every other calculation of long-run propensities in the chapter. If the rate of per capita real income growth were taken as 5 percent ($v^* = .05$), for example, then the long-run propensity would equal .89, virtually the same value appearing in equation (5.8).

Suppose now that disposable income rises steadily to a peak at time t_0 but then falls. Label this peak level Y^*_{Pk0}. During the stage in which income rises smoothly, consumption adheres to the proportional function (5.8), and it does so until Y^*_{Pk0} obtains. How does consumption respond in the next stage, when income falls? Does it decline along the proportional function? No! As income falls, relative income, Y^*_t / Y^*_{Pk} in equation (5.6), no longer remains constant, and its constancy is the crucial link in the chain establishing proportionality. To ascertain how consumption behaves in a downswing, the computational logic must allow relative income to vary.

From equation (5.5) with the appropriate parameter assignments, the marginal propensity to consume adopts the format

$$\frac{\partial C^*_t}{\partial Y^*_t} = 1.066 - .330 \frac{Y^*_t}{Y^*_{\text{Pk}}} \tag{5.9}$$

This propensity, which depends upon relative income, differs from the fixed .90 value in equation (5.8) because the underlying premise is now the nonconstancy rather than the constancy of that income. According to (5.9) the propensity rises as income declines from the previous peak, and it reaches a maximum of 1.07 at zero income. It equals .74 at the instant that income begins to decline from the peak, because then Y^*_t / Y^*_{Pk} still equals Y^*_t / Y^*_{t-1}, roughly unity. In other words, when income begins to fall, the marginal propensity to consume shifts from .90 to .74, and consumption descends along a function whose income slope increases with the income decline. The graphics of this response appear in Figure 5.3.

As income rises steadily, consumption follows the proportional line until the income level Y^*_{Pk0} is reached. The ensuing decline in income causes the consumption function to change shape—to become flatter—and consumption falls along the nonproportional line segment GHI. On this path saving decreases more dramatically than it would if consumption declined via the proportional function.

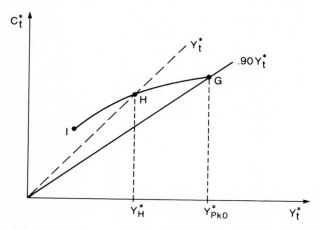

Figure 5.3

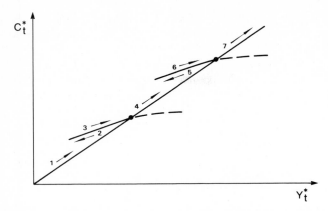

Figure 5.4 *Source*: Duesenberry, *Theory of Consumer Behavior*, p. 114.

This more pronounced saving contraction is exhibited in two ways. First, the marginal propensity to save along the nonproportional segment roughly equals .26 while its proportional counterpart amounts to .10. Thus, for each dollar of lost income, saving falls 26 cents along the nonproportional function and only 10 cents along the proportional one. Second, saving may become negative under nonproportionality, whereas it cannot become negative under proportionality. In Figure 5.3 saving at any level of income is represented by the distance between the diagonal line Y_t^*, the usual 45° construct, and the corresponding consumption function. Under nonproportionality, saving remains positive to the right of point H and equals zero at H. To the left of H it becomes negative—consumers dissave at income levels below Y_H^*. By contrast, dissaving never occurs under proportionality.

Recovery of the economy from a slump leads consumption to retrace its steps along the nonproportional function until savings are restored to their preslump level. Restoration becomes complete upon return to point G. Further income increases make consumption expand along the proportional function until another recession occurs. Consumption then falls along a new nonproportional function, one which lies above that traversed in the earlier bust because consumers now defend a higher standard of living. Stated differently, habits associated with the new peak income prompt more spending than previously from given levels of income.

Figure 5.4 maps the route of consumption, the numbered arrows indicating the sequence and direction of movement.[18] Since consumption does not descend along the proportional function but instead observes the flatter nonproportional functions, Duesenberry refers to this response as a "ratchet effect." If recovery proceeds vigorously, with income rising rapidly in the short run, then the corresponding nonproportional consumption function may extend rightward,

---

[18] Duesenberry, *Theory of Consumer Behavior*, pp. 114–115.

crossing the proportional ray with diminishing steepness in the spirit of equation (5.9). The dashes in Figure 5.4 illustrate. Eventually, however, consumption returns to the proportional line.

Modigliani, referencing consumption habits,[19] expresses the average propensity to save in terms of a cyclical income index $(Y_t^* - Y_{\mathrm{Pk}}^*)/Y_t^*$, which must be negative in a slump or recovery since $Y_t^* < Y_{\mathrm{Pk}}^*$ then. The functional form selected for the average saving propensity reads

$$\frac{S_t^*}{Y_t^*} = a_M + b_M \frac{Y_t^* - Y_{\mathrm{Pk}}^*}{Y_t^*} \tag{5.10}$$

which yields the consumption function

$$C_t^* = (1 - a_M - b_M)Y_t^* + b_M Y_{\mathrm{Pk}}^* \tag{5.11}$$

In this equation, which is the linear counterpart of Duesenberry's equation (5.5), previous peak income determines the intercept $b_M Y_{\mathrm{Pk}}^*$. As long as current income remains cyclically below the peak, consumption must increase or decrease along a stationary nonproportional locus. As the peak income rises, however, the nonproportional function shifts upward, and thus layers of these functions can be envisioned.

What about the special case of steadily rising income? Again, $Y_{\mathrm{Pk}}^* = Y_{t-1}^*$, and since $(Y_t^* - Y_{t-1}^*)/Y_{t-1}^*$ equals a constant v^*, $Y_{t-1}^* = Y_t^*/(1 + v^*)$. Substitution into equation (5.11) gives

$$C_t^* = \left(1 - a_M - b_M \frac{v^*}{1 + v^*}\right) Y_t^* \tag{5.12}$$

For steady increases in income, the consumption function exhibits proportionality, and for a faster income growth (greater v^*), its marginal propensity assumes a lower value. In stationary state the propensity becomes $1 - a_M$. Applying equation (5.10) to annual U.S. data for 1921 to 1940, Modigliani obtains $a_M = .098$ and $b_M = .125$. Therefore, his short-run and long-run marginal propensities to consume amount to .78 and (roughly) .90, reproducing the Duesenberry values and the Kuznets long-run propensity.

Modigliani's work bears marked resemblance to Duesenberry's in terms of saliencies; it also has strong kinship in terms of subtleties. For instance, like Duesenberry, Modigliani argues that the nonproportional function may pass through the proportional ray and assume a lower slope to the right of the intersection point. Furthermore, should income remain depressed below the previous peak for a considerable period, it is possible in both efforts for the nonproportional function to shift downward as households grow to accept, and thus defend, an inferior standard of living. In short, the "target" income relevant to consumption decisions becomes redefined at a level below the previous peak. Both authors also acknowledge that the effect of income on consumption might

---

[19] Modigliani, "Fluctuations," pp. 386–387.

be more properly captured by a weighted average of current income, previous peak income, and incomes for the intervening years. Consequently, their functions (5.5) and (5.11) might be viewed as approximations to more complicated specifications.[20]

Although the schematics by Duesenberry and Modigliani can reconcile the short-run and long-run consumption functions, they cannot explain the negative relationship between current consumption and current income sometimes in evidence. Points like G and I in Figure 5.2 might be located to the left of the proportional ray in Figure 5.4, but not in consecutive periods unless the target income level rose while current income fell or the target income level fell while current income rose. The first option is impossible theoretically, and the second is implausible.

Consumption functions (5.5) and (5.11) represent consumer habits and the associated standard of living by means of an income variable. Other variables, however, might be used for that purpose, and Duesenberry himself argues that previous peak real consumption per capita could be adopted instead. So does Tom Davis. In a 1952 paper Davis advises that since consumption habits cannot be formed unless consumption actually occurs, the surrogate should be a consumption variable, notably, previous peak consumption.[21] With this modification the Duesenberry and Modigliani functions (5.5) and (5.11) become, respectively,

$$C_t^* = (1 - A_D)Y_t^* - B_D\frac{Y_t^{*2}}{C_{Pk}^*} \tag{5.13}$$

and

$$C_t^* = (1 - A_M - B_M)Y_t^* + B_M C_{Pk}^* \tag{5.14}$$

where C_{Pk}^* is the previous peak real consumption per capita.

In the long-run setting, consumption—like income—grows steadily through time. Let γ^* be the rate of per capita consumption growth: $\gamma^* = (C_t^* - C_{t-1}^*)/C_{t-1}^*$. Then $C_t^* = (1 + \gamma^*)C_{t-1}^*$. Under long-run conditions previous peak consumption must be consumption of the previous period, $C_{Pk}^* = C_{t-1}^*$, and it follows that $C_{Pk}^* = C_t^*/(1 + \gamma^*)$. Substitution into equations (5.13) and (5.14) yields $C_t^* = \Psi Y_t^*$ and $C_t^* = \Xi Y_t^*$, respectively, where Ψ denotes some constant determined from a quadratic equation and Ξ denotes $(1 + \gamma^*)(1 - A_M - B_M)/(1 + \gamma^* - B_M)$. The long-run consumption functions are proportional.

Using annual data drawn from the period 1929–1940 for the United States, Davis finds that $1 - A_D = 1.16$, $B_D = .20$, $1 - A_M - B_M = .79$, and $B_M = .17$. The marginal propensity corresponding to the short-run function (5.13), $(1 - A_D) - 2B_D Y_t^*/C_{Pk}^*$, amounts to .72 if Y_t^*/C_{Pk}^* is equated to 1.11, a value

---

[20] On these matters see Duesenberry, "Income-Consumption," p. 74, and Modigliani, "Fluctuations," pp. 386–388, along with the addenda to "Fluctuations" by Wassily Leontief and Modigliani, p. 443.

[21] Davis, "The Consumption Function," pp. 274–275.

approximating the $(1 + \gamma^*)Y_t^*/C_t^*$ prevailing at the onset of recession. The marginal propensity relevant to equation (5.14) equals .79, of course. Long-run propensities for the modified Duesenberry[22] and Modigliani functions both stand at .95.

Under Davis' refinement, current consumption depends upon past consumption, or, more precisely, past peak consumption. Since Duesenberry and Modigliani offered their functional forms as approximations to specifications which might include weighted values of a series of past incomes, the thought arises that perhaps a series of past consumptions should be included in the consumption function. At least consumption of the immediately preceding period might be an argument. Indeed, this proves to be the case.

5.4 DISCONTINUOUS AND CONTINUOUS HABIT PERSISTENCE

T. M. Brown is another advocate of habit persistence. In a 1952 article, he reports detecting sluggishness in consumer behavior and argues that this inertia may be due to habits acquired from past consumption. Brown writes, "Habits... associated with real consumption previously enjoyed become 'impressed' on human physiological and psychological systems and this produces an inertia or 'hysteresis' in consumer behaviour."[23] Thus Brown, like Davis, links habits to previous consumption rather than to previous income.

Two versions of habit persistence are considered by Brown: discontinuous and continuous. Discontinuous persistence says that only habits associated with previous milestones or landmark events affect current behavior; by contrast, continuous persistence says that habits associated even with pedestrian prior events influence present actions.[24] To represent the discontinuity option, Brown proposes the linear relationship

$$C_t = a_0 + a_1 Y_t + a_2 C_{Pk} \tag{5.15}$$

where C and Y designate, respectively, real consumption expenditures and real disposable income, albeit not in per capita terms. C_{Pk} denotes previous peak real consumption expenditures. Its multiplicand a_2 serves as a sluggishness coefficient and gauges the strength of consumer inertia: a greater coefficient means greater inertia. Formulating a function to capture the continuity option requires a

---

[22] The second root from the quadratic applicable to the modified Duesenberry function equals .21. It is discarded because it lies below the short-run propensity .72.

[23] T. M. Brown, "Habit Persistence and Lags in Consumer Behaviour," *Econometrica*, **20** (July 1952), p. 359.

[24] Given this dichotomy the hypotheses of Duesenberry, Modigliani, and Davis—manifested by equations (5.5), (5.11), (5.13), and (5.14)—can be viewed as discontinuous persistence. However, since Duesenberry and Modigliani allude to the possibility that a series of past values may affect current behavior, such exclusive categorization seems to misrepresent their position. More general mathematical formulations could render their hypotheses continuous persistence.

determination of both the number of past consumption terms to be included as arguments and the weight to be assigned to each. For the general case Brown suggests that their number could be established by data availability, while their weights may decline as the terms become more distant. However, since consumption in the immediately preceding period might be viewed as embodying all past experience, he settles on

$$C_t = A_0 + A_1 Y_t + A_2 C_{t-1} \tag{5.16}$$

where A_2 is the sluggishness coefficient. This equation is found in preliminary research to be empirically superior to the discontinuous formulation (5.15).[25]

The intercept in equation (5.16) is $A_0 + A_2 C_{t-1}$. While A_0 remains stationary through time, $A_2 C_{t-1}$ does not. It may rise or fall, and consequently this equation may drift upward *or* downward. Downward shiftability is a wrinkle not found in the customary response envisioned by Smithies, Duesenberry, Modigliani, or Davis, and it adds a new dimension for explaining the inverse relationship between current consumption and current income occasionally observed. Figure 5.2 can help in the exposition. For present purposes the notation there should be read without asterisks and t_0 should be interpreted as zero. At time zero the lower function operates, its intercept being $A_0 + A_2 C_{-1}$. Point G results, and consumption equals C_0. Assume that $C_0 > C_{-1}$. In the next period, $t = 1$, the relevant consumption function has an intercept $A_0 + A_2 C_0$ and must lie above the previous locus. Income reduced to Y_1 does not outweigh the stimulus to consumption arising from habits, and thus point I obtains. Consumption at $t = 1$ stands at C_1.

To consider the opposite scenario, recalibrate $t_0 + 1$ as zero and t_0 as unity in Figure 5.2. At time zero the upper function operates and point I arises. However, consumption associated with I falls below consumption in the previous period ($C_0 < C_{-1}$), perhaps because income declined at time zero. This reduced consumption then generates a lower consumption function binding at time one (the locus actually identified with $t = t_0$ in the figure). Increased income in that period only partly offsets the depressing influence of habits, and point G emerges. Current consumption therefore falls when current income rises.

This scenario—$C_1 < C_0 < C_{-1}$ and $Y_1 > Y_0 < Y_{-1}$—exactly matches the events for the period 1953:2–1953:4 recorded in Table 5.5, quarter 3 serving as time zero. The drop in income during quarter 3 caused consumption to fall that period and forced downward the consumption function pertinent to quarter 4. Even though income rose in quarter 4, the downward thrust of the function was sufficient to depress consumption again.

Nonproportional function (5.16) can explain the sometimes negative association between consumption and income. But can it be reconciled with the long-run proportionality observed by Kuznets? To answer this question, suppose that

[25] Brown, "Habit Persistence," pp. 360–361, 370. The econometric tests supporting continuity over discontinuity include a variable which allows for structural changes, and they separate disposable income into wage and nonwage components.

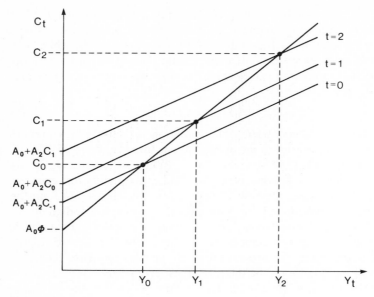

Figure 5.5

consumption has been growing steadily through time at the rate γ. Then $C_t = (1 + \gamma)C_{t-1}$ and $C_{t-1} = C_t/(1 + \gamma)$. Substitution into equation (5.16) yields, after simplification,

$$C_t = A_0\Phi + A_1\Phi Y_t \qquad (5.17)$$

where $\Phi = (1 + \gamma)/(1 + \gamma - A_2)$. As consumption rises smoothly through time, the intercept in the nonproportional function (5.16) moves upward in such a way that the observed consumption-income points generate equation (5.17). Figure 5.5 illustrates. Since $\Phi > 1$ for any finite growth rate γ, the long-run function exhibits a greater marginal propensity ($A_1\Phi$) than does its short-run cousin, but it is clearly nonproportional and hence stands at odds with the Kuznets result. The fundamental reason for this inconsistency is that function (5.16) postulates a stationary intercept component, A_0. The presence of A_0 there, however, might be explained as enabling a test of the proposition that the true short-run intercept does not contain a fixed element. Consequently, should A_0 prove to be no different from zero in empirical experimentation, then long-run function (5.17) could be regarded as proportional. Observe that because Φ decreases as γ increases, so does the long-run marginal propensity.

Applying annual Canadian data for the periods 1926–1941 and 1946–1949 to equation (5.16), Brown estimates the short-run marginal propensity at .34, a value substantially below those found by the proponents of habit persistence already mentioned but hardly out of line with findings of the wealth theorists to be discussed anon. Brown's long-run propensity equals approximately .43, about half

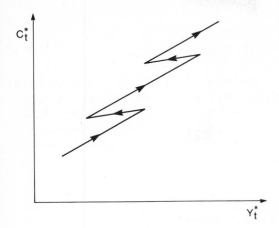

C_t^*

Y_t^*

Figure 5.6 *Source*: Smyth and Jackson, "Ratchet Models," p. 90.

of Kuznets'. The sluggishness coefficient registers .22. For the record, A_0 exceeds zero on statistical grounds and unhappily makes relation (5.17) nonproportional.[26]

Two additional studies based on habit persistence deserve reference. H. S. Houthakker and Lester Taylor in a 1966 effort follow the continuous persistence route and derive the function

$$C_t^* = b_0 + b_1 \Delta Y_t^* + b_2 Y_{t-1}^* + b_3 C_{t-1}^*$$

where all variables are real per capitas.[27] Reexpressing this equation yields

$$C_t^* = b_0 + b_1 Y_t^* + (b_2 - b_1) Y_{t-1}^* + b_3 C_{t-1}^* \qquad (5.18)$$

Apart from the use of per capita magnitudes, equation (5.18) differs from Brown's equation (5.16) by the presence of a lagged income term.

In a 1978 paper David Smyth and John Jackson present a consumption model of discontinuous habit persistence wherein consumers do not retrace their steps as income recovers from a slump.[28] Figure 5.6 illustrates, with arrowheads, the response sequence imagined. Consumption there experiences a "reverse lightning bolt" effect, in contrast to the ratchet effect of Duesenberry and Modigliani portrayed in Figure 5.4. Underlying this lightning bolt is an equation written in

[26]An ancillary estimation experiment with equation (5.16) generates results of the same character as those from the original test. The short-run and long-run propensities amount to .40 and .59, respectively, while the sluggishness coefficient equals .32. See Brown, "Habit Persistence," pp. 361, 364, 369–370.

[27]H. S. Houthakker and Lester D. Taylor, *Consumer Demand in the United States, 1929–1970: Analyses and Projections* (Cambridge, Mass.: Harvard University Press, 1966), pp. 8–16, 56–57, 173–179.

[28]David J. Smyth and John D. Jackson, "A Theoretical and Empirical Analysis of Ratchet Models as Alternatives to Permanent Income and Continuous Habit Formation Consumption Functions," *Journal of Economics and Business*, **30** (Winter 1978), pp. 89–97. These authors, unlike the other advocates of habit persistence quoted, define consumption as a service flow, a concept to be addressed in the next section.

terms of real per capitas:

$$C_t^* = d_0 + d_1 Y_t^* + \sum_{i=2}^{5} d_i D_{i-1, t}^* \tag{5.19}$$

where the d factors represent coefficients and the D^* series are (or are based on) variables known as "dummies," variables which assume only zero and unit values. This equation performs well empirically, but the use of the D^* quantities leaves much to be desired. While they may capture the effects of discontinuous persistence, they say nothing about which *economic* measures embody habits and nothing about how those determinants should enter the consumption function. They beg those questions.

5.5 THE COMING OF WEALTH THEORIES

Habit persistence postulates go a step beyond the Keynesian absolute income hypothesis to argue that consumer behavior is subject to inertia and that this sluggishness arises from habits acquired through previous experiences. Current consumption therefore depends not only upon current income but also upon past consumption or past income. An alternative explanation for this sluggishness ties consumer response formally to utility maximization, and an early presentation of this approach came from William Hamburger in his 1951 doctoral dissertation and in two ensuing papers dated 1954 and 1955.[29] Hamburger argues that a household determines current consumption as part of a lifetime plan of consumption. In particular, it chooses a consumption stream over time in order to maximize utility, and current consumption represents only one element in that stream.

The household's utility function reads

$$u_t = u(c_t, c_{t+1}, c_{t+2}, \ldots, c_{t+\iota}) \tag{5.20}$$

where u_t and c_t denote utility and real consumption, respectively, in the current period. $c_{t+\iota}$ denotes real consumption planned for the final period of the household's expected life. In studies predating Hamburger's, consumption was treated as the amount *spent* on consumer items, namely, services, nondurables, and durables. This interpretation, says Hamburger, misses the mark because consumption occurs only when these items are "used up." While services and nondurables can be construed as being entirely used up in the period of their purchase, durables cannot. They enjoy much longer life, and only a portion of them disappears in any period. Consonant with this use, or service flow, concept, he visualizes consumption in a period to be the expenditures on services and

---

[29] William Hamburger, "Consumption and Wealth" (Ph.D. dissertation, University of Chicago, 1951); "Determinants of Aggregate Consumption," *Review of Economic Studies*, **22** (October 1954), pp. 23–34; and "The Relation of Consumption to Wealth and the Wage Rate," *Econometrica*, **23** (January 1955), pp. 1–17. See also Mayer, *Permanent Income*, p. 26.

nondurables that period plus the value of services provided by durables that period. The latter might be equated to the level of depreciation.

To complete the household's optimization problem, a budget constraint must be postulated to accompany the utility function. Since that function stretches into the future, so must the constraint. It therefore reflects the individual's total lifetime receipts, which stem from two sources: property wealth and human wealth. Property, or nonhuman, wealth consists of tangible assets such as financial instruments and goods. Human wealth, by contrast, encompasses intangibles embodied within a person. The "stock" of these traits serves as the source of an individual's current and future labor income and hence merits the wealth designation.[30]

Direct measurement of the income from human wealth would involve the difficult task of calculating discounted values of expected future labor earnings. Hamburger therefore measures it indirectly by treating it as proportional to the household's current wage rate. Eventually he derives a consumption function of the form

$$C_t^* = a_H W_t^* + b_H Q_t^* \qquad (5.21)$$

where C_t^* indicates real per capita use consumption at time t; W_t^*, real per capita property wealth at t; and Q_t^*, the average real wage rate per worker at t. Coefficients a_H and b_H capture the effects of several factors on consumption. For instance, uncertainty about prospective yields causes individuals to discount expected returns from human wealth more heavily and thus reduces the importance of the proxy wage rate variable while strengthening that of nonhuman wealth. b_H would therefore be smaller and a_H larger. Similarly, decisions to leave estates would generate a_H and b_H coefficients lower than their values in the absence of bequests. *Ceteris paribus*, households consume less under an estate motive.

5.6 THE PERMANENT INCOME HYPOTHESIS

Concepts such as intertemporal utility maximization, use consumption, and human wealth presented in Hamburger's work find reexpression in the later efforts of Milton Friedman and Franco Modigliani, both of whom served as supervisors of Hamburger's dissertation. Consider first Friedman's endeavor.[31]

The household is initially imagined to enjoy complete certainty about future receipts, interest rates, and the like. In this circumstance two reasons can be

---

[30]Actually, Hamburger, in "Determinants," p. 24, defines human wealth not in terms of a stock of traits but rather in terms of a flow of income: specifically, the discounted expected disposable labor income. The posture adopted here of regarding wealth as the source of income instead of as income itself coincides with the usual treatment. See, for example, Barry N. Siegel, *Aggregate Economics and Public Policy*, 3d ed. (Homewood, Ill.: Richard D. Irwin, Inc., 1970), p. 10.

[31]Milton Friedman, *A Theory of the Consumption Function* (Princeton, N.J.: Princeton University Press, 1957), especially Chapters II–III.

identified for selecting a saving stream through time: to reduce fluctuations in expenditures which would otherwise occur because of fluctuations in receipts and to earn interest on loans. Since saving is the obverse of consumption, the household's preference function can be expressed equivalently in terms of a consumption stream. In its most general format, this function has an indefinite number of consumption arguments reflecting infinite life of the household. Rather than implying immortality, however, this formulation merely means that the household incorporates into its own spending decision the future expenditures of those receiving its bequests.[32]

For simplicity, abandon this general preference expression and suppose instead that the individual's utility depends only upon real consumption c planned for the current period and real consumption c_1 planned for the next period:

$$u = u(c, c_1) \qquad (5.22)$$

where the time subscript t is suppressed. u exhibits traditional properties. It has positive but declining marginal utilities and positive cross-marginals: an increase in c increases the marginal utility of c_1 and an increase in c_1 increases that of c. The opposite applies to decreases. Moreover, u is homogeneous of degree one.

In the present period the household chooses the consumption stream c and c_1 to maximize utility subject to a budget constraint which says that the total amount consumed over the planning interval must equal the total receipts arising over that interval. To articulate this constraint, future receipts must be discounted to the present because the household has a time preference. A receipt of \$1 in period 1 is not the same as a receipt of \$1 currently; in fact, \$1 next period is worth only \$$[1/(1 + r)]$ to the consumer now, r being the real rate of interest—the nominal rate minus the rate of price change. Similar reasoning applies to consumption; consumption of c_1 units next period is equivalent to consumption of $c_1/(1 + r)$ units currently. The budget constraint, translating all future variables into present value terms, thus reads

$$c + \frac{1}{1 + r}c_1 = w_e \qquad (5.23)$$

$$w_e = q + \frac{1}{1 + r}q_1$$

where q and q_1 denote planned real receipts from both human and nonhuman wealth for the current period and for the subsequent period, respectively.[33] Note the expectational orientation of the q variables; w_e, which Friedman labels wealth, thus has an expectational nature too.

---

[32] Ibid., p. 14, and Mayer, *Permanent Income*, p. 36.

[33] On the use of real magnitudes, see Milton Friedman, "Windfalls, the 'Horizon,' and Related Concepts in the Permanent-Income Hypothesis," in *Measurement in Economics: Studies in Mathematical Economics and Econometrics in Memory of Yehuda Grunfeld* (Stanford, Calif.: Stanford University Press, 1963), p. 8.

Maximization of (5.22) subject to (5.23) can be accomplished by solving the constraint for c_1 and by inserting the resulting expression into the utility function. Utility then becomes dependent upon c alone, and hence the rules of simple two-variable differentiation apply for solving the optimization problem.[34] Accordingly,

$$u = u\big[c, (1 + r)w_e - (1 + r)c\big]$$

and differentiation totally with respect to the single independent variable c renders

$$\frac{du}{dc} = \frac{\partial u}{\partial c} + \frac{\partial u}{\partial c_1}\frac{dc_1}{dc}$$

$$\frac{du}{dc} = \frac{\partial u}{\partial c} - (1 + r)\frac{\partial u}{\partial c_1}$$

The stationary point occurs where $du/dc = 0$ or, equivalently, where[35]

$$\frac{\partial u}{\partial c} = (1 + r)\frac{\partial u}{\partial c_1} \tag{5.24}$$

Constrained utility maximization requires that spending be spread through time to equate the marginal utilities corrected for time preference. If some stream c and c_1 made, say, $\partial u/\partial c > (1 + r)\partial u/\partial c_1$, a revision of plans by reducing future consumption c_1 and increasing current consumption c would increase total utility. While utility would be sacrificed by decreasing c_1, that decrease would be more than offset by the gain in utility attributable to increased c. From (5.24)

$$\frac{\partial u/\partial c}{\partial u/\partial c_1} = 1 + r \tag{5.25}$$

Since the utility function is homogeneous of degree one, each marginal utility must be homogeneous of degree zero: each depends only upon the *ratio* of the consumption variables. Specifically, $\partial u/\partial c = f_A(c_1/c)$ and $\partial u/\partial c_1 = f_B(c_1/c)$.

---

[34] This solution method has intuitive appeal. Since a household must adhere to the budget constraint, it does not search through all possible pairs of c and c_1; it only peruses those satisfying the constraint. Forcing the constraint into (5.22) acts to limit that search. In terms of three-dimensional graphics, the household seeks the maximum of only those utility values which lie directly above the budget line. This maximum is typically less than the maximum—say, some point G—attainable in the absence of the restriction. Only if the constraint happened to pass immediately under G would that point obtain. In this accidental circumstance the constraint would be costless in the sense of imposing no forfeiture of utility.

An alternative to the method of solution by substitution outlined in the text is the Lagrange technique, which lends itself to the general case where the function to be optimized involves any number of arguments. Both procedures are reviewed in Section 8 of Appendix A.

[35] Equation (5.24) describes the first-order condition for a utility maximum. The second-order condition $d^2u/dc^2 < 0$ is automatically satisfied since the utility function has diminishing marginal utilities and positive cross-marginals. These first- and second-order conditions are sufficient for a maximum of u.

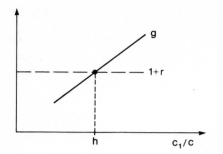

Figure 5.7

From the properties of u, when c_1/c rises, f_A rises and f_B falls. Therefore f_A/f_B, written more simply as g, rises, as Figure 5.7 illustrates. Concavity is ignored.

For a maximum of utility under the constraint, equation (5.25) requires that the ratio of marginal utilities equal $1 + r$, and this equality—as Figure 5.7 indicates—determines the optimum value h of the consumption ratio.[36] However, as r changes, so does h, and thus the optimum consumption ratio depends upon r. Formally stated, equation (5.25) becomes

$$g\left(\frac{c_1}{c}\right) = 1 + r$$

which yields $c_1/c = h(r)$, or $c_1 = h(r)c$. Inserting this expression for c_1 into the budget constraint (5.23) leaves

$$c + \frac{1}{1+r}h(r)c = w_e$$

or

$$c = i_A(r)w_e \qquad (5.26)$$

with $i_A(r) = [1 + h(r)/(1 + r)]^{-1}$. Therefore, c_1 becomes

$$c_1 = i_B(r)w_e \qquad (5.27)$$

where $i_B(r) = h(r)i_A(r)$.

Two features of the consumption function (5.26) deserve emphasis. First, current planned consumption depends proportionally upon wealth, the proportionality term reflecting the interest rate but remaining independent of wealth. Second, consumption depends through w_e not only upon expected current receipts but also upon receipts which the household expects to receive in the future. From this formulation it should be clear that current consumption could remain unchanged despite a change in current receipts if expected future receipts were to change in a compensatory manner. Consumption need not respond to present happenings.

---

[36] Intersection of g with the $1 + r$ locus must occur and hence an optimum consumption ratio must exist if the maximum and minimum values of the marginal utilities equal infinity and zero. These "boundary" conditions are sufficient for intersection.

Income can be viewed theoretically as a return on wealth. That income associated with the wealth term w_e is called "permanent income," $y_P = rw_e$. Permanent income necessarily shares attributes of wealth, and thus it too involves expectations of receipts. Planned consumption, renamed "permanent consumption" and notated c_P to underscore both its expectational aspect and its use definition, can therefore be reexpressed from (5.26) as

$$c_P = i_A(r)\frac{1}{r}(rw_e)$$

or as

$$c_P = j(r)y_P \tag{5.28}$$

where $j(r) = i_A(r)/r$. Permanent consumption is proportional to permanent (disposable) income.

Refinements to (5.28) are possible. The optimization process described occurred in the presence of certainty. Under uncertainty, however, the household may wish to save—to accumulate nonhuman wealth—for a third reason: to guard against emergencies. Not all forms of wealth serve equally well for this purpose, and hence the amount of nonhuman wealth accumulated may be based on the mix of wealth which the household presently possesses, a mix represented perhaps by the ratio v of nonhuman wealth to permanent income. Furthermore, the amounts saved and consumed depend upon demographic factors such as age and family size, because they shape the preference function. Although a set x of demographic variables is implicit in $j(r)$, it may be made explicit. These refinements convert equation (5.28) for the household to

$$c_P = k(r, v, x)y_P \tag{5.29}$$

Permanents are planned quantities, not actual quantities. However, they relate to actuals in a linear manner; namely,

$$c = c_P + c_T \tag{5.30}$$

$$y = y_P + y_T \tag{5.31}$$

where c and y designate measured (or actual) consumption and disposable income, respectively, and c_T and y_T designate transitory consumption and disposable income, respectively. All variables represent reals. The transitory components are random variables which may assume positive or negative values, and thus, according to equation (5.30), actual consumption deviates from planned current consumption by a chance factor. The same is true for actual income via (5.31).

The random and permanent components of a variable are presumed to be unrelated, as are the transitory elements of consumption and income. With ρ denoting the theoretical correlation coefficient between the variables written as its subscripts, these hypotheses transform into

$$\rho_{c_P c_T} = \rho_{y_P y_T} = \rho_{c_T y_T} = 0 \tag{5.32}$$

The first two correlations follow from the accidental nature of the transitory variables, and their imposition seems benign. The third, however, appears more crucial, for it says that a household will on average *not* consume unexpected income. At first blush this assumption may seem unreasonable, but it gains credibility when one recalls that consumption means service flow. An increase in transitory income could lead to an increase in durable purchases, which are mostly saving, thereby leaving consumption largely unchanged. Furthermore, positive associations between the transitory components in some instances would be offset by negative associations in others, and consequently the postulate $\rho_{c_T y_T} = 0$ may not be inappropriate.

A principal conclusion of the permanent income hypothesis is contained in equation (5.29); namely, a household's permanent consumption is proportional to its permanent income. The aggregate counterpart of this relation can be obtained by summing across individuals, giving

$$C_P = \kappa Y_P \tag{5.33}$$

where C_P and Y_P denote, respectively, real permanent consumption and real permanent disposable income in the aggregate. κ assumes a clumsy form, but it is essentially a weighted average of the proportionality terms $k(r, v, x)$ of all individuals. Specifically,

$$\kappa = \int_x \int_v \int_r m(r, v, x) k(r, v, x) \, dr \, dv \, dx$$

where each integral signifies a summation over the corresponding variable. $m(r, v, x)$ summarizes the distribution of households by r, v, and x; it indicates the fraction of households facing an interest rate r, a wealth mix v, and utility factors x. Given its composition, κ may vary through time. Since the aggregate consumption function (5.33) is proportional, it can be converted to per capitas, nominals, or both.

5.7 FROM PERMANENTS TO MEASUREDS AND BEYOND

Aggregate relationship (5.33) represents an interesting theoretical construct, but it leaves much to be desired from a practical standpoint because data on permanents, especially at the aggregate level, do not exist. That relationship is simply not operational. One way to overcome this obstacle calls for the assumption that permanent income consists of some function of current and past *measured* incomes. That linkage seems reasonable because permanent income refers to expected receipts, and expectations arise from current and past actual experiences. Moreover, since the mind's eye has clearer sight of newer experiences, it seems sensible to stipulate that this function gives heavier weight to more recent events than to occurrences further back in time. But what exact form should the function take?

Friedman offers an initial answer to this question by postulating that departures of actual income from permanent income cause the permanent level to be revised in the direction of the discrepancy. In short, permanent income observes an adaptive adjustment mechanism:[37]

$$\frac{dY_{P_t}}{dt} = \beta(Y_t - Y_{P_t}) \tag{5.34}$$

where $0 < \beta < 1$. The t again denotes time, while Y_{P_t} and Y_t symbolize, respectively, aggregate real permanent and aggregate real measured disposable income at t. If actual income exceeds planned income, then the planned level is revised upward; the reverse also holds. Transforming this equation renders permanent income a function of measured incomes:

$$Y_{P_t} = \beta \int_{-\infty}^{t} e^{-\beta(t-\theta)} Y_\theta \, d\theta \tag{5.35}$$

More precisely, permanent income is an exponentially weighted average of current and all past measured incomes with the weights summing to unity:

$$\beta \int_{-\infty}^{t} e^{-\beta(t-\theta)} \, d\theta = 1$$

Relationship (5.35) exemplifies a distributed lag, a function which "distributes" the value of a dependent variable across current and lagged values of another variable.

Although making permanent income measurable, expression (5.35) has an annoying trait: it forces permanent income to fall between the highest and the lowest values of actual income attained to date. This characteristic becomes particularly awkward in periods of, say, economic expansion, because current permanent income then remains systematically below current actual income. To remedy this deficiency Friedman introduces a trend factor for measured income: $Y_t = Y_0 e^{\alpha t}$, Y_0 indicating the value of measured income at time zero and α signifying the secular rate of growth. With this adjustment (5.35) can be written as

$$Y_{P_t} = \beta \int_{-\infty}^{t} e^{-(\beta-\alpha)(t-\theta)} Y_\theta \, d\theta \tag{5.36}$$

where $0 < \beta - \alpha < 1$. Now the weights can sum in excess of unity

$$\beta \int_{-\infty}^{t} e^{-(\beta-\alpha)(t-\theta)} \, d\theta = \frac{\beta}{\beta - \alpha}$$

and hence permanent income can lie beyond the range of the measured quantities. Converting (5.36) to its discrete-time counterpart, which preserves the weight sum at $\beta/(\beta - \alpha)$, gives

$$Y_{P_t} = \xi \left[Y_t + e^{-(\beta-\alpha)} Y_{t-1} + e^{-2(\beta-\alpha)} Y_{t-2} + \cdots \right] \tag{5.37}$$

[37]See Friedman, *Consumption Function*, pp. 142–152, for material pertinent to the present section.

with $\xi = \beta[1 - e^{-(\beta-\alpha)}]/(\beta - \alpha)$. Clearly, $0 < e^{-(\beta-\alpha)} < 1$; similarly,[38] $0 < \xi <$ 1. Equation (5.37) qualifies as a Koyck distributed lag.[39]

The aggregate counterpart of taxonomy (5.30) can be written as $C_t = C_{Pt} + C_{Tt}$, with C_t, C_{Pt}, and C_{Tt} denoting, respectively, real measured, real permanent, and real transitory consumption in the aggregate at time t. From this relationship and from equation (5.37), consumption function (5.33) yields

$$C_t = \kappa\xi\left[Y_t + e^{-(\beta-\alpha)}Y_{t-1} + e^{-2(\beta-\alpha)}Y_{t-2} + \cdots\right] + C_{Tt} \qquad (5.38)$$

C_{Tt}, of course, is a random disturbance.

Equation (5.38) says that current measured consumption depends upon current *and* past measured incomes. Current income has influence in a muted way and only to the extent that it alters the perception of permanent income. Past experience, captured by the lagged terms, serves to attenuate the effect of current income on permanent income and thus on current consumption; that is, past incomes reflect the inertia of consumers in adjusting permanent income to current events. Notice that while the marginal propensity to consume permanent income is κ, the propensity to consume current measured income is only $\kappa\xi$.

Using annual real per capita data for the United States drawn from the period 1905–1951 (excluding the periods 1917–1918 and 1942–1945), Friedman estimates κ, β, and α at .88, .40, and .02, respectively, making the marginal propensity to consume current measured income .29. Thus, under the permanent income hypothesis, current measured income has a much smaller effect on current consumption than it does under the absolute income hypothesis.[40]

---

[38]Each weight coefficient in (5.37) emerges from the continuous weight function by integration over the corresponding period. For example, the coefficient applicable to Y_{t-n} results by integrating $\beta e^{-(\beta-\alpha)(t-\theta)}$ between $t - n$ and $t - n - 1$ to obtain $e^{-n(\beta-\alpha)}\beta[1 - e^{-(\beta-\alpha)}]/(\beta - \alpha)$.

It can be quickly shown that the discrete-time weights in (5.37) sum to $\beta/(\beta - \alpha)$. Consider first the more interesting case in which (5.37) would contain a finite number of terms ending at time $t - n$. Let λ stand for $e^{-(\beta-\alpha)}$. Also let V stand for the weight sum: $V = \xi(1 + \lambda + \lambda^2 + \cdots + \lambda^{n-1} + \lambda^n)$. Multiply V by λ and then subtract λV from V. Thus, $V = (1 - \lambda^{n+1})\beta/(\beta - \alpha)$. Since λ falls below unity and n is typically large, the sum V approximates $\beta/(\beta - \alpha)$. For the case of an endless distributed lag, as in (5.37), n becomes infinite and V becomes $\beta/(\beta - \alpha)$.

[39]Koyck proposed for discrete time an infinite lag structure where the coefficients ω_i, known as "reaction coefficients," decline geometrically: $\omega_i = \omega_0\mu^i$, with $\omega_0 > 0$ and $0 \leq \mu < 1$ and with i being the integer number of periods the corresponding lagged term is distant from the present. Relating permanent income to current and past measureds à la Koyck engenders

$$Y_{Pt} = \omega_0 Y_t + \omega_0\mu Y_{t-1} + \omega_0\mu^2 Y_{t-2} + \cdots$$

$$Y_{Pt} = \omega_0\left[Y_t + \mu Y_{t-1} + \mu^2 Y_{t-2} + \cdots\right]$$

This expression clearly duplicates equation (5.37) with $\omega_0 = \xi$ and $\mu = e^{-(\beta-\alpha)}$. See L. M. Koyck, *Distributed Lags and Investment Analysis*, Contributions to Economic Analysis, no. IV (Amsterdam: North-Holland Publishing Company, 1954), pp. 11–12, 19–22.

[40]If consumption were defined as total expenditures, in accord with Keynes, rather than as a service flow, the marginal propensity would likely be greater than .29, but it would likely still remain far below Keynesian levels. Section 5.9 pursues this point.

With the help of modest algebra, equation (5.38) can be reexpressed in a more tractable manner. Since the equation holds at each point in time, at $t - 1$ it read

$$C_{t-1} = \kappa\xi\left[Y_{t-1} + \lambda Y_{t-2} + \lambda^2 Y_{t-3} + \cdots\right] + C_{T,t-1} \qquad (5.39)$$

where λ again represents $e^{-(\beta-\alpha)}$ for simplicity. Multiplication of (5.39) by λ yields

$$\lambda C_{t-1} = \kappa\xi\left[\lambda Y_{t-1} + \lambda^2 Y_{t-2} + \lambda^3 Y_{t-3} + \cdots\right] + \lambda C_{T,t-1}$$

which when subtracted from (5.38) leaves

$$C_t - \lambda C_{t-1} = \kappa\xi Y_t + (C_{Tt} - \lambda C_{T,t-1})$$

or

$$C_t = \kappa\xi Y_t + \lambda C_{t-1} + Z_t \qquad (5.40)$$

where[41] Z_t stands for the transitory composite $C_{Tt} - \lambda C_{T,t-1}$. For illustrative purposes, this random element may be taken as zero, disclosing

$$C_t = \kappa\xi Y_t + \lambda C_{t-1} \qquad (5.41)$$

Current real measured consumption depends upon current real measured disposable income and real measured consumption lagged one period. The marginal propensity to consume measured income is $\kappa\xi$, as noted above. λ serves as a sluggishness coefficient. A greater λ connotes a stronger tie to the past, a feature manifested in equation (5.37) by a slower decline in the factors λ, λ^2, λ^3,..., across past income values. Furthermore, since $\xi = \beta(1 - \lambda)/(\beta - \alpha)$, a greater λ often means a smaller ξ and a smaller propensity to consume current income. Given Friedman's estimates for β and α, λ equals .68.

Separation of current consumption into a current income component and a past consumption component via (5.41) has intuitive appeal. In the previous period households observed the optimization procedure, and on the basis of their permanent income collectively consumed C_{t-1}, transitory consumption ignored. C_{t-1} therefore reflects the level of permanent income operative in the prior period, and λC_{t-1} identifies that portion of current consumption attributable to the previous conception of permanent income. But the current period ushers in new experiences and causes a revision in the perception of permanent income. This revision prompts an adjustment in consumption, and that adjustment is captured by the current income component $\kappa\xi Y_t$. On an intuitive level, therefore, equation (5.41) can be interpreted as dividing current permanent income into its previous level and its change from that level and as identifying the separate effect of each on current consumption.

---

[41] If the distributed lag (5.37) were finite with the term for time $t - n$ being the most distant, then the derivation process would place an extra element $-\kappa\xi\lambda^{n+1}Y_{t-n-1}$ on the right side of (5.40). However, since λ lies below unity and n is large, the extra term would be negligible through λ^{n+1}. Thus, it could be disregarded.

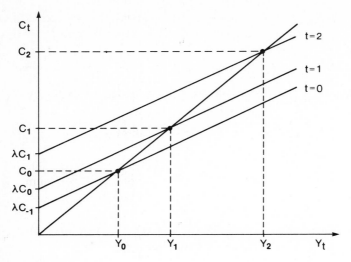

Figure 5.8

Equation (5.41) constitutes a short-run function. Like the Brown paradigm (5.16) and the Houthakker-Taylor formulation (5.18), it can shift upward or downward through time and hence can explain the negative relationship between current consumption and current income sometimes observed. What about the long-run function? Consonant with the earlier treatment, the long run may be viewed as the trend case wherein variables expand smoothly through time. Specifically, $C_t = (1 + \gamma)C_{t-1}$, or $C_{t-1} = C_t/(1 + \gamma)$. Insertion into (5.41) produces, after manipulation,

$$C_t = \kappa\xi\delta_F Y_t \tag{5.42}$$

where $\delta_F = (1 + \gamma)/(1 + \gamma - \lambda)$. In the long run the consumption function defined in terms of *measured* quantities becomes proportional. Since α and γ move together, δ_F must exceed unity, and the long-run marginal propensity to consume $\kappa\xi\delta_F$ must exceed its short-run counterpart $\kappa\xi$. Slower growth begets a smaller long-run propensity, and in stationary state, with measured income and consumption exhibiting no growth ($\alpha = \gamma = 0$), the long-run propensity pertinent to measured income equals κ, the propensity to consume permanent income.[42]

Figure 5.8 presents the long-run consumption function (5.42) along with its family of short-run functions (5.41). Aside from the definition of consumption,

---

[42] Proportionality of the measured quantities can be established by an alternative route. Since income grows smoothly in the long run, $Y_t = (1 + \alpha)Y_{t-1}$, or $Y_{t-1} = Y_t/(1 + \alpha)$. More generally, $Y_{t-n} = Y_t/(1 + \alpha)^n$. Substitution of this relationship into (5.38) yields, with transitory consumption ignored,

$$C_t = \kappa\xi\left[1 + \lambda/(1 + \alpha) + \lambda^2/(1 + \alpha)^2 + \cdots\right]Y_t$$

The bracketed expression reduces to $(1 + \alpha)/(1 + \alpha - \lambda)$, and the twin of (5.42) emerges.

this configuration differs from Brown's depicted in Figure 5.5 inasmuch as the long-run variant now passes through the origin.

The distributed lag used to quantify permanent income in (5.37) allows it to locate outside the range of measured income. Alternative structures having the same property can be suggested and serve to demonstrate the importance of the permanent income specification for a consumption function defined in terms of measured values. For example, suppose that permanent income is written as

$$Y_{Pt} = E_0 + E_1 t + E_2\big[Y_t + \sigma Y_{t-1} + \sigma^2 Y_{t-2} + \cdots\big] \qquad (5.43)$$

instead of as (5.37). $0 < \sigma < 1$, $E_2 = 1 - \sigma$, and $E_2 \Sigma_{i=0}^{i=\infty} \sigma^i = 1$; thus the value assumed by the expression $E_2[\ ]$ must fall between the maximum and minimum actual incomes. $E_1 t$ reflects a trend in the movement of measured income and bears a strong kinship to the trend factor imposed by Friedman in (5.36). E_0, a constant, captures other agents which on balance remain stationary through time. Clearly, because of E_0 and $E_1 t$ individually or combined, permanent income may transcend the range identified by the actuals.

Repetition of the computational steps followed in establishing (5.41) generates from (5.43)

$$C_t = \kappa\big[(1 - \sigma)E_0 + \sigma E_1\big] + \kappa(1 - \sigma)E_1 t + \kappa E_2 Y_t + \sigma C_{t-1} \qquad (5.44)$$

Importantly, this equation differs from (5.41) in that it includes a stationary intercept and a time trend besides current income and past consumption. Its long-run version, derived using $C_t = (1 + \gamma)C_{t-1}$, is

$$C_t = \kappa\big[(1 - \sigma)E_0 + \sigma E_1\big]\delta_A + \kappa(1 - \sigma)E_1 \delta_A t + \kappa E_2 \delta_A Y_t \qquad (5.45)$$

where $\delta_A = (1 + \gamma)/(1 + \gamma - \sigma)$. Due to the inclusion of E_0 and $E_1 t$ in the permanent income relation (5.43), the long-run consumption function becomes nonproportional unless for equation (5.44) *both* the stationary intercept and the coefficient of time are shown empirically not to differ from zero. The specification of permanent income is critical for the form of the consumption function expressed in terms of measureds, and alternative specifications may beget markedly dissimilar consumption functions.[43]

---

[43] Ralph Husby, studying the possible income dependence of the marginal propensity to consume and thus requiring income to enter the consumption function nonlinearly, postulates permanent income per capita in a manner analogous to (5.43) but with the trend term absent ($E_1 = 0$) and with quadratics of all income terms present. E_0 remains intact. From this format his consumption function takes the appearance $C_t^* = b_0' + b_1' Y_t^* + b_2' Y_t^{*2} + b_3' C_{t-1}^*$, all variables being "real" per capitas. Observe that b_0' and the quadratic $b_2' Y_t^{*2}$ result solely because of the permanent income specification. For the long run, where $C_t^* = (1 + \gamma^*)C_{t-1}^*$, the consumption function becomes $C_t^* = b_0' \delta_H + b_1' \delta_H Y_t^* + b_2' \delta_H Y_t^{*2}$, $\delta_H = (1 + \gamma^*)/(1 + \gamma^* - b_3')$. See Ralph D. Husby, "A Nonlinear Consumption Function Estimated from Time-Series and Cross-Section Data," *Review of Economics and Statistics*, **53** (February 1971), pp. 76–79. See also James H. Gapinski, "The Husby Consumption Analysis: A Comment," *Review of Economics and Statistics*, **56** (August 1974), pp. 401–402, and Husby's reply, p. 403.

5.8 THE LIFE CYCLE HYPOTHESIS

Developed by Albert Ando, Richard Brumberg, and Franco Modigliani, the life cycle hypothesis shares many features of the permanent income hypothesis,[44] a circumstance hardly surprising in view of the mutual interests and association of Hamburger, Friedman, and Modigliani. Life cycle presumes that a household maximizes utility by choosing a consumption stream over time, consumption being treated as a service flow rather than as total expenditures. This intertemporal optimization process, like that envisioned under Friedman, is essentially unimpaired by uncertainty about future events; Modigliani and associates argue that while uncertainty may affect the *composition* of saving—namely, the types of assets accumulated—it should not exert much impact on the overall *level* of saving and consumption. Furthermore, life cycle prompts the household to consume in proportion to current and future resources. However, resources are now explicitly segmented into those associated with human wealth and those associated with nonhuman wealth. The permanent income hypothesis avoids such a precise split. Another contrast exists. Under life cycle the individual does not plan to leave an estate; this postulate, however, can be relaxed without any substantive change in conclusions.[45]

Life cycle optimization contains manipulative steps analogous to those cited for permanent income and gives for an individual of age τ

$$c_t^\tau = \Omega_t^\tau \left[y_{Lt}^\tau + \text{dis}(y_L^\tau) + w_{t-1}^\tau \right] \tag{5.46}$$

Real consumption by the individual at time t, c_t^τ, is proportional to real resources at t: current disposable labor income, y_{Lt}^τ; the discounted value of disposable labor income expected to be forthcoming over the individual's remaining earning life, $\text{dis}(y_L^\tau)$; and net worth or property wealth carried over from the previous period, w_{t-1}^τ. Current and discounted future labor incomes represent the return from human wealth, while net worth represents nonhuman wealth. Proportionality term Ω_t^τ, in agreement with the permanent income case, includes utility factors and the real rate of return on assets but excludes current and future receipts. Equation (5.46) highlights the role of the utility factor age: the position of a household in its life cycle determines the resources available and the consequent consumption behavior.

---

[44] See the seminal work by Franco Modigliani and Richard Brumberg, "Utility Analysis and the Consumption Function: An Interpretation of Cross-Section Data," in K. K. Kurihara, ed., *Post Keynesian Economics* (New Brunswick, N.J.: Rutgers University Press, 1954), pp. 388–436, and the later effort by Albert Ando and Franco Modigliani, "The 'Life Cycle' Hypothesis of Saving: Aggregate Implications and Tests," *American Economic Review*, **53**, part I (March 1963), pp. 55–84. The relationship between the life cycle and permanent income hypotheses is discussed by Robert Ferber, "Consumer Economics, A Survey," *Journal of Economic Literature*, **11** (December 1973), pp. 1306–1307, and by Mayer, *Permanent Income*, pp. 29–31.

[45] The Modigliani and Brumberg paper "Utility Analysis" initially does permit bequests but later assumes them away for simplicity, pp. 390–391, 394; the Ando and Modigliani effort "Life Cycle" likewise rules them out for simplicity, pp. 56–57. Mayer summarizes the estate issue in *Permanent Income*, pp. 28–29.

Summing (5.46) first within then across age groups and, to avoid data problems, assuming that aggregate discounted future labor income is proportional to the current level give

$$C_t = \chi_1 Y_{Lt} + \chi_2 W_{t-1} \qquad (5.47)$$

C_t and Y_{Lt} denote, respectively, aggregate real consumption and aggregate real disposable labor income in the present period, while W_{t-1} denotes aggregate real property wealth at the end of the previous period.[46] Thus, the life cycle hypothesis leads to a short-run consumption function which reflects, through W_{t-1}, stock adjustment, whereas permanent income's consumption function (5.41) reflects, through C_{t-1}, flow adjustment.

Since a change in a stock constitutes a flow, transformation of equation (5.47) to produce a wealth change variable might lead to the emergence of a lagged flow term in the final specification. To check this possibility set that equation back one period and subtract the result from (5.47) to yield

$$C_t - C_{t-1} = \chi_1 (Y_{Lt} - Y_{L,t-1}) + \chi_2 (W_{t-1} - W_{t-2}) \qquad (5.48)$$

Reexpress $W_{t-1} - W_{t-2}$ by recalling that aggregate real disposable income Y_t divides into real consumption and real saving S_t and that saving equals the change in property wealth:

$$Y_t = C_t + S_t$$
$$Y_t = C_t + W_t - W_{t-1} \qquad (5.49)$$

Retreating one period, (5.49) reveals

$$W_{t-1} - W_{t-2} = Y_{t-1} - C_{t-1} \qquad (5.50)$$

and equation (5.48) thus converts to

$$C_t = \chi_1 \Delta Y_{Lt} + \chi_2 Y_{t-1} + (1 - \chi_2) C_{t-1} \qquad (5.51)$$

where $\Delta Y_{Lt} = Y_{Lt} - Y_{L,t-1}$. For the aggregate setting, current consumption depends upon the current change in disposable labor income and upon lagged values of consumption and total disposable income.

In the long run Y_{Lt} and Y_t grow at the rate ν while C_t expands at the rate γ. Consequently, equation (5.51) simplifies to

$$C_t = \Gamma Y_t \qquad (5.52)$$

where $\Gamma = [(\pi \chi_1 \nu + \chi_2)/(1 + \nu)][(1 + \gamma)/(\chi_2 + \gamma)]$; π denotes the constant fraction of disposable labor income in total disposable income. In the long run the consumption function is proportional.

The inelegance of equation (5.51) arises from the presence of labor income rather than total income in the original relationship (5.47). Suppose that (5.47)

---

[46]According to Betsy B. White, aggregation in the spirit of Ando and Modigliani to obtain equation (5.47) fails to capture the age distributions of income and property wealth; hence, says she, that functional form does not reflect the essence of the life cycle model. See her "Empirical Tests of the Life Cycle Hypothesis," *American Economic Review*, **68** (September 1978), pp. 547–549.

had been formulated alternatively as

$$C_t = \chi_1' Y_t + \chi_2' W_{t-1} \tag{5.53}$$

Moving this expression back one period, subtracting the result from (5.53), appealing to (5.50), and simplifying make[47]

$$C_t = \chi_1' Y_t + (\chi_2' - \chi_1') Y_{t-1} + (1 - \chi_2') C_{t-1} \tag{5.54}$$

The long-run counterpart of (5.54) is

$$C_t = \Lambda Y_t \tag{5.55}$$

where $\Lambda = [(\chi_1' \nu + \chi_2')/(1 + \nu)][(1 + \gamma)/(\chi_2' + \gamma)]$. Of course, result (5.55) replicates equation (5.52) for $Y_{Lt} = Y_t$. Then $\pi = 1$, $\chi_1 = \chi_1'$, and $\chi_2 = \chi_2'$ in (5.52); hence $\Gamma = \Lambda$.

5.9 SHORTSIGHTEDNESS: SIMILARITIES WITHIN A PRINCIPAL DIFFERENCE

A common denominator of the Hamburger, Friedman, and Ando-Brumberg-Modigliani hypotheses is that the household optimizes by choosing a consumption stream over time; it looks far into the future and bases current decisions on distant future events. While uncertainty, even in large doses, may cloud upcoming occurrences, longsightedness prevails. Some adjustment in the consumption relation might eventuate because of uncertainty—for instance, an argument reflecting the makeup of wealth types might be inserted—but the presence of uncertainty does not dissuade the household from maintaining an intertemporal perspective.

Is it reasonable to propose that households engage in intertemporal maneuvers under uncertainty? R. J. Ball and Pamela Drake do not believe so.[48] They assert that because of uncertainty about the future, individuals tend to be shortsighted. Households, reflecting their precautionary inclination, do not formulate a lifetime plan of consumption but instead tie spending decisions to present circumstances. In contrast to the prophetic utility functions (5.20) and (5.22), Ball and Drake postulate for household i

$$u_{it} = u_i(c_{it}, w_{it}) \tag{5.56}$$

u_{it} denotes the utility level of i at time t; c_{it}, i's real consumption at t; and w_{it}, i's stock of real nonhuman wealth at (the end of) t. Consumption may be interpreted either as expenditures inclusive of all spending on consumer durables or as service flow. Utility function (5.56) can vary across individuals, but for any individual it remains unchanged through time. It exhibits positive and declining marginal

[47]Equation (5.54) would arise even if equation (5.53) had an additional but stationary term χ_0', since χ_0' would vanish in the subtraction stage. See Michael C. Lovell, *Macroeconomics: Measurement, Theory, and Policy* (New York: John Wiley & Sons, Inc., 1975), pp. 131–133.

[48]R. J. Ball and Pamela S. Drake, "The Relationship between Aggregate Consumption and Wealth," *International Economic Review*, 5 (January 1964), pp. 63–81.

utilities along with positive cross-marginals; furthermore, it is homogeneous of degree one.

The household's human and nonhuman wealth provides the source of its real disposable income y_{it}, which is allocated between real consumption and real saving s_{it}: $y_{it} = c_{it} + s_{it}$. Since saving means wealth accumulation,

$$y_{it} = c_{it} + w_{it} - w_{i,t-1} \tag{5.57}$$

This equation serves as the household's budget constraint, and hence the posed optimization problem entails maximizing (5.56) subject to (5.57). Solving (5.57) for w_{it} and substituting the result into (5.56) gives, with suppression of the obvious subscripts,

$$u = u(c, y - c + w_{-1})$$

Total differentiation with respect to the lone decision variable c produces

$$\frac{du}{dc} = \frac{\partial u}{\partial c} + \frac{\partial u}{\partial w}\frac{dw}{dc}$$

$$\frac{du}{dc} = \frac{\partial u}{\partial c} - \frac{\partial u}{\partial w}$$

Equating the last equation to zero locates the stationary point of u which satisfies the constraint:[49]

$$\frac{\partial u}{\partial c} = \frac{\partial u}{\partial w} \tag{5.58}$$

For a maximum of utility under the budget restriction, income should be allocated between consumption and wealth until the marginal utilities of both equalize.

Since the utility function manifests homogeneity of degree one, the marginal utilities in (5.58) must be homogeneous of degree zero and therefore must depend only upon the ratio of c and w. Succinctly, $\partial u/\partial c = H(w/c)$, and $\partial u/\partial w = I(w/c)$. As w/c increases, H rises while I falls, producing a pattern depicted in Figure 5.9 without curvature. What emerges from equality (5.58) then is the wealth-consumption ratio necessary to maximize utility,[50] namely η. Reimposing subscripts leads to

$$\frac{w_{it}}{c_{it}} = \eta_i \tag{5.59}$$

This optimum ratio differs across individuals because the utility function (5.56) so differs. It does not vary through time because for any individual the utility function does not. In other words, each period a given household faces the same utility function, the same budget constraint, and the same optimization problem.

---

[49] The second-order condition $d^2u/dc^2 < 0$ holds automatically from the properties of the utility function.

[50] Intersection of the H and I loci occurs without question under the boundary conditions cited in footnote 36.

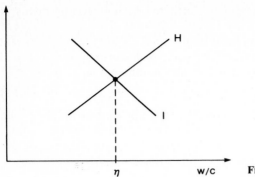

η w/c   **Figure 5.9**

Each period, therefore, it reaches the same decision. If the utility function did exhibit temporal sensitivity, then the optimum wealth-consumption ratio would betray that sensitivity, and η_i would be replaced by η_{it}.

From equation (5.59) $w_{it} = \eta_i c_{it}$, which, when summed across all individuals at time t, gives

$$\sum_i w_{it} = \sum_i \eta_i c_{it} \tag{5.60}$$

As before, let W_t and C_t denote aggregate real nonhuman wealth and aggregate real consumption at t, respectively. Also, let ε_{it} be the proportion of aggregate consumption attributable to household i at t, $\varepsilon_{it} = c_{it}/C_t$. Then equation (5.60) becomes

$$W_t = \sum_i \eta_i \varepsilon_{it} C_t$$

Removing C_t from the summation leads to

$$W_t = \zeta C_t \tag{5.61}$$

where $\zeta = \sum_i \eta_i \varepsilon_{it}$. ζ varies through time if the mix of households and the proportions of individual consumption in total consumption do not change in an exactly compensating manner. Regarding temporal variability ζ has the same status as does Friedman's κ in equation (5.33).

The individual's budget constraint (5.57) may be aggregated to repeat equation (5.49): $Y_t = C_t + W_t - W_{t-1}$, Y_t denoting aggregate real disposable income. Substitution of (5.61) into this relationship yields, after simplification,

$$C_t = \frac{1}{1 + \zeta} Y_t + \frac{\zeta}{1 + \zeta} C_{t-1} \tag{5.62}$$

Current consumption, taken either as total consumer spending or as service flow, depends upon current disposable income and consumption lagged one period. This function, derived from a shortsightedness hypothesis, has exactly the same form as the relation (5.41) obtained from longsightedness!

Given the strong similarity of the Friedman model (5.41) and the Ball-Drake paradigm (5.62), it seems fair to ask if there is any way to distinguish between them empirically. To put the question differently, suppose that one were commissioned to fit the consumption function

$$C_t = B_1 Y_t + B_2 C_{t-1} \qquad (5.63)$$

Is there any way to establish whether the empirical results support (5.41) or (5.62)? Yes, there is. The coefficients in the Ball-Drake equation sum to unity; those in Friedman's do not. Write the Friedman sum as

$$X = \kappa \frac{\beta}{\beta - \alpha} (1 - \lambda) + \lambda$$

Routine exercise reveals that $X \gtrless 1$ when $\kappa \beta / (\beta - \alpha) \gtrless 1$. Under Friedman's values for κ, β, and α, or alternatively under the common assumption that permanent income lies within the range defined by measured incomes ($\alpha = 0$), the "less than" case would apply. Thus one method for determining whether the empirical results obtained from (5.63) support the Friedman or the Ball-Drake hypothesis is to test if the coefficient sum equals or falls below unity.

Conducting this test, Ball and Drake find that the coefficient sum $B_1 + B_2$ does not differ significantly from unity for consumption measured either as total spending inclusive of durables purchases or as service flow. Their evidence thus supports (5.62) over (5.41). One estimation, based on annual U.S. data for the period 1929–1960 (excepting 1942–1945), relies on the expenditure view of consumption and places the marginal propensity to consume at .41 and the sluggishness coefficient at .58. Under the flow view the numbers become .25 and .74, respectively, for the same period. The wealth-consumption ratio ζ amounts to 1.41 in the first instance and to 2.92 in the second, the higher estimate there matching theoretical dictates.[51]

Consumption function (5.62) obviously can explain the negative relationship between current consumption and current income sometimes evidenced by the data. Also, through the usual steps beginning with $C_t = (1 + \gamma)C_{t-1}$, it reveals a long-run consumption function which is proportional:

$$C_t = \Upsilon Y_t \qquad (5.64)$$

where $\Upsilon = [1 + \zeta - \zeta/(1 + \gamma)]^{-1}$. For a finite growth rate, the long-run marginal propensity exceeds its short-run corollary. Slower growth witnesses a greater long-run propensity, which for the stationary state equals unity. In that case income is totally consumed and saving is zero.

A graphical portrayal of the Ball and Drake collection of consumption functions, (5.62) and (5.64), appears in Figure 5.8, notational changes being presumed.

---

[51]B_1 and B_2 each generate a ζ estimate, since $\zeta = 1/B_1 - 1$ or $\zeta = B_2/(1 - B_2)$. Each ζ value reported is the simple average obtained from both expressions.

5.10 RECAPITULATION AND A COMMENT ON PARTIAL ADJUSTMENT

Empirical developments since the debut of Keynes' absolute income hypothesis suggested that factors other than current income were responsible for current consumption. Inertia seemed to characterize consumer behavior, and this inertia appeared to be tied to the persistence of habits acquired through prior consumer experiences. To capture this effect, James Duesenberry and Franco Modigliani offered previous peak income as an additional argument in the consumption function. Tom Davis refined this formulation by replacing the "new" variable with previous peak consumption. Thus current consumption, at least for some time periods, was understood to be linked to current income and to consumption in the previous period. Hypotheses of continuous habit persistence proposed by T. M. Brown and by H. S. Houthakker and Lester Taylor underscored the importance of the previous period's consumption as a complement for explaining current behavior.

The emergence of longsighted wealth theories, which attributed inertia to the limited effect of current events on expected lifetime resources, provided additional support for including consumption of the prior period in the consumption function. Milton Friedman's permanent income model, when implemented by a Koyck-type distributed lag, forced that determinant to light in a straightforward fashion. The life cycle paradigm by Albert Ando, Richard Brumberg, and Franco Modigliani along with a variant of it did likewise after slight coaxing. Even abandoning the longsightedness approach in favor of the temporally myopic framework developed by R. J. Ball and Pamela Drake, wherein inertia may be related to consumer precaution under uncertainty, kept the role of lagged consumption intact.

Of course, factors besides current income and previous consumption belong in the consumption function. Real money balances and the distribution of income are ready candidates; so are prices for capturing possible effects of money illusion.[52] Moreover, disaggregation of consumption into its major constituents brings into view a panorama of potential determinants. Expectations regarding inflation may matter and may affect the separate consumption categories differently.[53] Purchases of consumer durables might behave more like spending on capital goods than like expenditures on nondurables, and thus for them, as the

---

[52] See, respectively, Don Patinkin, *Money, Interest, and Prices*, 2d ed. (New York: Harper & Row, Publishers, Incorporated, 1965), pp. 19–20, 205–209, 651–664; Philip Musgrove, "Income Distribution and the Aggregate Consumption Function," *Journal of Political Economy*, **88** (June 1980), pp. 506–512, 520–523; and William H. Branson and Alvin K. Klevorick, "Money Illusion and the Aggregate Consumption Function," *American Economic Review*, **59** (December 1969), pp. 834–837, 840–842.

[53] F. Thomas Juster and Paul Wachtel, "Inflation and the Consumer," *Brookings Papers on Economic Activity*, no. 1 (1972), pp. 91, 93, 101–102, 106.

next chapter suggests, the lagged *stock* of durables might be a key causal agent. Such considerations, however, do not reverse a principal thrust of the evolving theory of consumer behavior: current income and consumption of the previous period are important factors influencing current consumption.

This discussion should close with a brief reference to one of the simpler consumption models, that of partial adjustment. Suppose that consumers desire a particular level of real consumption for the current period, $\tilde{C}_t$, and that this target is linearly related to the current level of real disposable income, Y_t, both magnitudes being defined at the aggregate level. Then

$$\tilde{C}_t = \phi_1 + \phi_2 Y_t \tag{5.65}$$

consumption referring to either expenditures or service flow. Households try to adjust actual real consumption C_t to $\tilde{C}_t$, but because of inertia—arising for any reason whatever—their efforts systematically fall short of the mark. Formally,[54]

$$C_t - C_{t-1} = \psi(\tilde{C}_t - C_{t-1}) \tag{5.66}$$

where $0 < \psi < 1$. Consumers, who last period enjoyed C_{t-1}, currently want to reach $\tilde{C}_t$; they therefore intend to alter their consumption by the amount $\tilde{C}_t - C_{t-1}$. Because of inertia, however, they actually change it $\psi(\tilde{C}_t - C_{t-1})$. Consequently, in the aggregate

$$C_t = \psi(\phi_1 + \phi_2 Y_t - C_{t-1}) + C_{t-1}$$
$$C_t = \psi\phi_1 + \psi\phi_2 Y_t + (1 - \psi)C_{t-1} \tag{5.67}$$

Again current income and lagged consumption determine current consumption.

Due to nonproportionality of the relationship for desired consumption [equation (5.65)], the long-run function corresponding to the short-run function (5.67) is nonproportional with a marginal propensity to consume of $\psi\phi_2(1 + \gamma)/(\psi + \gamma)$, γ being the rate of consumption growth. For any finite rate this propensity exceeds the short-run's $\psi\phi_2$, and the implied consumption configuration resembles that of Brown displayed in Figure 5.5. As before, associated with a greater growth rate γ must be a smaller long-run propensity. If desired consumption were postulated as proportional to income—$\phi_1 = 0$ in (5.65)—or if the term $\psi\phi_1$ in (5.67) empirically tested to be no different from zero, then the long-run function would be proportional. In that case graphics akin to Figure 5.8 for the Friedman paradigm would hold.

---

[54] Early applications of the partial adjustment mechanism were directed at investment behavior to describe changes in stocks rather than flows. It has, however, found service in consumption analysis. See Hollis B. Chenery, "Overcapacity and the Acceleration Principle," *Econometrica*, **20** (January 1952), p. 13, and Richard M. Goodwin, "Secular and Cyclical Aspects of the Multiplier and the Accelerator," in *Income, Employment and Public Policy*, p. 120. See also Balvir Singh, Helmar Drost, and Ramesh C. Kumar, "An Empirical Evaluation of the Relative, the Permanent Income, and the Life-Cycle Hypotheses," *Economic Development and Cultural Change*, **26** (January 1978), p. 283.

Notice that equation (5.65) applies the Keynesian hypothesis to desired consumption, ϕ_2 being the corresponding marginal propensity to consume. In equation (5.67), which shows the relationship among actuals, the marginal propensity is $\psi\phi_2$, which must be less than ϕ_2. Partial adjustment, consonant with other hypotheses considered in this chapter, tempers the marginal propensity to a value smaller than that associated with Keynes' absolute income hypothesis. Only if adjustment were instantaneous, with $\psi = 1$, would the Keynesian propensity ϕ_2 carry over unaltered to the actual relationship (5.67). In that circumstance, of course, (5.65) and (5.67) would be identical. Keynes' formulation can therefore be interpreted as an instantaneous adjustment model.

CHAPTER

SIX

INVESTMENT, INERTIA, AND TEMPORAL MOTION

Investment has long been recognized as a principal source of cyclical fluctuations in macro systems. Chapters 3 and 4 demonstrated this point and to do so reviewed some investment theoretics. The present chapter extends that review. After considering two forms of an income variable possibly appropriate for the investment function, it examines the relationship between the marginal product of capital and the marginal efficiency of investment. It then looks at the function implicit in that relationship. The analysis shows that inertia, observed in Chapter 5 to influence consumption, affects investment as well, and the consequence of this joint sluggishness for the temporal response of macro models is explored. Along the way the discussion probes the role of finance in the investment decision. Lessons and thoughts borne of dynamics conclude the presentation.

Like consumption, investment could be treated in a disaggregated fashion, and the set of relevant causal agents would undoubtedly vary with the basis of disaggregation. Separate components might be identified for plant, equipment, and inventories, and they might be studied for individual economic sectors such as manufacturing, mining, and farming. The present exposition, however, limits itself to a single investment stream, most closely allied with plant and equipment, and disregards sectorial boundary lines. Recall that the total amount of capital goods produced in any period is referred to as "gross investment." These "machines" are used, first, to replace any deteriorating units and, second, to alter the existing machine stock. The former constitutes replacement investment; the latter, net investment. Should capital production fall below the number of units scheduled to expire, then net investment would become negative to the extent of the deficiency.

163

One concept that plays a significant part in what follows is capacity. It enjoys numerous definitions in the literature, but since this chapter addresses the stock of capital and the changes in that stock, capacity is taken as the amount of capital extant.[1] "Full capacity" therefore means that the actual stock resides at an optimum level. "Excess capacity" or "overcapacity" signifies an actual stock greater than the optimum, while "deficient capacity" or "undercapacity" refers to an actual stock less than the optimum.

6.1 CONTRAPUNTAL PRINCIPLES OF PROFITS AND ACCELERATION

In 1937 J. R. Hicks offered several recommendations for generalizing Keynes' general theory; one of them called for treating the income (output) level as a determinant of investment. According to Hicks, consumption demand might stimulate investment and, since consumption depends upon income, income should be inserted into the investment function.[2] Consequently, two versions of the Keynesian formulation might be envisioned: investment dependent upon interest or, more broadly, investment dependent upon interest and income together.

Including the level of income in the investment function can be justified on different grounds. J. Tinbergen contended in 1938 that profits have an important influence on investment, his argument running as follows.[3] Investment is undertaken for profit. Since capital goods exhibit long life, investment decisions must be based on profits expected to be earned in the future. A clue to future profits comes from current and past experience, and hence profits of at least the current period belong in the investment function. But profits serve another purpose. Investment projects must be financed. Some firms, however, may have difficulty obtaining funds from external sources—borrowing or equity (share) issue—and must therefore rely on their own internal resources to meet investment needs. Other firms might be preferred customers in credit markets, but they may for a variety of reasons have prejudice against borrowing. For them too, internal funds would make up an important source of investment finance. The wellspring of

---

[1] This interpretation coincides with that of L. R. Koyck, who discusses the connection among alternative capacity definitions in *Distributed Lags and Investment Analysis*, Contributions to Economic Analysis, no. IV (Amsterdam: North-Holland Publishing Company, 1954), pp. 41–43, 48. For additional comment see A. D. Knox, "The Acceleration Principle and the Theory of Investment: A Survey," *Economica*, New Series, **19** (August 1952), pp. 277–278.

[2] J. R. Hicks, "Mr. Keynes and the 'Classics'; A Suggested Interpretation," *Econometrica*, **5** (April 1937), p. 156.

[3] A hint of this thesis appears in J. Tinbergen, "Statistical Evidence on the Acceleration Principle," *Economica*, **5** (May 1938), pp. 167, 176. His line of reasoning is reported more fully in later publications, a thorough summary of it being presented in Jan Tinbergen and J. J. Polak, *The Dynamics of Business Cycles: A Study in Economic Fluctuations* (Chicago: University of Chicago Press, 1950), pp. 166–168, 172. See also Daniel Hamberg, *Models of Economic Growth* (New York: Harper & Row, Publishers, Incorporated, 1971), pp. 32–34.

these moneys, of course, is profits. Furthermore, the profit condition of a firm may affect its credit rating and its attractiveness to potential shareholders. Hence an improved profit position may make external funds more accessible to the firm. In short, profits enter the investment function because they serve as a barometer of future earnings, because they provide internal funds necessary to finance investment projects, and because they can unlock external funds.

Why should *income* enter the function? Because in the aggregate, income and profits display a close association. Since investment depends upon profits and since profits remain synchronous with income, income can replace profits in the investment expression. The notion that net investment depends upon the level of profits or, equivalently, upon the level of income is known as the "profits principle" (alias "profit principle"), terminology coined by Tinbergen in 1938.

While the propositions advanced by Hicks and by the profiteers for including the income level in the investment function seem meritorious, the resulting formulation suffers an obvious weakness. It implies that net investment remains positive and constant when income stays fixed.[4] Capital goods are continually acquired at an undiminishing rate even though total production in the economy does not change. Overcapacity must eventually arise, but this circumstance does not dampen entrepreneurial fervor for acquiring capital. A more reasonable hypothesis would hold that because of the accumulation phenomenon, net investment in the face of stagnant output should decline until it vanishes completely.

The profits principle seemingly stands at odds with the view, discussed in Section 4.1, that it is the *change* in output which affects net investment. The latter hypothesis dates back to the 1903 writing of T. N. Carver, who argued that "the value of producers' goods tends to fluctuate more violently than the value of consumers' goods." While suggesting that the relationship was proportional, Carver noted that only the *permanent* change in consumer output mattered for the investment decision.[5]

In 1917 J. Maurice Clark christened the relationship between net investment and output change "the acceleration principle." For illustrative purposes he offered a simple example in which net investment was proportional to the current change in consumption goods, but he warned the reader to "supply for himself an

---

[4] Knox, "Acceleration Principle," p. 295.

[5] T. N. Carver, "A Suggestion for a Theory of Industrial Depressions," *Quarterly Journal of Economics*, **17** (May 1903), pp. 498–499. Further support for the permanency basis of the investment decision is provided by Robert Eisner in "Investment: Fact and Fancy," *American Economic Review*, **53** (May 1963), pp. 237–240, 246, and in "A Permanent Income Theory for Investment: Some Empirical Explorations," *American Economic Review*, **57** (June 1967), pp. 364, 387.

That permanency makes up an essential precondition of the investment decision is almost self-evident. An output surge perceived to be temporary would likely elicit the increased use of labor and, perhaps, activate obsolete machinery, since these practices would be less costly than the acquisition of new equipment which would cause other units to become prematurely idle when output returned to its customary level. Similarly, a brief output slump would not dictate the cancellation of replacement activity since any capital shrinkage would only have to be rectified when output resumed its normal pace.

allowance for the elements that are not included in the formula." One such element was a lag between the change in demand for finished products and the resulting net investment. This lag, arising from gestation and from excess capacity which may characterize industries as they extricate themselves from recessed economic activity, thus admits the possibilities of deficient and redundant capital. Another factor to be recognized was asymmetry of the investment response. In Clark's words, "The investment in long-lived instruments cannot be reduced as readily as it can be increased. It is reduced, if at all, by the slow process of starving the maintenance account." In any period the production of capital cannot become negative, and consequently net investment can be negative by no more than the amount of depreciation.[6]

From these early studies by Carver and Clark emerges the conclusion that a relationship exists between net investment and the actual change in output. This relationship may involve a lag, and it may be proportional. The studies suggest, however, that the proportionality coefficient need not be constant. A given actual change in output could represent a different amount of perceived permanent change over different phases of the cycle. Thus investment tied by a proportional formula to the actual output change would show a variable coefficient. Bounds would also translate into a coefficient which is variable, as the coefficient must be able to accommodate an output change to prevent net investment from driving through its floor or through some ceiling traceable to production limits in the capital goods industries.[7]

A variable proportionality coefficient could arise for other reasons as well. Excess capacity, which may characterize the normal operating state of some industries, allows entrepreneurs flexibility in their reaction to demand changes, and they may respond differently to equal increments and decrements.[8] In this regard it should be remembered that any coefficient linking the capital stock to output may not be technically fixed but instead may be a behavioral parameter which entrepreneurs adjust in accord with economic circumstances.[9] The analysis in Section 4.1 makes this point clear. There the multiple bridging capital and output, Λ in equation (4.5), contains a factor-price ratio. Should this ratio become altered, then so would the investment coefficient, as equation (4.6)—rewritten as the product of two expressions, one being the output change—discloses. Credit conditions affect the coefficient too.[10] At times credit may be "easy," with ample

[6]J. Maurice Clark, "Business Acceleration and the Law of Demand: A Technical Factor in Economic Cycles," *Journal of Political Economy*, 25 (March 1917), pp. 220–226, 234–235. Asymmetry of investment behavior, of course, later became a mainstay of the cycle theory by Hicks. Equation (4.15) summarizes.

[7]John Maurice Clark, *Preface to Social Economics: Essays on Economic Theory and Social Problems* (New York: Farrar & Rinehart, Inc., 1936), p. 351.

[8]Hollis B. Chenery, "Overcapacity and the Acceleration Principle," *Econometrica*, 20 (January 1952), pp. 9–10; Simon Kuznets, "Relation between Capital Goods and Finished Products in the Business Cycle," in *Economic Essays in Honor of Wesley Clair Mitchell* (New York: Columbia University Press, 1935), pp. 231, 235; and Tinbergen, "Statistical Evidence," p. 166.

[9]Koyck, *Distributed Lags*, p. 44.

[10]Gottfried Haberler, *Prosperity and Depression: A Theoretical Analysis of Cyclical Movements*, 3d ed. (Geneva: League of Nations, 1941), p. 101, and Kuznets, "Relation," p. 227.

investment funds available; at other times conditions might be "tight," with investment finance limited. Again a given output change would be matched by varying amounts of net investment.

In its general form the acceleration principle says that net investment is *a* function of the actual change in output. This version has much appeal.[11] Only with the imposition of constant proportionality does the principle become dubious. Then it ignores the effects of perceptions, bounds, factor prices, and credit conditions, and instead it insists that the investment process, once begun, eliminates excess or deficient capacity in a single step. If lags between investment and the causative output change are absent, it asserts even more; it says that excess or deficient capacity never develops. Full capacity always prevails![12] The rendition of the principle requiring constant proportionality, with or without lags, is termed either the simple accelerator, as Section 4.1 notes, or the accelerator in rigorous form. A simple accelerator may be acceptable for some model building since it does provide laudable convenience, to which cycle models considered in Chapter 4 can attest. But from the standpoint of faithfully representing the investment process, a simple accelerator falls wide of the mark.

A net investment function postulated as dependent upon the level of output displays a theoretical blemish. A function postulated as a fixed proportion of the actual change in output also proves suspect theoretically. Variable proportionality, however, offers more promise for representing the investment decision, and hence further investigation of its basis seems warranted. As will be seen shortly, that investigation carries with it extra benefits. It leads to unification of the profits principle and the acceleration principle, thereby resolving the issue of whether the income level or the income change belongs in the net investment function. Moreover, it suggests additional variables to be included in the specification of the investment function for empirical purposes.[13] The beginnings of that inquiry lie in Keynes' exposition of investment, to which the discussion now returns.

6.2 MARGINAL PRODUCT AND MARGINAL EFFICIENCY

Keynes referred to the investment function as the marginal efficiency of capital schedule, and he defined the marginal efficiency as a rate of discount: namely,

> ... that rate of discount which would make the present value of the series of annuities given by the returns expected from the capital-asset during its life just equal to its supply price ... [this being] the price which would just induce a manufacturer newly to produce an additional unit of such assets, i.e., what is sometimes called its replacement cost.[14]

[11] Haberler, *Prosperity and Depression*, p. 97.

[12] Koyck, *Distributed Lags*, p. 46, and Tinbergen, "Statistical Evidence," p. 166.

[13] The econometric work reported in footnote 2 of Chapter 4 indicates that a net investment function containing either the income level alone or the income change alone performs poorly. A chief reason for this weak showing is the parochialism of the specifications; they ignore important investment determinants.

[14] John Maynard Keynes, *The General Theory of Employment, Interest, and Money* (New York: Harcourt, Brace & World, Inc., 1936), p. 135. See also pp. 136–137.

The supply price component of this definition may be viewed as that price given by the marginal-cost curve characterizing the capital goods industry. It contrasts with Keynes' demand price of capital, which will be referenced shortly.

Marginal efficiency declined with increasing investment, supposed Keynes, both because the prospective yield (the series of annuities) would decrease as the stock of capital expanded and because the supply price would rise. Combining these two explanations, however, blurs the distinction between stock and flow, a distinction which, when recognized, implies that Keynes' investment function or even its elaboration under Hicks and the profiteers ignores an important determinant. Clarification of the Keynesian position involves interfacing a theory of capital with a theory of investment along the following lines.[15]

In contemplating a change in the stock of capital, entrepreneurs really face two questions. What is the optimum stock, and (if the actual stock differs from the optimum) at what speed should the actual be changed? The first question can be answered by equating the marginal product of capital to the real capital rental, a principle reminiscent of that urged by the paradigm of the firm reviewed in Section 4.1. By acknowledging that the real rental equals the rate of interest, this optimum rule simplifies to a call for equality between the marginal product and the interest rate. That relationship can be established with only modest effort.

Let Z denote the net present value of the prospective yield associated with the capital stock; namely,

$$Z = R + \frac{R}{1+r} + \frac{R}{(1+r)^2} + \cdots + \frac{R}{(1+r)^n} - sK \qquad (6.1)$$

where $R = pY - wL$. Annuity R represents that portion of expected revenue anticipated to accrue each period to entrepreneurs from the use of capital. In particular, p and Y denote the price and quantity of output, respectively, corresponding to the combination of K units of capital and L units of labor in a production process summarized by the function $Y = F(K, L)$, which displays a positive but diminishing marginal product for each input. Output consists of a single type of good which may be either consumed or accumulated, and hence p must be identical to s, the price of capital. w signifies the money wage while r and n indicate the rate of interest and the life of capital, respectively.

Equation (6.1) may be rewritten as $Z = RX - sK$, X being the sum $1 + (1+r)^{-1} + \cdots + (1+r)^{-n}$. Dividing X by $1 + r$ and subtracting the result from X itself leads to

$$X = \frac{1}{r} \frac{(1+r)^{n+1} - 1}{(1+r)^n}$$

[15] Useful companions to the present discussion are Gardner Ackley, *Macroeconomic Theory* (New York: The Macmillan Company, ©1961), pp. 461–485; Ackley, *Macroeconomics: Theory and Policy* (New York: The Macmillan Company, ©1978), pp. 615–631; Robert L. Crouch, *Macroeconomics* (New York: Harcourt Brace Jovanovich, Inc., 1972), pp. 66–73, 77–83; Hamberg, *Models*, pp. 25–30; and Edward J. Shapiro, *Macroeconomic Analysis*, 4th ed. (New York: Harcourt Brace Jovanovich, Inc., 1978), pp. 163–173.

Since r is small, $(1 + r)^n = 1 + nr$ and $(1 + r)^{n+1} = 1 + r(n + 1)$ as approximations. Therefore $X = (\delta + r)^{-1}$ approximately, δ denoting the rate of straight-line depreciation. Consonantly, equation (6.1) becomes

$$Z = \frac{1}{\delta + r} R - sK \qquad (6.2)$$

Maximization of net present value with respect to capital requires that $\partial Z/\partial K = 0$. Thus, under competition,[16]

$$\frac{p}{\delta + r} \frac{\partial Y}{\partial K} - s = 0$$

or

$$\frac{\partial Y}{\partial K} = \frac{(\delta + r)s}{p} \qquad (6.3)$$

Furthermore, under competition net present value should be zero in equilibrium, rendering from equation (6.2)

$$R = (\delta + r)sK \qquad (6.4)$$

and

$$pY = wL + (\delta + r)sK \qquad (6.5)$$

The coefficient of K in equation (6.5) identifies the cost of using capital, and it is entirely analogous to labor's coefficient w. Each machine provides services, a unit of which may be taken as the amount of productive activity forthcoming from it in a single period. One machine generates one unit of service each period, while K machines supply K units. Accordingly, $(\delta + r)s$ can be regarded as the price per unit of capital service, also suitably called user cost à la Keynes since it measures in a sense the amount of capital consumed through the act of production.[17] But another interpretation attaches to $(\delta + r)s$. Entrepreneurs may be viewed as facing two options for the acquisition of K machines. They can purchase them outright at a cost of sK dollars, or they can rent them by paying equal installments of R dollars per period over the equipment's life. When would the two acquisition schemes be equivalent to entrepreneurs? When the costs are identical; more precisely, when the discounted value of the rental payments R equals sK. In terms of the net present value function (6.1), this equivalence happens when $Z = 0$ or when, via equations (6.2) and (6.4), the rental payment equals $(\delta + r)sK$. It follows that $(\delta + r)s$ stands for the unit capital rental. Equation (6.3) therefore says that the optimum capital stock is determined by

---

[16] $\partial^2 Z/\partial K^2$ equals $[p/(\delta + r)]\partial^2 Y/\partial K^2$, which must be negative because of diminishing marginal returns. Equation (6.3) therefore does locate the maximum of Z.

[17] Keynes, *The General Theory*, pp. 52–53. Amplification of Keynes' argument appears in Alvin H. Hansen, *A Guide to Keynes* (New York: McGraw-Hill Book Company, Inc., 1953), pp. 54–56.

equating the marginal product of capital to the real user cost—synonymously, the real unit rental.[18]

Output Y refers to the total quantity of goods manufactured in a period. Some of that output must be dedicated to replacing worn-out equipment if capital's equilibrium is to be preserved, and equation (6.5) can be rewritten to highlight this replacement phenomenon:

$$p(Y - \delta K) = wL + rsK \tag{6.6}$$

where $Y - \delta K$ represents net output, output available after the depreciation toll has been exacted. rs may be called the "net user cost" or "net unit rental" to distinguish it from the gross concepts introduced by equation (6.5). Obviously, these "nets" differ from their gross counterparts by the value of depreciation, again δs. In real terms the nets equal the interest rate r.

Allowance for replacement also modifies the optimum rule (6.3). R in equation (6.2) becomes $p(y + \delta K) - wL$, $y = Y - \delta K$, and repetition of the earlier arithmetic leaves

$$\frac{\partial y}{\partial K} = r \tag{6.7}$$

To determine the optimum stock of capital, equate the (net) marginal product of capital, hereafter notated MPK, with the interest rate.[19]

If entrepreneurs were to find themselves in a situation where capital's marginal product equaled the interest rate, they would have no reason to expand

---

[18]Derivation of equations (6.3)–(6.5) follows the outline given by Edmund S. Phelps, who labels R as quasi-rent. See his "Substitution, Fixed Proportions, Growth and Distribution," *International Economic Review*, **4** (September 1963), pp. 270, 272. Manipulations less rigorous than Phelps' can be found in John H. Makin, *Macroeconomics* (Hinsdale, Ill.: The Dryden Press, 1975), pp. 133–135. An expression for user cost more comprehensive than $(\delta + r)s$ is established by Dale W. Jorgenson, "Capital Theory and Investment Behavior," *American Economic Review*, **53** (May 1963), pp. 248–249.

Provided that capital's price in the production process is understood to be $(\delta + r)s$, equations (6.3) and (6.5) also emerge from the usual profit maximization procedure. Let π and q denote profits and some input price of capital, respectively. Thus $\pi = pY - wL - qK$. When competition prevails, $\partial \pi / \partial K = 0$ implies $\partial Y / \partial K = q/p$, and an equilibrium of zero profit makes $pY = wL + qK$. If $q = (\delta + r)s$, then equations (6.3) and (6.5) result.

Households, like entrepreneurs, may be regarded as facing the two options of buying their durables outright or of renting them, and consequently an expression akin to the unit rental $(\delta + r)s$ might be adopted for determining the amount of a consumer durable "used up" each period. This tack, which involves adding to the value of the good's depreciation each period (δs) the magnitude of interest income lost each period because s dollars were spent acquiring the good (rs), would embellish that suggested in Section 5.5 for calculating the durables component of use consumption.

[19]Further discussion of the optimum rule (6.7) and of gross and net rentals is presented by Paul A. Samuelson, "The Evaluation of 'Social Income': Capital Formation and Wealth," in F. A. Lutz and D. C. Hague, eds., *The Theory of Capital* (London: Macmillan & Co., Ltd., 1963), pp. 37–39.

Since $y = F(K, L) - \delta K$, it follows that $y = f(K, L)$. With single subscripts denoting first partial derivatives and double subscripts denoting second partials, $f_K = F_K - \delta$ and $f_{KK} = F_{KK}$. The former result says that the net marginal product curve lies below the gross curve $\partial Y / \partial K$ by a constant amount δ. Substitution of $F_K = f_K + \delta$ into equation (6.3) elicits $f_K = r$, thereby checking the derivation of (6.7) outlined in the text. Furthermore, since $\partial^2 Z / \partial K^2 = [p/(\delta + r)] f_{KK}$, equation (6.7) must identify the maximum of Z.

or to contract the existing stock. Net investment would be zero. If, however, the marginal product were to differ from the interest rate, entrepreneurs would alter the stock. Since capital manifests a diminishing marginal product, a marginal product in excess of the interest rate implies that capital should be expanded. Net investment would then be positive. A marginal product below the interest rate implies redundant capital and negative net investment. Thus capital theory advises whether the stock should be adjusted and, if so, it gives the *direction* of that adjustment. It does not, however, prescribe the *speed* at which the process should evolve. In other words, it says nothing about the magnitude of net investment. Capital theory is static, and therefore it can only locate equilibrium positions. Any question regarding a movement between equilibria falls instead within the jurisdiction of investment theory. The investment theory by Keynes, modified slightly, now comes to the fore.

Define the marginal efficiency of investment as that rate of discount which equates the discounted expected annuity stream associated with a unit of capital to the unit's supply price. This definition, which merely renames Keynes' marginal efficiency of capital, translates into the expression

$$s = u + \frac{u}{1 + m} + \frac{u}{(1 + m)^2} + \cdots + \frac{u}{(1 + m)^n} \qquad (6.8)$$

for a single machine. As before, each annuity term u takes the form of revenue accruing to the entrepreneur, namely, total revenue expected from the sale of goods generated by the machine minus the anticipated extra costs, such as labor expense, corresponding to its use. s and n denote the supply price and the life of capital, respectively, while m represents the marginal efficiency of investment MEI. It is the unknown in the equation. As investment expands, added stress is placed upon the capital goods industry, causing, according to Keynes, the supply price to rise. Consequently, MEI declines with increasing investment. Given this relationship investment in any period proceeds to the point where the marginal efficiency equals the interest rate. Why?

On an intuitive level the marginal efficiency registers in percentage terms the marginal revenue associated with an extra unit of capital. The interest rate, on the other hand, measures in percentage terms the cost of acquiring the machine; it gives the marginal cost. Hence the rule MEI $= r$ resembles the familiar criterion for profit maximization: equalize marginal revenue and marginal cost.

Another way to understand the optimum investment norm involves comparing the cost of acquiring a machine with the present value of its expected annuity stream. Any machine whose present value v exceeds its cost s would add to profit; any whose present value equals cost would "break even"; and any whose value falls below cost would diminish profit. Write the present value as

$$v = u + \frac{u}{1 + r} + \frac{u}{(1 + r)^2} + \cdots + \frac{u}{(1 + r)^n} \qquad (6.9)$$

From equations (6.8) and (6.9) it is clear that MEI$\gtrless r$ and $v \gtrless s$ are equivalent statements. Thus the Keynesian rule—invest to the point where for the marginal machine MEI $= r$—is tantamount to the norm of purchasing all machines compatible with profit maximization. Incidentally, Keynes referred to the present value v as the "demand price of capital." The position $v = s$ thus connotes equality between the demand price and the supply price, a conventional interpretation of equilibrium.[20]

Argumentation thus far advocates one rule for determining the optimum stock of capital, MPK $= r$, and another for determining the optimum speed of approach to the optimum stock, MEI $= r$. Both are obviously related through the rate of interest, but their connection becomes complete under a definition of the marginal product of capital offered by Abba Lerner. To him the marginal product can be defined as the marginal efficiency of investment when net investment equals zero.[21] With this linkage the puzzle of stock versus flow becomes quickly resolved.

Suppose that entrepreneurs own an optimum capital stock. Capital's marginal product equals the prevailing interest rate r_a, net investment I rests at zero, and the marginal product and marginal efficiency are identical. In short, MPK $=$ MEI $= r_a$, with $I = 0$. Suppose now that interest falls to r_b and that the new lower level is believed to be permanent. In the new economic climate, the marginal product of existing capital exceeds the relevant interest rate r_b, rendering that stock level deficient and causing net investment to turn positive. It proceeds to the point where MEI $= r_b$. This act of investment, however, gives birth to new capital and enlarges the existing stock. Because of the new higher stock level, the marginal product assumes a value lower than before, in keeping with the assumption of diminishing returns to inputs. Since the marginal product equals the marginal efficiency at zero net investment, this reduced marginal product establishes a new marginal efficiency schedule which lies below that applicable in the previous period. Net investment ensues, again to the point where MEI $= r_b$. More capital results, the marginal product falls once more, a new marginal efficiency curve appears, and net investment occurs. This process continues until the new optimum stock is reached. Then MPK $=$ MEI $= r_b$ and $I = 0$.

---

[20] Hansen, *A Guide*, p. 120, and Keynes, *The General Theory*, p. 137.

[21] Abba P. Lerner, *The Economics of Control* (New York: The Macmillan Company, 1944), p. 335. The subsequent analysis draws from that volume, pp. 330–340, and from Lerner's "On the Marginal Product of Capital and the Marginal Efficiency of Investment," *Journal of Political Economy*, **61** (February 1953), pp. 8–11.

The Lerner definition agrees nicely with the interpretation of marginal product found in production theory. Production theory contends that the marginal product of capital should have the dimension of output units per capital unit (for example, chairs per machine). In the present macro context, only chairs are produced, and consequently the marginal product reduces to chairs per chair or, equivalently, to a pure number in precise accord with Lerner's interpretation of the marginal product as a rate of discount ("On the Marginal Product," pp. 1–2). Furthermore, maintenance of any optimum capital stock located with the aid of the marginal product requires net investment to be zero. This stipulation enters Lerner's concept as well. Finally, under respecification of the annuity stream in equation (6.8) to exclude any immediate return, the Lerner definition, by the mathematics used to compress X in establishing equation (6.2), leads to (approximate) equality between the marginal product and u/s_0. With u serving as the unit rental and s_0 representing the supply price of capital at zero net investment, the similarity to equation (6.3) becomes apparent.

The description of this adjustment response can be made more articulate with the aid of graphics. Panel A of Figure 6.1 relates the marginal product of capital to the capital stock, while Panel B matches the marginal efficiency of investment to the level of net investment. For clarity, the investment scale has been greatly magnified; equivalent distances on the capital and investment axes represent far fewer machines in the latter case. Panel C depicts the association between the supply price of capital and the amount of capital produced in the period, gross investment I_G. I_R notates replacement investment. It warrants repeating here that the shape of the supply curve Q governs that of the marginal efficiency curves. For the moment ignore the angular dashed lines in Panels B and C. Also for the moment assume that replacement investment remains constant even though the capital stock may change.

Entrepreneurs begin in equilibrium with interest at r_a and capital at K_a. MPK $= r_a$, and $I = 0$, meaning that MPK $=$ MEI. Consequently, MPK $=$ MEI $= r_a$. Interest falls to r_b. At the existing stock of capital K_a, MPK exceeds the ruling interest r_b, provoking entrepreneurs to expand the capital stock. The new optimum is K_b.

In their effort to reach this new optimum, entrepreneurs first expand net investment by following the schedule MEI_1 to the point where MEI $= r_b$. I_1 machines result, enlarging the capital stock from K_a to K_1. Corresponding to this new higher stock is a lower MPK. Since MEI duplicates MPK at zero net investment, this lower MPK unveils a new MEI schedule, MEI_2, which lies below MEI_1. Entrepreneurs again press investment to the MEI $= r_b$ point, this time generating net investment of I_2. Those I_2 machines enlarge the capital stock further, to K_2, and MPK falls once more. A new MEI schedule, MEI_3, arises—it lies below the earlier two—and investment proceeds afresh, to I_3. This iterative process terminates when K_b is reached. Then MEI_N operates, $I = 0$, and MPK $=$ MEI $= r_b$.

Observe that during the convergence sequence net investment becomes progressively smaller: $I_3 < I_2 < I_1$. This shrinkage results from the depressing effect which the stock of capital exerts on the marginal product of capital. As a review of the expansion procedure shows, the stock of capital at the *beginning* of any period affects the amount of net investment undertaken in that period, and the relationship is negative: a greater capital stock engenders a smaller amount of net investment. It follows that the Keynesian investment function, $I(r)$ or $I(r, Y)$, lacks completeness and should be broadened to include the negative influence of the capital stock.[22] Rewritten, these functions become $I(r, K)$ or $I(r, Y, K)$, with $\partial I/\partial K < 0$ in either case.

In some instances, of course, the capital stock may fail to exert any influence on net investment. Equipment adjustments could take appreciable time, and an inquiry which focuses on a short time horizon might legitimately treat the capital

---

[22] In regard to the output variable of the net investment function, the theses presented by Hicks and by the profiteers and the argument to be advanced at the end of this section provide no strong reason for distinguishing between gross and net concepts. Hence that distinction is dropped, and Y should be interpreted henceforth as identifying output in either gross or net terms.

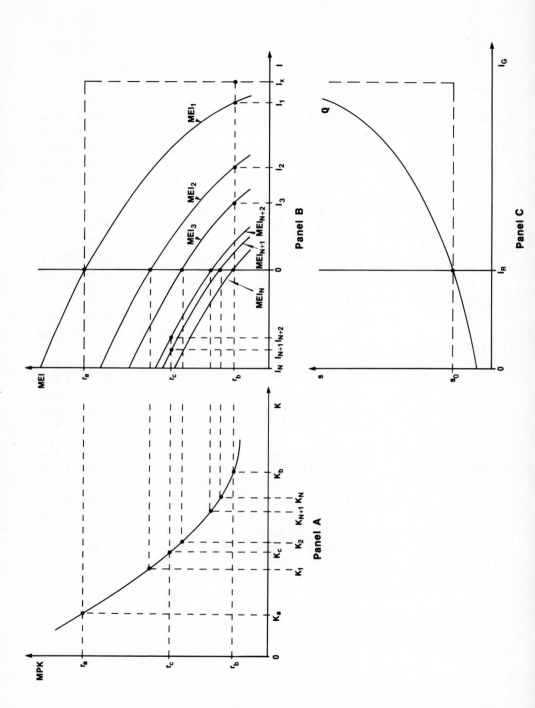

174

stock as constant, thereby barring it from the investment function. Keynes' own preoccupation with the short run supports his exclusion of the capital argument. It can also be disregarded in other situations, one of which is described below. Nevertheless, as a general formulation the investment function, on the present analysis anyway, should include a capital stock variable.

What if the interest rate rises? Then the accommodation apparatus works in reverse but with the possibility of a new wrinkle. For example, let interest increase from r_b to r_c in Figure 6.1, causing the optimum stock to fall from K_b to K_c. The operative marginal efficiency schedule MEI_N exhibits a ceiling[23] which now prevents equality with interest rate r_c. Greatest accommodation of the optimum investment rule occurs at zero gross investment, and there net investment assumes the maximum negative level permitted by depreciation, I_N. This action shrinks the stock from K_b to K_N. In the process MPK rises, as does the MEI schedule, to MEI_{N+1}. With MEI_{N+1} in place, the MEI $= r$ norm becomes effective, leading to I_{N+1} and to K_{N+1}. Then MEI_{N+2} appears along with I_{N+2}; clearly, $I_{N+2} > I_{N+1} > I_N$. Net investment rises as the capital stock falls, thus preserving the vestige of an inverse relationship between the two variables. It should be recognized, however, that contact with the floor $I_G = 0$, especially over successive periods, would contaminate the relationship and cause it to depart from the one applicable to positive net investment. Consequently, the investment function may display one set of coefficients for expansions and another for contractions. Here rests theoretical justification for the challenge to symmetric investment functions.

Consider now the angular dashed lines in Panels B and C of Figure 6.1. If substantial unemployment pervades the economy, expansion of machine production might occur without any increase in machine price until some absolute limit to productive capacity is reached, at which point price in effect becomes prohibitively high. In that situation the marginal efficiency schedule does not decline with increasing investment but instead remains horizontal until it falls vertically at I_x. Such reshaping of the price and marginal efficiency schedules revises the capital adjustment process and alters the implication for the net investment function. For the expansion case, with interest falling, capital accumulation causes the L-shaped MEI to shift downward, but each period net investment repeats at I_x: it is not moderated by the increase in capital stock. A similar sequence applies to the contraction case, where each period net investment would be negative to the fullest extent possible. Tempering would not occur.

Two conclusions emerge from this illustration of an L-shaped MEI. First, the approach to the optimum capital stock happens more rapidly than otherwise, and

---

[23]A finite maximum to the MEI schedule need not arise. If the supply price at zero gross investment equaled u, then from equation (6.8) the marginal efficiency at that point would be infinite and the ceiling would vanish.

Figure 6.1 *Source*: Ackley, *Macroeconomic Theory*, pp. 483–484.

it unfolds in uniform steps. Second, capital ceases to be a determinant in the investment function. This conclusion is significant because the case of an L-shaped MEI assumes credibility under substantial and persistent unemployment, the very circumstance stressed by Keynes. For this special case, and especially in a short-run context, the Keynesian investment function cannot be faulted for its omission of a capital stock argument.

The discussion to this point has been kept nuisance-free by the assumption that replacement investment remains constant in the face of a changing capital stock. That assumption, while convenient, forces an inconsistency. A greater stock implies that a greater number of machines deteriorate each period, and hence maintenance of the larger stock must require more replacement investment. The exact opposite holds for a smaller stock. Allowing replacement investment to vary, however, means that the price of capital associated with zero net investment varies, and therefore the marginal product of capital *schedule* must shift in accord with Lerner's definition. An adjustment process more elaborate than the one portrayed by Figure 6.1 finds that in Panels C and B the vertical lines which mark replacement investment and zero net investment shift and that the consequent movement of the capital price at zero net investment prompts the marginal product curve in Panel A to drift as well.

Such embellishment, however, does not alter the conclusion reached by the streamlined analysis that the capital stock exerts a negative influence on net investment. In fact, the "noise" actually strengthens that relationship. Even an L-shaped marginal efficiency curve shows it, although in this case the marginal product schedule does not shift since capital's supply price remains the same at all levels of replacement investment. It should be mentioned, however, that the effect on net investment of a changing level of replacement investment would probably be small. With a capital stock of K, replacement amounts to δK. Net investment equal to ΔK amends the replacement level to $\delta K + \delta \Delta K$, making the change in replacement investment equivalent to only the fraction δ of net investment.

Capital's marginal product schedule can shift for a variety of reasons besides a change in the replacement level of the capital price. Alterations in other input quantities would cause a shift, as would technological advance. Both of those events influence output, and hence the marginal product drift could be linked instead to output movement. Expectations also play a significant role. The annuities which form the basis of entrepreneurial capital and investment decisions are *prospective* magnitudes dependent upon anticipated future output levels and the like, and in this regard Carver's admonition to focus on permanents again applies. The "decision" or permanent marginal product involves expectations, and modifications to them would move the curve.

Any agent which shifts the marginal product schedule must simultaneously propel the entire family of marginal efficiency loci in the same direction. Accordingly, an upward surge in the marginal product curve stimulates net investment *ceteris paribus*, while a downward thrust depresses it. One of those agents is the level of output, and it must enter the net investment function with a positive effect. Its increases beget investment increases; its decreases beget decreases.

The interrelationship between the marginal product of capital and the marginal efficiency of investment joins Hicks and the profiteers in mandating that the *level* of output belongs in the net investment function.[24] The interrelationship also mandates, however, that output be accompanied by the stock of capital. It is this match of output and capital which leads to harmony between the profiteers and the accelerationists.

6.3 THE FLEXIBLE ACCELERATOR

Net investment formulation $I = I(r, Y, K)$ may be written linearly in alternative ways, one of which relates the interest rate to investment through coefficients in the equation. Specifically, $I = ABY - AK$, A and B being positive parameters dependent upon r. Equivalently,[25]

$$I_t = A[BY_t - K_{t-1}] \qquad (6.10)$$

with I_t, Y_t, and K_{t-1} denoting, respectively, net investment in period t, output in period t, and the stock of capital at the end of period $t - 1$. If the interest rate remains constant, then so do A and B. That assumption serves as a premise of much that follows.

In equation (6.10) BY_t lends itself to interpretation as the desired stock of capital. The bracketed expression then gives the discrepancy between the desired and actual stock levels which entrepreneurs plan to eventually eliminate, and $A[\ ]$ indicates the amount of that discrepancy which they eliminate in the present period. On theoretical grounds A cannot exceed unity. Discussion in the last section revealed that as firms move toward the optimum stock, net investment becomes progressively tempered but does not change direction. Net investment is always positive or always negative until it finally becomes zero; overshooting of the optimum stock never occurs. If A exceeded unity, then any attempt to correct a discrepancy between the desired and actual stock levels would prove excessive in that period, thereby requiring a reverse movement immediately afterward. If A equaled unity, then any discrepancy would be canceled in a single period. Only if A fell below unity would adjustment to the optimum stock proceed across multiple periods without ever causing overcorrection. Partial adjustment would occur in each period.

While an A of unity imposes single-step accommodation, it does allow equation (6.10) to embrace a familiar principle. With $A = 1$ (6.10) simplifies to

$$I_t = BY_t - K_{t-1} \qquad (6.11)$$

---

[24]It should be emphasized that the explanation for output's presence in the investment function provided by the combination of marginal product and marginal efficiency cites the technical association between capital's marginal product and output in the production process. This explanation differs from those offered by Hicks and by the profiteers.

[25]A similar derivation of equation (6.10) from the interaction of the marginal product and the marginal efficiency appears in Richard M. Goodwin, "Secular and Cyclical Aspects of the Multiplier and the Accelerator," in *Income, Employment and Public Policy: Essays in Honor of Alvin H. Hansen* (New York: W. W. Norton and Company, Inc., 1948), pp. 119–120.

which when taken back one period becomes

$$I_{t-1} = BY_{t-1} - K_{t-2} \tag{6.12}$$

Transposed, equation (6.12) advises that $I_{t-1} + K_{t-2} = BY_{t-1}$. The left-hand side of this latter expression adds net investment in period $t - 1$ to the stock of capital at the end of period $t - 2$. That sum, however, must be the stock of capital at the end of $t - 1$: $I_{t-1} + K_{t-2} = K_{t-1}$. Hence, $K_{t-1} = BY_{t-1}$, and equation (6.11) transforms into

$$I_t = B(Y_t - Y_{t-1}) \tag{6.13}$$

which is the simple accelerator! In light of the relationship between the simple accelerator and equation (6.10), it seems prudent to include unity in the set of permissible A values. Consequently, $0 < A \le 1$.

This link to the simple accelerator might be usefully pursued further. Rewrite equation (6.10) by adding zero within the brackets:

$$I_t = A[BY_t - K_{t-1} + BY_{t-1} - BY_{t-1}] \tag{6.14}$$

Factoring $B(Y_t - Y_{t-1})$ and simplifying give

$$I_t = \left\{ AB\left[1 + \frac{1}{g_t} - \frac{1}{Bg_t} \frac{K_{t-1}}{Y_{t-1}} \right] \right\} (Y_t - Y_{t-1}) \tag{6.15}$$

where $g_t = (Y_t - Y_{t-1})/Y_{t-1}$. This disguised form of (6.10) compares straightforwardly with the simple accelerator (6.13). While (6.13) has a constant coefficient B, (6.15) boasts a coefficient which varies in a complicated way with the current growth rate of output g_t and with the previous capital-output ratio. In other words, its coefficient is flexible, and thus equation (6.10) merits the label of flexible accelerator. It has also been called the "capital stock adjustment principle," CSAP.[26]

To cast some light on the different behavior patterns generated by the flexible accelerator (6.10) with $A < 1$ and the simple accelerator (6.13), suppose that in period t_0, firms, which had enjoyed perpetual equilibrium regarding their capital stock, experience a permanent increase in output to Y_b: $Y_{t_0} = Y_{t_0+1} = \cdots = Y_b$. For this scenario the simple accelerator (6.13) implies $I_{t_0} = B(Y_b - Y_{t_0-1})$, $I_{t_0+1} = B(Y_b - Y_b) = 0$, $I_{t_0+2} = 0$, and so forth. Net investment turns positive in period t_0, completely eliminates the deficiency in the capital stock, returns to zero, and then remains there forever. Opposing this pattern, the flexible accelerator gives from (6.14) $I_{t_0} = AB(Y_b - Y_{t_0-1}) + A[BY_{t_0-1} - K_{t_0-1}]$. The second term must be zero because, with capital equilibrium prevailing in period $t_0 - 1$, $I_{t_0-1} = 0$, and from (6.10) $BY_{t_0-1} = K_{t_0-2}$. However, $I_{t_0-1} = 0$ implies that $K_{t_0-1} = K_{t_0-2}$, the consequence being that $BY_{t_0-1} = K_{t_0-1}$. Therefore $I_{t_0} = AB(Y_b - Y_{t_0-1})$, which must fall short of the amount produced by the simple accelerator in t_0. In $t_0 + 1$ the flexible accelerator induces $I_{t_0+1} = AB(Y_b - Y_b)$

[26]Hamberg, *Models*, pp. 30–31, and R. C. O. Matthews, *The Business Cycle* (Chicago: The University of Chicago Press, 1959), pp. 40–41.

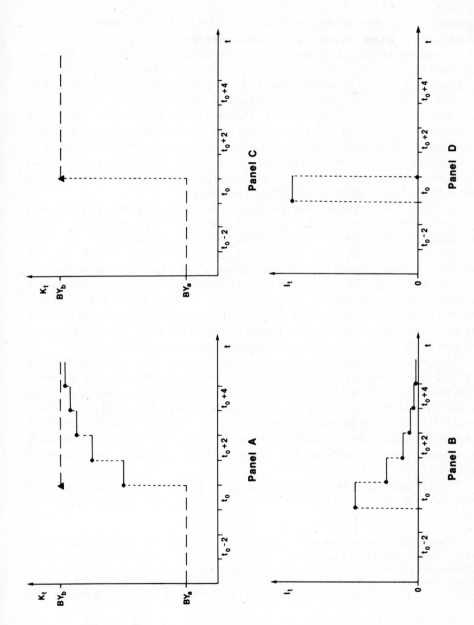

Figure 6.2

179

$+ A[BY_b - K_{t_0}]$. Now the first term equals zero, rendering $I_{t_0+1} = A[BY_b - K_{t_0}]$. Positive net investment in t_0 makes $K_{t_0} > K_{t_0-1}$, and since $K_{t_0-1} = BY_{t_0-1}$, $I_{t_0+1} < I_{t_0}$. In $t_0 + 2$, $I_{t_0+2} = A[BY_b - K_{t_0+1}]$; obviously, $I_{t_0+2} < I_{t_0+1} < I_{t_0}$. Therefore, under the flexible accelerator net investment becomes positive in period t_0 but to a lesser degree than it does under the simple accelerator. Positive net investment continues through time at a diminishing rate until the new optimum capital stock is attained. Net investment then expires.

Figure 6.2 depicts these movements of net investment along with the corresponding ones for the capital stock. Panels A and B pertain to the flexible accelerator with its coefficient $A < 1$; Panels C and D relate to the simple accelerator, coefficient $A = 1$. The capital and investment axes have identical scales, and the horizontal dashed lines and triangular points trace the equilibrium stock of capital defined [consonant with equation (6.10)] as that stock at the end of a period which equals a multiple B of the output in the period. Y_a denotes the output level ruling uninterruptedly prior to period t_0.

As Panels A and B make clear, the flexible accelerator engenders a protracted adjustment process mirroring that displayed in Figure 6.1. Entrepreneurs expand their capital stock slowly, and the size of the increments diminishes through time. Throughout this evolution the actual stock of capital remains below the new optimum; in short, capacity is deficient during adjustment. In a similar manner an equivalent decline in the desired level of capital would trigger a symmetric accommodative procedure during which excess capacity would persist. These response configurations contrast markedly with the one-step jump to full capacity imposed by the simple accelerator. Panels C and D highlight that characteristic. In Panel C the paths of the actual and equilibrium stocks coincide.

Deficient or excessive capacity may occur under the simple accelerator provided that it acknowledges a gestation lag. In that case the changed optimum stock recorded in Panel C would not activate the response mechanism immediately, and during the interim nonoptimum capacity would exist. Once excited, however, the mechanism would force optimality in a single period. A gestation lag would have an analogous effect on the flexible accelerator, but there nonoptimality would continue well beyond the activation of the adjustment apparatus.[27]

Flexible accelerator (6.10) can be derived by a route alternate to the passage from $I(r, Y, K)$ to $A[\ ]$ via linearity.[28] In Section 4.1 a firm was visualized as

---

[27]Mathematical representation of this lag phenomenon can be readily derived. Given a lag of i periods, economic information available for the investment decision in period t does not affect capital formation until period $t + i$. Stood on its head, this relationship says that net investment in period t depends upon magnitudes discernible i periods earlier. Hence the flexible accelerator (6.10) becomes $I_t = A[BY_{t-i} - K_{t-i-1}]$, while the simple accelerator (6.13) becomes $I_t = B\Delta Y_{t-i}$, $\Delta Y_{t-i} = Y_{t-i} - Y_{t-i-1}$.

[28]An inornate remedy for the weakness of the profits principle cited in Section 6.1 entails expressing profits as a rate rather than as a level. That procedure implies a flexible accelerator too. With output serving as surrogate for profits, net investment is made a function of the output-capital ratio, and imposition of linearity leads to $I_t = h_0 Y_t / K_{t-1} - h_1$, h_0 and h_1 being positive parameters. Consequently, $I_t = A_1[B_1 Y_t - K_{t-1}]$. See Knox, "Acceleration Principle," p. 295.

maximizing profit with respect to capital and labor under the stricture of a production function. The resulting expression for capital, equation (4.5), held the capital stock to be proportional to output (demand) and the proportionality term to be dependent upon the ratio of money wage to unit capital rental. A similar expression might apply to the macro setting, but for credibility the output variable should refer to the level of production which entrepreneurs regard as normal or permanent; namely,

$$K_t = DY_{P_t} \tag{6.16}$$

where D denotes a proportionality term and Y_{P_t} represents permanent output in period t.

Permanent output may be specified with an eye to the formula cited in the discussion of Friedman's consumption theory, equation (5.37). In particular,

$$Y_{P_t} = \omega\left[Y_t + \gamma Y_{t-1} + \gamma^2 Y_{t-2} + \cdots\right] \tag{6.17}$$

where $\omega = (1 - \gamma)\beta/(\beta - \alpha)$ and $\gamma = e^{-(\beta - \alpha)}$. β and α are constants having the same roles as their namesakes do in equation (5.36), and they subscribe to the earlier numerical restrictions written compactly as $0 \le \alpha < \beta < 1$. Therefore, $0 < \gamma < 1$. According to equation (6.17) entrepreneurs determine the permanent level of output by reviewing current and past experiences and by attaching less significance to those events which lie more distant from the present. Because permanent output reflects actual output's trend rate of growth, α, it has no obligation to fall within the range of the highest and lowest output levels recorded to date.

Inserting (6.17) into (6.16) yields

$$K_t = D\omega\left[Y_t + \gamma Y_{t-1} + \gamma^2 Y_{t-2} + \cdots\right] \tag{6.18}$$

Renotating this equation for period $t - 1$, multiplying that version by γ, and subtracting the result from (6.18) eventually produces

$$K_t = D\omega Y_t + \gamma K_{t-1} \tag{6.19}$$

Like its comrade λ in consumption function (5.41), γ in stock function (6.19) represents a sluggishness coefficient; it measures the strength of past lessons on current behavior. A capital stock increase in any period leads to a smaller increase in the next period *ceteris paribus*, and this sequence coincides with the profile portrayed in Panel A of Figure 6.2.

To convert equation (6.19) explicitly to a net investment function, subtract K_{t-1} from both sides and obtain

$$I_t = (1 - \gamma)\zeta Y_t - (1 - \gamma)K_{t-1} \tag{6.20}$$

or equivalently

$$I_t = (1 - \gamma)[\zeta Y_t - K_{t-1}] \tag{6.21}$$

where $\zeta = D\beta/(\beta - \alpha)$. In stationary state, output repeats itself through time, and its trend rate α must be zero. Additionally, capital remains constant at an optimum level of $\zeta Y_t \ (= DY_t)$ determined by setting $K_t = K_{t-1}$ in equation

(6.19).[29] Thus, the ζY_t term in equation (6.21) can be interpreted as the desired stock of capital. Furthermore, $1 - \gamma$ may be viewed as investment's speed-of-adjustment coefficient.[30] Greater $1 - \gamma$ implies greater investment; smaller $1 - \gamma$, smaller investment. This measure varies inversely with the sluggishness coefficient γ, connoting that a stronger tie to the past, symbolized by K_{t-1} in equation (6.19), calls forth a smaller (slower) current response I_t. Observe that equation (6.21) duplicates the specification of the flexible accelerator presented in equation (6.10).[31]

The flexible accelerator "marries" the profits principle and the acceleration principle. It represents the former inasmuch as it includes the level of output in the set of arguments. But it also evidences acceleration properties, as equation (6.15) reveals and as the special case of equation (6.10) with a unitary speed-of-adjustment coefficient confirms; then the flexible accelerator gives way to the simple accelerator. More fundamentally, its very philosophy, summarized by the expression for desired capital BY_t or DY_{P_t}, has an unmistakably accelerationist ring: more or less capital is needed because more or less output must be produced. By blending both competing principles, however, the flexible accelerator avoids weaknesses linked to either. Under its purview a constant level of output cannot be associated with both a constant positive amount of net investment and a continually increasing stock of capital. Panels A and B of Figure 6.2 show that stationary output coupled with an increasing capital stock mean continually decreasing positive net investment. Furthermore, within its jurisdiction the instantaneous accommodation and full-capacity dictates of the simple accelerator no longer apply and instead are replaced by a protracted adjustment sequence which features deficient or excessive capacity. Asymmetric investment response can be included in the flexible accelerator's repertoire by allowing the speed-of-adjustment coefficient to vary over the phases of a cycle.[32] This same end might be achieved if the income coefficient moved cyclically. Thus, while the flexible accelerator ignores important elements of the investment process, it does represent a considerable stride toward a satisfactory description of that process.

---

[29] An alternative calculation calls for equating all output terms in equation (6.18) to Y_t, thereby giving $K_t = D\omega J Y_t, J = 1 + \gamma + \gamma^2 + \cdots$. Since $J - \gamma J = 1, J = 1/(1 - \gamma)$ and $K_t = \zeta Y_t$. Discussion of the optimum stock and an outline for deriving (6.21) from (6.16) appear in Koyck, *Distributed Lags*, pp. 69–70.

[30] This terminology follows Koyck, although $1 - \gamma$ might also be called a "reaction coefficient." See Chenery, "Overcapacity," p. 13, and Koyck, *Distributed Lags*, pp. 11, 22–23.

[31] If entrepreneurs ignored current output Y_t in formulating their notion of permanent, then the output variable in equations (6.19)–(6.21) would exhibit lags. For instance, if Y_{t-j} were the most recent output term included in (6.17), then (6.21) would read $I_t = (1 - \gamma)[\zeta Y_{t-j} - K_{t-1}]$; the timing of the capital argument would remain unchanged. If $\gamma = 0 (A = 1)$, the simple accelerator to emerge from the method used in producing equation (6.13) would contain a lag of j periods: $I_t = \zeta \Delta Y_{t-j}$.

It should be recognized that the restriction $0 \leq \alpha < \beta < 1$ strictly speaking rules out the extreme points for γ, $\gamma = 0$ and $\gamma = 1$. Nevertheless, either extreme might be allowed on occasion to enhance interpretation. This strategy, exemplified earlier by the inclusion of $A = 1$ in equation (6.10) despite theoretical dictates, finds service again later.

[32] Chenery, "Overcapacity," p. 15, and Koyck, *Distributed Lags*, pp. 70–71.

6.4 ON THE FINANCIAL SIDE OF INVESTMENT

As recited in Section 6.2, the marginal efficiency of investment may be likened to the marginal revenue associated with an additional unit of capital. Similarly, the interest rate resembles the marginal cost of acquiring that good; it measures the cost of obtaining the funds needed to purchase the machine. In short, it is the marginal cost of funds MCF.

Implicit in the treatment of the investment process depicted in Figure 6.1 rests the assumption that the MCF schedule remains infinitely elastic at the market rate of interest. This assumption is questionable, however, because it says that firms can obtain all investment funds at a fixed rate regardless of how risky they become by virtue of their borrowing practices. Such a presumption stands at odds with the operation of credit markets, which typically do not blind themselves to risk. The prime, or lowest operative, rate of interest applies only to "best bets," and less secure customers or customers that become less secure face premiums which are added to the prime. Risk matters, but a horizontal MCF schedule misses that point. It also misses the possibility that entrepreneurs introduce a subjective component into their appraisal of alternative funding schemes.

Both of these considerations find expression in the argument advanced cogently by James Duesenberry and by L. R. Koyck.[33] It proceeds thus. A firm's investment funds can be drawn from four sources: depreciation allowances, retained earnings, external borrowing, and equity issue. The first two are internal to the firm; the remaining two, external. Each source attaches a cost to the funds provided. The use of depreciation allowances for investment purposes involves opportunity cost measured, perhaps, by the interest rate on government securities which the firm might have otherwise purchased. Use of retained earnings incurs opportunity cost too. However, failure to distribute earnings may upset shareholders, who typically have a favorable inclination toward receiving dividends, and concern of managers about shareholder sentiment—more personally, about their own jobs—may cause them to assign an extra charge for allocating retained earnings to investment activity. Thus the cost which they perceive for tapping this pool of funds is not only a forgone opportunity but also the conceivable displeasure of stockholders. The charge for the latter may rise with the portion of earnings withheld.

Borrowing externally entails obvious cash cost reflecting the risk premium. In addition, it carries an imputation based on management's fear of bankruptcy. As borrowing expands, so does the imputation, and executives with severe prejudice against debt would likely assign a large penalty to borrowed funds even if only a small quantity were involved. Equity sale means that yield per share falls unless the return from funds obtained by the issue is high. Since corporate officials value

---

[33]James S. Duesenberry, *Business Cycles and Economic Growth* (New York: McGraw-Hill Book Company, 1958), pp. 87–99, and Koyck, *Distributed Lags*, pp. 58–61. The ensuing discussion appeals primarily to Duesenberry's presentation.

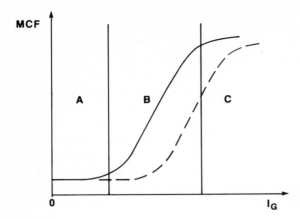

Figure 6.3 *Source*: Duesenberry, *Business Cycles*, p. 96.

their record of yield per share, they might envision a high imputation for moneys obtained from this origin.

Investment finance can therefore be regarded as flowing sequentially from various sources at increasing cost, and the marginal cost of funds schedule which results might assume an S shape. Figure 6.3 depicts this possibility, I_G again denoting gross investment. With respect to the solid curve, region A identifies investment which can be financed from internal funds—depreciation allowances and retained earnings. Regions B and C do likewise for external borrowing and equity sale, respectively. As the level of internal funds changes through alterations in profit, the size of region A changes and the MCF schedule shifts. An increase in internal dollars pushes the schedule rightward as the dashes indicate; a decrease pulls it leftward. Because of its subjective content, the MCF schedule may display markedly different shapes across firms. Nevertheless, those separate curves might be imagined to generate a configuration for the macro system having properties which rival those portrayed in the figure.

Confronting the economy's S-shaped MCF schedule with its MEI curve determines the optimum level of net investment I in any period. Figure 6.4 provides an illustration with the rate of interest r taken as a measure of opportunity cost. For the moment disregard MCF'. Perhaps the most striking conclusion to emerge from this confrontation regards the level of net investment. Net investment is smaller than it would be if the MCF schedule stayed perfectly elastic at the rate of interest; specifically, $I_1' < I_1$. Subjective and objective factors pertaining to the availability of investment funds combine to dampen net investment. However, if internal funds were to increase *ceteris paribus*, the MCF schedule would shift rightward and investment would move from I_1' in the direction of I_1. If funds continued to increase, I_1' would eventually coincide with I_1. Any further expansion of internal money, however, would foster no additional investment since MEI would then intersect MCF in its horizontal segment, as schedule MCF' shows.

Three morals emerge from this exercise. First, internal funds or, alternatively, profits constitute an important determinant of net investment. More funds lead to

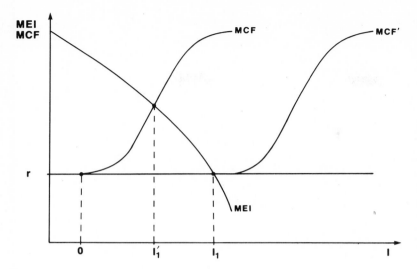

Figure 6.4

more investment provided that the latter remains below some upper limit. This proviso forms the basis of the second conclusion: Internal funds or profits exert a *permissive* influence on investment.[34] A shortage of funds prevents the attainment of I_1, but no amount of funding can stimulate investment beyond I_1. According to this analysis, finance, while a regulator of investment, is not its root cause. That lies elsewhere. To the disciples of acceleration, it rests with the relationship between capital and output in the production process. The third moral is that finance and capacity factors can affect investment simultaneously and contradictorily. For example, an increase in internal funds would shift the MCF curve rightward while an increase in capital stock shifts the MEI schedule leftward. In this circumstance the resulting level of net investment may be larger than, smaller than, or the same as the previous mark, depending upon the strength of the individual influences.

Net investment is determined at the junction of the MEI and MCF schedules. What governs their positions? Based on earlier discussion reasonable locators for MEI include output Y and capital stock K, and therefore in functional notation MEI may be written as MEI(I, Y, K). Locators for MCF include internal funds U to measure the length of the floor and "the" interest rate to measure its height. Debt might be represented by business liabilities V, while equity yield z may enter too. Thus MCF becomes MCF(I, U, r, V, z).

Initiating equality gives

$$\text{MEI}(I, Y, K) = \text{MCF}(I, U, r, V, z)$$

---

[34] Various authors subscribe to the permissive thesis. See, for instance, Eisner, "Theory for Investment," p. 386; Hamberg, *Models*, p. 35; Knox, "Acceleration Principle," p. 294; and Koyck, *Distributed Lags*, p. 61.

Solving this relationship for net investment produces

$$I = G(Y, K, U, r, V, z)$$

which under linearity becomes[35]

$$I_t = E_0 + E_1 Y_t + E_2 K_{t-1} + E_3 U_t + E_4 r_t + E_5 V_t + E_6 z_t \qquad (6.22)$$

At first blush formula (6.22) looks to be far removed from the flexible accelerator (6.10). It is not. It has the same parentage, the MEI = MCF rule, although it does carry the stamp of a more enthusiastic interpretation of MCF. The closeness of these formulations becomes clear when one recalls that function (6.10) exhibits the effect of interest parametrically. If this determinant were augmented by the other locators associated with an S-shaped MCF and if linearity were invoked, then equation (6.10) would be transformed into equation (6.22).[36]

6.5 AN INERTIAL MULTIPLIER-ACCELERATOR MODEL

The Samuelson-type model considered in Section 4.3 allows the multiplier and the accelerator principles to operate without restraint. Households spend solely on the basis of current income, and firms correct any capital imbalance in a single period. Rejecting such naiveté, numerous theories presented in Chapter 5 hold that consumers alter their spending patterns only sluggishly. Arguments advanced in preceding sections of the present chapter claim that entrepreneurs also have a "go slow" attitude. For consumers and entrepreneurs alike, current stimuli affect current behavior only in a muted way, and intuition asserts that such inertia should moderate the temporal response of a macro system. Intuition further

---

[35] On this derivation see Duesenberry, *Business Cycles*, pp. 110–111, and W. H. Locke Anderson, "Business Fixed Investment: A Marriage of Fact and Fancy" in Robert Ferber, ed., *Determinants of Investment Behavior* (New York: National Bureau of Economic Research, distributed by Columbia University Press, 1967), pp. 415–417. In actual practice the choice of locators for the MEI and MCF schedules would be dictated by particulars of the situation being studied. Equation (6.22) is merely suggestive, and it deliberately ignores lagged effects except capital's.

[36] Equations manifesting an affinity to expression (6.22) or to its adumbrated version (6.10) have been associated with several econometric macro systems such as the models of the Brookings Institution, Chase Econometric Associates, Hickman and Coen, Klein and Goldberger, Pindyck and Rubinfeld, and the Wharton School of the University of Pennsylvania. See Chase Econometric Associates, Inc., "Equations" (mimeograph, Bala Cynwyd, Pa., May 1977), equations E-1.1, E-2.1; Michael K. Evans, *Macroeconomic Activity: Theory, Forecasting, and Control* (New York: Harper & Row, Publishers, Incorporated, 1969), pp. 433–434, 498; Gary Fromm and Paul Taubman, *Policy Simulations with an Econometric Model* (Washington, D.C.: The Brookings Institution, 1968), p. 132; Bert G. Hickman, Robert M. Coen, and Michael D. Hurd, "The Hickman-Coen Annual Growth Model: Structural Characteristics and Policy Responses," *International Economic Review*, **16** (February 1975), p. 24; and Robert S. Pindyck and Daniel L. Rubinfeld, *Econometric Models and Economic Forecasts* (New York: McGraw-Hill Book Company, 1976), pp. 374–375, 378–379.

argues that as the pull of inertia intensifies, the behavior of the system should become less volatile.

Inertia's role in attenuating cyclical movement can be demonstrated by combining the flexible accelerator with some consumption function which permits sluggishness, say, that of Ball and Drake,[37] by systematically increasing the strength of inertia, and by examining the time paths generated. This inertial multiplier-accelerator model can be tied directly to the Samuelson-type paradigm provided that the flexible accelerator format discussed in Section 6.3 is altered in two respects. Its focus should be shifted away from total output and toward consumption, and its capital stock argument should be algebraically converted to a flow variable. The resulting equation would then be strictly comparable to the simple accelerator of Samuelson.

Let the capital stock be proportional to the level of consumption which entrepreneurs treat as permanent:

$$K_t = \theta C_{P_t} \tag{6.23}$$

where K_t and C_{P_t} denote, respectively, the capital stock at the end of period t and permanent consumption in t. The latter observes the Friedman distributed lag described by equation (5.37), and thus

$$C_{P_t} = \psi \left[C_t + \phi C_{t-1} + \phi^2 C_{t-2} + \cdots \right] \tag{6.24}$$

with C_t representing actual consumption in period t. $\psi = (1 - \phi)\beta/(\beta - \alpha)$, where β and α continue their earlier duties. $0 < \phi < 1$. Through the usual procedure (6.23) and (6.24) yield an equation for net investment:

$$I_t = (1 - \phi)\mu C_t - (1 - \phi)K_{t-1} \tag{6.25}$$

with $\mu = \theta\beta/(\beta - \alpha)$.

If machines have infinite durability, then gross investment and net investment are identical, and the capital stock existing at the termination of any period consists of all investment undertaken to that date:

$$K_{t-1} = I_{t-1} + I_{t-2} + I_{t-3} + \cdots$$

Equation (6.25) therefore becomes

$$I_t = (1 - \phi)\mu C_t - (1 - \phi)[I_{t-1} + I_{t-2} + I_{t-3} + \cdots]$$

Setting this expression back to period $t - 1$ and subtracting the result from the original formula produces

$$I_t = (1 - \phi)\mu(C_t - C_{t-1}) + \phi I_{t-1} \tag{6.26}$$

which enables a straightforward comparison with Samuelson's simple accelerator, equation (4.8).

---

[37]A match of the flexible accelerator with a sluggish-free consumption function and the macro implications of that pairing can be found in Goodwin, "Secular and Cyclical Aspects," pp. 109, 115, 120–132.

With the renovation of the flexible accelerator complete, the inertial multiplier-accelerator model may be postulated. Specifically,

$$C_t = (1 - \nu)Yd_t + \nu C_{t-1} \tag{6.27}$$

$$Yd_t = Y_t - T_t \tag{6.28}$$

$$T_t = \chi Y_t \tag{6.29}$$

$$I_t = (1 - \phi)\mu(C_t - C_{t-1}) + \phi I_{t-1} \tag{6.30}$$

$$G_t = G_o \tag{6.31}$$

$$Y_t = C_{t-1} + I_{t-1} + G_{t-1} \tag{6.32}$$

All variables represent reals. Yd_t and Y_t denote, respectively, disposable income and total income in period t, while T_t and G_t refer to taxes and government purchases in t, respectively. Equation (6.27) reproduces Ball and Drake's short-run formulation (5.62); hence the coefficients sum to unity. Additional parameter restrictions read $0 \leq \nu \leq 1$, $0 \leq \phi \leq 1$, $0 < \chi < 1$, and $\mu \geq 0$. For the sake of completeness, ϕ values of zero and unity are now permitted.

Equations (6.28) and (6.29) can be absorbed by (6.27), consolidating the inertial system to

$$C_t = (1 - \nu)(1 - \chi)Y_t + \nu C_{t-1} \tag{6.33}$$

$$I_t = (1 - \phi)\mu(C_t - C_{t-1}) + \phi I_{t-1} \tag{6.34}$$

$$G_t = G_o \tag{6.35}$$

$$Y_t = C_{t-1} + I_{t-1} + G_{t-1} \tag{6.36}$$

Against this set of equations stand the Samuelson-type equations of Section 4.3, reproduced here as

$$C_t = cY_t \tag{6.37}$$

$$I_t = b(C_t - C_{t-1}) \tag{6.38}$$

$$G_t = G_o \tag{6.39}$$

$$Y_t = C_{t-1} + I_{t-1} + G_{t-1} \tag{6.40}$$

These two models differ in that the inertial consumption and investment functions generalize the corresponding Samuelson functions. When the sluggishness parameters ν and ϕ vanish, equations (6.33) and (6.34) revert to (6.37) and (6.38), with $1 - \chi$ serving as c and μ as b. Thus, the inertial paradigm contains the Samuelson-type system as the special case where $\nu = \phi = 0$.

Other properties of the sluggishness model can be deduced. When $\nu = 1$, all induced effects are lost. This assignment makes $C_t = C_{t-1}$, and hence a permanent change in government purchases, while affecting output after a period delay, propagates no change in consumption and therefore none in investment. Output reacts only to the extent of the change in government expenditures, and it does so in a single jump. For the case of a stationary-state equilibrium, where variables duplicate their previous magnitudes, $\nu = 1$ sets the equilibrium government expenditures multiplier on output equal to unity. The corresponding dynamic multiplier equals zero at first and unity thereafter. When $\phi = 1$ (and $\nu < 1$), the inertial system exhibits multiplier effects alone.

Since ν and ϕ both restrain behavior, it seems reasonable to expect that if a particular temporal response configuration is to be preserved, then a trade-off relationship should exist between them. For example, an increase in ν should be compensated by a decrease in ϕ. Notice, however, that ν really exerts a double effect in bridling the model. It curtails consumption, but because investment depends upon consumption, it restrains investment as well. ϕ, by contrast, only affects investment. It follows that a given value for ν should impose a stronger tempering influence on the system than would an equal value for ϕ.

In stationary state the inertial model generally implies an output value of $Y_E = G_o/\chi$. Clearly, this expression remains independent of ν and ϕ. Furthermore, it resurrects the formula applicable to the Samuelson-type model; namely, $Y_E = G_o/(1 - c)$, equation (4.13). For equal values of χ and $1 - c$, both systems produce the same equilibrium, and that equilibrium holds regardless of the assignments for ν and ϕ, the case of $\nu = 1$ excepted.

Although ν and ϕ typically do not alter the equilibrium of the inertial system, they do affect its temporal movement. This feature can be seen from output's reduced-form equation, which surfaces through a process of iterative substitution backward through time. For instance, inserting consumption's (6.33) and investment's (6.34) into output's (6.36) expresses output not only in terms of lagged values of itself, as is true for the Samuelson-type model, but also in terms of lagged values of consumption and investment. However, substitution of (6.33) and (6.34) for those prior consumption and investment quantities and continual repetition of the procedure eventually relate current output exclusively to its own previous values. That relationship can be written as

$$Y_t = (1 - \nu)(1 - \chi) \sum_{k=1}^{\infty} \eta_k Y_{t-k} + G_{t-1} \qquad (6.41)$$

where $\eta_1 = 1 + \mu(1 - \phi)$ and $\eta_k = \nu\eta_{k-1} - \mu(1 - \phi)^2\phi^{k-2}$ for $k \geq 2$. It is evident from equation (6.41) that the movement of actual output depends upon the four parameters ν, ϕ, χ, and μ. Consequently, the task of establishing demarcation lines separating the different response patterns for output becomes a problem in four dimensions. For the Samuelson-type system the problem involved two dimensions, and its solution was summarized by Figure 4.5. Only when $\nu = \phi = 0$ would that figure apply to the inertial model.

To keep the task of establishing demarcations manageable while still allowing a demonstration of the role of ν and ϕ in bridling the system, χ and μ are set at selected values. The precise magnitudes chosen include as a subset all those used in generating for the Samuelson paradigm the time paths portrayed in Figure 4.3. Thus $\chi = .32$ to enable $1 - \chi = .68$; $1 - \chi$, recall, is the inertial counterpart of Samuelson's c. μ, the inertial twin of his b, alternatively equals 5.00, 3.60, 1.55, 1.47, 1.00, and .10. In the Samuelson context with $c = .68$, a b of 5.00 would generate direct explosion. So did b's 3.60. A b of 1.55 gave explosive oscillation, while 1.47 witnessed regular oscillation. The 1.00 value propagated damped cycles, and .10 prompted unidirectional convergence. For the cases illustrated in Figure 4.3, government purchases maintained a value of 250 prior to time zero, and over that millennium equilibrium output equaled 781.25. At time zero government purchases rose to 275 and remained there forever. Equilibrium output likewise rose, to 859.38 instantaneously, and held that level permanently. An identical sequence of events now applies to the inertial model.

Figure 6.5 presents the lines of demarcation identifying various kinds of output movements generated by the inertial system under the six combinations of χ and μ values treated. Region A marks unidirectional convergence; region B, damped oscillation; region C, explosive oscillation; and region D, direct explosion.[38] Several results of this experiment deserve elaboration.

First, for $\mu = 5.00$, all four output configurations arise. As μ drops to 3.60, the C-D line, that dividing regions C and D, collapses to a single point at the origin. A further decline to 1.55 causes explosive oscillation to almost disappear, and at a μ of 1.47 it does. There the B-C line becomes the origin point. For μ values of 1.00 and .10, only stable movements prevail, namely, unidirectional adjustment and damped oscillation.

Second, the B-C and C-D lines display negative slopes as expected: a decrease in the magnitude of one inertial parameter necessitates an increase in the value of the other to sustain a given temporal configuration. In addition, both the B-C and C-D lines are asymmetric around an imaginary 45° line through the origin consonant with the greater restraining power of ν. For example, in the case of $\mu = 5.00$, damped oscillation requires a ϕ of approximately .9 when $\nu = 0$, while it mandates a ν of about .7 when $\phi = 0$.

Third, the locus splitting regions A and B has a positive slope, implying that both inertial parameters must move in the same direction to maintain a particular time profile. It appears that once the system achieves some critical degree of tranquillity, additional restraint at the hands of ϕ produces oscillatory behavior unless further braking action comes from ν. Observe that the A-B line rotates clockwise around the point (1, 1) as μ declines.

Finally, for any ϕ value below unity, an increase in ν always means greater attenuation of the system's movement. For any ν value an increase in ϕ carries the same implication but with the exception just noted.

This exercise lends support to intuition by showing that inertia can substantially temper the dynamic movement of a macro system. Yet it also reveals, by the

---

[38] Due to the general clumsiness of equation (6.41) traceable to its infinite number of lagged output terms, Figure 6.5 emerged by appealing to a numerical method. Succinctly, the inertial model with assigned χ and μ was operated temporally for each of many pairs of ν and ϕ, and the patterns of the resulting paths were recorded. This catalog supplied the coordinates for the demarcation curves.

When $\phi = 1$, equation (6.41) reduces to $Y_t = (1 - \nu)(1 - \chi)[Y_{t-1} + \nu Y_{t-2} + \nu^2 Y_{t-3} + \cdots] + G_{t-1}$. With $\nu < 1$, a permanent increase in government purchases elicits continually diminishing increments from the bracketed expression, and unidirectional movement to the new stationary state results. This sequence imitates the pure multiplier response described in Sections 4.3 and 4.4. When $\phi = 1$ and $\nu = 1$, one-step adjustment occurs.

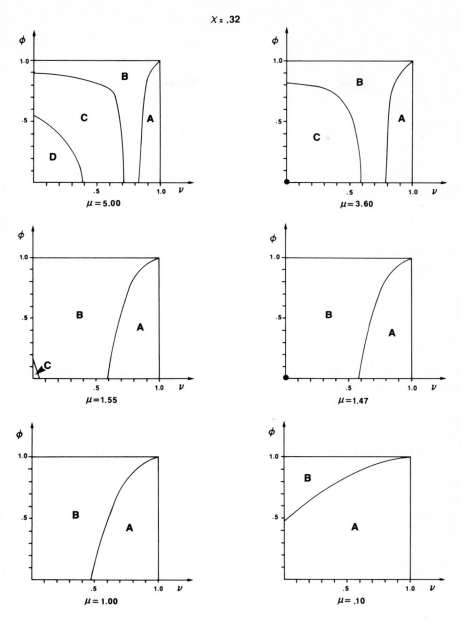

Figure 6.5

191

results for $\mu = .10$, that inertia can be the cause of a cyclical response. The possibility of oscillations arising from "curative" measures will be encountered again in conjunction with policy feedback models, to be discussed in Chapter 8.

6.6 LESSONS AND THOUGHTS FROM DYNAMICS

The excursion into dynamics which has been the purpose of Parts 2 and 3 leads to several principal conclusions. Among them is the observation that the existence of an equilibrium says little, if anything, about disequilibrium movements. A temporal response might take a system past equilibrium without ever looking back, or it might fashion cumulative or replicative oscillations. Alternatively, it could produce diminishing cycles or unidirectional approach to equilibrium. Various temporal configurations are possible, but existence may give no clue about the one pertinent to any particular circumstance. Existence and stability are two different issues.

Despite their dissimilarity, adjustment paths which direct an economy to a new equilibrium have a common denominator: they are long. A shock disrupting a previous state sets into motion a sequence of events which does not work to completion immediately. Something happens, then something else happens, and only after that can another something happen. Single-step accommodation does not occur except in rare situations; as a rule adjustment takes time.

The response of a system to some perturbation depends partly upon the length of lags characterizing its relationships. For some lags unidirectional movement may result; for others, oscillations may prevail. Its response also depends upon parameter values, and in that regard inertia exhibited by economic units tends to act as a tempering agent. In effect, it serves to reduce the size of parameters causing volatility.

Several thoughts concerning policy emerge from this discourse on dynamics. Since the time required for attainment of a new equilibrium is typically long, exclusive focus on equilibria in discussing policy questions would generally be inappropriate. For policy designed to moderate cyclical fluctuations, it is the departure from equilibrium that matters. Such countercyclical action must attempt to alter disequilibrium paths, although in the process it may amend equilibria as well.

Redirecting the economy is not easy. A countercyclical maneuver begun now may not impact the system until much later, and this delay could cause the initiative to be destabilizing. For instance, a stimulus implemented at a seemingly tactful moment might have full effect only when the economy reaches the peak of a cycle. Analogously, a depressant might come to bear only in a trough. Thus a stabilization move, if improperly timed, could exacerbate a boom or bust, or it could create an imbalance where none would have existed. But even if action were properly timed, it still could be destabilizing because of magnitude. A strong impact when a nudge is required might intensify rather than cure the economy's illness. On the other hand, a nudge when a decided shove is warranted may have little useful effect. A countercyclical initiative therefore faces the grim possibility that, while it may prompt a small favorable response, it may actually make conditions worse! Lags which vary through time and shocks which refuse to arrive by an orderly schedule only complicate the policy effort.

Determination of the proper timing and magnitude of countercyclical action encounters numerous difficulties. Advance warning of an impending cyclical crisis must be provided if a suitable remedy is to be designed and implemented before the crisis unfolds. Existing detection devices, however, frequently display disagreement about forthcoming developments, and the data which they do supply may arrive too late to be useful. The composite index of leading indicators has had a checkered career as a forecasting tool. Its false signals have been distracting, and its lead at troughs has frequently been very short. Popular econometric models occasionally offer forecasts pointing in different directions because of structural dissimilarities across systems and because of disparate opinions among the forecasters themselves regarding the future behavior of variables exogenous to their models. Prognosis of a strong or weak economy may turn on the optimism or pessimism about exogenous forces.

Calculating the appropriate magnitude of policy requires information on dynamic multipliers; that comes from the interface of theoretical and statistical procedures. Different theoretical bases engender different specifications to be estimated, while different statistical techniques and observational sets engender different parameter estimates for a given specification. Variety reigns, and it is manifested through the widely divergent sets of dynamic multipliers displayed by estimated macro systems for any particular policy action. Belief in multiplier values can amount to a considerable act of faith.

Countercyclical policy must be difficult, for otherwise economies would have ended their roller coaster rides long ago. At the heart of the problem rests the uncertainty which surrounds policy decision. Planners must anticipate the unknown, make sense of statistical riddles, and trust that errors committed along the way cancel. One means for dealing with this uncertainty is simply to avoid making decisions in the first place by substituting, where possible, automatic rules for discretion. In at least some instances, however, discretion may be the better part of policy, and hence it seems prudent to examine how uncertainty might affect the decisions of planners. These themes form the subject of Part 4.

FOUR

MECHANISM OF POLICY

POLICY DECISIONS UNDER CERTAINTY AND UNCERTAINTY

"If I seem to be limping, it's because someone dropped a rebate on my foot," intoned Charles Schultze after the tax rebate had been deleted from the Carter administration's economic stimulus package of 1977.[1] At the time of his remark, Mr. Schultze was chairman of the Council of Economic Advisers and, somewhat ironically, one of the President's closest economic confidants.

During the presidential campaign of 1976, the Democrats repeatedly cited the weak condition of the economy and blamed its feeble performance on the Republicans. When Mr. Carter assumed office, the electorate, or at least economists in that electorate, eagerly awaited the precise stimulative measures which the new administration would propose. The wait was short. Only 11 days after taking the oath of office, Mr. Carter announced his economic recovery package. It called for a two-year boost amounting to $31.2 billion, $11.4 billion of which was embodied in a comprehensive rebate: specifically, a $50 rebate for each taxpayer and dependent. The date was January 31.

From the first days of February until mid-April, economic experts of the administration spoke and testified about the importance of the stimulus package and its cornerstone, the rebate. Then came April 14 and the announcement from the White House that the cornerstone was being removed. To some observers this stark reversal was the result of political pressure, if not wisdom, since the rebate faced a gloomy future at the hands of an unsympathetic Senate. Scuttling the rebate eliminated possible political embarrassment which would ensue from a defeat on this key issue. But other observers, including the White House corps of

---

[1]Juan Cameron, "Jimmy Carter Gets Mixed Marks in Economics I," *Fortune*, June 1977, p. 100.

economists, confessed publicly that the rebate was amputated because of economic considerations. The improvement which the economy experienced over the first quarter of 1977 meant that the rebate was no longer needed.

> *Question*: Up until a matter of hours ago, members of the Administration were arguing before public bodies, before Congress, for this [rebate], and now it has been dropped... . What do you think this does to your credibility in arguing for the jobs program, elements of your anti-inflation program, the energy program and so on, before the Congress and the public?

> *Mr. Schultze*: You know, there are a lot of elements of credibility. I would hope that one of them is the ability to absorb and adjust to reality. And we think that is what this does. We think that is credible.

> *Question*: Isn't it kind of an overnight adjustment you made?

> *Mr. Schultze*: When facts, analyses, judgment, in a very difficult situation come together, they very often do come together quickly in the sense of the sort of things that have been kind of underlying your mind, and when you finally start to debate them among yourselves and weigh it, that final decision does tend to come quickly.[2]

This brief chronicle of the rebate that never was serves to demonstrate that policy formulation is a perplexing business, one which requires nimbleness of its practitioners. Programs designed to improve the functioning of the economy, perhaps by moving it closer to some preassigned target, may have to be modified to accommodate changing conditions. The strength of controlling forces such as government expenditures, taxes, or the money supply might have to be amended as well. The economy responds to a multitude of phenomena, and planners must be prepared to react quickly to any change.

In truth, policy is—and can only be—fashioned from incomplete information. It is composed under uncertainty, and the exchange involving Mr. Schultze made this point clear. Mr. G. William Miller clinched it during a conference with reporters held in mid-March 1980. Then the Secretary of Treasury, Mr. Miller was asked to defend an abrupt and belated revision to the federal budget drafted by President Carter for the fiscal year beginning with October 1980. The original budget called for a modest deficit; the reworked version promised an absolute balance, avowedly to combat inflation.

> *Mr. Pine*: Mr. Secretary, in late January, the President proposed a fiscal 1981 budget that had about a $16 billion deficit, which he said was appropriate for the economic situation we faced and also appropriate politically. Just four weeks after that, the Administration began a major policy review which led to Friday's reversals in budget balancing proposals. That is an awfully short time for a change of policy and I wondered whether the Administration simply misjudged the inflation rate back then a month or two ago or misjudged the political climate of the country or both.

> *Secretary Miller*: I think what we have seen is, since the budget was locked up in December and presented in January, a great deal of change in the conditions that affect the economy.... These changed conditions made it very important that we not just sit on our hands because the risk would be very great if we did, and so we have elected to act and act forcefully....

---

[2]Press conference of Michael W. Blumenthal, Charles L. Schultze, and Thomas B. Lance (mimeograph, The White House, April 14, 1977), pp. 11–12.

Mr. Pierpoint: But do you think that the situation now is going to convince consumers and our countrymen that, in fact, you have got a handle on inflation? Why should we believe you now when your economists have been so wrong in the past?

Secretary Miller: Well, all of the economists have been wrong. I think that we have to recognize that there isn't an econometric model of any type that has been able to predict what has happened because we are living in a regime that we have never had before in America, a period of high inflation rates in peacetime for sustained periods. We have never had them. So we don't know how the economy behaves and we are finding out, sadly, that it behaves toward overdoing it rather than more prudence.[3]

The following sections treat the problem of policy formulation in simple terms: a planner focuses on preselected numerical targets and designs policy in light of them. The case of certainty is considered first. The consequences of uncertainty then evolve from that discussion.[4]

7.1 AN ANALYTICAL FRAMEWORK

The policy maker is presumed to have, in some way, identified specific economic variables which merit close attention. Further, numerical targets for those variables are presumed to have been previously determined. Values of the variables which differ from the target levels are less desirable to the planner, whose hierarchy of preferences may be described by a utility function. This function, known also as a disutility or loss function, assumes the form of a quadratic and involves a weighted sum of the squared deviations of the economic variables from their target levels:

$$U = -h(Y - Y^*)^2 - i(B - B^*)^2 \qquad (7.1)$$

U denotes utility; Y and B denote, say, real income and the real budget deficit, respectively. The deficit in turn consists of the difference between real government expenditures on goods and services G and real net taxes T (taxes minus transfer payments). Stated mathematically, $B = G - T$. Quantities Y and B can be termed "state variables" inasmuch as they measure the state of the economy. Target Y^* might represent some income level associated with a small amount of unemployment, while target B^* might represent a minor budgetary imbalance.

---

[3] *Face the Nation*, CBS News interview with G. William Miller (mimeograph, Washington, D. C., March 16, 1980), pp. 2–4, 6. See also U.S. President, Address on Economic Policy (mimeograph, The White House, March 14, 1980), pp. 1–3.

[4] This exposition embraces four major contributions to the theoretics on policy: those of William Brainard, "Uncertainty and the Effectiveness of Policy," *American Economic Review*, **57** (May 1967), pp. 411–425; Robert A. Mundell, "The Appropriate Use of Monetary and Fiscal Policy for Internal and External Stability," in Warren L. Smith and Ronald L. Teigen, eds., *Readings in Money, National Income, and Stabilization Policy*, rev. ed. (Homewood, Ill.: Richard D. Irwin, Inc., 1970), pp. 611–616; Henri Theil, "Linear Decision Rules for Macrodynamic Policy Problems," in Bert G. Hickman, ed., *Quantitative Planning of Economic Policy* (Washington, D.C.: The Brookings Institution, 1965), pp. 18–41; and J. Tinbergen, *On the Theory of Economic Policy*, Contributions to Economic Analysis, no. I (Amsterdam: North-Holland Publishing Company, 1952), Chapters 1–5.

Unlike Y^*, however, B^* can be positive, zero, or negative. h and i are nonnegative weights reflecting the planner's subjective appraisal of the relative importance of the variables under consideration.

Utility function (7.1) displays several notable properties. First, it restricts the dependent variable to nonpositive values. The maximum value attainable is zero and occurs only when $Y = Y^*$ and $B = B^*$. Second, it manifests symmetry with respect to misses of a target: Y values above Y^* create as much discomfort for the planner as do Y values which fall below Y^* by an equivalent amount. Finally, it has indifference curves shaped like ellipses and centered around the point (B^*, Y^*). This property may be transparent since (7.1) is actually a variant of the general equation describing an ellipse; it can be readily exposed, however, with the aid of the marginal rate of substitution MRS.

For any indifference curve,

$$dU = 0 = \frac{\partial U}{\partial Y} dY + \frac{\partial U}{\partial B} dB$$

Thus,

$$\frac{dY}{dB} = -\text{MRS}$$

where $\text{MRS} = (\partial U/\partial B)/(\partial U/\partial Y)$. Elaborating MRS leaves

$$\frac{dY}{dB} = -\frac{i(B - B^*)}{h(Y - Y^*)}$$

whose sign depends upon the magnitudes of B and Y relative to their target levels. When both exceed the targets or when both fall short of them, dY/dB must be negative. Contrariwise, when B and Y pair a "high" value with a "low" one, it must be positive. It must also be symmetric. Given Y, it assumes the same absolute value for B magnitudes equally above and below the target. Similarly for Y given B.

Figure 7.1 illustrates these indifference curves for function (7.1) restated in terms of U': $U' = -U$. Curve U_1' has a negative slope in quadrants I and III, where Y and B lie on the same side of their target levels. In quadrants II and IV, where the variables lie on opposite sides of the targets, the curve shows a positive

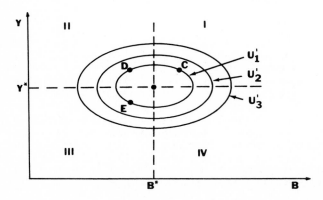

Figure 7.1

slope. Points C and D relate to the same Y value and evidence the same slope except for sign. So too for points D and E, which relate to identical B values. The three ellipses shown obey the relationship $0 < U_1' < U_2' < U_3'$; when $i = h$, they degenerate into circles.[5]

A planner governs state variables indirectly through forces which can be governed directly—through autonomous quantities exemplified by the money supply and the base level of net taxes. Such measures might be referred to as "instruments." Instruments interact with state variables in a manner dictated by the structure of the economy, and that structure may be represented by reduced-form equations. In the spirit of Chapter 2, they are written as

$$Y = \phi + \zeta M_o - \gamma T_o \tag{7.2}$$

and

$$B = \lambda - x\zeta M_o - (1 - x\gamma)T_o \tag{7.3}$$

The planner intends to utilize two instruments: the nominal money supply M_o and the base level of real net taxes T_o. $M_o > 0$ while $T_o < 0$. Equation (7.2) repeats equation (2.14) in simpler terms, and thus $\zeta = [v/(mp_t)]/[1 - c(1 - x) + vk/m] > 0$ and $\gamma = c/[1 - c(1 - x) + vk/m] > 0$. Equation (7.3) arises by first substituting equations (2.3) and (2.5) into the expression for B and then using formula (7.2) to articulate Y. Clearly, $x\zeta > 0$. $1 - x\gamma > 0$, as is easily shown.[6]

The problem facing the policy maker therefore translates into one of a constrained maximum: maximize U with respect to M_o and T_o subject to (7.2) and (7.3). Inserting both constraints into (7.1) gives

$$U = -h[\phi + \zeta M_o - \gamma T_o - Y^*]^2 - i[\lambda - x\zeta M_o - (1 - x\gamma)T_o - B^*]^2$$

Differentiation of U with respect to M_o and T_o produces

$$\frac{\partial U}{\partial M_o} = -2h\zeta Q + 2ix\zeta R$$

and

$$\frac{\partial U}{\partial T_o} = 2h\gamma Q + 2i(1 - x\gamma)R$$

---

[5] Equation (7.1), written in the standard fashion for an ellipse centered around (B^*, Y^*), becomes

$$\frac{(Y - Y^*)^2}{U'/h} + \frac{(B - B^*)^2}{U'/i} = 1$$

If $h > i$ (that is, if the planner gives higher priority to the income target), then the major axis of the ellipse lies parallel to the B axis. The ellipse is long in the B direction and short in the Y direction. The length of the major axis is $2\sqrt{U'/i}$. Larger U', therefore, correspond to ellipses farther away from the center.

Reversing signs in (7.1) flips the utility function into positive numbers, with the maximum for U translating into the minimum for U'. Consequently, problems seeking to maximize U are depicted graphically as trying to attain the lowest U', either the center itself ($U' = 0$) or an ellipse stationed near the center.

[6] $x\gamma = xc/(1 - c + cx + vk/m)$, which can be restated as $1/[1 + (1 - c)/(cx) + vk/(mcx)]$. This fraction must be less than unity, and hence $1 - x\gamma$ must be positive.

where $Q = \phi + \zeta M_o - \gamma T_o - Y^*$ and $R = \lambda - x\zeta M_o - (1 - x\gamma)T_o - B^*$. These partials, when set to zero, occasion, respectively,[7]

$$-h\zeta Q + ix\zeta R = 0 \qquad (7.4)$$

and

$$h\gamma Q + i(1 - x\gamma)R = 0 \qquad (7.5)$$

Solving (7.5) for Q in terms of R and substituting the result into (7.4) generate $R/\gamma = 0$. Obviously, $R = 0$ and $Q = 0$. Thus, for a maximum of U under the constraints,

$$Y^* = \phi + \zeta M_o - \gamma T_o \qquad (7.6)$$

and

$$B^* = \lambda - x\zeta M_o - (1 - x\gamma)T_o \qquad (7.7)$$

which in turn give

$$M_o^* = \frac{(1 - x\gamma)}{\zeta}(Y^* - \phi) - \frac{\gamma}{\zeta}(B^* - \lambda) \qquad (7.8)$$

and

$$T_o^* = -x(Y^* - \phi) - (B^* - \lambda) \qquad (7.9)$$

The optimum values of the instruments—M_o^* and T_o^*—depend upon both targets. Of course, when (7.8) and (7.9) hold, $Y = Y^*$ and $B = B^*$.

Observe that the maximization process posts values for M_o and T_o which are identical to those forthcoming directly from the reduced forms (7.2) and (7.3) after the target values are substituted for the dependent variables. This result means that the planner can maximize utility without any reference to the utility function: simply use the reduced forms to solve for the values of the instruments. The reason for this curiosity is that the instrumental variables do not appear in the utility function. According to that function, the planner has absolutely no concern for the value of the instruments. Only income and the deficit matter, and it is immaterial whether their target levels are achieved with high or low M_o or T_o.

This policy problem lends itself to ready graphical representation. Reduced forms (7.2) and (7.3) may be manipulated to express Y in terms of B, leaving

$$Y = \phi + \frac{\gamma}{1 - x\gamma}(B - \lambda) + \frac{\zeta}{1 - x\gamma}M_o \qquad (7.10)$$

$$Y = \phi - \frac{1}{x}(B - \lambda) - \frac{1}{x}T_o \qquad (7.11)$$

---

[7]The stationary point does identify a maximum. $\partial^2 U/\partial M_o^2 = -2h\zeta^2 - 2i(x\zeta)^2 < 0$ and $\partial^2 U/\partial T_o^2 = -2h\gamma^2 - 2i(1 - x\gamma)^2 < 0$. To show that $(\partial^2 U/\partial M_o^2)(\partial^2 U/\partial T_o^2) > [\partial^2 U/(\partial M_o \partial T_o)]^2$, the latter inequality may be rewritten as $[h\zeta^2 + i(x\zeta)^2][h\gamma^2 + i(1 - x\gamma)^2] > [h\gamma\zeta - i(1 - x\gamma)x\zeta]^2$. Expanding the right-hand side yields negative and positive terms, but the latter all cancel with terms on the left-hand side assuring that the inequality holds.

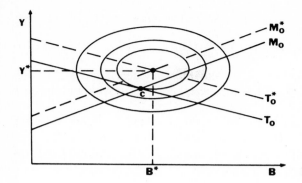

Figure 7.2

Equation (7.10) reveals the combinations of Y and B compatible with a given value of M_o. Equation (7.11) does likewise for T_o. These equations confront the planner's preferences in Figure 7.2, and for arbitrary M_o and T_o values, point C obtains. By raising M_o to M_o^* and lowering T_o to T_o^*, the targets are reached. So is the maximum level of utility, zero.

Thus far the optimization analysis displayed a convenient balance in that the targets and instruments were equal in number. Two equations emerged containing two unknowns: equations (7.4) and (7.5) in M_o and T_o. Equality of targets and instruments may not always occur, however. The number of instruments is largely decided by the structure of the economy and by the existing body of law. The number of targets, however, responds to subjective factors. A planner facing reelection may become concerned about farmers or about the inner cities as the election approaches. Instruments and targets may appear and disappear over time, and at any instant their numbers may be unequal. In what way do unequal numbers affect the solution mechanism?

Consider first the situation where there are more instruments than targets. For concreteness, suppose that $i = 0$ in (7.1), the planner now being concerned only with income. Differentiating U with respect to M_o and T_o yields, respectively,

$$-h\zeta Q = 0 \qquad (7.12)$$

and

$$h\gamma Q = 0 \qquad (7.13)$$

or

$$Y^* = \phi + \zeta M_o - \gamma T_o \qquad (7.14)$$

One equation results, (7.14), containing two unknowns, M_o and T_o.

In this case one instrument is actually redundant. Accepting the current tax level as given, the policy maker merely sets

$$M_o^* = \frac{1}{\zeta}(Y^* - \phi') \qquad (7.15)$$

If the money supply is taken as given, the solution becomes

$$T_o^* = -\frac{1}{\gamma}(Y^* - \phi'') \tag{7.16}$$

In either instance $Y = Y^*$ and $U = 0$. It should be evident from (7.14) that adjustments to both M_o and T_o from existing levels could occur without impeding goal attainment.[8]

If the number of instruments falls below the number of targets, then the targets will generally be missed. The planner retains both goals in (7.1) but now has only one instrument available, the money supply. Differentiation of U leads to

$$-h\zeta Q' + ix\zeta R' = 0 \tag{7.17}$$

where $Q' = \phi' + \zeta M_o - Y^*$ and $R' = \lambda' - x\zeta M_o - B^*$, the first two terms in Q' and R' representing the reduced forms for Y and B, respectively. Equation (7.17) produces that M_o which maximizes U:[9]

$$M_o^* = \frac{h}{h + ix^2}\frac{Y^* - \phi'}{\zeta} + \frac{ix^2}{h + ix^2}\frac{\lambda' - B^*}{x\zeta} \tag{7.18}$$

But inserting this value into the reduced forms for Y and B yields

$$Y = Y^* - \frac{ix}{h + ix^2}\left[x(Y^* - \phi') + (B^* - \lambda')\right] \tag{7.19}$$

and

$$B = B^* - \frac{h}{h + ix^2}\left[x(Y^* - \phi') + (B^* - \lambda')\right] \tag{7.20}$$

Thus $Y \neq Y^*$ and $B \neq B^*$ generally. Unlike the earlier cases where the number of instruments equaled or exceeded the number of targets, the targets are not met.

Figure 7.3 depicts this situation. The equation of the tangent line appears by solving the reduced forms for Y in terms of B; namely,

$$Y = \phi' - \frac{1}{x}(B - \lambda') \tag{7.21}$$

From this formulation it follows that the line cannot be repositioned by changing the value of the instrument. The optimum occurs at point C, and although utility is maximized there, it is restricted to a level below zero. In contrast to earlier situations, the constraints are now effective. If by chance the *targets* were to satisfy equation (7.21), then they would be attained by M_o^* in (7.18) and U would

---

[8]Put differently, equation (7.14) identifies multiple combinations of M_o and T_o leading to $Y = Y^*$. The graph of U against M_o and T_o manifests stationary points over the entire length of the line $\phi + \zeta M_o - \gamma T_o - Y^* = 0$ drawn in the M_o, T_o plane. At each point $U = 0$. Consonant with this functional shape, the test for a maximum in all directions fails. While $\partial^2 U/\partial M_o^2 < 0$ and $\partial^2 U/\partial T_o^2 < 0$ hold, $(\partial^2 U/\partial M_o^2)(\partial^2 U/\partial T_o^2) > [\partial^2 U/(\partial M_o \partial T_o)]^2$ does not. Equality prevails instead.

[9]Since U has M_o as the lone unknown, the second-order condition for a maximum is $\partial^2 U/\partial M_o^2 < 0$. This inequality is satisfied.

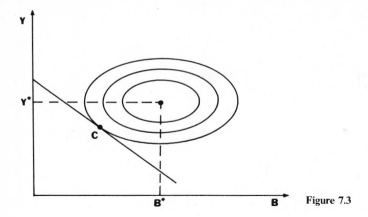

Figure 7.3

be zero. In that case Figure 7.3 would place the "tangent" line over the point (B^*, Y^*). However, since numerical goals involve subjective considerations, their satisfaction of (7.21) would be unlikely.

Failure to achieve the targets can be corrected by amending the dimensionality of the decision problem in order to equalize the number of instruments and state variables. Another instrument might be added to the policy set, for example, by levying a new tax. Alternatively, and perhaps more easily, a goal might be abandoned. The budget target might be forfeited, $i = 0$, thereby collapsing M_o^* in (7.18) to $(Y^* - \phi')/\zeta$ and Y in (7.19) to Y^*. Or the income target might be sacrificed, $h = 0$, forcing M_o^* in (7.18) to $(\lambda' - B^*)/(x\zeta)$ and B in (7.20) to B^*. Abandoning neither target means that the weights $h/(h + ix^2)$ and $ix^2/(h + ix^2)$ in (7.18) are both positive and sum to unity; accordingly, M_o^* lies between the two special solutions.

7.2 PAIRING INSTRUMENTS AND TARGETS

The optimization procedure examined in the previous section for the case of an equal number of targets and instruments determined the value of each instrument needed to attain the target levels for the state variables. That analysis generated the equilibrium solution.

An interesting question which immediately arises relates to the path to be followed in reaching the equilibrium position. It addresses the stability of the solution. If M_o and T_o differ from the values indicated by (7.8) and (7.9), then their values should be changed. But how? Since changes in M_o or T_o affect Y and B, the rule for adjusting the instruments might be couched in terms of their effects on the state variables. The rule, in fact, parallels the law of comparative advantage in international economics. Just as a country should concentrate on (or be paired with) that commodity which it produces relatively more efficiently, so too should an instrument be paired with that state variable on which it exerts the stronger relative effect.

Table 7.1 Multipliers in absolute value

	ΔM_o	ΔT_o
ΔY	ζ	γ
ΔB	$x\zeta$	$1 - x\gamma$

Table 7.1 shows in absolute value the multipliers which appear in the reduced-form equations (7.2) and (7.3). A unit change in the supply of money changes Y by ζ units and B by $x\zeta$ units. A unit change in the tax level changes Y by γ units and B by $1 - x\gamma$ units. The relative effect of M_o on Y is therefore $\zeta/(x\zeta)$, while the relative effect of T_o on Y is $\gamma/(1 - x\gamma)$. Based on comparative advantage, M_o should be paired with Y if its relative effect on Y exceeds T_o's relative effect on Y, that is, if

$$\frac{\zeta}{x\zeta} > \frac{\gamma}{1 - x\gamma}$$

Under this condition T_o should be matched with B. Conversely, if

$$\frac{\zeta}{x\zeta} < \frac{\gamma}{1 - x\gamma}$$

then M_o should be paired with B and T_o with Y.

What is the direction of the inequality? Clearly, the comparison reduces to one between $1/x$ and $1/(1/\gamma - x)$ or, more simply, between x and $1/\gamma - x$. Subtraction gives

$$x - (1/\gamma - x)$$

or

$$2x - \frac{1 - c + cx + vk/m}{c}$$

from the expression for γ. Simplification leaves

$$x - \frac{1 - c + vk/m}{c}$$

which is usually negative.[10] Hence,

$$\frac{1}{x} > \frac{1}{1/\gamma - x}$$

and

$$\frac{\zeta}{x\zeta} > \frac{\gamma}{1 - x\gamma}$$

In adjusting the values of M_o and T_o, M_o should be assigned to Y and T_o to B.

---

[10] This difference is negative, $-.20$, for the parameter estimates presented in equations (2.16)–(2.19).

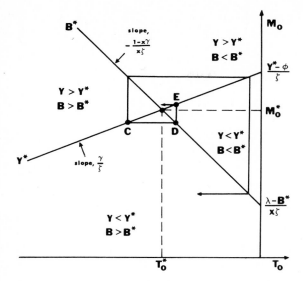

Figure 7.4

This inquiry into the pairing, or assignment, problem may be elaborated with the aid of a graph. The Y^* line in Figure 7.4 shows the combinations of M_o and T_o needed to maintain Y at Y^*; its coordinates are derived by substituting Y^* for Y in reduced form (7.2) and solving for M_o. The B^* line, obtained similarly from (7.3), shows the various combinations of M_o and T_o needed to maintain B at B^*. Intersection of the two lines locates the equilibrium position determined by the earlier optimization procedure. It is easily established that $Y > Y^*$ for points above the Y^* line and that $Y < Y^*$ below the line. $B < B^*$ above the B^* line, while $B > B^*$ below.

The policy maker begins with instrumental values at point C. M_o and T_o are suitable to render $Y = Y^*$, but they leave $B > B^*$. The pairing principle advises that the budget error should be rectified by adjusting the tax level—raising T_o. Point D results. Now, however, Y falls short of its target. This shortfall in income, again by the principle's dictate, should be corrected by monetary policy, with M_o rising and producing point E. Thus, by assigning M_o to Y and T_o to B, the equilibrium position is eventually attained. The cobweb converges. Had the linkage been reversed, with M_o tied to B and T_o to Y, an explosive cobweb would have resulted. The clockwise path demonstrates.

From a pictorial standpoint the solution to the pairing problem depends upon the absolute value of the slopes associated with the target lines. Figure 7.4 reveals the B^* line to be steeper

$$\frac{1 - x\gamma}{x\zeta} > \frac{\gamma}{\zeta}$$

but this circumstance implies the comparative advantage inequality

$$\frac{\zeta}{x\zeta} > \frac{\gamma}{1 - x\gamma}$$

Graphically, what matters for pairing is the slopes.

7.3 INSTRUMENTS AS TARGETS

In situations where the policy maker is totally unconcerned about the magnitudes assumed by the instrumental variables, the utility optimization effort converts to the straightforward task of solving the appropriate reduced-form equations for the instruments, provided, of course, that they are sufficiently plentiful. Planners may be indifferent to the levels of the instruments. On the other hand, they may not always be. Changes in the base tax, for instance, impact households and businesses, and the impacts can be profound particularly on those living in poverty. Planners might also be unwilling to permit the money supply to roam free. In short, planners may have some target levels in mind not only for state variables but also for instrumental variables. Allowing the latter to have target values increases the computational work required to answer the optimization question, but the results forthcoming coincide with intuition.

Repeating the earlier framework, the policy maker concentrates on two state variables, income and the budget deficit, and manipulates two policy instruments, the money supply and the base tax. Now, however, the planner has preferences regarding the values assumed by the instruments. These preferences reflect themselves in the utility function

$$U = -h(Y - Y^*)^2 - i(B - B^*)^2 - j(M_o - M^*)^2 - k(T_o - T^*)^2 \quad (7.22)$$

Like h and i, j and k are nonnegative; M^* and T^* denote the target levels for the money supply and the base tax, respectively. Given this formulation, it becomes clear that the optimization problem does not reduce to an exclusive focus on reduced forms. Even if M_o and T_o were adjusted to make $Y = Y^*$ and $B = B^*$, $U = 0$ would not occur unless by coincidence $M_o = M^*$ and $T_o = T^*$ as well. Introduction of preferences for instruments means that preferences for state variables might have to be sacrificed, and thus it might be anticipated that $Y \neq Y^*$ and $B \neq B^*$ in general.[11]

Inserting the reduced forms (7.2) and (7.3) into the utility function (7.22) gives

$$U = -h[\phi + \zeta M_o - \gamma T_o - Y^*]^2 - i[\lambda - x\zeta M_o - (1 - x\gamma)T_o - B^*]^2$$
$$-j[M_o - M^*]^2 - k[T_o - T^*]^2$$

---

[11]This case bears a close resemblance to the example of two targets and one instrument considered in Section 7.1. As long as there exists a target for a single state variable, the presence of a target for each instrument means that the total number of targets must exceed the total number of instruments. Instruments, therefore, should not be redundant, and targets should be missed.

Differentiating U and locating the stationary point yields[12]

$$h\zeta(Y - Y^*) - ix\zeta(B - B^*) + j(M_o - M^*) = 0$$
$$- h\gamma(Y - Y^*) - i(1 - x\gamma)(B - B^*) + k(T_o - T^*) = 0$$

Eventually tedious algebra produces

$$M_o^* - M^* = \alpha_{MY}(Y^* - Y_{MT}) + \alpha_{MB}(B^* - B_{MT}) \qquad (7.23)$$

and

$$T_o^* - T^* = \alpha_{TY}(Y^* - Y_{MT}) + \alpha_{TB}(B^* - B_{MT}) \qquad (7.24)$$

where

$$\alpha_{MY} = \frac{h\varepsilon}{j\omega}\left[\zeta - \frac{\mu\gamma}{k\eta}\right] \qquad \alpha_{MB} = -\frac{i\varepsilon}{j\omega}\left[x\zeta + \frac{\mu(1 - x\gamma)}{k\eta}\right]$$

$$\alpha_{TY} = \frac{1}{k\eta}[\mu\alpha_{MY} - h\gamma] \qquad \alpha_{TB} = \frac{1}{k\eta}[\mu\alpha_{MB} - i(1 - x\gamma)]$$

$\omega = 1 + h\zeta^2/j + i(x\zeta)^2/j$, $\eta = 1 + h\gamma^2/k + i(1 - x\gamma)^2/k$, $\mu = h\zeta\gamma - ix\zeta(1 - x\gamma)$, and $\varepsilon = 1/[1 - \mu^2/(j\omega k\eta)]$. Y_{MT} and B_{MT} denote the values for Y and B, respectively, under the condition that the instruments assume their target levels; namely,

$$Y_{MT} = \phi + \zeta M^* - \gamma T^* \qquad \text{and} \qquad B_{MT} = \lambda - x\zeta M^* - (1 - x\gamma)T^*$$

Evidently, all the planner's preferences would be satisfied under two provisos: $Y^* = \phi + \zeta M^* - \gamma T^*$ *and* $B^* = \lambda - x\zeta M^* - (1 - x\gamma)T^*$. Then, $M_o^* = M^*$ and $T_o^* = T^*$ in (7.23) and (7.24). It is unlikely, however, that both provisos would be met, and satisfaction of only one would be insufficient to prevent the frustration of goals. When only one condition holds, $M_o^* \neq M^*$ and $T_o^* \neq T^*$.

Since the target levels are likely to be inconsistent with the structure of the economy, it is useful to examine how the planner adjusts the instruments to accommodate that inconsistency. What happens when $Y^* \neq Y_{MT}$ or $B^* \neq B_{MT}$? The answer lies in the signs of the α coefficients. It is possible to demonstrate that

$$\alpha_{MY} > 0 \qquad \alpha_{MB} < 0 \qquad \alpha_{TY} < 0 \qquad \text{and} \qquad \alpha_{TB} < 0$$

Thus when $Y^* > Y_{MT}$, $M_o^* > M^*$ and $T_o^* < T^*$. Should the income target exceed the income value permitted under the target levels of the instruments, both instruments adjust in the expected manner. The money supply rises above its target level while the base tax falls below its target level. Both adjustments exert a stimulative effect on income. When $Y^* < Y_{MT}$, the reverse happens. Departure of the deficit from its target also leads to the expected adjustment. When the desired deficit falls below that resulting from the target levels of the instruments,

---

[12]A maximum does exist at the stationary point since $\partial^2 U/\partial M_o^2 = -2h\zeta^2 - 2i(x\zeta)^2 - 2j < 0$, $\partial^2 U/\partial T_o^2 = -2h\gamma^2 - 2i(1 - x\gamma)^2 - 2k < 0$, and $(\partial^2 U/\partial M_o^2)(\partial^2 U/\partial T_o^2) > [\partial^2 U/(\partial T_o \partial M_o)]^2$. The latter inequality collapses to $[h\zeta^2 + i(x\zeta)^2 + j][h\gamma^2 + i(1 - x\gamma)^2 + k] > [h\gamma\zeta - i(1 - x\gamma)x\zeta]^2$ which, as footnote 7 indicates, must be true.

$B^* < B_{MT}$, the money supply is revised upward—above its target level. So is the level of taxes. The increased money supply increases income and, through an induced increase in taxes, lowers the deficit below what would have resulted under the money target. Similarly, the increase in autonomous taxes raises net tax receipts, thereby lowering the deficit. When $B^* > B_{MT}$, the opposite scenario occurs.

To confirm the previous speculation that $Y \neq Y^*$ and $B \neq B^*$ generally, insert (7.23) and (7.24) into the reduced forms for Y and B, (7.2) and (7.3), and obtain

$$Y = Y_{MT} + [\zeta\alpha_{MY} - \gamma\alpha_{TY}](Y^* - Y_{MT}) + [\zeta\alpha_{MB} - \gamma\alpha_{TB}](B^* - B_{MT})$$

$$B = B_{MT} - [x\zeta\alpha_{MY} + (1 - x\gamma)\alpha_{TY}](Y^* - Y_{MT})$$
$$- [x\zeta\alpha_{MB} + (1 - x\gamma)\alpha_{TB}](B^* - B_{MT})$$

$Y = Y_{MT}$ when $Y^* = Y_{MT}$ and $B^* = B_{MT}$. Under the same conditions $B = B_{MT}$. Consequently, $Y = Y_{MT} = Y^*$ and $B = B_{MT} = B^*$ given compatibility of goals and the economic structure. Failure of compatibility implies that $Y \neq Y^*$ and $B \neq B^*$ generally.

Equations (7.23) and (7.24) admit two special cases deserving mention. Elimination of a state target abridges each equation by the corresponding term. For example, should the planner no longer be concerned about the status of the budget, i becomes zero, as do α_{MB} and α_{TB}. Note, however, that unlike the situation under (7.1) when the instruments outnumber the state targets, neither instrument becomes redundant. Both are used and both have optimum values assigned to them. This result arises simply because the policy maker *is* concerned about the values assumed by the instruments.

If, instead, an instrument is dropped from consideration, then the corresponding equation—(7.23) or (7.24)—vanishes, and the one remaining becomes abbreviated. Should money cease to be an instrument, (7.23) would disappear, as would the terms involving μ in the bracketed expressions for α_{TY} and α_{TB} of (7.24). Similar adjustments occur when taxes vanish as an instrument.

Parameter μ gauges a relative effect. ζ and γ are the absolute-value money and tax multipliers on income, while h is income's weight in the utility function. $x\zeta$ and $1 - x\gamma$ are the absolute-value money and tax multipliers on the budget, while i is the budget's weight in the utility function. Thus μ measures the differential impact on income and budget produced by unit changes in money and taxes, the separate effects weighted to reflect the planner's judgment about the importance of each state variable.

7.4 CONSEQUENCES OF UNCERTAINTY: RANDOM EXOGENOUS VARIABLES

The scene observed by the planner was portrayed as rather tranquil. At the time that a policy decision had to be made, the values for all exogenous variables and parameters were known with certainty, and the job to be undertaken, while not necessarily easy, involved the straightforward manipulation of instruments to attain a position as close as possible to the designated targets. This quiescent setting provided an opportune framework for an introductory examination of policy decisions, but the burden of knowledge which it presumed cannot be borne in actual circumstances.

The reduced-form equations for Y and B, (7.2) and (7.3), capture a host of economic pressures that are changeable. ϕ and λ, for instance, contain autonomous consumption and investment, which respond to numerous factors including severe weather conditions, boycotts, policies of foreign countries, regulations by the domestic government, and even animal spirits. Consequently, a more advanced look at policy decisions should take account of the possibility that exogenous variables—like ϕ and λ—shift randomly through time. A similar argument applies to multipliers. Multipliers—like ζ, $-\gamma$, $-x\zeta$, and $-(1 - x\gamma)$—consist of structural parameters, and those parameters may be affected by external events too.

Uncertainty about exogenous variables and multipliers is intensified because reduced forms are derived from models which, regardless of their sophistication, must involve subjectiveness. The specification of reduced forms, therefore, varies from model to model, and the model chosen to represent the true structure of the economy for policy purposes may in fact do so remotely. Still more confusion comes from the method used to derive values for the exogenous variables and multipliers. The method is estimation, and characteristically, different estimation procedures generate different values for given measures. So do different data sets and different versions of the same set (for example, preliminary versus revised versus rebenchmarked series). The consequences for the estimates may be small; they could be large, however.

There are then several reasons why the planner might not adhere to a premise that everything is known except the values of the instruments. Much is changeable, much is changing, and much is unknown. For clarity of exposition the uncertainty faced by a planner enters the ensuing analysis in stages. It first affects only exogenous variables.

The utility function and the economic constraint are taken to be

$$U = -h(Y - Y^*)^2 \tag{7.25}$$

and

$$Y = \phi' + \zeta M_o \tag{7.26}$$

Convenience dictates a focus narrowed to one state variable and one instrument. ϕ' is random and may be called an innovation. In the presence of this uncertainty, the earlier decision process becomes inappropriate because, if applied to (7.25) and (7.26), it would render M_o^* a function of ϕ'. With ϕ' random, however, the planner would gain only some idea of the optimum M_o; the optimum value itself would remain unknown and random. The decision procedure must be revised, and it must be revised along the lines of mathematical expectation.[13] It now says to maximize the *expected value* of utility subject to the structural constraint.

---

[13] The concept and arithmetic of mathematical expectation are reviewed in Section 12 of Appendix A.

To determine the expected value of utility, write (7.25) via (7.26) as

$$U = -h[\phi' + \zeta M_o - Y^*]^2$$

Expansion yields

$$U = -h[\phi'^2 + 2\zeta M_o\phi' + \zeta^2 M_o^2 - 2Y^*\phi' - 2\zeta M_0 Y^* + Y^{*2}]$$

To this expression mathematical expectation (conditional upon M_o) is applied, leaving

$$EU = -h[\sigma_{\phi'}^2 + (E\phi')^2 + 2\zeta M_o E\phi' + \zeta^2 M_o^2 - 2Y^* E\phi' - 2\zeta M_o Y^* + Y^{*2}]$$

where $E\phi'$ and $\sigma_{\phi'}^2$ denote, respectively, the mean and variance of the ϕ' probability distribution. $\sigma_{\phi'}^2$ surfaces by the addition of zero in the form $(E\phi')^2 - (E\phi')^2$. Differentiating EU with respect to M_o under the assumption that $E\phi'$ and $\sigma_{\phi'}^2$ do not depend upon M_o produces

$$\frac{\partial EU}{\partial M_o} = -2h\zeta[E\phi' + \zeta M_o - Y^*]$$

Consequently,

$$M_o^* = \frac{1}{\zeta}(Y^* - E\phi') \tag{7.27}$$

Equation (7.27) duplicates the result obtainable under certainty with one exception; namely, ϕ' is replaced by its mathematical expectation.[14] Furthermore, in continued analogy with the certainty case, $EY = Y^*$, as insertion of (7.27) into (7.26) and calculation of the expected value reveal. The planner in selecting the optimum level of the instrument expects to hit the target of the state variable.

If the planner expresses an interest in the value of the instrument, then the analysis becomes similar to that in Section 7.3. Specifically, the utility function reads

$$U = -h(Y - Y^*)^2 - j(M_o - M^*)^2$$

whose mathematical expectation is to be maximized subject to (7.26). This expectation is

$$EU = -h[\sigma_{\phi'}^2 + (E\phi')^2 + 2\zeta M_o E\phi' + \zeta^2 M_o^2 - 2Y^* E\phi' - 2\zeta M_o Y^* + Y^{*2}]$$
$$-j[M_o - M^*]^2$$

and eventually

$$M_o^* - M^* = \frac{h\zeta}{j + h\zeta^2}[Y^* - (E\phi' + \zeta M^*)] \tag{7.28}$$

appears. Equation (7.28) can be recognized as the twin of certainty's (7.23) when

---

[14] The comparable certainty case is found in Section 7.1. It entails (7.1) with $i = 0$ and (7.2) expressed as (7.26). Differentiation of U with respect to M_o yields (7.12), Q trivially redefined, and leads to (7.15).

the latter is suitably amended to allow for the details considered here. Those details streamline (7.23) to

$$M_o^* - M^* = \frac{h\zeta}{j + h\zeta^2}\left[Y^* - (\phi' + \zeta M^*)\right] \qquad (7.29)$$

and clearly (7.28) differs from (7.29) only because $E\phi'$ replaces ϕ'. Inserting (7.28) into the reduced form for Y and taking expectation give $EY \neq Y^*$. As under certainty, concern about the level of the instrument leads to some forfeiture of the state target: the planner does not expect to reach the income goal.

Uncertainty regarding an exogenous variable seems to have minor practical consequence for the decision-making process. The planner merely needs to replace the random variable with its expectation and then can proceed as before, treating everything except the instrumental value as known. This replacement phenomenon, referred to as "certainty equivalence," has been elevated to the status of a theorem: decisions under uncertainty are equivalent to decisions under certainty provided that the random elements are replaced by their mathematical expectations.[15] Certainty equivalence does not apply generally, however. It requires particular features of the probability distributions to be unaffected by the policy instruments and, as will be demonstrated shortly, uncertainty to be confined to additive terms. Moreover, it does not survive under all forms of the utility function.

7.5 ENTER UNCERTAINTY REGARDING MULTIPLIERS

When uncertainty attaches to an additive exogenous factor alone, it modifies only the "starting point" of the reduced-form equation. The instrument does not interact with the element contaminated by uncertainty, and the impact of uncertainty remains unaltered by policy action. Circumstances change appreciably when a multiplier becomes contaminated. The instrument then interacts with the random component, and any adjustment in policy strength alters the impact of uncertainty.

The planner endeavors to maximize the mathematical expectation of

$$U = -h(Y - Y^*)^2$$

subject to

$$Y = \phi' + \zeta M_o$$

[15] When policy decisions span several periods and lags pervade the economic structure, differences between the certainty case and the certainty equivalence case become somewhat more pronounced. Under certainty, multiple-period decisions can be made at a single point in time because the outcome for each future period can be accurately determined in advance. Under certainty equivalence, multiple-period decisions are tentative at first and are then revised through time as new information on the random elements develops.

ϕ' *and* ζ are random, and ζ—like ϕ'—may be nicknamed an innovation. Calculating the expectation of U leaves

$$EU = -h\Big[\sigma_{\phi'}^2 + (E\phi')^2 + 2M_o\rho\sigma_{\phi'}\sigma_\zeta + 2M_o E\phi' E\zeta + M_o^2\sigma_\zeta^2$$
$$+ M_o^2(E\zeta)^2 - 2Y^*E\phi' - 2M_o Y^*E\zeta + Y^{*2}\Big] \qquad (7.30)$$

In extracting this equation two covariance relationships are adopted: $\Pi_{\phi'\zeta} = E(\phi'\zeta) - E\phi'E\zeta$ and $\Pi_{\phi'\zeta} = \rho\sigma_{\phi'}\sigma_\zeta$, where $\Pi_{\phi'\zeta}$ denotes the covariance of ϕ' and ζ and where ρ denotes the correlation coefficient for the same two variables. Each σ, of course, represents a standard deviation; each measures the planner's uncertainty about the value to be assumed by the corresponding variable. A larger σ implies more uncertainty, while a zero σ implies certainty.

Under the assumption that selected properties of the ϕ' and ζ probability distributions remain invariant to the policy instrument (an assumption analogous to that used for certainty equivalence), the derivative of EU taken from (7.30) registers as

$$\frac{\partial EU}{\partial M_o} = -2h\Big[\rho\sigma_{\phi'}\sigma_\zeta + E\phi'E\zeta + M_o\sigma_\zeta^2 + M_o(E\zeta)^2 - Y^*E\zeta\Big]$$

making

$$M_o^* = \frac{(Y^* - E\phi')E\zeta - \rho\sigma_{\phi'}\sigma_\zeta}{\sigma_\zeta^2 + (E\zeta)^2} \qquad (7.31)$$

Equation (7.31) bears a similarity to equation (7.27), which was derived under identical conditions save for the uncertain multiplier. Several new terms present themselves, however. A more striking resemblance arises when $\rho = 0$—when the random movements of the exogenous variable and multiplier are unrelated to each other on balance. Then

$$M_o^* = \frac{Y^* - E\phi'}{\sigma_\zeta^2/E\zeta + E\zeta}$$

Rewriting (7.27) to reflect a token substitution produces for certainty equivalence

$$M_o^* = \frac{Y^* - E\phi'}{E\zeta}$$

Since $\sigma_\zeta^2/E\zeta > 0$, it follows that uncertainty regarding the multiplier leads to reduced policy action. Multiplier uncertainty begets conservatism in policy decisions.

This conclusion must be amended somewhat if the random motions of ϕ' and ζ are related on balance. For $\rho > 0$, M_o^* is further reduced below the level dictated by certainty equivalence. Why? When $\rho > 0$, high ζ values tend to be paired with high ϕ' as they disrupt Y. The policy maker attempts to compensate for the effect of these reinforced shocks by reducing the magnitude of policy action. On the other hand, when $\rho < 0$, high ζ tend to be paired with low ϕ', and consequently the random elements themselves diminish their unsettling effect on Y. This inherent offset weakens the conservative bias of policy action, allowing M_o^* to adjust in the direction of its certainty equivalence counterpart.

The timidness bred by an uncertain multiplier is transmitted to the state variable. Here

$$EY = E\phi' + M_o E\zeta \tag{7.32}$$

or with $\rho = 0$

$$EY = E\phi' + \frac{Y^* - E\phi'}{\left(\sigma_\zeta/E\zeta\right)^2 + 1}$$

Under certainty equivalence $EY = Y^*$, which may be expressed as

$$EY = E\phi' + \frac{Y^* - E\phi'}{1}$$

Since $(\sigma_\zeta/E\zeta)^2 > 0$, EY must lie below its value under certainty equivalence. When an uncertain multiplier prevails, the target value is expected to be undershot: $EY < Y^*$.

Several cases of multiplier uncertainty may be usefully explored with the aid of graphics. Since Y is a linear function of two random variables, its reduced form can be worked into

$$\sigma_Y^2 = \sigma_{\phi'}^2 + \sigma_\zeta^2 M_o^2 + 2\rho\sigma_{\phi'}\sigma_\zeta M_o \tag{7.33}$$

From this expression equation (7.30) simplifies to

$$U'' = \sigma_Y^2 + (EY - Y^*)^2 \tag{7.34}$$

$U'' = -EU/h$. Formula (7.34) generates a circle in σ_Y and EY, centered at the point $(0, Y^*)$ and having the radius $\sqrt{U''}$. Figure 7.5 illustrates for $0 < U_1'' < U_2'' < U_3'' < U_4''$.

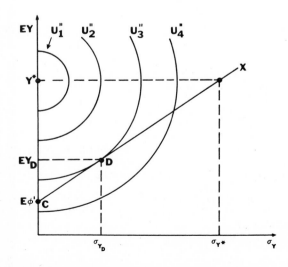

Figure 7.5 *Source*: Brainard, "Uncertainty and Policy," p. 416.

Let $\sigma_{\phi'} = 0$ and $\sigma_\zeta > 0$, meaning that the intercept term in the reduced form is known and that uncertainty affects only the multiplier. Relationship (7.33) then collapses to[16] $\sigma_Y = \sigma_\zeta M_o$. Solving this proportionality for M_o and inserting the result into (7.32) yields

$$EY = E\phi' + \frac{E\zeta}{\sigma_\zeta}\sigma_Y \qquad (7.35)$$

Equation (7.35) describes the X line appearing in Figure 7.5. It has an intercept $E\phi'$ and slope $E\zeta/\sigma_\zeta$. $M_o = 0$ would produce $\sigma_Y = 0$ and $EY = E\phi'$, point C in the figure. Increments to M_o continually raise EY, but they also continually heighten the uncertainty about Y. As can be seen from the figure, the increments first raise and then lower the planner's utility. The optimum policy magnitude, determined by (7.31) with $\sigma_{\phi'} = 0$, is represented by point D. There $EY < Y^*$. While the target is missed, the level of uncertainty associated with the optimum policy is only σ_{Y_D}. Had the policy maker selected a policy level to force $EY = Y^*$, uncertainty would have been σ_{Y^*}. The planner takes a conservative stance and thereby gains some certainty about the value to be assumed by the state variable. Note, from equation (7.35) and Figure 7.5, that as doubt about ζ dissipates, the optimum point rotates counterclockwise, enabling EY to rise and σ_Y to fall. Should $\sigma_\zeta = 0$, then $\sigma_Y = 0$ and $EY = Y = Y^*$. Complete certainty reappears.

Next let $\sigma_{\phi'} > 0$ and $\sigma_\zeta > 0$, but let $\rho = 0$. Both intercept and multiplier involve uncertainty, although their behavior patterns are unrelated on balance. The X line in Figure 7.5 now becomes parabolic, a transformation which is easily shown. From (7.33) $M_o = \pm\sqrt{\sigma_Y^2 - \sigma_{\phi'}^2}/\sigma_\zeta$, and thus (7.32) may be rewritten as

$$EY = E\phi' \pm \frac{E\zeta}{\sigma_\zeta}\sqrt{\sigma_Y^2 - \sigma_{\phi'}^2} \qquad (7.36)$$

Graphing (7.36) produces the X curve in Figure 7.6. $M_o = 0$ corresponds to $\sigma_Y = \sigma_{\phi'}$ and to $EY = E\phi'$; point C illustrates. As M_o increases from zero, the upper portion of the parabola is traversed.[17] Point D represents the optimum

---

[16] This expression verifies a statement made at the beginning of the section: when uncertainty contaminates the multiplier, its impact depends upon the magnitude of policy action. Another statement made there, that the impact of uncertainty remains unaffected by policy when randomness applies only to the additive exogenous factor, is verified by setting $\sigma_\zeta = 0$ in (7.33). Then σ_Y loses all ties to M_o.

[17] A slightly more detailed view of the parabola might be helpful. When $\sigma_Y = \sigma_{\phi'}$, $M_o = 0$. But as σ_Y rises above $\sigma_{\phi'}$, M_o assumes two roots (one positive and one negative), both of which increase in absolute value with σ_Y. Therefore, EY begins at $E\phi'$ for $\sigma_Y = \sigma_{\phi'}$ and then rises and falls around $E\phi'$ as σ_Y increases.

Negative quantities of money are economically meaningless, and regrettably the choice of money as the policy instrument proves awkward in examples of this type. The awkwardness, however, does not impair the analytics. A more propitious choice of instrument for such situations would be the base net tax T_o, since it could be allowed to adopt negative, zero, or positive values. The modifications required to accommodate this switch would be minor.

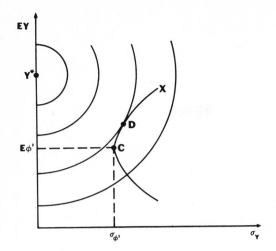

Figure 7.6 *Source*: Brainard, "Uncertainty and Policy," p. 416.

policy magnitude. Again, $EY < Y^*$, but the uncertainty concerning Y is less than that which would have occurred had the planner forced $EY = Y^*$.

Finally, let $\sigma_{\phi'} > 0$, $\sigma_\zeta > 0$, and $\rho \neq 0$. Both intercept and multiplier are random, and their movements tend to be related. The X curve remains parabolic, but now its specific shape depends upon the value of ρ. Equation (7.33) gives $M_o = [-\rho\sigma_{\phi'} \pm \sqrt{\rho^2\sigma_{\phi'}^2 + \sigma_Y^2 - \sigma_{\phi'}^2}\,]/\sigma_\zeta$, and thus from (7.32)

$$EY = E\phi' + \frac{E\zeta}{\sigma_\zeta}\left[-\rho\sigma_{\phi'} \pm \sqrt{\rho^2\sigma_{\phi'}^2 + \sigma_Y^2 - \sigma_{\phi'}^2}\,\right] \qquad (7.37)$$

Consider the case where ρ assumes a small positive value. $M_o = 0$ is again associated with $\sigma_Y = \sigma_{\phi'}$ and with $EY = E\phi'$, but this time it corresponds to a point on the upper portion of the parabola, point C of curve X in Figure 7.7. M_o increasing from zero leads to a movement along this upper segment away from point C. Point D represents the optimum policy level, and as before it calls for the policy maker to move the economy in the direction of the target. This result may not always hold, however. It is possible that the shocks to ϕ' and ζ are so reinforcing in their disruption of Y that the planner's primary concern becomes one of reducing uncertainty. The planner would sacrifice the target altogether and direct the economy *away* from the preselected goal in order to acquire certainty. This possibility departs sharply from the outcome in the comparable certainty or certainty equivalence situation—where instruments remain absent from the preference function and at least match the state targets in number. In those instances the economy is propelled *to* the target: $Y = Y^*$ or $EY = Y^*$. Figure 7.7 portrays the "wrong way" movement with parabola X', which is drawn for a large positive ρ. Point C continues to identify the location of $M_o = 0$, but now the optimum

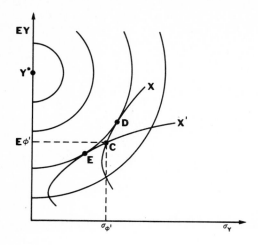

Figure 7.7 *Source*: Brainard, "Uncertainty and Policy," p. 416.

resides at *E*. Clearly, $EY_E < EY_C < Y^*$. The case for $\rho < 0$ proceeds similarly *mutatis mutandis*.[18]

Uncertainty regarding the multiplier leads to another conclusion which differs from that under certainty or certainty equivalence. In Section 7.1 it was shown for the certainty perspective that when instruments do not enter the utility function, their number may be excessive, a condition easily remedied by arbitrary elimination of the extraneous tools. The same conclusion would apply under certainty equivalence. With multiplier uncertainty, however, all instruments would likely be used even if the planner had no preferences for their levels. The logic should be clear intuitively. An uncertain multiplier produces an optimum policy which fails to hit the mark, $EY < Y^*$, and which fails to eliminate uncertainty, $\sigma_Y > 0$. In short, the optimum leaves much room for improvement. The state variable might be brought closer to its target, the degree of uncertainty might be reduced, or both. Additional instruments, some perhaps used in the wrong direction, would enable such improvements to occur.

The nonredundancy of instruments under multiplier uncertainty may be formally demonstrated by redefining the policy problem as one of maximizing the

---

[18]When $\sigma_Y = \sigma_{\phi'}$, $M_o = 0$ and $M_o = -2\rho\sigma_{\phi'}/\sigma_\zeta$. Correspondingly, $EY = E\phi'$ and $EY = E\phi' - 2\rho\sigma_{\phi'}E\zeta/\sigma_\zeta$. For $\rho > 0$, $EY = E\phi'$ must therefore lie on the upper segment of the parabola. This initial position, point C in Figure 7.7, is independent of ρ, and hence it applies to all parabolas drawn for positive ρ.

The vertex of the parabola occurs where EY becomes single valued, namely, where $\sqrt{\rho^2\sigma_{\phi'}^2 + \sigma_Y^2 - \sigma_{\phi'}^2}$ vanishes. Since $\rho^2\sigma_{\phi'}^2 > 0$, this radical expires at some $\sigma_Y < \sigma_{\phi'}$, and at that point $EY = E\phi' - \rho\sigma_{\phi'}E\zeta/\sigma_\zeta$, which for positive ρ lies below $E\phi'$. As ρ assumes more positive values, the vertex falls diagonally. However, since each parabola must pass through C, a larger ρ appears to rotate the upper portion of the curve clockwise through that point. The adjustments required for $\rho < 0$ should be transparent.

mathematical expectation of

$$U = -h(Y - Y^*)^2$$

subject to

$$Y = \phi + \zeta M_o - \gamma T_o$$

where ϕ, ζ, and γ are innovations. By virtue of a now familiar assumption that select features of the probability distributions do not depend upon the policy instruments, the optimization process ultimately provides[19]

$$M_o^* = (\Gamma E\zeta - \Omega E\gamma)\Lambda(Y^* - E\phi) - (\Gamma\rho_{\phi\zeta}\sigma_\zeta - \Omega\rho_{\phi\gamma}\sigma_\gamma)\Lambda\sigma_\phi \qquad (7.38)$$

and

$$T_o^* = (\Omega E\zeta - \Phi E\gamma)\Lambda(Y^* - E\phi) - (\Omega\rho_{\phi\zeta}\sigma_\zeta - \Phi\rho_{\phi\gamma}\sigma_\gamma)\Lambda\sigma_\phi \qquad (7.39)$$

$\Gamma = \sigma_\gamma^2 + (E\gamma)^2$, $\Phi = \sigma_\zeta^2 + (E\zeta)^2$, $\Omega = \rho_{\gamma\zeta}\sigma_\gamma\sigma_\zeta + E\gamma E\zeta$, and $\Lambda = 1/(\Phi\Gamma - \Omega^2)$, with the subscripts of a correlation coefficient ρ indicating the variables to which it applies. According to equations (7.38) and (7.39), both instruments are used; neither is redundant.

7.6 SUMMING UP

Several results have been stressed in this discussion of policy decisions. Given certainty, the targets for state variables are achieved when the instruments do not enter the planner's utility function and when they equal or exceed the targets in number. If instruments outnumber targets, then the extra instruments may be inconsequentially deleted from the policy set. If instruments are outnumbered, then targets are missed. Misses also occur when the instruments enter the planner's utility function. In that circumstance they automatically become outnumbered; none are superfluous.

The pairing of instruments and targets is an aspect of policy decisions which merits the close attention of planners, because pairings formed casually may exacerbate an already unsatisfactory condition of the economy. Some guidance to proper linkage can be gained from international economics; the principle of comparative advantage suggests tying an instrument to a target on the basis of the strength of relative effect.

Uncertainty about exogenous variables can lead to largely the same conclusions as does certainty; the only difference is that mathematical expectations join the formulas in place of those elements made random. This certainty equivalence

---

[19] The stationary point does reveal a maximum. Establishing the validity of the cross-partial condition $(\partial^2 EU/\partial M_o^2)(\partial^2 EU/\partial T_o^2) > [\partial^2 EU/(\partial M_o \, \partial T_o)]^2$ is most easily accomplished by considering only the circumstance most conducive to a failure of the inequality; namely, $\rho_{\gamma\zeta} = 1$. In that case the condition reduces to $(\sigma_\gamma E\zeta - \sigma_\zeta E\gamma)^2 > 0$, which must be true.

theorem does not apply generally, however, and uncertainty with respect to exogenous variables could beget conclusions appreciably at odds with their certainty counterparts.

Uncertainty about multipliers provides results which contrast with those for certainty or certainty equivalence. Policy action may now be less ambitious than otherwise. Targets for state variables are typically missed even when the utility function remains instrument-free, and instruments may be used in seemingly perverse directions. Moreover, all instruments are likely to find service in the pursuit of policy objectives. Redundancy almost ceases to be an issue.

For ease of exposition this discussion has focused on rather simple cases. Increased complexity might lead to a revision or reversal of some conclusions, but it seems clear that for any degree of complexity considered, policy decisions under multiplier uncertainty are characteristically different from those under certainty or certainty equivalence. The interaction between instruments and uncertain multipliers means that policy maneuvers must necessarily influence the impact of uncertainty; hence uncertainty must be an integral factor in the decision process and cannot be lightly dismissed. It is this integral role of uncertainty which makes planners like Charles Schultze and William Miller easy to recognize. They walk with a limp, and they never sit on their hands.

EIGHT

POLICY DISCRETION AND RULES

Is discretion the better part of policy? Should authorities be free to choose the course of policy, or should they be tied to rigid rules of conduct? Are active countercyclical measures superior to a passive posture which cries "Sit on your hands" or "Don't do something, just stand there"[1]? These questions have been hotly debated, and that debate forms the basis of the present chapter.

It may be advisable to observe at the outset that the distinction between discretion and rules is not absolute. A planner who faces no mandated rule for conducting policy would nevertheless adhere to fundamental tenets set forth in economic theory, for to do otherwise would invite economic ruin along with its political repercussions. Conversely, the planner who is instructed to follow a rule may still exercise discretion if only by selecting from some designated menu of possibilities the specific value for a policy instrument or by deciding the exact succession of steps to follow in achieving that value. Discretion typically involves rules, and rules typically involve discretion.[2] The distinction between them is more a matter of emphasis than it is a contention of mutual exclusion.

Throughout what follows, "active countercyclical policy" refers to the manipulation of an instrument with the intent of reducing fluctuations in an endogenous economic series. It may also be called "stabilization policy" or "compensatory policy." "Passivism," by contrast, means that an instrument holds faithfully to a smooth path—be it rising, falling, or constant through time—and that no attempt is made to attenuate fluctuations.

8.1 A CHALLENGE TO FUNCTIONAL FINANCE

The Keynesian revolution of classical thinking established a clear role for active countercyclical policy. To correct unemployment the government could increase spending or decrease taxes, and to correct inflation it could do the reverse.

---

[1] Milton Friedman and Walter W. Heller, *Monetary vs. Fiscal Policy* (New York: W. W. Norton & Company, Inc., 1969), p. 34.
[2] Milton Friedman, *A Program for Monetary Stability* (New York: Fordham University Press, 1959), p. 84.

Reflecting this Keynesian spirit, Abba Lerner in 1941 advanced the principles of functional finance, which held that fiscal policy measures should be judged solely in terms of their effects.[3] These principles struck a blow at the popular belief in "sound finance," whose cornerstone was the postulate of a balanced budget. To Lerner the condition of the budget was an afterthought. What really mattered was the condition of the basic economy, and consequently policy makers should be willing to sacrifice a balanced budget and to switch between deficit and surplus in order to improve economic performance.

Functional finance consists of three propositions. First, the government should use its spending and taxing powers to avoid unemployment and inflation. Second, it should borrow or lend by issuing or retiring bonds to affect the rate of interest and thereby to achieve some desirable level of investment. Third, the government should create or destroy money to accommodate the first two principles. In this schema monetary control clearly has a secondary role; it plays servant to the instruments identified in principles one and two.[4]

At the heart of functional finance lies a macro model in which the effect of policy can be closely controlled and in which any policy error can be quickly corrected. "Doing something" can help without causing irreparable harm, and therefore active countercyclical maneuvers are unquestionably recommended. But do they exhibit such precise control over the economy? Milton Friedman, responding to Lerner in 1947, expressed considerable doubt. He cautioned that delays contaminate policy action. In particular, there exists a lag between the need for action and the recognition of that need, a lag between recognition and the taking of action, and a lag between action and its effect on economic variables. These lags may be long and variable, and consequently they may cause policy to impact at precisely the wrong time. As he noted,

> ... governmental attempts at counteracting cyclical fluctuations through "functional finance" may easily intensify the fluctuations rather than mitigate them. By the time an error is recognized and corrective action taken, the damage may be done, and the corrective action may itself turn into a further error.[5]

Discretionary action to combat cycles was therefore seen by Friedman as an agent of instability. In a 1948 paper he proposed reforming the fiscal and

---

[3] Born under the name "rational public finance" and affectionately nicknamed the "economic steering wheel," functional finance had its rechristening completed by 1943. Its maturation process can be traced through the following sequence of publications by Abba P. Lerner: "Full Employment and Total Democracy," *Social Change* (second quarter 1941), pp. 5–12; "The Economic Steering Wheel or the Story of the People's New Clothes," in *The University Review* (Kansas City, Mo.: University of Kansas City, June 1941), reprinted as Chapter 1 of *Economics of Employment* (New York: McGraw-Hill Book Company, 1951), pp. 7–12; and "Functional Finance and the Federal Debt," *Social Research*, **10** (February 1943), pp. 38–41.

[4] Abba P. Lerner, *The Economics of Control* (New York: The Macmillan Company, 1944), p. 314.

[5] Milton Friedman, "Lerner on the Economics of Control," *Journal of Political Economy*, **55** (October 1947), p. 414. Used by permission of The University of Chicago Press. Composed and printed by The University of Chicago Press, 1947. See also p. 413.

monetary framework of policy to eliminate all discretionary responses to cyclical movements.[6] The plan contained four points, the first of which asserted that the main function of monetary authority was to create money to finance a budget deficit and to destroy it to suit a budget surplus. Under this reform, budget imbalances would be matched dollar for dollar by changes in the money supply, and changes in the money supply could arise only in response to budget imbalances. In conjunction with this tenet, Friedman recommended that reserve requirements be raised to 100 percent, thus eliminating excess reserves and the discretionary management of those reserves. Furthermore, the Federal Reserve System should not engage in open market purchases or sales of securities.

Points two, three, and four of the reform package deal with government spending and taxing powers. They argue that government policies involving expenditures on goods and services, transfer expenditures, and tax receipts should reflect deep-seated community wants and should not be amended to meet the calling of countercyclical pressures. For instance, government purchases should be determined by "the community's desire, need, and willingness to pay for public services." Since that preference would likely change only slowly through time, such a principle would result in a rather stable flow of purchases. Similarly, transfer programs should reflect the level of payment which "the community feels it should and can afford to make." Finally, tax policy should be set to assure that at some full-employment level of output, the budget would balance or would exhibit a slight deficit. The deficit option, coupled with point one, would lead to a secular increase in the money supply.

The thrust of Friedman's program is decidedly long run. While transfer expenditures and tax receipts would respond to cyclical movements in the economy, no policy changes would be permitted for the express purpose of rectifying those movements. The state of the government's budget would change, but it would respond only passively to economic conditions. No deliberate, active change would be tolerated. Therein lies a key difference between the vision of Friedman and that of Lerner. To the latter the budgetary state is the means to an end; to the former it is an end from the means.

Despite its long-run tone, the four-point plan might have favorable short-run consequences. For example, it might temper or offset cyclical fluctuations. However, in Friedman's view its principal merit for the short run is that it would likely cause less harm than would discretionary action. It is less likely to be destabilizing.

A decade after this program debuted, Friedman offered a much simpler scheme which advocated that the money supply grow at a fixed rate through time.[7] The money aggregate which he favored for this constant growth rate rule consisted of currency, demand deposits, and time deposits at commercial banks:

---

[6]Milton Friedman, "A Monetary and Fiscal Framework for Economic Stability," *American Economic Review*, **38** (June 1948), pp. 245–250, 254–255.

[7]Friedman, *A Program*, pp. 89–99. See also his address to the American Economic Association, "The Role of Monetary Policy," *American Economic Review*, **58** (March 1968), p. 16.

succinctly, currency plus all commercial bank deposits. The money construct adopted was not crucial, however, provided that the rate chosen for its growth was set accordingly. The criterion to be followed in determining that rate manifested, as might be expected, a secular orientation: the maintenance of a stable price level in the long run. The "new" quantity theory of money, a sophisticated restatement of the classical view discussed in Chapter 1, contended that the supply of money bore a proportional relationship to money income but added that the proportionality term—the reciprocal of velocity—could vary in a systematic manner.[8] Hence, for prices to remain constant, the money supply should grow at a rate equal to the difference in the growth rates of output and velocity. With M and V denoting the money stock and velocity, respectively, and with P and Y representing price and real income, respectively, $M = PY/V$. Thus, $m = p + y - v$, where the lowercase letters notate the growth rates of the corresponding variables. Price stability, $p = 0$, results when $m = y - v$. For the money aggregate preferred by Friedman, the requisite annual growth rate ranged from 3 to 5 percent.[9]

Should the simple rule allow the money stock to vary seasonally? Friedman saw no strong objection to seasonal variation, but his inclination led him in the opposite direction—to dispensing with it. Hence the constant growth rate rule might be stated thus: The supply of money should grow month by month at that predetermined rate which would assure the maintenance of price stability in the long run. Its rationale was more empirical than theoretical. It would have avoided, Friedman concluded, the major policy mistakes of the past; stated differently, policy action which failed to obey the rule proved to be destabilizing.

---

[8]Milton Friedman, "The Quantity Theory of Money—A Restatement," in Milton Friedman, *Studies in the Quantity Theory of Money* (Chicago: University of Chicago Press, 1956), p. 11.

[9]Precedent for the reforms advanced as the four-point program and for the constant growth rate rule can be found in work by Henry Simons dating back to 1936, the year when Keynesian economics made its formal appearance. Simons decried discretionary action as "utterly inappropriate in the money field" and called for a "definite and simple" rule "clear enough and reasonable enough to provide the basis for a new 'religion of money.'" He espoused a 100 percent policy for required reserves and argued that "the powers of the monetary authority should have to do primarily or exclusively with fiscal arrangements—with the issue and retirement of paper money (open-market operations in government securities) and perhaps with the relation between government revenues and expenditures." Simons considered, as a possible monetary rule, holding the quantity of money constant, although he observed that "once well established and generally accepted... , any one of many different rules (or sets of rules) would probably serve about as well as another." He also suggested pacing monetary action to provide price stability. Friedman's constant growth rate rule may therefore be interpreted as that revision of Simons' zero growth rate rule intended to achieve price stability in the long run. See Henry C. Simons, "Rules versus Authorities in Monetary Policy," *Journal of Political Economy*, **44** (February 1936), pp. 2–3, 4–5, 19–21, 29–30. Quotations used by permission of The University of Chicago Press. Composed and printed by The University of Chicago Press, 1936.

Friedman acknowledges the influence of Simons on his own work and discusses the similarities and differences in their viewpoints in his paper, "The Monetary Theory and Policy of Henry Simons," *Journal of Law and Economics*, **10** (October 1967), pp. 1–4, 6, 12.

It can be demonstrated with the aid of elementary statistics that compensatory policy may destabilize.[10] Let Z_t denote the level of, say, real output at time t in the absence of countercyclical action. Let W_t denote the effect on real output at t of a specified countercyclical measure regardless of its implementation date. Thus W_t may reflect action taken prior to t, at t, or even after t, if the government credibly announces its intentions in advance. Finally, let Y_t represent real output at t under the countercyclical policy. Y_t can be linked to Z_t and W_t additively, and therefore

$$Y_t = Z_t + W_t \qquad (8.1)$$

The temporal evolution of a series may be separated into two components: movement along a trend line and fluctuations around that line. Each variable in equation (8.1) is assumed, for simplicity, to have a horizontal trend, and the magnitude of its fluctuations is taken to be gauged by the variance or, analogously, by the standard deviation. Since Y_t is the sum of two random variables, it follows that

$$\sigma_Y^2 = \sigma_Z^2 + \sigma_W^2 + 2\rho_{ZW}\sigma_Z\sigma_W \qquad (8.2)$$

where σ^2 and σ denote, respectively, the variance and standard deviation of the variable in the subscript. ρ_{ZW} represents the coefficient of correlation for Z_t and W_t, while $\rho_{ZW}\sigma_Z\sigma_W$ can be recognized as their covariance. A greater σ_Y^2 implies greater fluctuations in the Y_t series, and a smaller σ_Y^2 implies smaller fluctuations. σ_Z^2 and σ_W^2 lend themselves to like interpretations, but σ_W^2 has a second meaning. Stronger countercyclical action typically leads to greater policy impact and to larger fluctuations in the W_t series. Hence σ_W^2, and similarly σ_W, serves as an index of the strength of countercyclical action. A greater σ_W^2, or σ_W, indicates a stronger stabilization maneuver and conversely.

The coefficient of correlation for Z_t and W_t ranges from -1 to $+1$. Negative ρ_{ZW} imply that large W_t values tend to associate with small Z_t values, while small W_t's tend to pair with large Z_t's. Positive ρ_{ZW} signal a customary match of either high values for both variables or low values for both. Zero ρ_{ZW} means no systematic pairing of Z_t and W_t. In the present context ρ_{ZW} can be viewed as an index of the timing of policy effects. For countercyclical policy to reduce fluctuations, it should have large impact when output would otherwise be low and small impact when it would otherwise be high. Thus, proper timing for stabilization corresponds to negative ρ_{ZW}. But does proper timing guarantee that countercyclical policy stabilizes? No!

Rewrite equation (8.2) as

$$\frac{\sigma_Y^2}{\sigma_Z^2} = 1 + \frac{\sigma_W^2}{\sigma_Z^2} + 2\rho_{ZW}\frac{\sigma_W}{\sigma_Z} \qquad (8.3)$$

---

[10] Milton Friedman, *Essays in Positive Economics* (Chicago: University of Chicago Press, 1953), pp. 121–126. Material used by permission of The University of Chicago Press. Copyright 1953 by The University of Chicago.

For compensatory policy to be stabilizing, $\sigma_Y^2/\sigma_Z^2 < 1$, or

$$\rho_{ZW} < -\frac{1}{2}\frac{\sigma_W}{\sigma_Z} \tag{8.4}$$

To be stabilizing, policy must have a magnitude geared to the timing of its effects. Even if timing were proper on balance, with $\rho_{ZW} < 0$, policy action might be too strong, causing output to fluctuate more than it would in the absence of policy. For instance, suppose that because of the economy's structure, timing is modestly proper: $\rho_{ZW} = -.20$. Then for an initiative to be stabilizing, its magnitude must be such that σ_W does not exceed 40 percent of σ_Z; namely, $\sigma_W < .40\sigma_Z$. If $\sigma_W > .40\sigma_Z$, then policy would be destabilizing, while if $\sigma_W = .40\sigma_Z$, it would have the same effect as no compensatory action at all.

Notice that if policy has a 50-50 chance of impacting in the proper direction ($\rho_{ZW} = 0$), then inequality (8.4) cannot be satisfied for *any* magnitude of policy, and countercyclical efforts must be destabilizing. Why is policy destabilizing if it carries a 50-50 rating? The answer comes from equation (8.2). Policy influences the system both through its magnitude and through its timing. Its magnitude, σ_W^2, necessarily intensifies the system's volatility, raising σ_Y^2 above σ_Z^2. Timing may increase or decrease instability, or it may be neutral. For a 50-50 action, neutrality prevails, and the destabilizing component of policy applies alone. Timing must be more favorable than the 50-50 risk because only then can countercyclical action hope to offset the instability which it itself adds to the system. Policy must first cancel the instability which it causes before it can address the volatility of the uncorrected series, Z_t. For it to do so, its effects must be in the right direction on balance.

To determine the magnitude of a countercyclical maneuver, authorities may adhere to a criterion of minimizing, rather than merely reducing, fluctuations; formally, they might minimize σ_Y^2 with respect to σ_W. From (8.2)

$$\frac{d\sigma_Y^2}{d\sigma_W} = 2\sigma_W + 2\rho_{ZW}\sigma_Z$$

which when set to zero gives [11]

$$\sigma_W = -\rho_{ZW}\sigma_Z \tag{8.5}$$

Under neutrality the optimum magnitude for countercyclical action is zero, a result which confirms the previous reasoning. Under perverse timing ($\rho_{ZW} > 0$), equation (8.5) cannot be satisfied, and the optimum policy magnitude is again zero.

Equation (8.5) highlights several characteristics of the optimum initiative given proper timing. That action should be designed to yield fluctuations in its impact typically smaller than those which it intends to correct. Concisely, $\sigma_W < \sigma_Z$. Only under perfect timing should policy be made strong enough to

---

[11] The second-order condition for a minimum of σ_Y^2 is satisfied since $d^2\sigma_Y^2/d(\sigma_W)^2$ always exceeds zero.

match fluctuations, $\sigma_W = \sigma_Z$, and under no circumstance should it exceed that critical strength. Furthermore, the worse is the timing, the smaller should be the magnitude of action. Authorities circumvent poorer timing and the greater uncertainty implied for the efficacy of policy by becoming more cautious. Uncertainty breeds conservatism, as Section 7.5 described.

The lesson here should be quite evident. Countercyclical action involves both a magnitude component and a timing component. For policy to be stabilizing, planners must mesh the magnitude component, which they control, with the timing component, which they largely do not. Even if policy impacts in the right direction on balance, it may be too strong, thereby worsening economic conditions. The constant growth rate rule may be preferable to an activist policy because, mathematically, σ_W would then be smaller.[12] Moreover, since this inquiry applies to instruments drawn from either the monetarist or the fiscalist camp, the balanced budget strategy of sound finance may be desirable over the budgetary adjustments prescribed by functional finance.[13]

The argument that countercyclical policy has an inherent destabilization risk has merit. However, it may be stood on its head to support the case for stabilization efforts provided that those efforts are conservative. In terms of equation (8.5), when proper timing prevails, the σ_W of cautious active policy could lead to less output fluctuation than could the smaller σ_W of a purely passive stance. It may therefore be possible to construct active, but conservative, policy rules superior to the lockstep plan of a constant growth rate or of a perpetually

---

[12] Friedman's four-point proposal of 1948 involves some countercyclical budgetary fluctuations, and hence for it $\sigma_W > 0$, his rough estimate being $\sigma_W = \sigma_Z/2$. The possibility therefore arises that the program would be too strong (if $\rho_{ZW} > -.25$). See Friedman, *Essays*, pp. 126–131.

It deserves mention that Friedman does not denounce all countercyclical action; he does advise, however, that such efforts be directed only at large cyclical swings, for which the timing parameter would tend to be within hailing distance of the perfect mark, -1. It is fine tuning, the attempt by authorities to correct modest fluctuations, to which he objects. Elaboration appears in his *Essays*, p. 131, and in Friedman and Heller, *Monetary vs. Fiscal Policy*, pp. 47–49.

[13] As the appellation suggests, a monetarist believes that the stock of money crucially affects economic performance and that it constitutes the government's main policy weapon. By contrast, a fiscalist (or post-Keynesian) contends that government spending and taxation activities are vital and make up the chief instruments. The labels usually do not intend absoluteness. A monetarist can in good conscience hold that fiscal measures affect the economy, and a fiscalist can without shame acknowledge a role for money. The difference in perspectives is typically one of degree, the issue being which instrument matters *more* or *much* rather than which matters *only*.

Monetarism has its roots in the classical school and in the revitalization of classicalism at the University of Chicago. Fiscalism traces back to Keynes and especially to his polar case of depression economics. From these competing traditions come different attitudes about short-run stabilization practices. Confident that the economic system can by itself adjust rather quickly to exogenous shocks, monetarists lean toward passivism. Fiscalists hold that the economy may lack powers necessary for rapid self-correction and hence urge active countercyclical measures. See Leonall Andersen, "The State of the Monetarist Debate," *Federal Reserve Bank of St. Louis Review*, **55** (September 1973), pp. 2–8; Friedman and Heller, *Monetary vs. Fiscal Policy*, pp. 16–17, 46–47, 94–95; Friedman, "Quantity Theory," pp. 3–4; and Kenneth D. Garbade, *Discretionary Control of Aggregate Economic Activity* (Lexington, Mass.: D. C. Heath and Company, 1975), pp. 38–39.

balanced budget. These active rules might permit discretion by giving authorities some license in choosing parameter values. They would nevertheless discipline discretion and eliminate or substantially encumber the ad hoc brand of policy conduct which Friedman challenged with his reform programs. The hot issue of discretion *versus* rules would then cool to the temperate subject of discretion *through* rules, and the operative question would become "Which rule?" rather than "Why rule?"[14]

8.2 FEEDBACK CONTROLS AND THEIR EFFECTS

As countercyclical policy impacts the economic system, it generates information which might be useful for its evaluation and possible reformulation. The new data could be fed back into the planning mechanism, and through this process policy could be continually adapted to the needs of changing economic conditions. Such feedbacks test the direction of the wind and steer stabilization policy into that wind. A passive structure, by contrast, prefers to remain ignorant of new information and steers a fixed course regardless of the wind's direction.

"Feedback controls," known also as "formula flexibility," are often linked to A. W. Phillips, who identified three types.[15] One is a proportional variant and may be written as $\gamma(Y_{t-1} - Y^*)$ with $\gamma < 0$. This feedback determines the current (time t) magnitude of a stimulus policy instrument by citing the latest information on the difference between the actual value of some economic variable Y and the target value for that variable Y^*. Here real output and its temporally fixed full-employment level assume those respective roles. If actual output previously fell below the full-employment mark, then policy stimulus would be increased from some norm. Conversely, if output exceeded its full-employment level, then stimulus would be decreased from the norm. By increasing or decreasing the absolute value of the control parameter γ—by making γ more or less negative— authorities respectively strengthen or weaken the response of policy to the economy's previous behavior.

"Integral control" constitutes the second type of feedback. It relates the magnitude of stimulus policy to the cumulative discrepancy between an endogenous variable and its target level: $\beta\Sigma_i(Y_i - Y^*)$, $\beta < 0$. The summation applies to past periods, but its range can be defined in different ways. For instance, the sum may be written to include a given number of periods n, and consequently i would

---

[14]Further discussion of this point appears in Garbade, *Discretionary Control*, pp. 2–3, 50–51, and in Thomas J. Sargent and Neil Wallace, "Rational Expectations and the Theory of Economic Policy," *Journal of Monetary Economics*, **2** (1976), p. 169.

[15]A. W. Phillips, "Stabilisation Policy in a Closed Economy," *Economic Journal*, **64** (June 1954), pp. 290–305. See also Howard Pack, "Formula Flexibility: A Quantitative Appraisal," in Albert Ando, E. Cary Brown, and Ann F. Friedlaender, eds., *Studies in Economic Stabilization* (Washington, D. C.: The Brookings Institution, 1968), pp. 5–29, 37–38, and A. W. Phillips, "Stabilisation Policy and the Time-Forms of Lagged Responses," *Economic Journal*, **67** (June 1957), pp. 265–277.

run from $t - n$ to $t - 1$. Within the n periods some discrepancies may be positive while others may be negative. If they are negative overall, then the stimulus would be heightened relative to the benchmark; if positive, it would be lessened. Alternatively, the summation might be written in the style of Phillips to include *all* previous periods in which actual output departed from its target. In this case i runs from h to $t - 1$, h denoting a prior period when equilibrium prevailed at the target level. The particular choice for h proves to be immaterial. Since h corresponds to a full-employment stationary state, selection of an earlier or later date would merely mean more or fewer zeros in the summation.

The third feedback mechanism, known as "derivative control," keys counter-cyclical action to the previous change in an endogenous variable. It may be written as $\mu(Y_{t-1} - Y_{t-2})$, $\mu < 0$. If output previously fell, then derivative policy contributes stimulus; if output rose, then the policy vents stimulus. Notice that derivative control is really a negative accelerator. Discussions of the Samuelson-type model in Section 4.3 and of the more general inertial model in Section 6.5 made clear that increasing the acceleration coefficient magnifies volatility. In effect, the simple accelerator acts as a *destabilizing* feedback. The derivative control, by reversing acceleration effects, hopes to diminish volatility.

All three feedback controls influence output's temporal movement, but their exact consequences differ. The proportional apparatus moves equilibrium output toward the target. Actual output, in converging to the equilibrium, is therefore brought closer to the target as well. Integral control defined to include a constant number of periods alters equilibrium like a superproportional policy expanding the control parameter's force by a factor of n. Phillips' integral control has a different effect. Since this version must continually change value as long as actual output remains away from the target level, it assures that if actual output stops changing, it does so at the target. In general, the n-period integral cannot provide that assurance. Proportional and integral controls may impart cyclical fluctuations to actual output; attenuation or elimination of those oscillations results from the derivative control.

The properties of these feedback rules can be further examined with the aid of a simple macro system:

$$C_t = C_o + cYd_t \tag{8.6}$$

$$Yd_t = Y_t - T_t \tag{8.7}$$

$$I_t = I_o \tag{8.8}$$

$$G_t - T_t = \gamma(Y_{t-1} - Y^*) + \beta\Sigma_i(Y_i - Y^*) + \mu(Y_{t-1} - Y_{t-2}) \tag{8.9}$$

$$G_t = G_o \tag{8.10}$$

$$Y_t = C_{t-1} + I_{t-1} + G_{t-1} \tag{8.11}$$

C_t, Yd_t, and I_t denote consumption, disposable income, and investment at time t, respectively. G_t and T_t stand for government purchases and net taxes (taxes minus transfers) at t, respectively; therefore, $G_t - T_t > 0$ signifies a budget deficit, while $G_t - T_t < 0$ connotes a surplus. $G_t - T_t = 0$ means a balanced budget. As before,

Y_t denotes total output at time t, and the constant Y^* identifies output's full-employment level. Furthermore, the summation index i again ranges from $t - n$ to $t - 1$ or from h to $t - 1$ depending upon whether the integral control assumes an n-period form or a Phillips form. C_o, I_o, and G_o represent exogenous magnitudes. All variables refer to reals. With regard to the parameters, $0 < c < 1$, while γ, β, and μ are each nonpositive.[16] The system begins in stationary state with employment being full, and hence $Y^* = [C_o + I_o + (1 - c)G_o]/(1 - c)$.

If countercyclical policy were strictly prohibited ($\gamma = \beta = \mu = 0$), then the budget would always balance consonant with the doctrine of sound finance. For that case, only the multiplier would operate. Should autonomous investment, say, fall and remain at the lower level permanently, actual output would decline unidirectionally from Y^* to a new lower equilibrium, and in the process unemployment would rise. The budget would perpetually stay balanced, but it would do so at the cost of increased unemployment. With active policy the opposite scenario would take place. Budget balance would be sacrificed in an effort to mitigate the employment loss which would otherwise occur. Functional finance would obtain.

Under proportional policy alone, with $\gamma < 0$ and $\beta = \mu = 0$, the stationary-state equilibrium output corresponding to some new level of autonomous investment I'_o becomes

$$Y_E = \frac{H - c\gamma Y^*}{1 - c - c\gamma} \tag{8.12}$$

where $H = C_o + I'_o + (1 - c)G_o$. I'_o may exceed or fall short of the original mark I_o. The effect of proportional policy on equilibrium is judged by the derivative $dY_E/d\gamma$; specifically,

$$\frac{dY_E}{d\gamma} = -\frac{c(1 - c)}{(1 - c - c\gamma)^2}(Y^* - Y_E^-) \tag{8.13}$$

where Y_E^- indicates equilibrium in the absence of countercyclical policy, $Y_E^- = H/(1 - c)$. Obviously, $dY_E/d\gamma \gtrless 0$ as $Y^* \lessgtr Y_E^-$. For instance, if equilibrium output under the new level of autonomous investment lies below the target in the absence of proportional policy, then the application of policy, by reducing γ from zero, must raise the equilibrium toward the target. The converse also holds, and thus applying policy always moves the equilibrium toward the target. Furthermore, since the sign of $dY_E/d\gamma$ remains independent of γ, strengthening policy from any initial magnitude propels the equilibrium in the right direction. From equation (8.12) and l'Hopital's rule, however, it is apparent that only an infinitely strong action, $\gamma = -\infty$, can make the equilibrium coincide with the target.

---

[16]Signs for feedback parameters clearly depend upon the nature of the instrument being controlled. In equation (8.9) the parameters are nonpositive since the instrument is the deficit, an expansionary device. If that equation were reexpressed to explicitly solve for taxes, a contractive agent, then the parameters would become nonnegative. Moreover, as discussion in Section 8.4 will show, control parameters may not all point in the same direction; they may have opposing signs. For convenience, this generalization is ignored in the present section and in the next.

What about the budget deficit under proportional control? With investment permanently changed from I_o to I_o', the stationary-state equilibrium deficit becomes

$$G_t - T_t = \frac{\gamma}{1 - c - c\gamma} \Delta I_o \qquad (8.14)$$

with $\Delta I_o = I_o' - I_o$. A negative ΔI_o implies a budget deficit in equilibrium; a positive ΔI_o implies a surplus. If I_o declined, forcing Y_E^- below Y^*, policy action of a given strength would raise equilibrium output back toward its target, and this movement would occur in conjunction with a budget deficit. The reverse would happen if I_o rose.

Intensifying policy alters the equilibrium deficit. Because

$$\frac{d(G_t - T_t)}{d\gamma} = \frac{1 - c}{(1 - c - c\gamma)^2} \Delta I_o \qquad (8.15)$$

increasing the power of action decreases the equilibrium deficit when the autonomous shock fuels aggregate demand , and it increases the deficit when the shock siphons demand. Specifically, $d(G_t - T_t)/d\gamma \gtreqless 0$ as $\Delta I_o \gtreqless 0$. Infinitely strong policy designed to drive equilibrium output to equality with the target would result in a deficit of $-\Delta I_o/c$, again by l'Hopital.

Figure 8.1 provides a graphical description of the effect of proportional policy. The model initially resides in stationary state at Y^* with the budget balanced. Values for the exogenous variables and parameters come from the estimated equations (2.16) and (2.18) and from the related discussion. In particular, $C_o = 6.90$, $c = .80$, $I_o = 211.75$, and $G_o = 250$. It follows that $Y^* = 1343.25$. At time zero autonomous investment falls by 25 units to 186.75 and remains there forever. Equilibrium output without policy drops to 1218.25, and since only the multiplier process operates, actual output adjusts monotonically to that level. Convergence becomes complete at time 46. Path A illustrates. The degree of unemployment at any point during the adjustment period is measured by the difference between the Y^* and A lines. As noted above, the budget stays balanced throughout the adjustment process; its locus continually coincides with the horizontal axis.

Path B traces the behavior of actual output under proportional policy when the control parameter γ equals $-.20$. The equilibrium rises from the 1218.25 level without policy to 1273.81, to which actual output converges unidirectionally. Adjustment terminates at time 18. Locus C describes the trajectory of actual output under a stronger proportional policy, $\gamma = -.40$. The equilibrium is now stationed closer to the target, at 1295.17, but this more potent maneuver causes some overshooting of that equilibrium. It produces fluctuations when none would have occurred in the absence of countercyclical policy, demonstrating that curative measures themselves may cause a system to experience oscillations. Convergence obtains at time 26. From the standpoint of unemployment, both proportional policies are preferable to sound finance's balanced budget, and the stronger policy is preferable to the weaker one. Neither gives rise to inflationary pressure since neither causes overfull employment, $Y_t > Y^*$.

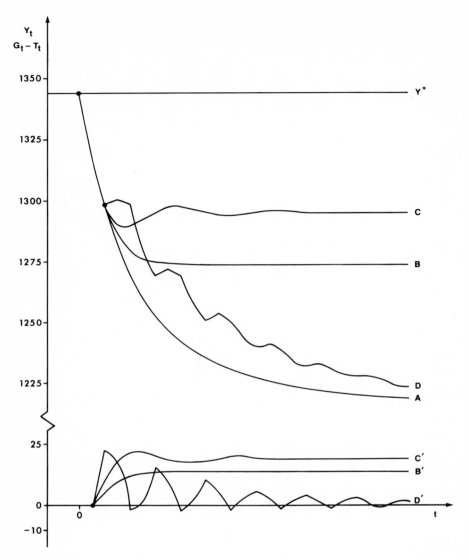

Figure 8.1

Trajectory B′ records the behavior of the budget deficit when $\gamma = -.20$; trajectory C′ does likewise for $\gamma = -.40$. A surplus never occurs, and for the long run the deficit amounts to 13.89 and 19.23, respectively, in accord with equation (8.14).

Proportional policy may not always improve the temporal response of a system, as Table 8.1 reveals for the economic conditions articulated above. UD denotes unidirectional convergence of output to the new equilibrium, while DO

Table 8.1 Pattern of adjustment and time at convergence for system (8.6)–(8.11) when feedback controls are used separately

Control parameter: γ, β, or μ	Proportional	Integral			Derivative
		5-period	10-period	Phillips	
− .10	UD: 39	DO: 139	EO	DO: 210	UD: 57
− .20	UD: 18	EO	EO	DO: > 250	UD: 66
− .30	DO: 23	EO	EO	EO	UD: 73
− .40	DO: 26	EO	EO	EO	UD: 81
− .50	DO: 28	EO	EO	EO	UD: 87
− .60	DO: 38	EO	EO	EO	UD: 94
− .70	DO: 45	EO	EO	EO	UD: 100
− .80	DO: 59	EO	EO	EO	UD: 107
− .90	DO: 81	EO	EO	EO	DO: 122
−1.00	DO: 118	EO	EO	EO	DO: 221
−1.10	DO: 219	EO	EO	EO	DO: > 250
−1.20	DO: > 250	EO	EO	EO	EO
−1.30	EO	EO	EO	EO	EO

and EO designate damped and explosive oscillations, respectively. A number following a colon identifies the time at which convergence occurs; the clock begins at zero, the moment of investment's shock.[17] Notice that as γ becomes more negative, the time required for convergence first decreases and then increases. In addition, output's behavior pattern becomes increasingly more turbulent, and eventually explosive oscillations arise.

Consider next the integral control, $\beta < 0$ and $\gamma = \mu = 0$. Its n-period variant yields a stationary-state equilibrium output of

$$Y_E = \frac{H - c\beta n Y^*}{1 - c - c\beta n} \tag{8.16}$$

Comparison of equations (8.12) and (8.16) indicates that n-period integral policy amends equilibrium like a magnified proportional policy: β equal to only one-nth of γ has the same equilibrium effect as does γ. Differentiating (8.16) with respect to β yields

$$\frac{dY_E}{d\beta} = -\frac{nc(1 - c)}{(1 - c - c\beta n)^2}(Y^* - Y_E^-) \tag{8.17}$$

[17]The pattern of adjustment registered in Table 8.1 and in its analogue, Table 8.2, to be presented shortly, was determined from the output series Y_t. Convergence time, however, came from the budget deficit $G_t - T_t$ because the apparatus used to generate the system's movement listed that series in greater precision than it did output. Rounding errors, which can appreciably affect the choice for convergence date even though they remain inconsequential for a general mapping of adjustment behavior, were kept smaller by using the deficit.

where Y_E^- again notates equilibrium output in the absence of policy, $Y_E^- = H/(1-c)$. Not surprisingly, $dY_E/d\beta \gtreqless 0$ as $Y^* \lesseqgtr Y_E^-$. The application of policy always thrusts the equilibrium toward its target; infinitely strong policy attains the target.

But n-period integral control contains a second policy parameter, namely, n. From equation (8.16)

$$\frac{dY_E}{dn} = -\frac{\beta c(1-c)}{(1-c-c\beta n)^2}(Y^* - Y_E^-)$$ (8.18)

and consequently $dY_E/dn \gtreqless 0$ as $Y^* \gtreqless Y_E^-$. Increasing n necessarily brings Y_E closer to Y^*, and infinitely forceful policy makes $Y_E = Y^*$.

Under the n-period integral, the budget deficit in stationary state amounts to

$$G_t - T_t = \frac{\beta n}{1-c-c\beta n}\Delta I_o$$ (8.19)

Differentiation with respect to the policy levers gives

$$\frac{d(G_t - T_t)}{d\beta} = \frac{n(1-c)}{(1-c-c\beta n)^2}\Delta I_o$$ (8.20)

$$\frac{d(G_t - T_t)}{dn} = \frac{\beta(1-c)}{(1-c-c\beta n)^2}\Delta I_o$$ (8.21)

Here $d(G_t - T_t)/d\beta \gtreqless 0$ as $\Delta I_o \gtreqless 0$, meaning that as autonomous investment assumes a permanently lower level, the application of policy increases the equilibrium budget deficit. Conversely, as autonomous investment assumes a permanently higher level, the application of policy decreases the equilibrium deficit. Since $d(G_t - T_t)/dn \lesseqgtr 0$ as $\Delta I_o \gtreqless 0$, expanding the number of terms encompassed by the summation increases the equilibrium deficit for a permanent decline in investment. Again the converse holds. In short, applying n-period integral policy, which always reduces the gap between the equilibrium and target output levels, increases a deficit if the autonomous shock represents decreased aggregate demand and decreases it if the shock constitutes increased demand. This property applies regardless of which policy parameter is adjusted. For policy of unlimited potency, again manifested through either β or n, $G_t - T_t = -\Delta I_o/c$.

Integral control of the Phillips type, where the summation index stretches over a growing number of terms as the economy adjusts to a perturbation, automatically allows for strengthened policy action until the target is reached and maintained. With this mechanism, equilibrium output under policy must equal the target. Analysis of the proportional and n-period integral controls showed that forcing equilibrium to coincide with the target by means of γ, β, or n would generate an equilibrium budget deficit of $-\Delta I_o/c$. Since that coincidence happens under Phillips' integral, intuition argues that in this case the equilibrium deficit should be $-\Delta I_o/c$. It is.

Integral feedback of either form can quickly become too strong. Table 8.1 indicates that a 5-period integral policy produces damped oscillations and convergence at time 139 when $\beta = -.10$, but for $\beta \leq -.20$ explosive oscillations result. A 10-period integral produces explosive cycles even for $\beta = -.10$. The Phillips integral appears to be only somewhat less volatile, prompting explosive cycles for $\beta \leq -.30$. Integral policy seems to be most exemplary of Friedman's worry that active policy can make matters worse. Leaning against the wind intensifies the storm.

Unlike its cousins, derivative control, $\mu < 0$ and $\gamma = \beta = 0$, has no effect on the stationary-state output and deficit. It does, however, influence the actuals. As Table 8.1 reports, increasing the force of the derivative lever always postpones the time for convergence while causing the response profile to become more unruly.

Path D in Figure 8.1 shows the movement of output under the derivative control when $\mu = -.90$. This trajectory remains above path A except for those periods immediately following the investment shock and, of course, at convergence. In both circumstances coincidence prevails. Path D demonstrates that while a derivative feedback can lessen the employment loss as the economy snakes toward a recessed equilibrium, this gain eventually disappears. The principal intent of the derivative, as recited above, is to diminish cyclical fluctuations caused by the proportional and integral controls or by other forces, such as an accelerator, which might be at work in a system. Path D' traces the behavior of the budget deficit when $\mu = -.90$; a surplus occasionally appears as the budget proceeds to its stationary-state balance.

8.3 FEEDBACKS IN COMBINATION

By combining the three types of feedback controls described in Section 8.2, authorities may be able to take advantage of their separate virtues while disabling their individual vices. Table 8.2 records, for the same economic "givens" underlying the previous table, selected results of changing the control parameters over a grid of values. In Table 8.2, and throughout this section, integral policy refers exclusively to the Phillips variety since it can force attainment of the target, whereas the n-period control generally cannot. Notation of Table 8.1 again applies, but now the damped oscillation prefix DO vanishes to preserve readability. All numerical entries should therefore be interpreted as corresponding to damped oscillatory movement. Convergence, when it occurs, does so at Y^*.

With the integral lever β fixed at $-.30$, decreasing the proportional parameter γ from zero for a given value of the derivative coefficient μ first shortens and then lengthens adjustment time. Decreasing the derivative parameter for a given value of proportionality does likewise in that β regime except when the proportional factor equals $-.10$. Then a continual shortening of adjustment time results. With the proportional parameter set at $-.30$ and with the integral factor free to vary subject to any particular derivative value, convergence time again follows a "U" pattern, with minor aberrations occurring for μ levels of $-.60$ and $-.70$. The U also emerges from variations in the derivative parameter when the integral factor holds steady at any value save $-.10$. In that case, only the right-hand segment of the U arises.

Several findings summarized in Table 8.2 bear on the merits of feedback policy relative to those of passivism. First, parameter combinations for the

Table 8.2 Pattern of adjustment and time at convergence for system (8.6)–(8.11) when feedback controls are used jointly

		Derivative control parameter, μ								
γ	β	0.0	−.10	−.20	−.30	−.40	−.50	−.60	−.70	−.80
−.10	−.30	> 250	> 250	> 250	222	195	175	167	164	162
−.20	−.30	> 250	194	148	124	117	114	113	111	122
−.30	−.30	168	115	92	82	80	79	83	93	169
−.40	−.30	123	78	59	55	55	59	81	132	> 250
−.50	−.30	110	67	33	36	52	73	114	233	> 250
−.60	−.30	122	76	56	57	73	108	200	> 250	EO
−.70	−.30	165	109	89	92	122	204	> 250	EO	EO
−.30	−.05	104	99	95	88	79	75	78	93	157
−.30	−.10	33	46	50	63	66	71	74	91	155
−.30	−.20	76	68	63	68	72	76	80	93	161
−.30	−.30	168	115	92	82	80	79	83	93	169
−.30	−.40	> 250	> 250	153	109	93	87	82	95	177
−.30	−.50	EO	EO	> 250	193	122	95	86	98	186
−.30	−.60	EO	EO	EO	> 250	216	121	93	99	203

feedback controls can be found which improve economic performance, perhaps substantially, over that associated with the passive posture of an unrelenting balanced budget, $\gamma = \beta = \mu = 0$. For instance, the coefficient trios of $\gamma = -.50$, $\beta = -.30$, and $\mu = -.20$ and of $\gamma = -.30$, $\beta = -.10$, and $\mu = 0$ enable a return of actual output to its target at time 33. Figure 8.2 illustrates. Curve B represents the former combination while curve C represents the latter; primes mark the corresponding trajectories for the budget deficit, whose stationary-state value equals 31.25. Path A repeats the output scenario tracked in Figure 8.1 for a perpetually balanced budget, albeit now the locus is abbreviated for graphical convenience. Both output paths with countercyclical policy evidence some inflationary pressure on their way back to the long-run full-employment mark, but despite this "unfavorable" aspect of the adjustment processes, it seems safe to conclude that paths B and C are preferable to sound finance's A. Functional finance proves to be superior.

Second, multiple combinations of policy coefficients can give rise to roughly the same type of movement. Table 8.2 notes, for example, that 4 parameter groupings generate damped oscillatory returns to the target with convergence times ranging from 50 to 55 while 8 groupings do so with times ranging from 50 to 60. Policy makers thus have some latitude in using their feedback controls to achieve a particular end. However, as Figure 8.2 advises, similar return paths may exhibit differences of importance to authorities. Relative to path C, configuration B reveals smaller employment losses in the short run at the expense of inflationary pressure and a greater budget deficit. A planner with considerable aversion toward unemployment but with little compunction about inflation would likely select B over C. Another planner might have the reverse preference and opt for C,

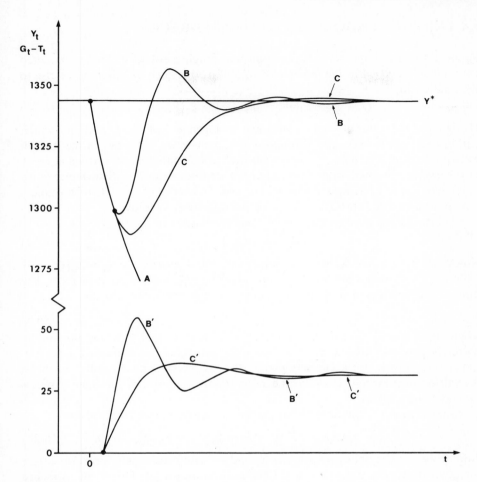

Figure 8.2

while a third may be indifferent between alternatives. The final choice of path and, more basically, the determination of policy mix would depend upon the operative preference function, a conclusion which agrees with the discussion in Chapter 7.

Third, as the EO entries in Table 8.2 attest, feedbacks can be destabilizing; "too much" *is* possible. This possibility, however, resembles more a qualification than an indictment. Feedbacks can dramatically improve economic performance, and this improvement can be obtained by cautious assignment of parameter values. The ability of countercyclical action to worsen the storm may be interpreted as an ever-present warning to planners to be conservative in setting the values of policy coefficients.

8.4 FURTHER ENDORSEMENT OF FEEDBACKS

Support for an active stabilization policy through feedbacks can be extracted from models steeped in the monetarist tradition. One such paradigm gives rise to the relationship[18]

$$Q_t = \xi_0 + \xi_1(m_t - m_{t-1,t}) + \xi_2 Q_{t-1} + u_t \qquad (8.22)$$

Q_t denotes the value at time t of some endogenous, or state, variable which authorities plan to influence through policy maneuvers. m_t signifies the growth rate of money at t, and $m_{t-1,t}$ represents the public's anticipation formed at $t - 1$ of the monetary growth rate to prevail at t. u_t denotes a random disturbance (alias "innovation") at t having a mean of zero and a variance of σ_u^2. The disturbances remain uncorrelated through time. All ξ parameters are positive.

Policy makers observe the proportional feedback rule

$$m_t = \lambda_1 + \lambda_2 Q_{t-1} \qquad (8.23)$$

which has $\lambda_1 > 0$ and $\lambda_2 < 0$ and which may be rewritten as $m_t = \lambda_2[Q_{t-1} - (-\lambda_1/\lambda_2)]$ to reveal a proportional control of the type seen in equation (8.9). The public's expectation of subsequent monetary action obeys the schema

$$m_{t-1,t} = \delta_1 + \delta_2 Q_{t-1} \qquad (8.24)$$

where $\delta_1 > 0$ and $\delta_2 < 0$. However, $\delta_1 \neq \lambda_1$ and $\delta_2 \neq \lambda_2$. While the public correctly perceives that monetary authorities set policy according to a proportional rule, it does not accurately perceive the parameters of the policy formula. As will become evident in the next section, the assumption of mistaken expectations is hardly trivial.

Substitution of equations (8.23) and (8.24) into equation (8.22) leaves

$$Q_t = [\xi_0 + \xi_1(\lambda_1 - \delta_1)] + [\xi_2 + \xi_1(\lambda_2 - \delta_2)]Q_{t-1} + u_t \qquad (8.25)$$

Authorities fix the policy parameters λ_1 and λ_2 with eyes trained on some target for Q_t in stationary state, that target being the constant Q^*. Due to the presence of random noise u_t, however, stationary state must now be defined not as the temporal constancy of an endogenous variable but rather as the temporal constancy of its probability distributions.[19] Hence stationary state now connotes $EQ_t = EQ_{t-1} = \ldots$ and $E(Q_t - EQ_t)^2 = E(Q_{t-1} - EQ_{t-1})^2 = \ldots$. Taking the

---

[18] The following system represents an adaptation of one of the models presented in Sargent and Wallace, "Rational Expectations and Policy," pp. 169–172. It is extended in Section 8.5.

[19] A stochastic time series which exhibits unchanging probability distributions is commonly said to be in "stochastic steady state." The label "stationary state" seems to be apt here, however, because it continues terminology used thus far in this volume to reference time-invariant equilibria and because it avoids possible confusion with the notion of deterministic steady state, the steady *growth* of a nonstochastic time series, to be encountered in Part 5. See Gregory C. Chow, *Analysis and Control of Dynamic Economic Systems* (New York: John Wiley & Sons, Inc., 1975), pp. 40–43, and Michael R. Darby, *Macroeconomics: The Theory of Income, Employment, and the Price Level* (New York: McGraw-Hill Book Company, 1976), p. 112.

expectation of Q_t in equation (8.25) occasions

$$EQ_t = [\xi_0 + \xi_1(\lambda_1 - \delta_1)] + [\xi_2 + \xi_1(\lambda_2 - \delta_2)] EQ_{t-1} \qquad (8.26)$$

since $Eu_t = 0$. With $EQ_t = EQ_{t-1} = Q^*$, equation (8.26) implies that

$$Q^* = \frac{\xi_0 + \xi_1(\lambda_1 - \delta_1)}{1 - [\xi_2 + \xi_1(\lambda_2 - \delta_2)]} \qquad (8.27)$$

Officials may also desire to minimize the variance of the endogenous variable around its target in stationary state. From (8.25) and (8.26) the variance of Q_t becomes

$$E(Q_t - EQ_t)^2 = [\xi_2 + \xi_1(\lambda_2 - \delta_2)]^2 E(Q_{t-1} - EQ_{t-1})^2 + Eu_t^2 \qquad (8.28)$$

and therefore[20]

$$\sigma_Q^2 = \frac{\sigma_u^2}{1 - [\xi_2 + \xi_1(\lambda_2 - \delta_2)]^2} \qquad (8.29)$$

where σ_Q^2 denotes the stationary-state variance of Q_t around Q^*. According to equation (8.29) planners minimize σ_Q^2 by forcing the bracketed term to zero: specifically, by setting $\lambda_2 = \lambda_2^*$ with

$$\lambda_2^* = \delta_2 - \frac{\xi_2}{\xi_1} \qquad (8.30)$$

Then $\sigma_Q^2 = \sigma_u^2$. Inserting λ_2^* into equation (8.27) determines the optimum value of λ_1:

$$\lambda_1^* = \delta_1 + \frac{Q^* - \xi_0}{\xi_1} \qquad (8.31)$$

This combination of λ_1 and λ_2 guarantees for stationary state that Q_t equals the target level Q^* except for noise and that it fluctuates around this target to the minimum extent possible.[21]

How do these results for the feedback mechanism (8.23) compare with those obtainable under the constant growth rate rule? In the present context that rule corresponds to the assignment $\lambda_2 = 0$, because then $m_t = \lambda_1$ from (8.23). With $\lambda_2 = 0$, Q^* still can be attained on average provided that authorities set λ_1 at

$$\lambda_1^{**} = \delta_1 + \frac{Q^*(1 - \xi_2 + \xi_1\delta_2) - \xi_0}{\xi_1} \qquad (8.32)$$

---

[20]An elegant derivation of equations (8.27) and (8.29) can be found in Chow, *Analysis and Control*, pp. 40–42. His equation (1) exactly matches equation (8.25) above.

[21]Notice that for authorities to set λ_1 and λ_2 optimally, they must be informed about the parameters of the public's anticipation function: authorities know the public's expectation formula even though the public does not know the authorities' policy formula. Learning on the part of the public is treated anon.

as equation (8.27) dictates. Thus, under Friedman's criterion authorities retain control over the mean; they relinquish it, however, over the variance.[22] When $\lambda_2 = 0$, equation (8.29) becomes

$$\sigma_Q^2 = \frac{\sigma_u^2}{1 - (\xi_2 - \xi_1\delta_2)^2} \tag{8.33}$$

which involves no policy parameters. Planners forfeit all ability to dampen the fluctuations of the endogenous variable.

This inferiority of the constant growth rate rule to the proportional feedback control (8.23) can be demonstrated graphically. Figure 8.3 sketches σ_Q^2 against λ_2 using equation (8.29). Clearly, σ_Q^2 is parabolic around $\lambda_2 = \lambda_2^*$, becoming infinite at $\lambda_2^* \pm 1/\xi_1$. For $\lambda_2 = 0$, σ_Q^2 comes from equation (8.33).[23] Observe that for *any* value of λ_2 between zero and $2\lambda_2^*$, the variance of Q_t falls below that associated with the constant growth rate rule. Policy makers have a range of strategies over which countercyclical action proves to be more stabilizing than the monetary lockstep. Outside that range, of course, the feedback would be destabilizing relative to Friedman's mechanism, but again this property only qualifies the central conclusion. Feedback policy, applied cautiously, is superior to the passivism of lockstep.

A similar proposition emerges from a model which involves both proportional and derivative feedback controls.[24] The equation for the endogenous variable reads

$$q_t = \eta q_{t-1} + \sum_{i=0}^{\infty} \xi_i x_{t-i} + u_t \tag{8.34}$$

q_t refers to the deviation at time t of a state variable Q_t from its target level Q_t^*, and x_t notates the deviation at t of some policy instrument X_t, either monetary or fiscal, from that level X_t^* which would keep the system at target in the absence of noise. The random disturbance u_t maintains the properties described in connection with equation (8.22). Moreover, $0 < \eta < 1$, and the nonnegative ξ_i follow a Pascal distribution, a special case of which is the Koyck lag configuration. One parameter in the Pascal can be treated as measuring the length of the policy lag, since the mean lag of the instrument's effect on the state variable changes directly with it. Denote that parameter by α. A larger α signifies that a policy action

---

[22] For a more general statement of the relationship between the means and variances of endogenous variables and the intercepts and slopes in proportional feedback controls, see Chow, *Analysis and Control*, pp. 166, 208.

[23] Equation (8.29) can be rewritten as $[\lambda_2 - (\delta_2 - \xi_2/\xi_1)]^2 = -\xi_1^{-2}(\sigma_u^2/\sigma_Q^2 - 1)$, which corresponds to a parabola in λ_2 and σ_u^2/σ_Q^2. Its axis of symmetry locates at $\lambda_2 = \delta_2 - \xi_2/\xi_1$; its directrix, at $\sigma_u^2/\sigma_Q^2 = 1 + .25\xi_1^{-2}$. Focal and vertex points have $(\lambda_2, \sigma_u^2/\sigma_Q^2)$ coordinates of $(\delta_2 - \xi_2/\xi_1, 1 - .25\xi_1^{-2})$ and $(\delta_2 - \xi_2/\xi_1, 1)$, respectively, the latter confirming λ_2^* in equation (8.30) as the site of the minimum σ_Q^2 and σ_u^2 as that minimum.

[24] Stanley Fischer and J. Phillip Cooper, "Stabilization Policy and Lags," *Journal of Political Economy*, **81** (July/August 1973), pp. 847–877. Material used by permission of The University of Chicago Press. © 1973 by The University of Chicago.

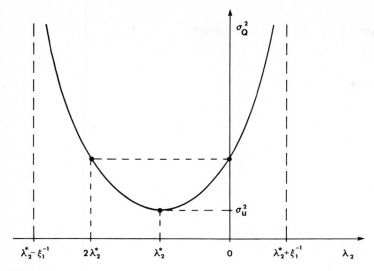

Figure 8.3

experiences a longer delay before the "bulk" of its impact reaches the system; conversely, a smaller α means that a shorter delay is experienced.[25]

Policy variable x_t obeys the rule

$$x_t = \phi_1 q_{t-1} + \phi_2(q_{t-1} - q_{t-2}) \tag{8.35}$$

which may be written more fully as

$$X_t - X_t^* = \phi_1[Q_{t-1} - Q_{t-1}^*] + \phi_2[(Q_{t-1} - Q_{t-1}^*) - (Q_{t-2} - Q_{t-2}^*)] \tag{8.36}$$

---

[25] The Pascal distribution generates weights according to the expression

$$\zeta_i = \omega\{(\nu + i - 1)!/[(\nu - 1)!\,i!]\}(1 - \alpha)^\nu \alpha^i$$

$i = 0, 1, 2, 3,$ and so forth. ω, α, and ν are parameters with $\omega > 0$ and $0 < \alpha < 1$; ν is some positive integer. When $\nu = 1$, the weights become $\zeta_0 = \omega(1 - \alpha)$, $\zeta_1 = \omega(1 - \alpha)\alpha$, $\zeta_2 = \omega(1 - \alpha)\alpha^2$, $\zeta_3 = \omega(1 - \alpha)\alpha^3, \ldots$ in the tradition of Koyck. When $\nu = 2$, they become $\zeta_0 = \omega(1 - \alpha)^2$, $\zeta_1 = 2\omega(1 - \alpha)^2\alpha$, $\zeta_2 = 3\omega(1 - \alpha)^2\alpha^2$, $\zeta_3 = 4\omega(1 - \alpha)^2\alpha^3, \ldots$. In that case the weights may rise to a maximum before declining to zero: they may traverse an inverted "V." Parameter ω, which serves to adjust the sum of the weights, equals $1 - \eta$ for the problem at hand. Mapped against the order of lag i, the weight coefficients of a distributed lag beget a function resembling a probability distribution, whose mean is known as the "mean lag." The mean lag takes the form of a value for i, but it need not be an integer. In regard to the Pascal for ζ_i, it equals $\nu\alpha/(1 - \alpha)$. Further discussions of the Pascal and of mean lags appear in Fischer and Cooper, "Stabilization Policy," pp. 852–854, 873–874; Robert S. Pindyck and Daniel L. Rubinfeld, *Econometric Models and Economic Forecasts* (New York: McGraw-Hill Book Company, 1976), p. 213; Robert M. Solow, "On a Family of Lag Distributions," *Econometrica*, **28** (April 1960), pp. 394–397; and Henri Theil, *Principles of Econometrics* (New York: John Wiley & Sons, Inc., 1971), pp. 264–266. A review of the Koyck distribution appears in footnote 39 of Chapter 5 of the present text.

The proportional feedback component essentially duplicates that in equation (8.9). The derivative component, however, concentrates on the change in error rather than on the change in level. Its construction is more general than the one envisioned in (8.9) and reduces to the earlier format if the target remains stationary through time.[26] When $\phi_1 = \phi_2 = 0$, $x_t = 0$ or, equivalently, $X_t = X_t^*$, and the instrument follows a predetermined path without deviation regardless of the economy's condition. This situation describes the passivism of either Friedman's constant growth rate rule for the money stock or sound finance's edict of a balanced budget.

Authorities select the values for ϕ_1 and ϕ_2, and they do so in accordance with the principle advanced earlier—by minimizing the long-run variance of q_t. The solution to this puzzle appears in Figure 8.4, which presumes that $\eta = .5$ and $\alpha = .8$ and that a Koyck weight profile applies. The locus drawn identifies those combinations of ϕ_1 and ϕ_2 which generate a q_t variance equal to that associated with passivism. Any point outside this isovariance ellipse corresponds to a variance larger than that obtainable on it, while any point within the ellipse identifies a variance smaller than that on it. Point A marks the minimum-variance strategy. Of particular importance for the present discussion is the observation that countercyclical policy remains superior to passivism over a grid of parameter values. Even if one feedback coefficient became positive, that superiority could persist, a characteristic which implies that a stabilization package need not have all its feedback elements operating in the same direction to be effective. Some may actually be procyclical. Again, while active stabilization policy can be inferior to passivism, *cautious* countercyclical action must be superior.

This conclusion continues to hold even when long and variable policy lags, the root cause of Friedman's refusal to test the wind, are considered. The isovariance locus retains its basic shape, passing through the origin and embracing some positive values of either (but not both) of the feedback coefficients. The area within the ellipse shrinks, but more importantly it does not shrink to zero. Therefore, while authorities lose options for compensatory policy, they can still select a feedback strategy which produces fluctuations in q_t smaller than those associated with a lockstep plan.

The proportional control embedded in equation (8.36) may be generalized to encompass r instruments and s state variables:

$$X_{jt} = X_{jt}^* + \sum_{k=1}^{s} \phi_{jkt}(Q_{k,t-1} - Q_{k,t-1}^*) \tag{8.37}$$

$j = 1, 2, \ldots, r$. This equation arises formally from a two-step optimization procedure in which planners minimize disutility, or loss, functions subject to constraints imposed by the economy's structure. The target magnitudes for the instrument and state variables evidence certainty equivalence, while the policy parameters, which may vary through time, reflect both the structure of the

[26]Pack, "Formula Flexibility," pp. 14–15.

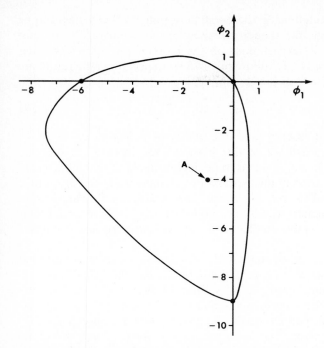

Figure 8.4 *Source*: Fischer and Cooper, "Stabilization Policy," p. 860.

economy and the priorities of the planners, a property consistent with discussion in Chapter 7. This general formulation of proportional feedbacks leads to the same findings deduced from equations (8.34) and (8.35): namely, that cautious countercyclical policy is superior to a passive stand ($\phi_{jkt} = 0$ for all j, k, and t) and that a stabilization program preferable to lockstep may contain both pro-cyclical and countercyclical forces simultaneously.[27]

8.5 RATIONAL EXPECTATIONS: COMPLETING THE CIRCLE?

Arguments reviewed in the two preceding sections cogently support active feedback policy over a passive stance. In fact, they are so forceful that it is difficult to imagine how they could be successfully attacked. Difficult, that is, until the issue of expectations rears its head.

---

[27]See Kenneth D. Garbade, "Economic Stabilization in the Presence of Limited Discretion," *Southern Economic Journal*, **43** (January 1977), pp. 1243–1259. Also see his *Discretionary Control*, pp. 46–54, 158–180. Chow conducts a similar inquiry in *Analysis and Control*, pp. 152–160, 163–166, 289–295. Furthermore, using a small estimated macroeconomic model, he studies the countercyclical effects of varying the money supply and government purchases when both instruments follow the proportional feedback rule and, alternatively, when both follow the constant growth rate rule. Feedbacks prove to be markedly superior. Chow, *Analysis and Control*, pp. 100–104, 203–220.

The importance of expectations to the question of policy effectiveness can be brought to the fore through the model premised on equation (8.22). In that paradigm the public forms its expectations on the basis of formula (8.24) even though policy makers unswervingly follow rule (8.23). Expectations therefore are always incorrect, the magnitude of bias being

$$m_{t-1,t} - m_t = (\delta_1 - \lambda_1) + (\delta_2 - \lambda_2)Q_{t-1} \qquad (8.38)$$

As equations (8.22) and (8.25) reveal, the ability of policy to influence Q_t depends entirely upon the existence of this bias; yet the implication that the public never learns from its mistakes seems to be unreasonable. If the public erred in its anticipations, it might modify the expectation mechanism, δ_1 and δ_2, until it "guessed right." In that event the policy parameters λ_1 and λ_2 would vanish from (8.25), and countercyclical action would have no effect on Q_t. There would then be little reason to argue for active feedbacks or, equivalently, for any departure from passivism.

The notion that the public enjoys unbiased expectations is known as "rational expectations." In introducing this concept, John Muth remarked that "expectations, since they are informed predictions of future events, are essentially the same as the predictions of the relevant economic theory." Rational expectations are those psychological anticipations which duplicate mathematical expectation; they exhibit no systematic error.[28] In a deterministic context, where the anticipated and true policy magnitudes involve no random elements, rational expectations become synonymous with perfect foresight, the continually accurate forecast of future actual values. Equations (8.23) and (8.24), if the latter were understood to have λ_1 and λ_2 replace δ_1 and δ_2, respectively, would exemplify that synonymity.[29] They would be identical.

Rational expectations cast a pall over active feedback policy and simultaneously breathe new life into passivism generally and into the constant growth rate rule particularly. However, the reason for the resurrection of Friedman's lockstep differs from the cause of its birth. The argument then held that less harm would have occurred by the rule than by activism. That argument was empirical.

---

[28]John F. Muth, "Rational Expectations and the Theory of Price Movements," *Econometrica*, **29** (July 1961), p. 316, and Brian Kantor, "Rational Expectations and Economic Thought," *Journal of Economic Literature*, **17** (December 1979), p. 1425.

[29]Edmund Phelps equates rational expectations with perfect foresight, while Sargent and Wallace sever the two concepts by introducing a stochastic error term having zero mean into their counterpart of equation (8.23). For them rational expectations correspond to the mathematical expectation of that randomized feedback control. See Edmund S. Phelps, "Obstacles to Curtailing Inflation," in James H. Gapinski and Charles E. Rockwood, eds., *Essays in Post-Keynesian Inflation* (Cambridge, Mass.: Ballinger Publishing Company, 1979), p. 189, and Sargent and Wallace, "Rational Expectations and Policy," pp. 173–175.

Perfect foresight receives much attention in the literature on putty-clay capital, a subject to be addressed in Chapters 10 and 11.

Under rational expectations it becomes deductive: since active feedback policy proves to be ineffective, why depart from lockstep?[30]

The hypothesis of rational expectations makes clear that countercyclical policy ties its fortune to ignorance, because only if the public adheres to incorrect anticipations can it be effective. If authorities cannot disguise their true stabilization plan, then the public, behaving in its own interest, exactly offsets the intended consequences of policy. The public always stymies the planner.[31]

It must be remembered, of course, that acquiring knowledge takes time. A new policy strategy, even if announced well in advance, gains credibility and acceptance only after it has been applied consistently. Thus rational expectations really describe the final form of expectations. Until this Age of Enlightenment arrives, the operative anticipation framework likely reflects both the old policy strategy which the public had already come to accept and the new one which it now faces.[32]

This transformation of expectations may be described thus. Consonant with equations (8.23) and (8.24), the old and new policy rules are $m_t = \delta_1 + \delta_2 Q_{t-1}$ and $m_t = \lambda_1 + \lambda_2 Q_{t-1}$, respectively. During transformation the public's expectation mechanism mirrors both policy positions, the new one becoming dominant as time passes. Mathematically,

$$m_{t-1,t} = [\delta_1 + \delta_2 Q_{t-1}]e^{-\theta t} + [\lambda_1 + \lambda_2 Q_{t-1}](1 - e^{-\theta t}) \qquad (8.39)$$

or, expressed in terms of the bias,

$$m_{t-1,t} = [\lambda_1 + \lambda_2 Q_{t-1}] + [(\delta_1 - \lambda_1) + (\delta_2 - \lambda_2)Q_{t-1}]e^{-\theta t} \qquad (8.40)$$

the parameter θ being positive. As the public grows wiser, the new policy posture acquires strength in the expectation scheme at the expense of the old; equivalently, the bias shrinks. $e^{-\theta t}$ can be viewed as a learning curve with θ measuring the learning rate.[33] A zero θ would indicate no learning, and expectations would remain biased forever. In this circumstance the results gathered from equations (8.27) and (8.29) attesting to the potency of countercyclical policy would apply without amendment. An infinite θ, by contrast, says that learning is instantaneous. The public always knows the compensatory tactic of authorities and always responds to frustrate it, as equation (8.25) warns. This θ identifies a world

[30]David C. Colander, "Rationality, Expectations and Functional Finance," in *Essays in Post-Keynesian Inflation*, p. 207; Thomas J. Sargent and Neil Wallace, "'Rational' Expectations, the Optimal Monetary Instrument, and the Optimal Money Supply Rule," *Journal of Political Economy*, **83** (April 1975), pp. 241–250; and Sargent and Wallace, "Rational Expectations and Policy," pp. 174–175.

[31]Sargent and Wallace, "Rational Expectations and Policy," pp. 174, 179–180.

[32]John B. Taylor, "Monetary Policy during a Transition to Rational Expectations," *Journal of Political Economy*, **83** (October 1975), pp. 1010, 1012–1013.

[33]Temporal weight function $e^{-\theta t}$ approximates the properties of a learning curve postulated by Kenneth J. Arrow in "The Economic Implications of Learning by Doing," *Review of Economic Studies*, **29** (June 1962), p. 159.

of pure rational expectations. For θ values in between, ignorance and wisdom coexist in a temporally changing mixture.

Under the adaptive rationality of (8.39) or (8.40),[34] equation (8.25) becomes

$$Q_t = [\xi_0 + \xi_2 Q_{t-1}] - \xi_1 [(\delta_1 - \lambda_1) + (\delta_2 - \lambda_2) Q_{t-1}] e^{-\theta t} + u_t \quad (8.41)$$

As already noted, the bias evaporates through time, and with it so does the effectiveness of active stabilization policy. Eventually, policy becomes completely powerless. It must be emphasized, however, that throughout the public's learning period, policy does influence endogenous economic magnitudes, and the brief filed earlier in support of countercyclical feedbacks over passivism points to their superiority during transition. Furthermore, the speed of learning may not lie beyond the control of authorities. Do they advertise a new philosophy before it takes effect? Do they ever depart from their avowed rule? Their own behavior could regulate the pace at which the public grasps the true strategy.[35]

Active stabilization policy may be defended on the ground that rational expectations constitute an asymptotic result rather than an instantaneous happening. It may also be defended on the ground that the public may allow the government to retain a curative dimension in the belief that the government can achieve stabilization more efficiently than can private markets. Authorities might be perceived as enjoying an advantage over the private sector in countercyclical affairs, and consequently the public might deliberately refrain from frustrating policy maneuvers since it is in the public's interest to exercise such restraint. The public "rationally expect[s] that the government is the correct agent to undertake the stabilizing role, and it is merely accomplishing a result which the free market would have achieved in a more costly fashion."[36] Viewed thus, the bias in anticipations signifies wisdom, not ignorance, and active countercyclical policy through feedback controls withstands the attack by rational expectationists. It can do more, however. It can mount an offensive of its own, using the same rational expectations weapon to reassert the superiority of feedbacks over lockstep.[37]

---

[34]Adaptive rationality may be defined as an expectation hypothesis which allows for experiential learning and which can eventually lead to that expectation which would be formed on the basis of perfect knowledge. Refer to James G. March, "Bounded Rationality, Ambiguity, and the Engineering of Choice," *Bell Journal of Economics*, **9** (Autumn 1978), pp. 592–593.

[35]See Taylor, "Monetary Policy," pp. 1015–1017, 1021, but also see Sargent and Wallace, "Rational Expectations and Policy," pp. 180–182.

[36]Colander, "Rationality," p. 206. This sentiment is echoed by Stanley Fischer, "On Activist Monetary Policy with Rational Expectations," in Stanley Fischer, ed., *Rational Expectations and Economic Policy* (Chicago: University of Chicago Press, 1980), pp. 211–212, 225.

[37]Edmund Phelps and John Taylor show that under rational expectations, a proportional feedback control for the money supply typically leads to smaller output variance than does a constant growth rate rule provided that prices exhibit stickiness in the sense that for any given period they are set and become inflexible before the money supply is decided. The assumption of stickiness explains why the finding by those authors disagrees with that by Sargent and Wallace, who in "'Rational' Expectations and the Rule" postulate flexible prices. Edmund S. Phelps and John B. Taylor, "Stabilizing Powers of Monetary Policy under Rational Expectations," *Journal of Political Economy*, **85** (February 1977), pp. 164–166, 174, 180–183. (*continued*)

Leaning against the wind may be preferable to standing statuelike even when expectations are rational. But *is* it preferable? Further exchanges between the adversaries will undoubtedly eventuate.

Besides endorsing the conclusion reached by Phelps and Taylor, Bennett McCallum notes another circumstance in which a proportional monetary feedback control can reduce output fluctuations despite rational expectations. That circumstance features the presence of an asset whose price is known to all agents in the economy. Peter Howitt, extending the argument of Phelps and Taylor along the line advanced by Colander and by Fischer, establishes that the costs of securing and processing information, combined with uncertainty about the economy's structure, can justify the use of a proportional monetary feedback device, rational expectations notwithstanding. Peter Howitt, "Activist Monetary Policy under Rational Expectations," *Journal of Political Economy*, **89** (April 1981), pp. 249–250, 253–255, 263–264, 267, and Bennett T. McCallum, "Rational Expectations and Macroeconomic Stabilization Policy: An Overview," *Journal of Money, Credit and Banking*, **12** (November 1980), pp. 734–738.

The threat posed by rational expectationists to active stabilization through feedbacks suffers a setback on the empirical front at the hands of Stephen Figlewski and Paul Wachtel, whose econometric tests involving data on anticipations soundly reject the rational expectations hypothesis. Stephen Figlewski and Paul Wachtel, "The Formation of Inflationary Expectations," *Review of Economics and Statistics*, **63** (February 1981), pp. 2–4.

FIVE

EQUILIBRIUM DYNAMICS AND POLICY

CELEBRATED PARADIGMS OF ECONOMIC GROWTH

The models discussed in Chapter 4 were concerned with fluctuations in output around equilibrium paths. Growth models focus on the equilibrium paths themselves and particularly on those associated with the steady growth of output. Their dynamics address equilibrium movements.

Although a growth paradigm may come replete with postulates about labor supply, investment, and saving, its fundamental behavior pattern is usually determined by properties of the underlying production process. For instance, the Harrod-Domar model posits the factor proportion (the capital-labor ratio) as fixed and consequently evidences no systematic responsiveness in the equilibrium growth rate. By contrast, neoclassical growth appeals to a variable proportion and enjoys a systematically adjustable equilibrium rate. The Cambridge model of Kaldor shows similar responsiveness. It contains a technical progress function, which presumably differs from a production function but which actually bears kinship to the Cobb-Douglas. Of the growth systems considered, Robinson's alone fails to accept the production function or its close cousin. The equilibrium growth rate adjusts grudgingly only under special circumstances.

Models discussed in this chapter represent main thrusts in the growth literature.[1] Their presentation here treats output, investment, and saving as net of

[1]Among the treatises devoted exclusively to economic growth, two merit reference as excellent complementary reading: Daniel Hamberg, *Models of Economic Growth* (New York: Harper & Row, Publishers, Incorporated, 1971), and Luigi L. Pasinetti, *Growth and Income Distribution*: *Essays in Economic Theory* (London: Cambridge University Press, 1974). The Hamberg volume's influence on the current effort should be apparent.

depreciation; more precisely, these measures presume that a complete allowance has already been made for capital consumed in the process of production. Net output thus equals the total amount of output generated (gross output) minus that portion of the total dedicated to the replacement of expiring machines. Analogous interpretations apply to the other two concepts. The presentation also takes notational liberties when that practice does not threaten clarity. For instance, the expression $\lim_{\kappa \to \infty} z(\kappa) = \infty$ may be written as $z(\infty) = \infty$, with the limiting procedure being understood. Furthermore, time subscripts may not always be imposed on variables which exhibit temporal movement.

Since growth theory invokes properties of the technical progress component of a production process, it seems judicious to review them at the outset. Examination of particular growth systems follows immediately afterward.

9.1 DIMENSIONS OF TECHNICAL PROGRESS

Technical progress can be defined in the spirit of Robert Solow as "any upward shift in the production function."[2] This definition has enjoyed immense popularity for many years despite a principal difficulty associated with its use. Progress so regarded arises from an increase (decrease) in any variable which exerts a positive (negative) effect on output but which, for whatever reason, is not explicitly included as an argument in the production function. Consequently, the contribution of progress to output, and hence the importance of progress in the production process, varies with the choice of arguments. In the extreme case where all determinants of output were known and were properly formulated and measured, the production function would never shift. Progress of this sort would not occur. Since a production function can be expressed in terms of its contours, or isoquants, so can technical progress; that is, progress may be taken as any shift in isoquants toward the origin. The two definitions are equivalent.[3]

At least three dimensions of progress can be distinguished. The first references the means by which progress enters the productive system; it focuses on

---

[2] This section excerpts heavily from James H. Gapinski, "Technical Progress, Factor Substitutability, and Models of Production: I," *De Economist*, **122** (1974), pp. 411–418. The conception of progress cited appears in Robert M. Solow, "Technical Change and the Aggregate Production Function," *Review of Economics and Statistics*, **39** (August 1957), p. 312.

[3] Treating progress as a time-shift exhibited by the production function or by the attendant isoquants renders it a measure of ignorance, as Robert M. Solow observes in "Investment and Technical Progress," in K. J. Arrow, S. Karlin, and P. Suppes, eds., *Mathematical Methods in the Social Sciences, 1959* (Stanford, Calif.: Stanford University Press, 1960), p. 90. Progress could be defined more elegantly as, for example, the addition to the stock of knowledge resulting from research and development activity. Such a view links progress to a change in something specific rather than to a change in "everything else." Murray Brown and Alfred H. Conrad follow this alternative tack in "The Influence of Research and Education on CES Production Relations," in Murray Brown, ed., *The Theory and Empirical Analysis of Production*, Studies in Income and Wealth, vol. 31 (New York: National Bureau of Economic Research, 1967), pp. 343–347, 353. Others do as well.

what is needed for isoquants to shift at all. In this first respect progress is either disembodied or embodied. The second dimension addresses the pattern of the isoquant shift. It compares the shapes of isoquants before the shift to their shapes after. Progress is either neutral or nonneutral. The third aspect notes the ability of entrepreneurs to control the shift. Progress is either exogenous or endogenous. Each dimension warrants elaboration.

Disembodied or Embodied

"Disembodied progress" refers to technical advances which float down upon the productive system. They enter without requiring adjustment to the input mix and also, in particular, without requiring acquisition of new capital goods. They are essentially phenomena which improve "the organization and operation of inputs without reference to the nature of the inputs themselves."[4] All machines, regardless of their age, share equally in the progress; they are homogeneous from the standpoint of technical developments.

Consider the production function

$$Y_t = B(K_t, L_t, t) \qquad (9.1)$$

where Y_t denotes the quantity of output forthcoming at time t from K_t units of capital and L_t units of labor. The time argument serves as an index of the technology level. It establishes the height of the production surface and, equivalently, the proximity of the individual isoquants to the origin. This surface and its isoquants shift each period independently of capital purchases, because all machines, even those already installed, take advantage of new technological breakthroughs. Each machine always reflects the current state of the art.

"Embodied progress" refers to technical advances which enter the productive system only through the acquisition of new units of input. While they may be embodied in capital, labor, or any other factor or combination of factors, they are usually regarded as embedded only in capital: new capital is the sole vehicle of progress. According to this view, capital must be classified by vintage—by date of construction. Machines built in 1982 must be distinguished from those built in 1981 because they reflect a higher level of technology. From the standpoint of progress, capital goods are heterogeneous across vintages; within a vintage, however, they are homogeneous.

The heterogeneity of capital attributable to progress gives rise to what can be called "vintage production functions." Basically, each layer of capital has its own production function that resembles equation (9.1) except in one important respect: a vintage identifier, rather than the time variable t, measures the technology level. Capital goods are built to capture the latest state of the art, but

---

[4]Solow, "Investment," pp. 90–91. See also G. C. Harcourt, *Some Cambridge Controversies in the Theory of Capital* (London: Cambridge University Press, 1972), pp. 47–48, and Edmund S. Phelps, "The New View of Investment: A Neoclassical Analysis," *Quarterly Journal of Economics*, **76** (November 1962), p. 549.

after their construction they are unable to share in future technical breakthroughs. Consequently, the height of each vintage production function becomes fixed when the corresponding capital is built, and it does not change afterward. The functions for newer vintages lie above those for less modern equipment, and the accompanying isoquants lie closer to the origin than their "older" counterparts do. It is in this sense that isoquants shift. Shifts occur only when new capital is acquired.[5]

Neutral or Nonneutral

Of the many possible ways to classify the pattern of progress as neutral or nonneutral (alias unbiased or biased, respectively), two are extremely popular: those of Sir John Hicks and Sir Roy Harrod. Both Hicks and Harrod developed their taxonomies with an eye to the distribution of income, and both regarded progress as neutral if it did not alter the distribution and as nonneutral if it did. Hicks, however, looked at the initial effects of progress, while Harrod addressed its long-run effects.[6] The setting continues to be that of two inputs: capital and labor.

Hicks' classification concentrates on the impact which technical progress has on the marginal rate of technical substitution MRTS at a given factor proportion, MRTS being taken as the ratio of the marginal product of labor to that of capital. Progress is neutral if it leaves MRTS unchanged at the given capital-labor ratio. Any change in MRTS at that factor proportion signals nonneutral progress. More precisely, if progress results in a decreased MRTS at that proportion, then it is capital-using. If it results in an increased MRTS, then it is capital-saving.[7]

Under Hicks neutrality, isoquants shift toward the origin in a parallel fashion. With competitive forces awarding factors their marginal products, such a shift leads to no change in the equilibrium factor proportion if the ratio of factor prices remains unchanged.[8] Capital is not substituted for labor, and labor is not substituted for capital. Hicks nonneutrality appears as nonparallel shifts in isoquants, and it does lead to a change in the equilibrium factor proportion at a given factor-price ratio. Capital-using progress prompts an increase in the capital-labor ratio; capital is used relative to labor. Capital-saving progress evokes a decrease in the ratio; capital is saved relative to labor.

[5] Phelps, "New View," p. 552, and Solow, "Investment," pp. 91–92.

[6] C. E. Ferguson, *The Neoclassical Theory of Production and Distribution* (London: Cambridge University Press, 1971), pp. 217, 219–221.

[7] J. R. Hicks, *The Theory of Wages* (New York: The Macmillan Company, 1932; reprinted, New York: Peter Smith, 1948), pp. 121–122. For a restatement of the Hicksian scheme, see Joan Robinson, *Essays in the Theory of Employment* (New York: The Macmillan Company, 1937), pp. 132–133, and R. F. Harrod, "Essays in the Theory of Employment" (review), *Economic Journal*, **47** (June 1937), p. 328.

The presence of only two factors—capital and labor—means that capital-using progress is also labor-saving and that capital-saving progress is also labor-using.

[8] If the factor-price ratio changes, then so does the equilibrium factor proportion. Hicks neutrality merely says that the equilibrium proportion does not change because of technical progress.

Harrod defined progress as neutral if it left the capital-output ratio unchanged at a constant rate of interest.[9] Reference to the interest rate in this definition proves to be slightly cumbersome. With progress treated as a shift in isoquants, it seems desirable to follow the example of Hicks' taxonomy and to redefine Harrod neutrality solely in terms of production function characteristics. An established alternative may be stated thus: Harrod-neutral progress is progress which does not alter the capital-output ratio at a constant marginal product of capital. In the same vein technical progress is capital-using (capital-saving) if it increases (decreases) the capital-output ratio at the constant marginal product of capital.[10]

The imposition of a specific pattern of progress restricts the isoquant shifts, and this extra information may enable the generality of the production function to be reduced. Let function (9.1) be linearly homogeneous in K_t and L_t. If progress is Hicks neutral, then[11]

$$B(K_t, L_t, t) = T_t^1 C(K_t, L_t)$$

T_t^1 is a function of the technology index t alone,[12] and progress affects the quantity of output only through T_t^1. If progress is Hicks neutral, then the production function becomes decomposable with respect to the technology index. The reverse also holds: If $B(K_t, L_t, t)$ is decomposable, then progress must be Hicks neutral.

Under Harrod neutrality[13]

$$B(K_t, L_t, t) = D(K_t, T_t^2 L_t)$$

Harrod neutrality has the effect of augmenting the quantity of labor and only the

---

[9]Harrod, "Essays" (review), p. 329; R. F. Harrod, *Towards a Dynamic Economics* (London: Macmillan & Co., Ltd., 1948; reprinted, London: Macmillan & Co., Ltd., 1952), pp. 22–23; and Joan Robinson, "The Classification of Inventions," *Review of Economic Studies*, **5** (February 1938), pp. 139–140.

[10]The alternative statement of neutrality was suggested by Harrod himself in "Essays" (review), p. 329, and adopted formally by others such as Hamberg, *Models*, p. 70; Robert M. Solow, "Some Recent Developments in the Theory of Production," in Brown, *Theory and Empirical Analysis*, p. 29; and H. Uzawa, "Neutral Inventions and the Stability of Growth Equilibrium," *Review of Economic Studies*, **28** (February 1961), p. 118.

On Harrod nonneutrality see Hamberg, *Models*, footnote 29, p. 71; Harrod, *Towards a Dynamic Economics*, pp. 26–27; and Robinson, "Classification," p. 140.

[11]Proof can be found in R. Sato and M. J. Beckmann, "Neutral Inventions and Production Functions," *Review of Economic Studies*, **35** (January 1968), p. 59, and in Uzawa, "Neutral Inventions and Stability," p. 120. Although function (9.1), with its disembodiment postulate, provides the framework for illustrating this property and those to follow, equivalent illustrations could be presented using a vintage production function and embodiment.

[12]Technology functions T_t^2, T_t^3, and T_t^4, to be encountered momentarily, also depend solely upon t.

[13]Sato and Beckmann, "Neutral Inventions," p. 59, and Uzawa, "Neutral Inventions and Stability," pp. 119–120.

quantity of labor. As before, the reverse applies; if $B = D$, then progress must be Harrod neutral.

Let progress now augment both factors. Production function (9.1) can therefore be written as[14]

$$Y_t = E\left(T_t^3 K_t, T_t^4 L_t\right)$$

where E is linearly homogeneous. When T_t^3 and T_t^4 increase at the same proportionate rate, T_t^3/T_t^4 stays constant at, say, λ. Hence $Y_t = T_t^4 E(\lambda K_t, L_t)$ or, more simply,

$$Y_t = T_t^4 E^1(K_t, L_t)$$

Hicks neutrality and technical progress which augments both factors at the same rate are synonymous.

When T_t^4 varies while T_t^3 remains fixed at λ_3,

$$E(\lambda_3 K_t, T_t^4 L_t) = E^2(K_t, T_t^4 L_t)$$

Harrod neutrality results. Similarly, when T_t^3 varies with T_t^4 being stationary at λ_4,

$$E(T_t^3 K_t, \lambda_4 L_t) = E^3(T_t^3 K_t, L_t)$$

Progress is entirely capital-augmenting. In this form it represents another version of neutrality, one named after Solow in honor of his pioneering work which linked the existence of aggregate production measures under capital embodiment to capital augmentation.[15] Rivaling its Hicks and Harrod counterparts, Solow neutrality does not alter the distribution of income.[16]

These three brands of neutrality can be readily exchanged among themselves when the Cobb-Douglas applies.[17] With T_t notating the technology function, the relation describing Y_t may be written as

$$T_t K_t^{\xi_1} L_t^{\xi_2} = \left(T_t^{1/\xi_1} K_t\right)^{\xi_1} L_t^{\xi_2} = K_t^{\xi_1}\left(T_t^{1/\xi_2} L_t\right)^{\xi_2} \tag{9.2}$$

Hicks neutrality appears first; Solow neutrality, second; and Harrod neutrality, third. If the technology function were postulated to be the exponential $T_t = T_0 e^{T^* t}$, then progress at the Hicks-neutral rate T^* would translate into progress at the Solow-neutral rate T^*/ξ_1 or at the Harrod-neutral rate T^*/ξ_2.

---

[14] The subsequent arithmetic involving the various E functions reviews a discussion by Solow, "Some Recent Developments," pp. 28–30. Superscripts like that in E^1 identify members of the E family; they do not signify partial differentiation.

[15] For instance, see Solow, "Investment." The issue of aggregation under embodiment is treated in Sections 10.1 and 10.3.

[16] Hamberg, *Models*, footnote 9, pp. 148–149, and Sato and Beckmann, "Neutral Inventions," p. 59.

[17] Robinson, "Classification," p. 141, and Solow, "Investment," footnote 2, p. 91.

Exogenous or Endogenous

Technical progress is most often treated as exogenously determined, its pattern and pace given to entrepreneurs independently of the economic climate. An opposing view claims that the pattern and pace can be controlled by entrepreneurs, who adjust them to variations in costs, factor shares, or the like. Changing economic conditions would therefore lead to changing characteristics of progress.[18]

Elements in the several dimensions of technical progress can be combined quite freely. For example, progress might be disembodied, endogenous, and Hicks capital-saving, or embodied, exogenous, and Solow neutral. It could be partly disembodied and partly embodied. In this chapter, however, it is generally taken to be disembodied, exogenous, and Harrod neutral.

9.2 THE MODEL OF HARROD

About the same time that Samuelson was marrying the accelerator and multiplier, so was Harrod, although for a somewhat different reason.[19] Unlike Samuelson, who largely emphasized cyclical fluctuations, Harrod directed his attention to the trend line around which those oscillations might lie. At the heart of Harrod's model rests a basic antinomy: saving depends upon the income *level* while investment depends upon the income *change*. Under these conditions, can saving equal investment through time? An affirmative answer emerges, provided that income grows steadily—at a constant rate.

In Harrod's model, saving observes a proportional function, one hardly inappropriate for the long-run time frame of growth analysis. Specifically,

$$S_t = sY_t \tag{9.3}$$

S_t and Y_t denote net saving and net output at time t, respectively, while s represents a constant which is positive but less than unity. Net investment at t, I_t, obeys the simple accelerator discussed in Section 4.1:

$$I_t = v\frac{dY_t}{dt} \tag{9.4}$$

---

[18] Works dealing with endogenous, or induced, progress include Akihiro Amano, "Biased Technical Progress and a Neoclassical Theory of Economic Growth," *Quarterly Journal of Economics*, **78** (February 1964), pp. 135–136; E. M. Drandakis and E. S. Phelps, "A Model of Induced Invention, Growth and Distribution," *Economic Journal*, **76** (December 1966), pp. 828–831; Hicks, *Theory*, pp. 124–127; Charles Kennedy, "Induced Bias in Innovation and the Theory of Distribution," *Economic Journal*, **74** (September 1964), pp. 542–545; Joan Robinson, *The Accumulation of Capital* (London: Macmillan & Co., Ltd., 1956), p. 170; and Robinson, *Essays in the Theory of Economic Growth* (New York: St. Martin's Press, Inc., 1962), pp. 51–52.

[19] R. F. Harrod, "An Essay in Dynamic Theory," *Economic Journal*, **49** (March 1939), pp. 14–33. That discussion receives amplification in Harrod, *Towards a Dynamic Economics*, especially lecture 3.

where v denotes the entrepreneurs' desired capital-output ratio. Acceleration coefficient v is a positive constant.

Equilibrium witnesses equality between investment and saving, and consequently

$$I_t = S_t \qquad (9.5)$$

Substituting (9.3) and (9.4) into (9.5) gives

$$\frac{dY_t}{dt} / Y_t = s/v$$

which after integration and application of antilogs becomes

$$Y_t = Y_0 e^{(s/v)t} \qquad (9.6)$$

Y_0 denotes the output level relevant to the initial period, time zero.

According to equation (9.6) an economy starting from a position of equilibrium ($I_0 = S_0$) must have output grow at the constant rate s/v for equilibrium to be maintained through time. Stated differently, equation (9.6) describes the equilibrium path of the economy. It can be easily shown that equilibrium truly exists along this steady growth path by inserting (9.6) into the saving and investment expressions to obtain, respectively,

$$S_t = sY_0 e^{(s/v)t} \qquad \text{and} \qquad I_t = sY_0 e^{(s/v)t}$$

Notice that $I_0 = S_0 = sY_0$. From Y_0 the initial values of I_t and S_t can be determined.

The rate s/v is output's equilibrium rate of growth. Harrod, however, adopts the terminology "warranted rate" because the equilibrium path is unstable: a departure from that path results in a cumulative movement away from it.[20] This instability becomes evident by comparing the warranted rate g_w with output's actual growth rate g_a. To facilitate this comparison g_a can be expressed in terms similar to g_w. Realized saving always equals realized investment. The former amounts to sY_t; the latter to $v_r dY_t/dt$, where v_r denotes the ex post acceleration coefficient. Hence, the actual rate simplifies to s/v_r.

Suppose that $g_a > g_w$. Then $v_r < v$, which in turn implies that realized investment falls short of planned investment. Entrepreneurs, unable to acquire as much capital as desired, attempt to compensate for the shortfall by increasing their equipment orders, an action which forces g_a further away from g_w. The exact opposite sequence applies when $g_a < g_w$. In that case $v_r > v$, and realized investment exceeds the planned level. The reduction in capital orders which ensues again thrusts g_a further from g_w.

Instability of equilibrium forms the basis of Harrod's two famous long-run anomalies: secular stagnation and secular exhilaration. In addition to (but quite

---

[20] Due to its instability the equilibrium growth path has been described as a knife edge. Harrod, however, objects to such imagery, preferring instead that of a shallow dome. See R. F. Harrod, "Harrod after Twenty-One Years: A Comment," *Economic Journal*, **80** (September 1970), pp. 740–741, and Robert M. Solow, "A Contribution to the Theory of Economic Growth," *Quarterly Journal of Economics*, **70** (February 1956), p. 65.

distinct from) the warranted rate, Harrod postulates a natural rate, which is the maximum rate of output growth allowed by increased labor supply and by technological progress in the presence of full employment. The progress envisioned leaves the capital-output ratio unchanged at a constant rate of interest; it is Harrod neutral. It is also disembodied and exogenous, and it occurs at the exponential rate ψ. The natural rate g_n therefore equals $\eta + \psi$, where η signifies the exponential rate of growth in the labor supply. g_n defines the ceiling rate which the economy can sustain, and along the corresponding path labor is fully employed. While the actual rate may exceed the natural rate, it cannot do so indefinitely.

Secular stagnation arises when $g_w > g_n$. Since the economy cannot perpetuate growth at any rate greater than the natural, the actual rate tends to remain below the warranted rate, triggering depressionary forces which usher in widespread unemployment. Secular exhilaration results when $g_w < g_n$; then the ceiling does not prevent attainment of g_w. Instead, the actual rate tends to exceed the warranted rate, and stimulative behavior by entrepreneurs leads to chronic inflation.

Differing warranted and natural rates mean long-term problems for the economy. By contrast, a tranquil state arises when the rates coincide ($g_w = g_n$). Then the economy grows along an equilibrium path which affords full employment *inter alia*. In the Harrod model, however, agreement of the warranted and natural rates would only be a chance occurrence; it would happen only by accident. The four components of those rates—s, v, η, and ψ—are parameters. While perhaps not completely unresponsive to current economic conditions, these parameters cannot be presumed to adjust to fully eliminate any discrepancy between the two rates. Succinctly, while some movement toward equality is possible, attainment of exact equality is unlikely. No automatic adjustment mechanism exists to assure convergence of the two rates.

Observe that the acceleration coefficient v really plays two roles. In the investment function it serves as a behavioral measure indicating entrepreneurial intentions about investment. But v must also be tied to the realities of the production process: entrepreneurial desires must coincide with the "facts" of production. If v does not mirror the production structure, then a given change in output would lead to excess or deficient capacity. Too much or too little capital would be acquired.[21] Such imbalance would eventually cause entrepreneurs to abandon the simple accelerator as their decision rule, and the time path of output derived from equation (9.4) would no longer correspond to equilibrium. For the accelerator to remain valid over the entire growth path, v must be both a behavioral and a technical coefficient. Being constant, v must equal a constant

---

[21]"Capacity" refers to the amount of capital extant. "Excess capacity" means that some machines are not used in generating current output; "deficient capacity" means that all are used although more are desired to satisfy current production needs. "Full capacity" connotes that all machines are used with no additional ones being sought to meet existing needs. This convention resembles that adopted in Chapter 6; it applies throughout Part 5.

K_t/Y_t, where K_t denotes the actual stock of capital at time t. This equality prevents excess or deficient capacity. An immediate corollary is that the equilibrium path must be characterized by full-capacity use of capital.[22] It follows that the blissful state of steady equilibrium growth at the natural rate, $g_w = g_n$, would evidence not only full employment of labor but also full-capacity use of capital.

As will be seen shortly, the principal rigidity of Harrod's model, which distinguishes it as a special case in a wide class of growth paradigms, is the constancy of v. Fixed v implies under linear homogeneity a fixed factor proportion. Thus the production function underlying Harrod's model displays no substitution between factors,[23] a property consistent with two possibilities. Either the production function is Leontief, with substitution being ruled out on technical grounds, or the function allows a variable proportion but the input-price ratio remains stationary. Both cases fall under the specter of Harrod.

Since $v = K_t/Y_t$, the warranted rate can be written as sY_t/K_t. But from the saving function and the equilibrium condition, time subscripts ignored, sY/K translates into I/K or, equivalently, into $\dot{K}/K$, where $\dot{K}$ denotes the time derivative dK/dt. Therefore,

$$g_w = s\frac{Y}{K} = \frac{I}{K} = \frac{\dot{K}}{K} \qquad (9.7)$$

The warranted rate is synonymous with the rate of capital accumulation.

9.3 PROFESSOR DOMAR'S EFFORT

A comprehensive view of investment admits that it has a dual nature. Additional dollars spent acquiring capital become circulated throughout the economy, causing income to rise by a multiple. This aspect of investment, along with its implications for employment, captivated Keynes and found key expression in his model of income determination, discussed in Chapters 1 and 2. The other side of investment is an expansion of capacity. Acquisition of capital means greater potential for producing goods; should that additional output not be forthcoming, excess capacity would result, causing entrepreneurs to rethink planned future acquisitions.

---

[22] D. Hamberg and Charles L. Schultze offer this reasoning in "Autonomous *vs.* Induced Investment: The Interrelatedness of Parameters in Growth Models," *Economic Journal*, **71** (March 1961), p. 59.

[23] A clear statement of this point appears in Solow, "Contribution," pp. 65, 83.

Since output, capital, and labor satisfy a production function, so do their values at time zero, and hence Y_0 is determined automatically from the initial input levels. For full capacity initially, Y_0 must equal K_0/v, a relationship which Hamberg calls the "Hicksian stock equilibrium condition." Hamberg, *Models*, p. 12.

The Keynesian model largely ignored the capacity-creating effect of investment.[24] Such posture was justifiable given the system's short-run focus and its concern with unemployment. Furthermore, the clumsiness of a constant capital stock in the face of positive net investment could be easily ignored by recognizing that changes in the stock relative to the existing level would be small. Thus stock constancy in the shadow of positive net investment was a tolerable approximation. This approximation becomes much less tolerable, however, in a long-run setting. There the presence of excessive or deficient capacity would undoubtedly prompt entrepreneurs to take corrective action, which would affect the temporal movement of the economy. As Harrod's model suggests, the issue of capacity cannot be lightly dismissed in a long-run framework.

Professor Domar develops a model addressing both the capacity-generating and the income-generating aspects of investment.[25] What specifically emerges is a growth path along which capital remains fully utilized. Encountered first is a definitional equation for the productivity ratio ι, more formally termed the potential social average investment productivity:

$$\iota = \frac{dP_t}{dt} / I_t \tag{9.8}$$

P_t denotes capacity output at time t, that output level which can be attained with full-capacity use of capital, and I_t denotes net investment at t. The ratio ι is presumed to be a constant of known value. Domar cautions that it should not be interpreted as a marginal concept which implicitly treats factors other than capital as constant. Instead, the assumption underlying the definition of ι is that the quantities of other factors would vary to accommodate the changed capital stock.

Definition (9.8) can be transparently manipulated to yield

$$\frac{dP_t}{dt} = \iota I_t \tag{9.9}$$

New capital in the amount of I_t raises capacity output by ιI_t. In other words, for new capital to be fully utilized, actual production Y_t must rise by ιI_t.

Full capacity is taken to characterize the economy initially; namely,

$$P_0 = Y_0$$

where Y_0 is output at time zero. Thus, maintenance of full capacity through time requires that

$$\frac{dP_t}{dt} = \frac{dY_t}{dt} \tag{9.10}$$

---

[24] If capacity expansion were incorporated into the discussion of Keynes' paradigm presented in Chapter 1, the aggregate production function—equation (1.12) modified by K_t replacing K_o—would shift upward with net capital acquisitions, as would the schedule for labor's marginal product.

[25] Evsey D. Domar, "Capital Expansion, Rate of Growth, and Employment," *Econometrica*, **14** (April 1946), pp. 137–147 and "Expansion and Employment," *American Economic Review*, **37** (March 1947), pp. 34–55.

However, thanks to the famous multiplier, dY_t/dt can be articulated further. The customary proportional saving function and equilibrium condition, $S_t = sY_t$ and $I_t = S_t$, respectively, give

$$I_t = sY_t \tag{9.11}$$

and then

$$\frac{dY_t}{dt} = \frac{1}{s}\frac{dI_t}{dt} \tag{9.12}$$

Substituting (9.9) and (9.12) into (9.10) makes

$$\frac{1}{s}\frac{dI_t}{dt} = \iota I_t$$

This expression underscores the dual nature of investment. The left-hand component identifies the multiplier or income-creating effect, while the right-hand element isolates the capacity-creating effect, which (paraphrasing Domar) might be designated the "ι effect." Capital is fully utilized only if these two effects prove to be equal.

Clearly,

$$\frac{dI_t}{dt}\bigg/I_t = \iota s$$

and eventually after integration

$$I_t = I_0 e^{\iota s t} \tag{9.13}$$

emerges. To maintain full-capacity use of capital through time, investment must grow at the exponential rate ιs, called by Domar the "required rate." Oddly, investment, which causes the capacity problem, also constitutes its cure provided that investment grows.

With the aid of (9.9), rewrite (9.10) as

$$\frac{dY_t}{dt} = \iota I_t$$

From (9.11) this formula becomes

$$\frac{dY_t}{dt} = \iota s Y_t$$

or

$$Y_t = Y_0 e^{\iota s t} \tag{9.14}$$

Full capacity occurs when investment and output grow at the required rate. Furthermore, from (9.14) and the proportional saving function, it is evident that saving too grows at the required rate. Given equilibrium initially, such growth preserves equilibrium through time. Observe that Y_0 sets the initial values for I_t and S_t via the saving and equilibrium relationships: $I_0 = S_0 = sY_0$.

Domar's model contains several striking similarities to Harrod's. Harrod seeks an equilibrium growth path, but for that path to truly represent equilibrium, it must also engender full-capacity use of capital. Domar looks for full capacity but, by appealing to the multiplier, admits equilibrium through the back door.

Both models, therefore, describe an equilibrium, full-capacity growth path. Both have investment, saving, and output growing at constant exponential rates; those rates even show the saving coefficient entering in exactly the same manner—as a multiplicative factor of another parameter. In addition, Domar, like Harrod, holds that the capital-output ratio is fixed,[26] and consequently a fixed factor proportion underlies the Domar model as well.

These similarities are remarkable, so much so that temptation arises to regard the two models as identical. A principal obstacle to making this equivalence, however, seems to be the different expressions for the warranted and required rates: s/v versus ιs. One rate involves $1/v$; the other, ι. This obstacle proves to be illusory. Full capacity in the Domar model means that ι can be reexpressed as $(dY_t/dt)/I_t$ by substituting (9.10) into (9.8). Written more simply, $\iota = \Delta Y/\Delta K = 1/(\Delta K/\Delta Y)$. Since Harrod's paradigm has $v = K/Y = \Delta K/\Delta Y$ (the latter equality arising from the constancy of v), $\iota = 1/v$, completing the match.[27]

9.4 THE NEOCLASSICAL VIEW OF GROWTH

"All theory depends on assumptions which are not quite true.... When the results of a theory seem to flow specifically from a special crucial assumption, then if the assumption is dubious, the results are suspect." So begins Robert Solow in a paper which challenges the Harrod-Domar postulate of a fixed factor proportion. In the long-run context, Solow continues, substitution should be the operative rule, not fixity. Thus enters the neoclassical growth model.[28]

---

[26] See the discussion of capital deepening in Evsey D. Domar, "The Problem of Capital Accumulation," *American Economic Review*, **38** (December 1948), pp. 777–779.

[27] The relationship between ι and v betrays complications when autonomous investment exists. Autonomous investment may compete with its induced counterpart in the sense of satisfying capital needs otherwise fulfilled under inducement; as a consequence v reduces merely to a behavioral coefficient whose value falls below $1/\iota$. Hamberg and Schultze have more on this point in their "Autonomous Investment," pp. 60–65.

Autonomous investment is ignored here because, as Harrod suggests in *Towards a Dynamic Economics* (p. 79), the complications which it poses evaporate in the long run. Moreover, the traditional treatment of models to be considered subsequently ignores it, and appreciation of the fundamental differences among them seems enhanced by the elimination of entangling nuances. Harrod himself reveals some impatience with subtleties. "I believe that we are on the way to certain basic truths, which are independent of complications that have to be introduced when we seek to build up a more detailed picture of the whole process.... We must start with some generality however imperfect. We shall never go ahead if we remain in a world of trivialities or fine points." *Towards a Dynamic Economics*, pp. 80–81.

[28] Solow, "Contribution," pp. 65–66. Solow's paper stands as one of the seminal expositions of the neoclassical growth model, and this section owes much to it. Another early treatment of that paradigm appears in T. W. Swan, "Economic Growth and Capital Accumulation," *Economic Record*, **32** (November 1956), pp. 334–361.

The relevance of neoclassical growth to a developed economy is argued by Hans Brems, "Reality and Neoclassical Theory," *Journal of Economic Literature*, **15** (March 1977), pp. 72–83. But also see the associated criticism and rejoinder, pp. 83–84. An unflattering portrait of the neoclassical system is given by Pasinetti, *Growth*, pp. 124–126.

This section first considers properties of the production function underlying the model. That function assumes a general form, and its features, which are critical for a growth solution, receive close examination. The remainder of the system is then presented, and the steady growth solution is derived. Stability analysis of that solution comes next, followed by a look at the behavior of prices in steady growth. An inquiry into the importance of Harrod neutrality for steady growth concludes the discussion. Section 9.5 presents the analytics for a special case: that based on a CES production function.

Consider the production function

$$Y_t = F(K_t, A_t L_t) \tag{9.15}$$

where A represents exogenous Harrod-neutral disembodiment: $A_t = A_0 e^{\psi t}$. As before, Y and K denote output and the capital stock, respectively; L denotes labor. AL signifies labor in efficiency units, natural units stretched or augmented by the technology factor. Function (9.15) obeys customary neoclassical dictates. It is continuous and twice differentiable in capital and labor, having positive first and negative second partials. In addition, it displays linear homogeneity and evidences a nothing-from-nothing feature: $F(0, AL) = F(K, 0) = F(0, 0) = 0$.

Since (9.15) is linearly homogeneous, it can be conveniently translated into ratio form. Let $\tilde{v} = Y/(AL)$ and $\kappa = K/(AL)$. Then $\tilde{v} = f(\kappa)$, with $f(\kappa) = F[K/(AL), 1]$. Regarding f,

$$f \geq 0 \quad \text{for} \quad \kappa \geq 0 \quad \text{with} \quad f(\infty) = \infty$$

$$f' > 0 \quad \text{and} \quad f'' < 0 \quad \text{for} \quad \infty > \kappa > 0$$

where the derivative properties[29] come directly from the relationships $F_K = f'$ and $F_{KK} = (AL)^{-1} f''$. To assure the existence of a meaningful growth solution, two limiting (or boundary) conditions, often attributable to Inada,[30] are imposed; namely,

$$f'(0) = \infty \quad \text{and} \quad f'(\infty) = 0$$

Taken together, these properties give rise to the production locus depicted in Figure 9.1.

Other aspects of the model quickly present themselves. The supply of labor increases at the exponential rate η from its time-zero level of L_0:

$$L_t = L_0 e^{\eta t} \tag{9.16}$$

Moreover, equilibrium prevails. Given the proportional saving function $S_t = sY_t$,

---

[29] Consonant with established practice, subscripts indicate the argument with respect to which a partial is taken. One subscript indicates the first partial; two, the second. When only one argument exists, the first and second derivatives are designated by a prime and a double prime, respectively. Higher-order derivatives are notated similarly. This convention applies throughout Part 5.

[30] Ken-ichi Inada, "On a Two-Sector Model of Economic Growth: Comments and a Generalization," *Review of Economic Studies*, **30** (June 1963), p. 120. However, also consult H. Uzawa, "On a Two-Sector Model of Economic Growth II," *Review of Economic Studies*, **30** (June 1963), p. 108.

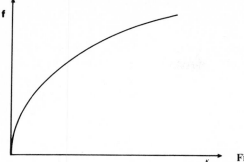

Figure 9.1

its constant s observing the constraint $1 > s > 0$, $I_t = sY_t$. Equivalently,

$$\dot{K}_t = sY_t \qquad (9.17)$$

where, as before, the dot abbreviates the time derivative, $\dot{K}_t = dK_t/dt$. Equations (9.15) to (9.17) contain the essence of the neoclassical system.

In order to begin extracting implications, divide (9.17) by K to obtain (without subscripts)

$$\frac{\dot{K}}{K} = s\frac{Y}{K} \qquad (9.18)$$

This expression, resurrecting (9.7), describes the warranted rate of Harrod, who associates steady equilibrium growth with a constant capital-output ratio. What happens when that ratio becomes constant in the neoclassical context?

The answer arrives with the help of production function (9.15), which gives $Y/K = F(1, AL/K)$. Since A grows at the exponential rate ψ, while from (9.16) L does likewise at the rate η, AL grows at the rate $\eta + \psi$. Constancy in Y/K therefore means that K expands at the rate $\eta + \psi$ too:

$$K_t = K_0 e^{(\eta + \psi)t} \qquad (9.19)$$

Accordingly, Y increases at the rate $\eta + \psi$ as well; namely,

$$Y_t = Y_0 e^{(\eta + \psi)t}$$

Furthermore, in view of (9.19) equilibrium condition (9.18) becomes

$$\eta + \psi = s\frac{Y}{K} \qquad (9.20)$$

Clearly, the left side is nothing but Harrod's natural rate; the right, his warranted rate. Equilibrium holds, and it says that the warranted and natural rates are equal. Steady equilibrium growth occurs at the natural rate! This circumstance contrasts sharply with the Harrod implication that such growth happens only by chance—only if the parameters accidentally assume the "right" values.

Working backward from (9.20) may be instructive. Equality of the warranted and natural rates implies that Y/K remains constant at $(\eta + \psi)/s$. Constancy in Y/K signals from (9.15) that K grows at the rate $\eta + \psi$ and therefore that Y does also. This expansion pattern satisfies equilibrium condition (9.18), and consequently warranted and natural rate equality must imply steady equilibrium growth at the natural rate.[31]

A constant capital-output ratio leads to impressive results in the neoclassical model, but an even more impressive property lies just ahead. That ratio gravitates toward its constancy mark, $s/(\eta + \psi)$; in other words, the warranted rate sY/K tends toward the natural rate $\eta + \psi$. In the neoclassical model there *is* an inherent tendency for the warranted rate to adjust to the natural rate, and a disruption of the system away from the natural rate activates forces which assure a return. To set the stage for stability analysis, observe that the warranted rate depends upon κ alone. sY/K becomes $sf(\kappa)/\kappa$, and hence any movement in sY/K must be caused by a change in κ. Investigating the temporal behavior of the warranted rate thus necessitates an inquiry into $\dot{\kappa}$.

From the definition of κ,

$$\frac{\dot{\kappa}}{\kappa} = \frac{sf}{\kappa} - (\eta + \psi) \tag{9.21}$$

$\dot{\kappa}/\kappa$ consists of the difference between the warranted and natural rates. From (9.21) it follows that

$$\dot{\kappa} = \kappa\left[\frac{sf}{\kappa} - (\eta + \psi)\right] \tag{9.22}$$

or more conveniently that

$$\dot{\kappa} = sf - (\eta + \psi)\kappa \tag{9.23}$$

The special case $\dot{\kappa} = 0$, implying constancy in the warranted rate and in the capital-output ratio, arises when

$$sf = (\eta + \psi)\kappa \tag{9.24}$$

that is, when the warranted and natural rates equalize. $\dot{\kappa} = 0$ therefore means steady equilibrium growth at the natural rate;[32] of course, so does satisfaction of (9.24).

Figure 9.2 draws both right-hand components of (9.23) against κ, enabling full inferences about $\dot{\kappa}$. For the moment ignore dashed lines sf_1 and sf_2. It should be clear that two κ values render $\dot{\kappa} = 0$: namely, $\kappa = 0$ and $\kappa = \kappa^*$. The former says that the stock of capital is zero, and by the nothing-from-nothing property it

---

[31]As mentioned in the analysis of Harrod's model, Section 9.2, $g_w = g_n$ connotes full employment of labor and full-capacity operation of capital. These characteristics are confirmed by the use of (9.16) and (9.19) in deriving (9.20).

[32]The immediate link between $\dot{\kappa} = 0$ and steady expansion at the natural rate can be shown another way. Differentiating the production function (9.15) totally with respect to time and appealing to Euler's theorem give

$$\frac{\dot{Y}}{Y} = \frac{f'}{f}\dot{\kappa} + (\eta + \psi)$$

$\dot{\kappa} = 0$ makes $\dot{Y}/Y = \eta + \psi$, confirming the link.

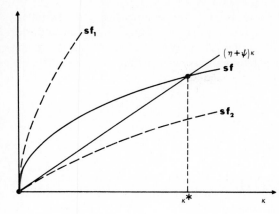

Figure 9.2 *Source*: Solow, "Contribution," pp. 70, 72.

intimates that output also is zero. Hence $\kappa = 0$ holds no interest. κ^*, being nontrivial (namely, positive and finite), does.

Consider some nontrivial $\kappa \neq \kappa^*$. What must be true for $\dot{\kappa}$? As Figure 9.2 attests, when $\kappa > \kappa^*$, $sf < (\eta + \psi)\kappa$ and consequently $\dot{\kappa} < 0$ from (9.23). κ falls toward κ^*, causing the warranted rate sf/κ to rise toward the natural rate. Conversely, when $\kappa < \kappa^*$, $sf > (\eta + \psi)\kappa$ and $\dot{\kappa} > 0$. κ rises, reducing the warranted rate.[33] Any departure of κ from κ^*—synonymously, any departure of the warranted rate from the natural rate—initiates movement which eliminates the discrepancy. Note, incidentally, that the solution $\kappa = 0$ is unstable: the slightest increase in κ eventually leads to $\kappa = \kappa^*$.

The role of Inada's boundary conditions in determining the steady growth solution κ^* can be seen from Figure 9.2. The right-hand condition $f'(\infty) = 0$ precludes sf loci which, like sf_1, persist in rising too rapidly[34] to intersect $(\eta + \psi)\kappa$

---

[33] That κ and the warranted rate move in opposite directions can be easily established. Since $g_w = sf/\kappa$, its rate of change becomes

$$\dot{g}_w/g_w = s(\dot{f}/f - \dot{\kappa}/\kappa)$$

Further manipulation yields

$$\dot{g}_w = g_w \frac{s}{\kappa}\left(\frac{f'}{f/\kappa} - 1\right)\dot{\kappa}$$

Since the marginal product of capital f' lies below its average product f/κ, the expression in parentheses must be negative. Consequently, as κ falls ($\dot{\kappa} < 0$), g_w rises ($\dot{g}_w > 0$), and conversely. The natural rate remains unchanged throughout the convergence process.

[34] Exclusion of the pattern sf_1 due to the right-hand Inada boundary is proven by showing that the difference $sf - (\eta + \psi)\kappa$ becomes negative as $\kappa \to \infty$. Write that difference as in (9.22): $[sf/\kappa - (\eta + \psi)]\kappa$. As $\kappa \to \infty$, the first term in brackets tends to ∞/∞, an indeterminate form but one which can be penetrated by l'Hopital's rule. That technique leaves

$$\left[\frac{s \lim_{\kappa \to \infty} f'}{1} - (\eta + \psi)\right]\lim_{\kappa \to \infty} \kappa = [s \cdot 0 - (\eta + \psi)]\infty = -\infty$$

The crucial element making $sf - (\eta + \psi)\kappa$ negative for large κ is $\lim_{\kappa \to \infty} f' = 0$, the right-hand Inada condition.

at a nontrivial κ. Its left-hand counterpart $f'(0) = \infty$ assures that sf immediately rises above $(\eta + \psi)\kappa$, preventing configurations like sf_2. Thus, Inada's boundaries guarantee that a solution to (9.24) exists at a nontrivial κ. However, being sufficient, they are in fact more restrictive than needed for that guarantee. Weaker conditions would serve equally well:

$$sf'(0) > \eta + \psi \qquad \text{and} \qquad sf'(\infty) < \eta + \psi$$

which may be written more compactly as

$$f'(0) > \frac{\eta + \psi}{s} > f'(\infty)$$

In sum, under neoclassical postulates steady equilibrium growth occurs at the natural rate $\eta + \psi$. Only one meaningful growth path exists, and along it labor remains fully employed and capital operates at capacity. Output, capital, and efficient labor all grow at the rate $\eta + \psi$; so does investment and saving from (9.17). Labor in natural units grows at the rate η while the output-capital ratio stands fixed at $(\eta + \psi)/s$. Fixed also are the capital-labor and output-labor ratios in efficient units, although in natural units both ratios grow at the rate ψ.

Now for prices. Faced by a variable factor proportion, entrepreneurs must be induced to choose one input combination over another, an inducement which comes from market pressures transmitted through the pricing mechanism. It therefore seems obligatory to examine the behavior of prices along the steady growth path.

Underlying the neoclassical production model is the marginal productivity theory of income distribution, according to which factors are paid their marginal products. Thus, $F_K = r$ and $F_L = w$, r and w being the interest rate and the real wage, respectively. The movement of interest can be quickly deduced. Since the production function F exhibits homogeneity of degree one in K and AL, F_K only depends upon the ratio $K/(AL)$. But since this ratio remains constant along the steady growth path, so does F_K. Interest too should be constant.

Labor's marginal product can be expressed as

$$F_L = A(f - \kappa f')$$

Along the growth path, κ and f are stationary, as is f' since $f' = F_K$. Consequently, the marginal product of labor grows at the rate of technical progress ψ. The real wage does also.

In the absence of technical progress, the previous analysis and conclusions change in a straightforward manner. Then, $\psi = 0$ and $A_t = A_0$. Steady equilibrium growth at the natural rate persists although the natural rate is now η alone. Output, capital, labor, investment, and saving grow at that rate, and hence the input-output ratios and factor proportion remain stationary. The marginal products of capital and labor hold constant, as do interest and wages.

Growth without progress provides a convenient framework for understanding why growth with progress relies on Harrod neutrality. Without progress, the steady growth path displays constancy in both the marginal product of capital (equivalently, the rate of interest) and the capital-output ratio. But as discussed in

Section 9.1, progress that is Harrod neutral leaves the capital-output ratio unchanged at a constant marginal product of capital (or interest rate). Thus, Harrod neutrality is consistent with the fundamental characteristics of growth without progress and therefore can be imposed harmoniously upon it. Since that brand of progress acts only to augment labor, its introduction in effect merely alters the rate of labor supply growth from η to $\eta + \psi$. Accommodating changes then trickle through the growth solution.

The relationship of Harrod neutrality to steady equilibrium growth at the natural rate can be shown formally.[35] Its compatibility has already been seen. To review, however, recall that AL grows at the exponential rate $\eta + \psi$. If K grows at this rate too, then so does Y by the linear homogeneity of the production function. Establishing necessity is slightly involved. Write the production function more generally as

$$Y = F(K, AL, t) \tag{9.25}$$

This format does not restrict the pattern of progress to Harrod neutrality; the argument t allows for any other pattern. Time-differentiating (9.25) gives

$$\dot{Y} = F_K \dot{K} + F_{AL}(\dot{A}L + \dot{L}A) + F_t$$

which under steady growth conditions becomes

$$(\eta + \psi)Y = (\eta + \psi)[F_K K + F_{AL} AL] + F_t$$

By Euler's theorem the linear homogeneity of (9.25) means that $Y = F_K K + F_{AL} AL$, reducing the bracketed expression in the previous equation to Y. Consequently, $F_t = 0$. Steady growth excludes progress which is not Harrod neutral. Thus, Harrod neutrality is compatible with steady growth at the natural rate, and in steady growth all progress must be Harrod neutral.

9.5 NEOCLASSICAL GROWTH UNDER THE CES

The neoclassical growth solution evolved last section under a linear homogeneous production function which, while postulated generally, nevertheless satisfied specific limit conditions. It is therefore of interest to examine the steady growth solution for a broad class of production functions whose members typically do not satisfy those conditions. That class, the CES production family, includes the Cobb-Douglas as a special (and the exceptional) case.

Steady equilibrium growth at the natural rate occurs, according to (9.24), when

$$sf = (\eta + \psi)\kappa$$

Hence experimentation requires deriving the properties of f for the CES and repeating the previous exercise under those properties.

---

[35] This exposition is adapted from Christopher Bliss, "On Putty-Clay," *Review of Economic Studies*, **35** (April 1968), pp. 110–111.

With Harrod neutrality the CES can be written as

$$Y_t = \gamma\left[\xi_1 K_t^{-\rho} + \xi_2(A_t L_t)^{-\rho}\right]^{-1/\rho} \tag{9.26}$$

Parameter γ is positive and finite, while parameters ξ_1 and ξ_2 are both positive and sum to unity. Parameter ρ locates between -1 and infinity excluding (here) either endpoint, and consequently the elasticity of factor substitution σ, $\sigma = 1/(1 + \rho)$, must be positive and finite.[36] Translated into the form $\tilde{v} = f(\kappa)$, expression (9.26) becomes

$$f = \gamma\left[\xi_1 \kappa^{-\rho} + \xi_2\right]^{-1/\rho}$$

Lengthy but straightforward calculations reveal that

$$f' = \gamma\xi_1\left[\xi_1 + \xi_2\kappa^\rho\right]^{-1/(\sigma\rho)}$$

$$f'' = -\sigma^{-1}\gamma\xi_1\xi_2\left[\xi_1 + \xi_2\kappa^\rho\right]^{-(2-\sigma)/(1-\sigma)}\kappa^{\rho-1}$$

As $\rho \to 0$, function (9.26) degenerates into the Cobb-Douglas[37]

$$Y_t = \gamma K_t^{\xi_1}(A_t L_t)^{\xi_2} \tag{9.27}$$

for which

$$f = \gamma\kappa^{\xi_1}$$

$$f' = \gamma\xi_1\kappa^{\xi_1-1}$$

$$f'' = \gamma\xi_1(\xi_1 - 1)\kappa^{\xi_1-2}$$

Thus $f > 0$, $f' > 0$, and $f'' < 0$ for all positive and finite κ regardless of the ρ value.

These features are rather pedestrian; special fascination, however, attaches to the extreme values of f and f', those for $\kappa = 0$ and $\kappa = \infty$. Three cases can be distinguished by the value of ρ.

Case I: $0 < \rho < \infty$ Convenience suggests writing f as

$$f = \frac{\gamma}{\left[\xi_1(1/\kappa)^\rho + \xi_2\right]^{1/\rho}}$$

where the exponents are positive. Clearly, $f \to 0$ as $\kappa \to 0$, while $f \to \gamma\xi_2^{-1/\rho}$ as

---

[36] That (9.26) reflects Harrod neutrality readily emerges. Manipulate the equation to yield $K/Y = [(\gamma^\rho/\xi_1)F_K]^{-\sigma}$. This relationship says that in the presence of technical progress the capital-output ratio remains unchanged at a constant marginal product of capital, precisely the criterion for Harrod neutrality. Hicks neutrality would be represented in effect by a temporally changing γ; Solow neutrality, by a changing ξ_1. Under those and other alternatives, K/Y would generally not remain constant at a fixed F_K.

[37] Details appear in Section 3 of Appendix C.

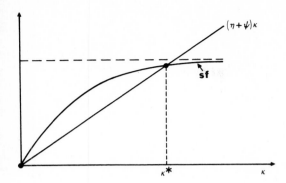

Figure 9.3

$\kappa \rightarrow \infty$. Write f' as

$$f' = \frac{\gamma \xi_1}{\left[\xi_1 + \xi_2 \kappa^\rho\right]^{1/(\sigma\rho)}}$$

$f' \rightarrow \gamma \xi_1^{-1/\rho}$ as $\kappa \rightarrow 0$, and $f' \rightarrow 0$ as $\kappa \rightarrow \infty$. Although the right-hand Inada condition is satisfied, its left-hand counterpart is not. Figure 9.3 presents sf and $(\eta + \psi)\kappa$ in this instance.

sf begins at zero with a positive and finite slope and increases monotonically to an asymptote. Provided that sf rises fast enough initially, a unique nontrivial solution exists, κ^*, in addition to the trivial one, $\kappa = 0$. The quickness proviso is $sf'(0) > \eta + \psi$ or, equivalently,

$$s > \xi_1^{1/\rho}(\eta + \psi)/\gamma \tag{9.28}$$

Case II: $\rho = 0$ Here $f(0) = 0$ and $f(\infty) = \infty$. Also, $f'(0) = \infty$ and $f'(\infty) = 0$. These properties duplicate those extant in Section 9.4, and hence the sf locus in Figure 9.2 again applies. Two solutions exist,[38] one being trivial.[39]

---

[38] Elaborating A in (9.27) gives $Y = \gamma A_0^{1-\xi_1} e^{(1-\xi_1)\psi t} K^{\xi_1} L^{1-\xi_1}$. Taking the time derivative and imposing the steady growth condition $\dot{Y}/Y = \dot{K}/K$ lead to $\dot{Y}/Y = \eta + \psi$. This expression differs from that cited by Hamberg, *Models*, p. 46; Solow, "Contribution," p. 85; and Swan, "Economic Growth," p. 338. Those authors divide the rate of progress by labor's output elasticity. However, they postulate the Cobb-Douglas as $Y = \gamma A_0 e^{ht} K^{\xi_1} L^{1-\xi_1}$, and consequently their Hicks-neutral rate h is equivalent to the Harrod-neutral rate ψ adjusted by labor's elasticity, $h = (1 - \xi_1)\psi$. Their expression $\dot{Y}/Y = \eta + h/(1 - \xi_1)$ thus coincides exactly with the one deduced here. Relationships in (9.2) summarize the connection between Hicks and Harrod neutralities under the Cobb-Douglas.

[39] That the trivial solution $\kappa = 0$ is extraneous, or "extra," when $\rho = 0$ becomes obvious by working directly with equation (9.21). In the present circumstance $\dot{\kappa}/\kappa = s\gamma\kappa^{-\xi_2} - (\eta + \psi)$. Since the warranted rate $s\gamma\kappa^{-\xi_2}$ declines monotonically from infinity at $\kappa = 0$ to zero at $\kappa = \infty$, it must equal the natural rate—and $\dot{\kappa}/\kappa$ must be zero—at a single κ; this κ must be nontrivial. Section 10.2, offering an alternative computational framework, establishes a single neoclassical growth solution for the Cobb-Douglas case.

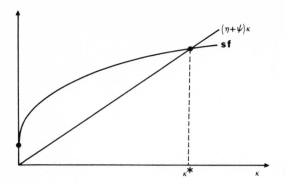

Figure 9.4

Case III: $-1 < \rho < 0$ Obviously, $-\rho > 0$. Now $f \to \gamma\xi_2^{-1/\rho}$ as $\kappa \to 0$, and $f \to \infty$ as $\kappa \to \infty$. For convenience f' can be reexpressed as

$$f' = \gamma\xi_1\left[\xi_1 + \xi_2(1/\kappa)^{-\rho}\right]^{-1/(\sigma\rho)}$$

which indicates that $f' \to \infty$ as $\kappa \to 0$ and $f' \to \gamma\xi_1^{-1/\rho}$ as $\kappa \to \infty$. Only the left-hand Inada condition survives. Graphics appear in Figure 9.4.

At zero κ, sf is positive and finite with infinitely positive slope. As κ rises, sf rises monotonically to infinity while its slope falls toward a positive limit. Existence of a nontrivial κ satisfying (9.24) requires that $sf'(\infty) < \eta + \psi$ or that

$$s < \xi_1^{1/\rho}(\eta + \psi)/\gamma \qquad (9.29)$$

The solution is unique.

Notice that inequalities (9.28) and (9.29) apply in addition to the usual restriction on s, $0 < s < 1$. These extra constraints arise, however, when $\rho \neq 0$, but not when $\rho = 0$. In the former circumstance the Inada boundary conditions are violated while in the latter they are not. Consequently, (9.28) and (9.29) can be viewed as restrictions which compensate for the inability of the CES to satisfy Inada.[40] More discussion regarding the notion of compensation can be found in Section 10.7.

---

[40] This point may be made evident by recalling that (9.24) has a nontrivial solution κ^* given the satisfaction of the inequality condition $f'(0) > (\eta + \psi)/s > f'(\infty)$. When $\rho = 0$, $f'(0) = \infty$ and $f'(\infty) = 0$. Both the left-hand and the right-hand Inada boundaries hold, and the inequality condition is automatically satisfied. When $\rho > 0$, $f'(\infty) = 0$ but $f'(0) = \gamma\xi_1^{-1/\rho}$. The left-hand Inada is violated, and for the inequality condition to hold s must exceed $\xi_1^{1/\rho}(\eta + \psi)/\gamma$: restriction (9.28) must be observed. Conversely, when $\rho < 0$, $f'(0) = \infty$ but $f'(\infty) = \gamma\xi_1^{-1/\rho}$. Right-hand Inada expires, and the inequality condition requires that s lie below $\xi_1^{1/\rho}(\eta + \psi)/\gamma$: restriction (9.29) must be obeyed.

An alternative, but related, interpretation of (9.28) and (9.29) can be wrought in terms of the output-capital ratio. Satisfaction of (9.24) means that Y/K must equal $(\eta + \psi)/s$. When $\rho = 0$, $Y/K = \gamma\kappa^{\xi_1-1}$ from (9.27), and an increase in κ from zero to infinity produces a monotonic decrease in Y/K from infinity to zero. Consequently, no barrier exists to prevent the equality of Y/K with $(\eta + \psi)/s$. *(continued)*

Stability analysis for the CES largely repeats that presented earlier and does not deserve separate exposition. It should suffice to mention that when two solutions exist, the nontrivial version is stable and the trivial one is not.

9.6 CAMBRIDGE GROWTH, KALDOR STYLE

The neoclassical growth model embraces the marginal productivity theory of income distribution, which presumes that perfect competition and profit maximization prevail in the presence of a linear homogeneous production function. Under these conditions total product is completely exhausted among the inputs, and income shares are tied to the factor proportion. Details follow.

At any time t the production function (9.15) yields via Euler's theorem

$$Y = F_K K + F_L L$$

or

$$1 = F_K \frac{K}{Y} + F_L \frac{L}{Y}$$

With factors paid their marginal products, these expressions become, respectively,

$$Y = rK + wL$$

and

$$1 = \frac{rK}{Y} + \frac{wL}{Y}$$

where again r is the interest rate and w the real wage. Output is completely distributed to capital and labor, and the output elasticities reappear as the factor shares. Because of linear homogeneity, those elasticities depend upon the factor proportion, and that dependency translates into a tight link of shares to the input ratio. In the case of steady equilibrium growth at the natural rate, where interest stays fixed while real wages grow at the rate of progress, income shares remain constant.

When $\rho > 0$, however, $Y/K = \gamma/[\xi_1 + \xi_2 \kappa^\rho]^{1/\rho}$ from (9.26). An increase in κ causes Y/K to fall to zero from the finite ceiling $\gamma \xi_1^{-1/\rho}$, and thus nontrivial κ are associated with Y/K in the abbreviated interval $\gamma \xi_1^{-1/\rho} > Y/K > 0$. For a nontrivial solution to (9.24), $(\eta + \psi)/s$ must locate in the same interval. $\gamma \xi_1^{-1/\rho} > (\eta + \psi)/s > 0$ and hence $s > \xi_1^{1/\rho}(\eta + \psi)/\gamma$. If $s \leq \xi_1^{1/\rho}(\eta + \psi)/\gamma$ in violation of (9.28), then κ converges to zero and Y/K converges to its ceiling $\gamma \xi_1^{-1/\rho}$. To expose these movements write (9.21) as $\dot{\kappa}/\kappa = sY/K - (\eta + \psi)$. $s \leq \xi_1^{1/\rho}(\eta + \psi)/\gamma$ implies that sY/K remains below $\eta + \psi$ for all nontrivial κ, causing $\dot{\kappa}/\kappa$ to be negative for those κ. Thus κ and Y/K behave as indicated. Similar analysis applies for $\rho < 0$. See J. D. Pitchford, "Growth and the Elasticity of Factor Substitution," *Economic Record*, **36** (December 1960), pp. 494–496, and Kazuo Sato, "Growth and the Elasticity of Factor Substitution: A Comment—How Plausible Is Imbalanced Growth?" *Economic Record*, **39** (September 1963), pp. 356–357.

Marginal productivity theory was not warmly received by all economists. For instance, Nicholas Kaldor of Cambridge, England, challenged the theory's doctrine of perfect competition as unrealistic. More fundamentally, he strongly objected to its cornerstone, the production function. A principal failing of the neoclassical function, claimed Kaldor, was its inability to correctly portray productive activity under capital embodiment, in his view the almost exclusive form of progress. To him, embodiment meant that a shift in the production function could not be divorced from movements along it, thereby rendering nonsensical the independence of input quantities and progress assumed by that construct.[41]

Presumably immune from the conceptual difficulty posed by embodiment is Kaldor's technical progress function, which expresses the rate of change in output per head in terms of the rate of change in capital per head:

$$\frac{\dot{y}}{y} = \zeta\left(\frac{\dot{k}}{k}\right) \tag{9.30}$$

with $y = Y/L$ and $k = K/L$. This function, displayed in Figure 9.5, has a positive intercept reflecting society's "dynamism" or creative spirit and willingness to embrace new ideas. It also shows positive first and negative second derivatives mirroring the belief that investment opportunities favorable to output exist and are exploited in accordance with a careful plan: namely, pursue first those opportunities which raise output most. A more formal statement of these properties reads

$$\zeta > 0 \quad \text{for} \quad \dot{k}/k \geq 0 \quad \text{with} \quad \zeta(\infty) = \infty$$

$$\zeta' > 0 \quad \text{for} \quad \infty > \dot{k}/k \geq 0 \quad \text{with} \quad \zeta'(\infty) < 1$$

$$\zeta'' < 0 \quad \text{for} \quad \dot{k}/k > 0$$

The technical progress function, however, is not without its own frailties. For instance, dynamism might not be independent of the rate of accumulation, and hence shifts in the function could be confounded with movements along it—the precise analogue of Kaldor's own complaint against the neoclassical construct. In any event, the technical progress function may not really be far removed from the neoclassical production function: when postulated linearly, it quickly converts into an expression having a Cobb-Douglas format!

Written linearly, ζ is

$$\frac{\dot{y}}{y} = \frac{\dot{a}}{a} + \varepsilon\frac{\dot{k}}{k} \tag{9.31}$$

where the constants $\dot{a}/a$ and ε satisfy the inequalities $\infty > \dot{a}/a > 0$ and $1 > \varepsilon > 0$. Under these restrictions the linear function cuts the 45° line in Figure 9.5 from

---

[41]Comprehensive treatment of Kaldor's innovations appears in his "Alternative Theories of Distribution," *Review of Economic Studies*, **23** (March 1956), pp. 83–100, and his "Capital Accumulation and Economic Growth," in F. A. Lutz and D. C. Hague, eds. *The Theory of Capital* (London: Macmillan & Co., Ltd., 1961), pp. 177–222.

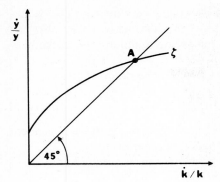

Figure 9.5 *Source*: Kaldor, "Capital Accumulation," p. 208. Used by permission of The International Economics Association and Macmillan, London & Basingstoke.

above at a positive and finite $\dot{k}/k$. Integrating both sides of (9.31) gives

$$\ln y = qt + \varepsilon \ln k + \ln Q_0$$

where q denotes $\dot{a}/a$ and $\ln Q_0$ represents the constant of integration. Antilogs followed by easy manipulation finally reveal

$$Y_t = Q_0 e^{qt} K_t^{\varepsilon} L_t^{1-\varepsilon} \tag{9.32}$$

This metamorphic character of the linear technical progress function,[42] which appears later as part of the Kaldor growth model, should lead to the suspicion that Cambridge growth à la Kaldor possesses key features in common with those of the neoclassical paradigm.

Rather than entertain polemics about the merits of the technical progress function versus those of the neoclassical production function, it seems advisable for the flow of discussion simply to recognize that renouncement of the production function concept, for whatever reason, is tantamount to rejection of the marginal productivity theory of distribution. That rejection creates a need for a replacement theory, and Kaldor attempts to provide it.

Total saving is presumed to consist of two components: saving from profits and saving from wages. In keeping with a long-run setting, each component is proportionally related to the corresponding income category, giving

$$S = s_R R + s_W W \tag{9.33}$$

R and W respectively denote real profits and real wages ($R + W = R + wL = Y$),

---

[42] Kaldor himself acknowledges the schizophrenic tendency of a linear technical progress function but hastens to add that the resulting Cobb-Douglas (9.32) is spurious. He claims that under embodiment a function connecting separate aggregate measures of output, capital, and labor cannot be validly constructed, and he suggests that the relationship for aggregate output Y_t must instead be posited as $Y_t = G(H_t)$, where H_t "specifies the distribution of capital according to age as well as (in a multi-commodity world) the distribution of both capital and labor between industries and firms." Kaldor, "Capital Accumulation," footnote 1, p. 215.

Despite Kaldor's contention, capital embodiment does not necessarily invalidate the concept of an aggregate production function. That issue receives airing in Sections 10.1 and 10.3.

while s_R and s_W represent the corresponding saving coefficients. The values assumed by these coefficients prove to be hardly inconsequential; they obey the restriction $1 > s_R > s_W \geq 0$. Parenthetically, the saving function used in the neo-classical model emerges from (9.33) when $s_R = s_W$.

From (9.33) total saving as a proportion of income becomes

$$\frac{S}{Y} = s_R \frac{R}{Y} + s_W \frac{W}{Y}$$

As before, S/Y might be designated by s; now, however, s is a variable dependent upon the factor shares. In the neoclassical model it is a parameter.

Keynesian equilibrium requires that $I = S$, which can be restated as

$$\frac{I}{Y} = s_R \frac{R}{Y} + s_W \frac{W}{Y} \tag{9.34}$$

This equality holds through time because of the adjustment of saving to investment through a change in factor shares. The adjustment process is easily described. Given full employment an increase in investment (investment being treated for the moment as exogenous) forces prices to rise relative to money wages. The profit share rises at the expense of the wage share and, since $s_R > s_W$, s rises, preserving equilibrium. Had $s_R \lessgtr s_W$, s would have remained unchanged, or it would have fallen, exacerbating the inequality between saving and investment. $s_R > s_W$ is therefore a stability condition. The opposite behavior pattern also applies. A fall in investment forces prices to fall relative to money wages, increasing the wage share at the expense of its profit counterpart. s therefore falls, restoring equilibrium.

Manipulation of equation (9.34) with the understanding that $W/Y = 1 - R/Y$ leaves

$$\frac{R}{Y} = \frac{1}{s_R - s_W} \frac{I}{Y} - \frac{s_W}{s_R - s_W} \tag{9.35}$$

In contrast to marginal productivity theory, the profit share depends upon the investment proportion, not upon the factor proportion. Equation (9.35) automatically produces

$$\frac{R}{K} = \frac{1}{s_R - s_W} \frac{I}{K} - \frac{s_W}{s_R - s_W} \frac{Y}{K} \tag{9.36}$$

where R/K represents the profit rate.

Empirical evidence cited by Kaldor supports the proposition that $s_R > s_W$. But it does more. It suggests that s_W can be regarded as zero.[43] Thus, (9.35) and (9.36) respectively translate into

$$\frac{R}{Y} = \frac{1}{s_R} \frac{I}{Y} \tag{9.37}$$

$$\frac{R}{K} = \frac{1}{s_R} \frac{I}{K} \tag{9.38}$$

---

[43] For the U.S. example, saving from profits amounted to 70 percent while that from personal income approximated only 5 percent. Kaldor, "Capital Accumulation," p. 194.

Entrepreneurs, by raising investment spending, can raise their profit, profit rate, and income share; the wage share is lowered in the process. Constraint $s_W = 0$ is adopted henceforth.[44]

For the income redistribution mechanism to work, prices and money wages must be flexible. This flexibility in turn requires that both profiteers and wage earners be willing to tolerate price and wage changes. For $I > S$ prices must rise relative to money wages in order to reduce real wages. But if as a result real wages were to be pushed below a subsistence level, workers would resist that reduction and frustrate the adjustment process. Similarly for $I < S$: entrepreneurs would resist any price movement which would drive their share below a minimum level, again frustrating adjustment. That minimum profit share might reflect the degree of monopoly power in the economy. Hence smooth functioning of the redistribution mechanism requires that two inequalities be observed:

$$w \geq w_{min} \quad \text{and} \quad \frac{R}{Y} \geq \left(\frac{R}{Y}\right)_{min}$$

Thus far investment has been treated as exogenous. It can be made endogenous in various ways; Kaldor, in fact, tried several.[45] One construction assumes that investment is induced both by an acceleration phenomenon and by a discrepancy between prospective and realized profit rates. Elaboration might be helpful. Acceleration generates capital accumulation which assures that productive capacity just matches prospective output, a match governed by the technical progress function. Solved for $\dot{K}$, that function determines the acceleration component, which may be associated with a changing capital-output ratio. Profit expectations then either add to or subtract from this rate of accumulation.

---

[44] Proportional relationships (9.37) and (9.38) can be derived without the restriction $s_W = 0$ under a reformulation of the saving function (9.33). The capital stock is owned by all those, wage earners included, who participate in saving activity; consequently, wage earners must receive a portion of profits, R_W. The balance of profits, R_C, accrues to the capitalists. Expression (9.33) can accommodate this view, although somewhat awkwardly:

$$S = s_W W + s_R R_W + s_R R_C$$

which claims that wage earners save from wages at one rate and from profits at another—one exactly equal to the capitalists'.

A more satisfactory postulate seems to be

$$S = s_W(W + R_W) + s_R R_C$$

which states that wage earners treat wage and profit income as homogeneous for saving purposes. This alternative can be shown to yield (9.37) and (9.38) under the reasonable long-run hypothesis that the interest rate equals the profit rate. The restriction $s_W = 0$ is not needed. This finding strengthens the credibility of (9.37) and (9.38) in the long-run setting. For more on this point, see Luigi L. Pasinetti, "Rate of Profit and Income Distribution in Relation to the Rate of Economic Growth," *Review of Economic Studies*, **29** (October 1962), pp. 270–272. Incidentally, Pasinetti assisted Professor Kaldor with the mathematical specification of his growth model.

[45] A first attempt appeared in Nicholas Kaldor, "A Model of Economic Growth," *Economic Journal*, **67** (December 1957), pp. 599–602, 604. The formulation presented here is patterned after that discussed in his 1961 "Capital Accumulation," pp. 212–216.

A prospective rate of profit exceeding the current rate would prompt added investment as entrepreneurs attempt to exploit profitable investment opportunities. The reverse also holds; a prospective rate below the current rate dampens investment. A convenient means of incorporating this rate discrepancy into the investment function might be found by factoring the profit rate R/K into $(R/Y) \cdot (Y/K)$. If Y/K has been rising historically, then entrepreneurs relying on past experience might expect it to continue to rise in the future. If the profit share R/Y were anticipated to remain largely unchanged at some norm value, then the prospective profit rate would lie above the current rate. Conversely, a declining Y/K would beget a prospective rate below the current. It follows, therefore, that a rising output-capital ratio would stimulate investment, while a falling ratio would repress it.

These considerations lead to the investment function

$$I_{+c} = \frac{1}{\varepsilon}\left[\frac{\dot{Y}}{Y} - (1 - \varepsilon)\eta - q\right]K + \pi \frac{d}{dt}\left(\frac{Y}{K}\right) \tag{9.39}$$

where the subscript $+c$ implies that the investment relationship involves a lag of c periods. η denotes $\dot{L}/L$, while π denotes a positive and finite constant. The first component on the right side of (9.39) constitutes the acceleration effect coming from the technical progress function, now taken to be linear in Figure 9.5. It results by solving (9.31) for $\dot{K}$. The second component represents the effect of expected profitability; it works wonders. At each point on the technical progress function, acceleration calls forth just enough capital to leave entrepreneurs satisfied that capacity changes remain consistent with prospective output changes. But at any point to the left of point A in Figure 9.5, $\dot{Y}/Y > \dot{K}/K$ and Y/K rises, prompting additional investment and increasing the warranted rate $\dot{K}/K$. To the right of point A, $\dot{Y}/Y < \dot{K}/K$, and investment is damped, causing $\dot{K}/K$ to fall. In short, the profitability component of investment provides a tendency for the system to gravitate toward point A, where $\dot{Y}/Y = \dot{K}/K$.

What is true at point A? From the linear technical progress function (9.31),

$$\frac{\dot{Y}}{Y} = \eta + \frac{q}{1 - \varepsilon}$$

Output grows steadily at the natural rate, and characteristically, since $\dot{K}/K = \dot{Y}/Y$, the warranted rate equals the natural rate.[46] For simplicity denote $q/(1 - \varepsilon)$ by ψ.

Remaining features of the steady growth solution readily emerge. From (9.38)

$$\frac{R}{K} = \frac{1}{s_R}\frac{\dot{K}}{K} = \frac{\eta + \psi}{s_R}$$

---

[46] Expression $\eta + q/(1 - \varepsilon)$ resembles the natural rate coming from a standard Cobb-Douglas framework for the neoclassical model and discussed in footnote 38. This finding should not be completely surprising given the kinship of the linear technical progress function with the Cobb-Douglas evidenced by (9.31) and (9.32). The q in (9.32) may be likened to the rate of exogenous Hicks-neutral disembodiment.

which is constant. Since $R/K = (R/Y)(Y/K)$ with R/K and Y/K constant, R/Y must be constant as well. So too must be W/Y, meaning in turn that with Y and L growing at rates $\eta + \psi$ and η, respectively, w grows at the rate ψ. Factor share constancy, of course, implies s constancy. Furthermore, drawing from (9.38) and the equilibrium condition $I/Y = S/Y = s$,

$$\frac{R}{K} = \frac{s}{s_R} \frac{Y}{K}$$

which gives

$$\frac{Y}{K} = \frac{\eta + \psi}{s}$$

What results then is steady equilibrium growth at the natural rate. Along that path, labor remains fully employed, consonant with the income distribution apparatus, and capital remains fully utilized, consonant with the accelerator. Factor shares and s are stationary, as are the profit rate and interest.[47] Real wages grow through time.

Existence of this solution[48] is assured by $\dot{a}/a > 0$ and $\varepsilon < 1$. The former inequality serves the same purpose as the left-hand Inada condition in the neoclassical framework; the latter acts like the right-hand condition. This growth solution is stable, stability deriving from the profit component of the investment function. Thus, despite its different mechanism of income distribution, Kaldor's model generates growth properties clearly analogous to those of the neoclassical system.

9.7 THE CAMBRIDGE OF ROBINSON

A hallmark of the neoclassical growth model is a production function with a variable factor proportion. The direct parallel in Kaldor's system is the technical progress function with its variable capital-output ratio. Professor Joan Robinson seems to be sympathetic to neither. Neither appears in her growth model, nor does anything resembling a replacement construct.[49]

---

[47] In equilibrium the profit rate equals the interest rate plus a subjective risk premium imposed by entrepreneurs. Interest is determined in the general case along Keynesian lines with the money supply interacting with the liquidity preference schedule. The growth model, however, posits interest as constant, implying that the risk premium must be constant too.

[48] Kubota shows that a slip in Kaldor's analysis, traceable to the formulation of investment, compromises the existence of a growth solution. See. K. Kubota, "A Re-examination of the Existence and Stability Propositions in Kaldor's Growth Models," *Review of Economic Studies*, **35** (July 1968), pp. 358–360.

The investment function has been a source of persistent trouble for Kaldor as one correction gave rise to another problem. Specifically, a fault in the 1957 function led to the 1961 version, which then proved harmful for a growth solution. Kaldor, "Capital Accumulation," pp. 212, 214.

[49] The ensuing discussion appeals to Robinson, *Essays in Growth*, pp. 22–87. See also Hamberg, *Models*, pp. 114–119, 121.

Drawing on Kaldor's theory of income distribution, Robinson postulates that $S = s_R R$, where the propensity to save from wage income, s_W, is assumed zero. In equilibrium $I = S$, and hence equations (9.37) and (9.38) again apply. The latter, which relates the rate of profit to the rate of accumulation, can be written equivalently as

$$\frac{I}{K} = s_R \frac{R}{K} \tag{9.40}$$

This equation comprises one of two key relationships in her analysis.

The second equation links desired investment—more precisely, the desired rate of accumulation—to the expected profit rate:

$$\frac{I}{K} = \chi(m) \tag{9.41}$$

m being the expected profit rate $\widehat{R/K}$. A variety of χ configurations is possible, but the preferred form seems to stipulate that a minimum expected profit rate m_{min} is necessary to induce investment and that investment is induced at a decreasing rate, a pattern consistent with hedging behavior of entrepreneurs faced by uncertainty about the future.[50] In mathematical terms

$$\chi > 0 \quad \text{for } \infty > m > m_{min} > 0 \text{ with } \chi(m_{min}) = 0 \text{ and } \chi(\infty) = \infty$$

Furthermore,

$$\chi' > 0 \quad \text{and} \quad \chi'' < 0 \quad \text{for } \infty > m > m_{min}$$

Additional χ properties are

$$\chi'(m_{min}) > s_R \quad \chi'(\infty) < s_R \quad \text{and} \quad \chi(m^*)/m^* > s_R$$

where m^* denotes the finite m greater than m_{min} at which $\chi' = s_R$. The derivative inequalities for the minimum and infinite expected rates act roughly like Inada boundary conditions in the present setting. Since expectations are assumed to be static, with the current profit rate expected to persist unchanged into the future, $m = R/K$. Figure 9.6 confronts investment function (9.41) with equilibrium equation (9.40).[51]

Investment plans and equilibrium are consistent at two points, A and B.[52] The former is unstable; the latter, stable. To the left of A, the rate of accumula-

---

[50] Robinson considers other χ configurations in her *Essays in Growth*, footnote 1, p. 49.

[51] Figure 9.6 graphs the two functions as defined in (9.40) and (9.41); they are the inverses of the functions plotted by Robinson, *Essays in Growth*, p. 48. This tack facilitates exposition.

[52] Formal proof tying the existence of points A and B to the stated properties of χ proceeds thus. Under static expectations $m = \widehat{R/K} = R/K$; consequently, the difference between $\chi(m)$ and $s_R R/K$ becomes $u = \chi(m) - s_R m$. Since $\chi(m_{min}) = 0$, $u(m_{min}) = -s_R m_{min} < 0$. Since $\chi(\infty) = \infty$, $u(\infty) < 0$ by l'Hopital's rule, given that $\chi'(\infty) < s_R$. The derivative of u is $\chi' - s_R$. Because $\chi'(m_{min}) > s_R$ and $\chi'(\infty) < s_R$, $u'(m_{min}) > 0$ and $u'(\infty) < 0$. Furthermore, with $u'' = \chi''$, $u'' < 0$ for $\infty > m > m_{min}$. Therefore u rises steadily from a negative value at m_{min}, reaches a maximum at (say) m^*, and then falls steadily. *(continued)*

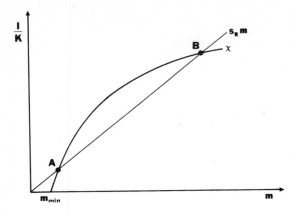

Figure 9.6 *Source*: Robinson, *Essays in Growth*, p. 48. © 1962 by Joan Robinson. Used by permission of St. Martin's Press, Inc.

tion exceeds that desired by entrepreneurs at a given profit rate, and thus they reduce investment. Between points A and B, the rate of accumulation falls short of that desired based on the profit rate; consequently, the rate of accumulation rises. To the right of point B, accumulation proceeds faster than desired at the stated profit rate, and hence it slows. The rate of accumulation associated with point B can be labeled the "warranted" or "equilibrium rate" because at that rate entrepreneurs are satisfied with the results of their actions.

This warranted rate of capital accumulation might be compared against the natural rate $\eta + \psi$. ψ signifies the growth rate of output per capita due to Harrod-neutral progress, whose own rate now varies if the tightness of the labor market changes.[53] Given initially near-full employment and a stock of capital

---

For points A and B to exist, u must become positive somewhere between extreme m values. If u assumes a positive value anywhere, it does so at its maximum, at m^*. A positive u is thus assured when $\chi(m^*)/m^* > s_R$. Regrettably, this m^* inequality is not especially descriptive.

The m^* inequality is needed because the left-hand condition $\chi'(m_{min}) > s_R$ can only narrow the discrepancy between χ and $s_R m$ for an initial increase in m; it cannot guarantee that χ eventually lies above $s_R m$. But if $m_{min} = 0$, then $\chi'(m_{min}) > s_R$ does guarantee that χ exceeds $s_R m$ for any initial m increase, making u positive and assuring the existence of points A (now the origin) and B. Put differently, when $m_{min} = 0$, $\chi(m_{min})/m_{min} = \chi'(m_{min})$ by l'Hopital, and with $\chi'(m_{min}) > s_R$, the m^* inequality must hold automatically. It ceases to be a separate constraint.

An example of the χ graphed in Figure 9.6 is $\chi = \beta_1(m - m_{min})^{\beta_2}$, $\infty > \beta_1 > 0$ and $1 > \beta_2 > 0$. Thus, $\chi' = \beta_1\beta_2(m - m_{min})^{\beta_2 - 1}$ and $\chi'' = \beta_1\beta_2(\beta_2 - 1)(m - m_{min})^{\beta_2 - 2}$. It follows that $\chi(m_{min}) = 0$ and that $\chi(\infty) = \infty$. Moreover, $\chi' > 0$ and $\chi'' < 0$ for $\infty > m > m_{min}$, while $\chi'(m_{min}) = \infty$ and $\chi'(\infty) = 0$. In addition, $m^* = m_{min} + (\beta_1\beta_2/s_R)^{1/(1 - \beta_2)}$. Satisfaction of inequality $\beta_2^{-1}/\{1 + m_{min}[s_R/(\beta_1\beta_2)]^{1/(1 - \beta_2)}\} > 1$ assures that points A and B exist, and when $m_{min} = 0$, this inequality holds without question.

[53] Robinson refers to the equilibrium rate of accumulation as the "desired rate," though admitting her temptation to use Harrodian terminology. She opted for new nomenclature because of Harrod's ambiguity about whether entrepreneurs are satisfied with the stock of capital or with its growth rate. Similarly, she designates $\eta + \psi$ as the "possible rate." Notice that the rate of progress is taken to be partly endogenous. Robinson, *Essays in Growth*, pp. 49, 51–52.

compatible with growth, steady growth occurs with coincident warranted and natural rates, $I/K = \eta + \psi$. Then, since $R = I/s_R$,

$$\frac{R}{K} = \frac{\eta + \psi}{s_R} \qquad \text{and} \qquad \frac{R}{Y} = \frac{s}{s_R}$$

with $s = I/Y$. Real wages rise at the rate ψ, fixed because of unchanging labor market conditions, and maintain constancy of the factor shares and s. Moreover, since $R/K = (R/Y)(Y/K)$,

$$\frac{Y}{K} = \frac{\eta + \psi}{s}$$

Kaldorian results reappear.

However, equality of the warranted and natural rates does not result from the operation of an automatic adjustment mechanism inherent in the model. Adjustment might occur, but only through the action of various ad hoc and basically incidental devices. For instance, when $I/K < \eta + \psi$, the economy limps along below full employment with unemployment possibly worsening. The consequent decline in living standards can lead to a lower rate of population growth, causing the natural rate to fall toward the warranted. Such Malthusian adjustment, however, must be regarded as a parenthetical attachment to the model rather than as an integral part of its core.

The converse situation, $I/K > \eta + \psi$, means that entrepreneurs cannot expand as quickly as they desire. Employment being full, inflation might emerge, triggering a rise in the interest rate and thereby dampening investment. So the warranted rate falls toward the natural. Curiously, except for its rise to restrain inflation and to restrict investment, the interest rate remains constant. It does not fall to stimulate investment when $I/K < \eta + \psi$.

Although embracing the same theory of income distribution, the growth models of Kaldor and Robinson differ fundamentally. Kaldor's paradigm contains within its nucleus a mechanism which eliminates any discrepancy between the warranted and natural rates. A changing capital-output ratio prompts changes in the rate of accumulation and propels the economy along the technical progress function to the point of steady growth at the natural rate. Robinson's model, by contrast, contains no built-in instrument of adjustment. It relies instead on either Malthusian misery or asymmetric monetary policy response—controls *attached* to the nucleus—to reduce the discrepancy between the warranted and natural rates. In this light Robinson's model bears the same relationship to Kaldor's as Harrod-Domar's bears to the neoclassicals'. The Robinson and Kaldor models might even be interpreted as Cambridge versions of the Harrod-Domar and neoclassical systems, respectively. That interpretation, however, stops far short of equating the Robinson paradigm to the Harrod-Domar or the Kaldor to the neoclassical.

9.8 NEOCLASSICAL GROWTH WITH A CAMBRIDGE SAVING FUNCTION

The neoclassical growth solution discussed in Section 9.4 presumes the existence of a proportional saving function $S = sY$, s being a parameter with $1 > s > 0$. This solution, which depends crucially upon the properties of the production function (9.15), can survive Kaldor's elaboration of the saving function, although in general greater articulation of those properties is required.

Using (9.33), rewrite the equilibrium condition $I = S$ as

$$\dot{K} = s_W W + s_R R \tag{9.42}$$

This expression contrasts with equilibrium equation (9.17) adopted earlier. Since marginal productivity theory demands that factor prices equal marginal products and that output be exhausted, $R = F_K K$ and $W = Y - F_K K$. Equation (9.42) thus converts into

$$\dot{K} = s_W(Y - F_K K) + s_R F_K K \tag{9.43}$$

Manipulation yields

$$\frac{\dot{K}}{K} \frac{K}{AL} = \frac{Y}{AL}\left[s_W + (s_R - s_W)\frac{F_K K}{Y}\right]$$

For constant Y/K under the progress and labor supply assumptions $A = A_0 e^{\psi t}$ and $L = L_0 e^{\eta t}$, the production function (9.15) implies that $\dot{K}/K = \eta + \psi$. Hence for a constant capital-output ratio, the equilibrium condition (9.43) becomes

$$s_W f + (s_R - s_W)\kappa f' = (\eta + \psi)\kappa \tag{9.44}$$

Equation (9.44) generalizes equation (9.24).

To solve (9.44) and thereby determine steady equilibrium growth at the natural rate, the characteristics of its left-hand component must be learned. Denote that component by z, which depends solely upon κ:

$$z = s_W f + (s_R - s_W)\kappa f'$$

Consequently,

$$z' = s_R f' + (s_R - s_W)\kappa f''$$
$$z'' = (2s_R - s_W)f'' + (s_R - s_W)\kappa f'''$$

Establishing the behavior of z with respect to κ generally requires more information about the production function than that needed when saving followed a proportional rule. Details of the third derivative f''' must come to the fore, and the second derivative f'' must be specified more completely. Three convenient cases readily suggest themselves, however.

Pure Neoclassicalism: $1 > s_R = s_W > 0$ Here the saving function *is* proportional, and $z = s_W f$. Equation (9.44) therefore degenerates into equation (9.24),

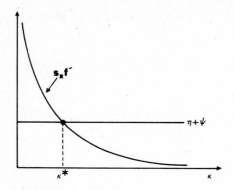

Figure 9.7

and the discussion centering on Figure 9.2 applies. Being repetitive, this case is offered merely for completeness.

Special Kaldorism:[54] $1 > s_R > s_W = 0$ Equation (9.44) becomes

$$s_R f' = \eta + \psi$$

and Inada's conditions $f'(0) = \infty$ and $f'(\infty) = 0$ guarantee the $s_R f'$ locus illustrated in Figure 9.7. A unique growth solution exists at the positive and finite κ^*, and that solution is stable. Stability can be shown by appealing to the time derivative of κ in a manner reminiscent of (9.22):

$$\dot{\kappa} = \kappa \left[\frac{\dot{K}}{K} - (\eta + \psi) \right]$$

Since $s_W = 0$, equation (9.43) gives $\dot{K}/K = s_R f'$, leading to

$$\dot{\kappa} = \kappa \left[s_R f' - (\eta + \psi) \right]$$

$\kappa > \kappa^*$ means that $s_R f' < \eta + \psi$, causing κ to fall ($\dot{\kappa} < 0$), while $\kappa < \kappa^*$ makes $s_R f' > \eta + \psi$, forcing κ to rise ($\dot{\kappa} > 0$).

General Kaldorism: $1 > s_R > s_W \geq 0$ with $\sigma = 1$ The Cobb-Douglas function (9.27) has $f = \gamma \kappa^{\xi_1}$ and $f' = \gamma \xi_1 \kappa^{\xi_1 - 1}$, rendering $z = s_{RW} \gamma \kappa^{\xi_1}$, $z' = s_{RW} \gamma \xi_1 \kappa^{\xi_1 - 1}$, and $z'' = s_{RW} \gamma \xi_1 (\xi_1 - 1) \kappa^{\xi_1 - 2}$, where $s_{RW} = s_R \xi_1 + s_W (1 - \xi_1)$ and $s_R > s_{RW} > s_W$. Therefore,

$z > 0$	for	$\infty > \kappa > 0$	with	$z(0) = 0$	and	$z(\infty) = \infty$
$z' > 0$	for	$\infty > \kappa > 0$	with	$z'(0) = \infty$	and	$z'(\infty) = 0$

---

[54] Uzawa considers an extreme version of this case, $s_R = 1$, in "Neutral Inventions and Stability," pp. 121–123. An $s_R = 1$ can be easily handled by the present analysis.

Moreover,

$$z'' < 0 \quad \text{for} \quad \infty > \kappa > 0$$

It follows that equation (9.44) replicates the solid lines for sf and $(\eta + \psi)\kappa$ in Figure 9.2. The unique κ^* is stable.

In sum, a Kaldorian saving function with $s_W = 0$ does absolutely no violence to the neoclassical growth solution. Additional properties of the production function are not required. When $s_W > 0$, extra information on that function typically must be provided, but as the Cobb-Douglas example demonstrates, the neoclassical growth solution is not precluded.

TEN

GROWTH UNDER VINTAGE CAPITAL

Believing that most, if not all, technical progress takes the form of capital embodiment, Professor Kaldor rejected the production function concept and in its place inserted the technical progress function, which became a mainstay of his growth theory. Such drastic action could have been avoided, however. Embodiment need not invalidate the production function; furthermore, it need not deny the conclusion that steady equilibrium growth occurs at the natural rate. Robert Solow, writing at about the same time that Kaldor was refining his own theory, offered a stunning affirmation of neoclassical postulates under such progress, and shortly thereafter Edmund Phelps extended that ratification.[1]

Section 10.1 draws on the work by Solow and Phelps to show that the neoclassical concepts of an aggregate capital stock and an aggregate production function can survive capital embodiment. An aggregate capital stock, of course, is a single measure of the total quantity of capital used in the production process. For the case of the two factors capital and labor, an aggregate production function is a function which focuses on the total amount of output generated from all units of the two inputs and expresses it in terms of the aggregate capital stock and a separate measure of the total labor quantity employed. Section 10.2 accepts the aggregate function with embodiment and completes the macro model. It then studies the growth properties of that system. Section 10.3 returns to the issue of the existence of aggregate production measures under embodiment. It

[1]Edmund S. Phelps, "The New View of Investment: A Neoclassical Analysis," *Quarterly Journal of Economics*, **76** (November 1962), pp. 551–560, and Robert M. Solow, "Investment and Technical Progress," in K. J. Arrow, S. Karlin, and P. Suppes, eds., *Mathematical Methods in the Social Sciences, 1959* (Stanford, Calif.: Stanford University Press, 1960), pp. 90–93, 103–104.

reviews the conditions upon which existence depends and verifies that the model treated in Sections 10.1 and 10.2 satisfies them. It also presents an example elaborating the negative point that aggregation cannot proceed when those conditions are violated. Simple alteration of the example to allow compliance leads to successful aggregation in a straightforward manner.

In Section 10.4 consideration is given to the hypothesis that capital has a "putty-clay" nature. The section compares implications of putty-clay with those arising from the view of capital held throughout the discussion to that point, and it notes the consequence of putty-clay for aggregation under embodiment. It concludes by calling for the study of growth properties in the context of labor-augmenting embodiment and putty-clay capital. That call is answered in Section 10.5, which develops a model founded on the two constructs. Expectations are taken to be static. Section 10.6 investigates the steady growth solution of the model, and Section 10.7 examines additional features of its steady state. Especially notable is the derivation of several comparative dynamic properties. Section 10.8 concludes the chapter by modifying the putty-clay model to admit expectations having an adaptively rational orientation. The steady growth solution is also reworked.

10.1 FROM VINTAGES TO AGGREGATES

Some advances in technology, as Section 9.1 observed, might enter the productive process only through capital built to take advantage of them. New capital embodies new discoveries and fully enjoys their benefits.[2] Old capital, by contrast, never benefits from new breakthroughs. Furthermore, since machines fashioned at different times carry different levels of technology, they must be identified by construction date—by vintage. Other technical advances might not be vintage specific. They have the ability to join the productive process independently of new capital, and they affect all vintages equally. Such progress is disembodied.[3]

A Cobb-Douglas production function which captures both embodied and disembodied progress may be written as

$$Y_{vt} = \gamma e^{\tau t + \phi v} K_{vt}^{\xi_1} L_{vt}^{\xi_2} \qquad (10.1)$$

Y_{vt} denotes the quantity of output forthcoming from vintage v capital at time t,

---

[2] Other factors, notably labor, could serve as vehicles of technical progress. This chapter and the next, however, take embodiment to mean progress embodied in capital. All embodiment is capital embodiment.

[3] For additional discussion of material presented in this section, see James H. Gapinski, "Technical Progress, Factor Substitutability, and Models of Production: I," *De Economist*, **122** (1974), pp. 412–413, and "Technical Progress, Factor Substitutability, and Models of Production: II," *De Economist*, **122** (1974), pp. 522–530. See also Phelps, "New View," pp. 551–555, and Solow, "Investment," pp. 90–93.

$v \le t$, K_{vt} represents the quantity of vintage v in use at t, and L_{vt} notates the labor input employed on vintage v at t. Disembodiment occurs at the rate τ, while embodiment transpires at the rate ϕ. Parameters γ, ξ_1, and ξ_2 satisfy the restrictions $0 < \gamma < \infty$, $\xi_1 > 0$, and $\xi_2 > 0$, with $\xi_1 + \xi_2 = 1$.

Several aspects of the production process deserve elaboration. First, all progress is expressed as Hicks neutral, and consequently τ and ϕ have the interpretation of Hicks-neutral rates. Both are nonnegative. In pictorial terms a positive rate of embodiment forces the production surface for a newer vintage to lie above that for an older one, and a positive rate of disembodiment causes the entire family of vintage surfaces to drift upward through time. Second, existing capital always enjoys complete utilization. Physical deterioration— depreciation—exacts its toll at the nonnegative exponential rate δ, and therefore $K_{vt} = I_v e^{-\delta(t-v)}$, where $t - v$ signifies the age of vintage v at time t. I_v gives the total amount of vintage v capital produced; it denotes *gross* investment at time v. Third, any vintage is malleable in the sense that it can accommodate a varying number of workers after its construction. Ex post the factor proportion, the capital-labor ratio, remains variable. Fourth, workers are homogeneous, each possessing the skill needed to operate any vintage.

Entrepreneurs assign labor to capital at time t by equalizing labor's marginal product across vintages, a rule which assures maximum aggregate output from a given supply of workers and the existing capital.[4] The marginal product of labor on vintage v at t reads

$$\frac{\partial Y_{vt}}{\partial L_{vt}} = \xi_2 \gamma e^{\tau t + \phi v} K_{vt}^{\xi_1} L_{vt}^{-\xi_1} \tag{10.2}$$

Although this marginal product is identical for all vintages, its common value may vary through time because the allocation process repeats each period subject to a labor supply and a capital profile which may change. Let m_t denote the common marginal product at t. Then

$$m_t = \xi_2 \gamma e^{\tau t + \phi v} K_{vt}^{\xi_1} L_{vt}^{-\xi_1} \tag{10.3}$$

which can be solved for L_{vt} to yield

$$L_{vt} = \left(\xi_2 \gamma e^{\tau t + \phi v} / m_t \right)^{1/\xi_1} K_{vt} \tag{10.4}$$

The supply of labor L_t is distributed across the capital vintages, and consequently it follows that

$$L_t = \int_{-\infty}^{t} L_{vt} \, dv \tag{10.5}$$

---

[4]An objective of the following exercise is to establish an aggregate production function. As Section 1.1 reported, a production function describes a boundary; it refers to the *maximum* output producible from a given combination of inputs. The rule of equal marginal products, being necessary for maximum aggregate output, is fundamental to the development of an aggregate production function.

Since capital deteriorates exponentially, a vintage completely expires only when it arrives at the ultimate long run, infinity. Hence the integral indicating total employment should embrace all capital ever built;[5] its lower limit should be $-\infty$. Obviously, equation (10.5) serves as the full-employment condition.

Inserting (10.4) into (10.5) gives

$$L_t = \int_{-\infty}^{t} \left(\xi_2 \gamma e^{\tau t + \phi v}/m_t\right)^{1/\xi_1} K_{vt}\, dv \qquad (10.6)$$

Removing from this integral each element independent of v leads to

$$L_t = \left(\xi_2 \gamma e^{\tau t}/m_t\right)^{1/\xi_1} J_t \qquad (10.7)$$

$$J_t = \int_{-\infty}^{t} e^{(\phi/\xi_1)v} K_{vt}\, dv \qquad (10.8)$$

J_t can be understood as the effective stock of capital. The surviving quantity of each vintage is weighted to reflect the level of technology embodied therein, and accordingly the more primitive vintages receive the smaller weights. Through this scaling procedure machines representing different levels of technology are converted into homogeneous efficiency units which permit aggregation.

Total output Y_t is the sum of production levels coming from the layers of capital in service:

$$Y_t = \int_{-\infty}^{t} Y_{vt}\, dv \qquad (10.9)$$

which from function (10.1) becomes

$$Y_t = \int_{-\infty}^{t} \gamma e^{\tau t + \phi v} K_{vt}^{\xi_1} L_{vt}^{\xi_2}\, dv \qquad (10.10)$$

Substituting (10.4) into (10.10) and again extracting elements from the integral leaves

$$Y_t = \gamma e^{\tau t}\left[\left(\xi_2 \gamma e^{\tau t}/m_t\right)^{1/\xi_1}\right]^{\xi_2} J_t \qquad (10.11)$$

The expression in brackets can be recognized from (10.7) as L_t/J_t, and thus (10.11) collapses to

$$Y_t = \gamma e^{\tau t} J_t^{\xi_1} L_t^{\xi_2} \qquad (10.12)$$

Equation (10.12) says that aggregate output is related to the aggregate capital stock and to aggregate labor. Moreover, it says that the relationship among the aggregate variables is well-behaved. In particular, it displays linear homogeneity and observes positive but declining marginal products, properties which carry

---

[5] A vintage would not be operated if the revenue to be obtained from the sale of its output were to fall short of variable cost. However, the properties of the Cobb-Douglas function (10.1) and the continual equality of marginal products assure that in each period all physically surviving vintages escape loss. This circumstance is examined further in Section 10.4.

over directly from the vintage function (10.1). Parameters γ, τ, ξ_1, and ξ_2 of the vintage function occupy the same positions in the aggregate formula. ϕ, however, does not; it becomes absorbed by the measure of aggregate capital. Rather than pivoting the aggregate function, it acts to correct the physical units of capital for the technology levels which they represent. This difference aside, the aggregate function duplicates the vintage specification, with the aggregate variables replacing their vintage counterparts. Embodied technical progress, notwithstanding its insistence that capital be identified by vintage and that each vintage have its own production function, need not invalidate the neoclassical constructs of an aggregate capital stock and an aggregate production function. Not only can an aggregate relationship exist, it can even be well-behaved.

If technical progress were exclusively disembodied, then the link between vintage and aggregate concepts would be transparent. When $\phi = 0$, the effective stock of capital in (10.8) becomes

$$J_t = \int_{-\infty}^{t} K_{vt} \, dv \tag{10.13}$$

meaning that the aggregate stock is simply the unweighted sum of all physically surviving machines. Aggregate function (10.12) then differs from the vintage function (10.1) only because it replaces the vintage quantities by their unweighted totals across all vintages.

10.2 NEOCLASSICAL GROWTH DESPITE EMBODIMENT

Moving from the aggregate production function (10.12) to a complete neoclassical growth model can be accomplished by positing two familiar equations, one to determine labor supply and one to define macroeconomic equilibrium. The full growth model which emerges can be written as[†]

$$Y_t = \gamma e^{\tau t} J_t^{\xi_1} L_t^{\xi_2} \tag{10.14}$$

$$L_t = L_0 e^{\eta t} \tag{10.15}$$

$$I_t = sY_t \tag{10.16}$$

Equation (10.14) renumbers function (10.12) and thereby embraces the definition of J_t given in (10.8). Expression (10.15) says that the supply of labor L_t grows exponentially at the rate η from its time-zero level of L_0, and the presence of L_t in both (10.14) and (10.15) signals perpetual full employment. Equation (10.16) postulates that saving is proportional to output, and it acknowledges that in equilibrium investment equals saving. Investment, saving, and output are gross quantities, and the constant s satisfies the restriction $0 < s < 1$.

[†]This model replicates the paradigm studied by various theorists including K. Sato, "On the Adjustment Time in Neo-classical Growth Models," *Review of Economic Studies*, **33** (July 1966), pp. 263–264. Portions of the present analysis closely parallel Sato's. Refer also to Phelps, "New View," pp. 553–554.

To establish the existence and stability of steady growth for this system, translate equation (10.14) into logs and differentiate the result totally with respect to time. This effort yields

$$\frac{\dot{Y}}{Y} = \tau + \xi_1 \frac{\dot{J}}{J} + \xi_2 \frac{\dot{L}}{L} \tag{10.17}$$

which ignores time subscripts for convenience. The dots identify time derivatives; for example, $\dot{Y}$ means dY/dt. Further articulation of $\dot{Y}/Y$ requires additional details for $\dot{J}/J$ and $\dot{L}/L$. The latter promptly reduces to η via equation (10.15), but the former is more difficult to penetrate.

Describing $\dot{J}$ requires formal appeal to the rule for differentiating a definite integral. That theorem eventually leads to[6]

$$\dot{J} = e^{(\phi/\xi_1)t}I - \delta J \tag{10.18}$$

Change in the aggregate capital stock is the net result of two opposing phenomena. One is the appearance of new machines due to the act of investment; these enter the stock measure bearing their technology weight to render them compatible with the homogeneous counting unit. The second happening is the expiration of some machines in accord with the preordained mortality table. Dividing equation (10.18) by J produces

$$\frac{\dot{J}}{J} = \frac{I}{\bar{J}} - \delta \tag{10.19}$$

where $\bar{J} = e^{-(\phi/\xi_1)t}J$. $\bar{J}$ can be regarded as the aggregate stock of capital in current efficiency units. Its full statement is

$$\bar{J} = \int_{-\infty}^{t} e^{(\phi/\xi_1)(v-t)}K_{vt}\, dv \tag{10.20}$$

which shows that the current period t serves as base: the unit weight corresponds to vintage t. For J, by contrast, the unit weight applies to vintage zero, as

---

[6] The general formula for differentiating a definite integral is

$$\frac{d}{dc}\int_{p(c)}^{q(c)} n(z,c)\, dz = \int_{p(c)}^{q(c)} \frac{\partial}{\partial c} n(z,c)\, dz + n(q,c)\frac{dq}{dc} - n(p,c)\frac{dp}{dc}$$

It calls for differentiating both the integrand $n(z,c)$ and the limits $q(c)$ and $p(c)$. With J being defined by (10.8), this formula leads to

$$\frac{d}{dt}J = \int_{-\infty}^{t} \frac{\partial}{\partial t}\left[e^{(\phi/\xi_1)v}I_v e^{-\delta(t-v)}\right] dv + e^{(\phi/\xi_1)t}I_t e^{-\delta(t-t)}\frac{dt}{dt}$$

$$- e^{(\phi/\xi_1)(-\infty)}I_{-\infty}e^{-\delta[t-(-\infty)]}\frac{d(-\infty)}{dt}$$

Simplification leaves

$$\dot{J} = -\delta \int_{-\infty}^{t} e^{(\phi/\xi_1)v}I_v e^{-\delta(t-v)}dv + e^{(\phi/\xi_1)t}I_t - 0$$

which yields equation (10.18).

equation (10.8) tells. Thus $\bar{J}$ and J differ in their choice of base; $\bar{J}$ uses the current period, while J adopts the zero period.

Substituting η and expression (10.19) into (10.17) and recognizing (10.16) yield

$$\frac{\dot{Y}}{Y} = \tau + \xi_1\left(s\frac{Y}{\bar{J}} - \delta\right) + (1 - \xi_1)\eta \tag{10.21}$$

From equation (10.21) it should be evident that steady equilibrium growth occurs if and only if $\bar{J}/Y$ remains constant through time. This constancy of the capital-output ratio as a proviso for steady equilibrium growth harkens back to the standard neoclassical requirement cited in the exposition following equation (9.18).

Under what circumstance does the capital-output ratio become constant? To answer this question, let π denote $\bar{J}/Y$. Log transformation and total differentiation evoke

$$\frac{\dot{\pi}}{\pi} = \frac{\dot{\bar{J}}}{\bar{J}} - \frac{\dot{Y}}{Y} \tag{10.22}$$

By recalling the linkage between $\bar{J}$ and J and by taking note of equations (10.16), (10.19), and (10.21), equation (10.22) can be converted into

$$\dot{\pi} = s(1 - \xi_1) - \Xi\pi \tag{10.23}$$

where Ξ equals $\tau + \phi/\xi_1 + (1 - \xi_1)(\eta + \delta)$ and thus must be positive. Figure 10.1 displays both right-hand components of (10.23). Since $s(1 - \xi_1) \neq \Xi\pi$ except at $\pi = \pi^*$, π must be changing through time as long as it remains away from π^*. Once it assumes that value, however, it stays constant. The lone constancy amounts to

$$\pi^* = s(1 - \xi_1)/\Xi \tag{10.24}$$

in view of relationship (10.23).

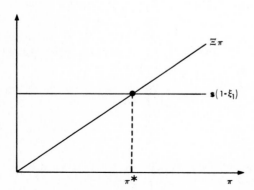

Figure 10.1

Insertion of π^* from (10.24) into (10.21) determines the steady growth rate for output:

$$\frac{\dot{Y}}{Y} = \eta + \frac{\tau + \phi}{1 - \xi_1} \qquad (10.25)$$

Output expands at a rate equal to labor's growth rate plus an adjusted sum of the progress rates. What equation (10.25) really argues, albeit in a clumsy way, is that output grows at Harrod's natural rate. To make this property obvious, rewrite the vintage production function (10.1) in terms of Harrod neutrality:

$$Y_{vt} = \gamma K_{vt}^{\xi_1} \left(e^{\psi t + \mu v} L_{vt} \right)^{\xi_2} \qquad (10.26)$$

where ψ and μ denote Harrod-neutral rates of disembodiment and embodiment, respectively. Comparison of functions (10.1) and (10.26) quickly establishes that $\tau = (1 - \xi_1)\psi$ and that $\phi = (1 - \xi_1)\mu$. Consequently, (10.25) collapses to[7]

$$\frac{\dot{Y}}{Y} = \eta + \psi + \mu \qquad (10.27)$$

Along the path of steady equilibrium growth, output does expand at Harrod's natural rate, which now includes both types of progress. Since only one constant π exists, only one steady growth path exists. A steady equilibrium growth path exists, and it is unique.

But is it stable? Yes. Figure 10.1 indicates that if $\pi > \pi^*$, then $s(1 - \xi_1) < \Xi\pi$. Therefore $\dot{\pi} < 0$ from (10.23), and π falls toward π^*. Conversely, if $\pi < \pi^*$, then π rises toward π^*. A discrepancy between the capital-output ratio and its steady growth value triggers a force which causes the discrepancy to vanish. This inherent tendency for π to gravitate to π^* means that $\dot{Y}/Y$ has a corresponding tendency to gravitate to the natural rate. Subtraction of $\eta + \psi + \mu$ from both sides of equation (10.21) produces

$$\frac{\dot{Y}}{Y} - (\eta + \psi + \mu) = -\frac{s\xi_1}{\pi\pi^*}(\pi - \pi^*) \qquad (10.28)$$

When π lies above its steady growth value, $\dot{Y}/Y$ lies below the natural rate, and as π falls toward its target, $\dot{Y}/Y$ rises toward its target. The reverse holds when π understates π^*. The path of steady equilibrium growth is stable.[8]

Since output expands at the natural rate $\eta + \psi + \mu$ in steady growth, so must the capital stock measured in current efficiency units. Given equation (10.16) investment and saving too must increase at that rate. From its relationship with

---

[7]A similar conversion was discussed in footnote 38 of Chapter 9. Equalities (9.2) also bear here.

[8]Inasmuch as the movement of $\dot{Y}/Y$ is firmly tied to that of π, either variable might be used to track the temporal response of the system should it depart from the steady growth path. Other measures could serve that purpose as well.

Behavior patterns outside of steady growth are studied in Chapter 11; the present system receives attention in Sections 11.1 and 11.6.

capital in current efficiency units, the stock of capital in efficiency units of period zero grows at the rate $\eta + \psi + \mu/\xi_1$: it expands faster than its twin does. Consequently, although the capital-output ratio remains constant for current-period efficiency, it rises for zero-period efficiency. In either case the capital-labor and output-labor ratios, labor being registered in natural units, increase.

Entrepreneurs distribute labor to capital by equalizing labor's marginal product across the vintages. An economic incentive for this allocation rule is the maximization of total output from all vintages. There is another inducement, however. Entrepreneurs might assign labor to a vintage in order to maximize the quasi-rent earned by that set of machines. Quasi-rent being revenue in excess of variable cost, it can be written for vintage v at time t as

$$Y_{vt} - w_t L_{vt}$$

where w_t denotes the real wage at t. Maximum quasi-rent for vintage v at t occurs when[9]

$$\frac{\partial Y_{vt}}{\partial L_{vt}} = w_t$$

namely, when the marginal product of labor employed on it equals the real wage. Since the same wage applies over all capital, a predisposition to maximize quasi-rents is tantamount to equalization of labor's marginal product across vintages. Equality therefore not only assures that total output achieves its maximum, but when tied to wages it also guarantees that each vintage earns maximum quasi-rent. Both benefits accrue every period.

This argument implies that the common marginal product m_t identified in equation (10.3) can double as the real wage. Expressed in terms of the aggregates L_t and J_t, m_t becomes

$$m_t = \xi_2 \gamma e^{\tau t} J_t^{\xi_1} L_t^{\xi_2 - 1}$$

from equation (10.7). Consonant with the temporal behavior of L_t and J_t in steady growth, real wages must grow at the combined rate of technical advance $\psi + \mu$. The two types of progress band together to set the tempo for wages in steady growth.

Careful comparison of this m_t equation with function (10.12) reveals a third interpretation for m_t: it is the marginal product of aggregate labor in the aggregate production function, $\partial Y_t/\partial L_t$. Such a property has considerable intuitive appeal, because if the aggregate production function validly portrays activity which in truth occurs at the vintage level, then its marginal product should equal the vintage marginal products when the latter are all equal. That m_t has this third role helps to corroborate the aggregation procedure. But it also helps to expose the behavior of aggregate capital's input price along the steady growth path. Rewritten to reflect capital in current efficiency units, production function (10.12)

---

[9]The second-order condition, which requires that $\partial^2 Y_{vt}/\partial L_{vt}^2 < 0$, holds without question under the Cobb-Douglas.

yields from Euler's theorem

$$Y_t = \frac{\partial Y_t}{\partial \bar{J}_t} \bar{J}_t + m_t L_t$$

In steady growth Y_t and $m_t L_t$ increase at the natural rate. Therefore, so must $(\partial Y_t/\partial \bar{J}_t)\bar{J}_t$. However, $\bar{J}_t$ itself grows at that rate, and consequently the input price of capital $\partial Y_t/\partial \bar{J}_t$ must remain constant. Similar reasoning concludes that the price of capital input J_t falls at the rate $\mu \xi_2/\xi_1$.

The steady growth properties deduced here bear a striking resemblance to those derived from the neoclassical model (9.15) to (9.17) when the aggregate production function (9.15) is taken to be the Cobb-Douglas.[10] That model admits progress of the disembodied sort only, and it defines investment, saving, and output as net of depreciation. The present system allows embodiment in addition to disembodiment, and it postulates the trio of variables in terms of gross quantities. It reduces to the old model when its parameters ϕ and δ are set to zero. The two paradigms have the same basic structure, and they have the same basic features in steady growth.

That the old model comprises the special case of the new when $\phi = \delta = 0$ can be easily shown. With $\phi = 0$, equation (10.18) notes that $\dot{J}_t = I_t - \delta J_t$ and therefore that $I_t = \dot{J}_t + \delta J_t$. Furthermore, with embodiment no longer present, J_t represents the unweighted sum of all physically surviving capital, as equation (10.13) attests. Thus J_t must be synonymous with the capital variable K_t in equation (9.15), still interpreted as the Cobb-Douglas, and $\dot{J}_t$ must duplicate the net investment variable $\dot{K}_t$ in equation (9.17). With these notational conversions accepted to underscore the assumption that $\phi = 0$, system (10.14) to (10.16) can be rewritten as

$$Yn_t + \delta K_t = \gamma e^{\tau t} K_t^{\xi_1} L_t^{\xi_2} \tag{10.29}$$

$$L_t = L_0 e^{\eta t} \tag{10.30}$$

$$\dot{K}_t + \delta K_t = s(Yn_t + \delta K_t) \tag{10.31}$$

where Yn_t denotes net output at t and δK_t indicates capital deterioration and replacement at t. Equation (10.31) in turn gives

$$\frac{\dot{K}_t}{K_t} = s\frac{Yn_t}{K_t} - \delta(1 - s) \tag{10.32}$$

When $\delta = 0$, equations (10.29) to (10.31) revert to equations (9.15) to (9.17) under the Cobb-Douglas prescription, and relation (10.32) simplifies to formula (9.18). The new system generalizes the old. It therefore follows that equation (10.23) and

---

[10]As Case II of Section 9.5 proves, a Cobb-Douglas form for (9.15) generates the *sf* curve in Figure 9.2 and guarantees the existence, uniqueness, and stability of steady growth at the natural rate. Recall from footnote 39 of Chapter 9 that the solution $\kappa = 0$ in Figure 9.2 is extraneous under the Cobb-Douglas.

Figure 10.1 can be used to describe the adjustment behavior of the old model provided that Ξ is compressed to $\tau + (1 - \xi_1)\eta$ or, equivalently, to $(1 - \xi_1)(\eta + \psi)$. These two analytical devices provide an alternative to the two adopted in Chapter 9: namely, the $\dot{\kappa}$ equation (9.23) and Figure 9.2.

Steady equilibrium growth at the natural rate can occur under embodiment. The steady state can be unique, and it can be stable. A key to these results is the derivation of the aggregate production function (10.12) from the vintage function (10.1). Being important, that derivation deserves further scrutiny.

10.3 BASICS OF AGGREGATION AMPLIFIED

In 1965 Franklin Fisher investigated in formal terms the possibility of constructing an aggregate capital stock and an aggregate production function when technical progress was capital-embodied. He presumed that labor was allocated each period across vintages until its marginal product equalized, thereby assuring maximum output and a proper framework for developing an aggregate production function. From this premise he proved that if every vintage production function was "capital-generalized constant returns," then a necessary and sufficient condition for the existence of an aggregate capital stock and an aggregate production function was that all embodiment be expressible as "capital-altering progress." He also remarked parenthetically that existence placed no restriction on the nature of disembodiment.[11] A year later J. K. Whitaker offered a similar analysis proving *inter alia* Fisher's claim that disembodiment in no way threatened the aggregate measures: they could be constructed under any type of disembodiment.[12]

According to Fisher, capital-altering technical progress is progress which transforms a quantity of capital into any monotonic function of that quantity for the purpose of determining the capital input to production. It converts the K_{vt} units of vintage v surviving at time t into the monotonic function $G^v(K_{vt})$, which then serves as the capital input in the vintage production function. G^v may vary across vintages, as its superscript v indicates, but the vintage production function which houses it does not. Monotonicity is imposed on G^v to preserve the one-to-one correspondence between K_{vt} and output. A popular variant of capital-

---

[11] Franklin M. Fisher, "Embodied Technical Change and the Existence of an Aggregate Capital Stock," *Review of Economic Studies*, **32** (October 1965), pp. 264–265, 267–274. A less technical presentation appears in his Irving Fisher Lecture "The Existence of Aggregate Production Functions," *Econometrica*, **37** (October 1969), pp. 554–564.

[12] J. K. Whitaker, "Vintage Capital Models and Econometric Production Functions," *Review of Economic Studies*, **33** (January 1966), pp. 7–10. See also Peter A. Diamond, "Technical Change and the Measurement of Capital and Output," *Review of Economic Studies*, **32** (October 1965), pp. 297–298.

altering progress is capital augmentation, wherein the alteration formula merely multiplies K_{vt} by a vintage weight independent of K_{vt} itself.[13] For example, $G^v = e^{(\phi/\xi_1)v}K_{vt}$.

Capital-generalized constant returns CGCR means the linear homogeneity of a production function whose arguments include any monotonic function of capital as the capital input. When that monotonic schedule results from technical progress, CGCR links with capital alteration. For the present two-factor circumstance, a vintage production function is CGCR under capital alteration if it exhibits constant returns to scale in G^v and L_{vt}. Should G^v assume a capital-augmenting pattern, then that vintage function simplifies to constant returns for the inputs in natural units; it becomes linearly homogeneous in K_{vt} and L_{vt}. Capital augmentation and constant returns stand as a special case of capital alteration and capital-generalized constant returns.

From this discussion it is evident that the existence of the aggregate capital stock J_t described by equation (10.8) and the aggregate production function (10.12) does not happen by accident, nor does it imply that aggregation must always happen. It occurs because the conditions identified by Fisher are satisfied. Entrepreneurs allocate labor across vintages to equalize its marginal product, as equation (10.3) confesses. Furthermore, the vintage function (10.1), being Cobb-Douglas, enables the assumed rule for embodiment $e^{\phi v}$ to be *expressed* as one of pure capital augmentation:

$$Y_{vt} = \gamma e^{\tau t}\left[e^{(\phi/\xi_1)v}K_{vt}\right]^{\xi_1}L_{vt}^{\xi_2} \tag{10.33}$$

Capital vintages are enhanced at the rate ϕ/ξ_1, and the weight schedule $e^{(\phi/\xi_1)v}$ converts the technologically heterogeneous capital goods into a homogeneous counting unit. The vintage function (10.1) therefore displays capital augmentation and linear homogeneity. Interpreted more broadly, it is CGCR under the capital-altering function $G^v = e^{(\phi/\xi_1)v}K_{vt}$.

Notice that the requisite tie of existence to capital alteration explains why the technology weights for J_t in definition (10.8) involve ϕ/ξ_1 and not ϕ alone. ϕ

---

[13] Fisher's exact definition of capital alteration may be restated thus. Technical progress is capital-altering if and only if there exist a function F, independent of v, and a set of monotonic functions $G^1, G^2, \ldots, G^p$ such that for all $v = 1, 2, \ldots, p$ and for all positive values of K_{vt} and L_{vt}, $f^v(K_{vt}, L_{vt}) = F[G^v(K_{vt}), L_{vt}]$. Under capital-altering progress differences in the vintage production functions f^v become differences in the alteration formula alone: the forms of the vintage production functions become identical across vintages. Notice that since $G^v(K_{vt})$ serves as the capital input, the marginal product of G^v should be positive ($\partial F/\partial G^v > 0$). Consonantly, for the "unaltered" capital variable K_{vt} to have a positive marginal product under the F function ($\partial F/\partial K_{vt} > 0$), G^v must be monotone-*increasing*.

The renowned specialization of capital alteration can be defined in the spirit of Fisher as follows. Technical progress is capital-augmenting if and only if there exist a function F, independent of v, and a set of positive constants $c_1, c_2, \ldots, c_p$ such that for all $v = 1, 2, \ldots, p$ and for all positive values of K_{vt} and L_{vt}, $f^v(K_{vt}, L_{vt}) = F(c_v K_{vt}, L_{vt})$. f^v again become uniform over the vintages. See Fisher, "Embodied Change," pp. 268, 270.

denotes the rate of *output* augmentation; only ϕ/ξ_1 represents the rate of *capital* augmentation.

Both the importance of the restriction that all embodiment be capital-altering and the absence of any restriction on the character of disembodiment can be demonstrated with a vintage CES which postulates that embodiment and disembodiment augment both inputs. For this exercise the general CES has a crucial advantage over its Cobb-Douglas version, because by its structure augmentation of a given factor cannot be reexpressed as augmentation of capital alone. Write the CES as

$$Y_{vt} = \gamma\left[\xi_1\left(e^{\tau_K t + \phi_K v}K_{vt}\right)^{-\rho} + \xi_2\left(e^{\tau_L t + \phi_L v}L_{vt}\right)^{-\rho}\right]^{-1/\rho} \quad (10.34)$$

where τ_K and ϕ_k denote the nonnegative rates of capital augmentation attributable to disembodiment and embodiment, respectively, and where τ_L and ϕ_L have like connotations for labor augmentation. Linear homogeneity prevails, as do the constraints on γ, ξ_1, and ξ_2 posited in connection with function (10.1). Additionally, $-1 < \rho < \infty$.

Optimal allocation of labor yields

$$m_t = \xi_2\gamma\Upsilon_{vt}^{-\rho}(\xi_1\Pi_{vt}^{-\rho}K_{vt}^{-\rho} + \xi_2\Upsilon_{vt}^{-\rho}L_{vt}^{-\rho})^{-1/\rho-1}L_{vt}^{-\rho-1} \quad (10.35)$$

with $\Pi_{vt} = e^{\tau_K t + \phi_K v}$ and $\Upsilon_{vt} = e^{\tau_L t + \phi_L v}$. Solving equation (10.35) for L_{vt} gives

$$L_{vt} = (\xi_1\Psi_{vt}\Pi_{vt}^{-\rho})^{-1/\rho}(1 - \xi_2\Psi_{vt}\Upsilon_{vt}^{-\rho})^{1/\rho}K_{vt} \quad (10.36)$$

where $\Psi_{vt} = (\xi_2\gamma\Upsilon_{vt}^{-\rho}/m_t)^{-\rho/(1+\rho)}$. Equations (10.35) and (10.36) correspond to (10.3) and (10.4), and consequently the hypothesis that some embodiment augments labor, via ϕ_L, does not impede the calculations. The arithmetic, however, has been confined thus far only to the vintage level.

Trouble arises when one aggregates the L_{vt} in (10.36) across vintages. Following (10.5) that procedure leaves

$$L_t = \int_{-\infty}^{t}\left[(\xi_2\gamma/m_t)^{1/(1+\rho)}\xi_1^{-1/\rho}\right]\Upsilon_{vt}^{-\rho/(1+\rho)}\Pi_{vt}$$

$$\cdot\left\{1 - \xi_2(\xi_2\gamma\Upsilon_{vt}^{-\rho}/m_t)^{-\rho/(1+\rho)}\Upsilon_{vt}^{-\rho}\right\}^{1/\rho}K_{vt}\,dv \quad (10.37)$$

This equation is compatible with formulation (10.6), but in contrast to its predecessor, it does not allow removal from the integral of all terms other than a simple capital weight and K_{vt} itself. Some streamlining is possible; however, since Υ_{vt} and Π_{vt} both depend upon v, the integrand can be compacted only by extracting the bracketed term from the integral's jurisdiction. Little is gained by this action since the remaining coefficient of K_{vt}, unlike that in equation (10.8), still does not reflect exclusively the level of technology embedded in vintage v. It reflects in addition the two disembodiment rates and the common marginal product of labor. Besides losing its interpretive value, the coefficient prohibits consolidation of equation (10.37) into a form analogous to equation (10.7), and the aggregation process cannot continue further.

The real obstacle to simplifying equation (10.37) comes from the nonlinear expression in braces. It depends upon v, and it must remain in the integral. But it depends upon v only because Υ_{vt} does—only because some embodiment augments labor. Void that assumption. Then ϕ_L becomes zero, and Υ_{vt} merely equals $e^{\tau_L t}$. The braced term in (10.37) thus becomes entirely independent of v, and further compression of the equation ensues, resulting in

$$L_t = e^{\tau_K t} \xi_1^{-1/\rho} \Psi_t^{-1/\rho} \{1 - \xi_2 \Psi_t \Upsilon_t^{-\rho}\}^{1/\rho} J_t \qquad (10.38)$$

with $\Upsilon_t = e^{\tau_L t}$ and $\Psi_t = (\xi_2 \gamma \Upsilon_t^{-\rho}/m_t)^{-\rho/(1+\rho)}$. Furthermore,

$$J_t = \int_{-\infty}^{t} e^{\phi_K v} K_{vt} \, dv \qquad (10.39)$$

Equation (10.38) rivals the earlier (10.7), and J_t now has exactly the same interpretation as it does in equation (10.8). ϕ/ξ_1 in (10.8) represents the rate of capital-augmenting embodiment implicit in (10.1); ϕ_K in (10.39) represents the rate of capital-augmenting embodiment explicit in (10.34).

Substituting function (10.34), with $\phi_L = 0$, into the aggregate output expression (10.9) and observing steps similar to those used earlier in the derivation of function (10.12) but now appealing to equations (10.36), (10.38), and (10.39) make

$$Y_t = \gamma \left[\xi_1 \left(e^{\tau_K t} J_t \right)^{-\rho} + \xi_2 \left(e^{\tau_L t} L_t \right)^{-\rho} \right]^{-1/\rho} \qquad (10.40)$$

Aggregate output can be written as a well-behaved function of aggregate capital and aggregate labor. The rate of capital-augmenting embodiment ϕ_K is absorbed by the capital index, but except for that adjustment the lone difference between the vintage function and the aggregate function is the use of aggregate measures in the latter.

It must be emphasized that the intractability of equation (10.37) occurred solely because some embodiment was dedicated to augmenting labor. With that property canceled, aggregation proceeded without impediment. It must also be emphasized that at no time did the nature of disembodiment matter. Disembodiment entered equation (10.37) through the Υ_{vt} and Π_{vt} functions. But since it depended upon time alone, it could be completely extricated from the integral once the ϕ_L problem was resolved. Its removal could occur if it augmented only capital, only labor, or both equally or unequally. Regardless of its form, disembodiment does not make capital heterogeneous, and thus no restrictions need be placed on it for constructing aggregates.

Other examples shed more light on the properties of the aggregation process. Let the capital-altering function retain its general format G^v. Besides augmentation cases such as $e^{(\phi/\xi_1)v} K_{vt}$ and $(\beta_v + \chi_v v) K_{vt}$, samples of G^v include $\beta_v + \chi_v K_{vt}$ and $\beta_v + \chi_v e^{K_{vt}}$. For the immediate rehearsals, however, G^v is understood to be any monotonic function of K_{vt}.

Take the vintage production function as a Cobb-Douglas which exhibits CGCR under G^v and which admits Hicks-neutral disembodiment. This generalization of expression (10.1) reads

$$Y_{vt} = \gamma e^{\tau t} \big[G^v(K_{vt}) \big]^{\xi_1} L_{vt}^{\xi_2}$$

Familiar steps eventually lead to

$$Y_t = \gamma e^{\tau t} J_t^{\xi_1} L_t^{\xi_2}$$

$$J_t = \int_{-\infty}^{t} G^v(K_{vt})\, dv$$

When the vintage function is a full CES defined to be CGCR under G^v and postulated to allow disembodiment which augments both inputs G^v and L_{vt}, it may be written as

$$Y_{vt} = \gamma \Big\{ \xi_1 \big[e^{\tau_K t} G^v(K_{vt}) \big]^{-\rho} + \xi_2 \big[e^{\tau_L t} L_{vt} \big]^{-\rho} \Big\}^{-1/\rho}$$

Manipulating this relation, which generalizes function (10.34) while recognizing that $\phi_L = 0$, yields

$$Y_t = \gamma \Big[\xi_1 \big(e^{\tau_K t} J_t \big)^{-\rho} + \xi_2 \big(e^{\tau_L t} L_t \big)^{-\rho} \Big]^{-1/\rho}$$

$$J_t = \int_{-\infty}^{t} G^v(K_{vt})\, dv$$

In these two examples the form of the capital measure J_t reflects that of the capital-altering function G^v. Moreover, the form of the aggregate production function reflects the form of its vintage counterpart. Both similarities appear to possess some degree of generality. They hold when the vintage production function displays linear homogeneity in K_{vt} and L_{vt} and when embodiment simultaneously dictates capital augmentation; that is, they arise under any linear homogeneous vintage function coupled with any definition of augmentation weights.[14] They also apply, as these two illustrations show, to the CGCR family of CES vintage functions under capital alteration.

10.4 THE PUTTY-CLAY HYPOTHESIS

A key to constructing an aggregate capital stock and an aggregate production function is the premise that entrepreneurs optimally allocate labor across vintages. Each vintage remains malleable after its construction and can accept different numbers of workers through time. This assumption of a variable proportion for capital in place is hardly foreign to the growth literature, but it does exclude interesting possibilities. One alternative is referred to as the "putty-clay hypothesis," whose formal debut by 1960 can be credited separately to Leif Johansen and to W. E. G. Salter. The hypothesis asserts that the factor proportion may be varied while capital is being designed but not at all after it has been built. Capital

---

[14]Whitaker, "Vintage Models," p. 8.

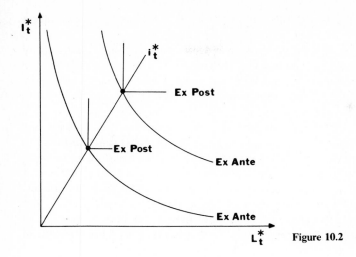

Figure 10.2

is putty ex ante; during its design stage it can be molded to accommodate any number of workers. Ex post, however, it is hard-baked clay. A vintage, once installed, can be operated only in fixed proportion with labor.[15]

Knowledge extant at a given moment determines the capital specifications which can be constructed, each stipulating the labor input required to operate a single machine and the output level to result from that factor combination. Since capital designs relate inputs to output, they can be represented by a blueprint (or ex ante) production function having features determined by the knowledge of the moment. Its elasticity of substitution is positive. Selection of a particular specification and construction of the prescribed machines change the relationship between inputs and output. The ex post production function which describes that association has a zero substitution elasticity.[16]

Figure 10.2 sketches isoquants for the two functions. I_t^* denotes the quantity of capital which entrepreneurs consider building at time t, and L_t^* signifies the labor input which they plan to employ on that capital. In keeping with some optimization principle, they search over the ex ante isoquants and determine the preferred factor proportion to be i_t^*. Vintage t is built according to that specifica-

---

[15] Leif Johansen, "Substitution versus Fixed Production Coefficients in the Theory of Economic Growth: A Synthesis," *Econometrica*, **27** (April 1959), p. 158, and W. E. G. Salter, *Productivity and Technical Change* (London: Cambridge University Press, 1960), p. 17. Salter's thesis, which had crystallized by the mid-1950s, did not insist upon an absolutely fixed proportion ex post (see his footnote 2, p. 17); however, since it includes putty-clay as a special case, he can be considered one of the founders of that hypothesis. G. C. Harcourt notes the kinship between the efforts of Johansen and Salter in his volume *Some Cambridge Controversies in the Theory of Capital* (London: Cambridge University Press, 1972), pp. 6, 66. See also pp. 54–55.

[16] This argument draws from the discussions by Murray Brown, *On the Theory and Measurement of Technological Change* (London: Cambridge University Press, 1968), pp. 65–68, and by Salter, *Productivity*, pp. 14–15, 17.

tion, and its operation afterward obeys the right-angled isoquants centered along stationary ray i_t^*.

Because of clay ex post, entrepreneurs give "hostages to fortune"[17] when they select a machine design. Since they have no ability to refit existing capital to take account of changing economic conditions in general or of rising wages in particular, they are likely to find that some installed vintage would generate negative quasi-rent if it were operated. To avoid this loss they scrap it; they remove it from service even though physical life remains. That vintage has become obsolete (obsolescence referring to the erosion of quasi-rent), and retirement occurs. The length of time that a vintage can earn nonnegative quasi-rents defines its economic life. It is established endogenously by market pressures and contrasts with physical life, which typically carries the status of a parameter. Since clay ex post precludes later correction of mistakes made during the planning period, expectations of future economic occurrences play a pivotal role in any decision regarding the capital to be built. Entrepreneurs look to the future in making current input decisions.

This view of the world differs appreciably from the one which contends that workers can always be swapped across installed vintages to achieve an optimal allocation of labor. The equi-marginal-product rule, when matched to the real wage, assures that labor always earns its marginal product on every vintage. Under linear homogeneity and the usual derivative properties of production functions, labor's average product equals or exceeds its marginal product, and the condition $\partial Y_{vt}/\partial L_{vt} = w_t$ therefore implies that $Y_{vt}/L_{vt} \geq w_t$ or, equivalently, that $Y_{vt} - w_t L_{vt} \geq 0$. Due to ex post malleability, a vintage can be continually reshaped to prevent the onset of negative quasi-rent. Each has an infinite economic life and accordingly leaves service only because of physical expiration.[18] But ex post malleability also means that entrepreneurs need not worry about the future in making decisions pertinent to new capital inasmuch as that capital can be redesigned later if economic conditions warrant. The factor proportion can be varied with equal ease whether capital rests on the design table or operates in the assembly line. Capital is putty ex ante and putty ex post, and the elasticity of substitution is the same for capital in either state. In graphical terms the corresponding ex ante and ex post isoquants coincide, and no angles appear.[19]

Putty-clay capital, unlike the putty-putty treated in the previous sections of this chapter, is inimical to the satisfaction of the equi-marginal-product rule for

[17]J. R. Hicks, *The Theory of Wages* (New York: The Macmillan Company, 1932; reprinted, New York: Peter Smith, 1948), p. 182.

[18]If the vintage production function assigns a finite maximum to the marginal product of labor at $L_{vt} = 0$, then $\partial Y_{vt}/\partial L_{vt} = w_t$ cannot be satisfied for all possible w_t, and a w_t which exceeds that maximum for a vintage would drive all labor from it, perhaps causing its retirement. This scenario, however, constitutes a special case. As long as "the corner" is not encountered, scrapping does not occur. See Eytan Sheshinski, "Stability of Growth Equilibrium in a Neoclassical Vintage Model," *International Economic Review*, **10** (June 1969), pp. 142–143. Additional comment appears in Gapinski, "Technical Progress: II," pp. 527–528.

[19]Alternatives to putty-putty and putty-clay are summarized by Gapinski in "Technical Progress: I," pp. 418–422.

labor allocation and therefore acts as an impediment to the construction of aggregate measures under embodiment. Should any of that embodiment be *labor*-augmenting, then aggregation would be frustrated twice.[20] Doubt about neoclassical aggregates necessarily raises doubt about the neoclassical conclusion that steady equilibrium growth occurs at the natural rate. But skepticism about this conclusion would arise even if aggregates could be established under embodiment, the analysis in Section 10.2 notwithstanding.

Consider a macro system composed of the aggregate CES function (10.40) and the aggregate stock measure (10.39), which reflects capital augmentation. As usual, the labor supply precept (10.15) and the equilibrium statement (10.16) complete the paradigm. The equation governing aggregate output's equilibrium growth rate may thus be written as

$$\frac{\dot{Y}_t}{Y_t} = \frac{\xi_1}{\gamma^\rho} \left[\frac{Y_t}{e^{\tau_K t} J_t} \right]^\rho \left\{ \left(s \frac{Y_t}{e^{-\phi_K t} J_t} - \delta \right) + \tau_K \right\} + \frac{\xi_2}{\gamma^\rho} \left[\frac{Y_t}{e^{\tau_L t} L_t} \right]^\rho \{ \eta + \tau_L \}$$

$$(10.41)$$

where the coefficients of the first and second braced expressions represent the shares of efficient capital $e^{\tau_K t} J_t$ and efficient labor $e^{\tau_L t} L_t$, respectively. Since L_t grows at the rate η, labor's share remains constant provided that Y_t expands at the natural rate $\eta + \tau_L$. By Euler's theorem a constant labor share mandates a constant capital share, and hence J_t must increase at the rate $\eta + \tau_L - \tau_K$. If it does, however, then the ratio multiplying s in the first set of braces does not remain immobile. Instead, it increases at the rate $\tau_K + \phi_K$, implying that steady growth at the rate $\eta + \tau_L$ cannot occur. It can occur, however, if $\tau_K + \phi_K = 0$. With technological regress being outlawed, this condition becomes $\tau_K = \phi_K = 0$. Technical progress must be entirely labor-augmenting *and* entirely disembodied.[21]

Steady equilibrium growth at the natural rate is hardly a general characteristic if aggregates are to hold under embodiment. Moreover, acknowledgment that the capital-altering function $G^v(K_{vt})$ may impose manipulations more complicated than augmentation seems to clinch the argument against generality. The reason why the aggregate model studied in Section 10.2 allows neoclassical growth is that it presumes augmentation and, through the vintage Cobb-Douglas, the ready and complete exchange of one type of augmentation for another. This explanation may be easily verified.

---

[20] It has been shown that the combination of putty-clay and embodiment generally does not yield an aggregate production function when the vintage functions are Cobb-Douglas. The failure of aggregation under the Cobb-Douglas is quite telling because that formulation, marked by its penchant for translating labor augmentation into a capital-augmenting equivalent, is favorably inclined to constructing aggregates, as the examples in Sections 10.1 and 10.3 indicate. See Edmund S. Phelps, "Substitution, Fixed Proportions, Growth and Distribution," *International Economic Review*, **4** (September 1963), pp. 275, 286–287.

[21] This result meshes nicely with the relationship between Harrod neutrality and steady equilibrium growth at the natural rate deduced at the end of Section 9.4 for the case of disembodiment alone.

As the CES (10.40) dissolves into the Cobb-Douglas, equation (10.41) becomes

$$\frac{\dot{Y}_t}{Y_t} = \xi_1\left(s\frac{Y_t}{\bar{J}_t} - \delta \right) + \xi_1\tau_K + \xi_2(\eta + \tau_L) \tag{10.42}$$

where $\bar{J}_t = e^{-\phi_K t}J_t$. Following the steps used to derive (10.24) from (10.22) and inserting into (10.42) the resulting constant $Y_t/\bar{J}_t$ give natural-rate growth:

$$\frac{\dot{Y}_t}{Y_t} = \eta + \tau_L + \frac{\xi_1}{\xi_2}(\tau_K + \phi_K) \tag{10.43}$$

The right-most term in (10.43) identifies that portion of labor augmentation attributable to the transformation of capital augmentation; proof comes from the vintage function (10.34) which, with $\phi_L = 0$ as assumed by (10.40) and (10.41), becomes the Cobb-Douglas

$$Y_{vt} = \gamma K_{vt}^{\xi_1}\left[e^{(\xi_1/\xi_2)(\tau_K t + \phi_K v)} e^{\tau_L t}L_{vt} \right]^{\xi_2} \tag{10.44}$$

A full-blown CES does not allow this free conversion among augmentation forms.[22]

Skepticism about the generality of the neoclassical growth solution when embodiment prevails urges further investigation of growth properties in that context. Can steady equilibrium growth at the natural rate happen under nonconvertible labor-augmenting embodiment when capital is putty-clay? In other words, can it happen when aggregation is twice frustrated? That question sets the focus for the remainder of the chapter.[23]

10.5 A MODEL WITH EMBODIED PROGRESS AND PUTTY-CLAY CAPITAL

The ex ante production function of an economy takes the form[24]

$$Y_t^* = \gamma\left[\xi_1 I_t^{-\rho} + \xi_2\left(e^{\mu t}L_t^* \right)^{-\rho} \right]^{-1/\rho} \tag{10.45}$$

Y_t^* denotes the output quantity which would be forthcoming from capital to be

---

[22] Intuition runs thus. Constructing aggregates under embodiment is associated with capital augmentation, while establishing steady equilibrium growth at the natural rate is associated with labor augmentation. The two objectives therefore conflict except when the vintage production function allows technical progress to be all capital-augmenting and all labor-augmenting simultaneously. The Cobb-Douglas does; the general CES does not. Such reasoning implies that if the CES is to allow both aggregation and steady natural-rate growth, progress must be entirely disembodied to permit the former and entirely labor-augmenting to permit the latter. This conclusion was the one emerging from the analysis of equation (10.41) above.

[23] Growth properties of a model beset by the single frustration of nonconvertible labor-augmenting embodiment is studied by Sheshinski in "Stability," pp. 142–147.

[24] Discussion comprising the balance of this chapter makes strong appeal to James H. Gapinski's "Growth Parameters and Neoclassical Estimates: Effect of an Adaptive Wage-Expectation Scheme,"

(*continued*)

constructed if I_t units of that capital were combined with L_t^* units of labor. Y_t^* and L_t^* are planned levels to be determined, while I_t is known before entrepreneurs begin their planning deliberations. Technical progress is completely embodied in capital; its embodiment nature should become evident shortly. It augments only labor, and it does so at the exponential rate μ. The ex ante elasticity of substitution, denoted by σ, equals $1/(1 + \rho)$. With ρ presumed to satisfy the inequalities $-1 < \rho < \infty$, it follows that $0 < \sigma < \infty$. Furthermore, $0 < \gamma < \infty$, while $\xi_1 > 0$ and $\xi_2 > 0$ with $\xi_1 + \xi_2 = 1$ as well.[25]

Output from capital vintages already installed can be described by a Leontief function, which features right-angled isoquants:[26]

$$Y_{vt} = \min(\varepsilon_v K_{vt}, \zeta_v L_{vt})$$

As before, Y_{vt} notates the quantity of output generated by vintage v capital at time t. K_{vt} signifies the quantity of vintage v in use at t, and L_{vt} represents the labor input employed on that vintage at t. Now, however, $v < t$: capital experiences an installation lag and consequently does not operate in the period of its construction. ε_v and ζ_v denote, respectively, constant production coefficients for the capital and labor inputs associated with vintage v, and the designation "min" means that Y_{vt} equals the smaller of the two arguments enclosed by parentheses. Labor is homogeneous across vintages.

Since capital operates at capacity and since redundant labor is avoided, the ex post production function becomes

$$Y_{vt} = \gamma \left[\xi_1 K_{vt}^{-\rho} + \xi_2 \left(e^{\mu v} L_{vt} \right)^{-\rho} \right]^{-1/\rho} \tag{10.46}$$

where $v < t$. With capital decaying physically at the exponential rate δ, $K_{vt} = I_v e^{-\delta(t-v)}$ and $L_{vt} = L_v^* e^{-\delta(t-v)}$. Therefore $Y_{vt} = Y_v^* e^{-\delta(t-v)}$.

Although a given vintage will survive physically forever, it will continue in service only as long as its quasi-rent remains nonnegative: specifically, as long as

$$\frac{Y_{vt}}{L_{vt}} \geq w_t \tag{10.47}$$

with $v < t$. w_t denotes the real wage at t. Any vintage for which the equality in (10.47) prevails may be called a "marginal vintage" of time t; it rests on the margin of being scrapped.

Southern Economic Journal, **39** (January 1973), p. 431; "Growth Parameters and Neoclassical Estimates of the Substitution Elasticity," *Southern Economic Journal*, **38** (January 1972), pp. 285–289; and "Steady Growth, Policy Shocks, and Speed of Adjustment under Embodiment and Putty-Clay," *Journal of Macroeconomics*, **3**, no. 2 (Spring 1981), pp. 148–160 (Copyright © 1981 by Wayne State University Press).

[25] These parameter restrictions apply through Section 10.8, although for convenience they may not be repeated in their entirety. For instance, $\rho > 0$ is taken to connote $\infty > \rho > 0$ and $\rho < 0$ abbreviates $-1 < \rho < 0$.

[26] Amplification of this formulation appears in James H. Gapinski and T. Krishna Kumar, "Embodiment, Putty-Clay, and Misspecification of the Directly Estimated CES," *International Economic Review*, **17** (June 1976), pp. 473–474.

These details reviewed, the decision regarding the labor requirement of new capital, L_t^*, can be examined. Entrepreneurs choose L_t^* to maximize the discounted expected quasi-rents associated with that vintage. They anticipate capacity utilization with no excess employment, and they expect the current real wage, which like gross investment I_t is known at the time of decision, to persist unchanged into the future: their expectations regarding the wage rate are static. Entrepreneurs confine their attention only to the values of L_t^* for which $Y_t^* \geq w_t L_t^*$, and for those "eligible" L_t^* new capital is expected to earn nonnegative quasi-rents over its entire physical life.[27]

The discounted expected quasi-rents of new capital can be written as

$$U_t = \int_t^\infty (Y_{tu} - w_t L_{tu}) e^{-r(u-t)} \, du$$

with $u > t$; r represents an exogenous and time-invariant interest rate. Simplification of the U_t expression leaves

$$U_t = (Y_t^* - w_t L_t^*)/(\delta + r) \tag{10.48}$$

whose maximization with respect to L_t^* generates

$$\frac{\partial Y_t^*}{\partial L_t^*} = w_t \tag{10.49}$$

The ex ante marginal product of labor equals the real wage. Since U_t is concave downward with respect to L_t^*, reflecting the concavity of (10.45), a global maximum of U_t exists whenever (10.49) is satisfied.[28]

The CES production process, by imposing limits on $\partial Y_t^*/\partial L_t^*$, restricts w_t to the same limits. In particular, if $\rho > 0$, then w_t must lie in the interval $0 \leq w_t \leq \gamma \xi_2^{-1/\rho} e^{\mu t}$. If $\rho = 0$, then $0 \leq w_t \leq \infty$, while if $\rho < 0$, then $\gamma \xi_2^{-1/\rho} e^{\mu t} \leq w_t \leq \infty$. Failure of w_t to fall within the appropriate bounds would render (10.49) unsolvable.

Equation (10.49) combines with function (10.45) to give

$$Y_t^* = (\gamma^\rho/\xi_1)^{1/\rho} (1 - w_t/\Omega_t)^{1/\rho} I_t \tag{10.50}$$

$$L_t^* = (\xi_2/\xi_1)^{1/\rho} e^{-\mu t} (\Omega_t/w_t - 1)^{1/\rho} I_t \tag{10.51}$$

where $\Omega_t = (\gamma^\rho/\xi_2)^\sigma e^{\sigma \rho \mu t} w_t^\sigma$. Notice that the differenced terms cannot be negative

---

[27]A value of L_t^* for which $Y_t^* < w_t L_t^*$ would never be considered, because new capital with such a labor requirement would be expected to earn negative quasi-rents throughout its physical life.

[28]Characteristics of (10.45) imply that the ex ante labor productivity Y_t^*/L_t^* exceeds the corresponding marginal product for positive and finite L_t^*. Satisfaction of (10.49) by any such L_t^* thus confirms that $Y_t^* \geq w_t L_t^*$.

if (10.49) holds.[29] As $\rho \to 0$, these equations reduce, respectively, to

$$Y_t^* = \left(\frac{\gamma \xi_2^{\xi_2} e^{\xi_2 \mu t}}{w_t^{\xi_2}} \right)^{1/\xi_1} I_t$$

$$L_t^* = \left(\frac{\gamma \xi_2 e^{\xi_2 \mu t}}{w_t} \right)^{1/\xi_1} I_t$$

Define $V(t, w_t)$ as the set of all those installed vintages operable without loss at time t when the wage stands at w_t:

$$V(t, w_t) = \{ v < t \mid Y_{vt} \geq w_t L_{vt} \} \tag{10.52}$$

which may be empty for large w_t. It follows that total labor demand at t is

$$\int_{V(t, w_t)} L_{vt} \, dv \tag{10.53}$$

An exogenously given labor supply L_t together with a requirement of full employment yield

$$L_t = \int_{V(t, w_t)} L_{vt} \, dv \tag{10.54}$$

With each past L_{vt} being known at t, (10.54) determines both w_t and $V(t, w_t)$, the latter because installed vintages are employed in decreasing order of quasi-rent. That having greatest labor productivity Y_{vt}/L_{vt} ($= Y_v^*/L_v^*$) is most profitable and hence enters service first.

Aggregate gross output at t can be expressed as

$$Y_t = \int_{V(t, w_t)} Y_{vt} \, dv \tag{10.55}$$

while equilibrium and a proportional saving function yield

$$I_t = s Y_t \tag{10.56}$$

s is constant, $0 < s < 1$.

Solution of the system proceeds straightforwardly. Given L_t and the labor requirements of past vintages, (10.54) determines w_t and $V(t, w_t)$. Then Y_t emerges from (10.55) and I_t from (10.56). With w_t and I_t known, Y_t^* and L_t^* are determined from (10.50) and (10.51), respectively, or from their Cobb-Douglas counterparts.

---

[29] Verification easily emerges. w_t/Ω_t is monotone-increasing in w_t for $\rho > 0$ and monotone-decreasing for $\rho < 0$. In either case w_t makes $w_t/\Omega_t = 1$ at the positive and finite endpoint of the interval compatible with (10.49). Departure from the endpoint makes $w_t/\Omega_t < 1$.

10.6 THE STEADY GROWTH SOLUTION

In steady growth aggregate gross output increases at a constant exponential rate. Under the equilibrium condition (10.56), gross investment must expand at the same rate,[30] and thus

$$Y_t = Y_0 e^{\alpha t} \tag{10.57}$$

$$I_t = I_0 e^{\alpha t} \tag{10.58}$$

It is assumed that steady growth admits an economic life of capital (θ) which remains constant. All vintages built before time $t - \theta$ are excluded from service because of cost considerations, while all vintages built at or after time $t - \theta$ are included:

$$V(t, w_t) = \{v \mid t - \theta \le v < t, \theta \text{ being constant}\} \tag{10.59}$$

Vintage profile (10.59) will be shown to be true under steady growth.

The exogenously determined labor supply L_t grows at an exponential rate η; namely,

$$L_t = L_0 e^{\eta t} \tag{10.60}$$

L_t must be equated to labor demand (10.53) each period if full employment is to be maintained through time. Therefore, in view of the vintage set (10.59)

$$L_0 e^{\eta t} = \int_{t-\theta}^{t} L_v^* e^{-\delta(t-v)} \, dv \tag{10.61}$$

By utilizing (10.57) and (10.59), the expression for aggregate gross output (10.55) becomes

$$Y_0 e^{\alpha t} = \int_{t-\theta}^{t} Y_v^* e^{-\delta(t-v)} \, dv \tag{10.62}$$

Since (10.61) and (10.62) hold continually through time, each may have both sides time-differentiated to obtain

$$L_t^* = (\eta + \delta)L_t + L_{t-\theta, t}$$

$$Y_t^* = (\alpha + \delta)Y_t + Y_{t-\theta, t}$$

$L_{t-\theta, t}$ and $Y_{t-\theta, t}$ expressed in terms of corresponding past values eventually disclose[31]

$$L_t^* = \Lambda L_0 e^{\eta t} \tag{10.63}$$

$$Y_t^* = \Phi Y_0 e^{\alpha t} \tag{10.64}$$

where $\Lambda = (\eta + \delta)/[1 - e^{-(\eta + \delta)\theta}]$ and $\Phi = (\alpha + \delta)/[1 - e^{-(\alpha + \delta)\theta}]$.

---

[30] The equality of growth rates serves to define steady growth in Christopher Bliss' "On Putty-Clay," *Review of Economic Studies*, **35** (April 1968), p. 109. In that paper, pp. 110–111, Bliss proves the importance of exponential Harrod neutrality for steady growth under putty-clay.

[31] Amplification of the arithmetic may be helpful. Consider (10.63). The general formula for differentiating a definite integral, presented in footnote 6, establishes the time derivative of the

(*continued*)

Substituting the steady growth expressions for I_t, L_t^*, and Y_t^* into the ex ante production function—equations (10.58), (10.63), (10.64), and (10.45), respectively—reveals that

$$\alpha = \eta + \mu \tag{10.65}$$

Because Y_t^* and I_t both grow at the rate α, Y_t^*/I_t is constant. But the linear homogeneity of the ex ante production function translates this constancy into one for $e^{\mu t} L_t^*/I_t$, and hence relationship (10.65) results. It says that in steady equilibrium growth, aggregate gross output and gross investment grow at Harrod's natural rate. Like the neoclassical growth model founded on a disembodied putty-putty production structure and studied in Sections 9.4 and 9.5, like the Cobb-Douglas paradigm based on an embodied putty-putty structure and examined in Section 10.2, this system, wherein embodiment combines with putty-clay, yields steady equilibrium growth at the natural rate.[32]

Entrepreneurial optimization regarding L_t^* makes $Y_t^*/L_t^* = \Omega_t$. But in steady growth the ex ante labor productivity grows at the rate μ. So, therefore, must Ω_t, implying that

$$w_t = w_0 e^{\mu t} \tag{10.66}$$

The real wage grows at the rate of technical progress, hardly an unfamiliar trait.

Yet outstanding are the determination of Y_0, I_0, w_0, and θ, along with the vindication of the assumption regarding $V(t, w_t)$ in (10.59). Given equilibrium

---

right-hand side of (10.61) as

$$-\delta \int_{t-\theta}^{t} L_v^* e^{-\delta(t-v)} \, dv + L_t^* - L_{t-\theta}^* e^{-\delta[t-(t-\theta)]}$$

or more simply as $-\delta L_t + L_t^* - L_{t-\theta}^* e^{-\delta\theta}$. This latter expression when equated to dL_t/dt from the left-hand side of (10.61) generates

$$L_t^* = (\eta + \delta) L_t + L_{t-\theta}^* e^{-\delta\theta}$$

But $L_{t-\theta}^* e^{-\delta\theta}$ may be expressed as

$$\left[(\eta + \delta) L_{t-\theta} + L_{t-2\theta}^* e^{-\delta\theta} \right] e^{-\delta\theta}$$

Therefore,

$$L_t^* = (\eta + \delta) L_t + (\eta + \delta) L_{t-\theta} e^{-\delta\theta} + L_{t-2\theta}^* e^{-2\delta\theta}$$

Repeating this procedure for the right-most term gives from (10.60)

$$L_t^* = (\eta + \delta) L_t [1 + e^{-(\eta+\delta)\theta} + e^{-2(\eta+\delta)\theta} + \cdots]$$

which reduces to (10.63).

[32] In his paper "Stability," pp. 143–145, Sheshinski establishes this same property under embodiment and putty-putty when the vintage production function assumes a form more general than the Cobb-Douglas. Sheshinski's model and the Cobb-Douglas variant cited in the text also include the rate of disembodiment within the natural rate, but they obviously contain exclusive embodiment as a transparent special case.

relation (10.56), determination of I_0 flows automatically from knowledge of Y_0; thus, Y_0, w_0, and θ are of primary concern.[33]

To find Y_0, rewrite Y_{vt} in (10.46) using the steady growth input quantities and insert the resulting expression into the aggregate output relation (10.62). Integration under the restriction $t = 0$ and recognition of (10.56) produce

$$Y_0 = \gamma L_0 (\Lambda/\Phi)(x/\xi_2)^{1/\rho} \qquad (10.67)$$

where $x = 1 - \xi_1(\gamma s)^{-\rho}\Phi^\rho$. As $\rho \to 0$, equation (10.67) collapses to

$$Y_0 = \Lambda L_0 (\gamma s^{\xi_1}/\Phi)^{1/\xi_2}$$

An expression for w_0 can be obtained from the full-employment equation (10.61) by substitution for L_v^* from (10.51). Integration using (10.58) and (10.66) eventually generates under (10.56) and (10.67)

$$w_0 = \gamma \xi_2^{-1/\rho} x^{1/(\sigma\rho)} \qquad (10.68)$$

As $\rho \to 0$, equation (10.68) tends to

$$w_0 = \xi_2 \left[\gamma(s/\Phi)^{\xi_1} \right]^{1/\xi_2}.$$

Only θ, the economic life of capital, remains to be determined. It has been assumed constant in steady growth, and this assumption must be validated. Notice, however, that determination of a constant θ would immediately substantiate the presumed composition of the vintage set in operation, (10.59). This point can be easily seen. A vintage of age θ operates but rests on the margin of being scrapped since its quasi-rent is zero:

$$Y_{t-\theta,t} = w_t L_{t-\theta,t} \qquad (10.69)$$

Y_v^*/L_v^* rises in steady growth, and because $Y_v^*/L_v^* = Y_{vt}/L_{vt}$, it follows that any vintage v capital with $v < t - \theta$ would earn a negative quasi-rent at t and therefore does not operate. By contrast, capital with $v > t - \theta$ would earn a positive quasi-rent at t and consequently does operate.

For equation (10.69) $Y_{t-\theta,t}/L_{t-\theta,t} = Y_{t-\theta}^*/L_{t-\theta}^*$. From (10.63) and (10.64) $L_{t-\theta}^* = L_0^* e^{\eta(t-\theta)}$ and $Y_{t-\theta}^* = Y_0^* e^{\alpha(t-\theta)}$, reducing (10.69) to

$$e^{\mu\theta} = \frac{Y_0^*}{L_0^*} \frac{1}{w_0}$$

with help from the w_t equation (10.66). But $Y_t^*/L_t^* = \Omega_t$. Thus Ω_0 combined with the w_0 formula (10.68) yields

$$e^{\mu\theta} = 1/x(\theta) \qquad (10.70)$$

---

[33] The neoclassical model treated in Section 9.4 enables Y_0 and w_0 to be written in terms of the parameters of the aggregate production function. For Y_0 the reason is easily found: $Y_0 = A_0 L_0 f(\kappa_0)$. For w_0 this linkage happens because of the aggregate marginal productivity condition: $w_0 = A_0[f(\kappa_0) - \kappa_0 f'(\kappa_0)]$. In the present case Y_0 and w_0 also acknowledge production parameters, but now they are ex ante parameters. Y_0 results from a summation across vintage production functions; w_0, from a summation across vintage labor requirement functions. These vintage functions reflect ex ante parameters, thereby accounting for the relationship.

Again $x(\theta) = 1 - \xi_1(\gamma s)^{-\rho}\Phi^\rho$, the more elaborate symbolism $x(\theta)$ being adopted to highlight the dependence of x upon θ. For convenience, $y(\theta) = 1/x$.

Equation (10.70) can be used to solve for θ, its only unknown. The existence of this θ solution and its uniqueness or lack thereof will be reflected in the solution values of all other endogenous variables since they all involve θ. Because (10.70) does not contain t, its θ solutions, if any, must be temporally constant. In what follows a prime represents the first derivative with respect to θ; a double prime, the second derivative. Three cases can be identified.

Case I: $0 < \rho < \infty$ Since $e^{\mu\theta}$ always remains positive, a necessary condition for the existence of any solution to (10.70) is that x must assume positive values. In the present case

$$x \to -\infty \text{ as } \theta \to 0 \quad\text{and}\quad x \to 1 - \xi_1(\gamma s)^{-\rho}(\alpha + \delta)^\rho \text{ as } \theta \to \infty$$

Moreover,

$$x' > 0 \text{ for } 0 \leq \theta < \infty \quad\text{and}\quad x' \to 0 \text{ as } \theta \to \infty$$

Therefore, x eventually becomes positive provided that $1 - \xi_1(\gamma s)^{-\rho}(\alpha + \delta)^\rho > 0$, or, equivalently, provided that

$$s > \xi_1^{1/\rho}(\alpha + \delta)/\gamma \tag{10.71}$$

Under this condition $x = 0$ at a positive and finite θ; namely,

$$\theta_a = -(\alpha + \delta)^{-1}\ln\left[1 - (\gamma s)^{-1}(\alpha + \delta)\xi_1^{1/\rho}\right]$$

Furthermore,

$$x < 0 \text{ for } 0 \leq \theta < \theta_a \quad\text{and}\quad x > 0 \text{ for } \theta_a < \theta \leq \infty$$

The behavior of y is now apparent. Under (10.71) x and, therefore, y are negative for $\theta < \theta_a$. But with $e^{\mu\theta}$ being positive, these y may be disregarded as uninteresting. For the remaining θ, y is positive and

$$y \to \infty \text{ as } \theta \to \theta_a \quad\text{and}\quad y \to \left[1 - \xi_1(\gamma s)^{-\rho}(\alpha + \delta)^\rho\right]^{-1} > 1 \text{ as } \theta \to \infty$$

In addition,

$$y' < 0 \text{ for } \theta_a \leq \theta < \infty \quad\text{and}\quad y' \to 0 \text{ as } \theta \to \infty$$

Finally,

$$y'' > 0 \quad \text{for } \theta_a \leq \theta \leq \infty$$

Figure 10.3 confronts y with $e^{\mu\theta}$. Clearly, there exists a unique, positive, and finite θ which satisfies (10.70). Inequality (10.71) is both necessary and sufficient for this result.

Case II: $\rho = 0$ Now y reduces to $1/\xi_2$, which exceeds unity but remains finite. Being independent of θ, it graphs as a horizontal line, intersecting $e^{\mu\theta}$ at a unique, positive, and finite θ. Since s vanishes from (10.70) in this case, the only s restriction is the customary $0 < s < 1$.

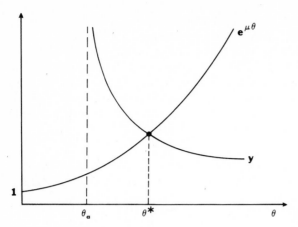

Figure 10.3

Case III: $-1 < \rho < 0$ Here

$$x \to 1 \text{ as } \theta \to 0 \qquad \text{and} \qquad x \to 1 - b \text{ as } \theta \to \infty$$

where $b = \xi_1(\gamma s)^{-\rho}[1/(\alpha + \delta)]^{-\rho}$. Also,

$$x' < 0 \text{ for } 0 \le \theta < \infty \qquad \text{and} \qquad x' \to 0 \text{ as } \theta \to \infty$$

Therefore, x remains positive for all θ if $1 - b > 0$ or if

$$s < \xi_1^{1/\rho}(\alpha + \delta)/\gamma \tag{10.72}$$

What about y? Under (10.72) it is positive for all θ with

$$y \to 1 \text{ as } \theta \to 0 \qquad \text{and} \qquad y \to (1 - b)^{-1} > 1 \text{ as } \theta \to \infty$$

Moreover,

$$y' > 0 \text{ for } 0 < \theta < \infty, \qquad y' \to \infty \text{ as } \theta \to 0, \qquad \text{and} \qquad y' \to 0 \text{ as } \theta \to \infty$$

Therefore, inequality (10.72) is sufficient for y to intersect $e^{\mu\theta}$ at least once with θ being nontrivial, namely, positive and finite. The solution at $\theta = 0$ is trivial and deserves no further discussion.

To establish that there is *only* one nontrivial solution, it must be shown that y is concave downward with respect to θ. The second derivative of y can be written as

$$y'' = B(\theta)\left[2\xi_1(\gamma s)^{-\rho}(-\rho)y\Phi^\rho + (-\rho) - e^{(\alpha+\delta)\theta}\right]$$

Because $B(\theta) = \xi_1(\gamma s)^{-\rho}(-\rho)y^2\Phi^{\rho+2}e^{-2(\alpha+\delta)\theta}$,

$$B > 0 \text{ for } 0 \le \theta < \infty \qquad \text{and} \qquad B \to 0 \text{ as } \theta \to \infty$$

Therefore, if the bracketed component of y'' were negative for all finite θ, then y'' would be too. This situation happens under the sufficient condition[34]

$$s < \left[\frac{1 + \rho}{1 - \rho}\right]^{-1/\rho}\xi_1^{1/\rho}(\alpha + \delta)/\gamma \tag{10.73}$$

---

[34]Write the bracketed part of y'' as $\chi(\theta) - e^{(\alpha+\delta)\theta}$, with $\chi(\theta) = -\rho[1 + \xi_1(\gamma s)^{-\rho}(1/\Phi)^{-\rho}]y$. As $\theta \to 0$, $\chi \to -\rho$, which lies between zero and unity. As $\theta \to \infty$, $\chi \to -\rho(1 + b)/(1 - b)$, which by

(continued)

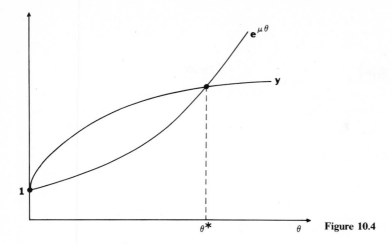

Figure 10.4

Since $(1 + \rho)/(1 - \rho) < 1$, satisfaction of (10.73) means satisfaction of (10.72). Therefore, (10.73) is sufficient both for existence and for uniqueness of a nontrivial θ solution to (10.70). Figure 10.4 summarizes the analysis for this case. Henceforth, θ^* will denote the unique solution to (10.70) for $\rho \geq 0$ and the unique nontrivial solution for $\rho < 0$.

10.7 FURTHER PROPERTIES OF STEADY GROWTH: COMPARATIVE DYNAMICS

The sufficient condition (10.73) is important. Eytan Sheshinski postulated a model rather similar to that examined in the previous two sections. It featured labor-augmenting embodiment and putty-clay capital. Furthermore, it assumed static expectations and a linearly homogeneous production function more general than the Cobb-Douglas. Specifically,[35] $Y_t^* = I_t j(\lambda_t)$, where $\lambda_t = e^{\mu t} L_t^*/I_t$ and where $j > 0, j' > 0$, and $j'' < 0$ for all $\lambda_t > 0$. In addition, $j(0) = 0$ and $j(\infty) = \infty$. Given these properties, Sheshinski imposed a sufficient condition for the existence and uniqueness of a steady growth θ, which was nontrivial. That condition, defined in terms of the ex ante elasticity of substitution, read $0 < \sigma \leq 1$. Doubt

---

(10.72) exceeds $-\rho$. Furthermore, $\chi' > 0$ for $0 \leq \theta < \infty$, while $\chi' \to 0$ as $\theta \to \infty$. Thus, χ begins at $-\rho$ for $\theta = 0$ and rises steadily to $-\rho(1 + b)/(1 - b)$ as θ rises.

If the maximum of χ were less than the minimum of $e^{(\alpha + \delta)\theta}$, then $\chi - e^{(\alpha + \delta)\theta}$ would always be negative. Since the minimum of $e^{(\alpha + \delta)\theta}$ is unity, the desired condition reads $-\rho(1 + b)/(1 - b) < 1$. Rewritten, this condition becomes $b < [1 - (-\rho)]/[1 + (-\rho)]$, which eventually gives inequality (10.73).

[35]E. Sheshinski, "Balanced Growth and Stability in the Johansen Vintage Model," *Review of Economic Studies*, **34** (April 1967), pp. 239–243. The rate of disembodiment, his β, is taken to be zero.

therefore lingered about existence, let alone uniqueness, of a nontrivial solution for $\sigma > 1$. By limiting the analysis to the specific class of CES production functions, an alternative sufficient condition, (10.73), arises under which a unique nontrivial θ solution exists for $\sigma > 1$. Steady growth then need not be precluded merely by the value which σ assumes.

It is useful to note at this point that the crucial θ equation, (10.70), can be recreated by appealing to Sheshinski's analysis. There two fundamental equations determine steady growth characteristics.[36] Rewriting them for the present rules of CES production and exponential deterioration leaves

$$s\gamma(\xi_1 + \xi_2\lambda^{-\rho})^{-1/\rho} = \Phi \tag{10.74}$$

$$\frac{\xi_1\lambda^\rho + \xi_2}{\xi_2} = e^{\mu\theta} \tag{10.75}$$

Since λ_t must be constant in steady growth, it enters without a time subscript. These two equations have two unknowns, λ and θ. Solving (10.74) for λ^ρ and substituting the result into (10.75) gives (10.70), verifying the earlier derivation.

Equation (10.74) serves another purpose; it can also be used to show that steady growth restrictions (10.71) and (10.73), which are imposed on s in addition to the usual condition $0 < s < 1$, are closely related to the inability of CES to satisfy the Sheshinski boundary conditions, $j(0) = 0$ and $j(\infty) = \infty$. Sheshinski's version of (10.74) with exponential deterioration and with $0 < s < 1$ produces the (λ, θ) solution locus depicted in Figure 10.5. A CES function generates a similar locus from (10.74) with $0 < s < 1$ only when $\rho = 0$; clearly, both boundary conditions are satisfied in that case. But when $\rho > 0$, the right-hand boundary is violated since $j(\infty) = \gamma\xi_1^{-1/\rho}$, and (10.74) has no meaningful (λ, θ) solution at all unless (10.71) is satisfied. When $\rho < 0$, the left-hand boundary falls since $j(0) = \gamma\xi_1^{-1/\rho}$, and the (λ, θ) locus of (10.74) becomes quite different from that in Figure 10.5 unless (10.73)—or, less restrictively, (10.72)—is satisfied. In a sense, the additional s restrictions (10.71) and (10.73) serve to compensate for the failure of the ex ante function (10.45) to satisfy the Sheshinski boundary conditions.

This notion of compensation can be recast in more familiar terms. The s inequalities (10.71) and (10.72) closely resemble inequalities (9.28) and (9.29) cited for the neoclassical CES model in Section 9.5, the only noteworthy difference for the present purpose being that δ now appears as an additional parameter. That exception, however, can be traced to the difference in measurement base, gross versus net. In the neoclassical framework the inequalities appeared when the *Inada* boundary conditions were violated; here they enter with the violation of *Sheshinski's*. Despite the seeming inconsistency, none exists. For the CES function (10.45), the derivative of $Y_t^*/(e^{\mu^t}L_t^*)$ with respect to $I_t/(e^{\mu^t}L_t^*)$—the latter being abbreviated κ_t—may be written as $f'(\kappa_t) = \gamma\xi_1[\xi_1 + \xi_2(1/\lambda_t)^\rho]^{-1/(\sigma\rho)}$, and the restrictions imposed on the $j(\lambda_t)$ derived from (10.45)

---

[36] Ibid., p. 242. The two appear between his equations numbered (18) and (19).

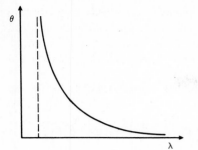

Figure 10.5

translate into the same restrictions on $f'(\kappa_t)$ only in the opposite direction. When $\rho > 0$, $j(\infty) = f'(0) = \gamma\xi_1^{-1/\rho}$; the right-hand Sheshinski condition evaporates, as does the left-hand Inada. When $\rho < 0$, $j(0) = f'(\infty) = \gamma\xi_1^{-1/\rho}$: left-hand Sheshinski and right-hand Inada fail. Consequently, inequalities (10.71) and (10.73), the latter subsuming (10.72), can be equivalently construed as compensating for the inability of function (10.45) to satisfy the Inada boundary conditions.

What about Y_0 and w_0? Are they positive and finite when $\theta = \theta^*$? The answer is affirmative. Recall that θ^* is positive and finite for all values of ρ considered. Therefore, it can be seen that both Y_0 and w_0 have the contemplated property for $\rho = 0$ from the limit versions of equations (10.67) and (10.68). For other ρ, Figures 10.3 and 10.4 make evident that $0 < x(\theta^*) < 1$, and thus the Y_0 and w_0 in equations (10.67) and (10.68) must be positive and finite.

It can also be shown that the restrictions on w_t required for the first-order condition (10.49) to be solvable are satisfied at θ^*. These restrictions at time zero read $0 \le w_0 \le \gamma\xi_2^{-1/\rho}$ for $\rho > 0, 0 \le w_0 \le \infty$ for $\rho = 0$, and $\gamma\xi_2^{-1/\rho} \le w_0 \le \infty$ for $\rho < 0$. Since w_0 is positive and finite at θ^* for any ρ considered, w_0 need only be compared with $\gamma\xi_2^{-1/\rho}$. Equation (10.68) says that

$$w_0 = \gamma\xi_2^{-1/\rho}x(\theta^*)^{1/(\sigma\rho)}$$

Because $0 < x(\theta^*) < 1$, $x(\theta^*)^{1/(\sigma\rho)}$ lies below unity for $\rho > 0$ and above unity for $\rho < 0$, and therefore the appropriate restrictions on w_t are all satisfied in steady growth.

With regard to θ^* itself, several comparative dynamic properties can be established under conditions (10.71) and (10.73). These features will prove to be especially helpful in Sections 11.4 and 11.6.

Consider first $d\theta^*/ds$. The θ equation (10.70) indicates that an s change affects θ^* only through y, whose response to s is

$$\frac{\partial y}{\partial s} = -\rho\xi_1\gamma^{-\rho}s^{-\rho-1}\Phi^\rho y^2$$

When $\rho > 0, \partial y/\partial s < 0$ for $\theta_a \le \theta \le \infty$: an increase in s shifts the y locus in Figure 10.3 downward, while a decrease shifts it upward. When $\rho = 0, \partial y/\partial s = 0$. In this case, with s vanishing, y remains invariant to s changes. When $\rho < 0$, $\partial y/\partial s > 0$ for $0 < \theta \le \infty$ although $\partial y/\partial s = 0$ for $\theta = 0$. Consequently, an increase in s pivots the y locus in Figure 10.4 upward around $y = 1$ at $\theta = 0$; a decrease does the opposite. It follows that

$$\frac{d\theta^*}{ds} \lesseqgtr 0 \qquad \text{as } \rho \gtreqless 0$$

Next, $d\theta^*/d\eta$. η impacts θ^* through the α in y. Clearly, $\partial y/\partial \eta = \partial y/\partial \alpha$, and

$$\frac{\partial y}{\partial \alpha} = \rho\xi_1(\gamma s)^{-\rho}\Phi^{1+\rho}\left[y/(\alpha + \delta)\right]^2\left\{1 - e^{-(\alpha+\delta)\theta}\left[1 + (\alpha + \delta)\theta\right]\right\}$$

the braced term lying between zero and unity inclusive. When $\rho > 0$, $\partial y/\partial \alpha > 0$ for $\theta_a \leq \theta \leq \infty$. Increased η thus drives the y locus upward and conversely. When $\rho = 0$, $\partial y/\partial \alpha = 0$ and y remains unaffected by an η change. Finally, when $\rho < 0$, $\partial y/\partial \alpha < 0$ for $0 < \theta \leq \infty$ with $\partial y/\partial \alpha = 0$ at $\theta = 0$. An increase in η pivots y downward around $y = 1$ at $\theta = 0$; a decrease swings it upward. Consequently,

$$\frac{d\theta^*}{d\eta} \gtreqless 0 \qquad \text{as } \rho \gtreqless 0$$

Now for $d\theta^*/d\mu$. Unlike amendments to s or η, μ changes influence θ^* by altering *both* sides of equation (10.70). Since $\partial y/\partial \mu = \partial y/\partial \alpha$, the effect of μ on y is identical to that described for η. The left-hand component of (10.70) rotates upward around unity at $\theta = 0$ as μ increases and rotates downward as μ decreases. Thus when $\rho = 0$, increased μ causes $e^{\mu\theta}$ to intersect the stationary y at a lower θ^*. When $\rho < 0$, the upward swing of $e^{\mu\theta}$ reinforces the downward tilt of y as μ rises, thereby assuring a fall in θ^*. Reverse movements apply to μ decreases. When $\rho > 0$, the pivoting motion of $e^{\mu\theta}$ counteracts the shift in y. Recourse to implicit differentiation is not especially enlightening about the net effect because the derivative assumes a clumsy form. Appeal to a numerical method, however, suggests that the net effect is negative. In sum,

$$\frac{d\theta^*}{d\mu} < 0 \qquad \text{for } \rho \gtreqless 0$$

What about $d\theta^*/d\xi_1$? θ^* again changes by way of y alone.

$$\frac{\partial y}{\partial \xi_1} = (\gamma s)^{-\rho}\Phi^\rho y^2$$

which must almost always be positive. Specifically, $\partial y/\partial \xi_1 > 0$ for $\rho > 0$ when $\theta_a \leq \theta \leq \infty$, for $\rho = 0$ regardless of θ, and for $\rho < 0$ when $\theta > 0$. The lone exception arises for $\rho < 0$ and $\theta = 0$; then $\partial y/\partial \xi_1 = 0$. Thus, an increase in ξ_1 shifts the y line upward when $\rho \geq 0$ and swings it upward around the pivot point at $\theta = 0$ when $\rho < 0$. A decrease in ξ_1 prompts the opposite movements. These responses imply that

$$\frac{d\theta^*}{d\xi_1} > 0 \qquad \text{for } \rho \gtreqless 0$$

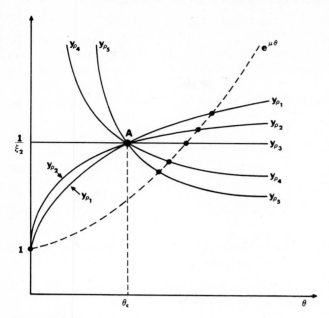

Figure 10.6

Lastly, $d\theta^*/d\rho$. The metamorphic behavior of y for different ρ values illustrated partially by Figures 10.3 and 10.4 promises an interesting exercise in establishing this comparative dynamic property. Differentiation of y yields

$$\frac{\partial y}{\partial \rho} = \xi_1 y^2 [\Phi/(\gamma s)]^\rho \ln[\Phi/(\gamma s)]$$

Perhaps the most important news conveyed by this derivative is that $\partial y/\partial \rho \gtreqless 0$ as $\Phi/(\gamma s) \gtreqless 1$, a condition which translates into a restriction on θ: $\partial y/\partial \rho \gtreqless 0$ as $\theta \lesseqgtr \theta_c$, where $\theta_c = -(\alpha + \delta)^{-1} \ln[1 - (\alpha + \delta)/(\gamma s)]$. The θ_c is meaningful only under the proviso $(\alpha + \delta)/(\gamma s) < 1$ or, equivalently, $s > (\alpha + \delta)/\gamma$.

Notice that $\partial y/\partial \rho = 0$ at θ_c independently of ρ. Notice also that at θ_c, $y = 1/\xi_2$ again independently of ρ. Hence, all y curves generated by alternative ρ values must pass through the same point at θ_c, say point A. As ρ decreases from positive values, the negatively sloped y locus rotates counterclockwise around point A, its horizontal asymptote rising toward $1/\xi_2$ and its vertical asymptote θ_a falling toward zero.[37] The y locus degenerates into the horizontal line $1/\xi_2$ as ρ approaches zero, and it continues rotating counterclockwise around point A as ρ further decreases, although now y assumes a positive slope. The solid lines in Figure 10.6 sketch this movement. There $\rho_5 > \rho_4 > \cdots > \rho_1$, with $\rho_3 = 0$.

---

[37]For all positive and finite ρ, $\theta_a < \theta_c$ and $\partial \theta_a/\partial \rho > 0$. Moreover, $\theta_a \to 0$ as $\rho \to 0$, and $\theta_a \to \theta_c$ as $\rho \to \infty$. Minimum value for the horizontal asymptote equals unity and occurs in the limit as $\rho \to \infty$.

With the behavior of y articulated, determination of $d\theta^*/d\rho$ merely requires locating the position of $e^{\mu\theta}$ in the family of y loci. The crucial question here is, Does $e^{\mu\theta}$ intersect the y loci before, at, or after θ_c? If intersection occurs before θ_c, then $d\theta^*/d\rho > 0$. If it happens at θ_c, then $d\theta^*/d\rho = 0$. If it happens after θ_c, then $d\theta^*/d\rho < 0$.

This question can be answered by comparing the values of $e^{\mu\theta}$ and y at θ_c:

$$e^{\mu\theta_c} = \left[1 - (\alpha + \delta)/(\gamma s)\right]^{-\mu/(\alpha+\delta)}$$

$$y(\theta_c) = 1/\xi_2$$

The comparison reveals that $d\theta^*/d\rho \gtreqless 0$ as $e^{\mu\theta_c} \gtreqless y(\theta_c)$, and easy calculations establish that

$$\frac{d\theta^*}{d\rho} \gtreqless 0 \text{ as } s \lesseqgtr \frac{\alpha + \delta}{\gamma\left[1 - \xi_2^{(\alpha+\delta)/\mu}\right]}$$

An abridged version of this general relationship may be obtained by recognizing that $\xi_1 < 1 - \xi_2^{(\alpha+\delta)/\mu}$ and by using ξ_1 to replace the bracketed expression in the s inequality. Doing so gives[38]

$$s > (\alpha + \delta)/(\gamma\xi_1) \tag{10.76}$$

as a sufficient condition for

$$\frac{d\theta^*}{d\rho} < 0$$

The dots lying along the dashed path for $e^{\mu\theta}$ in Figure 10.6 reveal this pattern. It should be emphasized that inequality (10.76) and the consequent implication for the derivative constitute a convenient, but nevertheless only a single, option within a general relationship. Other options are available.

Inequality (10.76) joins conditions (10.71) to (10.73) in providing another interpretation of the restrictions on s. That interpretation warrants consideration, as does a "loose end" displayed by Figure 10.6, namely, the insistence of the y curves to pass through point A. The s constraints are addressed first.

As Section 10.5 noted, entrepreneurs select the labor requirement of new capital by confining their attention to those L_t^* values for which $Y_t^* \geq w_t L_t^*$. Only if a vintage promises nonnegative quasi-rent during the design stage can it be expected to be operated without loss in the future. In steady growth this condition simplifies to $Y_0^* \geq w_0 L_0^*$, vintage zero becoming the frame of reference. Since $y = Y_0^*/(w_0 L_0^*)$, the simplification may be restated as $y \geq 1$. All y paths depicted in Figure 10.6 exhibit this property, and hence the s inequalities which form their underlay may be regarded as provisos assuring that vintage zero, when new,

---

[38] Because $(\alpha + \delta)/(\gamma\xi_1)$ must be greater than $(\alpha + \delta)/\{\gamma[1 - \xi_2^{(\alpha+\delta)/\mu}]\}$, any s which exceeds the former must also exceed the latter, but an s which falls below the former may still exceed the latter. Thus, (10.76) is sufficient. Unlike its predecessors (10.71) and (10.73), (10.76) does not depend upon ρ. It is compatible with them, however: parameter combinations satisfying (10.71) or (10.73) can also satisfy (10.76).

enjoys the prospect of nonnegative quasi-rent. Those inequalities are, of course, (10.71) and (10.73), the latter subsuming (10.72). For a date θ_c periods after its construction, vintage zero would have a quasi-rent of $(Y_0^* - w_0 e^{\mu \theta_c} L_0^*) e^{-\delta \theta_c}$. Rent would be positive if the relationship $y(\theta_c) > e^{\mu \theta_c}$ were satisfied; it is under the sufficient condition (10.76). Taken together, therefore, the s inequalities ensure that vintage zero passes the profitability test at the time of its construction and that it remains profitable θ_c periods later.[39]

The mystery of why each y curve passes through point A of Figure 10.6 can be explained by recalling from expression (10.49) that optimization requires equating the ex ante marginal product of labor to the real wage. At time zero, therefore, $\partial Y_0^* / \partial L_0^* = w_0$, and y may be rewritten as $(Y_0^* / L_0^*)/(\partial Y_0^* / \partial L_0^*)$: y represents the reciprocal of labor's ex ante output elasticity. From the CES (10.45) with $t = 0$, $y = 1 + (\xi_1 / \xi_2) \kappa^{-\rho}$, where κ now denotes the factor proportion I_0 / L_0^*. But since y may also be expressed from (10.70) in terms of θ, θ may be posited in terms of κ; namely,

$$\theta = -(\alpha + \delta)^{-1} \ln \left[1 - (\alpha + \delta)(\gamma s)^{-1} (\xi_1 + \xi_2 \kappa^\rho)^{1/\rho} \right]$$

which reduces to

$$\theta = -(\alpha + \delta)^{-1} \ln \left[1 - (\alpha + \delta)(\gamma s)^{-1} \kappa^{\xi_2} \right]$$

as $\rho \to 0$. Both equations indicate that as the factor proportion imagined for the capital being designed rises, the economic life rises as well. When the proportion becomes unity, θ becomes θ_c regardless of the ρ value. Moreover, because of the aforementioned link between y and κ generated by the CES, a proportion of unity means a y of ξ_2^{-1} for any ρ. It therefore follows that all y paths must assume the value ξ_2^{-1} at θ_c.

10.8 REFORMULATION UNDER ADAPTIVE RATIONALITY

Thus far entrepreneurs have adhered to a rather unimaginative form of wage expectations. Blind to history, they repeatedly assumed that the current wage would persist unchanged into the future, even though that assumption most likely proved to be wrong repeatedly. Steady growth provides a case of particular embarrassment for the expectation rule, because then wages grow *continually*. Entrepreneurs never learn from experience even though experience follows a very orderly sequence. In the language of Section 8.5, expectations remain perpetually biased.

---

[39] Footnote 40 of Chapter 9 observed that inequalities (9.28) and (9.29) enable the steady growth value of the output-capital ratio to lie within the limits imposed by the aggregate CES (9.26). Their counterparts (10.71) and (10.72) can be construed in a similar vein. From equations (10.56), (10.57), and (10.64), the steady growth value of the ex ante output-capital ratio Y_t^* / I_t becomes Φ/s. The bounds set for Y_t^* / I_t by the CES (10.45) imply the steady growth restrictions $0 < \Phi/s < \gamma \xi_1^{-1/\rho}$ when $\rho > 0$ and $\gamma \xi_1^{-1/\rho} < \Phi/s < \infty$ when $\rho < 0$. Inequality (10.71) is necessary for the former to hold while its cousin (10.72) is sufficient for the latter.

The rule of static expectations can be relaxed to admit more flexible patterns, ones which allow previous developments to shape beliefs about the future. A convenient choice compatible with growth analysis is a slightly modified version of the exponential expectation scheme popular among theorists of putty-clay.[40] That revision may be written as

$$\hat{w}_{tu} = w_t e^{\hat{\omega}_t(u-t)} \tag{10.77}$$

with $u \geq t$. The $\hat{w}_{tu}$ denotes the real wage expected at time t to prevail at time u, and $\hat{\omega}_t$ denotes the expected rate of wage change determined at t. Furthermore,

$$\hat{\omega}_t = \int_{t-a_2}^{t} \beta_{t-v}(\dot{w}_v/w_v)\,dv \tag{10.78}$$

where $\dot{w}_v$ stands for the time derivative dw_v/dv. In (10.78) $\beta_{t-v} = a_0 e^{-a_1(t-v)}$, and a_0, a_1, and a_2 are positive parameters. These additional restrictions are imposed: $a_0 = a_1/(1 - e^{-a_1 a_2})$, $a_1 < 1$, and $a_2 > -a_1^{-1}\ln(1 - a_1)$. These latter restrictions render $\int_{t-a_2}^{t}\beta_{t-v}\,dv = 1$ and $a_0 < 1$. Observe that the β_{t-v} weights decline smoothly over past experience. Equations (10.77) and (10.78) together claim that while wage expectations are exponential, the expected rate of change adapts to current and previous actual rates of change. Should the rate of change become permanently constant, then $\hat{\omega}_t$ would converge to that constant value. Expectations are adaptively rational: by virtue of experiential learning, they can become identical to the expectations which would have been formed on the basis of perfect knowledge.[41]

Using this adaptive variant to replace the static expectations of the model developed in Section 10.5 prompts alterations in the earlier equations. The precise adjustments involved hinge on the sign of $\hat{\omega}_t$. From (10.78) it is clear that at any particular instant $\hat{\omega}_t$ may be positive, zero, or negative, depending upon the record of actual wages, and in general $\hat{\omega}_t$ may assume different signs along a single time path. Three possibilities must therefore be explored. For simplicity, depreciation is ignored: δ equals zero.[42]

---

[40] Illustrations of exponential wage-expectations can be found in Seong Y. Park, "Substitution, Fixed Proportions, and Growth," *International Economic Review*, **9** (October 1968), pp. 307–308, and in Phelps, "Substitution and Distribution," p. 268. Since wages do grow exponentially in steady growth, exponential expectations are often referred to as "perfect foresight" while static expectations frequently carry the appellation "zero foresight."

[41] James G. March, "Bounded Rationality, Ambiguity, and the Engineering of Choice," *Bell Journal of Economics*, **9** (Autumn 1978), p. 592.

[42] The ensuing analysis of adaptive rationality follows a route less ambitious than that taken for static expectations. In addition to ignoring depreciation, it merely outlines the steady growth solution. This more modest tack can be justified by the limited motivation behind the inquiry into an alternative expectation scheme. The purpose is not to explore all nuances of an embellished model but rather to develop a mechanism which enables some assessment, here and in Chapter 11, of the sensitivity of temporal movement to the expectation assumption.

Of the three $\hat{\omega}_t$ possibilities to be studied, the first necessarily rivals the case examined by Park and by Phelps, both of whom dismiss the physical deterioration of capital. The preclusion of deterioration highlights the role of obsolescence since vintages then leave productive service only because of cost considerations. Park, "Substitution," p. 307, and Phelps, "Substitution and Distribution," p. 267.

$\hat{\omega}_t > 0$ With wages expected to rise in the future, entrepreneurs envision at time t that new capital will be on the scrapping margin at some later date $t + \hat{\theta}_t$. Hence the expected economic life of vintage t capital is $\hat{\theta}_t$, which can be calculated from

$$Y_{t,\,t+\hat{\theta}_t} = w_t e^{\hat{\omega}_t \hat{\theta}_t} L_{t,\,t+\hat{\theta}_t}$$

or explicitly from

$$\hat{\theta}_t = \hat{\omega}_t^{-1} \ln\left(\frac{Y_t^*}{w_t L_t^*} \right) \tag{10.79}$$

Because new capital is expected to be operated only through time $t + \hat{\theta}_t$, its discounted stream of future quasi-rents must be truncated then. Therefore

$$U_t = \int_t^{t+\hat{\theta}_t} \left[Y_t^* - w_t e^{\hat{\omega}_t(u-t)} L_t^* \right] e^{-r(u-t)}\, du$$

or, with the integral elaborated,

$$U_t = Y_t^* \frac{1 - e^{-r\hat{\theta}_t}}{r} - w_t L_t^* \frac{1 - e^{-(r-\hat{\omega}_t)\hat{\theta}_t}}{r - \hat{\omega}_t} \tag{10.80}$$

Expression (10.80) is more complicated than (10.48), especially since $\hat{\theta}_t$ depends upon L_t^*.

Maximizing U_t with respect to L_t^* while recognizing (10.79) gives

$$\frac{\partial Y_t^*}{\partial L_t^*} = \Gamma_t w_t \tag{10.81}$$

$$\Gamma_t = \frac{r}{r - \hat{\omega}_t} \frac{1 - e^{-(r-\hat{\omega}_t)\hat{\theta}_t}}{1 - e^{-r\hat{\theta}_t}} \tag{10.82}$$

For (10.81) to be satisfied, the decision wage $\Gamma_t w_t$ must lie within limits imposed by the ex ante production function (10.45). Since that function is unaffected by the choice of expectation scheme, the limits are identical to those cited for w_t in the discussion of equation (10.49). With $\Gamma_t > 1$ for $\hat{\theta}_t > 0$, the quantity of labor employed on vintage t capital is smaller *ceteris paribus* in the present case than under static expectations.[43] Anticipated wage increases lead entrepreneurs to build capital with a smaller labor requirement. Equations (10.81) and (10.82) replace (10.49).

Equations (10.79) and (10.81) contain two unknowns: $\hat{\theta}_t$ and I_t/L_t^*. It can be established for $r > \hat{\omega}_t$ that these equations yield a unique, positive, and finite solution for $\hat{\theta}_t$ and I_t/L_t^* provided that $\Omega_t/w_t > 1$, where again[44] $\Omega_t =$

---

[43] Γ_t is monotone-increasing in $\hat{\theta}_t$ beginning at unity for $\hat{\theta}_t = 0$. See Phelps, "Substitution and Distribution," pp. 285–286, and the graph of equation (2.7) on his p. 271.

[44] Proof appears in Park, "Substitution," pp. 308, 310–311, and in Phelps, "Substitution and Distribution," pp. 271–272. The restriction $r > \hat{\omega}_t$, imposed for expediency, hardly seems unreasonable for a developed economy in a growth setting. See, for instance, Howard C. Petith, "A Vintage Capital Paradox," *International Economic Review*, **19** (June 1978), p. 535.

$(\gamma^\rho/\xi_2)^\sigma e^{\sigma\rho\mu t} w_t^\sigma$. This proviso is automatically satisfied for $\rho = 0$. For other ρ it is satisfied when w_t lies in the open portion of the appropriate interval listed for equation (10.49).

Vintage quantities Y_t^* and L_t^* emerge from the production function (10.45) and the first-order condition (10.81):

$$Y_t^* = \left(\frac{\gamma^\rho}{\xi_1}\right)^{1/\rho}\left(1 - \frac{w_t}{\Gamma_t^{-\sigma\rho}\Omega_t}\right)^{1/\rho} I_t \tag{10.83}$$

$$L_t^* = \left(\frac{\xi_2}{\xi_1}\right)^{1/\rho} e^{-\mu t}\left(\frac{\Gamma_t^{-\sigma\rho}\Omega_t}{w_t} - 1\right)^{1/\rho} I_t \tag{10.84}$$

As $\rho \to 0$, these equations reduce to

$$Y_t^* = \left(\frac{\gamma\xi_2^{\xi_2} e^{\xi_2 \mu t}}{(\Gamma_t w_t)^{\xi_2}}\right)^{1/\xi_1} I_t$$

$$L_t^* = \left(\frac{\gamma\xi_2 e^{\xi_2 \mu t}}{\Gamma_t w_t}\right)^{1/\xi_1} I_t$$

Not much changes in these four expressions; the decision wage merely replaces the actual wage. No other adjustments to the system are required.

$\hat\omega_t = 0$ Expectations are static, and the earlier model requires no modification. Put differently, when $\hat\omega_t = 0$, $\Gamma_t = 1$ and the revised equations considered for $\hat\omega_t > 0$ revert back to their earlier formulations.

$\hat\omega_t < 0$ This case contains elements found in the previous two. Entrepreneurs expect wages to decline in the future, and hence for those values of L_t^* where $Y_t^* \geq w_t L_t^*$, new capital is expected to remain in service forever. This situation parallels that under static expectations. The discounted quasi-rent function can therefore be written as

$$U_t = Y_t^* \frac{1}{r} - w_t L_t^* \frac{1}{r - \hat\omega_t} \tag{10.85}$$

which replaces (10.48).

Maximization of (10.85) makes[45]

$$\frac{\partial Y_t^*}{\partial L_t^*} = \Gamma_t w_t \tag{10.86}$$

$$\Gamma_t = \frac{r}{r - \hat\omega_t} \tag{10.87}$$

---

[45] Consonant with the case of static expectations ($\hat\omega_t = 0$), U_t in (10.85) is concave downward with respect to L_t^*, reflecting the concavity of the CES (10.45). Satisfaction of (10.86) thus assures a global maximum of U_t. A similar assurance does not apply when $\hat\omega_t > 0$. It can be shown that for the CES, U_t in (10.80) is not concave downward over the entire range of I_t/L_t^* values associated with nonnegative quasi-rent. Consequently, the first-order condition (10.81) may not locate a U_t maximum. James H. Gapinski, "Substitution, Fixed Proportions, and Growth: Comment," *International Economic Review*, **12** (June 1971), pp. 325–328.

The limits assigned to the decision wage are identical to those already referenced. Clearly, $\Gamma_t < 1$, meaning that entrepreneurs opt for more labor intensive capital than they would under static expectations *ceteris paribus*. Equations (10.86) and (10.87) replace (10.49). All other requisite modifications replicate those for $\hat{\omega}_t > 0$ with the understanding that Γ_t is defined by (10.87) instead of by (10.82).

The steady growth solution under adaptive rationality may be quickly sketched. Since growth with technical progress invariably means rising wages, only the case for $\hat{\omega}_t > 0$ is contemplated.

Many of the equations offered in Section 10.6 are independent of the wage-expectation scheme adopted and continue to apply. Most notably, they include those for Y_t, I_t, $V(t, w_t)$, and L_t: equations (10.57) to (10.60). Also included are the full-employment condition (10.61) and the relationship between aggregate and vintage output levels (10.62). Consequently, so are the L_t^* and Y_t^* equations (10.63) and (10.64). Linear homogeneity of the ex ante production function (10.45) again yields $\alpha = \eta + \mu$, thereby confirming steady equilibrium growth at the natural rate. As before, Y_t^*/L_t^* grows at the rate μ.

Enter the new wrinkles. Labor productivity on the currently constructed capital is

$$\frac{Y_t^*}{L_t^*} = \Gamma_t^\sigma \Omega_t \tag{10.88}$$

If expectations are truly consistent with steady growth, then $\hat{\theta}_t$ should be constant at θ, reflecting the vintage composition (10.59), and $\hat{\omega}_t$ should be constant as well. The latter proposition might be accepted tentatively and retained if it could be verified as compatible with a steady growth solution. Under these conditions Γ_t remains stationary, $\Gamma_t = \Gamma$, implying from (10.88) that w_t grows at the rate μ. The $\hat{\omega}_t$ relationship (10.78) then gives $\hat{\omega}_t = \mu$, ratifying the constancy assumption for $\hat{\omega}_t$. Wage expectations *are* adaptively rational.

Expressions for Y_0 and I_0 stand unaltered by the expectation replacement. Y_0 comes from integration involving the ex post production function and relations for I_0 ($= sY_0$) and L_0^*; all these are quite independent of expectation formulas. I_0, of course, emerges directly from Y_0. The expression for w_0 changes; in particular, the right-hand side of (10.68) is now multiplied by Γ^{-1}, an amendment having intuitive appeal. Since the decision wage $\Gamma_t w_t$ serves the purpose previously satisfied by w_t alone, the right-hand portion of (10.68) now applies to Γw_0. Solving for w_0 produces the Γ^{-1} multiple. Finally, θ is determined from

$$\Gamma^{-1} e^{\mu\theta} = y(\theta) \tag{10.89}$$

This equation arises after substitutions into (10.79).

The derivation of θ^* from (10.89), while more involved than that from (10.70), is not difficult to picture. The movement of y has already been fully documented in Section 10.6; so has that of $e^{\mu\theta}$, which is transparent. Therefore, only the Γ^{-1} multiple needs attention. As reported earlier, Γ is monotone-increasing in θ beginning at unity for $\theta = 0$. Furthermore, for $r > \mu$, it approaches $r/(r - \mu)$ asymptotically. Thus Γ^{-1} begins at unity and continually declines toward the positive asymptote $(r - \mu)/r$. This relationship means that

$\Gamma^{-1}e^{\mu\theta}$ equals $e^{\mu\theta}$ when θ is zero or infinite and that it lies below $e^{\mu\theta}$ when θ is positive and finite. For the larger θ it acts much like $e^{\mu\theta}$. Consequently, it must cross the y line at a positive and finite θ for each of the three ρ cases considered. However, since $\Gamma^{-1}e^{\mu\theta}$ remains below $e^{\mu\theta}$ for nontrivial θ, θ^* values under adaptive expectations should exceed their static counterparts. Tables 11.6 and 11.7, when compared against Tables 11.4 and 11.5, will indicate that they do. Entrepreneurs, by taking account of future wage behavior, design capital with a smaller labor requirement than they would if, in accordance with static expectations, that future behavior were ignored. As a result, capital is able to earn nonnegative quasi-rents over a longer period. Tables 11.6 and 11.7 will also suggest that the comparative dynamic relationships between θ^* and each of s, η, μ, and ρ derived for static expectations hold in essence for adaptive rationality.

GROWTH AND POLICY: THE SPEED OF ADJUSTMENT

Shocks to the macro system initiated through policy action are intended to redirect temporal movement. Some policy shocks hope to deal with immediate problems; others are designed with longer-run objectives in mind. Policy actions, however, may have both short- and long-term consequences, as Milton Friedman remarked when unveiling the four-point program for monetary and fiscal reform discussed in Section 8.1. For instance, a change heralded as providing the thrust needed for achieving a higher growth path might generate noticeable effects even as the economy first begins adjusting to the perturbation. That adjustment process may be brief, with the system converging to a new growth state shortly after the initial impact. The long run would arrive quickly, and the limiting properties of growth models might serve as helpful guides in the formulation of policy action. If, however, adjustment proved to be lengthy, then the long-run consequences of policy initiatives would likely command little attention. Limit properties would be ignored in favor of a preoccupation with the short run.

In 1962 Edmund Phelps, investigating the speed of the adjustment process triggered by policy action, noted:

> The implications ... for investment policy depend, of course, on the decision rules used by the policymaker. Many (all?) sensible rules will involve, among other things, the responsiveness of output *in the short run* to a policy of greater thrift and investment. The short run assumes considerable importance when we observe that our model economy approaches its limiting path only asymptotically. Even to get close to that path may take considerable time. It is worthwhile therefore to inquire into the speed with which the economy adjusts to a change in the equilibrium path brought about by a change in the investment ratio.[1]

[1] Edmund S. Phelps, "The New View of Investment: A Neoclassical Analysis," *Quarterly Journal of Economics*, **76** (November 1962), p. 561.

Soon after this call was sounded, Ryuzo Sato published two papers which were destined to inspire a continuing debate. In 1963 and again in 1964, he demonstrated that the neoclassical growth model exhibited extremely slow convergence to the steady state and specifically that it required a full century for adjustment to become 90 percent complete. The long run almost never arrived. At the heart of Sato's work rested an aggregate Cobb-Douglas production function, technical progress exclusively of the disembodied variety, and variables defined as net of physical deterioration.[2]

Ryuzo Sato's predilection to ignore the possibilities of capital-embodied progress and capital mortality was challenged by Kazuo Sato, who in 1966 accordingly reworked his namesake's analysis while adhering to the Cobb-Douglas format. Kazuo Sato found that embodiment and deterioration acted to substantially accelerate the adjustment process forcing 90 percent convergence to occur within 25 to 38 years, a horizon well below the century mark. Furthermore, he gave new life to an earlier proof by Phelps that a given rate of embodiment would promote faster convergence than would an equal rate of disembodiment *ceteris paribus*. These conclusions were verified by R. L. Williams and R. L. Crouch in 1972.[3] Not all researchers, however, were entirely convinced about the necessity of faster convergence under embodiment, and one offered a dissenting view to that effect in 1975. That dissent was quieted shortly thereafter.[4]

Subsequent to Kazuo Sato's work, investigation of adjustment speed proceeded in several different directions. In 1966 John Conlisk broadened the model of both Satos to capture the effects of unemployment within the context of the aggregate Cobb-Douglas production process. By 1969 dedication to the Cobb-Douglas had ended. In that year A. B. Atkinson studied the speed of adjustment using an aggregate production function which allowed capital- and labor-augmenting disembodiment but which never permitted its elasticity of factor substitution to assume the Cobb-Douglas value of unity. In 1975 R. Ramanathan looked at the adjustment speed of a neoclassical growth model featuring the CES production function without technical progress, and in 1980 Ryuzo Sato modified his original model to admit a production relation having a variable elasticity of

---

[2] Ryuzo Sato, "Fiscal Policy in a Neo-Classical Growth Model: An Analysis of Time Required for Equilibrating Adjustment," *Review of Economic Studies*, **30** (February 1963), pp. 17, 22, and "The Harrod-Domar Model *vs* the Neo-Classical Growth Model," *Economic Journal*, **74** (June 1964), pp. 383–387.

[3] K. Sato, "On the Adjustment Time in Neo-classical Growth Models," *Review of Economic Studies*, **33** (July 1966), pp. 263–265, and R. L. Williams and R. L. Crouch, "The Adjustment Speed of Neoclassical Growth Models," *Journal of Economic Theory*, **4** (1972), pp. 552–555. Phelps' result can be found in "New View," p. 561. For the record, the two Satos are unrelated.

[4] In objecting to the necessity of quicker adjustment via embodiment, Richard Lansing appeared to misinterpret the parameter for the embodiment rate, and hence he misstated the parameter governing the speed of adjustment. P. Stoneman reviewed Lansing's analysis and reversed its principal conclusion. See Richard M. Lansing, "On Technical Progress and the Speed of Adjustment," *Economica*, New Series, **42** (November 1975), pp. 394–395, 400, and P. Stoneman, "Embodiment of Technological Change and the Speed of Adjustment," *Economica*, New Series, **44** (November 1977), pp. 421–422.

substitution.[5] Some authors, including Ramanathan in 1973 and in 1975,[6] followed yet another tack for studying adjustment speed. They abandoned the hypothesis that a macro system produces a single type of good and adopted instead the view that multiple types are generated, each in a different sector of the system.

Despite careful and extensive study of the subject, no consensus has been reached about what might be a reasonable estimate of the convergence time applicable to a developed economy. Rather, the precedents together seem to say, quite loudly in fact, that the estimate of adjustment time depends crucially upon the specification of the model and upon the parameter assignments for a given specification. Conlisk, for example, finds that his elaborated system engenders much faster convergence than do the narrower paradigms of the Satos. In particular, it allows 90 percent convergence within 11 to 28 years. Similarly, Ramanathan's two-sector model reveals that 90 percent adjustment could be achieved within 6 years. Ryuzo Sato, by contrast, reports that even with the flexibility afforded by a variable substitution elasticity, a century is still required to attain the 90 percent mark.

Since model structure appears to be a key to the study of adjustment time, it should be noted that the aforementioned efforts all stand on the neoclassical postulates of an aggregate capital stock and an aggregate production function. To them capital is putty-putty, and no formal attempt is made to study adjustment time from the vantage point of putty-clay.[7]

This chapter heeds the advice of Phelps and pursues in some detail the question of how fast an economic system adjusts to policy shocks, which are represented by changes in parameter values. In Section 11.1 the Cobb-Douglas growth model discussed in Section 10.2 is used to identify basic determinants of adjustment time. This system duplicates that adopted by Kazuo Sato and others and helps to convey the spirit of debate of the mid-1960s. Section 11.2 relates convergence time to the elasticity of substitution; it draws on works by Ryuzo Sato, Atkinson, and Ramanathan. Section 11.3 exchanges the assumption of putty-putty for the hypothesis of putty-clay, and it presents and evaluates a mechanism for investigating the convergence time of the model examined in

---

[5]Listed alphabetically, the references are A. B. Atkinson, "The Timescale of Economic Models: How Long Is the Long Run?" *Review of Economic Studies*, **36** (April 1969), pp. 137–144; John Conlisk, "Unemployment in a Neoclassical Growth Model: The Effect on Speed of Adjustment," *Economic Journal*, **76** (September 1966), pp. 551–562; and R. Ramanathan, "The Elasticity of Substitution and the Speed of Convergence in Growth Models," *Economic Journal*, **85** (September 1975), p. 612. An embellished description of Ramanathan's work appears in an undated manuscript (henceforth mimeo) by the same title, University of California at San Diego, pp. 1–3, 10–12. The reference to Ryuzo Sato is his "Adjustment Time and Economic Growth Revisited," *Journal of Macroeconomics*, **2** (Summer 1980), pp. 239–246.

[6]R. Ramanathan, "Adjustment Time in the Two-Sector Growth Model with Fixed Coefficients," *Economic Journal*, **83** (December 1973), pp. 1236–1244, as well as "Elasticity of Substitution," pp. 612–613, and mimeo, pp. 4–8, 13–22.

[7]Conlisk and K. Sato make note of putty-clay but only in a tangential manner. See Conlisk, "Unemployment," pp. 554–555, and K. Sato, "On the Adjustment Time," p. 266.

Sections 10.5 through 10.7. Expectations are presumed to be static. Section 11.4 continues the postulate of static expectations and studies the response of the putty-clay system after it is thrust from a path of steady equilibrium growth. Section 11.5 does the same given the formulation of adaptive rationality introduced in Section 10.8. Although both Sections 11.4 and 11.5 speak to the question of adjustment speed under putty-clay, a comprehensive treatment of that issue is reserved for Section 11.6. Section 11.7 remarks on the difficulty of redirecting behavior patterns. It also addresses the sensitivity of convergence time estimates and the implication of that sensitivity for the level of economic understanding needed to properly reckon convergence time.

11.1 SOME DETERMINANTS OF ADJUSTMENT TIME

Equation (10.23) describes the basic law of propulsion for the neoclassical growth model featuring both disembodied and capital-embodied technical progress in an aggregate Cobb-Douglas production framework. Capital is putty-putty. Renumbered and restated with subscripts for time t, that equation becomes

$$\dot{\pi}_t = s(1 - \xi_1) - \Xi\pi_t \tag{11.1}$$

where $\Xi = \tau + \phi/\xi_1 + (1 - \xi_1)(\eta + \delta)$. The π_t denotes the ratio of capital $\bar{J}_t$ to gross output Y_t, $\pi_t = \bar{J}_t/Y_t$; its dotted cousin represents time derivative $d\pi_t/dt$. The ξ_1 signifies the exponent of capital in the Cobb-Douglas function (10.14), or (10.1), and s notates the saving coefficient. Furthermore, τ and ϕ indicate the rates of disembodied and embodied Hicks-neutral progress, respectively, while η and δ mark the rates of labor growth and capital deterioration, respectively. Equation (11.1) presumes that labor always remains fully employed and that equality between planned gross saving and planned gross investment always holds. It restricts its attention to full-employment equilibrium paths.[8]

As Figure 10.1 revealed, the global stability of the steady growth path is assured since $\Xi > 0$. A π_t greater than the steady growth value $\pi^* = s(1 - \xi_1)/\Xi$ would activate pressure, causing π_t to fall monotonically toward that target until reaching it. Conversely, a π_t less than π^* would rise monotonically toward it. Notice that the slope of equation (11.1) regulates the speed of this adjustment process. A steeper slope means that a given discrepancy between π_t and π^* prompts a larger change in π_t per period, and hence a larger Ξ implies faster adjustment. The opposite also applies. Ξ might therefore be termed the "adjustment speed parameter."[9]

---

[8]The assumption that an economy stays in full-employment equilibrium even when it does not reside in steady state is not uncommon. Of the works cited in the introduction, the more noteworthy ones from this standpoint are Phelps, "New View," p. 554; Ramanathan, "Elasticity of Substitution," mimeo, p. 1; K. Sato, "On the Adjustment Time," pp. 263–264; Ryuzo Sato, "Adjustment Time," p. 240; Ryuzo Sato, "Fiscal Policy," p. 17; Ryuzo Sato, "The Harrod-Domar Model," pp. 381–382; and Williams and Crouch, "Adjustment Speed," p. 552.

[9]Ξ duplicates the measure of convergence tempo found in Phelps, "New View," p. 561; K. Sato, "On the Adjustment Time," p. 264; and Williams and Crouch, "Adjustment Speed," p. 555.

Adjustment *speed* can be transformed into adjustment *time* with the aid of equation (11.1). Exercising that formula eventually leaves[10]

$$\pi_t = \pi^* + (\pi_0 - \pi^*)e^{-\Xi t} \qquad (11.2)$$

where π_0 denotes the initial condition for π_t—the value of π_t at time zero. Let

$$\varepsilon = \frac{\pi_t - \pi_0}{\pi^* - \pi_0} \qquad (11.3)$$

The denominator gives the total "distance" between the initial and the steady growth values of π_t; the numerator records the distance actually traversed from time zero through time t. Thus ε can be interpreted as the proportion of the adjustment process completed through t. An ε of .90, for example, would signify that adjustment is 90 percent complete.[11] Using equation (11.3) to express π_t in terms of the convergence parameter ε and substituting the result into equation (11.2) yields

$$e^{-\Xi t} = 1 - \varepsilon$$

which when solved for time becomes

$$t_\varepsilon = -\Xi^{-1} \ln(1 - \varepsilon) \qquad (11.4)$$

Equation (11.4) indicates the amount of time needed for the adjustment process to become 100ε percent complete. As expected, adjustment time t_ε falls as the adjustment speed parameter rises.

From equation (11.4) it is clear that, for any ε, convergence time depends upon five factors: the rates of disembodiment and embodiment, capital's output elasticity, and the rates of labor growth and capital decay. The direction of each relationship may be summarized as

$$\frac{dt_\varepsilon}{d\tau} < 0 \qquad \frac{dt_\varepsilon}{d\phi} < 0 \qquad \frac{dt_\varepsilon}{d\xi_1} > 0 \qquad \frac{dt_\varepsilon}{d\eta} < 0 \qquad \text{and} \qquad \frac{dt_\varepsilon}{d\delta} < 0 \quad (11.5)$$

For instance, an increase in the rate of technical progress, be it disembodied or embodied, decreases adjustment time, while an increase in capital's output elasticity increases it. Furthermore, according to the specification of Ξ, the *nature* of technical progress matters. Since $\xi_1 < 1$, a hypothetical transfer of a 1 percent rate of technology advance from the disembodiment category to the embodiment roster would raise Ξ and would lower t_ε. Stated differently, a given rate of

---

[10] K. Sato, "On the Adjustment Time," p. 264.

[11] Although equation (11.3) uses the capital-output ratio as the device for clocking adjustment, other variables may be equally suited to the task. The output-capital ratio is an obvious alternative. Another choice might be the growth rate of output, whose departure from the natural rate corresponds exactly to the departure of the capital-output ratio from its own steady-state norm. Equation (10.28) articulates that connection. The level of output and the output-labor ratio represent still other candidates.

All these measures, and others, have found service in the literature, but the conclusions obtained have been rather insensitive to the device chosen. See, for example, Ryuzo Sato, "The Harrod-Domar Model," p. 384. See also Phelps, "New View," p. 561; K. Sato, "On the Adjustment Time," p. 264; and Williams and Crouch, "Adjustment Speed," pp. 554–555.

embodiment ϕ produces a shorter adjustment time than does an equal rate of disembodiment τ.

Table 11.1 catalogs from equation (11.4) the time needed to achieve alternative degrees of convergence under different combinations of parameter values. For purposes of later comparisons, the rates of progress listed in the table are expressed as Harrod-neutral equivalents using the conversions $\tau = (1 - \xi_1)\psi$ and $\phi = (1 - \xi_1)\mu$, where ψ and μ denote the rates of Harrod-neutral disembodiment and embodiment, respectively. Given this translation, the adjustment speed parameter may be rewritten as $\Xi = (1 - \xi_1)(\psi + \mu/\xi_1 + \eta + \delta)$, which preserves inequalities (11.5) although $dt_\varepsilon/d\tau$ and $dt_\varepsilon/d\phi$ must be understood as $dt_\varepsilon/d\psi$ and $dt_\varepsilon/d\mu$, respectively. Throughout the table, η equals .02, and all time listings are denominated in years.

Entries for Experiment I show that an increase in the rate of disembodied technical progress ψ from .01 to .04 decreases the time required for 70 percent convergence from 66.9 years to 33.4 years and for 90 percent convergence from 127.9 to 64.0 years. Convergence time falls to one-half of its value for $\psi = .01$. Experiment II demonstrates that an increase in the rate of embodiment μ from .01 to .04 cuts 70 percent adjustment time from 44.6 to 16.7 years and its 90 percent counterpart from 85.3 to 32.0 years, a reduction of more than one-half. Additionally, for the greatest rate of progress considered, adjustment time under embodiment is half that under disembodiment, say, 16.7 years instead of 33.4 years. This "half factor" does not hold generally, however. Experiments III and IV, which are identical to I and II, respectively, except for the rate of depreciation, show much smaller gains under embodiment.

Experiments I and III or II and IV illustrate the force of depreciation on convergence time. When the depreciation rate δ becomes 8 percent, adjustment time drops by at least half of that associated with no depreciation if progress is disembodied and by at least two-fifths if it is embodied. Since the growth rate of labor η enters the adjustment speed parameter with rank identical to that of δ, a change in η would have the same effect on convergence time as does an equal change in δ.

Finally, Experiments II, V, and VI announce that increasing capital's coefficient ξ_1 from .2 to .6 in equal installments of .2 increases convergence time sequentially by multiples of about two.

Ryuzo Sato's assumptions of exclusive disembodiment and net magnitudes find expression in Experiment I, and his parameter assignments made in 1963 and 1964 are most closely matched by those listed in line two for that exercise. Accordingly, the entry of 95.9 years for 90 percent adjustment lies within hailing distance of his century mark. Kazuo Sato's study in 1966 looked at disembodiment and embodiment separately and combined, but it always appealed to a depreciation rate of 8 percent. His parameter values are most closely approximated by those in line three for Experiments III and IV; to him adjustment occurs much more rapidly than Ryuzo Sato imagines. Experiments III and IV when set against I also convey the 1972 conclusion of Williams and Crouch, who adopted as their convergence criterion the half-life of disequilibrium, the time

Table 11.1 Adjustment time under select combinations of parameter values

δ	ξ_1	ψ	μ	Convergence parameter ε		
				.70	.80	.90
			Experiment I			
0	.40	.01	0	66.9	89.4	127.9
0	.40	.02	0	50.2	67.1	95.9
0	.40	.03	0	40.1	53.6	76.8
0	.40	.04	0	33.4	44.7	64.0
			Experiment II			
0	.40	0	.01	44.6	59.6	85.3
0	.40	0	.02	28.7	38.3	54.8
0	.40	0	.03	21.1	28.2	40.4
0	.40	0	.04	16.7	22.4	32.0
			Experiment III			
.08	.40	.01	0	18.2	24.4	34.9
.08	.40	.02	0	16.7	22.4	32.0
.08	.40	.03	0	15.4	20.6	29.5
.08	.40	.04	0	14.3	19.2	27.4
			Experiment IV			
.08	.40	0	.01	16.1	21.5	30.7
.08	.40	0	.02	13.4	17.9	25.6
.08	.40	0	.03	11.5	15.3	21.9
.08	.40	0	.04	10.0	13.4	19.2
			Experiment V			
0	.20	0	.01	21.5	28.7	41.1
0	.20	0	.02	12.5	16.8	24.0
0	.20	0	.03	8.9	11.8	16.9
0	.20	0	.04	6.8	9.1	13.1
			Experiment VI			
0	.60	0	.01	82.1	109.7	157.0
0	.60	0	.02	56.4	75.4	107.9
0	.60	0	.03	43.0	57.5	82.2
0	.60	0	.04	34.7	46.4	66.4

needed for a system to dissipate half of an initial shock. That criterion simply means $\varepsilon = .50$. For the parameter values in line three of Experiments III and IV, disequilibrium half-life is short, 8.9 and 6.6 years, respectively.[12]

Although expression (11.4) faithfully identifies the determinants of adjustment time considered by Phelps, Kazuo Sato, and Williams and Crouch, it misses a key agent studied by Ryuzo Sato, namely, the saving coefficient. He postulates that the economic system begins in a state of steady equilibrium growth and that, because of a change in the saving coefficient, it is forced away from that initial equilibrium. He then calculates the time needed for the system to enter the neighborhood of the new steady state.[13] Inasmuch as the perturbation takes the form of a change in the saving coefficient, it seems natural to relate convergence time to the original and new values of that parameter, s_1 and s_2, respectively.

To do so in the spirit of Ryuzo Sato, redefine ε in terms of the output-capital ratio ι_t, where $\iota_t = 1/\pi_t$:

$$\varepsilon = \frac{\iota_1^* - \iota_t}{\iota_1^* - \iota_2^*} \tag{11.6}$$

ι_1^* and ι_2^* denote the steady growth output-capital ratios under s_1 and s_2, respectively. Since ι_t must move in a direction opposite to that of π_t, the signs in definition (11.6) are the reverse of those in definition (11.3). Equation (11.2), written to explicitly reflect the saving proportions, becomes

$$\pi_t = \Xi^{-1}(1 - \xi_1)\left[s_2 + (s_1 - s_2)e^{-\Xi t}\right] \tag{11.7}$$

Inverting π_t from (11.7) gives an expression for ι_t, which when inserted into (11.6) eventually yields[14]

$$t_\varepsilon = \Xi^{-1}\ln\left[1 + \frac{s_1\varepsilon}{s_2(1 - \varepsilon)}\right] \tag{11.8}$$

This formula may be restated as

$$t_\varepsilon = -\Xi^{-1}\ln(1 - \varepsilon) + \Xi^{-1}\ln\left[1 - \frac{s_2 - s_1}{s_2}\varepsilon\right] \tag{11.9}$$

Equation (11.9) relates adjustment time to the adjustment speed parameter, to the convergence parameter, *and* to the values of the saving coefficient. The new information which it brings is that adjustment time for a decrease in s should be longer than for an equivalent increase. In particular, an s which begins at s_1 and

[12] Consult K. Sato, "On the Adjustment Time," p. 265; Ryuzo Sato, "Fiscal Policy," p. 22; Ryuzo Sato, "The Harrod-Domar Model," pp. 384–385; and Williams and Crouch, "Adjustment Speed," p. 555.

[13] This tack is followed by Ryuzo Sato in his original offerings "Fiscal Policy," pp. 16, 20, 22, and "The Harrod-Domar Model," pp. 383–387, and in his much more recent contribution "Adjustment Time," pp. 239–240, 242–243.

[14] Expression (11.8) generalizes the one derived by Ryuzo Sato in "Fiscal Policy," p. 20. Also refer to his paper "The Harrod-Domar Model," footnote 1, p. 383.

Table 11.2 Adjustment time and changes in the saving coefficient

δ	ξ_1	ψ	μ	s decreases from .20 to .10			s increases from .20 to .30		
				$\varepsilon = .70$	$\varepsilon = .80$	$\varepsilon = .90$	$\varepsilon = .70$	$\varepsilon = .80$	$\varepsilon = .90$
				Experiment I					
0	.40	.01	0	96.4	122.1	163.6	52.1	72.2	108.1
0	.40	.02	0	72.3	91.6	122.7	39.1	54.1	81.1
0	.40	.03	0	57.8	73.2	98.1	31.3	43.3	64.9
0	.40	.04	0	48.2	61.0	81.8	26.1	36.1	54.1
				Experiment II					
0	.40	0	.01	64.2	81.4	109.1	34.8	48.1	72.1
0	.40	0	.02	41.3	52.3	70.1	22.3	30.9	46.3
0	.40	0	.03	30.4	38.5	51.7	16.5	22.8	34.1
0	.40	0	.04	24.1	30.5	40.9	13.0	18.0	27.0
				Experiment III					
.08	.40	.01	0	26.3	33.3	44.6	14.2	19.7	29.5
.08	.40	.02	0	24.1	30.5	40.9	13.0	18.0	27.0
.08	.40	.03	0	22.2	28.2	37.7	12.0	16.7	24.9
.08	.40	.04	0	20.7	26.2	35.1	11.2	15.5	23.2
				Experiment IV					
.08	.40	0	.01	23.1	29.3	39.3	12.5	17.3	25.9
.08	.40	0	.02	19.3	24.4	32.7	10.4	14.4	21.6
.08	.40	0	.03	16.5	20.9	28.0	8.9	12.4	18.5
.08	.40	0	.04	14.5	18.3	24.5	7.8	10.8	16.2
				Experiment V					
0	.20	0	.01	31.0	39.2	52.6	16.8	23.2	34.7
0	.20	0	.02	18.1	22.9	30.7	9.8	13.5	20.3
0	.20	0	.03	12.8	16.2	21.7	6.9	9.6	14.3
0	.20	0	.04	9.9	12.5	16.7	5.3	7.4	11.1
				Experiment VI					
0	.60	0	.01	118.3	149.8	200.8	64.0	88.6	132.7
0	.60	0	.02	81.3	103.0	138.0	44.0	60.9	91.2
0	.60	0	.03	62.0	78.5	105.2	33.5	46.4	69.5
0	.60	0	.04	50.0	63.4	84.9	27.1	37.5	56.1

falls to $s_2 = s_1 - b$ $(b > 0)$ breeds longer adjustment than does an s which starts from s_1 and rises to $s_2 = s_1 + b$. If the saving coefficient does not change, then $s_1 = s_2$ and equation (11.9) collapses to equation (11.4). Inequalities (11.5) apply to (11.9) for any behavior of the saving coefficient.

Table 11.2 records from equation (11.9) adjustment times for the type of scenario considered by Ryuzo Sato. It presumes that the saving coefficient initially stands at .20 and that from there the coefficient either falls to .10 or rises to .30. As before, η equals .02 throughout, and all times carry an annual dimension. For either movement in s, the table manifests that the conclusions regarding the relationships of adjustment time to ψ, μ, δ, and ξ_1 reported by Table 11.1 continue to hold qualitatively. But it also shows that a decrease in s achieves 90 percent convergence over a period which exceeds by a multiple of 1.5 the period associated with an identical increase in s. For 80 percent and 70 percent convergence, the factors are 1.7 and 1.85, respectively. The adjustment process is not the same for equivalent changes in the saving coefficient.

11.2 LINKAGE WITH THE ELASTICITY OF SUBSTITUTION

A principal premise of the analysis in the last section is the aggregate Cobb-Douglas production function, whose elasticity of substitution σ equals unity. This specification, albeit convenient, necessarily prohibits formal inquiry into the effect which the substitution elasticity might have on adjustment time. However, from his Cobb-Douglas perspective, Ryuzo Sato speculates that convergence time should vary inversely with σ: it should decrease as σ increases.[15] He reasons from two polar cases. One is the example of the Harrod-Domar model, whose cornerstone of a fixed factor proportion, $\sigma = 0$, allows no adjustment to steady growth at the natural rate. The other is that of $\sigma = \infty$; then, says Sato, adjustment should be instantaneous since inputs are technically identical. Hence $dt_\varepsilon/d\sigma < 0$.

Although reasonable, Sato's surmise may fall short of the mark. A. B. Atkinson investigates convergence time for an aggregative model in which technical progress, exclusively disembodied, augments both capital and labor. Measuring adjustment time by changes in the capital share, he shows that it increases dramatically as σ rises from zero toward unity. For example, 30 percent adjustment takes roughly 55 years when $\sigma = .45$, but it requires approximately 80 years when $\sigma = .60$ and considerably more than 120 years when $\sigma = .75$. In each of these instances, σ remains constant at the designated value during the entire accommodative process, thereby implying that a CES function forms the basis of the numerical analysis. That $dt_\varepsilon/d\sigma > 0$ for $\sigma < 1$ should come without surprise, because as σ increases toward unity, the operative production function approaches the Cobb-Douglas, which forces the factor shares to remain absolutely constant. Logic argues that if σ passed unity and kept increasing, adjustment time would become progressively shorter at least over a range of σ values near one

---

[15] Ryuzo Sato, "Fiscal Policy," footnote 3, p. 21.

Table 11.3 Relationship of convergence time to the elasticity of substitution

ξ_1	g_0	s	σ	t_{90}
		Experiment I		
.25	.010	.10	2.1	54
.25	.010	.10	3.0	51
.25	.010	.10	4.0	50
.25	.010	.10	5.0	50
		Experiment II		
.25	.010	.15	2.1	58
.25	.010	.15	3.0	58
.25	.010	.15	4.0	59
.25	.010	.15	5.0	61
		Experiment III		
.25	.045	.10	.5	47
.25	.045	.10	1.1	37
.25	.045	.10	2.1	37
.25	.045	.10	3.0	37
.25	.045	.10	4.0	37
.25	.045	.10	5.0	37
		Experiment IV		
.25	.045	.15	1.1	38
.25	.045	.15	2.1	40
.25	.045	.15	3.0	41
.25	.045	.15	4.0	42
.25	.045	.15	5.0	43
		Experiment V		
.75	.045	.10	1.1	109
.75	.045	.10	2.1	133
.75	.045	.10	3.0	143
.75	.045	.10	4.0	> 150
.75	.045	.10	5.0	> 150

Source: Ramanathan, "Elasticity of Substitution," mimeo, pp. 10–11.

since increases in σ would then mean a movement *away* from the regime of rigid factor shares. Atkinson's work therefore suggests a nonmonotonic relationship between t_ε and σ. It does not specifically address that possibility, however.[16]

[16]Atkinson does conduct a test with $\sigma = 1.25$, but he considers no other values greater than one. Consequently, the inference about $dt_\varepsilon/d\sigma$ for $\sigma > 1$ can only be casual. See Atkinson, "Timescale," pp. 142–143.

R. Ramanathan pursues the relationship between t_ε and σ using a neoclassical growth model based upon the CES. The paradigm resembles that described in Section 9.5, but it ignores all technical progress and defines investment as gross of depreciation. A sampling of his results for 90 percent adjustment, measured by the growth rate of output,[17] appears in Table 11.3. There ξ_1 repeats the capital coefficient listed in equation (9.26),[18] and g_0 identifies the initial growth rate of output. Output's steady growth rate equals 5 percent, the growth rate of labor supply, and consequently the table relates to an economy whose beginning rate lies below the limiting value. The toll exacted by depreciation always stands at 4 percent; all times are years.

Experiments I and II together and III and IV together show that the direction in which adjustment time responds to the substitution elasticity depends upon the value of the saving coefficient. Apparently, $dt_{.90}/d\sigma \leq 0$ when $s = .10$, but $dt_{.90}/d\sigma \geq 0$ when $s = .15$. Sign also depends upon the value of ξ_1. As Experiments III and V indicate, the derivative is nonpositive for $\xi_1 = .25$ and nonnegative for $\xi_1 = .75$. By contrast, when the initial growth rate exceeds the limiting value (6 percent versus 5 percent), the derivative is always nonnegative regardless of the values assumed by s and ξ_1. These findings drive home the point intimated by Atkinson that in the context of a neoclassical model, with its reliance on an aggregate capital stock and an aggregate production function, the linkage between adjustment time and the elasticity of substitution cannot be determined without appealing to other magnitudes in the model. Ryuzo Sato's suspicion notwithstanding, the relationship may not always be inverse.[19]

An explanation for the tie between t_ε and σ is not offered by Ramanathan. Ryuzo Sato, however, talked about the effect of nonconstant factor shares on adjustment time,[20] and thus one hypothesis might be that σ affects t_ε through the shares. This hypothesis nicely explains Ramanathan's observed linkage between t_ε and σ for all exercises in which the initial growth rate exceeds the limiting value and definitely for some in which the initial rate falls below the limit. That it might not explain the linkage in all circumstances,[21] however, suggests that σ affects t_ε in a manner other than through the movement of shares alone.

In addition to supplying information on the connection between t_ε and σ, Table 11.3 extends to the full CES function a property demonstrated earlier for the Cobb-Douglas: adjustment time varies directly with the capital coefficient.

[17]Ramanathan, "Elasticity of Substitution," mimeo, pp. 1–3. The 90 percent criterion was the only convergence standard employed.

[18]The capital coefficient ξ_1 in the CES formulation (9.26) is the counterpart of the capital exponent in the Cobb-Douglas. Compare equations (9.26) and (9.27).

[19]The two-sector version of Ramanathan's CES model underscores this possibility. It shows that as the elasticity of substitution for the consumption-goods sector continually rises, adjustment time may fall then rise; rise then fall; or even fall, rise, and then fall again. In short, the relationship may not be monotonic. Ramanathan, "Elasticity of Substitution," mimeo, pp. 15–22.

[20]Ryuzo Sato, "Fiscal Policy," p. 21.

[21]To our mutual disappointment, telephone conversations with Ramanathan failed to produce an encompassing explanation whose validity was doubtless.

Comparison of Experiments III and V shows that for a given value of σ, greater ξ_1 implies greater adjustment time. This result survives under all values of s and g_0 considered by Ramanathan.

11.3 AN APPARATUS FOR EXAMINING ADJUSTMENT WHEN PUTTY-CLAY RULES

The studies of adjustment time reviewed thus far invoke the neoclassical constructs of an aggregate capital stock and an aggregate production function. This tactic has legitimacy either because technical progress is taken to be totally disembodied or because when embodiment enters consideration, the production process is postulated in compliance with the conditions required for aggregation. Noteworthy here is the proviso that capital allow a variable factor proportion ex post.[22] That requirement holds in the aforementioned studies since they all treat capital as putty-putty.

What about adjustment time under putty-clay? This question can be tackled by means of the model which occupied Chapter 10 from its fifth section onward. Consonant with the scenario contemplated by Ryuzo Sato, the system begins in a state of steady equilibrium growth. Authorities initiate a new policy action causing a parameter change, and the system is forced from its initial steady growth path. The trajectory which it subsequently follows will be called a "response path." In this section and the next, expectations are treated as static; adaptive rationality comes into play afterward.[23]

Analyzing the behavior of the putty-clay model wherein expectations are static encounters for the response paths a problem not found in the steady growth context. Now no appeal can be made to the simplification of the vintage set $V(t, w_t)$ given by equation (10.59), which states that only past vintages built at or after time $t - \theta$ remain in service. Instead, it becomes necessary to continually redetermine the vintage set, a formidable task since an equation describing its composition through time does not exist. In short, although the equations developed previously still hold, some have forms which are too general for precisely describing behavior patterns in the present circumstance.

One remedy to this problem comes from the simulation method, which "acts out" the operation of a system according to a computer program. To implement the simulation procedure, however, the model described in Section 10.5 must be

[22] Franklin M. Fisher, "Embodied Technical Change and the Existence of an Aggregate Capital Stock," *Review of Economic Studies*, **32** (October 1965), pp. 267–274, and J. K. Whitaker, "Vintage Capital Models and Econometric Production Functions," *Review of Economic Studies*, **33** (January 1966), pp. 7–10.

[23] The balance of this chapter draws from but elaborates the discussion in James H. Gapinski, "Steady Growth, Policy Shocks, and Speed of Adjustment under Embodiment and Putty-Clay," *Journal of Macroeconomics*, **3**, no. 2 (Spring 1981), pp. 160–175 (copyright © 1981 by Wayne State University Press).

converted from its continuous-time format to a discrete-time framework. Specifically,

$$L_t = L_0 e^{\eta t} \tag{11.10}$$

$$L_t = \sum_{V(t,\, w_t)} L_v^* \tag{11.11}$$

$$Y_t = \sum_{V(t,\, w_t)} Y_v^* \tag{11.12}$$

$$I_t = sY_t \tag{11.13}$$

$$Y_t^* = \left(\gamma^\rho / \xi_1\right)^{1/\rho} (1 - w_t / \Omega_t)^{1/\rho} I_t \tag{11.14}$$

$$L_t^* = \left(\xi_2 / \xi_1\right)^{1/\rho} e^{-\mu t} (\Omega_t / w_t - 1)^{1/\rho} I_t \tag{11.15}$$

L_t denotes the supply of labor at time t; it is exogenously given and grows at the rate η. L_v^* and Y_v^* signify, respectively, the planned labor input and the planned output for vintage v, while Y_t designates aggregate output at t. Vintage set $V(t, w_t)$, hereafter abbreviated V, consists of all surviving past vintages which can earn nonnegative quasi-rents at the real wage w_t. It obeys definition (10.52). Equations (11.11) and (11.12) restate relations (10.54) and (10.55) in terms of discrete sums, while the formula for I_t, representing investment at t, simply renumbers equation (10.56). Of course, s denotes the saving coefficient. Equations (11.14) and (11.15) copy equations (10.50) and (10.51) exactly, and as before $\Omega_t = (\gamma^\rho / \xi_2)^\sigma e^{\sigma \rho \mu t} w_t^\sigma$ and $\sigma = 1/(1 + \rho)$. All parameters in expressions (11.14) and (11.15) are defined by the ex ante CES function (10.45). In particular, ξ_1 symbolizes the coefficient of capital; μ, the Harrod-neutral rate of capital embodiment; and σ, the ex ante elasticity of substitution.

This system has several features which should be noted. Unlike the continuous-time model in Section 10.5, it explicitly posits the time path of labor supply and, of course, aggregates by discrete summation instead of by integration. Furthermore, it ignores depreciation. That omission highlights the role of cost considerations in determining the composition of the vintage set: vintages perish only because of obsolescence. The rate of depreciation δ appearing in conjunction with the ex post production function (10.46) becomes zero, and hence the labor employed on vintage v at time t, $v < t$, and the output forthcoming from that pairing reduce to L_v^* and Y_v^*, respectively. Three other characteristics deserve mention. First, the equality in expression (11.11) will usually mean that the vintage earning zero quasi-rent, or one such vintage if there are several, remains underutilized. For that vintage only, the labor and output quantities will be less in (11.11) and (11.12) than its L_v^* and Y_v^* values determined by (11.15) and (11.14) in some earlier period.[24] Second, a full-employment equilibrium always exists, as

---

[24] The case of underutilization is reviewed anon with the aid of Figure 11.1. Underutilization does not happen in continuous time because then no finite quantity of an instantaneous capital vintage exists; mathematically, the integral over a point is zero. Robert M. Solow et al. make this observation in "Neoclassical Growth with Fixed Factor Proportions," *Review of Economic Studies*, **33** (April 1966), p. 81.

(11.10), (11.11), and (11.13) attest. Third, the limiting forms of (11.14) and (11.15) apply when $\rho = 0$.

The simulation program generates a single run—a series of repeated steps which depict the temporal movement of the system—from selected values for the parameters, initial conditions, and exogenous variables. Initial conditions underlying any run consist of values for Y_v^* and L_v^* where $v < t^*$, t^* being the time at which a parameter change occurs. These initial values provide the history or relevant past of the economy upon which its present and future behavior depend. That present and future are described by the simulation at and beyond t^*, and each of those periods is shaped by the values for the exogenous variables: L_t and the other exponential functions of time, such as $e^{\sigma\rho\mu t}$. The initial conditions trace back 75 periods to assure a history sufficiently long to construct the vintage sets required temporally. The future extends 50 periods beyond t^* since that horizon encompasses the minimum time necessary for attaining a new steady growth state and should be distant enough to allow interesting configurations to emerge along the response path. For convenience, t^* is set to zero. A simulation run, therefore, begins at $t = 0$ with a legacy of 75 periods and proceeds forward for 51 periods[25] including the iteration at $t = 0$.

In more specific terms, the apparatus works thus. Labor productivity corresponding to each initial vintage is calculated, Y_v^*/L_v^* for $v < 0$, and these vintages are then arranged in descending order of labor productivity. Following arrangement, they enter service in sequence and fully employed, the one associated with highest productivity joining first. This process continues as long as the current (time zero) labor supply exceeds total employment. Eventually a vintage is added to V causing total employment to equal the current labor supply. Unlike its cousins, which must be completely utilized, this last vintage may be underutilized since its full-capacity operation might require more labor input than is still available. Regardless of its utilization status, however, its labor productivity becomes the current real wage. Simultaneously, V becomes determined for the current period.

Figure 11.1 graphs this process for time zero. Historical events have blessed the economy with capital vintages which, after arrangement by labor productivity, give the aggregate labor demand curve: namely, the locus of $\Sigma_v L_v^*$, where v applies to all surviving past vintages. Vintage v_1 has the greatest labor productivity and would be utilized first, providing employment for $L_{v_1}^*$ workers. v_2 would enter next, employing $L_{v_2}^*$ workers. Ultimately vintage v_n would enter, equating labor demand with supply. v_n, being the last to join, rests on the scrapping margin; thus $w_0 = Y_{v_n}^*/L_{v_n}^*$, thereby determining w_t at time zero. v_n and all vintages preferable to v_n automatically comprise V. As Figure 11.1 indicates, v_n is not used at capacity.[26]

---

[25] These historical and future time horizons are stretched in Section 11.6.

[26] This method for establishing w_t and V was suggested by Robert M. Solow in "Substitution and Fixed Proportions in the Theory of Capital," *Review of Economic Studies*, **29** (June 1962), pp. 212–213. (*continued*)

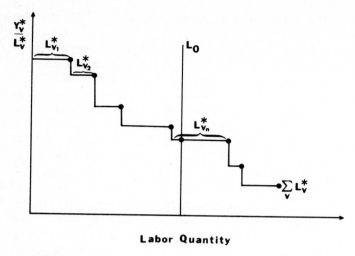

Labor Quantity

Figure 11.1

With V known, current aggregate output is calculated,[27] and current invest-ment then emerges from (11.13) . The potential output and labor requirement of new capital follow from (11.14) and (11.15). At this point the solution to the system for the current period is complete. The program proceeds to the next iteration, where the capital just created is added to the set of past vintages, and the sequential operations are then repeated for the enlarged set. This process continues until 51 iterations result.

Since equations (11.10) to (11.15) were to serve as a representation of the continuous-time system, a test of their ability to do so seemed warranted. If they gave rise to considerable error, the description of response paths obtained from the simulations would be worthless. These equations were therefore tested to see how closely they could duplicate the steady growth behavior described in Section 10.6. This test was the only one which could be performed since for any other temporal path the true composition of V remained unknown.

Testing first involved the choice of parameter values, with these selections being made: $\rho = 3.00, .33, 0, -.20$; $\eta = .02$; $\mu = .03$; $\gamma = 1.00$; $\xi_1 = .40$; and $s = .20$. Four parameter sets thus resulted, one for each ρ. Each set complied with the appropriate s condition, namely, (10.71) when $\rho > 0$ and (10.73) when $\rho < 0$.

If labor supply should intersect the labor demand curve at the full-capacity mark of v_n, then full employment would coincide with a *range* of wage values. Put differently, the wage would be indeterminate. This possibility is ignored by the simulation program, which always equates the wage to the labor productivity of the vintage that allows full employment.

[27]In terms of the example pictured in Figure 11.1, the Y_v^* values for vintages v_1 to, but excluding, v_n are summed. To this sum is added the fraction of $Y_{v_n}^*$ corresponding to the fraction of that vintage in service.

Table 11.4 θ_D **relatives for the steady growth simulations, static expectations**

		Decade				
ρ	θ^*	1	2	3	4	5
3.00	8	1.000	1.000	1.000	1.000	1.000
		(0.00)	(0.00)	(0.00)	(0.00)	(0.00)
.33	13	1.035	1.015	1.015	1.000	1.015
		(3.70)	(3.03)	(3.03)	(0.00)	(3.03)
0.00	18	.975	.961	.956	.950	.956
		(2.84)	(2.65)	(2.33)	(1.75)	(2.33)
−.20	23	1.000	.991	.970	.970	.970
		(0.00)	(1.75)	(2.05)	(2.05)	(2.05)

Consequently, a steady growth state existed for each set, and for each the economic life of capital in steady growth, θ^*, could be calculated from (10.70). Condition (10.76) was satisfied as well, indicating the applicability of the relationship between θ^* and ρ depicted in Figure 10.6. With L_0 fixed at 50 in all cases, the initial conditions for each parameter set were generated by inserting these parameters and the corresponding θ^* into the L_v^* and Y_v^* equations (10.63) and (10.64) and by allowing time to retreat from zero at integer steps. Values of the exogenous variables such as L_t emerged as time traveled forward from zero by integers. The initial conditions therefore assumed values at $t = -75, -74, \ldots, -1$, while the exogenous variables did so at $t = 0, 1, \ldots, 50$. Time carried an annual dimension.

These manipulations produced four steady growth simulations. Their purpose was to replicate the steady growth paths, and they did so quite well. In all runs the true values were approximated with an error generally below 4 percent even after 51 iterations. The number of operating vintages, denoted by θ_D with a time subscript being understood, acted as proxy for θ^*;[28] its record can be found in Table 11.4. There the time interval 0–50 is stratified into decades, decade 1 actually embracing the eleven periods 0–10 inclusive. Decades 2, 3, 4, and 5 encompass the inclusive periods 11–20, 21–30, 31–40, and 41–50, respectively. Each stratum discloses for a given ρ the θ_D relative, the mean θ_D expressed as a fraction of the integer form of θ^*. The θ^* is taken to be an integer because in discrete time vintages cannot be utilized for portions of periods.[29] Parentheses mark the coefficient of variation pertinent to θ_D. That measure, which divides the standard deviation by the mean and then translates the result into percent terms,

---

[28] For the steady growth case, the sums in (11.11) and (11.12) become $\Sigma_{t-\theta_D}^{t-1}$, where the integer θ_D can be recognized as both the number of vintages in service each period and the economic life of capital.

[29] The θ^* values produced by equation (10.70) are 7.52, 12.96, 17.03, and 22.30 for ρ levels of 3.00, .33, 0, and −.20, respectively.

gives normalized variation. Thus, a value of 3.70 indicates that the standard deviation of θ_D is 3.70 percent of its mean; a zero value signals constancy.

The relatives show that mean θ_D closely resembles the steady growth θ^*. Of the 20 decade entries listed, only 3 reflect errors exceeding 4 percent in absolute value. None exceed 5 percent and most lie at or below 3 percent. The error reported with greatest frequency is 0 percent. For $\rho = 3.00$, θ_D remains completely fixed at its steady growth value; for other ρ, it fluctuates nominally.

Since the discrete-time system functioned satisfactorily, its use in analyzing temporal movements prompted by policy shocks to the steady state did not seem to be inappropriate.

11.4 RESPONSE PATHS: THE CASE OF STATIC EXPECTATIONS

For system (11.10) to (11.15), the steady state corresponding to each ρ was disturbed by altering the values of s, μ, and η. Only one parameter changed at a time, and in each instance a simulation was performed. When one parameter varied, all others assumed their original steady growth magnitudes. The following changes occurred for each ρ: s decreased from .20 to .10 and increased from .20 to .30, μ decreased from .03 to .02 and increased from .03 to .04, and η decreased from .02 to .01 and increased from .02 to .03. All changes happened at time zero.[30]

Table 11.5 summarizes the system's behavior along the response paths. Its format basically mirrors that of Table 11.4, but two exceptions prevail. First, θ_D relatives are now based on the new integer θ^*, the one calculated from equation (10.70) using parameter values in force under the policy shock. This θ^* locates the new steady growth trajectory, and hence θ_D relatives founded on it serve to measure the distance of the system from that target path. Second, decade 1 is decomposed into two subintervals. Parameter changes may evoke at the outset interesting behavior which might be hidden at the decade level; the finer partitioning should guard against this possible information loss.

Several aspects of the response path behavior attract attention. Consider first a decrease in s. Given that perturbation, greatest initial disparity between mean θ_D and the new θ^* results for $\rho = 3.00$, whose discrepancy in the first half of decade 1 amounts to 38.7 percent in absolute value. $\rho = -.20$, however, shows a close second with 36.7 percent in the same interval. Overshooting occurs during the response process for all ρ, the peak θ_D relative always locating in decade 3. At

---

[30]A steady state existed in continuous time for each new parameter set resulting from these changes since each set fulfilled the appropriate s condition, either (10.71) or (10.73). Furthermore, the comparative dynamic properties of $d\theta^*/ds$, $d\theta^*/d\mu$, and $d\theta^*/d\eta$ derived in Section 10.7 were always substantiated. So was that for $d\theta^*/d\rho$, although the requisite comparison held the changed s, μ, or η constant at its new value. That $d\theta^*/d\rho < 0$ when $s = .10$ highlights the sufficiency of inequality (10.76); it is not satisfied in this case, $(\alpha + \delta)/(\gamma\xi_1)$ equaling .125. The more general inequality $s > (\alpha + \delta)/\{\gamma[1 - \xi_2^{(\alpha + \delta)/\mu}]\}$ is satisfied, however. Its right-hand term equals .087.

Table 11.5 θ_D relatives along the response paths, static expectations

Parameter change	New θ^*	Decade 1	2	3	4	5	Decade 1 $t = 0\text{–}4$	$t = 5\text{–}10$
		$\rho = 3.00$, original $\theta^* = 8$						
s decreases	15	.727	1.033	1.060	1.020	1.020	.613	.822
		(16.79)	(4.33)	(1.89)	(3.00)	(3.00)	(8.13)	(8.96)
s increases	6	1.076	1.000	1.000	1.000	1.000	1.167	1.000
		(12.12)	(0.00)	(0.00)	(0.00)	(0.00)	(12.78)	(0.00)
μ decreases	9	.889	.978	1.000	1.000	1.000	.889	.889
		(0.00)	(4.55)	(0.00)	(0.00)	(0.00)	(0.00)	(0.00)
μ increases	8	1.000	1.000	1.000	1.000	1.000	1.000	1.000
		(0.00)	(0.00)	(0.00)	(0.00)	(0.00)	(0.00)	(0.00)
η decreases	8	1.000	1.000	1.000	1.000	1.000	1.000	1.000
		(0.00)	(0.00)	(0.00)	(0.00)	(0.00)	(0.00)	(0.00)
η increases	8	1.011	1.013	1.000	1.000	1.013	1.000	1.021
		(3.55)	(3.70)	(0.00)	(0.00)	(3.70)	(0.00)	(4.56)
		$\rho = .33$, original $\theta^* = 13$						
s decreases	17	.968	1.224	1.259	1.112	1.041	.871	1.049
		(10.16)	(4.71)	(5.61)	(3.70)	(2.59)	(5.06)	(3.85)
s increases	12	.939	.875	.917	.950	.967	1.033	.861
		(11.40)	(4.76)	(0.00)	(4.30)	(4.22)	(8.22)	(4.56)
μ decreases	18	.773	.817	.889	.944	.944	.767	.778
		(2.07)	(3.12)	(0.00)	(0.00)	(0.00)	(2.90)	(0.00)
μ increases	11	1.198	1.109	1.000	1.000	1.000	1.218	1.182
		(2.93)	(3.28)	(0.00)	(0.00)	(0.00)	(3.66)	(0.00)
η decreases	13	1.007	1.000	1.000	1.000	1.000	1.015	1.000
		(2.20)	(0.00)	(0.00)	(0.00)	(0.00)	(3.03)	(0.00)
η increases	14	1.000	1.000	.993	.964	.964	1.000	1.000
		(0.00)	(0.00)	(2.16)	(3.70)	(3.70)	(0.00)	(0.00)
		$\rho = 0$, original $\theta^* = 18$						
s decreases	18	1.146	1.394	1.494	1.294	1.133	1.056	1.222
		(8.34)	(3.31)	(2.00)	(4.72)	(2.40)	(4.71)	(3.71)
s increases	18	.838	.744	.817	.867	.889	.911	.778
		(9.56)	(3.66)	(3.12)	(3.14)	(0.00)	(6.22)	(4.12)
μ decreases	26	.692	.731	.796	.846	.885	.692	.692
		(0.00)	(3.33)	(2.21)	(2.03)	(0.00)	(0.00)	(0.00)
μ increases	13	1.329	1.208	1.100	1.038	1.008	1.354	1.308
		(2.58)	(4.08)	(3.20)	(3.70)	(2.29)	(2.78)	(0.00)
η decreases	18	.944	.928	.939	.944	.944	.956	.935
		(2.51)	(2.74)	(1.78)	(0.00)	(0.00)	(2.33)	(2.21)
η increases	18	1.010	1.017	1.000	.972	.967	1.000	1.019
		(2.12)	(2.50)	(0.00)	(2.86)	(2.82)	(0.00)	(2.57)

(*continued*)

Table 11.5 θ_D relatives along the response paths, static expectations

Parameter change	New θ^*	Decade					Decade 1	
		1	2	3	4	5	$t = 0$–4	$t = 5$–10
				$\rho = -.20$, original $\theta^* = 23$				
s decreases	18	1.460	1.706	1.828	1.761	1.428	1.367	1.537
		(6.90)	(2.93)	(1.64)	(5.65)	(4.94)	(4.15)	(3.41)
s increases	26	.776	.673	.719	.785	.823	.831	.731
		(7.56)	(2.86)	(3.42)	(2.40)	(2.29)	(4.72)	(3.04)
μ decreases	38	.608	.645	.695	.742	.782	.605	.610
		(1.24)	(2.04)	(2.51)	(2.13)	(1.54)	(0.00)	(1.61)
μ increases	16	1.409	1.306	1.175	1.088	1.025	1.438	1.385
		(2.21)	(3.35)	(3.98)	(2.82)	(2.99)	(0.00)	(1.68)
η decreases	24	.913	.892	.908	.917	.917	.933	.896
		(3.05)	(2.29)	(1.83)	(0.00)	(0.00)	(2.19)	(2.33)
η increases	22	1.083	1.091	1.082	1.045	1.023	1.073	1.091
		(1.62)	(0.00)	(1.68)	(0.00)	(2.22)	(2.08)	(0.00)

that peak the difference between mean θ_D and the new θ^* varies inversely with ρ. For $\rho = 3.00$ it is 6.0 percent, while for $\rho = -.20$ it is 82.8 percent. Furthermore, response behavior appears to be more protracted for smaller ρ. The discrepancy in decade 5 stands at a mere 2 percent for $\rho = 3.00$ and at 4.1 percent for $\rho = .33$. But for $\rho = 0$ and $\rho = -.20$, it registers 13.3 percent and 42.8 percent, respectively. Why?

A reduction in s means that less output is allocated to investment and more to consumption; thus fewer new machines are available than otherwise. To preserve full employment in the face of this curtailment, vintages must be pressed into service in greater numbers, a reaction which is true regardless of the ρ value. However, as Section 10.7 indicated, for $\rho > 0$ reduced s implies that θ^* has risen. Therefore, as the vintage number increases to maintain full employment, it simultaneously rises *toward* the new target. By contrast, a reduced s connotes stationary or reduced θ^* for $\rho \leqslant 0$. Consequently, the enlarged number of vintages needed to preserve full employment along the response path represents a movement *away from* the target θ^*, especially for $\rho < 0$. This "wrong way" movement must be corrected later.

Increased s fosters the opposite adjustment response. More abundant new machines mean that full employment can be achieved with fewer vintages, and hence for all ρ the number of vintages in service falls initially. For $\rho > 0$ this movement evolves in the direction of the new θ^*; for $\rho \leqslant 0$ it represents a detour. Again there is a lengthier adjustment in the latter instances. Overshooting occurs for three of the ρ regimes, the trough being placed in decade 2. The exception arises for $\rho = 3.00$. There the adjustment process is completed by the second half of decade 1; the vintage number holds secure at 6 from that period forward.

A change in μ affects two characteristics of new capital: its labor requirement and, perhaps less importantly, its labor productivity. Decreased μ implies less efficient labor and, under the ρ considered, induces entrepreneurs to demand fewer workers for new machines. Hence full employment dictates that more vintages be used, and for any ρ the number of operating vintages increases. This action propels the economy toward its new θ^* independently of ρ since, according to Section 10.7, $d\theta^*/d\mu < 0$ independently of ρ. In short, the wrong-way travel characteristic of an s change for $\rho \leqslant 0$ does not apply. Then what might explain the longer adjustment for smaller ρ? As discussed earlier, μ impacts θ^* through counteracting forces when $\rho > 0$ and through uncontested or cumulative forces when $\rho \leqslant 0$. Consequently, the θ^* target moves more for smaller ρ; the adjustment process simply has further to go, a circumstance clearly shown by the θ_D relatives reported for the first half of decade 1. A μ decrease causes an absolute discrepancy of 11.1 percent for $\rho = 3.00$ compared to one of 39.5 percent for $\rho = -.20$. When μ increases, the opposite pattern of adjustment obtains. Notice that overshooting never occurs with the μ changes.

Alterations in η make labor more or less plentiful and by virtue of the full-employment mandate should respectively increase or decrease the number of vintages in service initially. The specific η changes allowed, however, provide little shock to the steady growth θ^* and generate benign response path behavior.

The foregoing discussion referenced the speed with which the economy adjusts to a disruption of steady growth. In general, the smaller ρ is, the slower the adjustment proceeds. For example, an s decrease causes in the third decade an absolute discrepancy of 6.0 percent between mean θ_D and the new θ^* when $\rho = 3.00$. When $\rho = .33$, however, it becomes 25.9 percent in that decade, swelling to 49.4 percent and 82.8 percent when $\rho = 0$ and $\rho = -.20$, respectively. Similarly, an s increase engenders in the third decade percent differences of 0, 8.3, 18.3, and 28.1 for ρ of 3.00, .33, 0, and $-.20$, respectively. A μ decrease has fourth decade percentages amounting to 0, 5.6, 15.4, and 25.8, respectively, while their counterparts for a μ increase equal 0, 0, 3.8, and 8.8. Likewise, an η decrease gives in the fifth decade percentages of 0, 0, 5.6, and 8.3, respectively. Other comparisons yield analogous sequences.[31]

Translating ρ into the ex ante elasticity of substitution σ converts the conclusion about convergence time t_ε into this postulate: Greater t_ε accompanies greater σ. This relationship differs from those derived under putty-putty conditions. It is the exact opposite of that surmised by Ryuzo Sato, and its uniform applicability over a host of parameter combinations appears to contrast with the invertible association detected by Ramanathan.[32] As already noted, forced revisions of the vintage set V constitute the basis of the link between convergence time and elasticity when putty-clay prevails. When putty-putty rules, V typically

---

[31]An η increase pledges some allegiance to this pattern inasmuch as it betrays a smaller percent difference for $\rho = 3.00$ than for $\rho = -.20$ in each decade. Across all ρ, however, exceptions exist. They occur rather randomly and appear to reflect simulation approximation error, whose presence may be dominant on occasion because of the timid reaction of θ_D to an η change. Evidence on the tie between approximation error and the exceptions is offered in footnote 35.

[32]Refer again to Ramanathan, "Elasticity of Substitution," mimeo, pp. 10–11, and Ryuzo Sato, "Fiscal Policy," footnote 3, p. 21.

contains all physically surviving capital,[33] and consequently the revisions of V witnessed under putty-clay would likely not be imitated under putty-putty. This differing behavior of V may explain why the two capital models give rise to different relationships between adjustment time and elasticity.

11.5 RESPONSE PATHS AND ADAPTIVE RATIONALITY

To examine response paths for putty-clay capital when expectations are adaptively rational, the discrete-time model at the heart of the simulation apparatus must be expanded to capture several properties introduced in Section 10.8. The new equation set reads

$$L_t = L_0 e^{\eta t} \tag{11.16}$$

$$L_t = \sum_{V(t, w_t)} L_v^* \tag{11.17}$$

$$Y_t = \sum_{V(t, w_t)} Y_v^* \tag{11.18}$$

$$I_t = s Y_t \tag{11.19}$$

$$\hat{\omega}_t = \sum_{i=0}^{4} \beta_i \left(\frac{w_{t-i} - w_{t-i-1}}{w_{t-i-1}} \right) \tag{11.20}$$

with $\beta_i = .30 - .05i$. Furthermore,

$$\Gamma_t = \begin{cases} \dfrac{r}{r - \hat{\omega}_t} \dfrac{1 - e^{-(r - \hat{\omega}_t)\hat{\theta}_t}}{1 - e^{-r\hat{\theta}_t}} & \text{if} \quad \hat{\omega}_t > 0 \tag{11.21a} \\[2ex] 1 & \text{if} \quad \hat{\omega}_t = 0 \tag{11.21b} \\[2ex] \dfrac{r}{r - \hat{\omega}_t} & \text{if} \quad \hat{\omega}_t < 0 \tag{11.21c} \end{cases}$$

An equation which applies only when $\hat{\omega}_t > 0$ bears the form

$$e^{\hat{\omega}_t \hat{\theta}_t} = \frac{\Gamma_t^{\sigma} \Omega_t}{w_t} \tag{11.22}$$

Completing the system are

$$Y_t^* = \left(\frac{\gamma^\rho}{\xi_1} \right)^{1/\rho} \left(1 - \frac{w_t}{\Gamma_t^{-\sigma\rho} \Omega_t} \right)^{1/\rho} I_t \tag{11.23}$$

$$L_t^* = \left(\frac{\xi_2}{\xi_1} \right)^{1/\rho} e^{-\mu t} \left(\frac{\Gamma_t^{-\sigma\rho} \Omega_t}{w_t} - 1 \right)^{1/\rho} I_t \tag{11.24}$$

---

[33] Formal argumentation appears in Section 10.4. Footnote 18 there considers a case of putty-putty in which V might not include all existing vintages.

Table 11.6 θ_D **relatives for the steady growth simulations, adaptive rationality**

		Decade				
ρ	θ^*	1	2	3	4	5
3.00	9	1.010	1.011	1.011	1.011	1.011
		(3.16)	(3.30)	(3.30)	(3.30)	(3.30)
.33	19	1.005	1.005	1.005	1.000	1.005
		(1.51)	(1.57)	(1.57)	(0.00)	(1.57)
0.00	26	1.000	1.000	.992	.996	.992
		(0.00)	(0.00)	(1.55)	(1.16)	(1.55)
$-.20$	34	.989	.991	.988	.979	.979
		(1.43)	(1.36)	(1.46)	(1.92)	(1.38)

In this enlarged model $\hat{\omega}_t$ denotes the expected growth rate of real wages, the anticipation being shaped at time t. $\hat{\theta}_t$ signifies the economic life expected for capital under construction at t, and r represents the rate of interest. It remains time invariant. Notice that the β weights in the $\hat{\omega}_t$ equation (11.20) assume positive values, decline smoothly, and sum to one in agreement with the properties of equation (10.78). Equations (11.21) capture the various possible definitions of Γ_t: those presented in equations (10.82) and (10.87) and the unit value pertinent to the special case where adaptive rationality becomes static. Equation (11.22) arises by substituting the Y_t^* and L_t^* expressions (10.83) and (10.84) into equation (10.79). Formulas (11.23) and (11.24) repeat those Y_t^* and L_t^* expressions, and when $\rho = 0$ their limiting specifications hold. As before, $\Omega_t = (\gamma^\rho/\xi_2)^\sigma e^{\sigma\rho\mu t} w_t^\sigma$. This collection of equations synthesizes the three cases for $\hat{\omega}_t$ examined in Section 10.8, and consequently it can accommodate any temporal sign behavior of $\hat{\omega}_t$. Full-employment equilibrium always exists.

The solution of this system closely follows that of its counterpart under static expectations. There are, however, several new aspects. At each t, w_t and V are determined from the full-employment condition (11.17). With V established, so too are Y_t from (11.18) and I_t from (11.19). The known w_t combines with the relevant past wages to determine $\hat{\omega}_t$ via (11.20). If $\hat{\omega}_t \leqslant 0$, then Γ_t comes from (11.21b) or (11.21c), respectively. If $\hat{\omega}_t > 0$, then Γ_t must be calculated simultaneously with $\hat{\theta}_t$ using (11.21a) and (11.22). With w_t, I_t, and Γ_t in hand, Y_t^* and L_t^* obtain from (11.23) and (11.24) or from their Cobb-Douglas variants.

Initial conditions for the simulation experiments were drawn from the steady growth paths generated by adaptive rationality in continuous time. Except for the use of these new initial conditions and the assignment of a .10 value[34] to the interest rate r, the experiments proceeded exactly as in the case of static expectations. Table 11.6, like Table 11.4, sketches the performance of the steady

---

[34] This assignment for r was made in the belief that inequality $r > \hat{\omega}_t$ would be satisfied when $\hat{\omega}_t > 0$, thereby assuring a unique nontrivial solution for $\hat{\theta}_t$. That inequality did always hold in each simulation, be it for steady growth or for a response path.

Table 11.7 θ_D relatives along the response paths, adaptive rationality

Parameter change	New $\theta*$	Decade 1	Decade 2	Decade 3	Decade 4	Decade 5	Decade 1 $t = 0-4$	Decade 1 $t = 5-10$
		$\rho = 3.00$, original $\theta* = 9$						
s decreases	17	.717	1.000	1.059	1.059	1.059	.624	.794
		(14.35)	(5.88)	(0.00)	(0.00)	(0.00)	(9.62)	(7.09)
s increases	7	1.065	1.000	1.000	1.000	1.000	1.171	.976
		(11.95)	(0.00)	(0.00)	(0.00)	(0.00)	(9.13)	(5.45)
μ decreases	10	.945	1.000	1.000	1.000	1.000	.900	.983
		(5.27)	(0.00)	(0.00)	(0.00)	(0.00)	(0.00)	(3.79)
μ increases	9	1.000	1.000	1.000	1.000	1.000	1.000	1.000
		(0.00)	(0.00)	(0.00)	(0.00)	(0.00)	(0.00)	(0.00)
η decreases	9	1.000	1.000	1.000	1.000	1.000	1.000	1.000
		(0.00)	(0.00)	(0.00)	(0.00)	(0.00)	(0.00)	(0.00)
η increases	10	.991	1.000	1.000	1.000	1.000	.980	1.000
		(2.90)	(0.00)	(0.00)	(0.00)	(0.00)	(4.08)	(0.00)
		$\rho = .33$, original $\theta* = 19$						
s decreases	23	.957	1.135	1.243	1.135	1.078	.896	1.007
		(6.99)	(3.18)	(1.71)	(3.18)	(1.61)	(4.95)	(2.97)
s increases	17	1.005	.894	.959	.982	1.000	1.071	.951
		(6.81)	(2.63)	(2.81)	(2.74)	(0.00)	(4.11)	(2.31)
μ decreases	25	.778	.824	.892	.924	.952	.768	.787
		(2.56)	(2.38)	(2.05)	(1.30)	(1.68)	(2.08)	(2.40)
μ increases	16	1.188	1.106	1.044	1.006	1.013	1.188	1.188
		(0.00)	(2.59)	(2.74)	(1.86)	(2.47)	(0.00)	(0.00)
η decreases	19	.976	.958	.974	.979	.995	1.000	.956
		(2.68)	(2.20)	(2.70)	(2.63)	(1.59)	(0.00)	(2.05)
η increases	20	.995	1.005	1.005	.990	.975	.990	1.000
		(1.44)	(1.49)	(1.49)	(2.02)	(2.56)	(2.02)	(0.00)
		$\rho = 0$, original $\theta* = 26$						
s decreases	26	1.105	1.254	1.350	1.323	1.169	1.054	1.147
		(4.94)	(2.81)	(1.99)	(4.54)	(2.18)	(2.92)	(2.30)
s increases	26	.916	.823	.842	.896	.935	.954	.885
		(4.67)	(2.29)	(3.79)	(1.97)	(2.64)	(3.02)	(2.51)
μ decreases	36	.727	.761	.808	.853	.894	.722	.731
		(1.47)	(1.79)	(2.41)	(2.09)	(1.86)	(0.00)	(1.79)
μ increases	21	1.225	1.167	1.067	1.024	.981	1.238	1.214
		(1.73)	(2.04)	(2.19)	(2.33)	(2.38)	(0.00)	(1.96)
η decreases	26	.969	.946	.954	.965	.965	.977	.962
		(1.53)	(1.99)	(1.61)	(1.20)	(1.20)	(1.93)	(0.00)
η increases	26	1.028	1.050	1.042	1.015	1.012	1.015	1.038
		(1.67)	(1.68)	(2.58)	(1.86)	(1.74)	(1.86)	(0.00)

Table 11.7 θ_D **relatives along the response paths, adaptive rationality**

Parameter change	New θ^*	Decade					Decade 1	
		1	2	3	4	5	$t = 0-4$	$t = 5-10$
				$\rho = -.20$, original $\theta^* = 34$				
s decreases	28	1.302	1.436	1.525	1.582	1.436	1.257	1.339
		(3.58)	(1.86)	(1.50)	(1.03)	(5.19)	(2.13)	(1.33)
s increases	37	.853	.786	.751	.819	.849	.881	.829
		(3.67)	(2.41)	(1.44)	(2.11)	(1.56)	(2.45)	(1.54)
μ decreases	49	.692	.714	.749	.786	.827	.690	.694
		(0.85)	(1.81)	(1.74)	(1.30)	(2.28)	(1.18)	(0.00)
μ increases	26	1.283	1.238	1.165	1.085	1.042	1.292	1.276
		(1.44)	(1.86)	(2.58)	(2.13)	(2.58)	(1.46)	(1.12)
η decreases	35	.930	.911	.911	.929	.937	.949	.914
		(2.01)	(0.94)	(0.94)	(3.15)	(2.28)	(1.20)	(0.00)
η increases	33	1.047	1.073	1.085	1.052	1.021	1.036	1.056
		(1.44)	(1.38)	(1.12)	(3.42)	(1.90)	(1.17)	(1.07)

growth simulations. Again, their "noise" level seems to be negligible. Maximum error experienced by mean θ_D in tracking the integer θ^* stands at an absolute value of 2.1 percent, and more than half of the 20 decade entries have errors below 1 percent.

Table 11.7 traces the system's behavior along the response paths; it presents θ_D relatives calculated with the new integer θ^* values as base. Familiar profiles emerge.

A decrease in s still causes overshooting, and the size of the absolute discrepancy between mean θ_D and the new θ^* at a peak θ_D relative continues to depend inversely upon ρ, registering 5.9 percent for $\rho = 3.00$ and 58.2 percent for $\rho = -.20$. The peaks, however, are now uniformly smaller than under static expectations. They also place themselves less consistently. For $\rho = .33$ and $\rho = 0$ they locate in decade 3, rivaling the earlier situation. But for $\rho = -.20$ the peak arises in decade 4, and for $\rho = 3.00$ it stretches across three decades. Increased s for $\rho = 3.00$ duplicates the previous quick convergence, and as before troughs occur for $\rho = .33$ and $\rho = 0$ in decade 2. However, $\rho = -.20$ remains a maverick, producing its minimum in decade 3. μ changes engender a repetition of the unidirectional adjustment witnessed under static expectations save for the trivial anomaly in decade 5 applicable to a μ increase for $\rho = .33$. All η changes persist in evoking subdued responses.

The relationship between adjustment time and the ex ante elasticity of substitution is again direct: greater t_ε accompanies greater σ. The third decade of an s decrease reveals absolute differences between mean θ_D and the new θ^* amounting to the percentages 5.9, 24.3, 35.0, and 52.5 for the ρ values 3.00, .33, 0, and $-.20$, respectively. In that decade increased s generates percentages of 0, 4.1, 15.8, and 24.9, and in the fourth decade increased μ makes the percentages 0, .6,

2.4, and 8.5. Decreased η registers fifth-decade figures of 0, .5, 3.5, and 6.3. Other examples produce similar patterns.[35]

Given the entries for decade 5, the length of the adjustment process under adaptive rationality does not seem to differ much from that under static expectations. This finding combined with those already reported say that while behavior along the response paths is not strictly identical for the two expectation schemes, the differences tend to be minor.

11.6 DETERMINANTS RECONSIDERED UNDER PUTTY-CLAY

According to the relationships summarized by inequalities (11.5) and quantified in Tables 11.1 and 11.2, a greater rate of embodiment μ means faster adjustment, and conversely, when capital is putty-putty. Does this property transfer to putty-clay capital? Table 11.2 also reports that putty-putty elicits an asymmetric response of adjustment time to symmetric changes in the saving coefficient s. Does this property transfer as well? How does the capital coefficient ξ_1 influence adjustment time under putty-clay? Its inequality (11.5) and the two tables show that capital's output elasticity, which becomes the capital coefficient in the CES, affects convergence time directly when putty-putty rules, and Table 11.3 confirms this point expressly for the CES. Does the direct association remain intact under putty-clay?

This third question prompts a fourth. Experiments III and V of Table 11.3 indicate that for putty-putty capital ξ_1 can alter the effect which the elasticity of substitution has on adjustment time. That effect may "flip" as ξ_1 moves from low to high values. An increase in elasticity may decrease convergence time when $\xi_1 = .25$ but may increase it when $\xi_1 = .75$. For the type of drill conducted in the previous two sections under putty-clay capital, such a reversal should not occur if the key to the relationship between adjustment time t_ε and the ex ante elasticity of substitution σ is a forced revision of the set of operating vintages. Since the same basic revision should occur for any value of ξ_1, the direct association between t_ε and σ should hold independently of ξ_1. But does it?

A final question addresses the consequence of putty-clay itself on adjustment time. Does the putty-clay nature of capital increase or decrease convergence time relative to that associated with putty-putty *ceteris paribus*? Since corrections to the vintage set cannot occur instantaneously and since those corrections happen for putty-clay but typically not for putty-putty, intuition might suggest lengthier adjustment under putty-clay.

---

[35] The exceptions for increased η associated with static expectations all but vanish under adaptive rationality. Only one remains, and it occurs in decade 5. This virtual extinction of anomalies given the improved accuracy of the simulation procedure, indicated by the generally smaller misses in the steady growth runs for adaptive expectations, supports the claim in footnote 31 that their presence reflects approximation error.

The investigation to follow is conducted only for static expectations. The similarity of results already obtained from the static and adaptive formats advises that little would be gained by working with both, and the computational simplicity of the static version strongly recommends it. Moreover, static expectations instruct the entrepreneur to make input decisions by looking solely at prevailing conditions, and in this regard they reproduce entrepreneurial behavior characteristic of a putty-putty regime. In its effect putty-putty implies static expectations. Therefore, that hypothesis should facilitate comparisons between capital models.

Inquiry proceeds along the lines described in Sections 11.3 and 11.4, although policy shocks are now quarantined to the saving coefficient consonant with the strategy of Ryuzo Sato. Shocks to labor's growth rate η are discarded because they evoked uninteresting behavior in the tests reported earlier by Table 11.5. Amendments to the embodiment rate are allowed, but these occur in a manner designed to yield information on the sensitivity of adjustment time to that rate. In particular, four μ values are posited: .01, .02, .03, and .04. For each, discrete-time steady growth paths are generated under the four ρ values 3.00, .33, 0, and $-.20$, using the previous steady growth magnitudes of all other parameters: namely, $\eta = .02$, $\gamma = 1.00$, $\xi_1 = .40$, and $s = .20$. Afterward, s either decreases from .20 to .10 or increases from .20 to .30 at time zero, thereby creating response paths. In short, s alternatively decreases and increases for each ρ under a given μ, and this sequence repeats for each[36] μ. The steady growth conditions (10.71) and (10.73) hold throughout.

The sensitivity of adjustment time to ξ_1 is assessed by repeating this entire procedure under two other ξ_1 values: .20 and .60. Since one of the purposes of this analysis is to check if different ξ_1 can flip the relation between t_e and σ, an appeal to greatly dissimilar ξ_1 seems to be essential. ξ_1 values placed close together might only establish that a reversal cannot occur in the small interval examined. If a reversal truly does exist under putty-clay, then its presence would more likely be detected by a wide band of ξ_1. A corollary criterion for selecting the ξ_1 levels comes from Table 11.3: they should straddle the midway mark .50.

Deciding upon a low value for ξ_1 posed no difficulty. $\xi_1 = .20$ nicely matched the .25 entry in Table 11.3, and it joined the other parameter magnitudes already adopted in easily satisfying conditions (10.71) and (10.73). The selection of a high ξ_1 proved to be more troublesome. Large ξ_1 values work toward violating condition (10.73) and, given the other parameter assignments, any value of ξ_1 larger than .42 does precisely that. But .42 falls below the ξ_1 midpoint, thereby compromising the search for a possible reversal. Rather than abandoning the search altogether or drastically modifying the experiment to enable ξ_1 values

---

[36] While at first blush a μ value of zero would seem to be a judicious choice since the corresponding response paths would manifest putty-clay effects alone, that candidate is disqualified because it would engender in steady growth a constant wage rate and an infinite economic life of capital. The comparative dynamic properties deduced in Section 10.7 would cease to operate, and the measure of adjustment time, θ_D, would become uninformative.

larger than .50 to accommodate (10.73),[37] a decision was made to sacrifice that sufficient condition. Inequality (10.72) could not be deserted, however, because by doing so y in equation (10.70) might quickly become infinite, dashing considerable hope of a steady growth solution. The less restrictive inequality (10.72) advised that the maximum ξ_1 which could be adopted without altering the experimental design was .63; thus the convenience .60 was chosen. The loss of assurance about the uniqueness of the steady growth path seemed to be an acceptable price to pay for an opportunity to explore the far side of the ξ_1 scale. Condition (10.71) was never threatened[38] by large ξ_1.

It should be mentioned that the set of parameter values, when expanded to include the new μ and ξ_1 magnitudes, gave rise to a much broader spectrum of θ^* levels than that observed in Section 11.4 for the compact set. To allow for this enlarged range, the simulation apparatus was reprogrammed to provide an initial capital profile covering 299 periods, $t = -299$ to $t = -1$, and to track the response paths for 101 periods, $t = 0$ to $t = 100$. The lengthy adjustment reported by Table 11.5 for the s changes under $\rho = 0$ and $\rho = -.20$ also urged that the horizon of response paths be stretched.

Results from this inquiry appear in Table 11.8, which indicates the decade when adjustment to the new steady growth path becomes virtually complete. As with Table 11.5, closeness to the steady state is measured by the discrepancy between mean θ_D in any decade and the new integer θ^*. Three convergence criteria ε are treated: .70, .80, and .90. An entry for, say, the 70 percent norm identifies the decade in which the absolute difference between mean θ_D and the new integer θ^* first becomes 30 percent or less of that θ^* *and* after which it never exceeds 30 percent. Decade 1 again refers to periods 0–10 inclusive; decade 2, to periods 11–20 inclusive; and so forth. Table 11.8 can be interpreted as the putty-clay counterpart of Table 11.2, which pertains to putty-putty under the Cobb-Douglas. It, however, encompasses three values of the substitution elasticity in addition to unity.

Table 11.8 clearly shows that a faster rate of embodiment accelerates the adjustment process under putty-clay. Some exceptions to this rule can be seen, but they locate principally for $\xi_1 = .20$ when the 90 percent standard is adopted. The noise level along the response paths for this ξ_1 appears to be too high to provide neat results when the standard for evaluation leaves little room to maneuver. Nevertheless, the thrust of the numbers cannot be denied: faster

---

[37]For example, inequality (10.73) would be observed by a ξ_1 in excess of .50 (in particular, by $\xi_1 = .52$) if μ were restricted to .04 and if s were only allowed to decrease from .20.

[38]Even though condition (10.73) expired under $\xi_1 = .60$, the solutions for θ^* which resulted obeyed the relevant comparative dynamic relationships presented in Section 10.7, namely, those involving s, μ, and ρ. Condition (10.76) continually held under $\xi_1 = .60$, and $d\theta^*/d\rho$ uniformly displayed a negative sign. It might be noted that when $\xi_1 = .20$, condition (10.76) frequently failed by a wide margin, and thus $d\theta^*/d\rho$ often found itself being positive. When $\xi_1 = .40$, the derivative became positive only once. Of course, failure of inequality (10.76), offered merely as an expedient special case, is not disabling for steady growth. The comparative dynamic property for ξ_1 established in Section 10.7 always held across the three ξ_1 values.

Table 11.8 Decades in which adjustment becomes virtually complete under putty-clay capital

ξ_1	ε	μ	s decreases from .20 to .10				s increases from .20 to .30			
			$\sigma = .25$	$\sigma = .75$	$\sigma = 1.00$	$\sigma = 1.25$	$\sigma = .25$	$\sigma = .75$	$\sigma = 1.00$	$\sigma = 1.25$
.20	.70	.01	1	4	5	7	1	1	1	4
.20	.70	.02	1	1	3	4	1	1	1	1
.20	.70	.03	1	1	1	3	1	1	1	1
.20	.70	.04	1	1	1	2	1	1	1	1
.20	.80	.01	2	4	6	8	1	1	3	5
.20	.80	.02	2	3	3	4	1	1	1	3
.20	.80	.03	2	1	3	3	1	1	1	2
.20	.80	.04	2	1	2	2	1	1	1	4
.20	.90	.01	2	5	7	9	1	3	5	8
.20	.90	.02	2	3	4	5	2	3	4	5
.20	.90	.03	2	3	10	3	1	> 10	3	> 10
.20	.90	.04	2	3	2	2	1	> 10	9	8
.40	.70	.01	1	7	> 10	> 10	1	1	1	9
.40	.70	.02	1	4	6	9	1	1	1	5
.40	.70	.03	1	1	4	6	1	1	1	3
.40	.70	.04	1	1	4	4	1	1	1	1
.40	.80	.01	2	8	> 10	> 10	1	1	7	> 10
.40	.80	.02	2	5	7	> 10	1	1	4	7
.40	.80	.03	2	4	5	7	1	1	3	5
.40	.80	.04	2	3	4	5	1	1	1	4
.40	.90	.01	2	9	> 10	> 10	2	5	> 10	> 10
.40	.90	.02	2	6	9	> 10	2	3	6	> 10
.40	.90	.03	2	5	6	9	1	3	6	8
.40	.90	.04	2	4	5	6	1	3	3	6
.60	.70	.01	1	10	> 10	> 10	1	1	8	> 10
.60	.70	.02	1	7	> 10	> 10	1	1	1	> 10
.60	.70	.03	1	5	9	> 10	1	1	1	10
.60	.70	.04	2	4	7	> 10	1	1	1	7
.60	.80	.01	2	> 10	> 10	> 10	1	4	> 10	> 10
.60	.80	.02	2	8	> 10	> 10	1	1	7	> 10
.60	.80	.03	2	6	10	> 10	1	1	5	> 10
.60	.80	.04	2	5	8	> 10	1	1	4	> 10
.60	.90	.01	2	> 10	> 10	> 10	2	7	> 10	> 10
.60	.90	.02	2	10	> 10	> 10	2	4	> 10	> 10
.60	.90	.03	2	7	> 10	> 10	2	3	8	> 10
.60	.90	.04	2	7	10	> 10	2	3	6	> 10

embodiment implies faster convergence. In this respect putty-clay has kinship with putty-putty.

It manifests kinship in two other ways. As Table 11.8 reveals, putty-clay betrays faster convergence for an increase in s than for an equivalent decrease. Furthermore, it evidences longer adjustment for larger ξ_1. Both properties match those illustrated in Table 11.2 for putty-putty.

What about the relationship between adjustment time and the elasticity of substitution? Table 11.8 confirms that it remains direct. An increase in σ increases adjustment time, and the few noisy renegades, occurring only when $\xi_1 = .20$ combines with large μ, do not invalidate the fundamental conclusion. Observe that this direct association gains strength as the embodiment rate decreases. As an illustration consider the s decrease for a ξ_1 of .40 and a convergence criterion of 80 percent. When μ equals .04, increasing σ from .25 to .75 requires 1 additional decade before convergence becomes nearly complete; yet it necessitates 6 extra decades when μ stands at .01. Such strengthening in the face of a diminishing embodiment rate implies that embodiment does not serve as a contributing cause of the positive association between t_ε and σ. On the contrary, it only acts to obscure that linkage. This obfuscatory role explains why the exceptions always coincide with the larger values of μ.

The root cause of this positive association, as asserted earlier, appears to be the revision of the vintage set induced by a policy shock. Further corroboration of that assertion comes from the inability of the ξ_1 values to occasion a flip in the relationship. All ξ_1 magnitudes, even those on opposite sides of the midway point, tie larger t_ε to larger σ. The pairing of smaller t_ε with larger σ witnessed in Table 11.3 for putty-putty does not happen. Since that table presumes a total absence of technical progress, the closest comparison possible between it and Table 11.8 involves a μ of .01 in the latter. Putty-clay then gives a direct relationship for any ξ_1, and for either s change, without the slightest exception!

The last question to be addressed regards the effect of putty-clay on the adjustment process. Does it lead to slower or to faster convergence than does putty-putty? Some information pertinent to this inquiry can be gathered by comparing the entries for Experiments II, V, and VI in Table 11.2 with the correspondent results comprising the columns for $\sigma = 1.00$ in Table 11.8. *Ceteris paribus* then applies to parameter values. Translating the precise estimates of adjustment time reported by Table 11.2 into the less exacting decade dimension of Table 11.8 should help to reduce any inconsistency arising from an appeal to different measurement devices,[39] ι_t versus θ_D. Consequently, subtraction of the

[39]Conversion of the point estimates in Table 11.2 into decade (interval) equivalents is the obvious first step if comparisons are to be made with the numbers in Table 11.8. K. Sato notes in his paper "On the Adjustment Time," p. 265, that alternative continuous-time variables drawn from the same model may give only slightly dissimilar appraisals of convergence time. However, the use of different measures across different models might yield larger dissimilarities, and they are the ones at issue here.

In transforming Table 11.2 any point estimate which lies in the interior of a period immediately preceding the start of the next decade is included in that following decade. For example, the value 70.1

(*continued*)

Table 11.9 Adjustment time for putty-clay relative to that for putty-putty: the case of the Cobb-Douglas

ξ_1	μ	s decreases from .20 to .10			s increases from .20 to .30		
		$\varepsilon = .70$	$\varepsilon = .80$	$\varepsilon = .90$	$\varepsilon = .70$	$\varepsilon = .80$	$\varepsilon = .90$
.20	.01	1	2	1	-1	0	1
.20	.02	1	0	0	0	-1	1
.20	.03	-1	1	7	0	0	1
.20	.04	0	0	0	0	0	7
.40	.01	≥ 4	≥ 2	nc	-3	2	≥ 3
.40	.02	1	1	1	-2	0	1
.40	.03	0	1	0	-1	0	2
.40	.04	1	0	0	-1	-1	0
.60	.01	nc	nc	nc	1	≥ 2	nc
.60	.02	≥ 2	nc	nc	-4	0	≥ 1
.60	.03	2	2	nc	-3	0	1
.60	.04	2	1	1	-2	0	0

decade equivalents for Table 11.2 postings from the corresponding entries in Table 11.8 for $\sigma = 1.00$ should provide a clue regarding the effect of putty-clay on convergence time.

Table 11.9 presents the results of this endeavor. A positive entry identifies the number of extra decades required by putty-clay for 100ε percent convergence. A listing of 2, for example, says that putty-clay reaches 100ε percent adjustment 2 decades later than putty-putty does. Contrariwise, a negative entry signifies the number of decades by which putty-clay achieves convergence ahead of putty-putty; a -3 indicates that putty-clay attains 100ε percent adjustment 3 decades in advance of putty-putty. A zero denotes a tie. Weak inequalities such as ≥ 4 refer to those instances where putty-clay alone locates adjustment time in the nondescript interval ">10," which could mean decade 11 or any subsequent one. When both capital models put convergence in the >10 zone, relative adjustment time cannot be calculated. An "nc" registers each of those cases.

Several interesting features emerge from Table 11.9. For the decrease in s, putty-clay usually requires longer adjustment time. When $\xi_1 = .20$ and $\mu = .02$, for example, it reaches the 70 percent mark 1 decade later than putty-putty does

---

finds its way into decade 8, which includes all values c in the interval $70.0 < c \leq 80.0$. This practice agrees with that adopted for expressing the continuous-time magnitudes of θ^* in discrete-time terms. It also leads to results which, from at least one perspective, stand "in the middle" of those obtainable via two other straightforward taxonomies, namely, rounding and truncating. The former would define decade 8 as $70.5 \leq c < 80.5$, while the latter would state it as $71.0 \leq c < 81.0$. A number such as 70.9 would therefore be included in decade 8 by the first alternative and in decade 7 by the second. Although these endpoint conversions hinge on the particular taxonomy adopted, the transformed pictures of Table 11.2 emerging from the three schemes do not differ much in toto.

and 2 decades later when $\xi_1 = .60$ and $\mu = .04$. However, the listings for decreased s give a slight hint that a catch-up phenomenon exists. Although putty-clay lags behind putty-putty at the 70 percent mark in the two examples cited, at the 80 percent point it pulls dead even for the first and draws to within a single decade for the second. The prevalence of nc appearances precludes a definitive statement regarding this catch-up possibility.

The s increase generates a pattern at odds with that for the decrease. Putty-clay now achieves 70 percent convergence ahead of putty-putty, but beyond that mark it slows relatively. It passes the 80 percent target about even with putty-putty, and by the 90 percent target it has fallen behind. Catch-up again operates, but it now benefits putty-putty, not putty-clay. The unequal effects which the s changes have on adjustment time for putty-putty and putty-clay individually as reported by Tables 11.2 and 11.8 carry over to the relative convergence time for the two capital models. Equivalent s changes beget different adjustment responses within a given model and across models.

Another hint, again slight, can be gleaned from Table 11.9: faster embodiment seems to reduce the disparity in adjustment times. For instance, an s decrease with $\xi_1 = .40$ causes putty-clay to reach 80 percent convergence at least 2 decades behind putty-putty when $\mu = .01$, but it prompts a tie when $\mu = .04$. As μ rises from .01 to .04 for an s increase with $\xi_1 = .40$, the lead of 3 decades enjoyed by putty-clay at the 70 percent standard dwindles to a lead of 1. Quicker embodiment not only speeds the adjustment process for putty-putty and putty-clay separately but also may give preferential treatment to the slower capital model, thereby attenuating discrepancies in convergence times.

Capital's ξ_1 parameter upholds its reputation for influencing convergence in a manner counter to that of the embodiment rate. An increase in ξ_1 tends to widen differences in the adjustment times of the two models. Although that effect remains somewhat veiled for increased s, it comes into full view for decreased s. There, with μ set at .04, putty-clay reaches the 70 percent norm tied with putty-putty when ξ_1 equals .20, but it falls behind by 1 decade when ξ_1 rises to .40. It slips further behind when ξ_1 becomes .60. Other examples can be readily found. Larger ξ_1 lengthen the adjustment sequence for either capital model, and they exaggerate the difference between the separate convergence times. In terms of effect, ξ_1 is the reverse of μ.

Because of the crudeness of the comparisons summarized in Table 11.9, the findings presented must be regarded as speculative. Furthermore, they are parochial since they pertain only to the Cobb-Douglas format. Nevertheless, they encourage the conclusions that the relative adjustment time for putty-clay and putty-putty, like the absolute times for both, depends upon parameter values including the convergence criterion and that putty-clay tends to exhibit slower convergence overall. Table 11.9 never shows putty-clay crossing the 90 percent mark ahead of putty-putty.[40]

---

[40] Similarly, the rounding and truncating taxonomies never show putty-clay leading at the 90 percent milestone. Of the differing results attributable to the choice of endpoint code, the only one

(*continued*)

11.7 A CONCLUDING THOUGHT

Policy action may have consequences in both the long run and the short run. It may alter the economy's secular growth trajectory while simultaneously propagating a new path which the economy immediately begins to traverse as it heads for the long run. The arrival there deserves notation because it is then that the full benefits of policy action may come to pass.

Redirecting behavior is often difficult. Old patterns are stubborn, and they may succumb only to large doses of economic inducement. Raising the saving coefficient for the purpose of securing, say, higher levels of per capita income requires an instantaneous forfeiture of consumption. Costs occur "up front," and the present generation might be more inclined to accept those costs if it saw an opportunity for sharing meaningfully in the benefits. Knowledge that future generations would be thankful for current sacrifices might be comforting, but it would provide much less gratification than would an awareness that present and future generations together stand to gain appreciably from them. Who gains how much from current draconian feats hinges upon the arrival time of the long run.

The analysis presented in this chapter shows that arrival time is a function of parameter magnitudes. A greater rate of technical progress shortens it; a greater capital coefficient lengthens it. Increased thrift leads to shorter time than does decreased thrift. These features hold under different conceptions of the economy's structure, but some properties, such as the effect of factor substitutability, do not.

Determining when the long run arrives seems to require a rather complete understanding of how the economy works. Specifics are needed. General issues concerning the characteristics of capital and the like must be resolved, but the tricky econometric business of parameter estimation must be settled as well. Simple theoretical paradigms designed to inspire thoughts and to foster policy prescriptions may be ill-equipped to meet the challenge. The practice of incorporating into the analysis selected complications may not help much either. The addition of embodied technological advance to the basic neoclassical framework serves to reduce adjustment time. So does a recognition of capital mortality. Grafting Keynesian unemployment equations onto the model or splitting a single product-sector into multiple components can further shorten adjustment time. Adoption of these complications should be applauded for enhancing the realism of the paradigm. Yet care must be taken to avoid drawing from such exercises the conclusion that even more complications borrowed from reality would enable the detection of still shorter adjustment times, for it is only a very small step from this conclusion to the sweeping statements that the real-world economy must adjust quickly and that the present generation must benefit handsomely from its own sacrifices. The *number* of complications added to the analysis does not matter. What matters is the *nature* of the complications added. Putty-clay represents a complication of the neoclassical model; yet it can increase adjustment time.

---

which deserves mention regards the catch-up phenomenon. Relative to the scheme underlying Table 11.9, rounding improves the brief for catch-up given an s decrease whereas truncating worsens it.

Continuing his 1962 discussion, Edmund Phelps remarked, "An alteration of the model does not change the world but only the conception and estimation of its parameters."[41] The economic world may insist upon some particular adjustment time, which may be short or which may be long. Selectively complicating economic models in the name of realism merely alters the perception of that time. It might move perception in the right direction, or it might not.

[41]Phelps, "New View," p. 562.

APPENDIX
A

QUANTITATIVE TOOLS OF ECONOMIC ANALYSIS

This appendix presents a general review of quantitative concepts and methods used in the volume. Although an exhaustive treatment of the material clearly lies beyond its scope, it does attempt to examine each topic in sufficient detail to enable the review to be self-contained. The examples considered come mainly from text itself, and when they do, they typically retain their original notation to underscore the connection between the discussions. Notation retention means that a given symbol may be encountered here several times in different contexts, but despite this circumstance no threat of confusion arises. Appendixes B, C, and D continue the inquiry into the quantitative side of economics; each has an orientation more narrow than that of the current effort.

A.1 THE LIMIT

At the heart of calculus rests the notion of "limit," which focuses on the *approach* of variables to designated values rather than on their *arrival* at those values. Consider a function $z = f(x)$, where z and x represent the dependent variable and the independent variable, respectively. Imagine that x, known also as the "argument of f," moves closer to some number b and that as it does, z moves closer to some number c. This quantity c is called the "limit of z."

To fashion a more formal statement of limit, the conception of closeness must be refined. Specifically, how close is close? Let δ be a positive value. Then x is close to b if $b - \delta < x < b + \delta$. Similarly, z is close to c if $c - \varepsilon < z < c + \varepsilon$, ε being positive. A more exact definition of limit then reads thus: c is the limit of

z as x approaches b if for any ε there is a δ which enables z to lie in the interval $c - \varepsilon < z < c + \varepsilon$ when x lies anywhere in the interval $b - \delta < x < b + \delta$ except at b itself.

In some instances z may expand without bound as x approaches b; its limit is infinity. One such possibility envisions a limit of positive infinity (∞) and says that z becomes infinitely positive as x approaches b if for any positive number C there is a δ which makes $z > C$ when x lies anywhere in the interval $b - \delta < x < b + \delta$ except at b. The case where z has a limit of negative infinity ($-\infty$) can be described similarly. In other instances x may be the variable approaching infinity, and for the example of positive infinity the statement of limit may be revised to read that c is the limit of z as x approaches positive infinity if for any ε there is a positive number B which enables z to lie in the interval $c - \varepsilon < z < c + \varepsilon$ when x exceeds B. The description of minus infinity proceeds analogously, as do those for infinite limits at infinity.[1]

Conventional notation for the limit underscores the concern about the approach phenomenon. One variant has $\lim_{x \to b} z = c$, which says that c is the limit of z as x approaches b. Another has $z \to c$ as $x \to b$, which says that z approaches c as x approaches b. Less conventional and somewhat removed from a strict interpretation of limit is the shorthand $f(b) = c$. The latter can be used, however, when the meaning remains clear. It is adopted, for example, to describe properties of both the neoclassical production function in Section 9.4 and the Robinson function for desired investment in Section 9.7. Likewise, it finds service during the discussion of the Sheshinski boundary conditions in Section 10.7. Standard symbolism is associated with, say, the drill regarding Inada's right-hand boundary condition in footnote 34 of Chapter 9, the analysis of Cases I and III in Section 10.6, and the derivation of the Cobb-Douglas production function in Section C.3.

The limit has rather straightforward computational properties. The following list uses A and b to denote constants and $f(x)$ and $g(x)$ to denote functions. It also adopts the notation $x \to b^+$ to mean that x approaches b through values greater than b; similarly, $x \to b^-$ means that x approaches b through values less than b. Of course, $x \to b$ signifies that x approaches b from either direction.

Property 1. $\lim_{x \to b} A = A$.

Property 2. $\lim_{x \to b}(Ax) = A \lim_{x \to b} x = Ab$.

Property 3. $\lim_{x \to b}[f(x) \pm g(x)] = \lim_{x \to b} f(x) \pm \lim_{x \to b} g(x)$.

[1]Reference for the definitions of limit is Murray H. Protter and Charles B. Morrey, Jr., *College Calculus with Analytic Geometry*, 3d ed. (Reading, Mass.: Addison-Wesley Publishing Company, Inc., 1977), pp. 58–61, 83–84, 103, 105. References for other material included in this section are Protter and Morrey, *College Calculus*, pp. 37–38, 89–93, 103, 105–106, along with Alpha C. Chiang, *Fundamental Methods of Mathematical Economics*, 2d ed. (New York: McGraw-Hill Book Company, 1974), pp. 154–155, and Albert G. Fadell, *Calculus with Analytic Geometry* (Buffalo, N.Y.: University of Buffalo, 1961), p. 586.

Property 4. $\lim_{x \to b}[f(x)g(x)] = \lim_{x \to b}f(x)\lim_{x \to b}g(x)$.

Property 5. $\lim_{x \to b}[f(x)/g(x)] = \lim_{x \to b}f(x)/\lim_{x \to b}g(x)$ for $\lim_{x \to b}g(x) \neq 0$.

Property 6. $\lim_{x \to b}f[g(x)] = f[\lim_{x \to b}g(x)]$.

Property 7. $\lim_{x \to \infty}1/x = 0$, $\lim_{x \to -\infty}1/x = 0$, $\lim_{x \to 0^+}1/x = \infty$, and $\lim_{x \to 0^-}1/x = -\infty$.

The text appeals to properties 6 and 7 to establish in Cases I and III of Section 9.5 the behavior of $f(\kappa) = \gamma[\xi_1\kappa^{-\rho} + \xi_2]^{-1/\rho}$ as $\kappa \to 0^+$ and as $\kappa \to \infty$. However, it omits the superscript in 0^+ because κ, being confined to nonnegative values, can obviously approach zero only from the positive direction.

Linked to the concept of limit is that of asymptote. An asymptote constitutes a line to which a function $f(x)$ tends as x tends to some number. If that line is vertical, then it can be called a "vertical asymptote." If it is horizontal, then it may be termed a "horizontal asymptote." An illustration of the former comes from equation (8.29), according to which σ_Q^2 becomes infinite as λ_2 moves from λ_2^* either to $\lambda_2^* - 1/\xi_1$ or to $\lambda_2^* + 1/\xi_1$. Both of those λ_2 destinations represent vertical asymptotes, as the dashed lines in Figure 8.3 make clear. Case I of Section 9.5 provides an example of a horizontal asymptote. There as $\kappa \to \infty$, $f(\kappa) \to \gamma\xi_2^{-1/\rho}$, and hence $sf(\kappa) \to s\gamma\xi_2^{-1/\rho}$. Quantity $s\gamma\xi_2^{-1/\rho}$ marks the horizontal asymptote which appears as the dashed line in Figure 9.3.

A.2 THE DERIVATIVE

It is a small step from the limit to the derivative.[2] Suppose that x changes from x_0 to $x_0 + \Delta x$, Δ standing for "change in," and that $z = f(x)$ changes accordingly from $f(x_0)$ to $f(x_0 + \Delta x)$. The ratio expressing this change in z relative to the change in x may be written as the difference quotient

$$\frac{f(x_0 + \Delta x) - f(x_0)}{(x_0 + \Delta x) - x_0}$$

and may be likened to the slope of z: $\Delta z/\Delta x$. As Δx becomes smaller and smaller, the difference quotient becomes more and more descriptive of the slope of z in the vicinity of x_0, and in the limit it gives the slope *at* x_0. This limit of the difference quotient is called the "derivative" and is symbolized by dz/dx, where d replaces Δ in $\Delta z/\Delta x$ to acknowledge that the changes being considered are infinitesimally small. Since x_0 represents any value of x, the derivative of z with respect to x may be expressed as

$$\frac{dz}{dx} = \lim_{\Delta x \to 0}\frac{f(x + \Delta x) - f(x)}{\Delta x}$$

[2]With regard to what follows, see Chiang, *Fundamental Methods*, pp. 137–141, 164–173, 176, 179–182; Fadell, *Calculus*, pp. 282–283; and Protter and Morrey, *College Calculus*, pp. 72–73, 115–123, 331–332.

Other common identifiers for the derivative of z with respect to x include $d(z)/dx$, df/dx, and $f'(x)$.

Because the derivative looks at the change in z when x changes by a very small amount—say, by a unit—it should be easy to accept that the derivative must be zero if z equals the constant A and must be the constant A if z equals Ax. Furthermore, it should be easy to imagine that a z equal to the sum or difference of two functions $f(x)$ and $g(x)$ has a derivative which amounts to the sum or difference, respectively, of the separate derivatives. These features can be stated more compactly.

Property 1. If $z = A$, then $dz/dx = 0$.

Property 2. If $z = Ax$, then $dz/dx = A$.

Property 3. If $z = f(x) \pm g(x)$, then $dz/dx = f'(x) \pm g'(x)$.

Less intuitive are the derivatives pertinent to the product and quotient of functions.

Property 4. If $z = f(x)g(x)$, then $dz/dx = f'(x)g(x) + f(x)g'(x)$.

Property 5. If $z = f(x)/g(x)$, then $dz/dx = [g(x)f'(x) - f(x)g'(x)]/[g(x)]^2$.

Property 2 can be viewed as a special case of the power rule. That rule gives the derivative of $z = Ax^p$, p being any real number, and reads

Property 6. If $z = Ax^p$, then $dz/dx = pAx^{p-1}$.

Another important precept of differentiation is known as the "chain rule":

Property 7. If $z = f[g(x)]$, then $dz/dx = \{df[g(x)]/dg(x)\}\{dg(x)/dx\}$.

When z is a function f of a function g of x, first calculate the amount by which f changes when g changes by a unit, and then multiply that amount by the amount g changes when x changes by a unit.

An example involving the power and chain rules along with other derivative properties can be found in Section 9.5. There $z = \gamma[\xi_1\kappa^{-\rho} + \xi_2]^{-1/\rho}$. Let $h(\kappa) = \xi_1\kappa^{-\rho}$, $i(\kappa) = \xi_2$, and $g(\kappa) = h(\kappa) + i(\kappa)$. Thus $z = \gamma[g(\kappa)]^{-1/\rho}$; that is, $z = f[g(\kappa)]$. The chain rule advises that to find $dz/d\kappa$, first differentiate $f[g(\kappa)]$ with respect to $g(\kappa)$. Doing so by the power rule leaves $df[g(\kappa)]/dg(\kappa) = -(1/\rho)\gamma[g(\kappa)]^{-1/\rho-1}$. Next, differentiate $g(\kappa)$ with respect to κ, and multiply the result into $df[g(\kappa)]/dg(\kappa)$. Since $g(\kappa)$ equals the sum of $h(\kappa)$ and $i(\kappa)$, $dg(\kappa)/d\kappa = dh(\kappa)/d\kappa + di(\kappa)/d\kappa$ by property 3. But by the power rule, $dh(\kappa)/d\kappa = -\rho\xi_1\kappa^{-\rho-1}$, and by property 1, $di(\kappa)/d\kappa = 0$. Therefore, $dg(\kappa)/d\kappa = -\rho\xi_1\kappa^{-\rho-1}$. It follows that

$$\frac{df[g(\kappa)]}{dg(\kappa)}\frac{dg(\kappa)}{d\kappa} = -\frac{1}{\rho}\gamma[\xi_1\kappa^{-\rho} + \xi_2]^{-1/\rho-1}(-\rho)\xi_1\kappa^{-\rho-1}$$

which simplifies to $dz/d\kappa = \gamma\xi_1[\xi_1 + \xi_2\kappa^\rho]^{-1/(\sigma\rho)}$ since $\sigma = 1/(1 + \rho)$.

$f'(x)$ gives the slope of $f(x)$ at the point x. Inserting different x values into $f'(x)$ produces a curve representing the slope, and that curve itself has a slope. The slope of the slope curve at any point can be found by taking the derivative of $f'(x)$. This derivative of $f'(x)$ with respect to x is called the "second derivative," distinguishing it from $f'(x)$, which bears the name "first derivative." Notation for the second derivative includes $d(dz/dx)/dx$, d^2z/dx^2, d^2f/dx^2, and $f''(x)$. Derivatives of orders higher than two are produced the same way. For example, the third derivative $f'''(x)$ arises by differentiating the second derivative; the fourth derivative $f^4(x)$, by differentiating the third.

The first and second derivatives of a function $z = f(x)$ can be used to describe its monotonicity and its concavity, respectively. Monotonicity refers to the ability to preserve or to reverse order (association). The function preserves order if $f(x_2) > f(x_1)$ when $x_2 > x_1$; it reverses order if $f(x_2) > f(x_1)$ when $x_2 < x_1$. From this description it should be evident that the function is order-preserving, alias monotone- (or monotonic-) increasing, over an x interval if $f'(x) > 0$ over that interval. By contrast, it is order-reversing, or monotone-decreasing, over the x interval if $f'(x) < 0$ for those x. Concavity refers to the curvature of $f(x)$. $f''(x) > 0$ over an x interval means that $f(x)$ bends upward over the interval: $f(x)$ is concave upward there. The converse also holds. $f''(x) < 0$ over an interval signifies that $f(x)$ bows downward there: $f(x)$ is concave downward. Figure A.1, which follows the usual practice of showing the positive directions by arrowheads affixed to the axes, presents four $f(x)$ curves for $b_1 \leq x \leq b_2$. Curve A is monotone-increasing and concave upward, while curve B is monotone-increasing but concave downward. Curves C and D are monotone-decreasing. C is concave upward; D, concave downward.

Monotonicity proves to be a key consideration in formulating an aggregate capital stock, as Section 10.3 argues. The functions $G^v(K_{vt})$ cited in that exposition are taken to be monotone. Concavity constitutes the central focus in establishing the uniqueness of a steady growth solution; Case III of Section 10.6 presents the details. The function in question is $y(\theta)$.

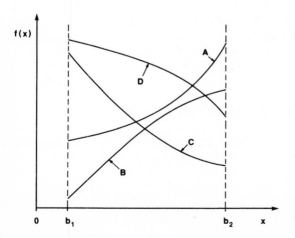

Figure A.1

A.3 INDETERMINATE FORMS AND l'HOPITAL'S RULE

Various expressions involving multiple zeros or infinities provide no clue about the values which they assume on balance and hence are called "indeterminate forms." Those expressions include $0/0$, ∞/∞, $0 \cdot \infty$, $\infty - \infty$, 1^∞, and variants producible by changing the sign of the infinite quantity. That the form 1^∞ qualifies as indeterminate may be easily seen by converting it to the common logarithm: $\infty \log_{10} 1 = \infty \cdot 0$.

On some occasions the indeterminacy of an expression can be broken by considering how fast each of the component parts approaches its tricky value. Intuition suggests, for instance, that the form ∞/∞ would reduce to zero if the denominator approached infinity faster than the numerator did and would expand to infinity if the opposite speed pattern held. Developed by G. F. A. l'Hopital, the formal rule for resolving indeterminacy captures this intuitive notion of relative speed by focusing not on the components themselves but rather on their derivatives. l'Hopital's rule may be stated thus: If $\lim_{x \to b}[f(x)/g(x)]$ equals $0/0$, ∞/∞, or any variation of the latter generated by sign changes, then $\lim_{x \to b}[f(x)/g(x)] = \lim_{x \to b} f'(x)/\lim_{x \to b} g'(x)$. Provided that the indeterminacy takes the form of a quotient, the limit of the quotient can be replaced by the quotient constructed from the limits of the separate derivatives. Should $\lim_{x \to b} f'(x)/\lim_{x \to b} g'(x)$ be an indeterminate form, the rule could be applied again, giving $\lim_{x \to b} f''(x)/\lim_{x \to b} g''(x)$, which must equal $\lim_{x \to b}[f(x)/g(x)]$. This process can be repeated further.[3]

l'Hopital's procedure finds frequent use in the text. Consider equation (8.12): $Y_E = (H - c\gamma Y^*)/(1 - c - c\gamma)$. Clearly, $\lim_{\gamma \to \infty} Y_E = -\infty/(-\infty)$, an indeterminate form. Applying l'Hopital's rule renders $\lim_{\gamma \to \infty} Y_E = \lim_{\gamma \to \infty}(-cY^*)/\lim_{\gamma \to \infty}(-c) = Y^*$. Similarly, applying the rule to equation (8.14), that is, to $G_t - T_t = \gamma \Delta I_o/(1 - c - c\gamma)$, leaves $\lim_{\gamma \to \infty}(G_t - T_t) = \lim_{\gamma \to \infty} \Delta I_o/\lim_{\gamma \to \infty}(-c) = -\Delta I_o/c$.

In some instances an indeterminate form such as $\infty - \infty$ can be translated into the quotient type, enabling l'Hopital to be applied to the transformation. Footnote 52 of Chapter 9 provides an illustration. $u = \chi(m) - s_R m$ with $\lim_{m \to \infty} u = \infty - \infty$. Rewrite u as $u = m[\chi(m)/m - s_R]$. Now $\lim_{m \to \infty} u = \infty[\infty/\infty - s_R]$. Directing l'Hopital's rule to the ∞/∞ term produces $\lim_{m \to \infty}[\chi(m)/m] = [\lim_{m \to \infty}\chi'(m)]/1$. But $\lim_{m \to \infty}\chi'(m) < s_R$, meaning that $\lim_{m \to \infty} u = -\infty$.

A.4 DIFFERENTIAL CALCULUS OF SEVERAL VARIABLES

Thus far the discussion has presumed that z depends upon a single variable. In the more general case, z depends upon a set of variables, and in that circumstance

[3] Inquiry into indeterminate forms and l'Hopital's rule can be found in Fadell, *Calculus*, pp. 467–468, 470–475, and in Protter and Morrey, *College Calculus*, pp. 564–568.

the derivative possibilities are more abundant. Derivatives then associate with each independent variable treated individually. Furthermore, an independent variable may actually depend upon another, and such interrelationship must be noted when performing differentiation. In short, when z becomes a function of several variables, it becomes necessary to distinguish between partial derivatives and total derivatives.[4]

Partial differentiation with respect to any one independent variable is differentiation which regards all other independent variables as constant. Since those other variables are treated as fixed, it should be evident that the derivative properties and rules discussed in Sections A.2 and A.3 apply to the partial derivative too. Notation changes, however. Let $z = f(x, y)$. Then the partial derivative of z with respect to x may be written as $\partial(z)/\partial x$, $\partial z/\partial x$, or $\partial f/\partial x$, where ∂ reads "partial." Other symbols are z_x and f_x. The second partial derivative of z with respect to x can be written as $\partial(\partial z/\partial x)/\partial x$, $\partial^2 z/\partial x^2$, $\partial^2 f/\partial x^2$, z_{xx}, or f_{xx}. Similar designations hold for higher-order partials. Inasmuch as $z = f(x, y)$ generalizes $z = f(x)$, the symbols for partial derivatives used in the former circumstance can be used in the latter as well. When $z = f(x)$, the derivative of z with respect to x *is* the partial, and consequently d or ∂ can serve equally well then. The text employs either symbol in single-argument cases depending upon the nature of the question at hand. Footnote 9 of Chapter 7 and the equation preceding formula (8.5) in Chapter 8 illustrate.

Imagine that $z = f(x, y)$ is graphed against x when y remains constant at y_0. More precisely, imagine that $z = f(x, y_0)$ is measured on the vertical axis and x on the horizontal. The slope of the z function is then given by f_x while the curvature is given by f_{xx}. Suppose now that y assumes a new value, y_1. The z function drawn against x shifts from its old position, and in the process its slope and curvature may change: f_x and f_{xx} may depend upon y. The extent of this dependency is determined by taking the partial derivatives of f_x and f_{xx} with respect to y.

The partial of f_x with respect to y may be written in several ways, including $\partial(\partial z/\partial x)/\partial y$, $\partial^2 z/(\partial y\,\partial x)$, $\partial f_x/\partial y$, or more simply z_{xy} or f_{xy}. This cross-partial derivative lends itself to important economic interpretation. Let $z = f(x, y)$ be a production function with x and y denoting capital and labor, respectively. f_x is the marginal product of capital, and therefore f_{xy} indicates the change in that marginal product due to a unit change in the labor input. It can be called a "cross-marginal product." Along the same lines, f_{xx} gives the slope of capital's marginal product curve and consonantly indicates the change in that marginal product resulting from a unit change in capital.

A convenient property, known as "Young's theorem," applies to cross-partials; namely, the sequence of cross-partial differentiation has no effect on the value

---

[4]More comprehensive exposition of material presented here appears in R. G. D. Allen, *Mathematical Analysis for Economists* (New York: St. Martin's Press, Inc., 1938), pp. 332–338; Chiang, *Fundamental Methods*, pp. 184–187, 205–207, 210–212, 323–324; and Protter and Morrey, *College Calculus*, pp. 621, 650–653, 655–656, 660–663.

of the cross-partial. Succinctly, $\partial f_x / \partial y = \partial f_y / \partial x$ or $f_{xy} = f_{yx}$. Differentiating capital's marginal product with respect to labor leads to exactly the same result as does differentiating labor's marginal product with respect to capital. An obvious example can be developed from the Cobb-Douglas production function (9.27): $Y_t = \gamma A_t^{\xi_2} K_t^{\xi_1} L_t^{\xi_2}$. The marginal product of capital f_K amounts to $\xi_1 \gamma A_t^{\xi_2} K_t^{\xi_1 - 1} L_t^{\xi_2}$; that of labor f_L to $\xi_2 \gamma A_t^{\xi_2} K_t^{\xi_1} L_t^{\xi_2 - 1}$. But $\partial f_K / \partial L_t = \xi_2 \xi_1 \gamma A_t^{\xi_2} K_t^{\xi_1 - 1} L_t^{\xi_2 - 1}$, while $\partial f_L / \partial K_t = \xi_1 \xi_2 \gamma A_t^{\xi_2} K_t^{\xi_1 - 1} L_t^{\xi_2 - 1}$. Clearly, $\partial f_K / \partial L_t = \partial f_L / \partial K_t$.

The various properties exemplified here in the production function context are referenced by footnote 6 of Chapter 1. They also apply straightforwardly to other situations such as those involving utility functions. For instance, equation (5.22) presents a simplified rendition of the utility function adopted by Friedman in his analysis of household consumption behavior: $u = u(c, c_1)$. Thus $\partial u / \partial c$ and $\partial u / \partial c_1$ denote the marginal utilities of c and c_1, respectively. $\partial^2 u / \partial c^2$ and $\partial^2 u / \partial c_1^2$ describe the movement of the separate marginal utilities, while $\partial^2 u / (\partial c \, \partial c_1)$ describes cross-marginal utility—the cross-marginals. The latter three derivatives act as grist for footnote 35 of Chapter 5.

A partial derivative presumes that all independent variables other than the one under consideration remain unchanged, and consequently it provides a "partial" picture of the changes which bear on the dependent variable. Another construct, named the "total differential," presents a broader view of those changes. For the function $z = f(x, y)$, the total differential—written dz or df—is $dz = f_x \, dx + f_y \, dy$. It has ready interpretation. f_x reports the change in z due to a unit change in x. Differential dx reports the full (but small) change in x. Consequently, $f_x \, dx$ gives the change in z attributable to the full change in x, and similarly $f_y \, dy$ gives the change attributable to the full change in y. Hence, dz represents the total change in z originating from all sources. Equation (4.6) can be seen to be a total differential in disguise. Expressed strictly, it would be $dK = f_Q \, dQ + f_{w/q} \, d(w/q)$. From (4.5) $f_Q = \Lambda$ and $f_{w/q} = Q \, \partial \Lambda / \partial(w/q) = \Omega(Q, w/q)$.

Independent variables x and y in the function $z = f(x, y)$ may be related. If so, then a change in x would change y, and therefore an x change would affect z directly through x and indirectly through y. This total derivative can be obtained from the total differential $dz = f_x \, dx + f_y \, dy$ by dividing through by the differential dx. That procedure leaves $dz/dx = f_x(dx/dx) + f_y(dy/dx)$, where each ratio of differentials carries the interpretation of a derivative. Since $dx/dx = 1$, the total derivative simplifies to $dz/dx = f_x + f_y(dy/dx)$.

A previous example involved Friedman's utility function in abridged form: $u = u(c, c_1)$, equation (5.22). According to budget constraint (5.23), c and c_1 are related, allowing c_1 to be written in terms of c. Specifically, $c_1 = (1 + r)w_e - (1 + r)c$. As c changes, it affects u directly and, through c_1, indirectly, producing the total effect

$$\frac{du}{dc} = \frac{\partial u}{\partial c} \frac{dc}{dc} + \frac{\partial u}{\partial c_1} \frac{dc_1}{dc}$$

This total derivative collapses to

$$\frac{du}{dc} = \frac{\partial u}{\partial c} - (1 + r) \frac{\partial u}{\partial c_1}$$

Section 10.2 posits $\pi = \bar{J}/Y$, where both $\bar{J}$ and Y depend upon t. Thus

$$\frac{d\pi}{dt} = \frac{\partial \pi}{\partial \bar{J}} \frac{d\bar{J}}{dt} + \frac{\partial \pi}{\partial Y} \frac{dY}{dt}$$

But $\partial \pi / \partial \bar{J} = 1/Y$ and $\partial \pi / \partial Y = -\bar{J}/Y^2$, rendering

$$\frac{d\pi}{dt} = \frac{1}{Y} \frac{d\bar{J}}{dt} - \frac{\bar{J}}{Y^2} \frac{dY}{dt}$$

Dividing through this equation by π and using dotted variables as shorthand for derivatives with respect to t yield equation (10.22). If $\bar{J}$ and Y had depended upon *two* variables t and v, then the total derivative of π with respect to t would have been written as

$$\frac{\partial \pi}{\partial t} = \frac{\partial \pi}{\partial \bar{J}} \frac{\partial \bar{J}}{\partial t} + \frac{\partial \pi}{\partial Y} \frac{\partial Y}{\partial t}$$

where the symbol ∂ in the t derivatives signifies that v had been treated as constant.

Function $z = f(x, y)$ says that a relationship exists among z, x, and y and that z can be construed to be dependent upon x and y. It makes z an explicit function of x and y. The linkage among these three variables may be expressed another way—implicitly—by means of the formula $g(x, y, z) = 0$, which claims that the three are related but which does not isolate the variable to be taken as dependent. $g(x, y, z) = 0$ is called an "implicit function." For it to always maintain its zero value, any movement in one variable must be exactly offset by movements in the others. From this property it is possible to determine how any two variables must change, and the key to that determination is again the total differential.

Write $g(x, y, z) = 0$ more generally as $g(x, y, z) = w$, where w is momentarily interpreted as a variable. Then the total differential of this general formulation reads $dw = g_x\, dx + g_y\, dy + g_z\, dz$. But because $g(x, y, z)$ really assumes a fixed value, $dw = 0$ and therefore $0 = g_x dx + g_y dy + g_z dz$. Suppose that one needs to know the way y must change when x changes; z is to be regarded as constant, making $dz = 0$. In this circumstance the total differential gives $0 = g_x\, \partial x + g_y\, \partial y$, where the symbol ∂ serves to emphasize that z is being held fixed. Solving this equation for $\partial y / \partial x$ yields $\partial y / \partial x = -g_x/g_y$. Had the implicit function not contained z but instead had been written simply as $g(x, y) = 0$, the implicit derivative would have been $dy/dx = -g_x/g_y$. Higher-order derivatives can be obtained from the implicit derivative by applying the total derivative to it.

An exercise in implicit differentiation might be helpful. Let $4x - y^2 + 2z^3 = 0$. To find $\partial y / \partial x$, treat the left-hand side as $g(x, y, z)$. Then $g_x = 4$ and $g_y = -2y$. Since $\partial y / \partial x = -g_x/g_y$, it follows that $\partial y / \partial x = -4/(-2y) = 2/y$. Similar calculations would produce $\partial z / \partial x = -2/(3z^2)$.

Implicit differentiation can be invoked to establish the slope of an indifference curve associated with the utility function $z = f(x, y)$. Since a given curve displays a constant level of utility z_0, its equation must be $z_0 = f(x, y)$. Applying the total differential occasions $dz_0 = f_x dx + f_y dy$. However, because $dz_0 = 0$,

$dy/dx = -f_x/f_y$. The slope of an indifference curve equals the negative of the ratio of marginal utilities, that ratio—f_x/f_y—being called the "marginal rate of substitution." Section 7.1 involves calculations of this type. So does Section C.1, although it focuses on isoquants and seeks the marginal rate of technical substitution g_L/g_K. Section 10.7 makes use of implicit differentiation to examine the comparative dynamic behavior of θ^* with respect to μ.

A.5 HOMOGENEOUS FUNCTIONS

A function $z = f(x, y)$ is homogeneous[5] of degree ϕ if the multiplication of each independent variable x and y by any positive and finite number λ leads to the multiplication of the dependent variable z by λ^ϕ. This proviso may be written succinctly as $\lambda^\phi z = f(\lambda x, \lambda y)$ or as $\lambda^\phi f(x, y) = f(\lambda x, \lambda y)$.

If $z = f(x, y)$ is homogeneous of degree zero, then z depends only upon the ratio of the independent variables. Set $\lambda = 1/y$. From the definition of homogeneity, $(1/y)^0 z = f(x/y, 1)$. Since the 1 in $f(x/y, 1)$ is a constant, $f(x/y, 1)$ may be rewritten as $g(x/y)$, which absorbs the 1 into the functional notation. Thus $z = g(x/y)$ or more completely $z = g(x/y) = f(x, y)$. When $z = f(x, y)$ is homogeneous of degree one, it is said to be linearly homogeneous, alias linear homogeneous. For that function doubling each independent variable doubles the dependent variable, while halving each halves it. Moreover, such a function can be expressed in intensive, or ratio, form. Again, set $\lambda = 1/y$. Accordingly, $z = f(x, y)$ becomes $(1/y)z = f(x/y, 1)$ or more simply $z/y = g(x/y)$, where $g(x/y) = f(x/y, 1)$. This intensive form converts to $z = yg(x/y)$.

Examples of homogeneous functions can be readily found in the text. The CES production function (4.3) is homogeneous of degree ζ. Given $Q = \gamma[\xi_1 K^{-\rho} + \xi_2 L^{-\rho}]^{-\zeta/\rho}$, multiply each input by λ to obtain $\gamma[\xi_1(\lambda K)^{-\rho} + \xi_2(\lambda L)^{-\rho}]^{-\zeta/\rho}$, which factors to $\lambda^\zeta \gamma[\xi_1 K^{-\rho} + \xi_2 L^{-\rho}]^{-\zeta/\rho}$ or to $\lambda^\zeta Q$. When $\zeta = 1$, the function becomes linearly homogeneous and causes the corresponding profit function (4.1) to become linearly homogeneous as well. With $\pi = pQ - wL - qK$, multiplying each input by λ generates $p\lambda Q - w\lambda L - q\lambda K$, equivalently, $\lambda \pi$. Production function (9.15), being linearly homogeneous, may be easily converted to intensive form by setting $\lambda = 1/(A_t L_t)$. Specifically, $Y_t = F(K_t, A_t L_t)$ occasions $\lambda Y_t = F[\lambda K_t, \lambda(A_t L_t)]$ and leads to $[1/(A_t L_t)]Y_t = F[K_t/(A_t L_t), 1]$, the right-hand component collapsing to $f[K_t/(A_t L_t)]$.

Three properties of the linearly homogeneous function $z = f(x, y)$ deserve special mention.

First, the partial derivatives $\partial z/\partial x$ and $\partial z/\partial y$ are homogeneous of degree zero. Write $z = f(x, y)$ as $z = yg(x/y)$. Invoking the chain rule and consolidating the result leave $\partial z/\partial x = g'(x/y)$, where $g'(x/y) = dg(x/y)/d(x/y)$. Similarly, by the product and chain rules, $\partial z/\partial y = g(x/y) - (x/y)g'(x/y)$. Both $\partial z/\partial x$

---

[5]An excellent account of homogeneous functions is given by Allen, *Mathematical Analysis*, pp. 315–320. See also Chiang, *Fundamental Methods*, pp. 403–407, 410–411.

and $\partial z/\partial y$ depend only upon the ratio x/y, and consequently they must be homogeneous of degree zero. Sections 5.6 and 5.9 rely on this feature to determine the household's optimum consumption point. That point is shown in Figures 5.7 and 5.9.

From the first property comes the second. Multiply $\partial z/\partial x$ by x and $\partial z/\partial y$ by y and sum the terms to obtain $xg'(x/y) + yg(x/y) - xg'(x/y)$, which obviously reduces to $yg(x/y)$. But $yg(x/y)$ is z. Thus, $z = (\partial z/\partial x)x + (\partial z/\partial y)y$, a relationship known as "Euler's theorem." If $z = f(x, y)$ represents a production function and if the inputs are paid their marginal products, then Euler's theorem advises that output z must be completely exhausted by payments to the factors. x units of, say, capital receive $(\partial z/\partial x)x$ units of output, while y units of, say, labor collect $(\partial z/\partial y)y$ units. This exhaustiveness characteristic comes to the fore in that part of Section 9.4 which discusses the connection between Harrod neutrality and steady equilibrium growth at the natural rate and in that part of Section 9.6 which addresses the marginal productivity theory of income distribution. It reappears in the examination of equation (10.41).

The third property of a linearly homogeneous function $z = f(x, y)$ is offered without proof: $z_{xx} = -(y/x)z_{xy}$ and $z_{yy} = -(x/y)z_{xy}$. These links between the second partials and the cross-partial lead directly to a characteristic which has particular import in the examination of maxima and minima of functions. That characteristic is $z_{xx}z_{yy} = z_{xy}^2$. When the function under consideration is linearly homogeneous, an equality (rather than an inequality) joins the product of the second partials to the square of the cross-partial. For profit function (4.1) linear homogeneity thus means that $\pi_{LL}\pi_{KK} = \pi_{LK}^2$.

A.6 MAXIMA AND MINIMA OF FUNCTIONS: ONE INDEPENDENT VARIABLE

Consider the function $z = f(x)$, whose locus for the x values $0 \leq x \leq x_6$ appears in Figure A.2. Point A marks the smallest value of z in the x interval, while point F designates its greatest value there. Those points are called the "global minimum" and the "global maximum" of z in the interval, respectively. At point B the value of z is greater than it is to the immediate left or right of B; point B can be termed a "local maximum." So can point F: F represents both a local and a global maximum. At point C, z assumes a value smaller than those in the neighborhood of C, and that point is referred to as a "local minimum." Points D and E are posted because even though z attains neither a maximum nor a minimum at either position, it does change curvature at each. D and E are known as "inflection points." Other inflection points which occur are not posted.[6]

---

[6]Authorities for the present section consist of Allen, *Mathematical Analysis*, pp. 186, 460–461; Chiang, *Fundamental Methods*, pp. 244–246, 248, 258; Protter and Morrey, *College Calculus*, pp. 147, 155, 159–160; and Taro Yamane, *Mathematics for Economists: An Elementary Survey*, 2d ed. (Englewood Cliffs, N.J.: Prentice-Hall, Inc., 1968), pp. 179–182.

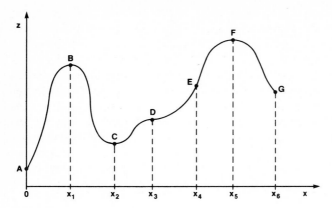

Figure A.2

From Figure A.2 it should be evident that a local maximum has $f'(x) = 0$ and $f''(x) < 0$. A local minimum has $f'(x) = 0$ and $f''(x) > 0$. Therefore, to detect local maxima or minima, locate the points where $f'(x) = 0$. For each point, referred to as a "stationary point" since z exhibits no change there, test whether $f''(x)$ is negative or positive. If it is negative, then the corresponding point is a local maximum; if it is positive, then the point is a local minimum. Should $f''(x) = 0$, then the stationary point may be a local maximum, a local minimum, or an inflection point, and further inquiry is required.[7] When $f''(x)$ remains negative throughout an x interval, no more than one stationary point can arise for those x, but in the event that the point does occur, it must correspond to both a local and a global maximum. The opposite situation holds for a persistently positive $f''(x)$.

The criteria for determining extrema can be categorized. For a local maximum, $f'(x) = 0$ constitutes a necessary condition, and $f'(x) = 0$ coupled with $f''(x) < 0$ constitute a sufficient condition. Likewise, $f'(x) = 0$ is necessary for a local minimum, while $f'(x) = 0$ and $f''(x) > 0$ together are sufficient. Another taxonomy applied to the criteria calls the restriction on the first derivative, $f'(x) = 0$, the "first-order condition." It lists the restriction on the second derivative, either $f''(x) < 0$ or $f''(x) > 0$ depending upon whether a maximum or a minimum is sought, as the "second-order condition." The function being optimized (maximized or minimized) is labeled the "objective function."

Equation (8.2) posits σ_Y^2 as dependent upon σ_W alone: $\sigma_Y^2 = \sigma_Z^2 + \sigma_W^2 + 2\rho_{ZW}\sigma_Z\sigma_W$. All other symbols denote constants. To find the minima of σ_Y^2, first

---

[7]In this case the ambiguity is settled by finding the first higher-order derivative to become nonzero at the x value under study. Let that derivative be of order m; namely, $f^m(x) \neq 0$. If m is odd, then the point is inflectional. If m is even with $f^m(x) < 0$, then the point is a local maximum, but if it is even with $f^m(x) > 0$, then the point is a local minimum.

Observe from Figure A.2 that an inflection point may have either $f'(x) = 0$ or $f'(x) \neq 0$.

locate the stationary points by differentiating σ_Y^2 and by restricting the derivative to zero. Doing so yields the first-order condition $d\sigma_Y^2/d\sigma_W = 2\sigma_W + 2\rho_{ZW}\sigma_Z = 0$, which may be restated as $\sigma_W = -\rho_{ZW}\sigma_Z$. This σ_W expression, equation (8.5), says that a single stationary point exists, and it gives the σ_W location of that point. Does σ_Y^2 attain a minimum there? Yes. The second derivative of σ_Y^2 is $d^2\sigma_Y^2/d(\sigma_W)^2 = 2$, which, being positive, fulfills the second-order condition. Thus σ_Y^2 reaches a local minimum when $\sigma_W = -\rho_{ZW}\sigma_Z$. But since the second derivative remains positive for all σ_W, σ_Y^2 must be everywhere concave upward, a circumstance implying that the lone stationary point must represent both a local and a global minimum.

The example of profit maximization premised on equation (1.2) proceeds similarly, as footnote 7 of Chapter 1 indicates. There, however, the derivatives are written as partials.

A.7 MAXIMA AND MINIMA: SEVERAL INDEPENDENT VARIABLES

When z becomes a function of several independent variables, the problem of locating extrema increases in complexity. Although the necessary condition generalizes straightforwardly, the sufficient condition does not; it must be broadened to include the cross-partial.[8]

Suppose that $z = f(x, y)$ has the shape given in Figure A.3. At point A, where $x = x_0$ and $y = y_0$, $f_x = 0$ and $f_y = 0$, meaning that z experiences no variation in the x and y directions, known as the "fundamental directions." But since $dz = f_x\, dx + f_y\, dy$, $f_x = 0$ and $f_y = 0$ also mean that at point A, $dz = 0$ for any dx and dy: z remains stationary even if changes in x and y prompt a movement from (x_0, y_0) in any nonfundamental direction. Succinctly, $f_x = 0$ and $f_y = 0$ locate a stationary point.

Establishing that point A corresponds to a local maximum requires an examination of the second partials. As Figure A.3 indicates, $\partial^2 z/\partial x^2 < 0$ and $\partial^2 z/\partial y^2 < 0$ are symptomatic of a maximum, but these conditions only say that z is concave downward in the fundamental directions. What about its curvature in all other directions?

Imagine that y is related to x by the linear constraint $y = y_0 + \iota(x - x_0)$, where ι denotes some constant. The constraint appears in Figure A.3 as a straight line passing through point (x_0, y_0), and it indicates how y changes from y_0 when x changes from x_0. The ι controls the direction of movement away from (x_0, y_0). To determine the curvature of z in the "ι" direction, take the total derivative: $dz/dx = f_x + f_y\, dy/dx$. Since $dy/dx = \iota$ from the constraint, it follows that

---

[8] The ensuing exposition draws on Allen, *Mathematical Analysis*, pp. 315, 355, 369, 497–498; Chiang, *Fundamental Methods*, pp. 327–332; and Yamane, *Mathematics*, pp. 187–190, 472–473.

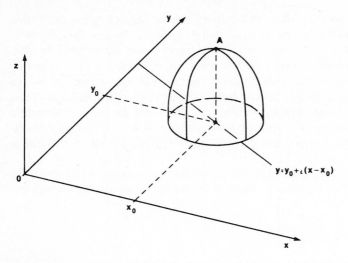

Figure A.3

$dz/dx = f_x + \iota f_y$. The second derivative, which describes curvature, becomes

$$\frac{d^2z}{dx^2} = \frac{\partial}{\partial x}\left(\frac{dz}{dx}\right) + \frac{\partial}{\partial y}\left(\frac{dz}{dx}\right)\frac{dy}{dx}$$

$$\frac{d^2z}{dx^2} = (f_{xx} + \iota f_{xy}) + (f_{xy} + \iota f_{yy})\iota$$

Simplification leaves

$$\frac{d^2z}{dx^2} = \iota^2 f_{yy} + 2\iota f_{xy} + f_{xx}$$

Factoring f_{yy} from the first two right-hand terms, completing the square of the resulting factor $\iota^2 + 2\iota f_{xy}/f_{yy}$, and consolidating elements make

$$\frac{d^2z}{dx^2} = f_{yy}\left(\iota + \frac{f_{xy}}{f_{yy}}\right)^2 + \frac{f_{xx}f_{yy} - f_{xy}^2}{f_{yy}}$$

This "ι" equation gives the curvature of z in the ι direction from point (x_0, y_0). At (x_0, y_0), however, $f_{xx} < 0$ and $f_{yy} < 0$, and consequently $d^2z/dx^2 < 0$ in the ι direction if $f_{xx}f_{yy} - f_{xy}^2 > 0$. This conclusion holds for any ι because ι enters its namesake equation as part of a squared factor. Thus, when z is concave downward in the x and y directions, the condition $f_{xx}f_{yy} - f_{xy}^2 > 0$ says that z is concave downward in all other directions as well.

Consonant with the first of the two taxonomies presented in the prior section, $f_x = f_y = 0$ constitutes a necessary condition for a maximum of $z = f(x, y)$. Equalities $f_x = f_y = 0$ combined with inequalities $f_{xx} < 0$, $f_{yy} < 0$, and $f_{xx}f_{yy} - f_{xy}^2 > 0$ constitute sufficiency. A necessary condition for a minimum of $z = f(x, y)$ is

$f_x = f_y = 0$. Equalities $f_x = f_y = 0$ joined by inequalities $f_{xx} > 0$, $f_{yy} > 0$, and $f_{xx}f_{yy} - f_{xy}^2 > 0$ form the sufficient condition. Observe that if z is concave upward in the fundamental directions, then the ι equation indicates that z is concave upward in all nonfundamental directions too when $f_{xx}f_{yy} - f_{xy}^2 > 0$. This inequality is the same one referenced for downward concavity. In keeping with the second taxonomy reviewed earlier, for either extremum $f_x = f_y = 0$ may be referred to as the first-order condition. Similarly, the three inequalities involving f_{xx}, f_{yy}, and f_{xy} make up the second-order condition in either case.

Profit function (4.1), $\pi = pQ - wL - qK$, again provides an informative illustration. Let Q be given by the production function $f(L, K)$, and let the usual properties apply: $f_L > 0, f_K > 0, f_{LL} < 0, f_{KK} < 0$, and $f_{LK} > 0$. Maximizing π with respect to L and K first requires locating the stationary points. Differentiate π to obtain $\pi_L = pf_L - w$ and $\pi_K = pf_K - q$. The π_L and π_K each assume a zero value once, and thus only one stationary point exists. It occurs at that combination of L and K where $f_L = w/p$ and $f_K = q/p$. The second partials of π are $\pi_{LL} = pf_{LL}$ and $\pi_{KK} = pf_{KK}$; these must be negative since $f_{LL} < 0$ and $f_{KK} < 0$. All that remains to be established is the satisfaction of the condition for a maximum in the nonfundamental directions. Specifically, does $\pi_{LL}\pi_{KK} > \pi_{LK}^2$ hold?

Since $\pi_{LK} = pf_{LK}$, it should be clear that the condition $\pi_{LL}\pi_{KK} > \pi_{LK}^2$ reduces to $f_{LL}f_{KK} > f_{LK}^2$, and hence the test for a profit maximum in all directions turns exclusively on the properties of the production function. For convenience, suppose that the function is the Cobb-Douglas variant of the CES (4.3); Section C.3 lists that version as $Q = \gamma K^{\zeta\xi_1}L^{\zeta\xi_2}$, ζ being the degree of homogeneity. Then $f_L = \gamma\zeta\xi_2 K^{\zeta\xi_1}L^{\zeta\xi_2-1}$, $f_K = \gamma\zeta\xi_1 K^{\zeta\xi_1-1}L^{\zeta\xi_2}$, $f_{LL} = \gamma\zeta\xi_2(\zeta\xi_2 - 1)K^{\zeta\xi_1}L^{\zeta\xi_2-2}$, $f_{KK} = \gamma\zeta\xi_1(\zeta\xi_1 - 1)K^{\zeta\xi_1-2}L^{\zeta\xi_2}$, and $f_{LK} = \gamma\zeta\xi_2\zeta\xi_1 K^{\zeta\xi_1-1}L^{\zeta\xi_2-1}$. Algebra shows that $f_{LL}f_{KK} \gtreqless f_{LK}^2$ as $(\zeta\xi_1 - 1)(\zeta\xi_2 - 1) \gtreqless \zeta\xi_1\zeta\xi_2$ or, with $\xi_1 + \xi_2 = 1$, as $1 - \zeta \gtreqless 0$. The lone stationary point corresponds to a profit maximum only when the production function exhibits decreasing returns to scale, $\zeta < 1$. When that function displays constant returns, $\zeta = 1$, or increasing returns, $\zeta > 1$, the condition $f_{LL}f_{KK} > f_{LK}^2$ does not hold. Its violation under constant returns was anticipated at the end of Section A.5.

The failure of function $z = f(x, y)$ to satisfy the stipulation $f_{xx}f_{yy} > f_{xy}^2$ under linear homogeneity deserves special note. Linear homogeneity causes $f(x, y)$ to graph as a cone whose vertex lies at the origin. A cone does not have a maximum in all directions, and that characteristic reflects itself in an equality relationship between $f_{xx}f_{yy}$ and f_{xy}^2. Footnote 5 of Chapter 4 addresses this circumstance. The other violation of $f_{xx}f_{yy} > f_{xy}^2$—that marked by a reversed inequality—means that $f_x = f_y = 0$ locates a "saddle point," a point where z falls in one direction but rises in another. Saddle points do not enter the textual discussion.

When z becomes a function of variables in addition to x and y, the necessary condition for a maximum or for a minimum expands transparently to $f_x = f_y = \cdots = 0$. The sufficient condition, however, becomes rather clumsy. The text does not consider maximization or minimization in the presence of more than two independent variables.

A.8 CONSTRAINED MAXIMA AND MINIMA

In the previous section the method for detecting extrema of $z = f(x, y)$ presumed that the independent variables x and y had no relationship between themselves. Although the analysis probing the underlay of condition $f_{xx}f_{yy} > f_{xy}^2$ did join x and y together, it did so only hypothetically to train attention on the nonfundamental directions. In fact, x and y were never connected. Many economic problems, however, manifest a relationship among the independent variables, and they require a different procedure for locating extrema.

Let $z = f(x, y)$ again be the function under investigation, and let its shape still be that portrayed in Figure A.3. A maximum of z continues to be sought, but now y is tied to x. That linkage is given by the function $y = g(x)$, which may be called a "side relation," a "subsidiary condition," or (as earlier) a "constraint." Figure A.4 illustrates the new situation. Constraint $y = g(x)$, assumed to be linear only for convenience, defines those x and y values over which the search for a maximum of z is to be conducted. There is no reason to consider any (x, y) point off the line, because such a point simply could not be obtained. A maximum occurs along the constraint at point B with $x = x_1$ and $y = y_1$, but this maximum is less than the unconstrained maximum A, where $x = x_0$ and $y = y_0$ as before. The constraint imposes a cost in the sense that preferred z values are forfeited.[9]

One procedure for handling this constrained maximization problem readily suggests itself. Substitute the constraint $y = g(x)$ into the function $z = f(x, y)$ and treat the resulting expression as a function of x alone. Then invoke the conditions for a maximum applicable to the case of a single independent variable: a maximum occurs when $dz/dx = 0$ and $d^2z/dx^2 < 0$. If a minimum were being sought, then the conditions would be $dz/dx = 0$ and $d^2z/dx^2 > 0$.

An illustration of this substitution method comes from the streamlined version of Friedman's consumption analysis presented in Section 5.6 and alluded to in Section A.4. The linearly homogeneous utility function (5.22) has $u = u(c, c_1)$, but the budget constraint (5.23) ties c_1 to c. In particular, $c_1 = (1 + r)w_e - (1 + r)c$, and thus the utility function may be rewritten as dependent upon c alone: $u = u[c, (1 + r)w_e - (1 + r)c]$. The total derivative of u with respect to c reads

$$\frac{du}{dc} = \frac{\partial u}{\partial c} + \frac{\partial u}{\partial c_1}\frac{dc_1}{dc}$$

$$\frac{du}{dc} = \frac{\partial u}{\partial c} - (1 + r)\frac{\partial u}{\partial c_1}$$

[9]See Chiang, *Fundamental Methods*, pp. 373–376. In regard to what follows, see Chiang, *Fundamental Methods*, pp. 376–378, 380–383, 388–390, and Allen, *Mathematical Analysis*, pp. 364–367.

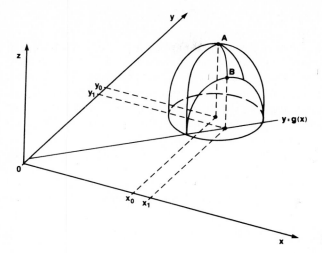

Figure A.4

To locate the stationary point, set $du/dc = 0$ and obtain

$$\frac{\partial u}{\partial c} = (1 + r)\frac{\partial u}{\partial c_1}$$

which is equation (5.24). To investigate concavity, differentiate du/dc:

$$\frac{d^2u}{dc^2} = \frac{\partial}{\partial c}\left(\frac{du}{dc}\right) + \frac{\partial}{\partial c_1}\left(\frac{du}{dc}\right)\frac{dc_1}{dc}$$

$$\frac{d^2u}{dc^2} = \frac{\partial^2 u}{\partial c^2} + (1 + r)^2\frac{\partial^2 u}{\partial c_1^2} - 2(1 + r)\frac{\partial^2 u}{\partial c_1 \partial c}$$

u has declining marginal utilities and, according to property 3 of linear homogeneity listed in Section A.5, positive cross-marginals. Therefore, d^2u/dc^2 must be negative, and the stationary point must correspond to a utility maximum. Footnote 35 of Chapter 5 makes that observation. Maximizing utility subject to a budget constraint proceeds along the same lines in the Ball and Drake framework. There the relevant equations are (5.56) to (5.58). Footnote 49 of Chapter 5 applies as well.

A second procedure for dealing with problems of constrained maxima or minima is known as the "Lagrange method of the undetermined multiplier." It too calls for restating the objective function, but it prescribes that the constraint be *added to* rather than *substituted into* the function. Again, $z = f(x, y)$ is the function to be maximized subject to the constraint, now being written as the implicit function $g(x, y) = 0$. Since $g(x, y)$ always equals zero, adding it—or any multiple of it—to $f(x, y)$ must yield a function whose values are identical to those of $f(x, y)$ but whose scope is confined only to that band of $f(x, y)$ lying directly over the constraint. Write the modified z function as $v = f(x, y) + \eta g(x, y)$. The Lagrange multiplier η represents an unknown to be determined in conjunction with the x and y which generate a maximum of $f(x, y)$ along the constraint. That constrained maximum of $f(x, y)$ must be the same as the maximum of v. Should η prove to be zero, then the constraint would be costless; it would contain the point (x_0, y_0), forcing the constrained maximum B to become the unconstrained maximum A in Figure A.4.

Differentiate v partially with respect to x, y, and η, and set the results to zero. That exercise gives

$$\frac{\partial v}{\partial x} = \frac{\partial f}{\partial x} + \eta \frac{\partial g}{\partial x} = 0$$

$$\frac{\partial v}{\partial y} = \frac{\partial f}{\partial y} + \eta \frac{\partial g}{\partial y} = 0$$

$$\frac{\partial v}{\partial \eta} = g(x, y) = 0$$

These equalities are necessary for a maximum.

Return to the task of maximizing $u = u(c, c_1)$ subject to $c_1 = (1 + r)w_e - (1 + r)c$. Define a new function v as $v = u(c, c_1) + \eta[(1 + r)w_e - (1 + r)c - c_1]$. Differentiation makes

$$\frac{\partial v}{\partial c} = \frac{\partial u}{\partial c} - \eta(1 + r) = 0$$

$$\frac{\partial v}{\partial c_1} = \frac{\partial u}{\partial c_1} - \eta = 0$$

$$\frac{\partial v}{\partial \eta} = (1 + r)w_e - (1 + r)c - c_1 = 0$$

Solving the second equation for η produces $\eta = \partial u/\partial c_1$, which when inserted into the first equation leaves $\partial u/\partial c = (1 + r)\partial u/\partial c_1$. This relation repeats the one deduced above by the method of substitution. Since $\eta = \partial u/\partial c_1$, $\eta \neq 0$, which indicates that the constraint causes utility to be less than the level obtainable in the absence of the constraint. The constraint is costly. Notice that the third equation, $\partial v/\partial \eta = 0$, actually reproduces the constraint and thereby assures that the c and c_1 values associated with the stationary point satisfy it.

When z and the constraint become functions of more than two independent variables, the necessary condition under Lagrange expands in an obvious way. For example, an additional independent variable w gives rise to the additional equation $\partial v/\partial w = 0$. The sufficient condition, even for the case of two independent variables, is awkward and is not pursued here since the text does not make use of the Lagrange method. Footnote 34 of Chapter 5 mentions the technique, however.

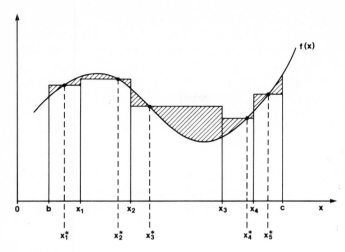

Figure A.5

A.9 THE INTEGRAL

That mathematical construct known as the "integral" can be regarded as the area under a curve, as a summation, and as an antiderivative.[10] What is an antiderivative? For a function $f(x)$ it is another function $F(x)$ which when differentiated yields $f(x)$.

Consider the function $z = f(x)$, which generates the curve appearing in Figure A.5. To calculate the area under this curve in the interval $b \le x \le c$, first divide that interval into, say, five subintervals by selecting the six values $x_0 = b, x_1, \ldots, x_5 = c$. The subintervals produced need not have uniform width. Next construct a rectangle for each subinterval by using the $f(x)$ value corresponding to some x value within the subinterval. Designate those x as $x_1^*, x_2^*, \ldots, x_5^*$. The total area M of these five rectangles is then $M = \Sigma_j f(x_j^*) \Delta x_j$, where $\Delta x_j = x_j - x_{j-1}$ for $j = 1, 2, \ldots, 5$.

As the shaded regions in Figure A.5 show, this strategy for calculating area leads to an error. The figure suggests, however, that this error would shrink if the x interval were partitioned into a greater number of smaller subintervals and that even further partitioning would cause even greater shrinkage. In the limit, the total area of the rectangles would exactly equal the area below the curve. Succinctly, $\lim_{\Delta x_j \to 0} \Sigma_j f(x_j^*) \Delta x_j = N$, where N denotes the true area under $f(x)$ between $x = b$ and $x = c$. This limit N is called the "definite integral" of $f(x)$ from b to c and may be notated as $\int_b^c f(x) \, dx$. In this symbolism Δx_j reappears as

---

[10]References for this exposition are Chiang, *Fundamental Methods*, pp. 430–434, 440–447, and Protter and Morrey, *College Calculus*, pp. 185–189, 198–199, 204–211, 718–723.

dx to highlight the fact that it is infinitesimally small. As Δx_j approaches zero, the number of subintervals crowded between $x = b$ and $x = c$ approaches infinity, and the number of terms embraced by the summation becomes infinite. The integral sign $\int$ replaces the summation sign to report that circumstance; its lower limit b and upper limit c mark those x values which begin and end the summation process, respectively. $f(x)$ is called the "integrand."

The integral can be seen simultaneously as an area beneath a curve and as a summation of many individual units of some "item." How can it be interpreted as an antiderivative?

Select any x value χ which lies between b and c. According to Figure A.6, the area under $f(x)$ between b and χ depends upon χ and therefore can be written as $F(\chi)$, $F(\chi) = \int_b^\chi f(x)\, dx$. Select a larger x value $\chi + \Delta x$ between b and c; it creates an area between b and $\chi + \Delta x$ amounting to $F(\chi + \Delta x)$, $F(\chi + \Delta x) = \int_b^{\chi + \Delta x} f(x)\, dx$. Thus the area between χ and $\chi + \Delta x$ must be $F(\chi + \Delta x) - F(\chi)$. From the previous discussion, it should be apparent that this area can be approximated using a rectangle fashioned by picking some x, say x^*, between χ and $\chi + \Delta x$ and by multiplying $f(x^*)$ into Δx. In short, $F(\chi + \Delta x) - F(\chi) \simeq f(x^*)\,\Delta x$, where the bent equality stands for approximation. Straightforward algebra then gives

$$\frac{F(\chi + \Delta x) - F(\chi)}{\Delta x} \simeq f(x^*)$$

As Δx grows smaller, x^* approaches χ and the approximation embedded in the difference quotient gains accuracy. This limiting process might be stated as

$$\lim_{\Delta x \to 0} \frac{F(\chi + \Delta x) - F(\chi)}{\Delta x} = f(\chi)$$

But the left-hand expression in this equality is simply $F'(\chi)$, the derivative of the

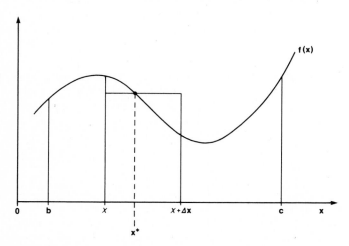

Figure A.6

function F at the point $x = \chi$. Thus, $F'(\chi) = f(\chi)$ or, since χ represents any value of x, $F'(x) = f(x)$. The integrand $f(x)$ is the derivative of another function $F(x)$, and because $F(x) = \int_b^x f(x)\, dx$, that other function is the integral. Integrand $f(x)$ is the derivative of integral $F(x)$, and integral $F(x)$ is an antiderivative of integrand $f(x)$. Recognize that $F(x)$ is *one* antiderivative of $f(x)$. Since the derivative of a constant equals zero, it must be true that if $F(x)$ constitutes an antiderivative, then so does $F(x) + C$, C being an arbitrary constant. If $dF(x)/dx = f(x)$, then $d[F(x) + C]/dx = f(x)$ too. With C, the constant of integration, taken into account, the link between the integral and the integrand may be expressed fully as

$$F(x) + C = \int_b^x f(x)\, dx$$

In contrast to the definite integral $\int_b^c f(x)\, dx$, which fixes both limits of integration, the integral $\int_b^x f(x)\, dx$ leaves the upper limit variable—that is, indefinite—and bears the name "indefinite integral." It may be written without limits, $\int f(x)\, dx$.

Properties of integrals can be set forth in terms of the indefinite integral. $f(x)$ and $g(x)$ represent functions, while A and p represent constants. $p \neq -1$. C continues to stand for the constant of integration.

Property 1. $\int Af(x)\, dx = A \int f(x)\, dx$.

Property 2. $\int [f(x) \pm g(x)]\, dx = \int f(x)\, dx \pm \int g(x)\, dx$.

Property 3. $\int Ax^p\, dx = Ax^{p+1}/(p+1) + C$.

The third property is called the "power rule."

Calculating the value of an integral over some x interval $b \leq x \leq c$ requires an appeal to the fundamental theorem of calculus:

$$\int_b^c f(x)\, dx = F(c) - F(b)$$

In the case of the power rule, this theorem advises that

$$\int_b^c Ax^p\, dx = A\frac{c^{p+1}}{p+1} - A\frac{b^{p+1}}{p+1}$$

It should be clear both from the theorem and from this example that the constant of integration associated with the indefinite integral vanishes from the definite integral through the process of subtraction. In effect, the constant enters twice, at points b and c, only to cancel itself. Furthermore, it should be clear that the integral over a single point is zero: $\int_b^b f(x)\, dx = F(b) - F(b) = 0$. Footnote 24 of Chapter 11 cites this characteristic. Finally, it should be evident that reversing the limits of integration reverses the sign of the integral. In particular, $\int_b^c f(x)\, dx = -\int_c^b f(x)\, dx$. This feature proves to be useful in the next section.

The concept of integral extends to the case where a function contains more than one independent variable. Let $z = f(x, y)$. Integration now proceeds iteratively. $f(x, y)$ is initially integrated with respect to one variable, the other being treated as a constant, and the result obtained is then integrated with respect to that other variable. The sequence of the iterative procedure does not matter. Integration could be taken first with respect to x and second with respect to y or first with respect to y and second with respect to x. The conclusion would be the same.

An iterative process of integration is symbolized by multiple integrals, which for the present example are $\int_y \int_x f(x, y)\, dx\, dy$ or $\int_x \int_y f(x, y)\, dy\, dx$. Here the "subscript" of an integral sign represents for the named variable the interval over which the calculation is made. Reading outward from the integrand gives the sequence of integration. Thus, $\int_y \int_x f(x, y)\, dx\, dy$ says integrate initially with respect to x and afterward with respect to y. The alternative $\int_x \int_y f(x, y)\, dy\, dx$ says the opposite.

As observed earlier, the integral can be interpreted as a sum. So can multiple integrals, and $\int_y \int_x f(x, y)\, dx\, dy$ may be viewed as summing $f(x, y)$ over the x and y intervals. Such is the interpretation to be given to the trio of integrals following equation (5.33).

A.10 TWO NATURAL FUNCTIONS: THE LOG AND THE EXPONENTIAL

The power rule of integration, introduced in the last section as property 3, presumes that $p \neq -1$. When $p = -1$, the integrand x^p (where $A = 1$ for convenience) reverts to $1/x$, and accordingly the integral involves division by zero. Thus $\int 1/x\, dx$ lies beyond the scope of the rule. Paradoxically, however, the function $1/x$ generates a curve which does project an area below it. Figure A.7 illustrates.

Let $\int_1^\chi 1/x\, dx$ denote the area under the $1/x$ curve in the interval $1 \leq x \leq \chi$. As χ declines, so does the area. When χ becomes unity, the x interval collapses to a point rendering the area zero, as the fundamental theorem of calculus advises. What happens as x moves leftward from unity toward zero? According to the

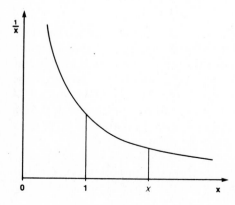

Figure A.7

fundamental theorem, $\int_b^c f(x)\,dx = -\int_c^b f(x)\,dx$ for $c > b$, and therefore intuition contends that when χ falls from untiy, the area under $1/x$ rises from zero while continually evidencing a negative sign: the integral becomes progressively more negative. Reversing the movement of χ thus leads to the conclusions that $\int_1^\chi 1/x\,dx$ rises from negative values as χ rises from zero, that it reaches zero when χ reaches unity, and that it turns positive and continues increasing as χ increases further. Throughout, $\int_1^\chi 1/x\,dx$ increases at a decreasing rate. Since χ represents an unspecified value of x, the indefinite integral may be rewritten as $\int_1^x 1/x\,dx$ or as $\int 1/x\,dx$ instead.[11]

Because $\int 1/x\,dx$ has neat characteristics, it is difficult to believe that the integral calculation cannot be made, and yet the power rule does fail in this case. Resolution of the paradox comes by way of definition: $\int 1/x\,dx$ is *defined* to be $\ln x + C$, C being the constant of integration. $\ln x$, known as the "natural logarithm of x," enjoys properties whose consonance with the foregoing remarks becomes apparent by treating C as zero. They are

Property 1. $\ln x \to -\infty$ as $x \to 0^+$.

Property 2. $\ln 1 = 0$.

Property 3. $\ln e = 1$, $e = 2.71828$.

Property 4. $\ln x \to \infty$ as $x \to \infty$.

Property 5. $d\ln x/dx = 1/x$.

Property 6. $d^2 \ln x/dx^2 = -1/x^2$.

Property 3, which involves the Napierian constant e, is derived anon. Property 5 evolves automatically from the relationship between an integral and its integrand, while property 6 arises by differentiating the first derivative. All six features are summarized by the solid z curve in Figure A.8. For the moment ignore the dashed z locus.

Applying the natural log to some function of x, $f(x)$, and invoking the chain rule produces an important result:

Property 7. $d\ln f(x)/dx = f'(x)/f(x)$.

This relationship finds frequent use in the text. For instance, equation (9.31) posits $\dot{y}/y = q + \varepsilon \dot{k}/k$, where y and k denote functions of time t and their dotted counterparts indicate time derivatives such as $\dot{y} = dy/dt$. The q and ε denote constants. Integrating both sides of this equation with respect to t leaves $\int \dot{y}/y\,dt = \int q\,dt + \varepsilon \int \dot{k}/k\,dt$. Integrand $\dot{y}/y$ is clearly $d\ln y/dt$, while integrand $\dot{k}/k$ is clearly $d\ln k/dt$. Their integrals, without integration constants, must therefore be

---

[11]More discussion of this and subsequent material appears in Fadell, *Calculus*, pp. 423, 426–427, 444–445; Protter and Morrey, *College Calculus*, pp. 302–303, 316–321, 324–335; and Yamane, *Mathematics*, pp. 83, 96–102, 253–254.

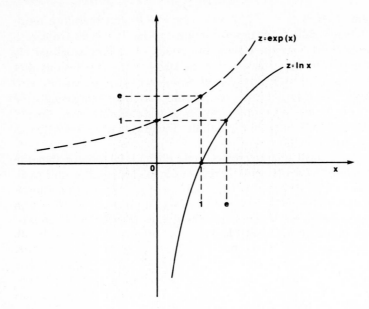

Figure A.8

$\ln y$ and $\ln k$, respectively. Directing the power rule to the constant q—treated as qt^0—gives $qt^1/1$. It follows that $\ln y = qt + \varepsilon \ln k + \ln Q_0$, $\ln Q_0$ representing the amalgam of all integration constants.

The standard arithmetic of logarithms applies to the natural log. In particular, $\ln(xy) = \ln x + \ln y$, $\ln(x/y) = \ln x - \ln y$, and $\ln x^y = y \ln x$. An example relying on the first and third formulas comes from equation (10.14): $Y_t = \gamma e^{\tau t} J_t^{\xi_1} L_t^{\xi_2}$. Here γ, τ, ξ_1, and ξ_2 signify positive constants; e denotes the Napierian parameter; and Y_t, t, J_t, and L_t represent functions of time. Taking natural logs leaves $\ln Y_t = \ln \gamma + \tau t \ln e + \xi_1 \ln J_t + \xi_2 \ln L_t$, which when differentiated with respect to time occasions in the absence of subscripts $\dot{Y}/Y = \tau + \xi_1 \dot{J}/J + \xi_2 \dot{L}/L$, which is equation (10.17).

Closely related to the natural log is the natural exponential function; in fact, this exponential is *defined* to be related to the log. Designate z to be a function of x, $z = f(x)$, and subject z to a functional operation g to yield x. In its effect g reverses the action of f; namely, $g(z) = g[f(x)] = x$. This $g(z)$ is called the "inverse function of $f(x)$." When $z = \ln x$, $g(z)$ is said to be the "exponential function" $\exp(z)$. Succinctly, $\exp(\ln x) = x$.

Since the behavior of $\ln x$ is known, so is that of $\exp(\ln x)$. As $x \to 0^+$, $\ln x \to -\infty$. Thus in the limit $\exp(-\infty) = 0$. At $x = 1$, $\ln x = 0$, making $\exp(0) = 1$. Furthermore, as $x \to \infty$, $\ln x \to \infty$. Accordingly, $\exp(\infty) = \infty$ in the limit.

The derivative of the exponential can be ascertained from the principle of inverse functions which argues that for $z = f(x)$ and its inverse $x = g(z)$, $f'(x)g'(z) = 1$. Since $z = \ln x$, $f'(x) = 1/x$; consequently, $g'(z) = x$. But

$x = g(z)$ and $g(z) = \exp(z)$. Thus $g'(z) = g(z) = \exp(z)$ or $d \exp(z)/dz = \exp(z)$. The derivative of $\exp(z)$ with respect to z is $\exp(z)$ itself! Because x represents the argument of the log function, it must be positive and, with $x = \exp(z)$, $d\exp(z)/dz$ must be positive too. x, however, may approach zero; as it does, $z = \ln x$ approaches minus infinity. In short, $d\exp(z)/dz > 0$ for $z > -\infty$, although $d\exp(z)/dz \to 0$ as $z \to -\infty$. Inasmuch as differentiating $\exp(z)$ with respect to z reproduces the original function $\exp(z)$, differentiating a second time must do the same; namely, $d^2 \exp(z)/dz^2 = \exp(z)$. Except for a limiting value of zero arising as z tends to minus infinity, the second derivative must be positive.

Figure A.8 traces with a dashed line exponential function $z = \exp(x)$, whose labels for the dependent and independent variables amend the preceding ones to conform to the convention of this appendix. $z = \exp(x)$ is monotone-increasing in x, rising from a lower limit of zero at minus infinity to a value of unity at zero and onward to a limit of infinity at infinity. It remains concave upward throughout.

Set $x = 1$ and mark by e the corresponding value of $\exp(x)$; that is, $\exp(1) = e$. Applying the log maneuver to both sides of this equation makes $\ln[\exp(1)] = \ln e$. But since the log and the exponential functions are inverses, $\ln[\exp(x)] = \exp(\ln x) = x$, yielding in the current circumstance $1 = \ln e$, a result presented as property 3 of the log. Recall that $e = 2.71828$.

$\exp(1) = e$, which may be regarded as $\exp(1) = e^1$, generalizes to $\exp(x) = e^x$. Taking logs produces $\ln[\exp(x)] = x \ln e$ or $x = x$, checking the generalized equality. Thus, $z = \exp(x)$ can also be written as $z = e^x$. That conclusion leads to another. Given the meaning of logarithm, the exponent x in $z = e^x$ can be stated as $x = \log_e z$, but imposing the natural log on $z = e^x$ renders $\ln z = x \ln e$ or $\ln z = x$. Consonantly, $x = \log_e z = \ln z$: the natural log is the logarithm to the base e. This finding serves to verify a previous comment that the standard arithmetic of logarithms holds for the natural log.

The inverse relationship between $\exp(x)$ and $\ln x$ proves to be helpful in the text. For example, Section 10.7 determines the sign of $d\theta^*/d\rho$ by comparing $e^{\mu\theta_c}$ with $y(\theta_c)$. The expression for $e^{\mu\theta_c}$ appearing there is derived by recognizing the formula for θ_c and by invoking the reversal action of inverse functions. Specifically, $\theta_c = -(\alpha + \delta)^{-1}\ln[1 - (\alpha + \delta)/(\gamma s)]$, converting $e^{\mu\theta_c}$ to

$$\exp\left[-\frac{\mu}{\alpha + \delta}\ln\left(1 - \frac{\alpha + \delta}{\gamma s}\right)\right] \quad \text{or to} \quad \exp\left[\ln\left(1 - \frac{\alpha + \delta}{\gamma s}\right)^{-\mu/(\alpha+\delta)}\right]$$

The latter expression reverses to $[1 - (\alpha + \delta)/(\gamma s)]^{-\mu/(\alpha+\delta)}$, producing the elaboration of $e^{\mu\theta_c}$ adopted in the text.

Write the exponential function e^x more generally as $z = a^x$, where a denotes some positive constant. To find the derivative dz/dx, transform $z = a^x$ into log form: $\ln z = x \ln a$. Then $d\ln z/dx = \ln a$. But $d\ln z/dx = (1/z)dz/dx$, and therefore $dz/dx = z \ln a$. When $z = a^x$, $dz/dx = a^x \ln a$. When $z = a^{f(x)}$, the chain rule gives $dz/dx = a^{f(x)}f'(x)\ln a$. Section C.3 subscribes to this property in deriving the Cobb-Douglas production function. Let $z = \xi_1 K^{-\rho} + \xi_2 L^{-\rho}$ be a function of ρ alone. Then $dz/d\rho$ (or $\partial z/\partial\rho$) $= \xi_1 K^{-\rho}(-1)\ln K +$

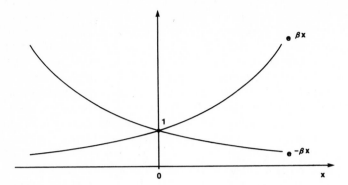

Figure A.9

$\xi_2 L^{-\rho}(-1)\ln L$, a finding needed to evaluate the numerator portion of the l'Hopital calculation there.

Assigning $a = e$ leads to $z = e^{f(x)}$ and to $dz/dx = e^{f(x)}f'(x) \ln e$. But since $\ln e = 1$, simplification occurs: when $z = e^{f(x)}$, $dz/dx = e^{f(x)}f'(x)$. For $f(x) = \beta x$ with β being a positive constant, $z = e^{\beta x}$, $dz/dx = \beta e^{\beta x}$, and $d^2z/dx^2 = \beta^2 e^{\beta x}$. Figure A.9 illustrates. The locus of $e^{\beta x}$ rivals that of $e^{\mu\theta}$ pictured in Figures 10.3, 10.4, and 10.6, which depict the solution patterns for equation (10.70). For $f(x) = -\beta x$ with β still denoting a positive constant, $z = e^{-\beta x}$, $dz/dx = -\beta e^{-\beta x}$, and $d^2z/dx^2 = \beta^2 e^{-\beta x}$. This function, also mapped in Figure A.9, assumes a central role in equations (8.39) and (8.40), where it is written as $e^{-\theta t}$.

The final aspect of the natural exponential examined here is its integral. Since $de^x/dx = e^x$, it must follow that $\int e^x dx = e^x + C$, C being the integration constant. Likewise, $\int e^{\beta x} dx = (1/\beta)e^{\beta x} + C$ and $\int e^{-\beta x} dx = -(1/\beta)e^{-\beta x} + C$ for the positive constant β. As an example consider the definite integral posted after equation (5.35): $\beta\int_{-\infty}^{t} e^{-\beta(t-\theta)}d\theta$, the constant β lying in the interval $0 < \beta < 1$. Integration proceeds with respect to θ, and therefore the t in the integrand is treated as fixed. Rewriting that integrand as $e^{-\beta t}e^{\beta\theta}$ and citing property 1 of integrals presented in Section A.9 leaves $\beta e^{-\beta t}\int_{-\infty}^{t} e^{\beta\theta} d\theta$. By the fundamental theorem of calculus, this expression becomes $\beta e^{-\beta t}[e^{\beta t}/\beta - e^{\beta(-\infty)}/\beta]$ and dissolves to unity.

A.11 LINEAR AND CONVEX COMBINATIONS

Let $z = f(x, y)$ take the form $z = \nu_1 x + \nu_2 y$, where ν_1 and ν_2 are constants. z is then said to be a "linear combination of x and y." When $\nu_1 \geq 0$, $\nu_2 \geq 0$, and $\nu_1 + \nu_2 = 1$, z is said to be a "convex combination of x and y."[12]

---

[12] Chiang, *Fundamental Methods*, pp. 641–642, and Saul I. Gass, *Linear Programming: Methods and Applications*, 2d ed. (New York: McGraw-Hill Book Company, 1964), p. 27.

A convex combination does not allow the dependent variable to assume a value either greater than the greatest value or smaller than the smallest value of all variables making up the combination. This property can be demonstrated via the foregoing example, which may be rewritten as $z = \nu_1 x + (1 - \nu_1)y$ with $0 \le \nu_1 \le 1$. When $\nu_1 = 0$, $z = y$; when $\nu_1 = 1$, $z = x$. Furthermore, when $x = y$, $z = x = y$ without regard to ν_1. Since $dz/d\nu_1 = x - y$, z must be monotone-increasing or monotone-decreasing in ν_1 except when $x = y$. In that exceptional case, z must be stationary in ν_1. Thus, although z may equal x or y or both for any permitted ν_1, it can never lie outside the range of values determined by x and y.

Convex combinations appear in the text several times. Equation (5.35) posits permanent income as a convex combination of current and past measured incomes, and equation (5.43) postulates one component of permanent income similarly. The M_o^* described by equation (7.18) qualifies as a convex combination of the arguments $(Y^* - \phi')/\zeta$ and $(\lambda' - B^*)/(x\zeta)$; the s_{RW} cited in remarks on general Kaldorism at the end of Section 9.8 does likewise, albeit with the arguments s_R and s_W.

A.12 MATHEMATICAL EXPECTATION AND ITS ARITHMETIC

Let $f(x)$ be a function having the property that $\int_{-\infty}^{\infty} f(x)\, dx = 1$ with $f(x) \ge 0$ for any x; that is, let $f(x)$ be a nonnegative function which generates an area of unity over all x. Consider now the x subinterval $b \le x \le c$ and the corresponding area $N = \int_b^c f(x)\, dx$. Figure A.10 portrays the situation. Since the total area under $f(x)$ equals one, N represents the fraction of the total lying in the subinterval. Similarly, $100N$ represents the percent of the total lying there. Suppose that N equals .20, making $100N$ equal to 20 percent. Then if x values were drawn randomly from a "black box," intuition would hold that they would fall between b and c inclusively 20 percent of the time. Worded differently, the probability that x takes a value in that interval would amount to 20 percent. Within this probability context $f(x)$ may be called the "probability density of x" or, perhaps more commonly, the "probability distribution of x." x itself may be called a "random variable." [13]

From the notion of density comes a host of concepts. The mathematical expectation (or expected value) of x, written Ex, is defined as

$$Ex = \int_{-\infty}^{\infty} xf(x)\, dx$$

It provides a measure of the central tendency of x, as Figure A.10 attests. Another

[13] Further discussion of topics considered in this section can be found in John E. Freund, *Mathematical Statistics* (Englewood Cliffs, N.J.: Prentice-Hall, Inc., 1962), pp. 117–121, 137–138, 143–145, 160–161, 173–174, 300–301; Paul G. Hoel, *Introduction to Mathematical Statistics*, 4th ed. (New York: John Wiley & Sons, Inc., 1971), pp. 35–36, 144; and William C. Merrill and Karl A. Fox, *Introduction to Economic Statistics* (New York: John Wiley & Sons, Inc., 1970), pp. 129–140.

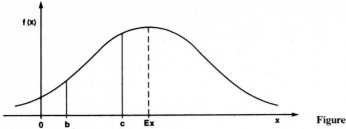

Figure A.10

name for Ex is the "mean of x." Simple calculations lead to

Property 1. $E(a_1 x + a_2) = a_1 Ex + a_2$,

a_1 and a_2 denoting constants, alias "scalars."

The "variance of x," notated $E(x - Ex)^2$ or, more simply, σ_x^2, obeys the formula

$$\sigma_x^2 = \int_{-\infty}^{\infty} (x - Ex)^2 f(x) \, dx$$

and measures the variation of x around its mean. The positive square root of σ_x^2, $\sigma_x \left(= \sqrt{\sigma_x^2} \right)$, is called the "standard deviation of x." It too gauges variation around the mean. Should x be a constant A, then $Ex = A$ and $\sigma_x^2 = \sigma_x = 0$.

In many instances a random variable x assumes one value while a second random variable y assumes another. This joint pattern of behavior is reported by the covariance of x and y: symbolically, $E[(x - Ex)(y - Ey)]$ or σ_{xy}.

$$\sigma_{xy} = \int_{-\infty}^{\infty} \int_{-\infty}^{\infty} (x - Ex)(y - Ey) g(x, y) \, dx \, dy$$

The nonnegative function $g(x, y)$, known as the "joint probability density of x and y," extends the idea of density in a straightforward manner. For instance, $\int_{b_2}^{c_2} \int_{b_1}^{c_1} g(x, y) \, dx \, dy$ gives the probability that x falls in the interval $b_1 \le x \le c_1$ when y falls in the interval $b_2 \le y \le c_2$. The relative behavior of x and y determines the sign of σ_{xy}. If x and y tend to locate on the same side of their individual means, then σ_{xy} must be positive. If they tend to locate on opposite sides of the means, then σ_{xy} must be negative. If x and y have no joint tendencies or if one (or both) of them is constant, then σ_{xy} must be zero.

Integrating the joint density $g(x, y)$ over y alone yields the density of x: $\int_y g(x, y) \, dy = g(x)$. Likewise, $\int_x g(x, y) \, dx = g(y)$. This characteristic combines with the covariance expression after expansion of the integrand to produce a useful result:

Property 2. $\sigma_{xy} = E(xy) - Ex \, Ey$,

where $E(xy) = \int_{-\infty}^{\infty} \int_{-\infty}^{\infty} xy \, g(x, y) \, dx \, dy$. Replacing y by x yields

Property 3. $\sigma_x^2 = E(x^2) - (Ex)^2$.

Covariance can be referenced again in connection with a quantity called the "correlation coefficient for x and y" and symbolized ρ_{xy}. By definition $\rho_{xy} = \sigma_{xy}/(\sigma_x\sigma_y)$: the correlation coefficient is the ratio of the covariance to the product of the standard deviations. Since for nonconstant x and y the standard deviations must be positive, ρ_{xy} mirrors the sign of σ_{xy}. Furthermore, it must be bounded by -1 and 1, $-1 \le \rho_{xy} \le 1$. When y behaves exactly as x does, $y = x$, and properties 2 and 3 make $\sigma_y = \sigma_x$ and $\sigma_{xy} = \sigma_x^2$. Thus $\rho_{xy} = 1$. By contrast, when y behaves exactly opposite to x, $y = -x$, and the two properties give $\sigma_y = \sigma_x$ along with $\sigma_{xy} = -\sigma_x^2$. Therefore $\rho_{xy} = -1$. The y patterns which depart from these extremes cause ρ_{xy} to depart from its own extremes. Should y bear no relation to x, then $\sigma_{xy} = 0$ and $\rho_{xy} = 0$. In that case x and y are uncorrelated. Solving the ρ_{xy} expression for σ_{xy} produces

Property 4. $\sigma_{xy} = \rho_{xy}\sigma_x\sigma_y$.

The text appeals to formulas presented here. For instance, equations (5.32) look at correlation coefficients and note their value when the variables under consideration have no relationship between themselves. Section 7.4 looks at the expected value of utility and makes use of properties 1 and 3 in forming the EU function from equations (7.25) and (7.26). It deserves mentioning that the application of mathematical expectation to derive EU treats the decision variable M_o as constant: EU involves conditional expectation, mathematical expectation calculated subject to a given value of some other variable. Planners ascertain EU for each M_o and select the M_o which maximizes it. Properties 2 and 4 find service in connection with equation (7.30).

Let z be a linear combination of two random variables x and y; namely, $z = \nu_1 x + \nu_2 y$, where ν_1 and ν_2 are scalars. Then

Property 5. $Ez = \nu_1 Ex + \nu_2 Ey$.
Property 6. $\sigma_z^2 = \nu_1^2\sigma_x^2 + \nu_2^2\sigma_y^2 + 2\nu_1\nu_2\sigma_{xy}$.

These two features generalize without trouble. For example, if z were expressed as $\nu_1 x + \nu_2 y + \nu_3 w$, then property 6 would contain $\nu_3^2\sigma_w^2 + 2\nu_1\nu_3\sigma_{xw} + 2\nu_2\nu_3\sigma_{yw}$ in addition to the terms already present. Covariances for all pairs of variables must be included.

Section 7.5 postulates $Y = \phi' + \zeta M_o$, ϕ' and ζ being random. From property 6, $\sigma_Y^2 = \sigma_{\phi'}^2 + M_o^2\sigma_\zeta^2 + 2M_o\sigma_{\phi'\zeta}$. This relationship along with property 4 give formula (7.33). Similarly, properties 4 and 6 extract equation (8.2) from equation (8.1).

A.13 REGRESSION ANALYSIS: ORDINARY LEAST SQUARES

Econometrics is the quantitative study which applies mathematics and statistics to economic questions. Since econometrics does draw upon both types of tools reviewed thus far, it seems to be an appropriate subject to consider in concluding this appendix. Regression analysis, the estimation and testing of equations from data, stands at its center and provides the specific focus here. While only the simplest of cases is examined, generalization of its characteristics would be immediate.

After carefully formulating their theory, researchers conclude that Y depends linearly upon X. They also conclude that Y is influenced by random shocks, and they therefore write $Y = \alpha + \beta X + u$, where Y and X represent the dependent variable and the independent (or explanatory) variable, respectively. u signifies a disturbance quantity; it captures random (stochastic) effects. α and β denote constants and are referred to as "parameters." This equation, which describes how the Y values are actually generated, is the true specification.

Although theory does reveal the true equation, it does not disclose values for the parameters. Those numbers are of interest, and consequently the researchers intend to estimate them. To do so, they gather a total of n pairs of X and Y values, pair i—(X_i, Y_i)—being called "observation i" and all n pairs together being called the "sample." The sample may relate to n individual economic units, perhaps households, at a single point in time; in that case it constitutes a cross section of data. It may, however, relate to a single economic entity, perhaps the entire economy, over n time periods; in that case it constitutes a time series of data. The data collection process ignores the u variable simply because data on it do not exit.

When plotted, the sample produces a scatter of points, and Figure A.11 illustrates it by marking each observation with a dot. Figure A.11 also illustrates two straight lines. Consider the one labeled $\alpha + \beta X_i$; it traces the deterministic (nonstochastic) part of the true specification. Since Y_i differs from the deterministic line by the disturbance u_i, the vertical distance between a data point and that

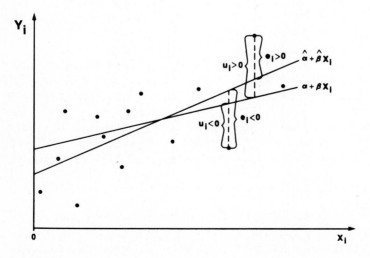

Figure A.11

locus measures u_i. For points above the line, $u_i > 0$; for those below it, $u_i < 0$. Notice that in effect u_i throws points randomly around the line.

The problem of estimating α and β appears in Figure A.11 as one of finding a line $\hat{Y}_i = \hat{\alpha} + \hat{\beta}X_i$, the "hat" in $\hat{Y}_i$ serving as a reminder that the equation produces estimated, not actual, values of the dependent variable. One criterion for guiding the search says that the line should lie as close as possible to the data points; formally, it says that the line should minimize the sum of the squared residuals, $\Sigma_i e_i^2$. Residual e_i, defined as the vertical distance between a data point and the line, equals $Y_i - \hat{Y}_i$. The estimation procedure complying with this least-squares dictate is referred to as the "ordinary least-squares (OLS) technique."

Write $\Sigma_i e_i^2$ as RSS, the residual sum of squares. Since $e_i = Y_i - \hat{\alpha} - \hat{\beta}X_i$,

$$\text{RSS} = \Sigma Y_i^2 + n\hat{\alpha}^2 + \hat{\beta}^2\Sigma X_i^2 + 2\hat{\alpha}\hat{\beta}\Sigma X_i - 2\hat{\alpha}\Sigma Y_i - 2\hat{\beta}\Sigma X_i Y_i$$

where the summation index i is understood. To minimize RSS with respect to $\hat{\alpha}$ and $\hat{\beta}$, find the stationary points:

$$\frac{\partial \text{RSS}}{\partial \hat{\alpha}} = 2n\hat{\alpha} + 2\hat{\beta}\Sigma X_i - 2\Sigma Y_i = 0$$

$$\frac{\partial \text{RSS}}{\partial \hat{\beta}} = 2\hat{\beta}\Sigma X_i^2 + 2\hat{\alpha}\Sigma X_i - 2\Sigma X_i Y_i = 0$$

These two so-called normal equations leave

$$\hat{\alpha} = \bar{Y} - \hat{\beta}\bar{X} \quad \text{and} \quad \hat{\beta} = \frac{\Sigma X_i Y_i - \bar{Y}\Sigma X_i}{\Sigma X_i^2 - \bar{X}\Sigma X_i}$$

The symbols with bars denote sample means—for instance, $\bar{Y} = \Sigma Y_i/n$—and are to be distinguished from the means in the sense of mathematical expectation. Observe that the $\hat{\alpha}$ expression sets $\bar{Y} = \hat{\alpha} + \hat{\beta}\bar{X}$, implying that the OLS regression line $\hat{Y}_i = \hat{\alpha} + \hat{\beta}X_i$ includes the point of the sample means. The second partials of RSS register as $\partial^2\text{RSS}/\partial\hat{\alpha}^2 = 2n > 0$ and $\partial^2\text{RSS}/\partial\hat{\beta}^2 = 2\Sigma X_i^2 > 0$ while the cross-partial amounts to $\partial^2\text{RSS}/(\partial\hat{\alpha}\partial\hat{\beta}) = 2\Sigma X_i$. It can be shown rather easily that $(2n)(2\Sigma X_i^2)$ exceeds $(2\Sigma X_i)^2$. Form $4n\Sigma X_i^2 - 4(\Sigma X_i)^2$, which when compared against zero simplifies to $\Sigma(X_i^2 - \bar{X}X_i) \gtreqqless 0$. The left-hand side of this expression may be rewritten as $\Sigma[(X_i - \bar{X})^2 + X_i\bar{X} - \bar{X}^2]$, becoming $\Sigma(X_i - \bar{X})^2$ since the last two terms cancel under the force of the summation. $\Sigma(X_i - \bar{X})^2$ must be positive, and therefore $(2n)(2\Sigma X_i^2)$ must exceed $(2\Sigma X_i)^2$. The sufficient condition for a minimum of RSS is satisfied.[14]

As their formulas make clear, $\hat{\alpha}$ and $\hat{\beta}$ depend upon X_i and Y_i, and accordingly they vary from sample to sample. Each is a random variable known as an "estimator"; its value produced from any particular sample is known as an "estimate." Each estimator has a mathematical expectation, but determining $E\hat{\alpha}$

[14]Derivation of the $\hat{\alpha}$ and $\hat{\beta}$ expressions can be found in Damodar Gujarati, *Basic Econometrics* (New York: McGraw-Hill Book Company, 1978), pp. 41–44, 63, and in J. Johnston, *Econometric Methods*, 2d ed. (New York: McGraw-Hill Book Company, 1972), pp. 13–16.

and $E\hat{\beta}$ entails recognizing that since Y_i depends upon X_i and u_i, $\hat{\alpha}$ and $\hat{\beta}$ collapse to functions of only those latter two variables. Calculations eventually lead to $E\hat{\alpha} = \alpha$ and $E\hat{\beta} = \beta$ provided that *inter alia* every disturbance term assumes a zero value on balance:[15] $Eu_i = 0$ for any i.

Let B be some estimator of a true value b, and define $EB - b$ as the estimator's bias. If $EB - b \gtrless 0$, then B is upward-biased, unbiased, or downward-biased, respectively. It follows that the OLS estimators $\hat{\alpha}$ and $\hat{\beta}$ are unbiased when the provisos hold. The provisos do not always hold, however, and footnote 10 of Chapter 2 alludes to a violation in its mention of specification bias. That type of bias occurs, for instance, when a regression equation omits an explanatory variable of the true specification. In that case all parameter estimators are usually biased.[16] The regression is wrong not only because it fails to calculate the coefficients of those true variables which it does not include but also because it tends to miscalculate the coefficients of those true variables which it does include.

The issue of bias surfaces in a second context. Equation (8.23) claims that planners follow the proportional rule $m_t = \lambda_1 + \lambda_2 Q_{t-1}$. The public, however, perceives that planners follow the rule $m_t = \delta_1 + \delta_2 Q_{t-1}$, and it sets its anticipation consonantly: $Em_t = \delta_1 + \delta_2 Q_{t-1}$, equation (8.24). As equation (8.38) indicates, the public's anticipation has a bias in the amount of $Em_t - m_t = (\delta_1 - \lambda_1) + (\delta_2 - \lambda_2)Q_{t-1}$.

Suppose that each disturbance u_i obeys a normal distribution having a mathematical expectation of zero and a variance of σ_u^2; notationally, $u_i \sim N(0, \sigma_u^2)$. In this circumstance the probability density reads $f(u_i) = (2.51\sigma_u)^{-1} \cdot \exp(-.50u_i^2/\sigma_u^2)$ for $-\infty < u_i < \infty$ and takes the form of the bell-shaped curve depicted in Figure A.10 after that curve has been shifted leftward to make Ex coincide with the vertical axis.[17] Then in the absence of anomalies, $\hat{\alpha} \sim N(\alpha, \sigma_{\hat{\alpha}}^2)$ and $\hat{\beta} \sim N(\beta, \sigma_{\hat{\beta}}^2)$.

The variances of the $\hat{\alpha}$ and $\hat{\beta}$ densities depend upon σ_u^2, but σ_u^2—like each u_i—is unknown. σ_u^2 may be estimated, however, and as Figure A.11 suggests the vehicle for doing so is the residual e_i, the regression's version of u_i. For the regression problem under review, an unbiased estimator of σ_u^2 proves to be $\hat{\sigma}_u^2 = \Sigma e_i^2/(n-2)$. The $\hat{\sigma}_u^2$ gives rise to $\hat{\sigma}_{\hat{\alpha}}^2$ and $\hat{\sigma}_{\hat{\beta}}^2$ and to their positive square roots $\hat{\sigma}_{\hat{\alpha}}$ and $\hat{\sigma}_{\hat{\beta}}$. These estimated standard deviations, dubbed "standard errors," enable the formulation of standardized $\hat{\alpha}$ and $\hat{\beta}$: $(\hat{\alpha} - \alpha_0)/\hat{\sigma}_{\hat{\alpha}}$ and $(\hat{\beta} - \beta_0)/\hat{\sigma}_{\hat{\beta}}$, α_0 and β_0 being arbitrary constants. Each standardized estimator has a known distribution and can be used to test if the corresponding regression coefficient differs significantly from some preselected level. For each that distribution is the Student's t. Developed by W. S. Gosset using the pen name "Student," it observes the equation $f(t) = \psi(1 + t^2/\omega)^{-(\omega+1)/2}$ for $-\infty < t < \infty$. Coefficient ψ de-

[15] Johnston, *Econometric Methods*, pp. 13, 18–20, 29–32, and G. S. Maddala, *Econometrics* (New York: McGraw-Hill Book Company, 1977), pp. 151–152.

[16] Johnston, *Econometric Methods*, pp. 168–169.

[17] Freund, *Mathematical Statistics*, pp. 129–130.

pends upon the degrees of freedom ω, which equals $n - 2$ in the present case. Like the normal, the t distribution has the shape of a bell centered at zero.[18]

Often concern centers on the question of whether an estimate differs significantly from zero, because if it does not, then the empirical evidence advises that the corresponding explanatory variable does not belong in the regression equation. For, say, $\hat{\beta}$ the common t test sets $\beta_0 = 0$ and concentrates on $\hat{\beta}/\hat{\sigma}_{\hat{\beta}}$: the regression coefficient divided by its standard error. If the absolute value of this ratio equals or exceeds 2 (approximately), then often the regression coefficient is significantly different from zero. If it falls below 2 (approximately), then the coefficient is not significantly different from zero.[19] Significance tests enter the discussion at several points, including the footnote 5 of Chapter 5; footnote of Table 5.3; the remarks concerning the intercept component A_0 in equation (5.16); and the comments on the intercept and the time coefficient of equation (5.44).

The t test of significance provides an indication of how well an estimator performs. The performance of the entire regression can be gauged too, and one barometer looks at how closely the regression line comes to the data points. If the line hits all data points—if all points fall on the line—then it has a "perfect" fit: it explains the dependent variable perfectly. In that deterministic event, of course, $\Sigma e_i^2 = 0$. A regression which leaves the data points scattered about the line but nevertheless near it has a "good" fit; it has high explanatory power. Σe_i^2, while not zero, is small. A wider scattering means a worse fit, a lower explanatory power, and a larger Σe_i^2.

Because Σe_i^2 ranges from a minimum of zero to a maximum of $\Sigma(Y_i - \overline{Y})^2$, a ready indicator of a regression's explanatory power or "goodness of fit" may be written as $r^2 = 1 - \Sigma e_i^2/\Sigma(Y_i - \overline{Y})^2$. The coefficient of determination r^2 clearly must vary between unity and zero, with unity signaling a perfect fit.[20] Footnote 2 of Chapter 4, however, reports low explanatory power for the investment regressions being discussed there.

The data points punctuating Figure A.11 exhibit a random pattern about the true line. Such a configuration may not always hold because disturbances may be systematically tied together; for instance, u_i might depend upon u_{i-1}. Referred to as "autocorrelation" or "serial correlation," a systematic relationship in the disturbances does not bias the OLS estimators, but it does bias their standard errors, thereby invalidating the standard t test.[21]

Detection of this anomaly involves the residuals. They estimate the disturbances, and therefore autocorrelated u_i should lead to autocorrelated e_i. One detection device, named after its formulators J. Durbin and G. S. Watson, satisfies the equation $DW = \Sigma(e_i - e_{i-1})^2/\Sigma e_i^2$. A DW value below 1 or above 3

[18] Freund, *Mathematical Statistics*, p. 202; Gujarati, *Basic Econometrics*, pp. 46, 71–73, 79–80, 399; and Johnston, *Econometric Methods*, pp. 24–28.

[19] Gujarati, *Basic Econometrics*, pp. 83–86.

[20] Ibid., pp. 47–49, and Johnston, *Econometric Methods*, pp. 34–35.

[21] Gujarati, *Basic Econometrics*, pp. 219–221, 224–226, and Johnston, *Econometric Methods*, pp. 243–249.

typically signals autocorrelation. Closely related to the Durbin-Watson statistic is a measure christened in honor of the work by John von Neumann. This von Neumann statistic reads $\text{VN} = [\Sigma(e_i - e_{i-1})^2/\Sigma e_i^2][n/(n-1)]$. It may be applied for small or large n, but in the latter case, say for $n \geq 30$, it has an approximately normal distribution with a mean of $2n/(n-1)$ and a variance of $4n^2(n-2)/[(n+1)(n-1)^3]$. Autocorrelation and both detection devices[22] are cited in footnote 5 of Chapter 5. Autocorrelation is also cited in footnote 2 of Chapter 4 and in the footnote of Table 5.3.

The true specification's deterministic component drawn in Figure A.11 indicates that no shift occurs in the relationship between X_i and Y_i over the n observations. In other words, the same parameter values hold for each observation. Economic relationships, however, may not be identical across the data points; for example, α_1 and β_1 might apply to one subsample while α_2 and β_2 might apply to another. To allow for a suspected shift in economic structure, the regression equation can be amended from $\hat{Y}_i = \hat{\alpha} + \hat{\beta}X_i$ to $\hat{Y}_i = (\hat{\alpha}_1 + \hat{\alpha}_D D_i) + (\hat{\beta}_1 + \hat{\beta}_D D_i)X_i$, where D_i denotes a "dummy" variable having zero values for all observations in the (α_1, β_1) subsample and unit values for all those in the (α_2, β_2) subsample. This equation, which splits into $\hat{Y}_i = \hat{\alpha}_1 + \hat{\beta}_1 X_i$ for the first stratum and into $\hat{Y}_i = (\hat{\alpha}_1 + \hat{\alpha}_D) + (\hat{\beta}_1 + \hat{\beta}_D)X_i$ for the second, is fitted to the n observations in the expanded form $\hat{Y}_i = \hat{\alpha}_1 + \hat{\beta}_1 X_i + \hat{\alpha}_D D_i + \hat{\beta}_D D_i X_i$, and the significance status and magnitude of $\hat{\alpha}_D$ and of $\hat{\beta}_D$ indicate if and how the economic structure has changed.[23] The $D_i X_i$, being the product of explanatory variables, is called an "interaction term." Footnote 25 of Chapter 5 refers to tests which employ a variable to allow for structural changes: that variable is a dummy of the D_i type. The D^* variables in equation (5.19) include an intercept dummy and an interactive dummy resembling D_i and $D_i X_i$, respectively.

[22] Gujarati, *Basic Econometrics*, pp. 235–238, 245, and Johnston, *Econometric Methods*, pp. 249–252, 432–433.

[23] Gujarati, *Basic Econometrics*, pp. 295–299, and Johnston, *Econometric Methods*, pp. 204, 206.

APPENDIX

B

MATHEMATICS OF THE COMPOSITE INDICES OF LEADING, COINCIDENT, AND LAGGING INDICATORS

For any series k, S_{kt} denotes the value assumed at month t, $t = 0, 1, 2, \ldots, n$. Percent changes for series k can be calculated with the average of the initial and terminal points used as base to allow symmetry;[1] specifically,

$$c_{kt} = 100 \frac{S_{kt} - S_{k, t-1}}{(S_{kt} + S_{k, t-1})/2}$$

with $t = 1, 2, \ldots, n$. If series k may assume zero or negative values or if it takes the form of a ratio or percentage, then c_{kt} is defined instead as the algebraic difference

$$c_{kt} = S_{kt} - S_{k, t-1}$$

To standardize (or amplitude amend) the changes c_{kt} for series k, they are divided by an adjustment factor a_k determined from some preassigned period, say, months i to j:

$$a_k = \frac{1}{j - i + 1} \sum_{t=i}^{j} |c_{kt}|$$

---

[1] This exposition is adapted from that in U.S. Department of Commerce, *Handbook of Cyclical Indicators: A Supplement to the Business Conditions Digest* (Washington, D.C.: U.S. Government Printing Office, May 1977), pp. 73–76.

The number of terms included in this summation equals $j - i + 1$, and hence a_k gives the average absolute difference or percent change in series k over the preassigned period. Dividing each c_{kt} by a_k yields the standardized rates sr_{kt}:

$$sr_{kt} = \frac{c_{kt}}{a_k}$$

Obviously, averaging the absolute values of sr_{kt} produces a number approximately equal ($\simeq$) to unity. In particular,

$$\frac{1}{n} \sum_{t=1}^{n} |sr_{kt}| = \left[\frac{1}{n} \sum_{t=1}^{n} |c_{kt}| \right] / a_k \simeq 1$$

If a_k were calculated over the period $t = 1, 2, \ldots, n$, averaging would exactly lead to unity.

Suppose that u series enter a composite index. For each month the standardized rates of all u series are consolidated by a weighted average:

$$ar_t = \sum_{k=1}^{u} sr_{kt} \frac{w_k}{\sum\limits_{k=1}^{u} w_k} \tag{B.1}$$

where coefficient w_k reflects the performance score of series k. This ar_t denotes the average rate for month t, and it reflects the amplitude adjusted movements of the u separate series.

For the leading and lagging indices, the next step in the calculations calls for standardizing the average rates ar_t. However, rather than tying these rates to unity —as are the sr_{kt}—the standardization process links them to the average rates for the coincident index. Let ar_t' represent the average rate for the coincident index in month t, ar_t' satisfying equation (B.1). Furthermore, let a' represent the average of the absolute average rates for the coinciders over the preassigned period:

$$a' = \frac{1}{j - i + 1} \sum_{t=i}^{j} |ar_t'|$$

Thus the standardized average rates for the leading and lagging indicators over the period $t = 1, 2, \ldots, n$ are

$$sar_t = \frac{ar_t}{b} a' \tag{B.2}$$

$b = (\sum_{t=i}^{j} |ar_t|)/(j - i + 1)$. Clearly, without a' the absolute standardized average rates would average roughly to unity, just as the sr_{kt} do. With a', however, they average roughly to the average of the absolute average rates applicable to the coincident indicators. For the coincident index the average rates ar_t' do not undergo standardization; namely, $sar_t = ar_t'$. In short, for the leading and lagging indices, the standardized average rates come from equation (B.2); for the coincident index, they equal the average rates determined from equation (B.1).

Values for any of the three composite indices CI evolve from the standardized average rates by appealing to the expression for symmetric percentages.

$$sar_t = 100 \frac{CI_t - CI_{t-1}}{(CI_t + CI_{t-1})/2}$$

Hence,

$$CI_t = CI_{t-1}\left(\frac{200 + sar_t}{200 - sar_t}\right) \tag{B.3}$$

The initial value of the index, that at $t = 0$, is arbitrarily set at 100, and from this base number equation (B.3) generates a profile of the index over the entire period $t = 0, 1, 2, \ldots, n$.

Since the three indices differ in their components, their values as computed from equation (B.3) have different secular trends. These trends can be equalized by amending the sar_t. Let *crt* denote the percent rate of trend implicit in the composite index values emerging from equation (B.3), and let *drt* represent the desired rate of trend—the percent rate of the average trend derived from the unweighted component series of the coincident index. Then

$$tasar_t = sar_t + (drt - crt)$$

gives the trend-adjusted standard average rate. Using $tasar_t$ instead of sar_t in equation (B.3) forces a composite index to evidence the trend rate *drt* rather than *crt*. This adjustment applies to the three composite indices, and thus they all exhibit the same trend rate. The process of modifying but not eliminating the trend is known as "reverse trend adjustment."

APPENDIX
C

FUNCTIONAL FORMS IN THE CES PRODUCTION FAMILY

C.1 THE ELASTICITY OF SUBSTITUTION AND THE CES FUNCTION

A two-factor production function relating the quantity of output Q to the quantities of capital K and labor L may be written as $Q = g(K, L)$. Its elasticity of (factor) substitution σ is defined as the percent change in factor proportion relative to the percent change in the marginal rate of technical substitution MRTS, output being held constant; namely,

$$\sigma = \frac{d(K/L)/(K/L)}{d(g_L/g_K)/(g_L/g_K)}$$

where g_i denotes the marginal product of input i. Since MRTS represents the negative of the isoquant slope, σ can be viewed as measuring the curvature of isoquants. Figure C.1 illustrates. A small, given percent increase in MRTS from point A yields point B with factor proportion k_2 for isoquant Q_1 and point C with proportion k_3 for isoquant Q'_1. The greater increase in factor proportion and the greater σ are therefore associated with the flatter isoquant. Extremes of $\sigma = 0$ and $\sigma \to \infty$ feature right-angled and straight-line isoquants, respectively.

In the general case σ assumes different values along any particular isoquant. The production function, however, can be written to restrict σ to the same value

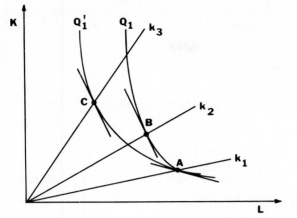

Figure C.1

at each point of every isoquant, and in that case the function takes the form

$$Q = \gamma \left[\xi_1 K^{-\rho} + \xi_2 L^{-\rho} \right]^{-\zeta/\rho} \qquad \text{(C.1)}$$

Parameters γ and ζ are positive and finite, while parameters ξ_1 and ξ_2 are positive and sum to unity. Parameter ρ can adopt any value in the range -1 to infinity including either extreme.

Equation (C.1), known as the constant elasticity of substitution (CES) production function, ties σ exclusively to ρ. That connection can be easily shown. Since (C.1) gives $g_K = \tau \xi_1 K^{-\rho-1}$ and $g_L = \tau \xi_2 L^{-\rho-1}$ with $\tau = \zeta \gamma^{-\rho/\zeta} Q^{1+\rho/\zeta}$,

$$\frac{g_L}{g_K} = \frac{\xi_2}{\xi_1} \left(\frac{K}{L} \right)^{1+\rho}$$

and

$$d\left(\frac{g_L}{g_K} \right) = \frac{\xi_2}{\xi_1} (1 + \rho) \left(\frac{K}{L} \right)^{\rho} d\left(\frac{K}{L} \right)$$

Consequently,

$$\frac{d(g_L/g_K)}{g_L/g_K} = (1 + \rho) \frac{d(K/L)}{K/L}$$

which, after insertion into the expression for σ, produces

$$\sigma = \frac{1}{1 + \rho}$$

Since ρ is a constant, so is σ. Equation (C.1) can also be shown to be homogeneous of degree ζ and to display positive but declining marginal products and positive cross-marginals for positive, finite input levels.[1] The three special CES cases cited in Section 4.1 readily emerge.[2]

C.2 THE LEONTIEF FUNCTION

For convenience write the CES in terms of positive exponents:

$$Q = \frac{\gamma}{\left[\xi_1 \dfrac{1}{K^\rho} + \xi_2 \dfrac{1}{L^\rho}\right]^{\zeta/\rho}} \tag{C.2}$$

As $\rho \to \infty$ (that is, as $\sigma \to 0$), the denominator tends to an indeterminate form, the precise variant depending upon the values of K and L. Translate (C.2) into

$$Q = \frac{\gamma K^\zeta}{\left[\xi_1 + \xi_2 \left(\dfrac{K}{L}\right)^\rho\right]^{\zeta/\rho}}$$

Clearly, $Q \to \gamma K^\zeta$ as $\rho \to \infty$ provided that $K < L$. Equation (C.2) also translates into

$$Q = \frac{\gamma L^\zeta}{\left[\xi_1 \left(\dfrac{L}{K}\right)^\rho + \xi_2\right]^{\zeta/\rho}}$$

and thus $Q \to \gamma L^\zeta$ as $\rho \to \infty$ provided that $K > L$. When $K = L$, equation (C.2) simplifies to $Q = \gamma K^\zeta$ or, equivalently, to $Q = \gamma L^\zeta$. These alternative limiting expressions can be written compactly:

$$Q = \min(\gamma K^\zeta, \gamma L^\zeta) \tag{C.3}$$

where the "min" operator says to select the smaller of the two arguments in parentheses. Equation (C.3) is a Leontief fixed-proportion production function with homogeneity of degree ζ.

---

[1] Proofs of some of these properties and identification of exceptions to them for particular parameter values are found in Murray Brown, *On the Theory and Measurement of Technological Change* (London: Cambridge University Press, 1968), pp. 45–50. The derivation of equation (C.1) appears in his Appendix A, which reproduces Appendix II of Murray Brown and John S. de Cani, "Technological Change and the Distribution of Income," *International Economic Review*, **4** (September 1963), pp. 305–309. Derivation of (C.1), with $\zeta = 1$, and description of its properties can also be found in K. J. Arrow, H. B. Chenery, B. S. Minhas, and R. M. Solow, "Capital-Labor Substitution and Economic Efficiency," *Review of Economics and Statistics*, **43** (August 1961), pp. 228, 230–231.

[2] Examination of the first two special cases under the assumption of $\zeta = 1$ appears in C. E. Ferguson, *The Neoclassical Theory of Production and Distribution* (London: Cambridge University Press, 1971), pp. 105–107. Ferguson also reviews other properties of the CES function along with the derivation of the function itself (pp. 101–105).

C.3 THE COBB-DOUGLAS FUNCTION

As $\rho \to 0$ (as $\sigma \to 1$), the CES specification (C.1) tends to $\gamma[1]^{-\infty}$. This indeterminacy can be penetrated by converting (C.1) into logarithms. Thus,

$$\ln Q = \ln \gamma - \frac{\zeta}{\rho} \ln[\xi_1 K^{-\rho} + \xi_2 L^{-\rho}]$$

For $\rho = 0$ the second term on the right reduces to $0/0$, and consequently l'Hopital's rule comes to the fore:

$$\lim_{\rho \to 0} \frac{\zeta}{\rho} \ln[\xi_1 K^{-\rho} + \xi_2 L^{-\rho}] = \lim_{\rho \to 0} \frac{\dfrac{\partial}{\partial \rho} \zeta \ln[\xi_1 K^{-\rho} + \xi_2 L^{-\rho}]}{\partial \rho / \partial \rho}$$

But

$$\frac{\partial}{\partial \rho} \zeta \ln[\xi_1 K^{-\rho} + \xi_2 L^{-\rho}] = -\zeta[\xi_1 K^{-\rho} + \xi_2 L^{-\rho}]^{-1}[\xi_1 K^{-\rho}\ln K$$

$$+\xi_2 L^{-\rho}\ln L]$$

which approaches $-\zeta[\xi_1 \ln K + \xi_2 \ln L]$ as ρ approaches 0. Therefore,

$$\lim_{\rho \to 0} \ln Q = \ln \gamma + \zeta\xi_1 \ln K + \zeta\xi_2 \ln L$$

Antilogs yield the limiting equation

$$Q = \gamma K^{\zeta\xi_1} L^{\zeta\xi_2} \tag{C.4}$$

which is a Cobb-Douglas with homogeneity of degree ζ.

C.4 THE LINEAR-ISOQUANT FUNCTION

As $\rho \to -1$ (as $\sigma \to \infty$), equation (C.1) tends to the form

$$Q = \gamma[\xi_1 K + \xi_2 L]^{\zeta} \tag{C.5}$$

For (C.5) the isoquant representing output level Q_1 is

$$K = \frac{\gamma^{-1/\zeta}}{\xi_1} Q_1^{1/\zeta} - \frac{\xi_2}{\xi_1} L$$

This equation describes a straight line with slope $-\xi_2/\xi_1$. Under constant returns ($\zeta = 1$), the production function (C.5) assumes linearity also.

APPENDIX
D

OUTLINE FOR SOLVING LINEAR DIFFERENCE EQUATIONS

D.1 THE SOLUTION MECHANISM

Consider a linear equation which expresses current real income in terms of past real incomes:

$$Y_t = a_0 + a_1 Y_{t-1} + a_2 Y_{t-2} + \cdots + a_{n-1} Y_{t-n+1} + a_n Y_{t-n} \qquad \text{(D.1)}$$

where the a factors represent constants and where t represents time. This reduced form is a difference equation in income. Its order is n, order being the number of periods spanned by the equation; specifically, $t - (t - n) = n$. Rewriting (D.1) to collect all income terms together leaves

$$Y_t - a_1 Y_{t-1} - a_2 Y_{t-2} - \cdots - a_{n-1} Y_{t-n+1} - a_n Y_{t-n} = a_0 \qquad \text{(D.2)}$$

If $a_0 = 0$, then the difference equation is termed "homogeneous"; if $a_0 \neq 0$, then it is termed "nonhomogeneous."

Solving (D.2) means converting it to a form which expresses current income solely in terms of time. At least two reasons can be offered for solving it. First, the solution enables temporal configurations of income to be determined analytically for entire ranges of parameter values. As it stands, equation (D.2) merely reveals, through a protracted iterative process, the temporal pattern which accompanies a given set of parameter values. Second, the level of income for any period after the disruption of equilibrium at $t = 0$ can be computed immediately from the solved equation. For example, Y_{50} emerges by simply setting $t = 50$. This Y_{50} can be determined from (D.2) only if all previous income levels are first calculated.

Since most difference equations encountered in macroeconomics are nonhomogeneous, that type warrants attention here. Consequently, the solution sought is the one for equation (D.2) when $a_0 \neq 0$. This solution should be general in order to apply to all situations—it should contain arbitrary constants, the values of which can be established on an individual-case basis.

The general solution to a nonhomogeneous difference equation is the sum of the general solution to its homogeneous part and any particular solution to the nonhomogeneous equation itself. The solution mechanism, therefore, entails solving the homogeneous component in terms of arbitrary constants and finding any solution to the original formulation of the equation.

Consider the homogeneous component of (D.2):

$$Y_t - a_1 Y_{t-1} - a_2 Y_{t-2} - \cdots - a_{n-1} Y_{t-n+1} - a_n Y_{t-n} = 0$$

Because this equation holds at each point in time, it can be advanced for convenience n periods forward without violating the equality:

$$Y_{t+n} - a_1 Y_{t+n-1} - a_2 Y_{t+n-2} - \cdots - a_{n-1} Y_{t+1} - a_n Y_t = 0 \qquad \text{(D.3)}$$

According to a fundamental theorem, a solution to a linear difference equation exists, and it is unique. This theorem implies that if a solution can be found, by whatever technique, then that solution must be *the* solution of the difference equation. As a trial solution, let $Y_t = \phi^t$, where ϕ denotes a constant. Substitution into (D.3) yields

$$\phi^{t+n} - a_1 \phi^{t+n-1} - a_2 \phi^{t+n-2} - \cdots - a_{n-1} \phi^{t+1} - a_n \phi^t = 0$$

or

$$\phi^t \left(\phi^n - a_1 \phi^{n-1} - a_2 \phi^{n-2} - \cdots - a_{n-1} \phi - a_n \right) = 0 \qquad \text{(D.4)}$$

Equation (D.4) can be satisfied in two ways, one of which ($\phi^t = 0$) is trivial because it means that income remains zero through time. The other possibility has more promise; namely,

$$\phi^n - a_1 \phi^{n-1} - a_2 \phi^{n-2} - \cdots - a_{n-1} \phi - a_n = 0$$

This equation, known as the "auxiliary equation," is a polynomial of degree n. It has n roots: $\phi_1, \phi_2, \ldots, \phi_n$. Given that the general solution to a difference equation of order n contains n arbitrary constants and that each ϕ root raised to the power t enters the solution as a linear combination, the general solution to (D.3) becomes

$$Y_t^G = A_1 \phi_1^t + A_2 \phi_2^t + \cdots + A_{n-1} \phi_{n-1}^t + A_n \phi_n^t \qquad \text{(D.5)}$$

where the A factors represent arbitrary constants.

Still needed is a particular solution to the nonhomogeneous equation (D.2). While any such solution would suffice, interpretation is facilitated by selecting that particular solution which corresponds to the equilibrium value of income. Under stationary-state conditions the particular solution, Y_t^P, therefore becomes

Y_E for all t, Y_E being a constant. From (D.2)

$$Y_E - a_1 Y_E - a_2 Y_E - \cdots - a_{n-1} Y_E - a_n Y_E = a_0$$

and

$$Y_E = \frac{a_0}{1 - a_1 - a_2 - \cdots - a_{n-1} - a_n}$$

The general solution to the nonhomogeneous equation (D.2) arrives by adding together the general solution (D.5) and the particular solution Y_E; namely,[1]

$$Y_t = A_1 \phi_1^t + A_2 \phi_2^t + \cdots + A_{n-1} \phi_{n-1}^t + A_n \phi_n^t + \frac{a_0}{1 - a_1 - a_2 - \cdots - a_{n-1} - a_n}$$

$$(D.6)$$

Equation (D.6) can be viewed as separating the movement of income into two segments. One represents equilibrium; the other, the deviation from equilibrium. In applying (D.6) to any specific situation, the A factors are determined from information pertinent to that situation. Examples might help.

D.2 SOLUTION FOR THE BASIC MULTIPLIER MODEL

The multiplier model presented in Section 3.2 offers expression (3.15) as the reduced-form equation for real income (output). That equation can be rewritten by noting the exogenous nature of real government expenditures and real money supply:

$$Y_t + \left[\frac{vk}{m} - c(1 - x) \right] Y_{t-1} = C_o + I_o + G_o - cT_o + \frac{v}{m} \left(\frac{M_o}{p_o} - L_o \right) \quad (D.7)$$

Equation (D.7) has the homogeneous component

$$Y_t + \left[\frac{vk}{m} - c(1 - x) \right] Y_{t-1} = 0$$

which translates into

$$Y_{t+1} + \left[\frac{vk}{m} - c(1 - x) \right] Y_t = 0$$

---

[1] This sketch ignores complications. For a comprehensive discussion of difference equations and their solution, see R. G. D. Allen, *Mathematical Economics*, 2d ed. (London: Macmillan & Co., Ltd., 1963), Chapter 6; Edward T. Dowling, *Theory and Problems of Mathematics for Economists*, Schaum's Outline Series (New York: McGraw-Hill Book Company, 1980), Chapters 19–20; and Taro Yamane, *Mathematics for Economists: An Elementary Survey*, 2d ed. (Englewood Cliffs, N.J.: Prentice-Hall, Inc., 1968), Chapter 9.

Let $Y_t = \phi^t$ be a trial solution. Then

$$\phi^{t+1} + \left[\frac{vk}{m} - c(1-x) \right] \phi^t = 0$$

and

$$\phi^t \left\{ \phi + \left[\frac{vk}{m} - c(1-x) \right] \right\} = 0$$

which is satisfied nontrivially by the auxiliary equation

$$\phi = c(1-x) - \frac{vk}{m}$$

The general solution to the homogeneous component of (D.7) therefore becomes

$$Y_t^G = A \left[c(1-x) - \frac{vk}{m} \right]^t$$

where A is an arbitrary constant.

The particular solution to the nonhomogeneous equation (D.7) identifies the stationary-state equilibrium. Consequently,

$$Y_E = \frac{C_o + I_o + G_o - cT_o + \dfrac{v}{m} \left(\dfrac{M_o}{p_o} - L_o \right)}{1 - c(1-x) + \dfrac{vk}{m}}$$

It follows that the general solution to equation (D.7) is

$$Y_t = A \left[c(1-x) - \frac{vk}{m} \right]^t + \frac{C_o + I_o + G_o - cT_o + \dfrac{v}{m} \left(\dfrac{M_o}{p_o} - L_o \right)}{1 - c(1-x) + \dfrac{vk}{m}} \tag{D.8}$$

Equation (D.8) reveals that the difference equation (D.7) generates unidirectional convergence to the new equilibrium provided that $0 < [c(1-x) - vk/m] < 1$. When is this condition satisfied?

Positiveness requires that

$$c(1-x) > \frac{vk}{m} \tag{D.9}$$

which is an inequality that lends itself to straightforward interpretation. $c(1-x)$ is the effect which a unit change in income exerts on total commodity demand when all feedbacks from other markets are eliminated. It measures the direct effect of the income change. But a change in income also influences commodity demand indirectly through interest rate effects on investment demand. The magnitude of this indirect effect is vk/m. As the LM equation (3.11) shows, a unit change in income changes interest by k/m units, which in turn changes investment by vk/m via equation (3.4). Inequality (D.9), therefore, says that positiveness occurs when the direct effect of an income change dominates the indirect effect. This condition is a familiar one for stability.[2]

For $c(1 - x) - vk/m$ to be less than unity, the inequality

$$\frac{k}{m} > -\frac{1}{v}[1 - c(1 - x)] \tag{D.10}$$

must hold. The left- and right-hand sides of (D.10) can be recognized as the slopes of LM equation (3.11) and IS equation (3.10), respectively. Hence the common case of a positively sloped LM and a negatively sloped IS assures that $c(1 - x) - vk/m$ falls below unity.

To apply (D.8) to the example tracked by Table 3.1, the arbitrary constant A must be determined. This calculation requires one initial condition. At $t = 0$, when a permanent increase in government expenditures from 250 to 275 disrupts the original equilibrium, income equals 1097.09. The new equilibrium is 1144.53, which is the relevant target. Thus, when $t = 0$, (D.8) occasions

$$1097.09 = A + 1144.53$$

making $A = -47.44$. The operative equation then becomes

$$Y_t = -47.44(.4729)^t + 1144.53 \tag{D.11}$$

For $t = 2$—for the second period after the increase in government expenditures —equation (D.11) produces $Y_2 = 1133.92$. For $t = 5$ and $t = 10$ it yields $Y_5 = 1143.41$ and $Y_{10} = 1144.50$. Rounding error aside, these values are identical to those generated by equation (3.17) and registered in Table 3.1.

D.3 SOLUTION FOR THE INTERACTION MODEL

Section 4.3 established equation (4.12) as the reduced form for real income. That expression may be restated as

$$Y_t - c(1 + b)Y_{t-1} + bcY_{t-2} = G_o \tag{D.12}$$

Equation (D.12) exhibits the homogeneous component

$$Y_t - c(1 + b)Y_{t-1} + bcY_{t-2} = 0$$

which translates into

$$Y_{t+2} - c(1 + b)Y_{t+1} + bcY_t = 0$$

Inserting $Y_t = \phi^t$ gives rise to the auxiliary equation

$$\phi^2 - c(1 + b)\phi + bc = 0 \tag{D.13}$$

Equation (D.13) is a quadratic, and consequently its roots can be computed from

---

[2]A clear example appears in Don Patinkin, *Money, Interest, and Prices*, 2d ed. (New York: Harper & Row, Publishers, Incorporated, 1965), pp. 235–236.

the famous discriminant:

$$\phi_1, \phi_2 = \frac{c(1 + b) \pm \sqrt{c^2(1 + b)^2 - 4bc}}{2}$$

The linear combination of ϕ_1' and ϕ_2', expressed with arbitrary constants, makes up the general solution to the homogeneous equation.

The particular solution imposes constancy in income, and from (D.12) it becomes

$$Y_E = \frac{G_o}{1 - c}$$

Thus, the general solution to the nonhomogeneous equation (D.12) is[3]

$$Y_t = A_1 \left[\frac{c(1 + b) + \sqrt{c^2(1 + b)^2 - 4bc}}{2} \right]^t$$
$$+ A_2 \left[\frac{c(1 + b) - \sqrt{c^2(1 + b)^2 - 4bc}}{2} \right]^t + \frac{G_o}{1 - c} \qquad (D.14)$$

Both arbitrary constants A_1 and A_2 can be determined by two initial conditions. In Section 4.3, G_o rises permanently from 250 to 275 at $t = 0$, and since $c = .68$, equilibrium income jumps to 859.38. For $t = 0$, however, income remains at the original equilibrium level of 781.25. It increases to 806.25 ($= 781.25 + 25.00$) for $t = 1$. When $b = .1$, these initial conditions produce from (D.14)

$$781.25 = \quad A_1 + \quad A_2 + 859.38$$
$$806.25 = .6421A_1 + .1059A_2 + 859.38$$

with $A_1 = -83.6559$ and $A_2 = 5.5259$. For this specific case, therefore, equation (D.14) reduces to

$$Y_t = -83.6559(.6421)^t + 5.5259(.1059)^t + 859.38$$

Setting $t = 2$, 5, and 10 renders $Y_2 = 824.95$, $Y_5 = 850.25$, and $Y_{10} = 858.38$, the same values plotted by Figure 4.3.

[3]Derivation from equation (D.14) of the regions depicted in Figure 4.5 is given by Yamane, *Mathematics*, pp. 338–346.

NAME INDEX

Abramovitz, Moses, 68n.
Ackley, Gardner, 4n., 21n., 168n., 175n.
Allen, R. G. D., 21n., 365n., 368n., 369n., 371n., 374n., 402n.
Amano, Akihiro, 257n.
Andersen, Leonall, 227n.
Anderson, W. H. Locke, 186n.
Ando, Albert, 154 − 156, 160, 228n.
Arrow, Kenneth J., 96n., 245n., 252n., 286n., 398n.
Atkinson, A. B., 326, 327, 334 − 336

Ball, R. J., 156 − 160, 187, 188
Beckmann, M. J., 255n., 256n.
Bliss, Christopher, 269n., 308n.
Blumenthal, Michael W., 198n.
Boschan, Charlotte, 83n., 84n., 85n.
Boskin, Michael J., 23n.
Brady, Dorothy S., 120n.
Brainard, William, 199n., 215n., 217n., 218n.
Branson, William H., 160n.
Brems, Hans, 263n.
Bronfenbrenner, Martin, 79n.
Brown, E. Cary, 228n.
Brown, Murray, 96, 252n., 301n., 398n.
Brown, T. M., 138 − 141, 152, 153, 160, 161
Brumberg, Richard, 154 − 156, 160
Burns, Arthur F., 68, 75n., 76, 83n., 87n.
Burress, Glenn E., 123n., 131n.

Cameron, Juan, 197n.
Canterbery, E. Ray, 129n.
Carter, Jimmy, 197, 198, 199n.
Carver, T. N., 165, 166, 176
CBS News, 199n.
Chase Econometric Associates, 186n.
Chenery, Hollis B., 96n., 161n., 166n., 182n., 398n.

Chiang, Alpha C., 360n., 361n., 365n., 368n., 369n., 371n., 374n., 377n., 384n.
Chow, Gregory C., 238n., 239n., 240n., 243n.
Christ, Carl F., 73n.
Clark, J. Maurice, 165 − 166
Clark, Lindley H., Jr., 23n.
Cloos, George W., 85n.
Coen, Robert M., 186n.
Colander, David C., 245n., 246n., 247n.
Conlisk, John, 326, 327
Conrad, Alfred H., 252n.
Cooper, J. Phillip, 240n., 241n., 243n.
Crouch, Robert L., 168n., 326, 328n., 329n., 332
Crum, W. L., 68

Darby, Michael R., 238n.
Davis, Tom E., 123 − 125, 137 − 139, 160
de Cani, John S., 96, 398n.
Diamond, Peter A., 296n.
Domar, Evsey D., 11n., 260 − 263, 282, 334
Dowling, Edward T., 402n.
Drake, Pamela S., 156 − 160, 187, 188
Drandakis, E. M., 257n.
Drost, Helmar, 161n.
Duesenberry, James S.:
  on consumption, 120n., 136 − 139, 141, 160
  consumption theory of, 131 − 136
  investment theory of, 183 − 186

Econometric Society, 131
Eisner, Robert, 165n., 185n.
Evans, Michael K., 21n., 27n., 186n.

Fadell, Albert G., 360n., 361n., 364n., 381n.
Feldstein, Martin, 23n.
Ferber, Robert, 123 − 125, 154n., 186n.

Ferguson, C. E., 254n., 398n.
Figlewski, Stephen, 247n.
Fischer, Stanley, 240n., 241n., 243n., 246n.
Fisher, Franklin, 296 – 297, 337n.
Fox, Karl A., 385n.
Freund, John E., 385n., 390n., 391n.
Friedlaender, Ann F., 228n.
Friedman, Milton:
   constant growth rate rule of, 223 – 224, 240,
     242, 244 – 245
   on consumption, 154,156, 158 – 161, 181,
     187
   consumption theory of, 143 – 153, 366,
     374 – 375
   on destabilizing nature of countercyclical
     policy, 221n., 225 – 227
   on functional finance, 222
   policy reforms of, 222 – 224, 325
   views of Henry C. Simons and, 224n.
Frisch, Ragnar, 94, 99 – 100, 106
Fromm, Gary, 73n., 74n., 186n.

Galbraith, John Kenneth, 3n., 79n.
Gapinski, James H., 24n., 93n., 129n., 153n.,
     244n., 252n., 287n., 302n., 304n.,
     305n., 322n., 337n.
Garbade, Kenneth D., 227n., 228n., 243n.
Gass, Saul I., 384n.
Goldsmith, Raymond W., 120, 122
Goodwin, Richard M., 161n., 177n., 187n.
Gordon, Robert A., 68n.
Gosset, W. S., 390
Gujarati, Damodar, 389n., 391n., 392n.

Haberler, Gottfried, 166n.
Hague, D. C., 170n., 274n.
Hamberg, Daniel:
   on growth models, 251n., 260n., 263n.,
     271n., 279n.
   on investment, 95n., 164n., 168n., 178n.,
     185n.
   on technical progress, 255n., 256n.
Hamburger, William, 142 – 143, 154, 156
Hand, John H., 24n.
Hansen, Alvin H., 169n., 172n.
Harcourt, G. C., 253n., 301n.
Harrod, Roy F.:
   on autonomous investment, 263n.
   basic antinomy of, 257
   growth model of, 257 – 260
   growth models and, 261 – 263, 266n., 282n.,
     334
   natural rate of, 258, 259, 265, 293, 309
   on technical progress, 254, 255
   warranted rate of, 258, 265, 281n.
Heller, Walter W., 23n., 221n., 227n.
Hickman, Bert G., 186n., 199n.

Hicks, J. R.:
   on investment, 164, 165 166n., 168, 173n.,
     177
   IS-LM apparatus of, 46
   on Keynesian economics, 21n., 22n., 48
   on saving in model of classics, 11n.
   stock equilibrium condition of, 260n.
   on substitutability of factors ex post, 302n.
   on technical progress, 254, 257n.
   theory of cycle by, 94, 106 – 108
Hoel, Paul G., 385n.
Houthakker, H. S., 141, 152, 160
Howitt, Peter, 247n.
Hurd, Michael D., 186n.
Husby, Ralph D., 153n.
Hymans, Saul H., 85n.

Inada, Ken-ichi, 264, 267, 271, 272, 279, 280,
    284, 314 – 315, 360

Jackson, John D., 141
Johansen, Leif, 300 – 301
Johnston, J., 389n., 390n., 391n., 392n.
Jorgenson, Dale W., 170n.
Juglar, Clement, 68
Juster, F. Thomas, 160n.

Kahn, R. F., 30n.
Kaldor, Nicholas:
   on embodied technical progress, 274, 286
   growth model of, 274 – 279
   growth models and, 279 – 280, 282
   on investment, 277 – 278, 279n.
   rejection of marginal productivity theory by,
     274, 275
   rejection of production function by, 251,
     274, 275, 286
   saving and, 275 – 277, 283 – 285, 385
   technical progress function of, 274 – 275
     Cobb-Douglas production function and,
     251, 274 – 275, 286
   theory of income distribution by, 275 – 277,
     280
Kantor, Brian, 244n.
Karlin, S., 252n., 286n.
Kennedy, Charles, 257n.
Keynes, John Maynard:
   absolute income hypothesis of consumption
     by, 21n., 119, 132, 142, 160
    as instantaneous adjustment model,
     161 – 162
   on classical economists, 4n., 221
   consumption function and, 119, 120, 123,
     125, 128, 129
    in model of classics, 10n.
   fiscal policy and, 19 – 20, 227n.

Keynes, John Maynard (*Cont.*):
  The General Theory, 3, 54*n.,* 119, 224*n.*
  on habit persistence in consumption, 131
  on hoarding, 13
  interest rate determination and, 279*n.*
  investment, dual nature of and, 260 – 261
  investment function and, 17*n.,* 18*n.,* 94, 164,
    167 – 168, 173, 175 – 176
  investment theory of clarified, 167 – 177
  on liquidity preference, 13*n.,* 19*n.*
  on liquidity trap, 15*n.*
  on marginal efficiency of capital, 17*n.,*
    167 – 168
  model of, 12 – 27, 261*n.*
  on money demand, 13 – 15
  on money-wage rigidity, 19*n.*
  multiplier concept and, 30*n.,* 260
  on normal interest rate, 13*n.* – 14*n.*
  on relation between money wage and real
    wage, 8*n.*
  on saving and interest rate, 17*n.*
  unemployment equations and, 357
  user cost and, 169
Kitchin, Joseph, 68
Klein, Lawrence R., 4*n.,* 21*n.,* 68*n.,* 73*n.,* 74*n.*
Klevorick, Alvin K., 160*n.*
Knox, A. D., 164*n.,* 165*n.,* 180*n.,* 185*n.*
Kondratieff, N. D., 68
Koyck, L. M.:
  on capacity definition, 164*n.*
  distributed lag of: in consumption,
    149 – 150, 160
    in countercyclical policy, 242
    as special case of Pascal distributed lag,
      240, 241*n.*
  on investment, 166*n.,* 167*n.,* 182*n.,* 183*n.,*
    185*n.*
Kristol, Irving, 23*n.*
Kubota, K., 279*n.*
Kumar, Ramesh C., 161*n.*
Kumar, T. Krishna, 305*n.*
Kurihara, K. K., 154*n.*
Kuznets, Simon S.:
  on consumption, 122*n.* – 123*n.,* 125,
    129 – 130, 133, 136, 139 – 141
  cyclical fluctuation named after, 68
  estimates by of consumption and income,
    120 – 121
  on investment, 166*n.*

Lance, Thomas B., 198*n.*
Lansing, Richard M., 326*n.*
Leontief, Wassily, 96, 98, 137*n.,* 260, 398
Lerner, Abba P., 172, 221 – 223
l'Hopital, G. F. A., 364
Lovell, Michael C., 156*n.*
Lundberg, Erik, 54
Lutz, F. A., 170*n.,* 274*n.*

McCallum, Bennett T., 247*n.*
Maddala, G. S., 390*n.*
Makin, John H., 170*n.*
March, James G., 246*n.,* 320*n.*
Matthews, R. C. O., 178*n.*
Mayer, Thomas, 131*n.,* 142*n.,* 144*n.,* 154*n.*
Mendershausen, Horst, 120*n.*
Merrill, William C., 385*n.*
Metzler, Lloyd A., 54*n.,* 94, 108 – 115
Miller, G. William, 198 – 199, 220
Minhas, B. S., 96*n.,* 398*n.*
Mintz, Ilse, 75*n.,* 79*n.*
Mitchell, Wesley C.:
  as founder of National Bureau of Economic
    Research (NBER), 75
  leading indicators and, 83*n.*
  measuring business cycles and, 75*n.,* 76,
    87*n.,* 93
  taxonomy of cycle phases by, 68, 76*n.*
Mitchell, William E., 24*n.,* 47*n.*
Modigliani, Franco:
  on adjustments under liquidity preference,
    16*n.*
  on consumption, 130*n.,* 131, 138*n.,* 139,
    143, 156
  consumption theories of, 136 – 138, 141,
    154 – 155, 160
Moore, Geoffrey H., 75*n.,* 76*n.,* 78*n.*
Morrey, Charles B., Jr., 360*n.,* 361*n.,* 364*n.,*
  369*n.,* 377*n.,* 381*n.*
Mundell, Robert A., 199*n.*
Musgrove, Philip, 160*n.*
Muth, John F., 244*n.*

Pack, Howard, 228*n.,* 242*n.*
Park, Seong Y., 320*n.,* 321*n.*
Pasinetti, Luigi L., 251*n.,* 263*n.,* 277*n.*
Patinkin, Don, 27*n.,* 33*n.,* 38*n.,* 45*n.,* 160*n.,*
  404*n.*
Petith, Howard C., 321*n.*
Phelps, Edmund S.:
  on construction of aggregate capital stock
    under embodied technical progress, 286,
    287*n.,* 290*n.,* 303*n.*
  on convergence time, 325 – 327, 328*n.,*
    329*n.,* 332, 358
  on putty-clay capital, 303*n.,* 320*n.,* 321*n.*
  on rational expectations, 244*n.,* 246*n.*
  on technical progress, 253*n.,* 254*n.,* 257*n.*
  user cost derivation and, 170*n.*
Phillips, A. W., 228 – 230
Pierpoint, Robert, 199
Pindyck, Robert S., 186*n.,* 241*n.*
Pine, Art, 198
Pitchford, J. D., 273*n.*
Polak, J. J., 164*n.*
Protter, Murray H., 360*n.,* 361*n.,* 364*n.,*
  369*n.,* 377*n.,* 381*n.*

Ramanathan, R., 326−327, 328n., 335n., 336−337, 345
Roberts, Paul Craig, 23n.
Robertson, Dennis, 54n.
Robinson, Joan:
  growth model of, 279−282
  investment function of, 280, 360
  rejection by of production function and technical progress function, 251, 279
  on technical progress, 254n., 255n., 256n., 257n.
Rockwood, Charles E., 93n., 129n., 244n.
Rubinfeld, Daniel L., 186n., 241n.

Salter, W. E. G., 300, 301n.
Samuelson, Paul A., 94, 99−106, 170n., 186−192, 229, 257
Sargent, Thomas J., 228n., 238n., 244n., 245n., 246n.
Sato, Kazuo:
  on convergence time, 326−327, 328n., 329n., 330, 332, 354n.
  neoclassical growth model with embodied technical progress and, 290n.
  on restrictions on saving coefficient in neoclassical growth model with CES production function, 273n.
Sato, Ryuzo:
  on convergence time, 326−327, 328n., 329n., 330, 332n.
    elasticity of substitution and, 327, 334, 336, 337, 345, 351
    saving coefficient and, 332, 334
  on technical progress, 255n., 256n.
Schepsman, Martin, 85n.
Schultze, Charles, 197−198, 220, 260n., 263n.
Schumpeter, Joseph A., 68, 69n., 70n.
Shapiro, Edward J., 168n.
Sheshinski, Etan, 302n., 304n., 309n., 313−315, 360
Shiskin, Julius, 79n.
Siegel, Barry N., 4n., 143n.
Simons, Henry C., 224n.
Singh, Balvir, 161n.
Smith, Warren L., 24n., 54n., 199n.
Smithies, Arthur, 120n., 128−131, 139
Smyth, David J., 141
Solow, Robert M.:
  on capital in continuous versus discrete time, 338n.
  on CES production function, 96n., 398n.

Solow, Robert M. (*Cont.*):
  on construction of aggregate capital stock under embodied technical progress, 286, 287n.
  on determination of wage rate and vintage set of capital under putty-clay capital, 339n.
  on growth model of Harrod, 258n., 260n., 263
  on neoclassical growth model, 263, 267n.
  on Pascal distributed lag, 241n.
  on technical progress, 252, 253n., 254n., 255n., 256
Stein, Herbert, 23n.
Stekler, H. O., 85n.
Stoneman, P., 326n.
Suppes, P., 252n., 286n.
Swan, T. W., 263n., 271n.

Taubman, Paul, 186n.
Taylor, John B., 245n., 246n.−247n.
Taylor, Lester, 141, 152, 160
Teigen, Ronald L., 24n., 54n., 199n.
Theil, Henri, 199n., 241n.
Tinbergen, Jan, 164−165, 166n., 167n., 199n.

U.S. Department of Commerce:
  on composite indices, 79n., 83n., 84n., 85n., 86n., 393n.
  on consumption, 122n.−123n., 124n., 126n.
  on cyclical fluctuations, 3n., 78n., 89n.
U.S. President, 199n.
Uzawa, H., 255n., 264n., 284n.

Wachtel, Paul, 160n., 247n.
Wallace, Neil, 228n., 238n., 224n., 245n., 246n.
Walter, Ingo, 24n.
Wardwell, C. A. R., 68
Whitaker, J. K., 296, 300n., 337n.
White, Betsy B., 155n.
Williams, R. L., 326, 328n., 329n., 332

Yamane, Taro, 369n., 371n., 381n., 402n., 405n.

Zarnowitz, Victor, 76n., 83n., 84n., 85n.

SUBJECT INDEX

Page numbers in *italic* indicate tables.

Absolute income hypothesis, 119, 142, 150, 160
  (*See also* Consumption theory of Keynes)
Acceleration coefficient:
  defined, 95
  in growth model of Harrod: dual nature of, 259−260, 263*n.*
    ex ante and ex post, 257−258
  relation of, to productivity ratio, 263
Accleration principle:
  asymmetric accelerator, 106−107, 165−166, 175, 182
  defined, 94, 167
  in investment function of Kaldor, 277−278, 279*n.*
  permanent output changes and, 165, 176
  versus profits principle, 165, 167, 182
  simple accelerator and, 94−95
    (*See also* Accelerator, simple)
  theoretical basis of, 95−98, 99*n.*, 366
  variable proportionality in, 166−167, 175
    flexible accelerator and, 178
    (*See also* Accelerator, flexible)
  view of Carver on, 165
  view of Clark on, 165−166
Accelerator, flexible:
  asymmetric investment response and, 182
  compared with simple accelerator, 177−180
  derivation of, 177−178, 180−182, 185−187
  in inertial multiplier-accelerator interaction model, 187−188
  links acceleration and profits principles, 182
  theoretical basis of, 177
  variable acceleration coefficient and, 178
  (*See also* Investment function)

Accelerator, simple:
  compared with flexible accelerator, 177−180
  conditions for validity of, 98
  defined, 95, 167
  destabilizing nature of, 105−106, 108
    as feedback control, 229
  evidence on, 95*n.*, 167*n.*, 391
  in growth model of Harrod, 257−258
  in inventories, 111
  as special case of acceleration principle, 94−95
  weakness of, 167
  (*See also* Investment function, simple accelerator form of)
Adaptive rationality:
  defined, 246*n.*
  efficacy of policy and, 246
  as generalized form of static expectations, 322, 347
  in putty-clay growth model (*see* Growth model with putty-clay capital, under adaptive rationality)
Adjustment speed, 326−327, 329
Adjustment-speed parameter:
  alternative expression of, 330
  defined, 328
  (*See also* Speed-of-adjustment coefficient)
Aggregate capital stock (*see* Capital stock, aggregate)
Aggregate production function (*see* Production function, aggregate)
Animal spirits:
  defined, 18*n.*
  in policy, 211
Antiderivative:
  defined, 377

Antiderivative (*Cont.*):
  integral as, 377−379
  (*See also* Integral)
Argument of function, defined, 359
Asymptote:
  defined, 361
  illustrated, 241, 271
  limit and, 361
Autocorrelation:
  in consumption, $122n.−123n., 124n.$, 392
  defined, 391
  in investment, $95n.$, 392
  (*See also* Regression analysis,
    autocorrelation in)
Average propensity to consume, defined,
  20
  (*See also* Consumption function)

Balanced budget:
  consequence of, 230
  defined, 33, 229
  functional finance and, 222, 227
    under feedback controls, 231−232,
      235−237
  multiplier, 32−34
  as policy strategy, 199−200, 222, 223,
    227−228, 230−232, 235−236
  under sound finance, 222, 227, 231
Baseline solution:
  control solution and, 72
  defined, 72
  in determining dynamic multipliers,
    72−73
Basic antinomy, 257
BB curve:
  bond market conditions and, 39−40
  confronted by IS and LM curves, 41
  negative slope of, 40−41
    estimated value of, $41n.$
    explained, 40−41
  shifts in, 42
BB equation:
  defined, 39
  derived from budget constraint, 38−39
Bond market, implied from IS−LM analysis,
  38−41
Bond price:
  case of British consol, 14
  defined, 14
  expression for, 14
  relation of, to interest rate, $14, 39n., 43n.$
Bonds:
  demand for, 38, 40−41
  supply of, 38
Boundary conditions:
  in consumption, $146n., 157n.$
  in growth model of Kaldor, 279
  in growth model of Robinson, 280
  of Inada: in neoclassical growth model, 264,
    360

Boundary conditions, of Inada: in neoclassical
  growth model (*Cont.*):
    determining growth solution, role of, in,
      267−268
    with saving function of Kaldor, 284
    violation of, 271, 272
  in putty-clay growth model, violation of,
    314−315
  of Sheshinski in putty-clay growth model,
    violation of, 314−315, 360
Budget, balanced (*see* Balanced budget)
Budget constraint, macro:
  bond market and, 38−39
  defined, 38
  real-balance propensities and, $45n.$
Buffers:
  in model of Hicks, 106−108
  shape of cycles and, 108
Business cycles, *88−91*
  harmonic motion within, 87−93
  (*See also* Cycle; National Bureau of
    Economic Research)
Business failures, cyclical phases of, *89*
Business formation, cyclical phases of, *89*

Capacity:
  defined, $164, 259n.$
  types of, $164, 259n.$
Capital:
  demand price of (*see* Demand price of
    capital)
  economic life of (*see* Capital, economic life
    of)
  heterogeneity of, under embodied technical
    progress, 253, 287
  homogeneity of, within vintage, 253
  marginal efficiency of (*see* Marginal
    efficiency of capital)
  marginal product of: average product of,
    and, $267n.$
  in classification of technical progress by
    Harrod, 255
  relation of, to marginal efficiency of
    investment, 172−177
  nature of: ex ante versus ex post, 300−302
  putty-clay (*see* Capital, putty-clay)
  putty-putty (*see* Capital, putty-putty)
  obsolescence of (*see* Capital, obsolescence
    of)
  scrapping of, $289n., 302n.$
  (*See also* Capital, obsolescence of)
  supply price of, 167−168
    compared with demand price of, 171−172
    defined, 167−168
    marginal efficiency of investment and,
      171, 173, 175
    schedule of, 173, 174
  theory of, 167−171
    interfaced with theory of investment,
      167−177

Capital (*Cont.*):
  user cost (unit rental) of [*see* User cost (unit rental) of capital]
  vintage of: in continuous versus discrete time, 338*n*.
    defined, 253, 287
    marginal, 305, 338, 339
  vintage set of (*see* Capital, vintage set of)
Capital, economic life of:
  comparison of, under static and adaptive expectations, 324, *341, 343 – 344, 347 – 349*
  defined, 302
  discrete-time proxy for, 341
  expected, 321, 347
  and obsolescence, 302
  versus physical life, 302, 305
  in steady growth, 308, 324
    comparative dynamic properties of, 315 – 318, 324, 342*n.*, 352*n.*, 368, 383
    determination of (*see* Growth model with putty-clay capital, determination of economic life of capital in)
    discrete-time proxy for, 341
    relation of, to factor proportion, 319
Capital, obsolescence of:
  defined, 302
  economic life of capital and, 302
  malleability of capital and, 289*n.*, 302
  marginal vintage and, 305, 338 – 340
  putty-clay capital and (*see* Capital, putty-clay, obsolescence of capital and)
Capital, putty-clay:
  consequence of, for capital aggregation, 302 – 303
  economic life of, defined, 302
    (*See also* Capital, economic life of)
  equi-marginal-product rule and, 302 – 303
  expectations and, 287, 302, 306, 319 – 320, 322, 323, 327 – 328, 337, 346 – 347, 351
  growth model of (*see* Growth model with putty-clay capital)
  hypothesis of, 300 – 301
  isoquants under, 301 – 302
  obsolescence of capital and, 302, 305, 307, 308, 320*n.*, 323, 338
  production functions under, 301 – 302
    ex ante, 301 – 302, 304 – 305
    ex post, 301 – 302, 305
Capital, putty-putty:
  defined, 302
  expectations and, 302, 351
  isoquants under, 302
Capital, vintage set of:
  composition of, under putty-putty, 302, 345 – 346
  defined, 307
  determination of, 307, 339 – 340, 347
  difficulty in formulating, 337
  response of, to policy shocks, 344 – 346

Capital, vintage set of (*Cont.*):
  in steady growth, 308, 323
Capital-altering progress (*see* Technical progress, capital-altering)
Capital-augmenting technical progress (*see* Technical progress, capital-augmenting)
Capital-generalized constant returns, defined, 297
Capital rental, 5, 95
  (*See also* User cost)
Capital stock:
  aggregate (*see* Capital stock, aggregate)
  effect of, on net investment, 173 – 176
Capital stock, aggregate:
  change in, 291
  construction of, under embodied technical progress, 287 – 290, 296 – 300
    conditions for, 296 – 297, 337, 363
    conflict of with steady growth, 303 – 304
    disembodied technical progress and, 296, 298, 299
    given CES vintage production function, 297 – 300
    labor allocation rule and, 288, 294, 302
    labor augmentation as obstacle to, 298 – 299, 302 – 303
    putty-clay capital as obstacle to, 302 – 303
  in current efficiency units: defined, 291
    growth rate of, in steady growth, 293
  defined, 275*n.*, 286
  under disembodied technical progress, 290, 296, 298, 299
  in period-zero efficiency units: defined, 289, 291 – 292
    growth rate of, in steady growth, 293 – 294
    price of, in steady growth, 294 – 295
  validity of, under embodied technical progress, 286, 289 – 290, 296 – 300
Capital stock adjustment principle as flexible accelerator, 178
  (*See also* Accelerator, flexible)
Certainty equivalence theorem, 213, 219 – 220, 242 – 243
  (*See also* Policy decisions)
Chain rule of differentiation:
  exemplified, 362
  stated, 362
Cobb-Douglas production function (*see* Production function, Cobb-Douglas)
Coefficient of determination, defined, 391
Coefficient of expectation:
  defined, 110
  similarity of, to acceleration coefficient, 114
Coefficient of variation:
  defined, 341
  tables of, *341, 343 – 344, 347 – 349*
  zero value for, meaning of, 342
Coincident indicators, composite index of (*see* Composite index, of coincident indicators)

Comparative advantage, law of:
  in international economics, 205
  in pairing instruments and targets, 205 – 208, 219
Composite index:
  of coincident indicators: components of, 85*n.*
    particulars in construction of, 85*n.*, 394, 395
  construction of, 79 – 82, 84 – 85, 393 – 395
  focus of, 80
  of lagging indicators: components of, 85*n.*
    particulars in construction of, 85*n.*, 394, 395
  of leading indicators: components of, 83 – 84
    particulars in construction of, 84 – 85, 394, 395
  performance of, 85 – 86, 193
  rationale for, 84
Concavity:
  curvature of function and, 363, 365
  defined, 363
  derivative and, 363, 365
  in steady growth solution, 312 – 313, 363
Constant elasticity of substitution (CES)
    production function (*see* Production
    function, constant elasticity of
    substitution)
Constant growth rate rule (*see* Policy rule,
    constant growth rate rule as)
Consumption:
  absolute income hypothesis of, 119, 142, 150, 160
    (*See also* Consumption theory of Keynes)
  cyclical phases of, *88, 90 – 91*
  data on, from U.S. Commerce, 125 – 128
  estate motive and, 144, 154
  estimates of, by Kuznets, 120 – 121
  as expenditure concept, 141*n.*, 142, 156, 158, 159, 161
  forecasts of, 123 – 125
  habit persistence notion of, 131, 138 – 139, 141 – 142, 160
    continuous versus discontinuous, 138 – 139, 141 – 142, 160
    (*See also* Consumption theory of Brown;
      Consumption theory of Davis;
      Consumption theory of Duesenberry;
      Consumption theory of Houthakker and
      Taylor; Consumption theory of
      Modigliani; Consumption theory of
      Smyth and Jackson)
  income distribution and, 160
  inertia in, 132, 135 – 136, 138 – 139, 151, 154, 161, 187
    causes of, 138, 142, 160
  inflationary expectations and, 160
  lags in (*see* Lags, in consumption)
  life-cycle hypothesis of, 154 – 155, 160
    (*See also* Consumption theory of Ando,
      Brumberg, and Modigliani)

Consumption (*Cont.*):
  longsightedness versus shortsightedness
    hypotheses of, 156, 158 – 160
  money illusion and, 160
  permanent (*see* Permanent consumption)
  permanent income hypothesis of, 143 – 153, 160
    (*See also* Consumption theory of
      Friedman)
  psychological law of, 20, 21*n.*, 119, 131
  ratchet effect in, 135, 141
  real-balance effect and, 160
  relative income hypothesis of, 132 – 136, 160
    (*See also* Consumption theory of
      Duesenberry; Consumption theory of
      Modigliani)
  reverse lightning bolt effect in, 141
    contrasted with ratchet effect, 141
  as service flow, 141*n.*, 142 – 143, 147, 148, 154, 156, 158, 159, 161
    unit rental for, 170*n.*
  shortsightedness hypothesis of, 156 – 160
    versus longsightedness hypothesis of, 156, 158 – 160
    (*See also* Consumption theory of Ball and
      Drake)
  types of, 24 – 25, 72, 142, 147, 160 – 161
    in permanent income hypothesis, 147
  uncertainty, effect of, on, 143, 147, 154, 156
  unit rental for, 170*n.*
  utility maximization and, 142 – 146, 154, 156 – 158, 366, 374 – 376
  wealth and, 143, 144, 147, 154, 156 – 157
    (*See also* Consumption theory of Ando,
      Brumberg, and Modigliani;
      Consumption theory of Ball and Drake;
      Consumption theory of Friedman;
      Consumption theory of Hamburger)
Consumption function:
  of Ando, Brumberg, and Modigliani, 154 – 155
    variant of, 155 – 156
  average propensity to consume in, 20, 119, 125
    constancy of, 120 – 122
  of Ball and Drake, 158
  of Brown, 139
  of classics, 10, 11*n.*
  of Davis, 137
  of Duesenberry, 133
  estimated (*see* Regression analysis, of
    consumption function)
  of Friedman, 147 – 148, 151
  of Hamburger, 143
  of Houthakker and Taylor, 141
  of Husby, 153*n.*
  in intertial multiplier-accelerator interaction
    model, 188

Consumption function (*Cont.*):
  of Keynes, 20, 119
  long-run versus short-run (proportional
    versus nonproportional), 120, 125,
    129–130, 133–140, 152–153,
    155–156, 158–159, 161
  marginal propensity to consume in, 20,
    24–25, 119, 124*n.*, 125, 129, 133,
    136–138, 140–141, 150–152, 159,
    161–162
    as function of income, 20, 128–129, 134,
      153*n.*
  of Modigliani, 136
  of partial adjustment model, 161
  ratchet effect in, 135
  real-balance effect in, 45
  reverse lightning bolt effect in, 141
  of Smithies, 129
  of Smyth and Jackson, 142
  trend term in, 128–129
Consumption theory of Ando, Brumberg, and
    Modigliani, 154–155, 160
  compared with theory of Friedman,
    154–155, 160
  definition of consumption in, 154
  estate motive in, 154
  stock adjustment in, 155
  uncertainty, effect of, in, 154
  wealth basis of, 154
  (*See also* Consumption theory of
    Modigliani)
Consumption theory of Ball and Drake,
    156–160, 375
  compared with theory of Friedman,
    158–160
  definition of consumption in, 156, 158, 159
  versus longsightedness theories, 156,
    158–160
  uncertainty, effect of, in, 156
  wealth in, 156–158
Consumption theory of Brown, 138–141, 160,
    391, 392
  continuous versus discontinuous habit in,
    138–139
  hysteresis basis of, 138
Consumption theory of classics, 10
Consumption theory of Davis, 137–138,
    160
  previous peak consumption in, 137
  relation of, to theories of Duesenberry and
    Modigliani, 137–138, 160
Consumption theory of Duesenberry,
    132–138, 141, 160
  compared with theory of Modigliani,
    136–137, 138*n.*, 160
  contrasted with theory of Keynes, 132
  previous peak income in, 132
  psychological basis of, 132
  ratchet effect in, 135, 141
  relative income in, 132

Consumption theory of Friedman, 143–155,
    160, 366, 374–376, 380, 384, 385, 387,
    391
  compared with theory of Ando, Brumberg,
    and Modigliani, 154–155, 160
  compared with theory of Ball and Drake,
    158–160
  definition of consumption in, 143, 147,
    148
  effect of income in versus that in theory of
    Keynes, 150
  estate motive in, 144
  expectational orientation of, 144, 146
  flow adjustment in, 155
  measured quantities in, defined, 147
  motives for saving in, 143–144, 147
  permanent consumption in, defined, 147
  permanent income in: adaptive adjustment
    mechanism for, 149
    as distributed lag, 149–150, 153, 181,
      384, 385, 391
    as return on wealth, 147
    with secular growth component, 149–150,
      153
  relationships among permanent and
    transitory quantities, 147–148, 150,
    387
  transitory quantities in, defined, 147
  uncertainty, effect of, in, 147
  wealth basis of, 144, 147
Consumption theory of Hamburger,
    142–143
  service flow view in, 142–143
  uncertainty, effect of, in, 143
  wealth basis of, 143
Consumption theory of Houthakker and
    Taylor, 141, 160
Consumption theory of Husby, 153*n.*
Consumption theory of Keynes, 20, 119–128,
    142, 150, 160, 162
  as absolute income hypothesis, 119, 142,
    150, 160
  effect of income in versus that in theory of
    Friedman, 150
  empirical tests and, 119–128
  implication of, for instantaneous adjustment,
    162
Consumption theory of Modigliani, 136–138,
    141, 160
  compared with theory of Duesenberry,
    136–137, 138*n.*, 160
  cyclical income index in, 136
  (*See also* Consumption theory of Ando,
    Brumberg, and Modigliani)
Consumption theory of partial adjustment,
    161–162
  definition of consumption in, 161
  theory of Keynes and, 162
Consumption theory of Smithies, 128–131
  structural shifts explained in, 128–129

Consumption theory of Smyth and Jackson, 141–142, 392
  definition of consumption in, 141*n.*
  reverse lightning bolt effect in, 141
Convergence, defined, 56
Convergence parameter:
  defined, 329
  relation of, to disequilibrium half-life, 330–332
Convergence time:
  for alternative capital models: catch-up phenomenon in, 355–356
    comparison of, 350, 354–356
  determinants of, 326–327, 329–337, 342–346, 348–350, 352–357
    compared across capital models, 345–346, 350, 352–354
  early studies of, 326–327
    basis of, 327
  estimates of, 231–237, 326–328, 330–335, 353, 355–356
    sensitivity of, 327, 328, 357–358
    tables of, *233, 236, 331, 333, 335, 353, 355*
    under feedback controls, 231–237
  lack of consensus about, 327, 357–358
  measures of, 233*n.*, 293*n.*, 329*n.*, 341, 342, 351*n.*, 352
  for neoclassical growth model with embodied technical progress, 328–334, 345–346, 350, 352–356
  for putty-clay growth model (*see* Growth model with putty-clay capital, convergence time for)
  speed of adjustment and, 326–327, 329
Convex combination:
  defined, 384
  properties of, 385
Correlation coefficient:
  defined, 387
  properties of, 387
  relation of, to covariance, 387
Covariance:
  defined, 386
  joint probability density and, 386
  relation of, to correlation coefficient, 387
  relation of, to variance, 386
Credit, easy versus tight, 166–167
Cross-section study:
  defined, 388
  of dissaving, 132
Crowding-out effect, defined, 45–46
Cycle:
  anatomy of, 67–68
  lags, role of, in, 60–65, 192
  phases of: by Mitchell, 68
    view of Schumpeter on, 68
  types of, 65–68
  view of Keynes on, 18*n.*
  (*See also* Cycle, theory of)

Cycle, theory of:
  by Frisch, 99–100, 106
    erratic shocks, role of, in, 99
    tendency for damped cycles in, 99
  by Hicks, 106–108
    asymmetric accelerator in, 106–107
    buffers in, 106–108
    ceiling in, 106, 108
    floor in, 106–108
    temporal movements in, 107–108
  with inertial multiplier-accelerator interaction, 188–192
    consumption function of Ball and Drake in, 188
    distributed lags in, 187
    as generalization of multiplier-accelerator (Samuelson-type) interaction theory, 188, 189
    inertia, effects of, in, 186–187, 190–192
    relation between inertial parameters in, 189–191
    temporal movements in, 190–191
  by Metzler, 108–115
    coefficient of expectation in, 110, 114
    inventory basis of, 108–110
    planned versus realized inventory change in, 110–111
    relation of, to multiplier-accelerator (Samuelson-type) interaction theory, 114
    simple accelerator in, 111, 114
    temporal movements in, 111–115
  with multiplier-accelerator (Samuelson-type) interaction, 99–106, 186–192, 404–405
    asymmetry in, 105–106
    destabilizing acceleration effect in, 105–106
    lag structure of, 99–100
    relation of inventory movements to output movements in, 102–104
    relation of, to theory of cycle by Metzler, 114
    solution to difference equation in, 404–405
    as special case in theory of inertial multiplier-accelerator interaction, 188, 189
    stabilizing multiplier effect in, 105
    temporal movements in, 102–105
  by Schumpeter, 68–70
    composite wave in, 69–70
Cyclical income index:
  defined, 136
  properties of, 136

Demand, aggregate, components of, 26
Demand price of capital:
  compared with supply price of capital, 172
  defined, 171–172

Derivative:
  concavity and, 363, 365
  cross-partial (*see* Derivative, cross-partial)
  defined, 361
  difference quotient and, 361, 378 – 379
  of higher orders: defined, 363
    notation of, 363
  implicit (*see* Derivative, implicit)
  integral and, 377 – 379
  of integral, 291*n.*
  of inverse functions, 382
  l'Hopital's rule and, 364
  as limit, 361
  of linearly homogeneous functions, 368 – 369
  in maxima or minima of functions (*see*
      Function, constrained maxima or
      minima of; Function, unconstrained
      maxima or minima of)
  monotonicity and, 363
  of natural exponential function, 382 – 384
  of natural log function, 381
  notation of, 361 – 362
  partial (*see* Derivative, partial)
  properties of, 362
    chain rule, 362
    power rule, 362
  in regression analysis, 389
  as slope, 361, 363, 365
  total (*see* Derivative, total)
Derivative, cross-partial:
  as cross-marginal product, 5*n.*, 365
  as cross-marginal utility, 144, 145*n.*, 366
  defined, 365
  interpretation of, 365 – 366
  notation of, 365
  second partial derivative and, 369
  Young's theorem of, 365 – 366
Derivative, implicit:
  defined, 367
  of higher orders, 367
  partial derivative and, 367
  slope of indifference curves and, 367 – 368
  slope of isoquants and, 368
  total differential and, 367
Derivative, partial:
  concavity and, 365
  cross-partial form of, 365
    (*See also* Derivative, cross-partial)
  defined, 365
  Euler's theorem and, 369
  of higher orders, 365
  implicit derivative and, 367
  for linearly homogeneous functions,
      368 – 369
  as marginal product, 5*n.*, 365
  as marginal utility, 144, 366
  in maxima or minima of functions (*see*
      Function, constrained maxima or
      minima of; Function, unconstrained
      maxima or minima of)

Derivative, partial (*Cont.*):
  notation of, 365
    for single argument, 5*n.*, 204*n.*, 226, 365,
      370 – 371
  properties of, 365
  in regression analysis, 389
  as slope, 365
  versus total derivative, 365, 366
  total differential and, 366
Derivative, total:
  defined, 366
  versus partial derivative, 365, 366
  total differential and, 366
Desired growth rate, defined, 281*n.*
Difference equation:
  defined, 400
  order of, 400
  solution procedure for: auxiliary equation in,
      401
    described, 400 – 402
    exemplified, 402 – 405
  types of, 400
Difference quotient:
  defined, 361
  derivative and, 361, 378 – 379
Differential:
  defined, 366
  ratio of, as derivative, 366
  total: defined, 366
    in establishing implicit derivative, 367
    interpretation of, 366
    partial derivative and, 366
    total derivative and, 366
Diffusion index:
  construction of, 79, 82 – 83
  focus of, 82
  types of, 82
Disequilibrium half-life:
  defined, 330 – 332
  relation of, to convergence parameter,
      330 – 332
Distributed lags (*see* Lags, distributed)
Dummy variables:
  in consumption, 139*n.*, 142, 392
  as interactive variables, 142, 392
  as shift variables, 139*n.*, 142, 392
Durbin-Watson statistic:
  in consumption, 122*n.* – 123*n.*
  defined, 391
  described, 391 – 392
Dynamic (disequilibrium) multipliers (*see*
      Multipliers, dynamic)
Dynamics:
  defined, 45, 51
  equilibrium and, 55, 251
  hallmark of, 51

Econometric models:
  described, 72

Econometric models (*Cont.*):
dynamic multipliers in, 72−75, 193
list of, 73
predictions by, 74−75, 86, 193, 198−199
Econometrics:
defined, 72*n.*, 387
multiplier estimation and, 33*n.*−34*n.*
(*See also* Regression analysis)
Economic life of capital (*see* Capital, economic life of)
Efficiency unit:
in constructing aggregate capital stock, 289
defined, 264
Elasticity, arc, 80
Elasticity of factor substitution:
for CES production function, 96, 270
derived, 396−397
defined, 396
as determinant of convergence time, 326−327, 334−337, 344−346, 349−350, 354
marginal rate of technical substitution and, 396
as measure of isoquant curvature, 396−397
under putty-clay capital: ex ante, defined, 301, 305
ex post, defined, 301
restriction by Sheshinski on, 313
Employment, cyclical phases of, *88*
(*See also* Full employment)
Endogenous variable, defined, 25
Equi-marginal-product rule:
for aggregation under embodied technical progress, 288*n.*, 296, 300
defined, 288
rationale for, 288, 294, 296
scrapping of capital and, 302
violation of under putty-clay capital, 302−303
Equilibrium multipliers (*see* Multipliers, equilibrium)
Erratic shocks, cycle theory of, 99−100, 106
Estimation (*see* Regression analysis)
Euler's theorem, stated, 369
Exogenous variable, defined, 25
Expectations:
adaptive rationality (*see* Adaptive rationality)
bias in, 238, 244−246, 384, 390
of consumption sales, 110
importance of, under putty-clay capital, 302
and investment, 164, 176, 277−278
liquidity preference schedule and, 13−15, 19*n.*
perfect foresight, 111*n.*, 244, 320*n.*
rational (*see* Rational expectations)
static: defined, 280
in growth model of Robinson, 280
in putty-clay growth model (*see* Growth model with putty-clay capital, static expectations in)

Expectations, static (*Cont.*):
under putty-putty capital, 351
as special case of adaptive rationality, 322, 347
in study of convergence time, 327−328 337, 351
as zero foresight, 320*n.*
in study of convergence time, 327−328, 337, 346−347, 351
trade cycle and, 18*n.*
during transition to rational expectations, 245−246, 384
unimportance of, under malleability of capital ex post, 302
Extraneous solution, defined, 271*n.*
Extrema of functions (*see* Function, constrained maxima or minima of; Function, unconstrained maxima or minima of)

Factor proportion, defined, 96, 251, 288
Feedback controls of policy (*see* Policy rule, feedback control as)
Fine tuning, defined, 227*n.*
Flexible accelerator (*see* Accelerator, flexible)
Forecast discrepancies, causes of, 74−75, 193
Forecast errors in consumption, 123−125
Forecasts:
ex ante, 124
ex post, 123−124
and policy decisions (*see* Policy decisions, forecasts and)
Formula flexibility as feedback control, 228
Full employment:
in convergence time analysis, 328, 338−339, 344, 347
defined, 6
in growth model with putty-clay capital (*see* Growth model with putty-clay capital, full employment in)
and growth model of Robinson, 281−282
in model of classics, 6−8
natural growth rate and, 258−259
output: as ceiling output in model of Hicks, 106
defined, 42−43
as policy target, 199, 228
threats to, in model of Keynes, 16−20, 22
(*See also* Employment)
Function:
antiderivative as, 377
argument of, defined, 359
concave downward: defined, 363
illustrated, 363
concave upward: defined, 363
illustrated, 363
concavity of, defined, 363
(*See also* Concavity)

Function (*Cont.*):
   constrained maxima or minima of (*see*
      Function, constrained maxima or
      minima of)
   as convex combination: defined, 384
      properties of, 385
   estimation of (*see* Regression analysis)
   explicit, defined, 367
   fundamental direction of, defined, 371
   homogeneous: defined, 368
      properties of, 368−369, 374−375
   implicit, defined, 367
   inflection point of, defined, 369
   integral as, 377, 379
   integrand as, defined, 378
   inverse, defined, 382
   as linear combination, defined, 384
   linearly homogeneous: defined, 368
      Euler's theorem and, 369
      properties of, 368−369, 374−375
   loss, 199, 242
   mathematical expectation of (*see*
      Mathematical expectation)
   maxima or minima of (*see* Function,
      constrained maxima or minima of;
      Function, unconstrained maxima or
      minima of)
   monotone-decreasing: defined, 363
      illustrated, 363
   monotone-increasing: defined, 363
      illustrated, 363
   monotonicity of: defined, 363
      (*See also* Monotonicity)
   natural exponential: defined, 382
      derivative of, 382−384
      generalization of, 383−384
      integral of, 384
      Napierian constant and, 383
      properties of, 382−384
      relation of, to natural log function, 382
   natural log: defined, 381
      derivative of, 381
      integral and, 380−381
      Napierian constant and, 381, 383
      properties of, 381−383
      rationale for, 380−381
      relation of, to natural exponential
      function, 382
   objective, defined, 370
   as probability density, 385
   as probability distribution, 385
   quadratic loss (*see* Quadratic loss function)
   saddle point of, defined, 373
   stationary point of, defined, 370
   unconstrained maxima or minima of (*see*
      Function, unconstrained maxima or
      minima of)
Function, constrained maxima or minima of:
   Lagrange test for, 145n., 375−376
      Lagrange multiplier in, 375−376
      necessary condition in, 376

Function, constrained maxima or minima of,
      Lagrange test for (*Cont.*):
      sufficient condition in, 376
   problem of, described, 374
   substitution test for, 374−375
Function, unconstrained maxima or minima of:
   global, defined, 369
   local: defined, 369
      first-order condition for, 370, 373
      under homogeneity, 96n., 369, 373
      necessary condition for, 370, 372−373
      properties of, 370
      second-order condition for, 370, 373
      sufficient condition for, 370, 372−373
      test for, 370−373
   in regression analysis, 389
Functional finance (*see* Policy,
      countercyclical, functional finance as)
Fundamental theorem of calculus, stated,
   379

Great depression, the:
   average propensity to consume in, 120−122
   consumption and income in, 120−122,
      125−126
   dissaving in, 132
   stock market crash and, 3, 78−79
   unemployment in, 3, 75
Growth, steady:
   conflict of, with capital aggregation,
      303−304
   defined, 257, 308
Growth model:
   focus of, 251
   production function, role of, in, 251
   (*See also* Growth model, neoclassical;
      Growth model of Domar; Growth
      model of Harrod; Growth model of
      Kaldor; Growth model with putty-clay
      capital; Growth model of Robinson)
Growth model, neoclassical, 263−273,
   283−285
   adjustment mechanism inherent in,
      266−267
   with CES production function, 269−273
      Cobb-Douglas variant of (*see* Production
      function, Cobb-Douglas, in neoclassical
      growth model)
      restrictions on saving coefficient and,
      271−273
   compared with growth model of Kaldor,
      275, 278n., 279, 282
   compared with putty-clay growth model,
      309, 310n., 314−315, 319n., 345−346,
      350, 352−356
   with embodied technical progress,
      290−296, 328−334, 367, 382
      adjustment mechanism inherent in, 293,
      328
      basis for steady growth in, 303−304

Growth model, neoclassical, with embodied
 technical progress (*Cont.*):
 convergence time for, 328 – 334,
  345 – 346, 350, 352 – 356
 full capacity in, 288
 full employment in, 290, 328
 investment function in, 290
 malleability of capital in, 288
 physical deterioration function in, 288, 328
 production function in, 287 – 290, 328
 saving function in, 290, 328
 similarity of, to growth model without
  embodied technical progress, 295 – 296
 technical progress, types of, in, 287 – 288,
  293, 328, 330
 full capacity in, 266*n.*
 full employment in, 266*n.*
 Harrod neutrality and, 268 – 269, 369
 Inada boundary conditions, role of, in,
  267 – 268
 investment function in, 265
 marginal productivity theory of income
  distribution and, 268, 273, 283, 369
 prices in, 268
 production function in (*see* Production
  function, in neoclassical growth model)
 saving function in (*see* Saving function, in
  neoclassical growth model)
 with saving function of Kaldor, 283 – 285,
  385
  additional information on production
   function and, 283, 285
  Cobb-Douglas production function and,
   284 – 285, 385
 similarity of, to growth model with embodied
  technical progress, 295 – 296
 without technical progress, 268 – 269
 technical progress, type of, in, (*see* Technical
  progress, in neoclassical growth model)
Growth model of Domar, 260 – 263
 full-capacity requirement in, 261 – 262
 investment, dual nature of, in, 260 – 262
 production function in, 263
 productivity ratio in, defined, 261
 required growth rate in, defined, 262
 saving function in, 262
 similarity of, to growth model of Harrod,
  262 – 263
Growth model of Harrod, 257 – 260
 acceleration coefficient (*see* Acceleration
  coefficient, in growth model of Harrod)
 adjustment mechanism, absence of, from,
  259, 265
 compared with growth model of Robinson,
  282
 full capacity and, 259 – 260
 full employment and, 258 – 260
 inflation in, 259
 instability of equilibrium path in, 258
 investment function in, 257 – 258

Growth model of Harrod (*Cont.*):
 knife-edge path in, 258*n.*
 natural growth rate in, defined, 258 – 259
 production function in, 251, 260, 263
 saving function in, 257
 secular exhilaration in, 258 – 259
 secular stagnation in, 258 – 259
 similarity of, to growth model of Domar,
  262 – 263
 technical progress, type of, in, 259
 warranted growth rate in: alternative
  expressions for, 260
  defined, 258
Growth model of Kaldor, 274 – 279
 adjustment mechanism inherent in, 278, 279
 compared with growth model of Robinson,
  281 – 282
 compared with neoclassical growth model,
  275, 278*n.*, 279, 282
 full capacity in, 279
 full employment in, 279
 income distribution mechanism in, 275 – 277
 investment function in, 277 – 278, 279*n.*
 technical progress function as determinant
  of, 277, 278
 saving function in, 275 – 277
 technical progress function in, 251,
  274 – 275, 278*n.*, 286, 381 – 382
Growth model with putty-clay capital,
  304 – 324, 337 – 358
 under adaptive rationality, 287, 320 – 324,
  346 – 350
  adjustments to structure of required,
   320 – 323, 346 – 347
  full employment in, 323, 347
  properties of, 320, 346 – 347
  steady growth solution for, 323 – 324, 347
 comparative dynamic properties of,
  315 – 318, 324, 342*n.*, 352*n.*, 368, 383
  tables showing, *341, 343 – 344, 347 – 349*
 compared with neoclassical growth model
  (*see* Growth model, neoclassical,
  compared with putty-clay growth
  model)
 convergence time for (*see* Growth model
  with putty-clay capital, convergence
  time for)
 determination of economic life of capital in,
  310 – 313, 323 – 324, 360, 363, 384
  restrictions on saving coefficient and,
   311 – 315, 318 – 319, 342*n.*, 351 – 352
 discrete-time variant of: under adaptive
  rationality, 346 – 347
  under static expectations, 337 – 339
 full employment in, 307, 308, 323,
  338 – 339, 347
 investment function in, 307, 323, 338, 346
 optimization procedure in: under adaptive
  rationality, 321 – 323
  under static expectations, 306

Growth model with putty-clay capital (*Cont.*)
  physical deterioration function in, 305, 320, 338
  production functions in: ex ante CES, 304–305
    ex post, 305
  relation of Harrod neutrality to steady growth in, 308*n*.
  saving function in, 307
  static expectations in, 287, 306, 319, 327–328, 337, 351
    awkwardness of, 319
    bias of, 319
  vintage set in, 307, 308, 323, 337–340, 347
    (*See also* Capital, vintage set of)
Growth model with putty-clay capital, convergence time for:
  under adaptive rationality, 346–350
  compared with that under putty-putty capital, 350, 354–356
  determinants of, 342–346, 349–350, 352–354
    compared with those under putty-putty capital, 345–346, 350, 352–354
    elasticity of substitution as, 344–346, 349–350, 354
  difficulty in formulating vintage set and, 337
  elasticity of substitution and, 344–346, 349–350, 354
    linkage compared with that under putty-putty capital, 345–346, 349–350, 354
  policy shocks and, 342, 351
  along response path, 337
  similarity of, under alternative expectation regimes, 349–350
  simulation analysis of, 337–342, 346–349, 351–352, 379
  under static expectations, 342–346, 350–356
  steady growth simulations and, 341–342, 347–349
    accuracy of, 342, 349
  wrong-way movement and, 344–345
Growth model of Robinson, 279–282, 364
  adjustment mechanism, absence of, from, 282
  compared with growth model of Harrod and Domar, 282
  compared with growth model of Kaldor, 281–282
  full employment and, 281–282
  income distribution mechanism in, 280, 282
  inflation in, 282
  investment function in, 280, 360
  Malthusian misery in, 282
  monetary policy in, 282
  natural (possible) growth rate in, 281
  saving function in, 280
  warranted (desired) growth rate in, 281

Habit persistence hypothesis (*see* Consumption, habit persistence notion of; Consumption theory of Brown; Consumption theory of Davis; Consumption theory of Duesenberry; Consumption theory of Houthakker and Taylor; Consumption theory of Modigliani; Consumption theory of Smyth and Jackson)
Hicksian stock equilibrium condition, stated, 260*n*.
Hoarding:
  view of classics on, 8–9
  view of Keynes on, 13

Income:
  cyclical phases of, 88, *90–91*
  disposable: cyclical phases of, 88, 90
    data on, from U.S. Commerce, 125–128
    defined, 10*n*.
    estimates of, by Goldsmith et al., 120–122
    relation of, to gross national product (GNP), 26
  estimates of: by Goldsmith et al., 120–122
    by Kuznets, 120–121
  permanent (*see* Permanent income)
  types of, in permanent income hypothesis, 147
  (*See also* Output)
Income determination model:
  of classics, 4–12
  of Keynes, 12–23
    compared with model of classics, 48
    short-run nature of, 22
Income distribution:
  marginal productivity theory of: in neoclassical growth model, 268, 273, 283, 369
    properties of, 268, 273, 283, 369
    rejection by Kaldor of, 274, 275
  theory of Kaldor, 275–277
Indeterminate forms:
  defined, 364
  l'Hopital's rule and, 364
  list of, 364
Index (*see* Composite index; Diffusion index)
Indifference curves for quadratic loss function, 200–201, 215
  marginal rate of substitution and, 200
Inertia:
  as cause of cyclical response, 190–192
  in consumption (*see* Consumption, inertia in)
  dynamic response and, 163, 186–192, 357
  in investment, 163, 186
Inflation:
  constant growth rate rule and, 223–224
  cyclical phases of, *89–91*
  expectations of, and consumption, 160

Inflation (*Cont.*):
  feedback controls and, 231, 236−237
  functional finance and, 221−222
  in growth model of Harrod, 259
  in growth model of Robinson, 282
    monetary policy control of, 282
  as subject of testimony by Secretary of
    Treasury Miller, 198−199
Inflection point:
  defined, 369
  test for, 370
Initial conditions:
  in discrete-time putty-clay growth model,
    339, 341, 347, 352
  in neoclassical growth model with embodied
    technical progress, 329
Innovation variable in policy decisions,
    defined, 211, 213−214, 238
Instrumental variable of policy, defined, 201
Integral:
  definite: defined, 377
    fundamental theorem of calculus and, 379
    notation of, 377−378
  indefinite: defined, 379
    notation of, 379
  interpretation of: as antiderivative,
    377−379
    as area, 377−378
    as sum, 377−378
  multiple, 380
  of natural exponential function, 384
  natural log function and, 380−381
  properties of, 379−380
  relation of, to integrand, 378−379
    constant of integration and, 379
Interest rate:
  cyclical phases of, *89*
  defined, 27
  normal, and shape of liquidity preference
    schedule, 13−15
  prime: defined, 183
    risk premium and, 183, 279*n*.
  real: defined, 144
  relation of: to bond price, 14, 39*n*., 43*n*.
    to marginal cost of funds, 183
    to marginal efficiency of investment,
      171−172
    to unit capital rental, 168−170
    to user cost, 169−170
  as target of functional finance, 222
  temporal movement of, in multiplier model,
    dynamic version, 57−60, 63−65
Inventories, temporal movement of:
  over cyclical phases, *89, 90*
  in model of Frisch, 108−109
  in model of Hicks, 108−109
  in model of Metzler, 109, 111−115
  in model of multipler: dynamic version,
    56−62, 65
    static version, 56*n*.

Inventories, temporal movement of (*Cont.*):
  in model of multiplier-accelerator
    (Samuelson-type) interaction,
    103−104, 108−109
Inventory decision rule:
  in model of Frisch, 108−109
  in model of Hicks, 108−109
  in model of Metzler, 109−111
  in model of multiplier, dynamic version, 57,
    59
  in model of multiplier-accelerator
    (Samuelson-type) interaction,
    108−109
Inventory investment:
  cyclical phases of, *88*
  ex ante versus ex post, 110−111
  simple accelerator in, 111
Investment:
  autonomous and growth model of Harrod
    and Domar, 263*n*.
  cyclical phases of, *88, 91*
  dual nature of, in growth model of Domar,
    260−262
  expectations and, 164, 176, 277−278
  finance considerations in, 164−165,
    183−185
    combined with capacity considerations,
      185−186, 277−278
    permissive role of profits and, 184−185
    (*See also* Profits principle)
  inertia in, 163, 186
  in inventories (*see* Inventory investment)
  lags in (*see* Lags, in investment)
  marginal efficiency of: analogy of, with
    marginal revenue, 171, 183
    defined, 171
    relation of: to interest rate, 171−172
      to marginal cost of funds, 184−186
      to marginal efficiency of capital, 167,
        171
      to marginal product of capital, 172−177
      to supply price of capital, 171, 173, 175
    schedule of, 171, 173−174
    (*See also* Investment theory, of
      Duesenberry; Investment theory, of
      Keynes)
  output considerations in (*see* Acceleration
    principle; Accelerator, flexible;
    Accelerator, simple)
  real-balance effect and, 45
  theory of interfaced with theory of capital,
    167−177
  types of, 72, 163, 263*n*.
    gross versus net, 163, 187, 251−252, 295
    (*See also* Acceleration principle;
      Accelerator, flexible; Accelerator,
      simple; Profits principle)
Investment function:
  acceleration principle and, 94
  of classics, 9−10

Investment function (*Cont.*):
  estimated, 33, 95*n.*, 167*n.*, 391
  flexible accelerator form of, 177, 178,
      181–182
    in model of inertial multiplier-accelerator
        interaction, 187–188
  of Hicks, 106–107, 164
  implied from link of marginal efficiency and
      marginal cost of funds, 185–186
  implied from link of marginal efficiency and
      marginal product, 173
  of Kaldor (*see* Growth model of Kaldor,
      investment function in)
  of Keynes, 17–18
    marginal efficiency of capital schedule as,
        17*n.*
  in neoclassical growth model, 265
    with embodied technical progress, 290
  in putty-clay growth model, 307, 323
    discrete-time variant of, 338, 346
  real-balance effect in, 45
  of Robinson, 280, 360
  simple accelerator form of, 95
    in growth model of Harrod, 257–258
    in model of Frisch, 99
    in model of Hicks, 106–107
    in model of Metzler, 111, 114
    in model of multiplier-accelerator
        (Samuelson-type) interaction, 100,
        188
Investment theory:
  of Carver, 165
    permanent output change in, 165
  of Clark, 165–166
    asymmetry in investment response and,
        166
    possibility of deficient or excessive
        capacity in, 166
  of classics, 9–10
    role of interest rate in, 9
    stability of investment function in, 9
  of Duesenberry, 183–186
    marginal cost of funds schedule in, 184
      effect of profit on, 184
    sources of investment funds in, 183–184
  of Hicks, 106–107, 164, 165
    as generalization of theory of Keynes,
        164
  of Kaldor, 277–279
    acceleration consideration in, 277
    finance consideration in, 278
      stability of growth model of Kaldor and,
          278, 279
  of Keynes, 17–19, 164, 167–168, 173,
      175–176
    generalized under Hicks, 164
    instability of investment function in,
        18–19
    interest rate, role of, in, 17
    stock of capital and, 168, 173, 175–176

Investment theory (*Cont.*):
  of Tinbergen, 164–165
    link between profit and aggregate income
        in, 165
    multiple roles of profit in, 164–165
IS curve:
  commodity market conditions and,
      36–37
  confronted by LM curve, 37–38
    and BB curve, 41
  in model of multiplier, dynamic version,
      59–60, 403–404
  negative slope of, 35–36
    explained, 35–36
    unidirectional movement of output and,
        403–404
  shifts in, 41–42
    linked to shifts in LM curve, 45–46
    under real-balance effect, 45
IS equation:
  confronted by LM equation, 29
  defined, 28
  under real-balance effect, 45

Knife-edge growth path, 258*n.*
Koyck distributed lag, 149–150, 160,
    240–242

Labor demand curve:
  in model of classics, 6
  in model of Keynes, 22
  in putty-clay growth model, 307, 308, 323
    discrete-time variant of, 338, 339, 346
Labor market equilibrium:
  in model of classics, 7–8
  model of Keynes and, 22
  in putty-clay growth model, 307, 308, 323
    discrete-time variant of, 338–340,
        346–347
Labor supply curve:
  in model of classics, 6–7
  model of Keynes and, 22
  in putty-clay growth model, 307, 308, 323
    discrete-time variant of, 338, 339, 346
Lagging indicators, composite index of (*see*
    Composite index, lagging indicators of)
Lagrange method of undetermined multiplier
    (*see* Function, constrained maxima or
    minima of, Lagrange test for)
Lags:
  in consumption, 119, 133, 136–139,
      141–142, 150–151, 153–156,
      158–161, 187–188
  distinction between actual and equilibrium
      values and, 54
  distributed: defined, 149
    of Koyck, 149–150, 160, 240–242
    Pascal, 240–241

Lags, distributed (*Cont.*):
  in representing permanent consumption, 187
  in representing permanent income, 149 – 150, 153, 181, 384, 385, 391
  efficacy of policy and, 192 – 193, 222, 242
  in feedback controls, 228 – 230, 238, 241, 242
  as hallmark of dynamics, 51
  in investment, 62, 119, 165 – 166, 173, 177 – 178, 180 – 182, 186 – 188
    (*See also* Acceleration principle; Accelerator, flexible; Accelerator, simple)
  length of, and effect, 60 – 65, 192, 242
  of Lundberg type, 54
  in output, 54, 60, 189, 190*n.*, 229, 238, 240, 246
Leading indicators, composite index of (*see* Composite index, of leading indicators)
Learning curve in formation of expectations, 245
Leontief production function (*see* Production function, Leontief)
l'Hopital's rule:
  derivative and, 364
  exemplified, 364
  limit and, 364
  stated, 364
Life-cycle hypothesis (see Consumption theory of Ando, Brumberg, and Modigliani)
Limit:
  asymptote and, 361
  defined, 359 – 360
  derivative and, 361
  integral and, 377 – 379
  l'Hopital's rule and, 364
  notation of, 360
  properties of, 360 – 361
Linear-isoquant production function (*see* Production function, linear-isoquant)
Liquidity preference schedule:
  in analysis by Kaldor, 279*n.*
  described, 13
  liquidity trap in (*see* Liquidity trap)
  shape of: expectational basis of, 13 – 15, 19*n.*
    explained, 13 – 15
    opportunity cost basis of, 13
  shift in, 19*n.*
Liquidity trap:
  defined, 13, 15
  economics of Keynes under versus economics of classics, 48
  efficacy of monetary policy in, 19 – 20
  shape of LM curve in, 47
LM curve:
  confronted by IS curve, 37 – 38
    and BB curve, 41

LM curve (*Cont.*):
  Hicksian form of, 46 – 47
  in model of multiplier, dynamic version, 59 – 60, 403 – 404
  money market conditions and, 37
  positive slope of, 37
    explained, 37
    unidirectional movement of output and, 403 – 404
  shape of, in liquidity trap, 47
  shifts in, 42
    linked to shifts in IS curve, 45 – 46
    under real-balance effect, 45
LM equation:
  confronted by IS equation, 29
  defined, 29
  under real-balance effect, 45
Long run, defined, 120, 152, 289
Long-run versus short-run consumption function (*see* Consumption function, long-run versus short-run)
Longsightedness hypothesis (*see* Consumption, longsightedness versus shortsightedness hypothesis of; Consumption theory of Ando, Brumberg, and Modigliani; Consumption theory of Friedman; Consumption theory of Hamburger)
Loss function, 199, 242
  in policy decisions (*see* Policy decision, loss function in)
  (*See also* Quadratic loss function)
Luring-in effect, defined, 45 – 46

Marginal cost of funds:
  defined, 183
  interest rate and, 183
  relation of, to marginal efficiency of investment, 184 – 186
  schedule of, 183 – 184
  (*See also* Investment theory, of Duesenberry, marginal cost of funds schedule in)
Marginal efficiency of capital:
  defined, 17*n.*, 167 – 168
  relation of, to marginal efficiency of investment, 167, 171
  schedule of, 17*n.*, 168
    volatility of, 18 – 19
Marginal efficiency of investment (*see* Investment, marginal efficiency of)
Marginal product of capital (*see* Capital, marginal product of)
Marginal propensity to consume, defined, 20
  (*See also* Consumption function, marginal propensity to consume in)
Marginal propensity to save, 28 – 29
Marginal propensity to tax, 26

Marginal rate of substitution:
  defined, 200, 368
  for quadratic loss function, 200
Marginal rate of technical substitution:
  for CES production function, 96, 397
  defined, 95 – 96, 368, 396
  in definition of elasticity of factor
    substitution, 396
Mathematical expectation:
  conditional, defined, 387
  defined, 385
  as mean of random variable, 385 – 386
  for normal distribution, 390
  properties of, 385 – 387
  for Student's t distribution, 390 – 391
Maxima of functions (*see* Function,
    constrained maxima or minima of;
    Function, unconstrained maxima or
    minima of)
Mean, defined:
  as mathematical expectation, 385 – 386
  as sample property, 389
Measured consumption:
  defined, 147
  (*See also* Permanent consumption)
Measured income:
  defined, 147
  trend factor for, 149
  (*See also* Permanent income)
Minima of functions (*see* Function,
    constrained maxima or minima of;
    Function, unconstrained maxima or
    minima of)
Money:
  demand function for, estimated, 33
    34n.
  in policy action, role of: under functional
    finance, 222
    monetarist view of, 227n.
  precautionary demand for, 15
  quantity theory of (*see* Quantity theory of
    money)
  real balances, defined, 26 – 27
  speculative demand for, 13, 15
    inserted into model of classics, 15 – 17
  supply of: in model of classics, 9
    in model of Keynes, 15
  transactions demand for: in model of
    classics, 8
    in model of Keynes, 15
Money illusion:
  in consumption, 160
  demand for money and, 27
  money demand function estimated under,
    34n.
Monotonicity:
  defined, 363
  derivative and, 363
  formulating capital aggregate and, 296 – 297,
    363

Multiplier model of temporal response:
  alternative lag structures, effect of, in,
    60 – 65
  described, 54 – 65
  as special case: in theory of cycle by Hicks,
    107
    in theory of cycle by Metzler, 111
    in theory of cycle with
      multiplier-accelerator (Samuelson-type)
      interaction, 105
Multiplier process:
  development of, under Kahn, 30n.
  in growth model of Domar, 261 – 262
  stabilizing nature of, 63 – 65, 105, 107,
    190n., 231
Multipliers:
  dynamic (disequilibrium): compared with
    equilibrium multipliers, 70
    defined, 70
    in econometric models, 72 – 75
    estimates of, *71, 74*
    in inertial multiplier-accelerator
      interaction model, 188 – 189
    types of, 70
  equilibrium: autonomous and induced effects
    in, 32
    balanced budget, 32 – 34
    compared with dynamic multipliers, 70
    defined, 30, 70
    estimates of, *33*
    expressions for, *31, 206*
    of fiscal policy, 32 – 34
    in inertial multiplier-accelerator
      interaction model, 188 – 189
    of monetary policy, 33 – 34
  inaccuracy possible in, 44, 74, 193, 211
  Lagrange, 375 – 376
  uncertainty about and effect on policy
    decisions, 213 – 220

Napierian constant:
  natural exponential function and, 383
  natural log function and, 381, 383
National Bureau of Economic Research
    (NBER):
  business cycle reference dates (turning
    points) of, *78*, 122
    cycle duration and, *78*
  formation of, 75
  method of locating business cycle reference
    dates, 76
  mission of, 75
  view of, on business cycle, 75 – 76
Natural growth rate, defined, 258 – 259
Neoclassical growth model (*see* Growth
    model, neoclassical)
Nontrivial solution, defined, 267
Normal good, defined, 40 – 41
Normal rate of interest, 13 – 15

Obsolescence of capital (*see* Capital, obsolescence of)
Orders, new, cyclical phases of, *89*
Ordinary least squares, criterion of, 389
  (*See also* Regression analysis, ordinary least-squares criterion of)
Output:
  capacity, defined, 261
  full employment, defined, 42–43
  gross versus net, 170, 173*n.*, 251–252, 295
  lags in (*see* Lags, in output)
  relation of, to income, 4
  temporal movement of, 192, 400–402
    under constant growth rate rule, 239–240, 242–243
    over cycle phases, *88, 91*
    under feedback controls, 231–235, 239, 242–243
      used in combination, 235–237, 240–243
    for growth model of Domar, 262
    for growth model of Harrod, 258–259, 260*n.*
    for growth model of Kaldor, 278
    for inertial multiplier-accelerator interaction model, 189–192
    IS-LM depiction of, 59–60
    for model of Frisch, 99–100
    for model of Hicks, 107–108
    for model of Metzler, 111–115
    for model of multiplier: dynamic version, 56–65, 403–404
      static version, 53–54
    for model of multiplier-accelerator (Samuelson-type) interaction, 101–105, 405
    for neoclassical growth model, 265, 266*n.*, 267*n.*, 268, 271*n.*, 310*n.*, 336
      with embodied technical progress, 290–293, 303–304, 309*n.*, 329, 382
    for putty-clay growth model, 308–310, 315, 323, 341–342, 347–349
    under sound finance, 231–232

Parameter, defined, 27, 388
Pascal distributed lag, 240–241
Per capita measures, rationale for, in macro context, 128
Perfect foresight, 111*n.*, 244, 320*n.*
  defined, 244
Permanent consumption:
  defined, 147
  expectational nature of, 147
  as function of measured consumptions, 187
  versus measured and transitory consumption, 147–148, 150, 387
Permanent income:
  adaptive adjustment mechanism in, 149
  defined, 147

Permanent income (*Cont.*):
  expectational nature of, 147, 148
  as function of measured incomes, 148–150, 153, 181, 384, 385, 391
  versus measured and transitory income, 147–148, 387
  trend component of, 149–150, 153
Permanent income hypothesis of consumption, 143–153, 160
  (*See also* Consumption theory of Friedman, permanent income in)
Policy:
  countercyclical: defined, 221
    destabilizing tendency of, 222, 225–227
      with proper timing, 225–226
    difficulties inherent in, 192–193, 198, 222, 226
    feedback controls in (*see* Policy rule, feedback control as)
    fine tuning as, defined, 227*n.*
    functional finance as: basis of, 222
      early labels for, 222*n.*
      feedback controls and, 230, 235–236
      principles of, 221–222
      sound finance versus, 221–222, 227, 230, 235–236
      unemployment and, 221–222, 230
    for minimizing fluctuations, 226–227, 239, 242
    relation of magnitude of, to timing of, 226–227
    support for, 221–222, 227–228
      through feedback controls (*see* Policy rule, feedback control as)
    views of fiscalists and monetarists on, 227*n.*
  fiscal: for combating unemployment, 42–43
    difficulty of, 44
    functional finance basis of, 221–222
    instruments of, 20, 227*n.*
    passive stance of, basis of, 227
    view of fiscalists on, 227*n.*
    view of, from model of Keynes, 19–20, 227*n.*
    (*See also* Policy, countercyclical; Policy rule)
  monetary: accommodative, 45–46
    for combating unemployment, 43
    under functional finance, 222
    passive stance of, basis of, 227
    view of from model of classics, 11, 227*n.*
    view of from model of Keynes, 19–20
    (*See also* countercyclical, *above;* Policy rule)
  proposed reforms of, 222–224, 325
    constant growth rate rule as, 223–224
    countercyclical budgetary adjustments and, 227*n.*
Policy decisions:
  assignment problem in, 205–208, 219

Policy decisions (*Cont.*):
  under certainty, 199 – 210, 219, 385
  compared with those for certainty
      equivalence, 211 – 215, 217 – 220
  forecasts and, 86
    discrepancies in, 74 – 75, 193
  innovation variable in, defined, 211,
      213 – 214
  instruments in, defined, 201
  loss function in, 199 – 201, 208 – 209,
      211 – 215, 218 – 219, 242 – 243
  and numbers of instruments and targets,
      203 – 205, 208 – 215, 218 – 220
  optimization procedure and, 201 – 205,
      208 – 209, 211 – 219, 226 – 227, 239,
      242 – 243, 370 – 371
  on pairing instruments and targets,
      205 – 208, 219
  state variables in, defined, 199, 238
  under uncertainty, 34*n.*, 193, 198, 210 – 220,
      387
    certainty equivalence theorem and, 213,
      219 – 220, 242 – 243
    conservative tendency in, 214, 216 – 218,
      220, 226 – 228, 237, 240, 242 – 243
    wrong-way action and, 217 – 218
Policy rule:
  actual versus expected, 238, 244 – 246
  constant growth rate rule as, 223 – 224
    basis of, 224, 227, 244 – 245
    inferiority of, 227 – 228, 239 – 240,
        242 – 243, 246 – 247
    precedent for, 224*n.*
    under rational expectations, 244 – 247
    stable prices and, 223 – 224
    stated, 224
  feedback control as: accelerator version of,
      229
    budget and, 231 – 232, 235 – 237
    combination of, 235 – 237
    conservatism in, 227 – 228, 237, 240 – 243
    convergence time under, 231 – 237
    destabilizing tendency of, 190 – 192, 229,
        232 – 235, 237, 240, 242
    formula flexibility and, 228
    loss function and, 242 – 243
    properties of, 229 – 237, 364
    under rational expectations, 244 – 247
    support for, 230, 231, 234 – 237,
        239 – 240, 242 – 243, 246 – 247
    during transition to rational expectations,
        246
    types of, 228 – 229
    unemployment and, 230 – 231, 235 – 237
  formula flexibility as, defined, 228
  laissez faire as, 3
  lockstep plan as, defined, 227 – 228
  passive, 221
    monetarists and, 227*n.*
  of passivism, defined, 221

Policy rule (*Cont.*):
  versus policy discretion, 193, 221 – 224,
      227 – 228
  of sound finance: balanced budget and, 222,
      227, 231
    principle of, 222
    unemployment and, 230, 231
Policy shocks:
  defined, 325
  long- and short-run effects of, 325, 357
  purposes of, 325
  representations of, 327
Possible growth rate, defined, 281*n.*
Power rule:
  of differentiation: exemplified, 362
    stated, 362
  of integration: failure of and natural log
      function, 380 – 381
    stated, 379
Predetermined variable, defined, 29
Price movement:
  over cycle phases, *89 – 91*
  linking shifts of IS and LM curves, 46
  macro adjustment and, 44, 46
  in neoclassical growth model, 268
  in theory of income distribution by Kaldor,
      276, 277
Probability density, joint:
  covariance and, 386
  defined, 386
  as generalization of probability distribution,
      386
Probability distribution:
  defined, 385
  normal, 390
  probability density and, 385
  as special case of joint probability density,
      386
  Student's *t*, 390 – 391
  (*See also* Random variable)
Production function:
  in acceleration principle theoretics, 95 – 98,
      99*n.*
  aggregate (*see* Production function,
      aggregate)
  capital-generalized constant returns in,
      defined, 297
  Cobb-Douglas, 96, 382, 399
    aggregation conditions and, 297 – 298,
        303*n.*, 304*n.*
    derived, 360, 383 – 384, 399
    in neoclassical growth model, 269 – 272,
        278*n.*, 284 – 285, 287 – 290, 328
    neutral technical progress and, 256, 270,
        271*n.*, 278*n.*, 287 – 288, 293, 297,
        299 – 300, 303*n.*
    technical progress function and, 251,
        274 – 275, 278*n.*, 381 – 382
  constant elasticity of substitution (CES), 96,
      396 – 397

Production function, constant elasticity of
    substitution (CES) (*Cont.*):
    developers of, 96, 398*n*.
    limiting cases of derived, 398 – 399
    marginal rate of technical substitution of,
        96, 397
    properties of, 96, 367 – 368, 397 – 399
    defined, 4, 288
    under disembodied technical progress, 253
    elasticity of factor substitution of (*see*
        Elasticity of factor substitution)
    ex ante: defined, 301
        exemplified, 304 – 305
    ex post: defined, 301
        exemplified, 305
    in growth model of Harrod and Domar, 251,
        260, 263
    growth model of Kaldor and, 251, 274 – 275
    growth model of Robinson and, 251
    in growth models, 251
    Leontief, 96, 398
        derived, 398
        in growth model of Harrod and Domar,
            251, 260, 263
        under putty-clay capital, 301 – 302, 305
        simple accelerator and, 97, 98
    linear, derived, 399
    linear-isoquant, 96, 399
        derived, 399
    marginal rate of technical substitution of (*see*
        Marginal rate of technical substitution)
    in model of classics, 4 – 5
        properties of, 4 – 5, 365 – 366
    in neoclassical growth model, 251, 264, 270,
        360 – 362, 368
        boundary conditions for, 264, 268, 269
        with embodied technical progress,
            287 – 290, 328
    under neutral technical progress, 255 – 256
        of Harrod, 255 – 256
        of Hicks, 255, 256
        of Solow, 256
    under putty-clay capital (*see* Capital,
        putty-clay, production functions under)
    rejection of, by Kaldor, 251, 274, 275*n*.,
        286
    rejection of, by Robinson, 251, 279
    technical progress function and, 251,
        274 – 275, 278*n*., 286, 381 – 382
    in theory of capital, 168
    vintage: defined, 253 – 254
        exemplified, 287 – 288
Production function, aggregate:
    compared with vintage production function,
        289 – 290, 294, 299 – 300
    construction of, under embodied technical
        progress (*see* Capital stock, aggregate,
        construction of, under embodied
        technical progress)
    defined, 275*n*., 286

Production function, aggregate (*Cont.*):
    under disembodied technical progress, 290,
        296, 298 – 299
    validity of, under embodied technical
        progress, 274, 275*n*., 286, 289 – 290,
        296 – 300
Productivity ratio:
    defined, 261
    relation of, to acceleration coefficient, 263
Profit maximization:
    in acceleration principle derivation, 95 – 96
    conditions for, 5 – 6
Profit rate:
    defined, 276
    prospective versus realized, 278
        investment and, 278
Profit share:
    defined, 276
    minimum value of, 277
Profits, corporate:
    cyclical phases of, *88*
    linked to aggregate income, 165
    permissive role of, in investment, 184 – 185
Profits principle:
    versus acceleration principle, 165, 167,
        182
    defined, 95*n*., 165
    evidence on, 95*n*., 167*n*., 391
    theoretical basis of, 164 – 165
    weakness of, 165, 167
Propensity to consume:
    as consumption function of Keynes, 21*n*.
    marginal, defined, 20
    (*See also* Consumption function;
        Consumption theory of Keynes)
Putty-clay capital (*see* Capital, putty-clay)
Putty-putty capital (*see* Capital, putty-putty)

Quadratic loss function:
    defined, 199 – 200
    indifference curves for (*see* Indifference
        curves for quadratic loss function)
    properties of, 200 – 201
Quantity theory of money:
    basis of, 8 – 9
    restated by Friedman, 224
    stated, 8
Quasi-rent:
    condition for maximum of, 294
    defined, 170*n*., 294

Random variable:
    defined, 385
    estimator as, 389
    mean of: mathematical expectation as,
        385 – 386
        as sample property, 389
    probability distribution (density) of, 385

Random variable (*Cont.*):
  standard deviation of, defined, 386
  variance of, defined, 386
Ratchet effect:
  contrasted with reverse lightning bolt effect, 141
  defined, 135
Rational expectations:
  empirical findings on, 247n.
  hypothesis of, 244, 245
  perfect foresight and, 244
  policy rule under: constant growth rate rule as, 244–247
    feedback control as, 244–247
Reaction coefficient, 182n.
Real-balance effect:
  in bonds, 45n.
  in consumption, 45, 160
  defined, 45
  in investment, 45
  in money demand, 45
Recursiveness:
  defined, 51
  versus simultaneity, 51
Reduced-form equation, defined, 29
Regression analysis:
  autocorrelation in: consequence of, 391
    defined, 391
    detection of, 391–392
    exemplified, 95n., 122n.–123n., 124n., 392
    serial correlation as, 391
  coefficient of determination in, 391
  of consumption function, 33, 122n.–123n., 124, 129, 133, 136–138, 140–141, 150, 159, 391–392
  defined, 388
  dependent variable in, defined, 388
  described, 387–392
  disturbance term in, defined, 388
  dummy variables in, 392
  estimator in: bias in, 390
    defined, 389
    versus estimate, 389
  explanatory variable in, defined, 388
  independent variable in, defined, 388
  interaction term in, 392
  of investment function, 33, 95n., 167n., 391
  of long-run marginal propensity to consume, 101n.
  of money demand function, 33, 34n.
  in multiplier estimation, 33–34, 44, 73–74, 193, 211, 390
  observation in, defined, 388
  ordinary least-squares criterion of: normal equations under, 389
    stated, 389
  ordinary least-squares estimators in:
    derived, 389
    hypothesis tests of, 391

Regression analysis, ordinary least-squares estimators in (*Cont.*):
    properties of, 389–391
    standard errors of, 390
  parameter in, defined, 388
  of profits principle, 95n., 167n., 391
  of rational expectations hypothesis, 247n.
  regression line of: compared with true line, 388–389
    explanatory power of, 391
    goodness of fit of, 391
  residual in, defined, 389
  sample in: defined, 388
    types of, 388
  scatter of points in, 388
  of simple accelerator, 95n., 167n., 391
  structural shift allowance in, 392
    dummy variables and, 139n., 142, 392
  of tax function, 33
  true specification in: defined, 388
    deterministic (nonstochastic) component of, defined, 388
Relative income hypothesis of consumption, 132–136, 160
  (*See also* Consumption theory of Duesenberry; Consumption theory of Modigliani)
Required growth rate, defined, 262
Response path, defined, 337
Reverse lightning bolt effect, 141
  contrasted with ratchet effect, 141
Reverse trend adjustment:
  defined, 395
  described, 395

Sales, cyclical phases of, *88*
Saving:
  of government, defined, 28
  gross versus net, 251–252
  marginal propensity associated with, 28–29
  personal (private), 28
  relation of, to wealth, 147, 155, 157
  total, 28
  view of Kaldor on, 275–277
    incorporated into neoclassical growth model, 283–285, 385
  view of Pasinetti on, 277n.
Saving coefficient:
  evidence on, 276n.
  restrictions on: in neoclassical growth model with CES production function, 271–273
    in putty-clay growth model with CES ex ante production function, 311–315, 318–319, 342n., 351–352
    in saving function of Kaldor, 275–277
Saving function:
  in growth model of Domar, 262
  in growth model of Harrod, 257

Saving function (*Cont.*):
  in growth model of Robinson, 280
  of Kaldor, 275–277
  in model of classics, 9–10
  in model of Keynes, 17, 20–21
  in neoclassical growth model, 264–265, 283
    with embodied technical progress, 290, 328
Scalar, defined, 386
Secular exhilaration, described, 258–259
Secular stagnation, described, 258–259
Serial correlation as autocorrelation, 391
Short run, defined, 5, 125
Shortsightedness hypothesis (*see*
    Consumption, shortsightedness
    hypothesis of; Consumption theory of
    Ball and Drake)
Simple accelerator (*see* Accelerator, simple)
Simulation procedure:
  defined, 337
  described for putty-clay growth model, 337–340, 379
Simulation run, defined, 339
Simultaneity versus recursiveness, 51
Single-sector model, defined, 4
Slope:
  defined, 361
  derivative and, 361, 363, 365
  of a slope, 363
Sluggishness coefficient:
  in consumption, 139–141, 151, 159, 188
  in investment, 181, 188
  relation of, to speed-of-adjustment
    coefficient, 181–182
Solution:
  baseline, defined, 72
  nontrivial, defined, 267
Sound finance (*see* Policy rule, of sound
    finance)
Speed-of-adjustment coefficient:
  defined, 181–182
  relation of, to sluggishness coefficient, 181–182
  synonymity of, with reaction coefficient, 182n.
  variability of, 182
  (*See also* Adjustment speed parameter)
Speed of adjustment and convergence time, 326–327, 329
Stagflation:
  data on, 88–91
  defined, 23n., 93
Standard deviation:
  defined, 386
  relation of, to standard error, 390
  relation of, to variance, 386
Standard error:
  defined, 390
  relation of, to standard deviation, 390

Standardization process for constructing
    composite indices, 80–81, 84–85, 393–394
State variable in policy decisions, defined, 199, 238
Static expectations (*see* Expectations, static)
Statics:
  comparative, defined, 51
  defined, 24, 51
Stationary point, defined, 370
Stationary state:
  in calculating consumption propensities, 133n., 136, 152, 159
  defined, 55, 238
  in inertial multiplier-accelerator interaction
    model, 188–189, 190n.
  integral feedback control and, 228–229
  in interpreting flexible accelerator, 181–182
  in models of feedback control, 229–230, 238–239
Steady growth (*see* Growth, steady)
Steady state, defined, 55, 238n.
Stochastic steady state, defined, 238n.
Stock prices, cyclical phases of, *89, 91*
Supply, aggregate, accommodating aggregate
    demand, 22–23, 26
Supply price of capital (*see* Capital, supply
    price of)
Supply-side economics:
  focus of, 23n.
  Keynesian economics and, 23n.
Surplus, government, defined, 28
Synchronous ratio:
  defined, 87
  table of, *88–89*

Tax function, estimated, 33
Taxes, net, defined, 26, 229
Technical progress:
  capital-altering: defined, 296–297
    exemplified, 297, 299
    as generalization of capital-augmenting
      technical progress, 296–297
  capital-augmenting: defined, 256, 296–297
    exemplified, 297, 299
    as special case of capital-altering technical
      progress, 296–297
  defined, 252
  dimensions (types) of, 252–257
  disembodied: construction of aggregate
    capital stock under, 290, 296, 298, 299
    defined, 253, 287
  disembodied versus embodied, 253–254, 287
  embodied: construction of aggregate capital
    stock under (*see* Capital stock,
    aggregate, construction of, under
    embodied technical progress)
    defined, 253, 287

Technical progress, embodied (*Cont.*):
  heterogeneity of capital and, 253, 289, 297
  production function validity and (*see*
    Production function, aggregate, validity
    of, under embodied technical progress)
  view of Kaldor and, 274, 286
exogenous versus endogenous, 257
  in growth model of Robinson, 281
in growth model of Harrod, 259
in growth model of Robinson, 281
Harrod-neutral as labor-augmenting
    technical progress, 255 – 256
  in CES production function, 270
Harrod-neutral rate of versus Hicks-neutral
    rate of, 256, 271n., 293, 330
Hicks-neutral: in CES production function,
    270n.
  decomposability of production function
    under, 255
  as factor-augmenting technical progress,
    256
as measure of ignorance, 252n.
in neoclassical growth model, 264, 268 – 269
  with embodied technical progress,
    287 – 288, 293, 328, 330
neutral versus nonneutral (unbiased versus
    biased), 254 – 256
  classification of, by Harrod, 254, 255
  classification of, by Hicks, 254
neutrality of, under Cobb-Douglas
    production function (*see* Production
    function, Cobb-Douglas, neutral
    technical progress and)
production function, form of, and 253,
    255 – 256
in putty-clay growth model, 304 – 305, 338
Solow-neutral: as capital-augmenting
    technical progress, 256
  in CES production function, 270n.
steady growth requirement for, 269,
    303 – 304, 308n.
view of Kaldor on, 274, 286
Technical progress function:
  Cobb-Douglas production function and, 251,
    274 – 275, 278n., 381 – 382
  as determinant of investment, 277, 278
  properties of, 274 – 275, 381 – 382
  rejection of, by Robinson, 251, 279
  (*See also* Growth model of Kaldor, technical
    progress function in)
Temporal movement, classification of, 65 – 70
Transfer payments:
  defined, 26
  as negative taxes, 26
Transitory consumption:
  defined, 147
  (*See also* Permanent consumption)
Transitory income:
  defined, 147
  (*See also* Permanent income)

Trivial solution (*see* Nontrivial solution,
  defined)

Unemployment:
  causes of, in model of Keynes, 19
  cyclical phases of, *88*
  estimates of, for the great depression, 3, 75
  feedback control and, 230 – 231, 235 – 237
  functional finance and, 221 – 222, 230
  sound finance and, 230, 231
User cost (unit rental) of capital:
  defined, 169
  gross versus net, 170
  relation of, to interest rate, 169 – 170
  synonymity of, with unit capital rental,
    169 – 170

Variance:
  defined, 386
  relation of, to covariance, 386
  relation of, to standard deviation, 386
Velocity of circulation, 9, 224
Vintage:
  of capital (*see* Capital, vintage of)
  marginal: defined, 305
    in discrete time, 338, 339
  production function: defined, 253 – 254
    exemplified, 287 – 288
Vintage set (*see* Capital, vintage set of)
von Neumann statistic:
  in consumption, 122n. – 123n.
  defined, 392
  described, 391 – 392

Wage, money
  in model of classics, 8
    relation of, to real wage, 8
  in model of Keynes, 19
    psychological law and, 19n.
  relation of, to price in income distribution
    theory of Kaldor, 276, 277
Wage, real:
  behavior of, in income distribution theory of
    Kaldor, 276 – 277
  common marginal product of labor under
    embodied technical progress and, 294
  interpretation of, 5 – 6
  in model of classics, 8
    relation of, to money wage, 8
Wage rate:
  decision, defined, 321
  determination of: in model of classics, 8
    in putty-clay growth model, 307,
      339 – 340, 347
  as proxy for income from human wealth, 143
Walras' law:
  bond market and, 38, 42

Walras' law (*Cont.*):
  stated, 27
Warranted growth rate:
  in growth model of Harrod (*see* Growth
    model of Harrod, warranted growth rate
    in)
  in growth model of Robinson, 281
Wealth:
  consumption theories based on, 160
    emergence of, 142–143, 160
    (*See also* Consumption, wealth and)
  money as means of holding, 13*n*.

Wealth (*Cont.*):
  relation of, to saving, 147, 155, 157
  as source of income, 143, 147, 157
  types of, 143, 144, 154, 157

Young's theorem:
  exemplified, 366
  stated, 365–366

Zero foresight, static expectations and, 320*n*.